U.S. Dept. of the Army

Library of Congress Cataloging in Publication Data

United States. Dept. of the Army. Nuclear weapons and Nato.

"Department of Defense pamphlet."
1. North Atlantic Treaty Organization—Bibliography. 2. Europe—Defenses—Bibliography. 3. Atomic weapons—Bibliography. 4. Military policy—Bibliography. I. Title.

Z6725.E8U54 1975 [UA646.3] 016.35503 75-619148

PREPARED BY: Harry Moskowitz and Jack Roberts

For sale by the Superintendent of Documents, U.S. Government Printing Office
Washington, D.C. 20402 - Price $8.65

Stock Number 008-046-00082-4

FOREWORD

Given the realities of today's world, we must maintain adequate power to deter attack and to prevent our becoming vulnerable to coercion. This must be done consistent with economic feasibility and political acceptability.

Optimum decisions, affecting these complex and sometimes competing requirements, can only be derived from an appreciation of pertinent facts, situations and viewpoints. This analytical survey was prepared to identify some of the factors which contribute to this appreciation.

Items in this survey were selected primarily for the pertinent facts they provide, their ability to stimulate thinking and further understanding of the total problem. The inclusion of an item does not necessarily indicate Department of Defense concurrence.

ROBERT ELLSWORTH
Assistant Secretary of Defense
International Security Affairs

ANALYSTS' NOTE

This analytical survey of literature was prepared at the request of the Assistant Secretary of Defense (International Security Affairs), United States Department of Defense. It is based on unclassified publications (both friendly and unfriendly) available, for the most part, on the open shelves of The Army Library, Headquarters, Department of the Army, Pentagon.

The 800 abstracts included in this publication were selected from several thousand periodical articles, books, studies, and documents, and are reflective of the many issues and problems confronting NATO. The document also explores the various aspects of the defense of Western Europe, as well as the varied elements of East-West strategic balance, with NATO and the WTO (Warsaw Treaty Organization) as the crux of the balance and the ever-increasing military strength of the Soviet Union as the predominant factor. The strategic implications of oil, the rising tide of communism in Europe, the problems of detente, and the intricacies of SALT I and II are also delved into.

The document is supported with background notes of each member state of NATO. Texts of treaties, charts, and other useful*** Appendixes lend additional support to the main body of the manuscript.

No effort has been made to delete or exclude references by reason of their controversial nature. On the other hand, inclusion of entries does not represent an official endorsement of the views expressed.

The Research Analysts of the Army Library gratefully acknowledge the fense and the Department of State. Special appreciation is extended to T. N. Dupuy Associates, Dunn Loring, Virginia, for permission to reprint extracts from their 1974 edition of The Almanac of World Military Power.

Symbols:

*-Not available at time of listing

LI-Library of the Institution

***-The appendixes were the latest ones available at the time of preparation. However, subsequent political, and, in some cases, military events have altered some of the data. Therefore, appendixes dealing with Greece, Italy, Portugal, Turkey, etc., should be studied accordingly.

NUCLEAR WEAPONS AND NATO
ANALYTICAL SURVEY OF LITERATURE

CHAPTER I

NATO ON ITS TWENTY-FIFTH ANNIVERSARY

CHAPTER II

THE ATLANTIC ALLIANCE: AN OVERVIEW
(See also Appendixes; and for Warsaw Treaty Organization Chapter VIII)

CHAPTER III

NATO'S INTEGRATED STRUCTURE: FUNCTIONS AND ACTIVITIES OF SOME OF ITS COMPONENTS (See also Appendixes)

*For Middle East Problems see also DA PAM 550-16, Middle East: The Strategic Hub and North Africa, 1973.

CHAPTER IV

NATO'S DEFENSE POSTURE: PROBLEMS AND PROSPECTS
(See also Chapter V and Appendixes)

CHAPTER V

DEFENSE AND SECURITY OF WESTERN EUROPE, NATO, AND NATIONAL STRATEGIES WITHIN THE ALLIANCE
(See also Chapter IV and Appendixes)

CHAPTER VI

EAST-WEST DÉTENTE: PROSPECTS AND LIMITS OF CONCILIATION

CHAPTER VII

WEAPONS AND TECHNOLOGY, AND ARMS CONTROL, DISARMAMENT AND NUCLEAR PROLIFERATION (See also Appendixes)

CHAPTER VIII

*WARSAW TREATY ORGANIZATION: A POLITICO-MILITARY REVIEW AND FORECAST (See also Appendixes)

*For more detailed information see DA PAM 550-8, Communist Eastern Europe, 1971.

CHAPTER I

NATO ON ITS TWENTY-FIFTH ANNIVERSARY

A. A Review of Its Accomplishments (See also Appendixes)

THE ATLANTIC PARTNERSHIP 25 YEARS LATER, by N. Khomutov, in *International Affairs, Moscow*, no. 5 (1974) 37-45.

"Western Europe played central part in the plans for world domination conceived in US ruling circles while the Second World War was still on. Under these plans, Western Europe, united in one form or another and held close to the USA by the bonds of military-political bloc, was to become a reliable partner in the struggle against the world socialist system, the national liberation and democratic movements. The absurdity of the US ruling circles' claims to world domination was obvious from the very beginning. However, it took almost a quarter-century, marked by the victories of the socialist revolutions in a number of countries in Europe, Asia and Latin America, the collapse of the colonial system of imperialism and the emergence of dozens of young national states, for US ruling circles themselves to realise the flimsiness of their hegemonistic aspirations. The early 1970s were a watershed . . . In view of this, the USA is making efforts to work out new principles for trans-Atlantic relations in NATO and between the USA and the EEC and to embody them in an official declaration. However, the USA seeks to make its relations with Western Europe, including those within the NATO framework, a component part of a broader system of relations that would help to cement relations both between the USA and Japan, and also between Japan and Western Europe. US foreign policy strategists naturally feel that this kind of system should function under US control."

THE CHALLENGE OF SUCCESS, in *NATO's Fifteen Nations*, v. 19, no. 2 (April-May 1974) 50-56.

"The North Atlantic Treaty Organisation (NATO) has had 25 years of success in maintaining peace during a period of unrest, confrontation and consultation. Allied Forces Central Europe (AFCENT) has played a vital role in that success since 1951. But despite a quarter-century of peace, the Western World is currently faced with a number of challenges brought on by the very success of NATO. These include the continuing threat posed from the East by the Warsaw Pact forces; and the necessity to continue to maintain a credible military posture and a spirit of solidarity which have been the backbone of NATO's success since 1949."

THE CHALLENGE TO SOCIO-POLITICAL STRUCTURE; DETERRENCE, DEFENSE, SOLIDARITY, DÉTENTE, by Gen. A. J. Goodpaster, in *Vital Speeches of the Day*, v. 41, no. 2 (1 November 1974) 48-52.

Speech delivered before the Atlantic Treaty Association, Ottawa, Canada, 10 September 1974.—"In my report today I wish to review with you some of the key features of the situation within the military side of NATO at this time, noting some indications of satisfying progress and also some areas of concern. The broad perspective for my remarks is the observation that while we find ourselves in an era of change which borders at times on the chaotic, the objectives of NATO, against which our military posture and programs must be evaluated, remain steadfast and valid."

NATO LOOKS AHEAD, by Patrick Wall, in *The Atlantic Community Quarterly*, v. 12, no. 3 (Fall 1974) 352-357.

"After 25 years of existence, NATO now has to face up to some fundamental problems both as regards control, organization and posture. Patrick Wall discusses the Committee of Nine report of the North Atlantic Assembly as one approach to these problems."

NATO'S 25TH BIRTHDAY, by Joseph M. A. H. Luns, in *The Atlantic Community Quarterly*, v. 12, no. 1 (Spring 1974) 7-11.

"On April 4, the signatories of the North Atlantic Treaty celebrated the 25th anniversary of their Alliance. Secretary General Luns, in this article, finds reason for justifiable satisfaction at NATO's achievements but expresses concern with current problems and anxiety for the future."

THE NORTH ATLANTIC ALLIANCE COMMEMORATES ITS TWENTY-FIFTH ANNIVERSARY; ADDRESS BY SECRETARY GENERAL JOSEPH LUNS, in *NATO Review*, v. 22, no. 3 (June 1974) 5-7.

"We are gathered together this morning to commemorate the Twenty-fifth Anniversary of the Atlantic Alliance. In the course of this year there will certainly be other opportunities for celebrating with more pomp and circumstance NATO's twenty-five years of existence. But 4 April, the date of the signing of the Washington Treaty, does call for an appropriate tribute. In the circumstances, it is inevitable that we should reminisce. As we cast our minds back over the past twenty-five years, we have every reason to be proud. Proud of our Alliance which has kept the peace in Europe, which has never attacked anyone, which has never persecuted or insulted anyone and which, in settling its own problems, has never ridden rough-shod over its members. At the same time, while maintaining their sovereign independence, member countries, through the security afforded by the Alliance, have been able to achieve unprecedented prosperity."

POLICY, EQUIPMENT CHALLENGING NATO, by Herbert J. Coleman, in *Aviation Week & Space Technology*, v. 100, no. 10 (11 March 1974) 30 plus.

"North Atlantic Treaty Organization approaches its 25th anniversary in April as a troubled alliance trying to reconcile the lessons of the Middle East War with its flexible response attitude toward Warsaw Pact countries that outgun and outman it. Simultaneously, the alliance is trying to foresee its posture in the event of troop withdrawals by the U.S. and at the same time to formulate a policy that would preclude a renewal of the transatlantic bitterness caused by refusal to allow U.S. Air Force aircraft permission to use (NATO) bases in the massive resupply of arms to Israel. Problem areas for NATO, which may be ready for presentation to alliance ministers in April or May, but probably will not, are [listed]."

PROBLEMS OF NATO 1974: DEFENSE, DÉTENTE AND THE PEOPLE, in *World Survey*, no. 63, (March 1974) 16 p.

"This is the second of two surveys on the position of the Atlantic Alliance a quarter of a century after its birth. Having been concerned, since organizing the Atlantic Treaty Association [the author continues], of which I was the first Secretary General, with the formation of public opinion about NATO, I seek to analyze from that angle, the present problems of defence in the new atmosphere of relaxation between the Soviet bloc and the Western World, with due regard to their incompatible philosophies of life."

PROSPECT FOR THE ALLIANCE, by M. A. H. Luns, in *NATO Review*, v. 22, no. 1 (1974) 3-7.

"As we celebrate this 25th anniversary the justifiable satisfaction with past achievement is somewhat moderated by concern with current problems and anxiety for the future. It may be useful to try to examine the causes of this concern and anxiety rather more thoroughly."

(*)—TRANSATLANTIC CRISIS: EUROPE AND AMERICA IN THE '70S, ed. by Joseph Godson. London, Alcove Press Ltd., 1974. 143 p.

"This is a compilation, with some later additions and expansions, of a series of 19 articles which were published earlier this year in the International Herald Tribune. The series, conceived in connection with the Alliance's twenty-fifth anniversary, considers a number of the political, economic and security problems bearing on the European-North American relationship. As NATO Secretary General Joseph Luns points out in an introduction, 'The discussion by responsible and knowledgeable authors of so many facets of the Atlantic relationship should contribute to spreading greater understanding of the Alliance and of its indispensable role in maintaining peace.' . . . In addition, texts of the North Atlantic Treaty and of the Ottawa Declaration—signed last June after the contributions were written—are given as appendices."

TWENTY-FIVE YEARS OF NATO!, by Gen. H. J. Kruls, in *NATO's Fifteen Nations*, v. 19, no. 1 (February-March 1974) 19-21.

"A twenty-fifth anniversary. A milestone to look back into the past twenty-five years and to make up the account, of plusses and minuses, the achievements and setbacks. A milestone, too, for serious consideration of the present position and—what is most important—for a view into the future: the future of NATO seen in the mirror of the past and a realistic appreciation of the present."

CHAPTER II

THE ATLANTIC ALLIANCE: AN OVERVIEW
(See also Appendixes; and for Warsaw Treaty Organization Chapter VIII)

A. Atlantic Union and Partnership: Political, Military, and Economic Aspects

1. Miscellaneous Information

(*)—ALLIANCES: LATENT WAR COMMUNITIES IN THE CONTEMPORARY WORLD, ed. by Francis A. Beer. New York, Holt, Rinehart and Winston, 1970. 384 p.

"A collection of essays on alliances and international conflict, the nature of cooperation in such alliances as NATO, the Warsaw Pact, the South East Asia Treaty Organization, the Arab League, and the Organization of African States, and the characteristics of alliance disintegration."

ATA 19TH ANNUAL ASSEMBLY CONSIDERS FUTURE OF ATLANTIC RELATIONS, in *NATO Review*, v. 21, no. 5 (1973) 10–15.

"The 19th Annual Assembly of the Atlantic Treaty Association was held in Brussels from 10 to 14 September under the chairmanship of Professor Eugene V. Rostow. The theme was, 'The Atlantic Alliance, indispensable basis for security and détente'."

THE ATLANTIC UNION RESOLUTION, by Gale McGee, in *The Atlantic Community Quarterly*, v. 10, no. 4 (Winter 1972–1973) 541–544.

"Senator Gale McGee makes a strong case for the need of an Atlantic Federal Union. He points to many problems which can no longer be settled on the nation-state level and to Europe's loss of confidence in the U.S.—confidence which the United States would immediately recoup by once again showing leadership by applying internationally the federative principle it has applied so successfully on its own domestic political scene."

BEYOND DÉTENTE: TOWARD INTERNATIONAL ECONOMIC SECURITY, by Walter F. Mondale, in *Foreign Affairs*, v. 53, no. 1 (October 1974) 1–44.

"Economic issues are now front and center for the world's political leaders, topping the agenda of both domestic and foreign policy concerns. While the major international security issues of the last quarter-century are still with us—the competition in strategic nuclear arms, the struggle of differing political systems, the confrontation of massively armed alliances in Europe, the menace of great-power involvement in local conflict—these are now being overshadowed by the risk that the operation of the international economy may spin out of control. For if this happens there will be no graver threat to international stability, to the survival of Western democratic forms of government, and to national security itself. Last June West German Chancellor Helmut Schmidt spoke plainly at the NATO summit meeting. As he saw it, the most serious risks facing NATO were not military. The growing economic difficulties of its members, he said, 'include dangers that cannot be exaggerated. Inflation and the necessarily following recession pose the greatest threat to the foundations of Western society.' . . . From this examination of the specific immediate and long-term actions now required, it is possible to envision the general outlines of a system of international economic security."

EUROPE AND AMERICA: BETWEEN COOPERATION AND COMPETITION, by Curt Gasteyger, in *NATO Review*, v. 20, nos. 5–6 (May/June 1972) 12–15.

"Following the interest caused by the recent publication of his Atlantic Paper, 'Europe and America at the Crossroads,' the NATO Review publishes . . . [here] an article which Dr. Gasteyger has based on this . . . essay. The article, which expresses the views of its author . . . is included because of its constructive contribution to the current debate on important issues now facing the Alliance."

EUROPEAN SECURITY AND THE ATLANTIC SYSTEM, ed. by William T. R. Fox and Warner R. Schilling. New York, Columbia University Press, 1973. 276 p.

"Seven essays by as many authors, including Klaus Knorr, Annette Baker Fox and Andrew J. Pierre, on arms control in Europe. The emphasis is on Western Europe, the United States and differing national perspectives rather than the problems of European security as seen from the East."

IN THE SAME BOAT, in *The Atlantic Community Quarterly*, v. 11, no. 3 (Fall 1973) 314-318.

"The nine member states of the European Community have so far been unable to agree on a common response to Henry Kissinger's proposal for a 'New Atlantic Charter' and a revitalized Atlantic partnership. The absence of a European spokesman for negotiations on the interdependent issues of common defense, trade and monetary reform, and French opposition to multilateral discussions with the US, endangers the cohesion of the Western World."

LONG-RANGE PLANNING FACTORS IN THE BROSIO EXERCISE, by Lawrence L. Whetten, in *Military Review*, v. 51, no. 7 (July 1971) 50-59.

"More than any other multilateral organization, the North Atlantic Treaty Organization has successfully modified its objectives and achievements to accommodate changing international political requirements. NATO was originally conceived by many as a supplementary instrument for the United Nations endeavors to preserve the peace and contain the cold war. It was also envisioned as a means of expanding and normalizing interstate relations within the framework of reliable regional security and stability. Initially, it was designed to assure active participation of all Western Nations, particularly the United States, in a general alliance that would afford protection, social progress, and economic prosperity. Accordingly, it was intended both to block Soviet expansionism through collective security and to prevent the resurgence of German nationalism through creating a German political entity in a Western likeness and binding it closely to the emerging security structure. A review of the proceedings of the two Ministerial meetings in 1970 reveals the change in emphasis experienced in the two decades of NATO history. Stress is now placed on military disengagement, political détente, and common regional problems, such as environmental pollution, to an extent never before recorded. But like all dynamic organizations, stardom has been illusive. Major differences have existed among the partners about such fundamental questions as burden-sharing, conventional versus nuclear preparedness, force structures, and modernization programs."

MR. BROSIO'S LAST SPEECHES AS SECRETARY GENERAL, in *NATO Review*, v. 19, nos. 11-12 (November/December 1971) 15-17.

"The effect on NATO of some recent developments on the international scene, was analyzed by Mr. Manlio Brosio in speeches to the Atlantic Treaty Association (ATA) in London on 20 September and the North Atlantic Assembly in Ottawa a week later. These were the last major public speeches by Mr. Brosio before his succession by Mr. Joseph Luns as NATO's Secretary General on 1 October. The NATO Review reproduces below extensive extracts from these two speeches."

NATO FACTS AND FIGURES. Brussels, NATO Information Service, 1971. 354 p.

Part I—Origins and Evolution of the Alliance (Origins of the Alliance, Analysis of the North Atlantic Treaty, The Atlantic Alliance from 1949 to 1968, Defence Policy and Financing, Soviet Military Capability); Part II—Activities of the Council (Political Consultation, Machinery for Crisis Management, Economic Cooperation, Defense Support and Infrastructure, Scientific Cooperation, Cultural Cooperation, Civil Emergency Planning, Coordination of Air Traffic, Press and Information); Part III—Structure of NATO (Civil Organization, Military Organization, Financial Control); Part IV—Chronology, Statistics, Appendices. With maps, charts, and statistical tables.

NATO HANDBOOK. Brussells, NATO Information Service, February 1974. 79 p.

Contents: North Atlantic Council—Permanent Representatives (including those of Denmark, Iceland, and Norway, among others); The North Atlantic Treaty; Analysis of the Treaty; An Alliance for Peace; Development of the Alliance (Chronology); The Organization; Annexes; and Documentation.

NATO: THE TRANSATLANTIC BARGAIN, by Harlan Cleveland. New York, Harper and Row, 1970. 204 p.

[A] ". . . pragmatic political analysis of alliance management between the United States and its European allies."

NATO: TWO VIEWS, in *Army*, v. 25, no. 2 (February 1975) 10-19.

Alliance in Transition: Dispelling the Illusions, by Capt. George E. Dials. For the Central Region: Forward Defense Strategy, by M/Sgt. Dick Larsen.

NATO'S POLITICAL LIMITATIONS, by Lothar Ruhl, in *The Atlantic Community Quarterly*, v. 12, no. 4 (Winter 1974-1975) 463-469.

"NATO's subordination to the Governments of the fifteen Allied countries and its own dependence on their effective cooperation do not rule out a political function for the Alliance, in particular for the Secretary General, the Chairman of the Military Committee and the Supreme Allied Commander in Europe. However, they find it difficult to exercise this function."

NUCLEAR BALANCE IN EUROPE, by Walter F. Hahn, in *Foreign Affairs*, v. 50, no. 3 (April 1972) 501-516.

"Throughout its existence, the Atlantic Alliance has reflected a complex and dynamic process—a 'transatlantic bargain.' The former U.S. Ambassador to NATO, Harlan Cleveland, has described this 'bargain' as partly an understanding among the European members of the Alliance, but mostly a deal between them and the United States. NATO, he contends, is an arena of organized controversy. 'Each year the mix of NATO defense forces and the character of allied political collaboration change, adjusting to the shifting technology of war and to . . . the tides of domestic politics in each of the fifteen NATO countries. But while the bargain changes, the constant is a consensus among the allies that there has to be a bargain.' This notion helps explain how NATO has survived over the years of crises, both external and internal, that, measured by the historical yardstick of alliances, might long ago have ripped apart a less cohesive pact. Yet the optimism can be overdrawn. Beneath the periodically rough, periodically serene surface of the Alliance an undertow has steadily gained strength. The 'transatlantic bargain' is strained by 'transatlantic drift'—a growing divergence between the security interests and perceptions of the United States and those of its West European partners. Unless the Alliance soon addresses, and takes steps to redress, the basic causes of this drift, all of the temporary accommodations among the Alliance partners may finally fail to prevent an ultimate crisis of mutual confidence . . . Since NATO is first and foremost a security 'bargain,' we must look for fundamental causes of the drift not so much in external factors, but rather in fissures in the security consensus itself. A central cause has been the faltering faith of our European partners in what they have embraced as the pillar of their security: namely, the NATO strategic-nuclear deterrent . . . The imperative of effective leadership applies to NATO generally. The Alliance, as a unique and unprecedented enterprise in history, was created by enlightened and courageous leadership. It will take the same, if not greater, measures of imagination and boldness to chart a viable future."

REALITY OF A COMMON DEFENCE SYSTEM VALIDITY OF A JOINTLY-DEFINED POLICY, in *NATO Review*, v. 20, nos. 9-10 (September/October 1972) 7-11.

"In a speech made at Aix-la-Chapelle on 26 June, during a Seminar organized by the Atlantic Treaty Association (ATA), the Belgian Permanent Representative to NATO, Mr. André de Staercke, in response to a request by the Chairman of ATA, Sir Frank Roberts, expressed his views on what the governments of the Alliance expected from it and on the specific problems which could arise should a collective effort prove unavailing."

STATEMENT BY GENERAL L. L. LEMNITZER, GENERAL, U.S. ARMY (RET) FORMERLY COMMANDER-IN-CHIEF, U.S. EUROPEAN COMMAND SUPREME ALLIED COMMANDER EUROPE FROM 1963 to 1969, BEFORE THE COMMITTEE ON FOREIGN AFFAIRS, SUBCOMMITTEE ON EUROPE, 4 MARCH 1970. Washington, Department of the Army, 1970. 6 p. (Mimeo.)

General Lemnitzer, as a prelude to his major statement, discusses first why the NATO alliance was born. He appeared before the Committee "to discuss the relationship between U.S. military activities in NATO Europe and the security interests of the United States." He develops "the continuing and increased importance of NATO today."

(*)—STRATEGY FOR THE WEST: AMERICAN-ALLIED RELATIONS IN TRANSITION, ed. by Richard B. Foster and others. New York, Crane, Russak, 1974. 258 p.

"Thirteen papers from a colloquim held at Junales-Pins, France, in 1973, in which strategic analysts from six countries examine a wide range of strategic and politico-economic issues of current significance. Among these are the general implications of the developing American global strategy, specific interests and perspectives within Europe in the context of European-American-Soviet relations, and the impact of SALT and force reduction discussions on those relations. Contributors include Walter Laqueur, Johan J. Holst, Walter F. Han, Duilio S. Fanali and the editors."

TO CONSIDER NATO MATTERS. HEARING BEFORE THE JOINT COMMITTEE ON ATOMIC ENERGY, CONGRESS OF THE UNITED STATES, NINETY-THIRD CONGRESS, SECOND SESSION, FEBRUARY 19, 1974. Washington, Government Printing Office, 1975. 28 p.

A statement by General A. J. Goodpaster, U.S. Commander in Chief, Europe, on the problems in NATO, particularly in reference to nuclear energy. He also touches on burdensharing, MBFR, and SALT.

THE UNITED STATES AND EUROPE: PARTNERS IN A MULTIPOLAR WORLD?, in *Orbis*, v. 17, no. 1 (Spring 1973) 31-50.

"Today there is a new fluidity in relationships that contrasts sharply with the early 1960's. This is reflected in the increase in EEC membership, the growth of intra-European consultations on foreign policy and defense in such bodies as the Davignon Committee and the NATO Eurogroup, and efforts to evolve a new security relationship between NATO and the Warsaw Pact, as evidenced by preparations for the forthcoming Conference on Security and Cooperation in Europe (CSCE) and negotiations on Mutual and Balanced Force Reductions (MBFR). The Ostpolitik of the German Federal Republic reveals a new independence of policy in Bonn, together with a quest for security through bilateral diplomacy between the Federal Republic and the Soviet Union. At the same time, the enlargement of the European Community with the admission of Britain, Ireland and Denmark has raised hope of progress toward the harmonization of policies in other areas, notably defense and foreign affairs, if not necessarily the immediate development of formal institutions for political unity as optimistically envisaged in the Europe of the 1950's and even the early 1960's. Changes on both sides have affected the transatlantic relationship. Once viewed as axiomatic in American foreign policy, the assumption of an identity of interest between the United States and Europe has been questioned. The inability of the Europeans to achieve security via political unity has made the United States less willing to accept economic discrimination by the European Community. The deterioration of the U.S. trade position and the crisis of the dollar in the international monetary system have led Washington to view with deepening apprehension the emergence of an enlarged Economic Community as the world's largest trading bloc. This, in turn, has contributed to a rise of hostility in the United States to the idea of European unity itself and a questioning of the once presumed identity of interest."

THE WEU AND EUROPEAN DEFENSE CORPORATION, by Colin Gordon, in *Orbis*, v. 17, no. 1 (Spring 1973) 247-257.

"WEU [Western European Union] was established in 1955 after the ratification by the Federal Republic of Germany of the amended Brussels treaty. The original treaty, signed in 1948 by Britain, France and the Benelux countries, established a mutual defensive alliance of the traditional kind with one novel feature: it provided for peacetime joint planning and military collaboration. The following year it was virtually overtaken by the North Atlantic treaty, and with the activation of SHAPE by General Eisenhower at the beginning of 1951 the defense functions of the Brussels Treaty Organization were formally transferred to NATO, the Atlantic alliance now becoming a treaty organization . . . WEU is still worthy of serious consideration as the instrument for European defense rationalization and cooperation."

2. Europe, the United States, and the Alliance: Integration or Disintegration

AMERICA AND EUROPE IN THE 1970s: INTEGRATION OR DISINTEGRATION?, by Simon Serfaty, in *Orbis*, v. 17, no. 1 (Spring 1973) 95-109.

"Since 1949 it has been argued that the Atlantic Alliance is essential to the Western effort to deter the Soviet Union from, at worst, militarily invading Western Europe, and, at least, extending its influence to the point of totally excluding the United States from Europe. Concurrently, a secondary, and understandably less publicized, objective of the alliance has been that of containing Germany from within by serving as a safeguard against a revival of German militarism. Nations on both sides of the ocean had a stake in Atlantic cooperation. The case made in 1949 continues to be argued today: There can be no security for America if there is no security for Europe, because Europe's industrial base, population and institutions remain essential to the physical security and economic and spiritual health of America . . . It is time to cope with the realities of the 1970's and to encourage the evolution of new relationships, not because the old ones have failed, but because their very success has finally made it possible to discard them."

CREATIVITY TOGETHER OR IRRELEVANCE APART, by Henry A. Kissinger, in *The Atlantic Community Quarterly*, v. 11, no. 4 (Winter 1973-1974) 413-421.

"In his speech to the Pilgrims Secretary of State Kissinger analyzed the difficulties of 1973 and the possibilities of 1974 and beyond for Atlantic relationships. Our era of profound political, strategic, economic and psychological changes requires a revitalization of the relations between a unifying Europe and the U.S. Closer consultation, common vision and recognition of shared goals are essential to this wider 'special relationship.' Specifically, he proposed the creation of an Energy Action Group of Europe, North America and Japan to begin immediately formulating long-term cooperative measures."

ASPECTS OF THE NATO ALLIANCE. McLean, Va., Research Analysis Corp., November 1970. 102 p. (RAC-P-62.)

"This is a series of articles providing a perceptive view of NATO, Europe, and the US needs to respond to the challenge of change in the seventies. The common themes, in additon to the necessary linkage in the Atlantic world, are that security and defense reform and readjustments are possible and necessary. The compulsion to change was prompted by forces largely beyond single-power control, but the political-military decision makers can act to guide future US policy to continued success. Contains an extensive bibliography. Contents: America's 1969 option; A new role for NATO; Defense of the Atlantic community; Europe, the U.S., and NATO; NATO's role after Czechoslovakia; The Nixon era and NATO; Revival for NATO is needed now. Selected bibliography."

(*)—EUROPE AND AMERICA: THE NEXT TEN YEARS, by W. Randolph Burgess and James Robert Huntley. New York, Walker, 1970. 232 p.

"An examination of the urgent social, economic, political, diplomatic and strategic issues facing the Atlantic Community in the 1970's: revolt of the youth, environmental deterioration, scientific-technological-industrial gaps and challenges, trade and monetary relationships, restiveness of the Third World, East-West accommodation, defense and unification of Western Europe, and cohesiveness of the Atlantic Alliance."

PAROCHIALISM IN EUROPE; 'CREEPING GAULISM' IN AMERICA, by George Ball, in *Atlantic Community Quarterly* (Summer 1973) 161-170.

"The systems of political and economic cooperation between the US and Europe, which both have taken for granted since WW II, are now being questioned on both sides of the Atlantic, according to George Ball. For more than two decades, Europe has been able to concentrate on its internal affairs relieved of most of its colonial possessions and secure under the protection of America's nuclear umbrella. Out of this concentration on internal matters came the European Economic Community which has fostered unprecedented economic growth. As a result of their economic success, Ball says, Europeans have become blaseé about security (although most favor the continued presence of US troops on European soil) and so parochial that instead of assuming a world role commensurate with its resources, Europe now exerts little more than a regional influence. In its attitude toward the US, the former recognition of common interests has been replaced by a growing resentment . . ."

THE SECRETARY OF STATE PRESS CONFERENCE. MAJOR TOPICS: PRESIDENT'S TRIP TO EUROPE, NATO, MIDDLE EAST, MAY 24, 1975. Washington, Department of State, Bureau of Public Affairs, Office of Media Services, 24 May 1975. 8 p.

The basic purpose of the trip was to have an opportunity to exchange views with other leaders of NATO, to assess the current state of the alliance, to determine where the alliance should go in the period ahead, and to use this opportunity as well to discuss a number of special problems that have arisen.

B. Declaration of Atlantic Relations, 1974

THE ATLANTIC DECLARATION, by Ljubomir Radovanović, in *Review of International Affairs*, v. 25, nos. 584-585 (5-20 August 1974) 13-14 plus.

"With a delay of several months in their plans, the NATO Pact member-countries signed a new 'Atlantic Declaration' in Brussels on June 26, 1974, marking the 25th anniversary of the signing of the NATO itself (April 4, 1949). The 'Declaration' was initialled a week earlier in Ottawa, and was christened by the press as the 'Ottawa Declaration'. This is neither the first Atlantic Pact declaration nor the first to be signed in Ottawa. There have already been several special declarations, among which one in Ottawa, on given aspects of Atlantic policy, new measures in the practise of the Atlantic alliance, the regulation of cooperation in certain fields of allied relations. Even the substance of this Declaration offers nothing new, if we abstract it from the circumstances in which it emerged, for it reiterates what has already been included in the Pact itself, or in other NATO declarations and conclusions. The very fact, however, that it offers not a single new idea to distinguish it from those which have guided the NATO countries from the very beginning, at the peak of the cold war, despite the unquestionable and fundamental changes which have since occurred in international developments, makes this declaration, at the very least, a peculiar phenomenon. Its form is surprising given the present international situation in which different roads and methods of international agreements are used or expected than those which the psychosis of the cold war suggested to the big powers of this world. The impression is that this declaration is the result of American insistence which the West European members acquiesced to, but that it contains nothing new because agreement could not be reached on anything new."

DECLARATION OF ATLANTIC RELATIONS, 26 JUNE 1974, in *Survival*, v. 16, no. 5 (September/October 1974) 246-248.

"In April 1973 Henry A. Kissinger had called on America's Atlantic partners to work out a new Atlantic Charter that 'builds on the past without becoming its prisoner, deals with the problems our success has created, creates for the Atlantic nations a new relationship in whose progress Japan shares (full text in *Survival*, July/August 1973, pp. 188-192). After over a year of inter-alliance diplomacy the result falls somewhat short of these conceptual ambitions: it rather confirms existing commitments and practices than sets up a new relationship for the future. The 'Declaration of Atlantic Relations' is reprinted . . . [here]."

DECLARATION ON ATLANTIC RELATIONS APPROVED AND PUBLISHED BY THE NORTH ATLANTIC COUNCIL IN OTTAWA, 19 June 1974, in *NATO Review*, v. 22, no. 4 (1974) 6-8.

"The members of the North Atlantic Alliance declare that the Treaty signed 25 years ago to protect their freedom and independence has confirmed their common destiny. Under the shield of the Treaty, the Allies have maintained their security, permitting them to preserve the values which are the heritage of their civilization and enabling Western Europe to rebuild from its ruins and lay the foundations of its unity. The members of the Alliance reaffirm their conviction that the North Atlantic Treaty provides the indispensable basis for their security, thus making possible the pursuit of détente."

FINLANDIZATION IS NOT A CURSE WORD, by Anne Fried, in *Worldview*, v. 16, no. 1 (January 1973) 17-21.

"The story of one nation's determined pursuit of her own way in something short of the best of all possible worlds . . . In almost all the literature about the future of Europe, whether hopeful or doom-laden, it is assumed that a Europe of real independence or of genuine partnership with other nations is not possible. Europe, we are told, can only be shaped by the struggle between the two superpowers. More particularly, wherever the U.S. withdraws we can be sure the USSR will move in, thus creating the unhappy situation which the international press has come to describe as Finlandization. But what does Finlandization mean? What, really, does it have to do with Finland? Anyone familiar with Finnish character and political history suspects that talk about Finlandization reflects either a gross misunderstanding of a country's determination to maintain independence, neutrality and, if possible, peace in Europe, or deliberate anti-Soviet propaganda. Such propaganda is common abroad as well as in certain political circles in Finland. To answer a slogan with a slogan, one may challenge talk about Finlandization with the title of the first chapter of Max Jakobson's book 'Finnish Neutrality: The Rebellious Pawn.' . . . While Finlandization seems to Russia a dangerous example, it serves as a desirable model to East European states. To a Western diplomat I questioned about it, Finlandization, incorrectly used, implied a process of progressive deterioration in the degree of independence and autonomous choice exercised by Finland due to Soviet pressure. Correct use of the word would underscore the great strides Finland has made in the field of constructive neutrality, within the structure of the northern balance."

NATO: BACK TO OLD POSITIONS, by V. Matveyev, in *International Affairs, Moscow*, no. 9 (September 1974) 102-105.

"The Declaration on Atlantic Relations adopted in Ottawa by the Foreign Ministers of the NATO countries on June 19, 1974, and signed a week later in Brussels during a meeting of NATO heads of state and government is intended to serve, as its text shows, as a political guideline for the North Atlantic Treaty Organisation in the today's conditions. According to Britain's The Guardian, the new Atlantic Declaration has been drawn up with the aim of convincing the world that NATO still has significance and meaning in the era of détente. This is not an easy assignment. More than a year has passed since the United States first came up with the idea of drawing up and signing a declaration—an idea which immediately triggered off mixed reaction in West European capitals. It proved difficult to word even this document, which does not touch on the thorniest and most vital aspects of relations between the NATO countries. Many Western observers consider that the Declaration skirts round the intractable economic and political problems. Commenting on the Declaration in this vein, The Washington Post even claims that it is essentially devoid of any content. Even though the Declaration may, in fact, avoid the acute problems of the mutual relations between the Atlantic allies, one can hardly agree with the above-mentioned claim. An examination of the document permits certain conclusions to be drawn about the main directions of NATO activity in today's conditions and concerning the main political line pursued by the bloc's leaders."

NORTH ATLANTIC COUNCIL MINISTERIAL MEETING ADOPTS DECLARATION ON ATLANTIC RELATIONS, in *The Department of State Bulletin*, v. 71, no. 1828 (8 July 1974) 37-44.

"The North Atlantic Council held its regular ministerial meeting at Ottawa on June 18-19 . . . [Included] is the transcript of a news conference held by Secretary Kissinger after the meeting, together with the texts of a final communique issued at the close of the meeting and the Declaration on Atlantic Relations adopted by the ministerial meeting on June 19."

PRESIDENT NIXON VISITS NATO HEADQUARTERS AND THE SOVIET UNION, in *The Department of State Bulletin*, v. 71, no. 1831 (29 July 1974) 165-173.

"President Nixon left Washington on June 25 for a visit to Belgium and the Soviet Union. While in Brussels June 25-27, he met with NATO heads of government and signed the Declaration on Atlantic Relations."

C. NATO As a Deterrent Force for Peace: Pro and Con

ABOLISH NATO!—BUT THEN WHAT?, in *NATO's Fifteen Nations*, v. 15, no. 1 (February-March 1970) 80-86.

"An 'Anti-NATO Congress' was held in Amsterdam at the end of November organized by Left-Wing Youth Organizations from NATO states. About 1,500 participated, the most vociferous of them being from Africa, Portugal and Greece. It ended with a peaceful march which was almost a model of its kind, with those responsible calling on the marchers 'not to provoke the police and not to let themselves be provoked by the police.' Believing that even an opposition movement to NATO is worth taking notice of, an experienced British author was asked by this magazine to find out just what it was all about, to discover what Europe's young people really think about NATO, and to see what arguments against its existence are being formulated. It was not the intention to answer each of the anti-NATO arguments; rather, it was felt both fair and useful to evaluate the ideas of these members of the coming generation and see just what they would bring forward as a substitute for NATO and the work it is doing."

ADDRESS BY GENERAL L. L. LEMNITZER, U.S. ARMY (RET) AT THE LUNCHEON MEETING OF THE ROTARY CLUB OF BROOKLYN, HOTEL ST. GEORGE, BROOKLYN, NEW YORK, WEDNESDAY, 17 APRIL 1974. Washington, Department of the Army, 1974. 10 p. (Mimeo.)

This address by General Lemnitzer is part of his recent lecturing and public speaking engagements as "part of a personal effort to assist in setting the record straight and emphasizing the vital importance of our national security generally, and NATO specifically."

CAN LINE BE HELD AGAINST COMMUNISTS IN WEST EUROPE?, in *U.S. News & World Report*, v. 78, no. 22 (2 June 1975) 24-25.

"While Communism has spread in other parts of the world, it has been kept from moving into Western Europe and NATO . . . is credited with helping prevent any advance."

DETENTE AND NATO; NOW AND THE FUTURE, by Gen. A. J. Goodpaster, in *Vital*

Speeches of the Day, v. 40, no. 1 (15 October 1973) 24–27.

Delivered at the Washington Institute of Foreign Affairs, Washington, D.C., September 26, 1973. "The first point I want to emphasize in talking with you about the Alliance . . . how tremendously successful NATO has been . . . I would be the first to agree that we cannot attribute this historic achievement solely to NATO's military strength. We cannot replay history to determine for sure what would have happened without NATO. Nevertheless the twenty-eight years of peace, progress, and prosperity in Europe contrast sharply with the wars and threats of war which have plagued Southeast Asia, South Asia and the Middle East during this period. But this unparalleled record of success has brought with it new challenges, new problems, and new dangers. Let me discuss a few of these with you briefly this afternoon . . . I would like to say a few words on the subject of cost—the burden of maintaining these American forces in Europe—and on burden-sharing in general. As you know this is a complicated subject with many ramifications. Reduced to its simplest form, however, is essentially an argument that the US is making a greater effort than its NATO Allies—is doing more than its fair share in providing for the common defense."

DETERRENCE IN NATO—THE ROLE OF THE MILITARY COMMITTEE, by Maj. Frank A. Partlow, Jr., in *Military Review*, v. 54, no. 12 (December 1974) 3–8.

"NATO and deterrence are practically synonymous since the alliance has never been called upon to fight in its defense, and since it has not yielded one inch of alliance territory during its 25-year history, its ability to deter a potential aggressor is a proven fact. The purpose of this article is to analyze deterrence and relate the NATO Military Committee (MC) to its continued operation."

DO WE STILL NEED NATO?, in *Army in Europe*, (March 1973) 4–6.

"From the outset the Atlantic Alliance has been motivated by common purpose—collective defense to deter aggression and preserve peace. In the beginning, back in 1949, the fear of possible further Soviet expansion westwards led the free nations of Western Europe to seek alliance with North America and Canada to provide for a system of collective defense. Since then NATO has successfully provided security in Western Europe for over 20 years. The Alliance has guaranteed and maintained the integrity of NATO territory, thus creating a climate of stability and confidence in which member countries have been able to regain their economic strength. But, in the past, the threat was more evident than it is today. Is NATO still necessary or has it outlived its purpose? Through NATO the member countries have created a stable military and political balance between East and West. They see this balance as an indispensable condition for peace and an insurance against the risks of another World War. Should this balance be upset the dangers of tension and conflict could again arise."

NATO; A SUCCESSFUL PRODUCT OF POLITICAL-MILITARY ENGINEERING, by Gen. A. J. Goodpaster, in *Vital Speeches of the Day*, v. 40, no. 13 (15 April 1974) 389–393.

Speech delivered before the Central Florida Section, American Institute of Aeronautics and Astronautics, Orlando, Florida, February 25, 1974.—"I want to discuss with you a successful product of what might be called 'political-military engineering', the North Atlantic Treaty Organization . . . Not one NATO nation has found itself forced to yield to military or political pressures from the East. And ancient enmities that bred two devastating world wars have given way to consultation, cooperation and collective security . . . But this unparalled record of success has brought with it new challenges and new problems. This situation is, of course, no surprise to an engineer. Few, if any, products designed in 1951 do not encounter problems in the changed situation of 1974. Let me touch briefly on the most important of the changes as they relate to the military security situation."

THE NATO ALLIANCE: THE BASIS FOR AN ERA OF NEGOTIATION, by Kenneth Rush, in *The Department of State Bulletin*, v.68, no. 1773 (18 June 1973) 867–871.

"The central element of continuity in our relations with Europe is the Atlantic alliance. The existing institution which embodies this alliance is NATO. We are determined that 1973 will see not an erosion of this alliance and this institution, but rather their strengthening and adaptation to meet current realities. We are embarked upon a far-reaching re-orientation of our entire postwar foreign policy. We are seeking to lower the burden of our international responsibilities and military balance and increasing the stability of that balance. NATO is an essential element of this evolving global policy. Looking to the future we perceive two major roles for NATO. First, in this era of negotiations between East and West, NATO is assuming a role of 'détente management.' Once considered primarily a military alliance designed to control East-West tensions, NATO must increasingly assume the responsibility for reducing these tensions. Without attracting a great deal of attention, the alliance has already come a long way in this direction. NATO is playing a central role in the formulation of Western positions for both of this year's major multilateral negotiations with the East—the talks on mutual and balanced force reductions (MBFR) and the Conference on Security and Cooperation in Europe (CSCE)."

(LI)—NATO IN A WORLD OF DÉTENTE, by Maj. Leslie W. Stewart, Jr. Maxwell AFB, Air Command and Staff College, 1974. 40 p. (Research Study.)

"The military future of the North Atlantic Treaty Organization has been increasingly questioned in the current era of détente. Political moves by the United States and the Soviet Union, aimed at relaxing international tensions, have led many observers to the conclusion that NATO serves no useful military purpose. This study analyzes the arguments of NATO's critics, and points out the fallacies inherent in them. The paper concludes that NATO will continue to serve a military purpose in the foreseeable future, détente notwithstanding."

POLITICO-ECONOMIC WORLD DEVELOPMENTS AS THEY AFFECT NATO NATIONS IN THE 1970's, by Walt W. Rostow, in *Naval War College Review*, v. 23, no. 8 (April 1971) 4–13.

"Two underlying forces that are at work on the world scene are the diffusion of power away from Moscow and Washington and the decline of the aggressive revolutionary romantics. With an understanding of these forces the existing dangers that confront mankind must be probed seriously, with confidence and caution. The role of NATO and its member nations should be more internationalistic in both perspective and commitment to the building of a stable world order."

SHOULD NATO WORRY ABOUT THE SCRAMBLE FOR AFRICA?, by A. H. Murray, in *NATO's Fifteen Nations*, v. 17, no. 2 (April–May 1972) 16–22.

A "picture of the penetration of Russian and Chinese influence and Communism in Africa. When combining Professor Murray's picture with the events in North Africa and the Middle East, as well as with the shift of maritime power in the Indian and South Atlantic Oceans and the Mediterranean Sea, the countries of the Western World will have a solid foundation for considering the question of whether the NATO in its present shape will still be able to safeguard the security of its member-countries and preserve the way of life and freedom of its peoples."

D. The Past and the Future: An Assessment and a Forecast

(*)—THE ATLANTIC ALLIES AND THE FUTURE OF EUROPE. Paris, Atlantic Treaty Association, 1973. 40 p.

"For the third consecutive year, the Atlantic Treaty Association—composed of national voluntary organizations from all member countries of the Alliance and Malta—has published extensive extracts from speeches given at its annual spring Seminar. The first booklet appeared in 1970 under the title 'The Soviets in the Mediterranean'; the second, 'The Soviets and Northern Europe' was produced the following year. Now we have, 'The Atlantic Allies and the Future of Europe', which presents the main arguments advanced during the Aachen Seminar of 1972. The speakers to be included in this study are former NATO Secretary General Manlio Brosio who discussed Europe and the Atlantic Alliance Today; Dr. Schiffers, of the Federal German Ministry of Defence (Atlantic Economy and Security); Mr. André de Staercke, Belgium's Permanent Representative to NATO (the Effort of Defence and the Hope of Détente); Mr. Maurice Deshors, Counsellor at the French Embassy in Bonn (The French Position on European Security Problems); and General Bennecke, Commander-in-Chief of Allied Forces Central Europe (The Defence of NATO's Central Region). In addition, there is an annex on 'The Warsaw Pact Threat' based on a briefing which General Bennecke had given at his AFCENT Headquarters in Brunssum, The Netherlands."

ATLANTIC RELATIONS: PERSPECTIVES TOWARDS THE FUTURE, by Eugene V. Rostow, in *NATO Review*, v. 21, no. 2 (1973) 7–10.

"The central problem of the NATO allies in planning the future of Atlantic relations is both intellectual and emotional: to achieve a common appraisal of what security requires, now, and for the next decade or so; and then to convince public opinion that the appraisal is correct, and should be accepted, emotionally and politically, as the major premise for policy."

CAN NATO MEND ITS FENCES—AND DEFENSES?, by Gen. T. R. Milton, in *Air Force Magazine*, v. 57, no. 10 (October 1974) 49.

"This next year will be perhaps a decisive one for the great experiment in mutual security. Maybe the strains will be too much, in which case we are all on our own. But maybe not. The Cyprus affair brought out a certain evidence of the importance the thinking people of the West attach to this alliance. My guess is that NATO has a good long run ahead of it."

(*)—CRISIS IN EUROPEAN DEFENCE: THE NEXT TEN YEARS, by Geoffrey Lee Williams and Alan Lee Williams. London, Charles Knight, 1974. 334 p.

"Twin brothers—one a former M.P. who was parliamentary private secretary to Denis Healey at the Ministry of Defence, the other an academic interested in defense questions—discuss a wide range of issues. The 'crisis' is the possibility of U.S. withdrawal and the uncertainty as to what the European political-military response should be."

EUROPE IN THE '70S: STABILITY AND CONFLICTS, by Pierre Hassner, *Revue de défense nationale*, (May 1970) 723-736.

"The direction of the European situation in the 1970s is difficult to predict now because of the presence of such opposing tendencies as bipolarity and polycentrism, hostility and cooperation, stability and turmoil. Although Europe remains divided by a balance between two alliances dominated by the two superpowers, cooperation is continuing between the countries of eastern and western Europe; and while interstate conditions seem to be stabilizing, intrastate conditions are characterized by pressure for social and political change. Because of these opposing tendencies in Europe, four types of conflict can be envisaged for Europe during the 1970s, in ascending order of probability: (1) a military attack by one alliance upon the other; (2) a conflict resulting from the non-conformity of a smaller power with agreements sanctioned by the two cooperating superpowers; (3) after a breakdown of the alliances, conflicts between countries over questions of national interest; and (4) conflicts resulting from possibly radical social and political changes within countries. Europe is thus entering an uncertain period where internal conditions of the involved countries, as well as the attitudes of the two superpowers, will probably change . . ."

(*)—THE FUTURE OF NATO, by Andrew J. Goodpaster, in *Armies and Weapons (Switzerland)*, (15 January 1975).

"All NATO countries are currently faced with the economic impact of inflation and of a growing scarcity of essential resources. These factors are steadily driving up the cost of maintaining our force levels. We have tried to offset the limited numbers of our manpower and equipment with a high level of qualitative effectiveness, reflected, for example, in modern aircraft, anti-tank weapons and anti-air missiles, but this process also is becoming ever more expensive. We see frequent tendencies to bow to the temptation to rationalize away the threat, to give way to economic pressures, and cut back the support of military programmes. But that cannot be the correct answer. The first element of the right answer to this problem of costs was provided by General Eisenhower, who predicted that 'the cost of peace is going to be a sacrifice, a very great sacrifice individually and nationally. But total war is a tragedy; it is probably the suicide of civilization.' . . . The future of NATO is a challenge to every member nation, and in some ways a harder challenge than ever before. There are severe economic problems to be overcome; there is a need for vigilance in recognizing the dangers that continue to inhere in the world situation; there is a requirement for greater cooperation than ever before. To meet these challenges, those who lead and support NATO need to take the initiative in several specific areas."

THE FUTURE OF NATO, by Morris Janowitz, in *Survival*, (December 1971) 412-415.

". . . Should the question of reducing US forces in Europe become an issue in the 1972 presidential campaign, a disruption of normal US foreign policy might occur in Europe . . . the US should continue its efforts toward mutual force reductions in Europe, but . . . it must also make a firm commitment of a minimal force for the next five to ten years to provide its NATO allies with the political security necessary to deal with the Warsaw Pact countries. Open discussion of this question by all presidential candidates should do much to clear the air and dispel any undesirable effect that might tend to increase tensions with the Russians . . . European leaders look at our troop commitments not merely as force levels, but as indicators of emerging political trends in the US. Assuming a successful mutual force reduction conference does take place, a long-term commitment of 150,000 US troops for all of Western Europe would still be required . . . Furthermore, Janowitz suggests not only a hot line between the two pact headquarters, but also that a joint liaison office staffed by members of both forces be established in a neutral country, such as Switzerland; increased communications would reduce the threat of accidental war and help implement surveillance arrangements deemed necessary on both sides."

NATO—AN ANALYSIS OF ITS PRIORITIES, in *Defense and Foreign Affairs Digest*, v. 3, no. 2 (February 1975) 7-12.

"The North Atlantic Treaty Organization, meanwhile, has recently weathered its 25th year, has matured and evolved, and yet sits precariously on the precipitous whim of a public base which has not developed its consciousness. The success of NATO in holding war in abeyance has been the very sonorous theme which lulled its base of support—the European and North American taxpayer—into optimistic and naive susceptibilities. They may be asleep when the critical decisions are called for. But if the summer has stretched through autumn in the West, and drugged its subjects into winter hibernation, then the chills of energy crises, of prowlers at their doors and the bickering of bedpartners may have sparked the first signs of an awakening. There are harbingers of spring in the promise of common sense in NATO decision-making. The hibernation may be ending."

NATO AND EUROPEAN SECURITY: PROSPECTS FOR THE 1970'S, by Robert L. Pfaltzgraff, Jr., in *Orbis*, v. 15, no. 1 (Spring 1971) 154-177.

"For the next several years the United States, with its own domestic and foreign policy problems, will face a Western Europe that is uncertain about its future. The United States seeks a 'lower profile' in foreign affairs; the Europeans strive to minimize their involvement in regions outside Europe and to maintain military capabilities only at a level necessary for deterring a seemingly remote Soviet attack. Whether or not the Atlantic Alliance can survive a prolonged period of negotiations with the power against which it was designed is problematical. But the essential prerequisite for the success of the Nixon Doctrine, applied to Europe, is a recognition of its logical implications for European security, namely, that Western Europe must undertake a phased development of capabilities under European control commensurate with whatever arrangement emerges from the thickening web of East-West security negotiations. Two major trends in international politics can be expected to heighten the urgency of steps toward the Europeanization of Western Europe's defense. The first is the evolving strategic balance between the United States and the Soviet Union; the second is the anticipated reduction in the U.S. defense commitment to Europe and other regions symbolized by the Nixon Doctrine, and the contemplated withdrawal of U.S. troops. Organizational problems, as well as timing and phasing, make a shift of a portion of the U.S. defense burden to Europe formidable, but this is the requirement if a military balance adequate to European security is to be maintained in a period of declining U.S. commitment to, and interest in, foreign policy."

(LI)—NATO IN THE 1970'S: A PROGNOSIS, by Col. Raymond H. Ottoman. Maxwell AFB, Ala., Air War College, 1970. 95 p. (Professional Study no. 3975.)

"This study begins with a broad statement of NATO's position in European affairs in 1960 and then presents an explanation of the purpose, provisions and accomplishments of the Alliance. Some of the international political-military developments and trends of the 1960's that have occurred in selected NATO countries are examined and discussed. The pressures and interplay of strategy changes as well as some of the problems of nuclear weapons control are discussed in some detail. In the process, evidence is presented to support the author's contention that NATO may become altered in structure and appearance by the end of the 1970's."

NATO LOOKS AHEAD, by Patrick Wall, in *Defence*, v. 5, no. 3 (March 1974) 98-99 plus.

"After 25 years of existence NATO now has to face up to some fundamental problems both as regards control, organisation and posture. The solution to these problems will raise great political and military controversy which will not be made easier as it comes at a time when détente is a very acceptable policy as far as the general public of the NATO nations is concerned. The importance and urgency of finding an acceptable solution to these problems was emphasized in the papers presented to the 19th meeting of the North Atlantic Assembly at Ankara in October last year . . .

The Report raised fundamental issues such as the potential instability in Central Europe, the pressures inside NATO and between Europe and the USA. It asked questions about economic policy, burden sharing and the escalating cost of both men and materials, and it made far reaching proposals as to the future cohesion of the Alliance in the fields of policy, administration and economics, as well as that of military strategy. These suggestions had a preliminary hearing in the Assembly's various committees whose task it will be this year to consider them in depth. Having achieved its aims of setting various guidelines to the Assembly as a whole the Committee of Nine has been disbanded, leaving a challenge to all NATO nations and their governments."

(LI)—NATO: THEN AND NOW, by Maj. Jerry T. Bailey. Maxwell AFB, Ala., Air Command and Staff College, 1974. 65 p.

"The subject of the North Atlantic Treaty Organization has been much discussed since its founding in 1949. There have always been those for and those against NATO. From historical viewpoint and from the perspective of the impact of the Yom Kippur war on the Alliance, this study looks at both the pros and cons of this organization. It examines the Warsaw Pact forces and discusses NATO in relation to this threat. Some thoughts and alternatives on the future of the Alliance are offered. It concluded that unless the Soviets change their policy, the need for NATO will continue to exist."

THE PROSPECTS FOR NATO, by I. H. J. Gilmour, in *NATO's Fifteen Nations,* v. 19, no. 1 (February-March 1974) 22-25.

"A revolutionary and constructive experiment in international relations. That was how the signature of the North Atlantic Treaty in Washington on 4th April 1949 was described by NATO's distinguished first Secretary General. Now, 25 years and several crises later, a skeptical public is asking to see the results. The discomfiture of NATO over the recent Middle East crisis was obvious to all, and will not be easily forgotten. No realistic assessment of the prospects for NATO can ignore this sombre background, just as it cannot disregard the real successes of the past quarter century . . . We must recognize, therefore, that NATO has experienced, and will continue to experience, within the framework of a common overall objective, many major changes—some of them alterations in principle, others a shift in emphasis. Yet we should not lose sight either of the threads of continuity which run through NATO's history."

WHERE DOES THE ATLANTIC ALLIANCE STAND TODAY?, by Andre de Staercke, in *The Atlantic Community Quarterly*, v. 11, no. 4 (Winter 1973-1974) 448-455.

"'In a period of reduction of tension, external policy, as far as public opinion is concerned, is more and more identified with relations between adversaries and less and less with relations between friends.' With this quote in mind, Andre de Staercke examines what is happening inside the Atlantic Alliance—an Alliance which 'has led its partners to a freedom from danger and even to the ability of freeing them from the Alliance itself'."

WILL NATO SURVIVE DÉTENTE?, by Manlio Brosio, in *The Atlantic Community Quarterly*, v. 9, no. 2 (Summer 1971) 143-155.

"In this . . . article, the Secretary General of NATO, Mr. Manlio Brosio, discusses the intriguing question of whether NATO, and in what form, will survive the changes of the years. On balance, Mr. Brosio, while denying any affinity for crystal ball activities, sees a continuing necessity for close relations between Western Europe and North America, and believes the future will include either this organization or one more federal in character that has grown out of it."

E. Proposals for Greater Security

A BALTIC SQUADRON FOR NATO?, by Edward Wegener, in *U.S. Naval Institute Proceedings* (January 1974) 63-70.

"The question of NATO's need for a Baltic Squadron, says Adm. Wegener, is complex. The Baltic is an internal sea, connected with the ocean only by way of the Danish straits and Kiel Canal. The canal has little strategic importance, since it is closed by ice for about six months each year. While under NATO control, Denmark and Schleswig-Holstein, the territories dominating the Straits, constitute a key naval strategic position by preventing the Soviet Union's Baltic Fleet from passing the Baltic Approaches. If Russia should control the Straits, says Wegener, either by occupying Denmark or by integrating it into the Soviet power sphere, its Baltic fleet could then unite with its Northern Fleet to take action in the North or Arctic Seas or in the Atlantic, putting NATO naval forces at a 'disastrous' disadvantage. Furthermore, Soviet control of the Straits could adversely affect overall strategy, particularly with regard to defense of southern Norway, the NATO front in Central Europe along the Iron Curtain which would be outflanked from the North, and Sweden, which would be cut off from the open seas. Wegener is confident that amphibious operations will play a decisive wartime role in the Baltic. The amphibious potential of the Warsaw Pact countries in the area is threatening, he notes, but NATO general forces capable of repelling such amphibious landings are sadly lacking. Thus, any defense against amphibious attack will depend almost entirely upon NATO naval forces; and only the meager navies of Denmark and the Federal Republic of Germany—both of which are inferior to Communist bloc sea and air forces—are available to fill the role, with no provision for NATO reinforcements. An indication of the quantitative balance of forces, obtained from the ratio of naval personnel, says Wegener, stands at approximately 1:6, with the Eastern side possessing additional advantages in their higher quality of materiel and training levels. In light of these unfavorable circumstances, formation of a Baltic Squadron to strengthen NATO naval forces in case of war appears highly desirable..."

EUROPE AND AMERICA: A CRITICAL PHASE, by Carl Kaiser, in *Foreign Affairs*, v. 52, no. 4 (July 1974) 725-741.

"The Atlantic world has had internal crises and tensions before: the rejection of the European Defense Community by the French National Assembly in 1954, the French departure from the military organization of NATO, de Gaulle's veto of British membership in the European Community, France's boycott of the Community institutions, the controversy over the Multilateral Nuclear Force (MLF) and U.S. unilateralism under Secretary of the Treasury John Connally in 1971. But the present crisis is more fundamental since it appears to threaten the essence, indeed the survival, of cooperation both within Europe and in the Atlantic world. At the heart of the matter is the growing inability of governments and countries which are linked together by basic interests and which share a number of problems crucial to their future to approach and solve them in common. As a result, the following achievements are at stake: the search for an Atlantic structure in which the United States and Canada, on the one side, and the unifying European Community on the other, cooperate on a variety of problems including global ones; the further development if not survival of West European integration; the Western economy as the motor of the world economy, based on liberal rules of the market; the acceptance of mutual dependence and of the need for cooperative management of existing problems; the survival of democracy, at least in West European countries; a joint security policy backed by the presence of the United States in Europe; and a continuation of détente between a stable Atlantic world and the Communist bloc."

NATO IN A TIME OF CRISIS, by Brig. Gen. Richard C. Bowman, in *Air Force Magazine*, v. 58, no. 4 (April 1975) 49-54.

"The author examines the interrelated crises that confront NATO, assesses the balance of forces in Europe, and discusses what must be done to preserve the viability of NATO in a time of crisis."

NATO MILITARY POLICY: THE CONSTRAINTS IMPOSED BY AN INAPPROPRIATE MILITARY STRUCTURE, by S. L. Canby. Santa Monica, Calif., Rand Corp., February 1972. 13 p. (P-4783.)

"Discussion of the thesis that the NATO force, particularly its U.S. component, is inappropriately structured and unnecessarily expensive. Though NATO's declaratory objectives stress defense and deterrence, its force structure is attuned to offense and protracted war. Remedies include (1) concentrating conventional defense preparations in the critical center region, (2) accepting the greater likelihood of a short war as a basic operating assumption, (3) restructuring the force to emphasize defense (more anti-tank weapons, prepositioned supplies) and short-term warfighting capability (more use of local logistical resources), and (4) changing the current practice of replacing wartime losses with individuals to a policy of unit replacement. Besides making the force more appropriate to its mission, the proposed measures would substantially reduce costs."

(LI)—NATO: OUR ESSENTIAL BUT TROUBLED ALLIANCE, by Donald J. Tuttle. Maxwell AFB, Ala., Air War College, 1974. 14 p. (Professional Study.)

"The need for certain constants or 'institutional anchors' takes on added importance in today's fluid international situation. NATO constitutes one of these vital anchors. The author stresses that NATO remains a crucial underpinning of Western security and a vital part of the basic security system upon which a stable détente with the East must be founded. Détente is viewed as tentative and fragile, and, in order to minimize the security risks, a framework for continued cohesion must remain intact between ourselves and our Western European partners. The best, well-tested framework is NATO. Finally, the article offers some suggestions for improving and strengthening the alliance both in order to deter aggression and to provide more credible fighting capabilities should détente go away and war occur."

A NEW ATLANTIC CHARTER, by Henry A. Kissinger, in *The Atlantic Community Quarterly*, v. 11, no. 2 (Summer 1973) 151-160.

"What the Administration means by the phrase, 'The Year of Europe.' ... The United States proposes to its Atlantic partners that, by the time the President travels to Europe toward the end of the year, we will have worked out a new Atlantic Charter setting the goals for the future—a blueprint that: Builds on the past without becoming its prisoner. Deals with the problems our success has created. Creates for the Atlantic nations a new relationship in whose progress Japan should share."

NEW CHALLENGES, NEW PROBLEMS, NEW DANGERS, by Andrew J. Goodpaster, in *The Atlantic Community Quarterly*, v. 10, no. 4 (Winter 1972-1973) 457-469.

"General Goodpaster, Supreme Allied Commander Europe, draws the balance of the challenges and opportunities posed by NATO. He points to the difficulties of arriving at a successful MBFR arrangement, yet does not draw back from the attempt. He describes the recent increases in Soviet military and especially naval strength, but also emphasizes increased contributions to NATO's potential from both sides of the Atlantic. Finally, he presents a list of proposals for improvements in coordination and cooperation which would contribute significantly to increasing NATO's strength."

(*)—THE SECURITY OF WESTERN EUROPE: TOWARDS A COMMON DEFENCE POLICY, by Bernard Burrows and Christopher Irwin. London, Charles Knight, 1972. 180 p.

"A ... study by a former British ambassador to NATO and the Deputy Director of the U.K. Federal Trust. The authors believe in the need for greater defense coordination because of the East-West negotiations on security and the evolution of the Common Market, and call for the eventual establishment of a European Defense Agency."

TREATING NATO's SELF-INFLICTED WOUND, by R. W. Komer. Santa Monica, Calif., Rand Corp., October 1973, 16 p. (P-5092).

"The advent of nuclear parity makes conventional deterrence and defense much more important than before. Yet inflated manpower and weapon costs risk pricing them out of the market. When America's allies, and increasingly the U.S. itself, shrink from fielding a credible conventional defense, they are victims of a pervasive myth that effective nonnuclear defense against a Warsaw Pact attack is impossible, at least without massive military outlays. But the myth of inevitable Pact superiority is largely a self-inflicted wound. NATO's inferiority springs from its own failure to optimize its defense posture. The solution presented is to restructure NATO's existing force posture, freeing up needed resources by cutting back on marginal activities, emphasizing tradeoffs rather than ad-ons, and reallocating existing budgets rather than buying more forces." (See also under same title in Military Review, v. 54, no. 8 (August 1974) 53-63; and in Foreign Policy, no. 13 (Winter 1973-74) 38-48.)

F. Tensions in the Alliance; The Troubled Partnership

1. *Miscellaneous Aspects*

ALLIANCE POLITICS, by Richard E. Neustadt. New York, Columbia University Press, 1970. 167 p.

"This is one of the most illuminating books on crisis politics in NATO so far written. The author deals with Anglo-American relations during the Suez crisis and with the Skybolt Affair. A ... conclusion rounds out ... [the] book."

THE ATLANTIC DEFENSE RELATIONSHIP: CORE, TROUBLES, PROSPECTS, by H. Mendershausen. Santa Monica, Calif., Rand Corp., July 1974. 9 p. (P-5262).

"The Atlantic Alliance is viewed as having a sound core and a persistent malaise. The sound core consists of the common need to create a steady military counterweight to Soviet power. The malaise results from the unresolvable conflict between the unity requirements of the security bond and the political separateness of the states it is supposed to hold together. The conflict has run along several fissure lines, some geographic, some functional. The resulting irritating issues have eroded the core of the alliance and made it vulnerable. But since what ails the alliance is not so much international but domestic malfunctions, the author points out what appears to be a necessary condition for its survival; states must solve their domestic problems. Failure of the liberal order in the Western countries today threatens their security more fundamentally than do their differences over diplomacy, alliance strategy, and national defense efforts."

EUROPE AND THE ATLANTIC ALLIANCE, by Richard M. Nixon, in *The Atlantic Community Quarterly*, v. 11, no. 3 (Fall 1973) 293-313.

"In his latest foreign policy report to Congress, President Nixon states that the alliance between the U.S. and Western Europe has been a fundamental factor in the postwar era but that recent changes in this relationship present both challenges and opportunities for the nations of the Atlantic region."

EUROPE COOL TO U.S. SUGGESTIONS ON REVITALIZED CHARTER, by Curt Gosteyger, in *The Atlantic Community Quarterly*, v. 11, no. 3 (Fall 1973) 319-321.

"Many Europeans feel that U.S. proposals for an overall review of the troubled Atlantic connection to represent a bear hug in which Europe would come off worst. Given Western Europe's military vulnerability, the negative response of many Europeans to U.S. proposals for a comprehensive review of Atlantic relations is both shortsighted and fraught with danger."

NATO: ALLIANCE IN DISARRAY, by William E. Griffith, in *Reader's Digest*, v. 105, no. 628 (August 1974) 56-60.

"The North Atlantic Treaty Organization, that long-flourishing alliance between the United States and Western Europe, has fallen into disarray, and its effectiveness as a shield against Soviet expansionism has been seriously weakened. Never since NATO was founded—and this year marks its 25th anniversary—has Russia had such an opportunity to eventually bring all or much of Western Europe under its political and economic dominance, and without firing a shot. The Atlantic alliance has been coming apart at a dismaying pace . . . What has happened to bring this once-vigorous alliance to such a state—from which only the U.S.S.R. stands to profit?"

NATO AND THE YEAR OF EUROPE, by Michael Howard, in *Survival*, v. 16, no. 1 (January/February 1974) 21-27.

"President Nixon's statement that 1973 was to be 'the Year of Europe', and Dr. Kissinger's appeal for 'A new Atlantic Charter', aroused, on this side of the Atlantic, public comment that was almost uniformly unfavourable and diplomatic reactions no more than polite. This negative reaction was understandable but wrong. In fact the affairs of Europe, both East and West, are now genuinely entering a phase so critical that they call for the same kind of imaginative powers of decision as were needed in the immediate aftermath of the last war."

NATO NEEDS A FRESH BREEZE, by Robert Ball, in *Fortune*, v. 89, no. 2 (February 1974) 104-109 plus.

"The much-touted 'Year of Europe' brought a new low-water mark in transatlantic relations. Europe's refusal to line up with the U.S. in supporting Israel in the October war caused the most serious internal crisis NATO has ever faced. The reexamination of the purpose of this troubled partnership is now urgent business. The U.S. has received more than its money's worth out of the Atlantic Alliance, but Henry Kissinger's view of it as 'a shared organ for diplomacy' on a global scale must now be reconciled with Europe's narrower view of it as a regional security pact. This will require agreement on what Kissinger has called 'a permissible range of divergence' in policies. The most successful re-definition of the transatlantic relationship might evolve by joint efforts to reach specific objectives—for example, getting better value for the defense dollar, assuring continued growth of world trade, and promoting adequate supplies of energy and raw materials."

RIFT AMONG FRIENDS, REFLECTION ABOUT FOES; A DOGFIGHT IN THE ATLANTIC ALLIANCE, in *Time*, v. 102, no. 20 (12 November 1973) 64 plus.

"Like an earthquake, the fighting in the Middle East has sent tremors round the world and caused diplomatic seismographs to quiver in Washington and Moscow—and most of the capitals in between. Old alliances have been shaken, and new accommodations have proved less durable than they were advertised to be. In the following stories TIME examines the impact of the war on an old alliance, the NATO pact, and on a new understanding, the Soviet-American détente."

STRATEGY DRIFT IN THE ATLANTIC, by John W. Tuthill, in *The Atlantic Community Quarterly*, v. 9, no. 2 (Summer 1971) 156-173.

"A former U.S. Ambassador to OECD, currently Director General of the Atlantic Institute, examines the realities underlying the principal political and economic problems of the Atlantic Community as well as the dangers in seeking narrow solutions. He suggests a means of moving towards an adequate political framework."

2. *NATO's Problems of Cooperation and Consultation*

CONSULTATION AND THE ATLANTIC ALLIANCE, by Manlio Brosio, in *The Atlantic Community Quarterly*, v. 12, no. 3 (Fall 1974) 308-318.

"Drawing upon his vast experience, Manlio Brosio analyzes the difficulty and ambiguity, the delusions and the miseries of consultation. All of this does not prevent him from attempting to outline some future prospects in a positive, realistic sense."

CONSULTATION AND THE ATLANTIC ALLIANCE, by Manlio Brosio, in *Survival*, v. 16, no. 3, (May/June 1974) 115-121.

"There are periodic discussions about consultation within the Atlantic Alliance—especially in moments of crisis, when it is regretted that consultation has not worked. The first serious episode of this sort occurred in 1956, after the Suez War." The Limits of Consultation; The Instruments of Consultation; Substance and Range of Consultation; Lack of Political Will."

DISENCHANTMENT BETWEEN EUROPE AND AMERICA, by Carl A. Erhardt, in *Aussen Politik*, (Winter 1973) 377-392.

"The 'Atlantic Partnership,' a term coined by President Kennedy, referred to the eventual worldwide tariff reductions agreed to by the U.S. and the European Economic Community (EEC) in 1968. When Britain was admitted to the Community in 1973, goals were set to unify commercial, economic and monetary systems as well as to set up free trade zones. The idea of an Atlantic Partnership has changed considerably since 1968. Erhardt feels that Pres. Nixon's suspension of the convertibility of the dollar in 1971, in addition to his ten percent import levy, were very significant factors in the deterioration of U.S.-European relations. Europe was extremely sensitive about being uninformed and felt the U.S. had, without consulting anyone, disregarded the rules of the world currency system in deference to its own interests. By the end of that year, the Smithsonian Agreement had been reached among ten countries; it set up new guidelines for the most important currencies and devalued the dollar for the first time since 1934 . . . The October crisis in the Middle East represented another kind of crisis in U.S.-European relations. Europe felt that the U.S. actions in the Middle East could have involved its NATO allies in the conflict, yet they were not consulted beforehand. Erhardt believes this 'crisis of confidence,' resulting from the U.S. failure to keep Europe informed, breeds a further lack of understanding. In his view, the Middle East crisis indicated that the American attempt to maintain 'singular' interests on both sides of the Atlantic is, in fact, an 'unnatural' goal."

NATO POLITICAL CONSULTATION: FACT OR MYTH?, by Richard Neff, in *NATO Review*, v. 23, no. 1 (January 1975) 7-9.

"Within two months after NATO Heads of Government met in Burssels last June to sign a 'Declaration on Atlantic Relations,' two of those governments—Greece and Turkey—came near to war over Cyprus. Paragraph 11 of the Declaration had stipulated that all member governments 'are firmly resolved to keep each other fully informed and to strengthen the practice of frank and timely consultations by all means which may be appropriate on matters relating to their common interests as members of the Alliance . . .'. Despite this resolve, intra-Alliance consultation broke down within a matter of weeks as a result of the Cyprus dispute. Does this mean that the Declaration was a mere piece of paper, worthless in time of stress? Not at all, in the view of NATO officials. They allow that allied governments, by signing the Declaration, did undertake a commitment to consult among themselves and that, in fact, Greece and Turkey did not do so in the Cyprus case. Nevertheless, 'the renewed political will' that emerged in the rest of the Alliance as a result of the Declaration was undoubtedly one reason why the other allies consulted as well as they did about the dispute and why they were successful in cooling it at least to some degree."

NUCLEAR CONSULTATION PROCESSES IN NATO, by Thomas C. Wiegele, in *Orbis*, v. 16, no. 2 (Summer 1972) 462-487.

"This article represents an attempt to examine the processes by means of which allies in the North Atlantic Treaty Organization consult with each other on nuclear matters of common concern. After considering the idea of consultation both generally and in the alliance from the perspective of small group theory, it will explore the mechanisms that have been utilized by the alliance to discuss and formulate nuclear policies. Within this context, it will make an assessment concerning the effectiveness of the nuclear consultative processes."

U.S.A.-WESTERN EUROPE: A "NEW RELATIONSHIP," by Y. Davydov, in *International Affairs*, Moscow, no. 1 (1974) 35-41.

"The recent flaring-up of the military conflict in the Middle East resulted in an aggravation of U.S.-West European relations. Moreover, to a certain extent, it brought to light two contradictory tendencies in the approach toward U.S.-West European ties on both sides of the Atlantic. In the obtaining world political situation, Washington treated its West European allies in such a manner as if it still retained its indisputable hegemony over them, not so much expressing as determining their interests. Without consulting its NATO partners, and even without warning them, the U.S. Government, intending to intimidate the world with its inexorable position, placed its troops on the alert, including the troops in Europe. The U.S. support of the aggressive policies of Israel, and its desire to use the NATO system for these purposes led to the exacerbation of the 'energy crisis' in the capitalist world, which affected Western Europe, receiving 80 per cent of oil from the Middle East, much more than its ally on the other side of the Atlantic getting 10 per cent of the required oil from that area . . . The exacerbation of contradictions between Washington and West European capitals did not come out of the blue skies. Since the late 1960s, the relationship between the U.S.A. and Western Europe was becoming increasingly complicated. In 1973, the developments reached the point when the President of the U.S.A. deemed it necessary to postpone his autumn visits to a number of West European capitals, although the year of 1973 was announced by Washington as the 'year of Europe,' the year when the basis for 'new relations' between the U.S.A. and its partners was to be elaborated."

3. *NATO, The Middle East Crisis (1973), and Oil *(See also V-T)*

AMERICA, EUROPE, AND THE MIDDLE EAST, by Eugene V. Rostow, in *Commentary*, v. 57, no. 2 (February 1974) 40-55.

"The crisis in Atlantic relations revealed by the October war was more serious than the other crises in the history of the alliance—more serious even than Suez, traumatic as that was—because the struggle in the Middle East manifests a major and continuing Soviet threat to the security of Europe, which the allies did not face together, and are still not facing together. Unlike the war in Indochina, and a number of other issues on which the allies have differed in recent years, the long conflict over Israel's right to exist has become not only a difficult regional problem, but, in the American government's opinion, an important tool in the Soviet Union's effort to outflank NATO, divide Europe from America, and neutralize Western Europe. In Europe, however, this view of Middle Eastern affairs was often put aside or questioned. For the most part, the European governments preferred to consider the Arab-Israeli conflict almost entirely as a regional quarrel, perceived in terms of old controversies about the rightness or wrongness of a hundred disputed episodes since the days of Balfour, Truman, and Dulles. The divisions among the allies over the October war were not simply the consequence of faulty intelligence, and insufficient consultation. They were occasioned by deeper causes, less available to the poultices of diplomacy. They were not brought about by the latest round of the Middle East war. On the contrary, the latest round of the Middle East war was brought about by divisions in the alliance which have existed for a long time, but have only now become generally visible."

EFFECTS OF THE MIDDLE EAST WAR AND THE ENERGY CRISIS ON THE FUTURE OF THE ATLANTIC ALLIANCE. PROCEEDINGS, NATIONAL SECURITY AFFAIRS CONFERENCE, JULY 1974 PANEL VII. Washington, National War College, February 1975.

The Warsaw Pact—NATO Security Balance; The Role of the U.S. in NATO; Political and Economic Effects of the Middle East War; A New Level of Cooperation in NATO.

THE IMPACT OF THE MIDDLE EAST CRISIS ON THE ATLANTIC ALLIANCE, in *The Department of State Bulletin*, v. 70, no. 1812 (18 March 1974) 279-284.

"Statements by Arthur A. Hartman, Assistant Secretary for European Affairs and Rodger P. Davies, Deputy Assistant Secretary for Near Eastern and South Asian Affairs, made before a joint hearing of the Subcommittee on Europe and the Subcommittee on the Near East and South Asia of the House Committee on Foreign Affairs on February 19."

THE LEGITIMATE CLAIMS OF NATIONAL SECURITY, by Maxwell D. Taylor, in *Foreign Affairs*, v. 52, no. 3 (April 1974) 577-594.

"I have advanced certain proposals for a military establishment which could defend before the public the legitimacy of its claims for national support. It would comprise a strategic retaliatory force of finite size and maximum deterrent effectiveness; general-purpose forces stressing readiness for minor conflicts but with only a delayed capability for major war; and Reserve forces with their mission, size and structure adjusted to the other changes proposed. The total force would be supported in funds and manpower under broad guidelines expressed in terms of an annual percentage of the gross national product and of a manpower ceiling stated as a fixed figure or established by the number of acceptable volunteers . . . On the international front, the oil situation will be an even greater disaster to our NATO allies, Japan, and many developing countries caught in the power play of the oil producers. Without prompt relief, the plight of the European and Japanese economies may bring about runaway inflation and a global recession which could easily involve us. A military consequence would be a further decline in the effectiveness of the NATO alliance and an added reason, the shortage of oil, to doubt the capability of NATO for prolonged self-defense."

THE LESSONS FOR NATO OF RECENT MILITARY EXPERIENCE, by Elmo R. Zumwalt, in *The Atlantic Community Quarterly*, v. 12, no. 4 (Winter 1974-1975) 448-462.

"The former Chief of Naval Operations, Admiral Zumwalt, finds many pertinent lessons in what was learned from the recent Middle East War. The most fundamental, however, is not purely military in its application. This is that in this interdependent world one cannot separate military from political and, increasingly, economic considerations."

(LI)—MIDDLE EAST OIL: ACHILLE'S HEEL OF NATO, by Maj. Joe F. Coughran. Maxwell AFB, Ala., Air Command and Staff College, 1974. 63 p. (Research Study.)

"The United States' support of Israel in the October 1973 Arab-Israeli war in the Middle East triggered unprecedented oil price increases, production cutbacks, and embargoes against nations friendly to the Israelis. Long standing relationships between the oil producing nations and the international oil companies underwent fundamental changes and the West's dependence on Arab oil was clearly shown. This study discusses these events and changes and emphasizes their importance to the United States and its allies in Western Europe. Consideration is also given to the Soviet Union's role in the Middle East and its ability to influence the policies of Arab governments."

(LI)—USAF POSTURE IN EUROPE AFTER THE YOM KIPPUR WAR OF 1973, by Maj. John F. Fiddler. Maxwell AFB, Ala., Air Command and Staff College, 1974. 48 p. (Research Study.)

"The Middle-East crisis of 1973 was cause for international concern due to the resultant involvement of the Soviet Union and the United States. This created what some considered the most dangerous moment effecting world peace since 1945. This study traces the growing Soviet influence in the Middle-East from 1956 to 1973, and stresses the importance of rapid mobility in the event of a Soviet conventional probing action. The differing perceptions of the United States NATO allies are analyzed in order to determine a viable USAF posture in Europe for the next decade."

THE YEAR OF EUROPE?, in *Foreign Affairs*, (January 1974) 237-248.

". . . In the case of the Middle East, . . . it is understandable that those countries whose economies are almost completely dependent on the continued flow of Middle East oil have to place their own national interests above those of the U.S. or Israel. To the U.S. this may seem disloyal and undignified, but the Europeans' overriding national interests left them no choice. At the same time, America's concern with maintaining a balance in the Middle East, and its military 'alert' in response to a Russian threat, are also understandable, though it is not suprising that the failure to brief Europeans left them 'apprehensive.' The point is, it should have been possible for Europeans and Americans alike to understand each other's position and, at the very least, to avoid 'public recriminations' . . . Ironically, the European Community is being criticized, . . . for achieving a degree of consensus on a political issue—something the U.S. has been urging on the European nations in the interests of greater cohesiveness . . . One important lesson is that alliances 'cannot stand still' lest they dissolve under the pressures of changing conditions. Although the threat which gave birth to the Atlantic Alliance seems less urgent in the present atmosphere of détente, the Alliance remains a necessary condition of stability in Europe and an 'essential element' of a safe international system. But it must change to accommodate new realities as Europe becomes more politically unified, with a stronger voice in international affairs. To the U.S., this means an end to the kind of unquestioned leadership it exercised for two decades; the time has come when both partners should be equal, sharing the mutual advantages to be derived from the Alliance . . . American participation in the Alliance is vital to Europe, for nothing can replace the U.S. nuclear umbrella and the presence of American troops as guarantees of European security . . ."

4. *British-Icelandic Fishing Disputes: Implications for NATO*

BRITISH-ICELANDIC CONFLICT, by B. Svetlov, in *New Times (Moscow)*, no. 22 (June 1973) 24.

"NATO circles are again in a flurry. This time on account of the sharp deterioration of relations between Iceland and Britain, both of them members of the Atlantic bloc. The old fishing dispute, which has come to be known as the 'cod war,' has grown into a grave political conflict. Many Western observers agree with UPI correspondent Joseph W. Grigg that this conflict 'has faced the North Atlantic Treaty Organization with a major crisis.' . . . The significance of what is taking place off the Icelandic coast transcends the bounds of the dispute over the fishing rights. The sharp conflict on the northern flank of NATO testifies to deep contradictions within this bloc in which the 'equal partnership' NATO propaganda is prone to eulogize exists only on paper. The events in the North Atlantic are convincing world public opinion once again that this is so."

THE BRITISH OCCUPATION OF ICELAND, 1940–1946, by Donald Bittner, in *The Army Quarterly and Defence Journal*, v. 103, no. 1 (October 1972) 81–90.

"One of the least known incidents of World War II is the Allied occupation of Iceland. This occurred in two phases, the first the period of the British occupation from 10th May, 1940, to 22nd April, 1942, and then the American occupation which lasted from 22nd April, 1942, to 7th October, 1946, although the last American forces were not withdrawn from the island until April, 1947. The importance of Iceland lies in its location in the North Atlantic. Situated along the great circle route from Halifax to Scotland, whoever controls Iceland dominates the shortest and most direct convoy routes to Europe from the western hemisphere. This basic fact explains the island's importance to the Western Allies in World War II. For the British, engaged in a life and death struggle with Germany, with long supply lines stretching all over the globe and especially to North America, and for over a year standing alone against victorious Germany, Iceland assumed an even more important role than it had in previous wars. Iceland presented two basic problems to British military planners during World War II."

ICELAND—A COD SUMMIT, in *The Economist*, v. 249, no. 6789 (6 October 1973) 40 plus.

"Iceland and Ireland have, it seems, even more in common than a similarity in name and a recurring tendency to be at loggerheads with their neighbour island, Britain. The Prime Minister's unprecedented visit to Dublin on September 17th was nicely timed to divert interest from those menacing Liberals' party conference. And on Wednesday Mr. Heath was on the front pages again, sharing attention with the Harold Wilson show at the Labour party conference, thanks to his dramatic personal intervention in the cod war. Statesmanship or datesmanship? . . . The year-long dispute has cost both sides dear; against Iceland's loss of British markets and of the benefits of its EEC agreement may be balanced the cost to Britain of maintaining the watching presence of tugs and frigates. And before Iceland broke off negotiations in May the British, who had been taking around 200,000 tons of fish a year from the disputed waters, were offering to limit their annual catch to 145,000 tons. Iceland offered only 117,000; but in the first year of the conflict it saw the British trawlers take, despite all, the 170,000 tons to which they would have been limited by the International Court's interim ruling and left them undisturbed . . . More immediate external pressure for a settlement has been applied from another direction. It has been no coincidence that NATO's secretary-general, Mr. Joseph Luns, visited Iceland on September 17th, talked with Mr. Heath at Chequers last Sunday, and reported next day to an emergency meeting of the NATO council."

ICELANDERS AND THE SEA, by Unnstein Stefánsson, in *The UNESCO Courier*, (February 1974) 26–30.

"Few nations are so dependent on the bounties of the ocean for their economic prosperity . . . Fishing is Iceland's principal industry employing one sixth of the nation's labour force and accounting for over 80 per cent of total exports . . . The rich fishing grounds around Iceland have long been a favourite haunt of the fishing fleets of various foreign nations. The continuous intensification of the fishing has resulted in a severe reduction of the fish stocks. The death rate of some species has reached dangerous levels. This is particularly true of cod, where the mortality is at least 70 per cent and the proportion of small fish in the catch is rising rapidly. Thus a point had been reached some time ago where it was clear that the stocks were seriously overfished and the productivity of the seas around Iceland gravely endangered. On September 1, 1972 the Icelandic Government and the Althing (Parliament) decided to extend the Icelandic fisheries jurisdiction to 50 miles. This decision has not been accepted by all nations and has been the cause of some tensions and disputes with certain European fishing nations."

WHERE A "COD WAR" IS THREAT TO NATO, in *U.S. News & World Report*, v. 74, no. 24 (11 June 1973) 33.

"Iceland is a small island country steering a collision course toward some big nations—including the U.S. The major issues are these: Iceland is threatening to kick American forces out of a strategic air base in Kwflavik—a base used by the North Atlantic Treaty Organization (NATO) to keep watch on Russian movements in key shipping routes of the North Atlantic Ocean. There is growing concern that Iceland may even decide to pull entirely out of membership in NATO. Although smaller in size than South Carolina, with a population—210,000—barely bigger than that of Des Moines, Ia., and with no armed forces of its own, Iceland is considered a valuable link in the NATO defense line simply because of its strategic location. Also heating up is a battle between Iceland and Great Britain that is known as the 'cod war.' This is a dispute over fishing rights—but it threatens to involve Iceland's role in NATO."

5. *Problems of Cyprus: Implications for NATO*

CYPRUS, NATO AND THE GREEK FUTURE, by P. Lambropoulos, in *The Nation*, v. 219, no. 9 (28 September 1974) 267-269.

"Only a few years ago, anyone who advocated abandoning NATO would have aroused deep suspicions among large segments of the Greek people. Today, Karamanlis is becoming a national hero by withdrawing the Greek armed forces from that organization. The apparent reason for this shift of public opinion, at least as given in the American press, is said to be the Cyprus crisis. However that is not quite the whole story as one hears it in Greece from the people and the press. The flavor is also different in most of the European press. The change we witness today had been occurring over the past several years and its origins should be kept in mind if one is interested in understanding present and future developments in Greece."

CYPRUS—1974. HEARINGS BEFORE THE COMMITTEE ON FOREIGN AFFAIRS AND ITS SUBCOMMITTEE ON EUROPE, HOUSE OF REPRESENTATIVES, NINETY-THIRD CONGRESS, SECOND SESSION, AUGUST 19 AND 20, 1974. Washington, Government Printing Office, 1974. 85 p.

Not only does this hearing document the Cyprus crisis but it shows how the crisis provided a unique test for both the United States and the NATO Alliance to which both Greece and Turkey belong.

CYPRUS—SEPARATION: A SENSE OF BETRAYAL, in *Time*, v. 105, no. 8 (24 February 1975) 32-33.

The formation of a separate federal state in the Turkish-occupied northern sector and what it portends. According to this report, the "Greek-Cypriot sense of betrayal could hardly have been deeper."

GREECE AND TURKEY: SOME MILITARY IMPLICATIONS RELATED TO NATO AND THE MIDDLE EAST. PREPARED FOR THE SPECIAL SUBCOMMITTEE ON INVESTIGATIONS, OF THE COMMITTEE ON FOREIGN AFFAIRS, BY THE CONGRESSIONAL RESEARCH SERVICE, LIBRARY OF CONGRESS. Washington, Government Printing Office, 1975. 63 p. (94th Congress, 1st Session, Committee Print.)

---

*For Middle East Problems see also DA PAM 550-16, Middle East: The Strategic Hub and North Africa, 1973.

CHAPTER III

NATO'S INTEGRATED STRUCTURE: FUNCTIONS AND ACTIVITIES OF SOME OF ITS COMPONENTS
(See Also Appendixes)

A. Miscellaneous Aspects

LOOKING FOR A COMMON DEFENCE POLICY, in *NATO's Fifteen Nations*, v. 17, no. 5 (October-November 1972) 12-14 plus.

"Emphasis is also given [in Great Britain] to the necessity of preserving the existing NATO military command structure through which NATO's rather weak commitment should be made explicit, while the stringent defence commitment of the Western European Union should also be maintained."

NATO'S SILENT SERVICE, by Rear Adm. R. W. van Lynden, in *NATO Review*, v. 22, no. 5 (October 1974) 25-29.

"NATO infrastructure in principle comprises fixed installations (with certain exceptions) in support of the operation of NATO military forces in accordance with their wartime deployment and tasks which result from the NATO approved strategic concept. It supplements nationally built infrastructure installations, in particular in those cases where military forces other than the host country's are required to operate from the latter's territory and in cases where NATO as a whole is the user."

B. ACE Mobile Force (Land) (AMF (L))

THE ACE MOBILE FORCE (LAND) TODAY; A FORCE FOR TOMORROW, by Maj. Gen. J. Grover, in *NATO's Fifteen Nations*, v. 18, no.5 (October-November 1973) 69-76.

"During the late 1950's the Western Powers re-considered their appreciation of the Communist threat to NATO Europe. The policy of massive retaliation was one which might, in the case of a local threat, have severely limited the options open to the Allies in managing the crisis. Consequently a policy of 'flexible response' was adopted by the Allies, which ensured a graduated reaction to any confrontation. Of particular concern, then as now, were the more remote areas of NATO Europe; Northern Norway, Denmark, Greece, Turkey and Northern Italy, where there are common frontiers or waterways with Russia or her satellite states and where NATO forces are not strongly represented. The aggressor might have been tempted to mount a surprise, limited scale attack upon one of these flank countries before the major NATO defence forces could be adequately deployed. It was therefore felt that within the concept of flexible or graduated response, a multinational force was required which could be rapidly deployed to one of these flank countries during a period of tension and which would, by its composition and presence, make clear to any actual or potential aggressor that an attack against one member of the NATO Alliance would constitute an attack against all of the member countries. This force would demonstrate the unity of purpose upon which NATO is based, and the presence of soldiers from the many different member nations would cause the aggressor to think again. In March 1960, General Lauris Norstad, then Supreme Allied Commander Europe, announced the proposed formation of a small, strategically mobile, multinational task force."

AMF THE ACE MOBILE FORCE (LAND), by Maj. Keith C. Buchanan, in *NATO's Fifteen Nations*, v. 15, no. 1 (February-March 1970) 49-56.

"The ACE Mobile Force (Land) is an important example of the NATO deterrent. An international, conventional military force ready to move at short notice, it is a small but invaluable part of Allied Command Europe (ACE). Normally referred to as AMF(L), the force comes directly under the Supreme Allied Commander Europe (SACEUR) General Andrew J. Goodpaster of the United States Army . . . The force itself does not exist in one geographical location; the units are drawn from seven nations of NATO. These are

Belgium, Canada, Germany, Italy, Luxembourg, the United Kingdom and the United States."

C. Advisory Group for Aerospace Research and Development (AGARD)

AGARD (ADVISORY GROUP FOR AEROSPACE RESEARCH AND DEVELOPMENT), in *NATO's Fifteen Nations,* v. 17, no. 6 (December 1972–January 1973) 39–44 plus.

Contents: The Early Days, by F. L. Wattendorf; Today, by M. I. Yarymovych; The Twentieth Anniversary, by Patrick Greene. "AGARD, the Advisory Group for Aerospace Research and Development, has completed twenty fruitful years in serving NATO. It has proved to be a successful pioneering experiment in scientific and technical cooperation among the NATO nations, and has shown remarkable adaptation to changing times. Its role as catalyst stems directly from the conceptual vision of its unique founder, Dr. Theodor van Karman who, without doubt, was the leading international aerospace scientist of his generation. Therefore, in celebrating the Twentieth Anniversary of AGARD, and in planning for the future, it is of interest to recall the origin and early accomplishments of AGARD from the broad conceptual viewpoint of its distinguished founder. It is of special interest to NATO to show how AGARD ad hoc activities put the spotlight on needs within NATO which were subsequently filled by the establishment of important NATO organizational groups."

D. Allied Forces Central Europe (AAFCE)

CINCENT'S RESPONSIBILITIES FOR THE ACE MOBILE FORCE, by Col. Norman L. Dodd, in *NATO's Fifteen Nations,* v. 15, no. 3 (June–July 1970) 60–67.

"'The Commander-in-Chief Allied Forces Central Europe (CINCENT), General Juergen Bennecke, German Army, is responsible both for the co-ordination of the movement of the AMF to and from its deployment location and of its logistical resupply arrangements.' . . . Part of the strength of the North Atlantic Alliance is the amount of constructive work that is done by cooperation and co-ordination between the fifteen sovereign Nations. Not by compulsion, not by order, but by willing and helpful co-operation. The way in which the elements of the AMF are moved to a sparsely populated area of North Norway from such far away places as Calgary in Western Canada and Cameri in Italy, and their logistical resupply on arrival, are striking examples of this co-operation and of the flexibility of the Alliance."

A LOOK AT A NEW COMMAND IN THE CENTRAL REGION, in *NATO's Fifteen Nations,* v. 19, no. 6 (December 1974–January 1975) 58–64.

"It was in June 1974 that the NATO Military Committee authorized the establishment of a new NATO Headquarters in the Central Region of Europe. The new headquarters, called Allied Air Forces Central Europe, or AAFCE, is commanded by a United States Air Force four-star General and is directly responsible to Headquarters Allied Forces Central Europe (AFCENT). The manpower for the new headquarters is provided by six Alliance nations—Belgium, Canada, The Federal Republic of Germany, The Netherlands, The United Kingdom, and The United States. The establishment of HQAAFCE does not represent an increase in the total number of personnel assigned to the Central Region; it does, however, represent a reorganization and realignment of the manpower and resources previously located in HQAFCENT and the two tactical air forces—Second Allied Tactical Air Force with its Headquarters at Rheindahlen, and Fourth Allied Tactical Air Force with its headquarters at Ramstein."

NATO RESHAPING TACTICAL AIR POSTURE, by Laurence Doty, in *Aviation Week & Space Technology,* v. 102, no. 9 (3 March 1975) 12–13.

"Recent switch in military tactics of the Soviet Union from a basically defensive to a highly mobile offensive posture has prompted the unification of the two tactical air forces in central Europe into a single command under the North Atlantic Treaty Organization. The newly formed unit, designated Allied Air Forces Central Europe (AAFCE), is under command of U.S. Gen. John W. Vogt, who also commands the U.S. Air Forces in Europe (USAFE). Both organizations are headquartered at the air base here. The latest Soviet development on the Warsaw Pact borders has turned USAFE to the McDonnell Douglas air-superiority F-15 as the most effective deterrent to the revised Russian tactical stance."

E. Allied Air Forces Southern Europe (AIR SOUTH)

AIR SUPERIORITY IN THE SOUTHERN REGION, in *NATO's Fifteen Nations,* v. 18, no. 4 (August–September 1973) 50–52 plus.

"Today the responsibility for Allied air superiority in the Mediterranean area is primarily entrusted to Allied Air Forces Southern Europe

(AIRSOUTH). The air forces of Greece, Italy, Turkey, the United Kingdom and the United States are bolstered by additional help from the other NATO members' air forces and strong naval aviation in the Mediterranean. AIRSOUTH works in close coordination with AFSOUTH's other principal subordinate commands, LANDSOUTH, STRIKFORSOUTH, LANDSOUTH-EAST and NAVSOUTH, and contributes the major air element required for overall defense of the Southern Region."

F. Allied Command Atlantic (ACLANT)

ACLANT MOBILE LOGISTICS A REQUIREMENT FOR STANDARDIZATION, by Rear Adm. Robert W. Timbrell, in *NATO's Fifteen Nations*, v. 17, no. 1 (February-March 1972) 82–84 plus.

"There has also been some international cooperation in particular areas of the logistic field and interest shown in the results of NATO standardization activities. Included within these standardization activities is work concerned with replenishment at sea, a function of mobile logistics. Against this background of increasing interest in logistic affairs, it may be opportune to take a look at the present system of mobile logistics within [Canadian Atlantic Sub-Area] ACLANT. As agreed by NATO nations, logistics is a national responsibility and so it follows that thirteen separate systems exist within NATO."

ALLIED COMMAND ATLANTIC, by Adm. Robert Lee Dennison, in *NATO's Fifteen Nations*, v. 17, no. 1 (February-March 1972) 16–19.

"The idea of a North Atlantic security pact developed from recognition on both sides of the Atlantic that the security of the Western World was indeed indivisible. The United Nations had not fulfilled its promise to provide adequate guarantees of world peace and security . . . Then, as now, the principal mission of the Allied Command Atlantic was to ensure that the Atlantic remains a bond and not a barrier. This means our control of the seas and denial of their use by any enemy . . . Navies, unlike armies and air forces, operate under a cloak of invisibility so far as the general public is concerned. There could be considerable disruption of seaborne traffic without any overt move against NATO territories. The only deterrent against conquest is sufficient force to face it and the will to use such force when, where and if necessary."

THE ALLIED COMMAND ATLANTIC—SUBMARINE CHALLENGE, by Comdr. J. O. Naugle, in *NATO's Fifteen Nations*, v. 17, no. 1 (February-March 1972) 62–68.

"The Soviet Union has in recent years developed the capability to interdict NATO sea lanes of communications and challenge the organization's use of ocean areas vital to its security. This expanding military potential has come from many sources over the years but most recently it has appeared in the form of ships. . . . The Naval Forces of NATO must stand ready to counter the Soviet Bloc threat which is rapidly growing in size and capability. The Allied Command Atlantic (ACLANT) area, generally considered as the ocean area North of the Tropic of Cancer, is where this challenge has most recently been thrust forward, and where it must be met. To do this, a balanced mix of forces, submarine, surface and air is needed. Over the past twenty years an effective organization has been structured to make maximum effective use of these forces. Commander Submarines Allied Command Atlantic (COMSUB ACLANT) enjoys an unusual position in this organization. COMSUBACLANT is one of five major subordinate commanders to the supreme Allied Commander Atlantic (SACLANT). The position is held by Commander Submarine Force, U.S. Atlantic Fleet (COMSUBLANT). This command is a functional command."

G. Allied Command Channel (ACCHAN)

THE CHANNEL COMMAND, in *NATO's Fifteen Nations*, v. 18, no. 3 (June-July 1973) 22–48.

"Although the Command is the smallest of the three NATO Commands, it has an importance out of all proportion to its size, situated as it is on the axis of the shipping routes to North-West Europe, and to NATO North-West Europe in particular. Through Channel Command's waters must pass all the seaborne needs of the area and, in the unhappy event of war, the supplies so urgently needed for the support of SACEUR. This daily traffic places squarely in Channel Command's area the greatest density of merchant shipping in NATO and, indeed, in the whole world. The problems of a maritime command are markedly different from those of a land equivalent . . . Contents: Foreword, by Adm. Edward Ashmore; ACCHAN Command Structure, by Comdr. J. D. Atkinson; Channel Command—The Operational Forces, by John Marriott; Strategic Problems of Channel Command, by Rear Adm. J. H. Adams."

H. Allied Command Europe (ACE)

AIR ARM OF THE ALLIANCE, by Gen.

Andrew J. Goodpaster, in *NATO Review*, v. 19, nos. 9-10 (September/October 1971) 3-6.

"The air forces which form the third essential element of the Allied Command Europe (ACE) military team. The task of ACE Air Forces is to gain and maintain a favorable air situation throughout ACE airspace—over land and sea—and to perform other essential missions including reconnaissance, interdiction, close air support for surface forces, and the maintenance of a credible strike posture. However, prior to addressing the air element itself, a brief review of the objectives of the Alliance, which NATO's military instrument is charged to serve, is in order."

REMARKS AT THE NATO DEFENSE COLLEGE, ROME, ITALY, 13 JULY 1973, by Gen. A. J. Goodpaster, in *NATO's Fifteen Nations*, v. 18, no.6 (December 1973-January 1974) 24-29.

"In my lecture today on Allied Command Europe, I plan to cover only three points: the past, the present, and the future . . . For this discussion I shall take as my point of departure the broad security objectives of the Command and of the Alliance."

I. Allied Forces Northern Europe (AFNORTH)

AFNORTH — NATO'S ASSAILABLE FLANK?, by Maj. John F. Meehan, in *Military Review*, v. 55, no. 1 (January 1975) 3-10.

"The attention of the Western World is now focused on events in Central Europe where, for the first time in a decade, the possibility of dramatic changes in the status quo seems to be a probability. SALT II, the European security conference and the Mutual Balanced Force Reductions talks are the center of Western speculation. Much concern is expressed for the vitality of NATO under various scenarios that can be postulated as a result of these events. Ironically, a far greater threat to NATO's cohesion and survival may be found in a situation that has existed in its present form since NATO's founding. NATO's northern flank, under the command of Allied Forces, Northern Europe (AFNORTH), is responsible for the defense of strategic areas key to any East-West confrontation, yet the command does not have the necessary military resources to make credible its defense of these areas. The North Cape of Norway and the exits of the Baltic Sea are absolutely vital to NATO control of the Atlantic and continued North American access to Europe. The defense of these strategic areas is the responsibility of AFNORTH."

J. British Army of the Rhine (BAOR)

BAOR AND NATO, by John Garnett, in *International Affairs*, (October 1970) 670-680.

"Because it is impossible to predict the nature of any European military conflict, doctrinal difficulties surround the role of ground troops in Europe. Faced with this dilemma, the British government has been hard put to define the function of the British Army Of The Rhine (BAOR) in NATO. Its present deployment in Germany is an uneasy compromise between a small mobile force capable of controlling minor frontier disputes, and a large army capable of fighting a major war in Europe . . . In spite of this uncertainty, British forces do play a major role in the overall context of European and NATO politics. Since the end of WW II, Britain has had armed forces on the continent of Europe, primarily in West Germany and Berlin. The physical presence of these British troops in Europe has had the advantage of increasing British influence in European affairs in general and in NATO affairs in particular. It has also fulfilled the function of appearing to limit the power of Western Germany, some of whose nearest allies remain a little nervous. The major political significance of the British role, however, relates to the fact that the security of Western Europe depends upon the presence of a large number of troops in Europe. The presence of BAOR indicates to Britain's allies, and to the U.S. in particular, its continuing willingness to play a substantial role in the ground defense of Europe, and, by example, to encourage others to do likewise . . . As NATO moved between the doctrines of conventional warfare, tactical nuclear warfare, massive retaliation, and flexible response, the British military correspondingly changed . . . [BAOR's] emphasis . . ."

K. Central Army Group (CENTAG)

CENTAG SOUTHERN GERMANY'S DEFENDER, by Lt. Col. Wolfgang R. Gebel, in *NATO's Fifteen Nations*, v. 19, no. 5 (October-November 1974) 54-60.

"Fourteen years ago a group of German, French and American soldiers walked into an aging German Kaserne in Mannheim-Seckenheim and began functioning as a single, integrated headquarters named Central Army Group (CENTAG). Since that time many changes have affected the military and political structures of the NATO members. Those changes that have been witnessed by CENTAG include the build-up of the German Army, the Bundeswehr, to a strong and viable member of the Alliance; the withdrawal of France from the military structure of NATO—and thereby from CENTAG; and the relocation of the Canadians into the CENTAG area, thus reorganizing Central Army Group as a tri-national headquarters. The opposing line-up of Warsaw Pact forces across the Eastern border steadily strengthened during this period, gradually developing into a numerically superior force in the Central European Region. However, CENTAG's missions and responsibilities have remained essentially the same."

L. Committee on the Challenges of Modern Society (CCMS)

NATO'S NEW CHALLENGES TO THE PROBLEMS OF MODERN SOCIETY, by Harry C. Blaney, in *The Atlantic Community Quarterly,* v. 11, no. 2 (Summer 1973) 236-247.

"NATO's Committee on the Challenges of Modern Society (CCMS) is four years old now. Harry C. Blaney takes a look at it to see what it has accomplished. He thinks it has proven the feasibility of international cooperation in this field. To name just two things, its progress in controlling oil spills and in providing international cooperation on highway safety have been considerable. But what it has done is just a starter. To do the job properly will require much more of a national commitment than now exists."

M. Eurogroup

THE EUROGROUP, in NATO's *Fifteen Nations,* v. 20, no. 1 (February-March 1975) 19-22 plus.

This is a political overview of the NATO Eurogroup, including a brief background, origin, makeup, force improvements, major equipment, etc.

THE EUROGROUP, by Antonio de Marchi, in *Military Review,* v. 54, no. 7 (July 1974) 75-77.

"For many years after World War II, Western European countries were unsuccessful in coordinating certain operational concepts. Therefore, it is surprising to look at the viability of the Eurogroup, an agency that works very effectively. This agency is acquiring a strong European feature even though it works strictly within NATO. The Eurogroup was born in 1969 and is made up of the defense ministers of European countries. Its aim is to strengthen the Atlantic Alliance by a more trenchant unitarian activity of the member countries, by coordinating efforts in the military field, thereby avoiding useless and wasteful duplications, and by setting up common objectives as far as weaponry, logistics and training are concerned."

THE EUROGROUP, in *NATO Review,* v. 20, nos. 11-12 (November/December 1972) 8-12.

"The Eurogroup, a relatively recent form of co-operation among a number of European NATO member countries, has already done a considerable amount of valuable work. Much of this work is discussed in a pamphlet edited by the group and published in the 'Aspects of NATO' series. The following article, based on the pamphlet, explains what the Eurogroup is, and outlines some of its major achievements."

N. European Nuclear Force (ENF)

A EUROPEAN NUCLEAR FORCE: UTILITY AND PROSPECTS, by Paul C. Davis, in *Orbis,* v. 17, no. 1 (Spring 1973) 110-131.

"Recently a number of considerations have given new impetus to serious contemplation of a European Nuclear Force (ENF). These include a decline in European confidence that the United States will use its strategic nuclear forces to save Europe when the chips are down; the belief that a diplomatic and military balance between Western Europe and the USSR is essential to Europe's long-term security; fears that the two superpowers will implicitly agree (e.g., via SALT II weapons decisions) not to risk their homelands over Europe; British belief that Britain's nuclear weapons position will obsolesce and the United States may even end its nuclear assistance; and the view of some 'Europeans' that a unified Europe, if it is to be a 'state,' will require the full panoply of the instruments of state power. As the obstacles to a European Nuclear Force are huge, most recent studies of this problem have concentrated on the prospects and difficulties —the feasibility—of forming an ENF. They have dealt only briefly with its value, even though this is neither self-evident nor unrelated to its prospects. On the principle that 'necessity is the mother of invention,' this article will examine fully the necessity, or more exactly the utility, of a European Nuclear Force. In light of its promise and the structure and policies needed to give it utility, we will then briefly examine obstacles to its creation and possible ways around them. Finally, we will summarize ways in which it might best serve the NATO mission."

O. Iberian Atlantic Area Command (IBERLANT) (See also Analysts' Note)

IBERIAN ATLANTIC AREA COMMAND, in *NATO's Fifteen Nations*, v. 17, no. 1 (February-March 1972) 90-92 plus.

"In October of last year, the flags of the North Atlantic Treaty Organization member nations were raised to the peaks of flagpoles in front of NATO's newest headquarters—the Iberian Atlantic Area Command (IBERLANT)—at Oeiras, Portugal . . . The North Atlantic Council had formally approved the activation of IBERLANT in December 1966 and the inauguration of the interim headquarters was held at a villa in Rio de Mouro, Portugal, on February 22, 1967 . . . The newly commissioned headquarters for IBERLANT consists of an underground operations and communications center and an above ground administrative building."

IBERIAN ATLANTIC COMMAND WATCHES OVER CROSSROADS OF THE SEAS, by Peter Jenner, in *NATO Review*, v. 19, nos. 5-6 (May/June 1971) 6-10.

"Almost all the European countries which are dependent on imported oil have built up sufficient stocks to tide them over short, unexpected crises but a long interruption to supplies would have serious consequences. Thus in times of international tension or, ultimately, war, steps would have to be taken to protect Western shipping and thus enable the oil companies to maintain the flow of this vital source of energy. A good part of the responsibility for this task rests with NATO's Iberian Atlantic Command (IBERLANT). Sixty-five percent of all oil imports to European NATO nations pass through its area which comprises some 600,000 square miles of ocean, extending from the Tropic of Cancer to Portugal's northern border and stretching 700 nautical miles westward from the Straights of Gibraltar into the Atlantic. In addition, the Command is responsible, in co-operation with Portuguese military authorities, for the defence of continental Portugal."

P. Military Agency for Standardization (MAS)

NATO AGENCY WORKS FOR INCREASED MILITARY STANDARDIZATION, by Rear-Adm. H. H. Wesche, in *NATO Review*, v. 20, nos. 3-4 (March/April 1972) 21-22.

"Equipping and maintaining the armed forces, which would be available to NATO in times of emergency, remains a national responsibility. Naturally enough, therefore, a considerable effort is made at the Brussels Headquarters towards increasing the efficiency of these resources by encouraging the highest possible degree of standardization. The responsibility for this task rests principally with NATO's Military Agency for Standardization (MAS)."

Q. The Military Committee (MC)

THE NATO MILITARY COMMITTEE AND THE INTERNATIONAL MILITARY STAFF: SOME RATIONALE AND A PROPOSAL FOR REORGANIZATION, by Maj. Frank A. Partlow, Jr., in *RUSI Journal*, 119, no. 3 (September 1974) 29-38.

"The NATO military Committee (MC) is the highest military authority in the North Atlantic Treaty Organization. It is composed of the Chiefs of Staff of each of the member nations except France. France is represented by a military mission. At Chiefs of Staff level (MC/CS), the Committee meets at least twice a year and more often as necessary. In order for the MC to be able to meet on a continuous basis in Brussels with delegated powers of decision, each nation appoints a permanent Military Representative (MilRep) of its Chief of Staff as a member of the Military Committee in Permanent Session (MC/PS). The Military Committee is the corporate expression of national military thought and operates at the interface of the political and military aspects of the Alliance. This background is provided to indicate in broad terms the organisation and responsibilities of the NATO MC and the IMS which supports it. Using and expanding upon this basic framework, the present study will evaluate the performance of the Committee and the IMS measured against the responsibilities and tasks enumerated. Our purpose is to suggest recommendations for organisational or policy changes which can result in enhanced efficiency or increased effectiveness in the discharge of its role by the highest military authority in NATO. Our method is first to examine in some detail the performance of the Military Committee and IMS, their interaction with each other, their interface with other NATO elements, and the type and severity of operational constraints under which they operate. Appreciation of these factors will suggest and support our recommendations for organisational realignment."

R. Multilateral Force (MLF)

(LI)—SEABORNE MULTILATERAL FORCE: MIXED MANNING, by Capt. Thomas E. Fortson. Maxwell AFB, Ala., Air War College, 1971. 18 p. (Professional Study no. 4336.)

"The multilateral force (MLF) concept in NATO has been proposed in many forms, one a jointly shared and jointly controlled fleet armed with nuclear weapons. One of the major features of this proposed MLF was that each ship would be 'mix manned' throughout with personnel from at least three participating nations. 'Mix manning' in men-of-war can be found in the history of just about all navies. There was some doubt in the minds of military and political leaders of today that the complexness and type of manning may not be practical. President Kennedy, a proponent of MLF, offered a U.S. guided missile destroyer to perform a demonstration of the 'mix manning' concept. The type ship chosen had complex equipment to operate, comparable in complexness to the Polaris system. This paper describes the demonstration, some problem areas and possible solutions for future 'mix manned' ventures."

S. NATO Industrial Advisory Group (NIAG)

NIAG HELPS STIMULATE ALLIED RESEARCH AND DEVELOPMENT CO-OPERATION, by John Stone, in *NATO Review*, v. 20, nos. 1-2 (January/February 1972) 18-19.

"NATO is always on the look-out for means of promoting Allied co-operation in such fields as armaments research, development and production, because not only is this likely to lead to substantial cost savings but also to greatly increased efficiency. Against this background, it was decided to establish a NATO Industrial Advisory Group (NIAG) back in 1968 which would bring together at the headquarters, senior industrialists from NATO countries. These meetings, held two or three times a year, provide a forum for the free exchange of views on the various industrial aspects of NATO armaments questions, and foster a deeper feeling of international involvement in research, development and production, as well as creating closer co-operation among the industries of member countries. NIAG makes its recommendations to NATO's Conference of National Armaments Directors (CNAD). All NATO nations except Iceland and Luxembourg agreed to participate in NIAG's work."

T. NATO Maintenance and Supply Organization (NAMSO)

ALLIED CO-OPERATION SAVES ON COST OF MAINTENANCE AND SUPPLY; FIFTEEN YEARS OF NAMSO, by Peter Jenner, in *NATO Review*, v. 21, no. 2 (1973) 18-22.

"As the cost of providing the North Atlantic Alliance with a reasonable level of defence continues to spiral upwards, member nations look increasingly for ways of getting better value for their money. One way of achieving this aim is by stepping up the number of projects to be undertaken, on a co-operative basis, by several nations having compatible requirements. NATO's Conference of National Armaments Directors (CNAD)—the senior body under the Council concerned with defence equipment and related matters—recently took several decisions in this direction, one of which called for greater use to be made of NATO logistics support services in order to reduce unnecessary, and expensive, duplication. One of the main services suited for this task is the NATO Maintenance and Supply Organization (NAMSO). Currently celebrating its fifteenth anniversary, NAMSO was set up by the Council in April 1958 to provide spare parts and maintenance services for jointly employed weapons so as to achieve maximum logistic support at minimum cost."

U. NATO Multi-Role Combat Aircraft Management Agency (NAMMA)

NATO'S ROLE IN PROMOTING CO-OPERATION ON AIRCRAFT PROJECTS, by Peter V. Brown, in *NATO Review*, v. 19, nos. 9-10 (September/October 1971) 13-16.

"On 3 September 1969, the NATO Council approved the formation of a NATO Multi-Role Combat Aircraft Management Agency (NAMMA) at Munich to control and manage what now promises to be the largest co-operative venture ever undertaken in the Western world. Two months later, the NATO Conference of National Armaments Directors approved the Multi-Role Combat Aircraft (MRCA) as a 'NATO project.' . . . The MRCA will now follow on and give the three nations an opportunity to design and develop, as well as produce, an aircraft of advanced conception to fulfill various military roles of Close Air Support, Interdiction, Strike, Air Superiority and Training."

V. NATO Weapon Systems Department

(LI)—NATO'S INSTITUTE FOR PROFESSIONAL DEVELOPMENT, by Lt. Col. William M. Carrington. Maxwell AFB, Ala., Air War College, 1973. 15 p. (Professional Study.)

"This article describes the NATO Weapon Systems Department to include its mission; its concept of operations, its courses, and the United States Air Force role in its daily activities. This school, originally established in 1953, has graduated over 20,000 officers and civilians from its six resident courses. Its international staff prepares students for NATO assignments and instructs on the employent of weapons and weapon systems available to NATO. Its concept of operations revolves around the thesis that there are five levels of responsibility within NATO for the use of military weapon systems. The United States Air Force supports the professional education mission of this school by providing twenty-five percent of the instructional staff and fifty percent of the administrative and support staff."

W. National Military Representatives (NMRS)

LINKS TO THE NATO NATIONS; THE NATIONAL MILITARY REPRESENTATIVES AT SHAPE, by Lt. Frederic J. Bruber, in *NATO's Fifteen Nations*, v. 15, no. 3 (June–July 1970) 38–44.

"The total number of messages which are exchanged between SHAPE and the defense ministries is staggering. The National Military Representatives (NMRs) exist to smooth the way. The thirteen NMRs and the Chief of the French Military Mission (FMM) are the direct representatives of their respective ministries of defense to General Andrew J. Goodpaster, U.S. Army, Supreme Allied Commander Europe (SACEUR). They provide a comprehensible communications channel between the NATO military command and their national defense authorities . . . At SHAPE they are spokesmen for their respective countries, making sure that SHAPE plans are in accord with national capabilities and interests. They assist SHAPE in the same way, giving international staff officers essential background information on national matters, directing communications to the right people, and making sure that SHAPE projects receive immediate and careful attention at their respective ministries of defense. When the need arises, each NMR has direct access to General Goodpaster."

X. North Atlantic Assembly

19TH ANNUAL SESSION OF THE NORTH ATLANTIC ASSEMBLY, in *NATO Review*, v. 21, no. 6 (1973) 19–25.

"The North Atlantic Assembly held one of its most successful meetings when NATO parliamentarians convened in Ankara and Istanbul from 21–30 October for their 19th annual session." Economic Committee (Economic Relations, Energy Crisis); Military Committee (Summary of Work); Political Committee (Main Debate) Scientific and Technical Committee; Committee on Education, Cultural Affairs and Information; Plenary Session.

20TH ANNUAL SESSION OF THE NORTH ATLANTIC ASSEMBLY, by Keith Williams, in *NATO Review*, v. 23, no. 1 (January 1975) 20–24.

"The Twentieth Annual Session of the North Atlantic Assembly, held in London from November 11 to 16, was attended by full parliamentary delegations from fourteen NATO countries. As the Assembly is the only forum where parliamentarians from both Europe and North America meet regularly to discuss common problems, a strong North American delegation is essential to ensure a well balanced discussion on major topics, and this was certainly achieved." The Plenary Session; Economic Committee; Committee on Education, Cultural Affairs and Information; Military Committee; Political Committee; and Scientific and Technical Committee.

Y. Nuclear Planning Group (NPG)

NUCLEAR POLICY-MAKING IN NATO, by Harvey B. Seim, in *NATO Review*, v. 21, no. 6 (1973) 11–13.

"When the Ministers of Defence of the Nuclear Planning Group (NPG) assembled at The Hague last November, they provided convincing evidence of the continuing vitality of one of the most imaginative, most successful but least known partnership activities in NATO. Dealing with the full range of nuclear policy questions, the NPG is of obvious importance to the security of all Alliance members, nuclear and non-nuclear. Personal involvement of nationally responsible government leaders, civilian and military is the key that assures realism in the NPG work and the essential vigorous support of member governments. This partnership arrangement came into being seven years ago when Ministers of the Defence Planning Committee (DPC) agreed in December 1966 to establish the Nuclear Defence Affairs Committee

(NDAC), a permanent advisory committee whose function is to propose general policy on nuclear defence affairs. At the same time, a smaller body, the NPG, was created. Subordinate to the NDAC, its task is to accomplish the detailed work required for the development of policy proposals to be sent to the NDAC for endorsement and to the DPC for final approval. The NDAC and the NPG are the only DPC advisory bodies in which Defence Ministers of Permanent Representatives participate."

Z. Royal Air Force Germany

THE ROYAL AIR FORCE IN GERMANY, by Robin Goodfellow and Roger Goodwin, in *NATO's Fifteen Nations*, v. 18, no. 6 (December 1973–January 1974) 85–92.

"Now known as Royal Air Force Germany to avoid confusion with NATO's 2nd Allied Tactical Air force, of which it forms part, the Command is more fully integrated into the NATO structure than any other RAF organisation. Thus NATO's switch from a nuclear trip-wire posture to one of flexible response a few years ago plunged it into the most thorough-going re-appraisal of role and equipment seen in any Royal Air Force Command since the war . . . Our new aircraft and equipment enable us to offer NATO a far wider range of roles than before, while still fulfilling our national commitments . . . Like all other Royal Air Force formations assigned or earmarked for assignment to NATO, RAF Germany combines certain national tasks with its NATO role."

AA. Royal Air Force Strike Command

RAF STRIKE COMMAND; A VITAL FORCE FOR NATO, by Tony Brooks, in *NATOs Fifteen Nations*, v. 18, no. 3 (June–July 1973) 49–56.

"It is a fact of geography that the United Kingdom lies astride the boundaries of the three major NATO formations, Allied Command Europe, Allied Command Atlantic, and Allied Command Channel. Because of this the United Kingdom forms a rear base for the Supreme Allied Commander Europe (SACEUR), away from the immediate battle area in Europe, and a forward base for the operations of the Supreme Allied Commander Atlantic (SACLANT) and the Commander-in-Chief Channel (CINCHAN). Accordingly, the Royal Air Force Strike Command participates in operations for all major NATO commanders with many of its aircraft assigned, or earmarked for assignment to them. The United Kingdom forms the cohesive base from which, by exploiting the flexibility of air power, assistance in the co-ordination of the joint efforts of the major NATO commanders is given."

BB. The Science Committee

SCIENTIFIC CO-OPERATION IN NATO, by Andreas Rannestad, in *NATO Review*, v. 21, no. 2 (1973) 23–26.

"Collaboration and consultation between the member countries of the Alliance has been of concern to the North Atlantic Treaty Organization ever since it was established, and is specifically called for by Article 2 of the Treaty . . . The NATO Science Committee, composed of distinguished scientists from all member countries of the Alliance and chaired by the Assistant Secretary General for Scientific Affairs, has, from its first meeting in March 1958, examined ways for stimulating science in an international context and has supported scientific development through several mechanisms encouraging training, research, planning and dissemination of information."

CC. SHAPE Technical Center (STC)

SCIENTIFIC COOPERATION FOR THE ATLANTIC ALLIANCE; THE ROLE OF THE SHAPE TECHNICAL CENTRE, by 1st Lt. Frederic J. Gruber, in *NATO's Fifteen Nations*, v. 15, no.4 (August–September, 1970) 61–68.

The origins of the STC; Expert Scientific Support; The STC Programme of Work; Force Structure Studies; Command and Control; Communication Requirements; Engineering Services; Experimental Research; and Helping to Make the Alliance Work.

DD. Sixth Allied Tactical Air Force (SIXATAF)

SIXATAF; 20 YEARS AS NATO'S SOUTH-EASTERN AIR ARMS, by M/Sgt. Don Burgin, in *NATO's Fifteen Nations*, v. 18, no. 4 (August–September 1973) 41–48.

"On 14 October 1973 NATO's Sixth Allied Tactical Air Force (SIXATAF) celebrates 20 years of keeping open important avenues of access to Europe and Asia. Situated in a position which commands natural land and sea routes joining countries from the Danube to the Persian Gulf and from the Nile to the Black Sea, SIXATAF guards the skies over one of the world's most strategic areas, the Aegean Sea, Turkish Straits and Marmara Sea . . . Today the task of defending the airspace over this critical area is entrusted to SIX ATAF. It is a highly demanding task—more so every day. Turkey and Greece must protect common borders with Warsaw Pact countries extending from the western edge of Greece to Mount Ararat (Agri) in Eastern Turkey. Russia and her satellites are much like a giant shadow hanging over Greece and Turkey, a threat to freedom and security in Southeastern Europe and Anatolia."

THE SIXTH ALLIED TACTICAL AIR FORCE, by Maj. Alan G. Lisle, Jr., in *NATO's Fifteen Nations*, v. 15, no. 2 (April–May 1970) 58–64.

"Lieutenant General Joseph H. Moore, U.S. Air Force SIXATAF Commander, confirms the esprit of his NATO-commited forces. Describing them as disciplined, dedicated, and deadly, General Moore pictures the air forces assigned to his command as a potent force for peace in NATO's bastion on the Mediterranean." Contents: Spirit and Zeal; Established in 1953; The Greatest Threat; Prime Responsibilities; Improving Weaponry; An Extra Dividend; Variety of Communications; Peacetime Activities; Training and Testing; Allied Exercises; A Unique Exercise; Logistics; NATO Infrastructure; etc.

EE. Standing Naval Force Atlantic

STANDING NAVAL FORCE ATLANTIC, by Capt. Raymond W. Allen, in *NATO's Fifteen Nations*, v. 17, no. 1 (February–March 1972) 46–52.

"It was only a month after the admiral's speech [of April 1967 when he left his post as Supreme Allied Commander Atlantic] that the Standing Naval Force Atlantic concept was approved in principle by the NATO military chiefs of staff. Final approval and authority for activation of a Standing Naval Force was given by the Defense Planning Committee in December 1967, and on January 13, 1968, the first multi-national naval squadron to permanently operate in peacetime was activated. On that day, at the Royal Navy's training base in Portland, England, HNLMS Holland, the Norwegian frigate HNOMS Narvik, and the American destroyer USS Holder gathered to begin the Standing Naval Force Atlantic's first months of operation. Since then ships from the NATO member countries of Canada, Denmark, the Federal Republic of Germany, the Netherlands, Norway, Portugal, the United Kingdom, and the United States have participated annually."

FF. Standing Naval Force Channel (STANAV FORCHAN)

STANAVFORCHAN; NATO FORMS ITS SECOND INTERNATIONAL MARITIME FORCE, in *NATO Review*, v. 21, no. 4 (1973) 12–14.

"The North Atlantic Treaty Organization formed its second permanent international naval force at Ostend, on 11 May, when Admiral Sir Edward Ashmore, Allied Commander-in-Chief Channel, inaugurated the Standing Naval Force Channel . . . Announcing the formation of the force, Admiral Ashmore, who is also Commander-in-Chief of NATO's Eastern Atlantic Area, and Commander-in-Chief Fleet, stressed that the inauguration did not mean an escalation in the strength of NATO's maritime force. 'The formation ensures that what have been hitherto purely national activites, now become international, thus increasing understanding and effectiveness in NATO, and demonstrating in tangible form, the unity and common purpose of the North Atlantic Alliance,' he said."

GG. Striking Fleet Atlantic (STRIKFLTLANT)

NATO'S STRIKING FLEET ATLANTIC, by Vice Adm. Vincent Paul de Poix, in *NATO's Fifteen Nations*, v. 17, no. 1 (February–March 1972) 38–44.

"In November, NATO's Striking Fleet Atlantic will observe its 20th anniversary. It represents for all the world to see the finest example of naval coordination, cooperation and coalition. And yet, in spite of the fact that the Striking Fleet has existed for almost two decades, surprisingly little has been written about it, and its potential is generally unknown even in some NATO countries. This anonymity is attributable to several factors. First, there has not been a crisis in these twenty years that has required the response of the Striking Fleet. Consequently its capabilities have not received the publicity that a crisis situation generates. Another factor contributing to the Striking Fleet's anonymity is that, except for specified exercises, it is a constructive Fleet. In other words, it is not a constant force in being. The staff, for the most part, is drawn from the staff of the Commander of the U.S. SECOND Fleet. In accordance with initial NATO agreement, Commander of the Striking Fleet Atlantic and Commander U.S. SECOND Fleet are one and the same. Add to this the fact that when the Fleet is activated for exercises, these exercises are held in open ocean areas, far from the notice of civilian populations."

HH. Supreme Allied Commander Atlantic (SACLANT)

SACLANT HEADQUARTERS CELEBRATES 20TH ANNIVERSARY, in *NATO Review*, v. 20, nos. 5-6 (May/June 1972) 8-11.

"Many prominent NATO personalities gathered in Norfolk, Virginia, last April for a ceremony marking the 20th Anniversary of the Alliance's only major military headquarters in North America—the Headquarters of the Supreme Allied Commander Atlantic (SACLANT) ... The command's area of responsibility includes more than 12 million square miles of Atlantic Ocean stretching from the coastal waters of Europe to those of North America, and from the North Pole to Tropic of Cancer. The staff is constantly engaged in planning and conducting a large variety of exercises which afford the NATO navies opportunities to work together, enhance readiness, develop common tactics and to test equipment."

II. Supreme Allied Commander Atlantic Submarine Warfare Research Center (SAC LANTCEN)

ALLIED COMMAND ATLANTIC'S ANTI-SUBMARINE WARFARE RESEARCH CENTER, in *NATO's Fifteen Nations*, v. 17, no. 1 (February-March 1972) 70-75.

"Scientists and technicians at the Allied Command Atlantic's Antisubmarine Warfare Research Centre (SACLANTCEN) agree that, for the present, submarine technology is far ahead of antisubmarine warfare proficiency. This international staff, however, is concentrating on the future and their collective efforts may one day contribute markedly to a theory, concept, or even the mere fragment of an idea that may lead to a revolutionary breakthrough that could well swing the uneven balance in this crucial contest from the side of the elusive submarine to that of the persistent seeker. The men and women at SACLANT CEN in La Spezia, Italy, represent 13 North Atlantic Treaty Organization members. They do not design new and radical antisubmarine aircraft or ships, nor do they conjure up ultra-sophisticated weapons to destroy submarines. However, when the art of antisubmarine warfare (ASW) makes appreciable progress, the staff at the ASW Centre most likely will have had a hand in the gain."

THE MARITIME EQUATION—SACLANT IN THE 1970s, by Adm. Charles K. Duncan, in *NATO's Fifteen Nations*, v. 17, no. 1 (February-March 1972) 28-35.

"As the members of the North Atlantic Treaty Organization close the chapter on twenty-two years of intimate cooperation, we can look back proudly on solid and concrete accomplishments. Together, we have orchestrated our individual national policies to reinforce the goals of the alliance and have achieved a result which, if we had acted separately would have not been possible. Our alliance has kept the peace we all desire so much; it has been the protective shield that has permitted a generation of allied growth and enrichment. The Allied Command Atlantic has been a significant element in providing the protective maritime structure that, together with Allied Command Europe and the Channel Command, has given muscle to this defensive Alliance ... On a day-to-day basis, SACLANT exercises operational control of the Standing Naval Force Atlantic. It is the only military force available to NATO on a continuing basis ... Supplementing the day-to-day availability of the Standing Naval Force Atlantic are on call forces under the Maritime Contingency Forces Atlantic concept. Under these plans, specially tailored multi-national task forces can be called up to meet various contingencies in the Atlantic area. These forces are, of course, the primary tools that SACLANT has to carry out the NATO strategy of Flexible Response, short of general war."

THE SACLANT ANTI-SUBMARINE WARFARE RESEARCH CENTRE, in *NATO Review*, v. 21, no. 1 (1973) 20-24.

"The Centre's mission is to provide scientific and technical advice and assistance in ASW to the Supreme Allied Commander Atlantic (SACLANT). The research at the Centre, commonly called SACLANTCEN is directed to the detection, classification and identification, of submarines, with the major emphasis on underwater acoustics. Oceanographic research is conducted in direct support of ASW tasks, and, in the operational research area, SACLANTCEN conducts studies and investigations that support research on the most efficient use of ASW systems."

JJ. United States Air Forces in Europe (US AFE)

UNITED STATES AIR FORCE EUROPE, in *NATO's Fifteen Nations*, v. 15, no. 1 (February-March 1970) 66-69.

"The USAFE of the 1970s will bear little resemblance to the USAFE of previous decades. It will be a streamlined, tightly managed, NATO-committed force with an improved combat readiness capability to meet any aggressive act with a new brand of airpower. Its aircraft and men are combat-tested in Southeast Asia and poised in vigilant operational readiness in Europe."

(LI)—USAFE AND SPECIALIZED TACTICAL FIGHTER WINGS, by Maj. Noah E. Loy. Maxwell AFB, Ala., Air Command and Staff College, 1971. 89 p. (Research Study no. 1215-71.)

"Flexibility, survivability, and credibility are three mandatory characteristics for modern military forces. These three characteristics do not necessarily complement each other when an Air Force Commander tries to employ his forces within their definitional limits. The Commander-in-Chief, United States Air Forces in Europe (CINC USAFE) has this employment problem plus a real day-to-day enemy threat. After analyzing and comparing two general operational concepts with the enemy threat, this study concludes that CINC USAFE may increase the survivability and credibility of his forces without losing flexibility by implementing an operational concept that employs Specialized Tactical Fighter Wings."

USAFE'S ROLE IN NATO DEFENSE, by Maj. R. M. Chubbuck, in *NATO's Fifteen Nations*, v. 18, no. 2 (April-May 1973) 58-64.

"The Commander-in-Chief, USAFE, wears a variety of hats. As a NATO commander serving the Supreme Allied Command, Europe (SACEUR), he also acts as the Commander of the 4th Allied Tactical Air Forces, USAFE is also a component of, and responsible to, the Commander-in-Chief, U.S. European Command (USEUCOM) in support of all unified U.S. military plans and operations in the European area. At the same time, the CINC USAFE maintains a responsibility to the U.S. Air Force Chief of Staff Washington for the training and maintenance of assigned forces, for logistic support of all major USAF command units in Europe, and for all matters involving Air Force policy and administration. How does USAFE conduct such a varied and complex mission? The command covers approximately one-fourth of the globe, for as a component commander under USEUCOM, the CINCUSAFE exercises responsibility in the geographical area assigned to USEU COM. It is concentrated in Western Europe but extends through the Mediterranean, the Middle East land mass, the Persian Gulf and North Africa. USAFE maintains major bases in England, The Netherlands, Spain, Germany, Italy, Greece and Turkey. Overall, more than 300 units of all sizes and stretching from Scandinavia to Iran are included in USAFE's area of responsibility."

KK. United States Army, Europe (USAREUR)

U.S. ARMY EUROPE: READY, DISCIPLINED, PROFESSIONAL, by Gen. Michael S. Davison, in *Army*, v. 24, no. 10 (October 1974) 20-23 plus.

"A powerful and carefully balanced deterrent force.—Sometimes characterized by...critics as 'tail-heavy,' U.S. Army, Europe is in fact adding combat battalions to an already powerful force, even though it must rely on its own resources and support a mobilization base far from home."

LL. Working Group on Industrial Property

NATO AND INDUSTRIAL PROPERTY, by Sotirios Tsambiras, in *NATO Review*, v. 22, no. 1 (1974) 19-21.

"As a result of the efforts undertaken by a NATO Working Group on Industrial Property created in 1955, in which highly-specialised national experts participate, two agreements have been established concerning industrial property: the NATO Agreement for the Mutual Safeguarding of Secrecy of Inventions relating to Defence and for which Applications for Patents have been made, and the NATO Agreement for the Communication of Technical Information for Defence Purposes."

CHAPTER IV

NATO'S DEFENSE POSTURE: PROBLEMS AND PROSPECTS
(See Also Chapter V and Appendixes)

A. Miscellaneous Aspects

ADDRESS AT NATO DEFENSE COLLEGE, ROME, ITALY, ON JULY 20, 1972, by Gen. A. J. Goodpaster, in *NATO's Fifteen Nations*, v. 17, no. 6 (December 1972–January 1973) 28–30 plus.

"My remarks today will deal with some of the current changes and will, I hope, provide a summary of the major issues in SHAPE and Allied Command Europe with which you have been concerned during your course of instruction. First, I will focus on some of the measures that SHAPE and Allied Command Europe are taking to meet the Soviet challenges in the Central Region and on the flanks of NATO. Second, I will suggest some of the present and potential dangers within NATO itself that could threaten the solidarity of the Alliance and against which we must continue to guard. I will conclude my remarks with a brief assessment of the capabilities of our Alliance and of the prospects for its continued success."

THE AMERICAN-WEST EUROPEAN DEFENCE RELATIONSHIP, in *NATO Review*, v. 22, no. 5 (1974) 3–11.

"The two articles published . . . continue the series on aspects of the defence problems which are facing the NATO allies . . . The first article in this series appeared in issue No. 1, 1974, of the NATO Review and was by Kenneth Hung, Deputy Director of the IISS, who discussed the theory of deterrence. W. F. K. Thompson, Defence Correspondent of the Daily Telegraph, wrote the second article, which appeared in issue No. 2 and dealt with NATO's force posture in Allied Command Europe. A third article, by Dr. Wolfgang Hopker, German author of several books on Soviet naval power, was published in issue No. 3 and was entitled Soviet Global Strategy—a Challenge at Sea. Stefano Silvestri, Deputy Director of the Institute for International Affairs, Rome, contributed the fourth article on Defence Expenditures and National Economies, which appeared in issue No. 4. This series will be concluded in issue No. 6 by a consideration of the role of the Alliance's forces as part of NATO's overall objectives."

NATO IN A TIME OF CRISIS, by Brig. Gen. Richard C. Bowman, in *Air Force Magazine*, v. 58, no. 4 (April 1975) 9 plus.

"The author examines the interrelated crises that confront NATO, assesses the balance of forces in Europe, and discusses what must be done to preserve the viability of . . . NATO in a time of crisis."

NATO IN THE 1970S, by Air Chief Marshal Christopher Foxley-Norris, in *RUSSI Journal*, v. 4, no. 117 (December 1972) 3–9.

"I would like to address myself today, and analyse whether NATO's defence posture is adequate and, therefore, credible in the light of the political, military, and economic developments which have occurred, and may occur, during the seventies, between East and West, between the two sides of the Atlantic and among the European members of NATO."

NATO MUSCLE: MORE SHADOW THAN SUBSTANCE, by Steven L. Canby, in *Military Review*, v. 53, no. 2 (February 1973) 65–74.

"Why is NATO outspending the Warsaw Pact—in terms of both men and money—while buying less security? This so-called 'people-PEMA paradox' (PEMA being acronymic jargon for 'procurement of equipment and missiles, Army'), which so perplexed the McNamara analysts, can be resolved by examining the assumptions underlying NATO's organization for defense. The Pact, consciously or not, has developed operating procedures and a force structure appropriate to its strategic requirements in Europe; NATO, and particularly the American component, has not. Restructuring NATO could release the resources necessary to implement flexible response and forward defense and remove some politically difficult choices. The crucial questions boil down to whether NATO should opt for highly visible, high initial combat forces (as the Soviets do), or retain low visibility, low initial combat forces which are sustainable."

THE ROLE OF NATO MILITARY FORCES AS PART OF THE ALLIANCE'S OVERALL OBJECTIVES, by Louis G. M. Jaquet, in *NATO Review*, v. 22, no. 6 (December 1974) 6-13.

"This article concludes the series on aspects of the defence problems which are facing the NATO allies . . . The first article in this series appeared in Issue No. 1, 1974, of the NATO Review and was by Kenneth Hunt, Deputy Director of the ISSS, who discussed the theory of deterrence. W. F. K. Thompson, Defence Correspondent of the Daily Telegraph, wrote the second article, which appeared in issue No. 2 and dealt with NATO's force posture in Allied Command Europe. A third article, by Dr. Wolfgang Hopker, German author of several books on Soviet naval power, was published in issue No. 3 and was entitled Soviet Global Strategy—A Challenge at Sea. Stefano Silvestri, Deputy Director of the Institute for International Affairs, Rome, contributed the fourth article on Defence Expenditures and National Economies, which appeared in issue No. 4. A further two articles, on the American/West European Defence Relationship, were published in issue No. 5—Core, Troubles, Prospects by Horst Mendershausen of The Rand Corporation, California, and Old Worries and New Issues, by Curt Gasteyger of the Institut Universitaire de Hautes Etudes Internationales, Geneva."

(LI)—WEST EUROPEAN DEFENCE, by Wing Comdr. Clive A. Herbert. Maxwell AFB, Ala., Air War College, 1974. 139 p. (Professional Study.)

"The report surveys European defence history since World War II, and considers present factors and future possibilities affecting the Atlantic Alliance. It identifies some dissension between the U.S. and European allies, and predicts moderate withdrawals of the U.S. military forces from Europe, either unilaterally or under MBFR arrangement. It defines European vital interests and the most likely threats to those interests. It suggests three broad paths which West European defence may follow. The first is to retain the historic U.S. leadership in NATO, and to attempt to match the Warsaw Pact conventionally at the U.S.'s urging. The second is to retain NATO's strategy of forward, flexible response, including recourse to tactical nuclear weapons as and when required, but with increasing Europeanization of the NATO structure by Eurogroup. The third path would be taken only in the event of total U.S. withdrawals from Europe, and would necessitate a common Eurogroup/Community effort in strategic and tactical nuclear weaponry, and in replacing withdrawn U.S. conventional forces. A European Defence Community may evolve. The report examines the costs of the three paths, and advocates the middle path of Europeanization of NATO, producing a more equitable Atlantic Alliance."

B. Strategy for Defense

1. *Miscellaneous Aspects*

THE DEFENCE OF WESTERN EUROPE, ed. by John C. Garnett. New York, St. Martin's Press, 1974. 134 p.

Papers presented at the National Defence College, Latimer (England), in September, 1972. "This book is a . . . study of European defense problems. Its time-scale is the immediate and medium-term future and it was prompted by the need to relate current European defense thinking to the significant changes which are taking place in European politics and East-West relations. The steady erosion of the Cold War, the new politics of détente, the improving superpower relationship and the changing attitude of the United States towards her European allies have all combined to create an environment of flux which has far-reaching implications for European defense. The writers thought it timely, therefore, to make some reassessment of the Soviet threat and to examine the emerging European-American relationship as revealed by the Nixon Doctrine. Against this background they have tried to speculate about the military problems of NATO, the defense implications of the European Economic Community, and the problem of improving the effectiveness of the Western defense effort by collaboration in the field of weapon procurement. The writers have identified and analyzed some important problems, and, where possible, they have tried to suggest possible solutions."

THE DEFENSE OF WESTERN EUROPE, by Lord Gladwyn, in *Foreign Affairs*, v. 51, no. 3 (April 1973) 588-597.

"As long as a substantial American force remains in Germany, giving rise to the assumption that if the Soviet Union attacked the allies in the West it would be the signal for a nuclear holocaust, the defense of Western Europe is in all probability assured. Nevertheless, in spite of statements to the contrary, we are always given to understand that there may, in the not too far distant future, be some partial withdrawal of American power and that, insofar as this may weaken the 'credibility' of the major deterrent, it will be necessary for the European members of the Alliance somehow to fill the ensuing gap. Already an effort to meet this American-implied demand has been made by the constitution of the so-called 'Eurogroup' (though France is not a member) and that is very much to the good. But might it be possible for Western Europe, one day, and if necessary, to be primarily responsible, within the Alliance, for its own defense? Most informed persons would unhesitatingly say no. . . The accepted philosophy at the moment seems to be that if there should be any aggressive move by the Warsaw Pact forces, whether in the central, the northern or the southern areas of NATO, it would be countered by a move having the same sort of weight behind it."

A EUROPEAN VIEW OF NATO STRATEGY, by Lawrence L. Whetlen, in *Military Review*, v. 51, no. 9 (September 1971) 25-37.

"After 20 years of successful deterrence, the North Atlantic Treaty Organization is now at the most decisive watershed in its tortuous history. The Soviet's achievement of strategic parity with the United States and a vast modernization program within the Warsaw Pact have made the opposing alliance far stronger physically than at any time since World War II. Paradoxically, the East also has entered recently into a variety of diplomatic contacts with NATO, intending apparently to seek some modus vivendi. As this diplomatic offensive commenced, sentiments were repeatedly voiced in the West citing technological innovations, budgetary pressure, and domestic unrest as justification for reducing defense funds and withdrawing troops from overseas. In the first 20 years, NATO's deterrence depended upon the credibility of the U.S. strategic deterrence and the political determination of the NATO partners. Strategic parity, détente atmosphere, and internal pressures have forced consideration of alternative strategies for the next 20 years. What alternative would counterbalance an opponent who is unlikely to crush Western resistance with overt force, but could neutralize policies contrary to his interests with paralyzing pressure; harmonize with the atmosphere of the Strategic Arms Limitation Talks (SALT) negotiations, the Federal Republic of Germany-USSR Treaty, and the European security conference; and advance the Western aim of guaranteeing national security without capitulation or compromise of guiding principles?"

NATO'S FORCE POSTURE IN ALLIED COMMAND EUROPE, by W. F. K. Thompson, in *NATO Review*, v. 22, no. 2 (1974) 7-13.

"The NATO Review gives below the second in a series of articles on aspects of the defence problems which are facing the Western world ... Subjects to be discussed by other eminent writers will include: NATO's naval Strategy; defence expenditures and national economies; the U.S.-Western Europe defence relationship; and the role of NATO's forces as part of the Alliance's overall objectives. The first such article in this series, which appeared in the previous issue of the NATO Review, was by Kenneth Hunt, Deputy Director of the IISS and considered the theory of deterrence."

NUCLEAR BALANCE IN EUROPE, Walter F. Hahn, in *Foreign Affairs*, (April 1972) 501-516.

"Suggests a plan for more equitable burden-sharing in the Atlantic Alliance and a commensurate easing of American military investment and obligations. Unless the Alliance takes steps to solve the growing divergence between the security interests and perceptions of the U.S. and those of its West European partners, he predicts, all of the temporary accommodations among the Alliance partners may not prevent an ultimate crisis of mutual confidence. The disparity in current American and European perceptions comes from the faltering faith of the European partners in the strategic-nuclear deterrent as the pillar of their security, while American policy, except for the short-lived period of 'massive retaliation' of the mid-fifties, has consistently embraced a concept on which effective deterrence is equated with effective conventional forces . . ."

(*)—THE RATIONALE FOR NATO EUROPEAN COLLECTIVE SECURITY—PAST AND FUTURE, by Morton A. Kaplan. Washington, American Enterprise Institute for Public Policy Research, 1973. 90 p.

"Professor Kaplan begins by reviewing the origins of NATO, and the current political and military problems besetting it. He then outlines his 'dissuasion' strategy which, basically, would be an attempt to discourage the Soviet Union's Warsaw Pact allies from actively supporting a Soviet attack on NATO Europe, in the unlikely event of one occurring. Should there be such an attack, the NATO allies would distinguish between Eastern Europe and the Soviet Union as target areas, and would avoid the use of weapons which would cause considerable damage in Eastern Europe. These restrictions, however, would only be observed so long as the armed forces of these countries refrained from active cooperation in the Soviet attack."

REALISTIC DETERRENCE IN NATO. Carlisle Barracks, Army War College, May 1973. 113 p.

"NATO still lacks a military doctrine that is fully accepted by all the allies, and has failed to achieve a division of labor that might yield a viable conventional defense of Europe. The U.S. strategy of Realistic Deterrence has not solved this problem, but has offered one possible solution if combined force planning is investigated. The approach was to first analyze the strategy of Realistic Deterrence and that of NATO. A literature search method was used which focused on the unclassified material which accurately describes the two strategies. Criticisms by academic and military leaders were analyzed. Recommendations are offered to better make the NATO strategy succeed. These include: turn over forward defense to the FRG; isolate France from military planning; place U.S., U.K., Belgium, Netherlands units in reserve positions with the U.K. around Bremerhaven and the U.S. around Frankfurt; guarantee the U.S. nuclear deterrent in specific terms."

STRATEGY FOR EUROPE, by Air Vice Marshal Stewart W. B. Menaul, in *NATO's Fifteen Nations*, v. 18, no. 5 (October-November 1973) 24-26 plus.

Historical—Grand Strategy and Military Strategy; The Nuclear Age; Changing Relations Between America and Europe; A New Strategy for Europe; Grand Strategy; Military Strategy—Revised Concept.

2. *Nuclear Planning and Defense*

a. *Miscellaneous Aspects*

A COMMON WESTERN NUCLEAR DOCTRINE, by Lt. Col. Marc E. Geneste, in *Military Review*. v. 51, no. 9 (September 1971) 3-12.

"Any change in the Western defense system for the seventies must stem from a clear vision of strategy. The general concept should be sufficiently simple to be easily understood and accepted by all the members of the Western alliance. Unity of strategic doctrine is the prerequisite for any concept of a 'division of labor' and any improvement of our present system . . . Thus, the irony of our times drives us to a strange conclusion: the nuclear weapons should not be the first to be sacrificed on the altar of disarmament, they should be the last. The atom, which has been the 'holy terror' of our age, would then be the guardian of peace while we work at a better world."

A CREDIBLE NUCLEAR-EMPHASIS DEFENSE FOR NATO, by W. S. Bennett and others, in *Orbis*, v. 17, no. 2 (Summer 1973) 463-479.

"This is a proposal of long-term goals toward which changes in NATO's defense posture should be directed. Its primary aim is to increase the effectiveness of NATO defense against Warsaw Pact aggression and to make that increase manifest and credible to both NATO and Warsaw Pact decision-makers. Negotiation of the issues dividing East and West in Europe could then be approached by the NATO governments, secure in the knowledge that the West's military posture was adequate to repel any invasion."

CRISIS IN EUROPEAN DEFENCE; THE NEXT TEN YEARS, by Geoffrey Lee Williams and Alan Lee Williams. London, Charles Knight & Co., 1974. 334 p.

"This study examines the major defence issues and developments which Western Europe faces over the next ten years. The authors look in detail at the strategic and foreign policy interests of the two superpowers, the United States and the Soviet Union, and their influence on European security, and go on to examine the defense problems of Great Britain, West Germany and France. They define ways in which threats to peace might arise in Europe and the type of military conflict which might occur. They re-assess the value and the limitations of NATO, and consider the issues of maritime and nuclear power, in particular the future role of British and French nuclear forces."

THE DEVELOPMENT OF NATO'S NUCLEAR POTENTIAL 1949/74, by John Marriott, in *NATO's Fifteen Nations*, v. 19, no. 1 (February-March 1974) 39-44 plus.

"John Marriott traces the growth of NATO's nuclear weapons from the date the alliance was formed until today and also discusses NATO's present day nuclear weapons and methods of delivery."

NUCLEAR CONSULTATION PROCESSES IN NATO, by Thomas C. Wiegele, in *Orbis*, v. 16, no. 2 (Summer 1972) 462-487.

"This article represents an attempt to examine the processes by means of which allies in the North Atlantic Treaty Organization consult with each other on nuclear matters of common concern. After considering the idea of consultation both generally and in the alliance from the perspective of small group theory, it will explore the mechanisms that have been utilized by the alliance to discuss and formulate nuclear policies. Within this context, it will make an assessment concerning the effectiveness of the nuclear consultative processes."

OPTIONS MAKE GOOD PROPAGANDA BUT POOR DEFENCE FOR NATO, by Air Vice Marshal Robert Cameron, in *NATO's Fifteen Nations*, v. 15, no. 3 (June-July 1970) 20-23.

"'We've got options . . . Two to be exact. The same two we've always had. We can plan our defences around tactical nucs and make sure the enemy knows what's on our mind. Or we can fiddle around till a crunch comes and get licked'—is how one U.S. authority put it . . . NATO's failure to match its new strategy with an effective capability can be blamed on two main causes. First of all the allies, while acknowledging (for the record at least) the U.S. diagnosis of their strategic ill, refuse to buy the prescribed U.S. medicine, i.e., more conventional sinew. Secondly, a combination of emotion and big power politics is steadily emasculating the capability of NATO's nucs to play their essential role in the total defence posture . . . For all these reasons, and more particularly the mounting pressure in Congress for a substantial reduction of U.S. forces currently in Europe, talk of getting more troops for NATO, from any ally, has become rather academic. So what the alliance authorities had best be doing, is thinking up ways and means to defend NATO with progressively fewer resources—not more. And no matter how clever we are at making-do with the conventional capability we still have in the 70s, it is quite clear that successful deterrence will be more and more dependent on how credible we can make the nuclear posture."

(LI)—PROMPT NUCLEAR DEFENSE: A PRACTICAL CONCEPT FOR NATO IN THE SEVENTIES, by Col. William G. MacLaren, Jr. Maxwell AFB, Ala., Air War College, 1971. 19 p. (Professional Study no. 4187.)

"Remarks on the general concern expressed as to the future of the North Atlantic Treaty Organization lead to a short chronological tracing of the background of current NATO strategy. A brief description of the strategy of the Warsaw Pact and a capsule comparison of NATO forces vis-a-vis the Warsaw Pact introduces a discussion of the anomalies inherent in current NATO strategy. The concept of prompt nuclear defense, i.e., willingness from the first to defend immediately with nuclear weapons, is then presented. The concept is suggested as being one method to structure forces that could optimize technological change while also recognizing budgetary and manpower constraints foreseen in the coming decade. The responsiveness of this concept to the politico-military needs of NATO in the coming decade is also addressed."

TACTICAL NUCLEAR STRATEGY AND EUROPEAN DEFENCE: A CRITICAL APPRAISAL, by Michael J. Brenner, in *International Affairs, London* (January 1975).

"It is often noted that if we were ever to be visited by the horrors of nuclear warfare it would most likely result from military conflict in Europe. The location of several thousand tactical nuclear weapons (TNWs) assigned a key role in war-fighting scenarios in the central arena of great power confrontation is the obvious reason for this estimate. Yet there has been a remarkably uncritical acceptance of these formidable theatre forces and of the doctrines for their use. In contrast to the repetitive, systematic review of strategic weapons, the former receives only the intermittent attention of public officials and analysts. It is appropriate to examine the disposition of tactical nuclear forces, plans for their contingent use, and proposals for the reform of both at a time when a number of diplomatic and military developments are nudging the subject into more prominent view. First, the capabilities and purposes of the American nuclear arsenal as a whole are being re-examined by an Administration in Washington which is seriously concerned about the ramifying political effects of parity with the Soviet Union. Second, the initiative by the Secretary of Defence, James Schlesinger, to shift the focus of our strategic forces towards counterforce targeting has the demanding requirements of the American commitment to Europe's defence as a major point of anxious reference. Third, the Pentagon is making a strong push for re-equipping NATO with 'mini-nukes', a 'new family of precision guided miniaturised weapons', that could be linked to revised plans for their early use in the event of hostilities. Finally, the problematic outcome of the interbloc negotiations of Mutual and Balanced Force Reductions heightens the general uncertainty about the permanence and effectiveness of NATO's conventional forces. In combination, these circumstances indicate a renewed emphasis on tactical nuclear arms, underline the paradox inherent in the alliance's reliance on them for both deterrence and defence, and increase the very considerable dangers of their premature and uncontrollable use. Our criticism of existing arrangements, and reason for disquietude over the direction of proposed changes, is threefold."

b. *Nuclear Strategies of United States, Great Britain, and France (Including East-West Strategic Issues)*

ACTION AND REACTION IN THE NUCLEAR ARMS RACE, by Colin S. Gray, in *Military Review*, (August 1971) 16-26.

"... Disagrees with the action-reaction theory which dominates much strategic thinking today. The theory fails to give due credit to domestic pressures which have often played a major role in U.S. strategic decisions, such as the enormous missile expansion during the Kennedy Administration and the Sentinel decision during the Johnson Administration. Moreover, it is based on a dubious understanding of Soviet strategic doctrine and reactive patterns. In the early 1960s the Soviets did react to the relatively inferior position in which they found themselves. However, they were not seeking to offset U.S. strategic forces strictly in Western terms of deterrence. Instead, Soviet leaders seemed determined to neutralize any political leverage that an apparent strategic superiority might provide the U.S. Since 1964, Gray finds no persuasive evidence that major Soviet strategic decisions have been sensitive to U.S. programs. The Soviets value defense of the homeland for itself, and they view the ability to disrupt an aggressor's blow by preemptive strike as an important component of a stable deterrence. This strategy has apparently not been a reaction to offset the Sentinel and Safeguard. There is no reason to believe that the Soviet ICBM and SLBM programs would be any smaller in the absence of a U.S. ABM. They have also shown no greater urgency to counter MINUTEMAN III and Poseidon. Furthermore, their continued heavy emphasis on air defenses is not merely an antiquated fondness for defense; it reflects accurately the enormous megatonnage deliverable by SAC bombers and the tactical aircraft of the 6th Fleet and NATO forces ..."

(LI)—A EUROPEAN NUCLEAR IDENTITY WITHIN NATO, by Col. Robert F. McCarthy. Maxwell AFB, Ala., Air War College, 1972. 50 p. (Professional Study.)

"The author reviews historical attempts at an Allied Nuclear Force focusing on the reasons for failure of such proposals. He analyzes the evolution of nuclear-sharing arrangements in NATO, their progress, limitations and impediments to expansion of existing arrangements. A description of the present nuclear forces of Great Britain and France follows with a military assessment of the efficacy of each force. Various official statements and policies of NATO member-nations toward a European nuclear force are examined. The author concludes that the United States should modify its nuclear-sharing policies and support creation of an independently manned and controlled nuclear force within the NATO framework."

IS A EUROPEAN NUCLEAR FORCE DESIRABLE?, by Alan Lee Williams, in *The Atlantic Community Quarterly*, v. 10, no. 2 (Summer 1972) 185-187.

"It has been argued that British-French nuclear cooperation, possibly eventuating in a European nuclear force, would be beneficial, for a number of reasons. Alan Lee Williams, Director of the British Atlantic Committee, takes up the points of this argument one by one and finds them wanting: Is a British-French force even possible, technically speaking? Will it be able to deter the Russians? Is it a necessity to achieve a United Europe? Or would it actually be a hindrance? In effect, he shows that the pro-nuclear argument has not been thought through."

THE NEW NUCLEAR DEBATE: SENSE OR NONSENSE?, by Ted Greenwood and Michael L. Nacht, in *Foreign Affairs*, v. 52, no. 4 (July 1974) 761-780.

"There is a widespread and deep-seated dissatisfaction today with many of the fundamental premises underlying American strategic weapons policy. The dissatisfaction stems in part from disappointment with the terms of the arms-control agreements concluded between the United States and the Soviet Union at the Moscow summit meeting in May 1972. The treaty on the limitation of anti-ballistics missile systems is sometimes said to provide little more than a codification of the immoral relationship in which the population of each super-power is left hostage to the strategic nuclear forces of the other. The Interim Agreement on Strategic Offensive Weapons is faulted for conceding numerical superiority to the Soviet Union. The inability of political accords to keep pace with technological innovation, it is argued, is rendering strategic arms-control agreements obsolescent almost before the ink dries. In part, too, the dissatisfaction stems from the vigor of Soviet strategic weapons programs and from apparent Soviet intransigence at the second round of the strategic arms limitation talks (SALT II). Other aspects of Soviet policy—their stance during and subsequent to the 1973 war in the Middle East and their continued rigidity in dealing with the question of human rights within their own society—while perhaps logically distinct from strategic issues, nevertheless reinforce a general skepticism of Russian intentions."

NUCLEAR DIPLOMACY: BRITAIN, FRANCE AND AMERICA, Andrew J. Pierre, in *Foreign Affairs*, v. 49, no. 2 (January 1971) 283-301.

"The Atlantic nations are moving toward a new security relationship which may in time involve the role of European strategic nuclear forces. We are in a period of widespread questioning of the nature of future American participation in the defense of Western Europe. In the squalor of American cities, the increased racial and social tensions of our society and the demands for a shift in national priorities away from defense toward domestic problems lie the seeds of change. If we add to these the economic recovery of Europe, the U.S. view that the allies are not carrying a fair share of their own defense, the balance-of-payments deficit toward which the U.S. forces abroad make a substantial contribution, the squeeze on the Pentagon budget, the tendency resulting from the traumatic experience in Vietnam to shed responsibilities, we find the ingredients of a reduced U.S. military involvement in Europe. Western Europe will, however, remain dependent upon the American commitment to its security. As long as the western end of the Eurasian land-mass is not politically united, and so long as the need for 'security' from the East exists, the United States must continue to act as the balancer. The only alternative to the American nuclear umbrella is a full-scale European nuclear deterrent, and this is not feasible for as far ahead as we can see."

(*)—NUCLEAR DIPLOMACY: THE FIRST TWENTY-FIVE YEARS, by George H. Quester. New York, Dunellen, 1971. 327 p. (for the Center for International Affairs, Harvard University.)

"Historical analyses of the Soviet-American nuclear relationship since the end of World War II. The emphasis of this . . . book is analytical rather than policy-oriented."

NUCLEAR POLITICS: AMERICA, FRANCE, AND BRITAIN, by Wynfred Joshua and Walter F. Hahn. Beverly Hills, Sage Publications, 1973. 84 p. (The Washington Papers, vol. I, no. 8.)

". . . The possibility of an Anglo-French agreement on nuclear cooperation appears to be remote . . . For every point on which France and Britain agree, there are several more on which they disagree. The authors express a need for national nuclear forces, both fear a crisis conflict, and both are concerned about Soviet political pressures. Also, both of them realize the value of nuclear power in an industrial race, and both believe in the necessity for any ranking nation of the world to possess a nuclear capability. On the other hand. though both doubt the credibility of U.S. nuclear protection, France has been much more vocal on the issue. While France has disassociated itself from the NATO alliance, Britain has used its nuclear capability in support of both NATO and its own independence. France finds the unique U.S.-U.K. relationship distasteful and regards it somewhat jealously. And though both support national control of nuclear forces, France is almost obsessed with the idea of the indivisibility of nuclear forces. In addition to the fact that their areas of technical competence differ, France is less advanced technologically than England, due to U.S. assistance to the latter. And while France, out of experience, manages R&D well, it is having difficulties of recruiting and training crews as well as providing adequate computer support for its nuclear forces. Until France reaches a nuclear development comparable to Britain's, it appears that France would stand to gain the most from a cooperative effort between them. Politics is another stumbling block for the two. The U.K. is an active member of NATO and supports the alliance. France, however, feels that the organization is dominated by U.S. interests and has adopted a 'go-it-alone' policy . . ."

STRATEGIC "SUPERIORITY" IN SUPERPOWER RELATIONS, by Colin S. Gray, in *Military Review*, v. 51, no. 12 (December 1971) 8-21.

"The recent literature of strategic studies is marked by the considerable attention paid to the apparently remorseless impact of new technologies upon the interacting defense planning of the superpowers. This attention was belated and, in the context of the Strategic Arms Limitation Talks (SALT), was to be welcomed. However, the notion of an arms race driven essentially by action and over-reaction in new technologies has often been taken to extremes. This discussion seeks to focus upon the fact that the strategic arms race is a foreign policy exercise."

A TACTICAL NUCLEAR STRATEGY FOR NATO, by Col. Stanley D. Fair, in *NATO's Fifteen Nations*, v. 19, no. 2 (April-May 1974) 59-61.

"The thesis of his article is that the utility of tactical nuclear weapons, under the conditions of strategic parity between the United States and the Soviet Union, lies in their use to achieve early war termination."

TOWARD NUCLEAR SELF-SUFFICIENCY IN EUROPE, by Col. Norman L. Dodd, in *Army*, v. 24, no. 3 (March 1974) 40-44.

"Anglo-French nuclear cooperation cannot take place so long as Britain maintains its special relationship with the United States, but rising costs or a change in American policy could produce an integrated European deterrent force in the future."

c. *The Strategy of Flexible Response*

THE MYSTIQUE OF NATO'S NUKES, by Gen. T. R. Milton, in *NATO Review*, v. 58, no. 1 (January 1975) 26-27.

"NATO has a rather considerable atomic arsenal. What is more, there are aircraft on alert to carry out nuclear strikes. The purpose of this nuclear capability is to provide meaning to NATO strategy—the so-called Flexible Response strategy, or, to give its formal name, MC 15/3."

NATO'S FLEXIBLE RESPONSE, by Maj. E. H. Ozarne, in *Army in Europe*, (October 1973) 10-13.

"Allied Command Europe Mobile Force (Land). AMF(L), also referred to as the ACE Mobile Force, is one of the most important and certainly unique operations within the North Atlantic Treaty Organization. Infantry, artillery, combat support and administrative units of seven nations comprise the ACE Mobile Force, an organization of approximately Brigade strength headquartered at Mannheim-Seekenheim, Germany. Concern over protecting the common frontiers and waterways of NATO's more remote areas—Northern Norway, Denmark, Greece, Turkey, Northern Italy—is what first prompted the NATO Alliance to adopt a military policy of 'flexible response.' So the ACE Mobile Force was formed in the late 1950's to close the gaps in areas where NATO forces are not strongly represented."

NUCLEAR WEAPONS AND "FLEXIBLE RESPONSE," by Phillip A. Karber, in *Orbis*, v. 14, no. 2 (Summer 1970) 284-297.

"The Soviet-led invasion of Czechoslovakia challenged many of the basic Western assumptions that have achieved prominence in the last decade. This brutal and unexpected use of force raised fundamental questions about East European 'liberalization,' Soviet intentions, and NATO's capabilities to prevent such an occurrence in Western Europe. The invasion also carried two distinct, if unannounced, warnings—one to the East European communist states and one to the European members of NATO . . . The concept of 'flexible response' was devised to meet and defeat, with like force, a full range of Soviet attack possibilities. Emphasis was shifted to building the conventional forces within NATO necessary to meet a large-scale conventional attack by the Soviet Union and the Warsaw Pact. The doctrine of 'flexible response,' officially adopted by NATO in 1967, is based on three major assumptions: (1) that the West can field enough conventional forces in Central Europe to defeat an all-out conventional attack by the Warsaw Pact; (2) that there will be adequate warning of a strategic buildup so Western forces can be reinforced and tactical surprise will not provide substantial advantage to the attacker; and (3) that 'under the most extreme circumstances,' if the Warsaw Pact forces are winning, nuclear weapons will be employed by the West and the changeover to tactical nuclear weapons will favor the NATO forces."

THE USE OF NUCLEAR WEAPONS IN THE EUROPEAN THEATRE, by Air Vice-Marshal S. W. B. Menaul, in *NATO's Fifteen Nations*, (April-May 1975).

"We come back to the concept of flexible response—or as I prefer to call it, appropriate response. This in essence means the ability to select the firepower necessary to stem any Warsaw Pact assault on Western Europe whenever, wherever and at whatever level it may be launched. Whether the Soviets in due course attempt to achieve their political goals by threats of overt action, using conventional forces only, in the hope that NATO would thereby be induced to refrain from using theatre nuclear weapons, or by any combination of conventional and nuclear forces. NATO should be seen to have and should make sure the Soviets know they have the means to stop a Soviet advance into Europe and in the process to inflict catastrophic losses on the Warsaw Pact forces. The review of the NATO nuclear stockpile is overdue. It could with advantage be reduced in size and changed in structure provided new technology is introduced which would increase firepower at all levels while maintaining existing manpower or even reducing it."

d. *Nuclear Deterrence*

THE ALLIANCE AND EUROPE: PART I—CRISIS STABILITY IN EUROPE AND THEATRE NUCLEAR WEAPONS, by Wolfgang Heisenberg. London, The International Institute for Strategic Studies, 1973. 35 p. (Adelphi Papers 96.)

The Need for a New Debate; What Functions—Deterrence or Defence?; Four Possible Doctrines; Tactical Nuclear Weapons and the Political Process; Notes and Glossary.

DETERRENCE AND DEFENCE IN EUROPE: REVISING NATO'S THEATRE NUCLEAR POSTURE, by Colin S. Grey, in *Strategic Review*, v. 3, no. 2 (Spring 1975) 58–70.

Reprinted from RUSI Journal, December 1974.—"Discussion of a realistic deterrence and defense posture for NATO must address six general conditions for nuclear weapons employment: Protracted war, conventional emphasis; short war, conventional emphasis; tactical nuclear war-fighting emphasis; flexible response with tactical nuclear weapons modernization; flexible response, present conditions; and early nuclear use. In the NATO countries, a decision for the tactical nuclear war-fighting emphasis is beset by uncertainties inherent in the nature of war, notably: The scale of the threat; the combat potential of the threat; the effectiveness and survivability of conventional weapons systems; the effectiveness, survivability and control of tactical nuclear weapons in combat; the nature of the Soviet tactical nuclear stockpile and the probably tactical nuclear use doctrine; and the attitudes to be found in NATO capitals. From a consideration of these aspects of the problem, it appears that emphasis on a NATO tactical nuclear war-fighting commitment is essential to preserve a credible balance of military forces in Europe which will deter or stop Soviet aggression and that transition to such clear policy from the present ambiguous commitment is imperative."

NATO'S NUCLEAR STRATEGY, by Major E. Hinterhoff, in *NATO's Fifteen Nations*, v. 15, no. 5 (October–November 1970) 42–48.

"During the past few months there have been several meetings of NATO defence Ministers at which the use of nuclear weapons for deterrent and defence purposes was discussed. There is, of course, nothing sensational in this, as the use of nuclear weapons, both strategic and tactical, has been almost since the setting up of NATO part and parcel of its strategy. Of course, in view of the evolution of the nuclear balance between NATO, and for all practical purposes between the United States, and the Soviet Union, developing from an absolute monopoly held by the U.S. for several years, down to the present 'party' in ICBM's and superiority in megatonnage held by the Soviets, nuclear strategy has become of paramount importance. However, one of the important aspects of the latest meetings of the NATO Defence Ministers was the fact that on these occasions they have been discussing and approving the draft of the 'guidelines' for the use of tactical atomic weapons located in Western Europe and numbering, as disclosed by American official spokesmen, well over 7,000."

(*)—NUCLEAR WEAPONS AND THE ATLANTIC ALLIANCE, by Wynfred Joshua. New York, National Strategy Information Center, Inc., 1973. 55 p.

"In this monograph, Dr. Joshua argues that tensions within the Alliance appear to be deepening while the Soviet and Warsaw Pact forces continue to be modernized and strengthened. 'Thus NATO finds itself in a profound dilemma at the very time that its objectives of deterrence and defence remain as valid as ever. The problem for the West appears to centre on the need to restore confidence and cohesion in the Alliance in order to insure West European resilience against Soviet political coercion.' Dr. Joshua gives special attention in her study to the role of tactical nuclear weapons in the defence of Western Europe, and to the place of national nuclear forces. Her conclusion is that while the Alliance is 'beset with the problems of diminishing allied cohesion and growing Soviet military capabilities and political initiatives,' nevertheless, 'a viable strategy . . . can still be found'."

STABLE DETERRENCE: A STRATEGIC POLICY FOR THE 1970'S, by J. H. Kahan, in *Orbis*, v. 15, no. 2 (Summer 1972) 528-543.

"Now that the Soviet Union has reached a position of overall strategic equality with the United States, we no longer hear serious talk of the need for U.S. superiority, but find ourselves discussing criteria for 'sufficiency' and attempting to negotiate nuclear weapons limitations. Whatever the outcome of the Strategic Arms Limitation Talks (SALT), it seems virtually certain that the United States and the Soviet Union will remain roughly comparable in nuclear power over the next decade . . . The changed nuclear balance has thus introduced new political as well as military uncertainties into the U.S.-Soviet strategic relationship. Whether or not a limited agreement emerges from the current arms negotiations, the task before us is to design an effective future strategic policy. This article describes a policy of 'stable deterrence' and argues that it is the best way of managing our strategic posture and maximizing our nuclear security in the 1970's."

e. *The Tactical Nuclear Weapons Option*

A COMMON WESTERN NUCLEAR DOCTRINE?, by Marc E. Geneste, in *Military Review*, (September 1971) 3-21.

". . . The Western allies, despite their economic competition, must develop a unified strategic doctrine for the seventies. He believes that the growing Soviet and Chinese military might present a common problem for the West, which requires a common strategic solution . . . Tactical nuclear doctrine, in contrast to strategic nuclear doctrine which can remain national, requires total allied 'integration' in peacetime. A common tactical doctrine implies common agreement among the allies on the preconditions under which the alliance commander-in-chief could decide to employ tactical nuclear weapons. The tactical trigger is thus predelegated to the soldier for the common cause, with a set of rules established by the politician to control escalation . . . If the allies were to agree on new conditions under which strategic and tactical nuclear forces would be employed, a new alliance could arise out of the past troubles of NATO, and an adequate solution could be found for a common military threat."

NATO'S TACTICAL NUCLEAR OPTION: PAST, PRESENT AND FUTURE, by Dennis M. Gormley, in *Military Review*, v. 53, no. 9 (September 1973) 3-18.

"The purpose here is to examine the military and political role and viability of NATO's tactical nuclear option. The article includes certain proposals for changes in the Alliance's military forces. In the course of examining NATO's tactical nuclear option, primary attention will focus on the following questions: Does our huge stockpile of tactical nuclear weapons in Western Europe represent an effective military force that would minimize collateral (civilian) damage, if employed? Can greater reliance on the use of tactical nuclear weapons compensate for reductions in conventional NATO ground forces? Can NATO fight a controlled 'tactical' nuclear war in Europe without precipitating escalation to more destructive levels of nuclear conflict? Can NATO defend conventionally against supposedly superior Warsaw Pact ground forces?"

THE REALITIES OF TACTICAL NUCLEAR WARFARE, by James H. Polk, in *Orbis*, (Summer 1973) 439-447.

"Gen. Polk believes that America's concepts regarding NATO defense arrangements are 'dangerously impractical' and that the tactical nuclear weapons based in Europe, products of the 1950's technology, must be updated and modernized if they are to serve as a credible force. He deplores the notion, widely accepted both in the US and in the Soviet Union, that any use of tactical nukes would inevitably lead to all-out nuclear war and major disaster; this belief operates to Russia's advantage because the Bloc's conventional forces are superior to NATO's. Thus, in the one area of military power where NATO is superior, i.e., tactical nukes, NATO, as well as the US, is deterred from first-use for fear of precipitating a larger war . . ."

THEATRE AIR FORCES AND TACTICAL NUCLEAR WEAPONS, by E. Van Veen, in *NATO's Fifteen Nations*, v. 17, no. 4 (August-September 1972) 34-39 plus.

Parity; NATO's Nuclear Policy; Tactical Nuclear Weapons (The Present Stock, Nuclear Weapons of the Future); NATO's Constraints Policy; NATO's Theatre Air Forces; The Nuclear Weapon Delivery Vehicles; Preparedness; and Conclusion.

U.S. NUCLEAR WEAPONS IN EUROPE: ISSUES AND ALTERNATIVES, by Jeffrey Record with Thomas I. Anderson. Washington, Brookings, 1974. 70 p.

Contents: Tactical Nuclear Weapons—Definitions and Categories; Present U.S. Tactical Nuclear Posture in NATO; Asymmetries Between U.S. and Soviet Tactical Nuclear Posture; Weaknesses of the Present U.S. Posture; Alternative Postures; and Tables.

WILL TACTICAL NUCLEAR WEAPONS EVER BE USED?, by Philip W. Dyer, in *Political Science Quarterly*, (June 1973) 214-229.

"Claims that confusion surrounds the role of tactical nuclear weapons. No definitive policy has ever been formulated on their use, even though the US today possesses an impressive arsenal of them. After correlating a model of foreign policy decision making with applications of tactical nuclear forces, Dyer concludes that such weapons 'have no conceivable role in future ground warfare.' . . . In a 1956 NATO war game codenamed 'Operation Carte Blanche,' only the Allied side had these weapons for deployment. Moreover, it was discovered in this operation that a tactical nuclear conflict would cause as many German civilian casualties as would an all-out global war. Another problem that Dyer emphasizes is the trouble in differentiating between what is 'tactical' and what is 'strategic.' US tactical nuclear weapons have the capability of wiping out a large city hundreds of miles from the point of launch. Dyer questions whether any conflict in which such a weapon was employed could be effectively localized . . . Dyer notes that the deployment of US tactical nuclear weapons is linked to this country's commitment to NATO. If NATO must defend West Europe without necessarily touching off a strategic war then, ideally, tactical nuclear weapons should serve a purpose as part of this shield. In 1967, however, NATO adopted a non-nuclear strategy and has continued to 'muddle through without a systematic and logical strategic policy in line with its capabilities.' Debate on the feasibility of tactical nuclear weapons has been further obfuscated by uncertainty among the Atlantic allies . . ."

f. *The Soviet View of NATO's Nuclear Strategy*

NATO NUCLEAR PLANS: PAST AND PRESENT, in *International Affairs, Moscow*, no. 11 (1973) 105-106.

A review of the following book: The Nuclear Policy of the USA in NATO, by V.G. Mitayev. Moscow, International Relations Publishers, 1973. 207 p. "The Soviet-American agreements on the prevention of nuclear war and the limitation of strategic arms visibly symbolise the rapid change which has occurred in present-day international relations. This change did not come of itself; it was prepared and determined by the long and steadfast struggle of the Soviet Union against the forces of reaction and aggression, against the arms race and the policy of militarism and revanchism in Europe. One of the important aspects of this struggle was the foiling during the 1960s of the plans for providing nuclear weapons to North Atlantic bloc. A detailed study of American nuclear policy in NATO and the stand of the USSR on these questions is the subject of the monograph The Nuclear Policy of the USA in NATO by V. G. Mitayev. This work is of importance not only as a historical study, although an insight into the way of thinking and methods of action used by the enemies of an International détente in the recent past is useful in itself. The author stresses that the reactionary militarist circles in Western Europe still cherish the hope of getting hold of nuclear weapons in one way or another and are seeking loopholes for achieving this end."

C. Military Preparedness and the Armed Forces (See also Appendixes)

1. *Miscellaneous Aspects*

THE ALLIANCE AND EUROPE: PART II—DEFENCE WITH FEWER MEN, by Kenneth Hunt. London, The International Institute for Strategic Studies, 1973. 42 p. (Adelphi Papers 98.)

The Present Defence Posture—Some Problems (Strategy, Forward Defence, Warning and Reinforcements, Current Weaknesses in the Forces, Financial Constraints, Manpower and Weapons Costs, Manpower Problems, US Forces in Europe, Mutual Force Reductions, Military Technology); Possible Future Defence Postures (The Problem of Change; Some Ideas for Change—Restructuring, Rapid Reinforcements in Crisis, More Reliance on Reservists, Simple Reduction, US Forces in Reserve, Defence in Depth); Conclusions.

45 COMMANDO ROYAL MARINES; BRITAIN'S ARCTIC WARFARE UNIT ASSIGNED TO NATO, by John Marriott, in *NATO's Fifteen Nations*, v. 19, no. 3 (June-July 1974) 31-35 plus.

"Consequent upon Britain's withdrawal from the Far and Middle Easts in 1969, the British

Government offered to assign their 4 Royal Marine Commandos to NATO. The offer was gratefully accepted and 45 Commando was given the role of acting as an emergency re-inforcement of the Norwegian forces in Norway in the event of a Soviet invasion. Since it was apparent that any invasion would be in the far north, the British Government decided that the Commando should become a specialized unit in mountain and arctic warfare and on 1 December 1969 45 Commando was designated as Britain's Mountain and Arctic Warfare Unit."

THE MILITARY BALANCE 1973-1974—THE NORTH ATLANTIC TREATY, in *Air Force Magazine*, v. 56, no. 12 (December 1973) 71-79.

Includes some of the following information on the military posture: military service, total armed forces, defense budget, army, navy, and air force. See also the following which includes similar information: The Military Balance 1973-1974—Other European Countries, in Air Force Magazine, v. 56, no. 12 (December 1973) 86-88.

NATO AND U.S. FORCES: CHALLENGES AND PROSPECTS, by Gen. Andrew J. Goodpaster, in *Strategic Review*, v. 2, no. 1 (Winter 1974) 6-17.

"The two objectives of NATO are deterrence and defense. NATO conventional defense forces lie between the high-risk, 'trip-wire' concept and the low-risk, full-conventional capability. There design and readiness require close coordination with the use of tactical nuclear weapons and with political policy. To be effective, the Alliance must achieve unity of purpose and action. As it does so, its capacity to promote détente will increase. NATO faces the MBFR negotiations with inferior forces, inferior position and a defensive psychology, seeking to draw constructive and balanced force reductions from negotiations. In these negotiations, NATO is weakened by euphoria derived from the act of negotiating, and by the capacity of the other side to exploit the divergent interests of the allies. It may be necessary for NATO to consider problems beyond its immediate mission but which have an adverse effect on the solidarity of the Alliance. In recent years, the Warsaw Pact forces have greatly enlarged their numbers and armament in Central Europe while the NATO powers, despite weapons improvements, have declined in strength. Through joint exercises, every effort is made to maintain a high state of readiness for NATO forces. Despite its economic strength, Europe is politically and militarily weak. NATO remains essential to European security. The security of Europe and of the United States are so interrelated that U.S. forces in NATO are also defending the United States. The U.S. contributions of forces and funds to the NATO defense are a prudent investment in our own security."

NATO FORCE SUFFICIENCY STUDY—1970: EXECUTIVE SUMMARY. Menlo Park, Calif., Stanford Research Institute, September 1970. 23 p. (SSC-TN-8260-11.)

"After more than 20 years of outstanding success NATO faces a protracted period of serious stress. The political-military environment in Europe is in a profound flux, partly as a result of changing perceptions of the Soviet/Warsaw Pact threat, domestic economic problems, and changing national priorities of the European NATO Allies. Compounding the crisis is the recognition that the Soviet Union has achieved a position of strategic nuclear parity vis-a-vis the U.S. Within Europe, moreover, the Soviet Union would have a position of strategic superiority if the U.S. strategic deterrent were to be decoupled from the defense of Europe. Another factor intensifying NATO's predicament derives from Soviet diplomatic maneuvers to outflank NATO at its peripheries. This is an *Executive Summary* of a study that seeks to determine a sufficiency concept for NATO forces and to present a range of feasible NATO strategies for the 1970s. It discusses the alternative strategies that meet NATO requirements of deterrence and defense against armed aggression or the threat of armed attack, ranging from the broadest aspects of U.S. national security to the more specific matters of detailed force composition and utilization."

NATO MUSCLE: MORE SHADOW THAN SUBSTANCE, by Steven L. Canby, in *Military Review*, v. 53, no. 2 (February 1973) 65-74.

"Why is NATO outspending the Warsaw Pact—in terms of both men and money—while buying less security? This so-called 'people-PEMA paradox' (PEMA being acronymic jargon for 'procurement of equipment and missiles, Army'), which so perplexed the McNamara analysts, can be resolved by examining the assumptions underlying NATO's organization for defense. The Pact, consciously or not, has developed operating procedures and a force structure appropriate to its strategic requirements in Europe; NATO, and particularly the American component, has not. Restructuring NATO could release the resources necessary to implement flexible response and forward defense and remove some difficult political choices. The crucial questions boil down to whether NATO should opt for highly visible, high initial combat forces (as the Soviets do) or retain low visibility, low initial combat forces which are sustainable."

NATO'S CURRENT MILITARY PROBLEMS; AN ADDRESS BEFORE THE NATO DEFENSE COLLEGE, by Gen. Johannes Steinhoff, in *NATO's Fifteen Nations*, v. 18, no. 6 (December 1973–January 1974) 20–22.

"I have tried to characterize some of the important issues facing NATO in the military field. Although NATO is still a strong Alliance, we must view realistically its force capabilities, and these realistic assessments shall not be interpreted as undue pessimism. I was trying to differentiate in a very general way the causes for existing problems in certain member countries and, basically, when looking into these matters, one always comes back to the same conclusion: not enough money. I have also given you my thoughts on an approach to ease this problem and how best to use the available resources. I am firmly convinced that we should be able to organize our defence more efficiently, but only if we can develop co-operation in defence between the NATO countries to a degree hitherto unknown. This approach, in my opinion, promises so much that every effort should be made to overcome the inevitable obstacles."

PROFESSIONAL MILITARY EDUCATION; A BAND OF NATO AIR FORCES, by Irving H. Breslauer, in *NATO's Fifteen Nations*, v. 15, no. 4 (August–September 1970) 98–100 plus.

"In the past 20 years more than 1,000 NATO officers have attended Air University schools. The majority of these officers have attended Squadron Officer School and the balance have attended either Air Command and Staff College or the Air War College. Turkey and Denmark lead the NATO countries in the number of Air University school graduates with 167 and 147 respectively . . . Before the Allied student goes to SOS or either of the other two Air University schools, Air Command and Staff College (ACSC) and Air War College (AWC), he must go through a period of pre-training."

THE ROAD TO DÉTENTE, by Gen. Johannes Steinhof, in *The Atlantic Community Quarterly*, v. 10, no. 4 (Winter 1972–1973) 446–456.

"General Steinhoff, Chairman of the NATO Military Committee, makes clear that while the Western powers contine to strive for détente, their military leaders would be remiss in their duty if they did not point to increasing Soviet capabilities, leaving the question of intentions to the statesmen. He also considers certain kinds of Mutual and Balanced Force Reduction (MBFR) theoretically possible, though not necessarily politically acceptable. Overall, he emphasizes the need for continued public awareness of, and support for, proper military preparedness in the present period of détente."

STRATEGY AND CAPABILITIES OF ALLIED COMMAND EUROPE, by Gen. Andrew J. Goodpaster, Jr., in *Naval War College Review*, v. 23, no. 2 (October 1970) 11–18.

"One of the most important factors in Western Europe's economic and political recovery after the Second World War was confidence in the military strength and solidarity provided by NATO. Because of this, investments and long-term programs were undertaken in an optimistic spirit. One danger of the current cutbacks in military expenditures and commitments on the part of the United States is that this spirit of confidence will be lost, with a resulting deterioration in strength, growth, and solidarity."

TERRITORIAL DEFENSE IN NATO AND NON-NATO EUROPE, by H. Mendershausen. Santa Monica, Calif., Rand Corp., February 1973. 114 p. (R–1184–ISA.)

"Pressures working on defense structures of European NATO countries, particularly those of the Federal Republic of Germany (FRG), tend to favor a change to latent conscript forces oriented toward territorial defense on one hand, standing volunteer armies on the other. Political, financial, and military potentialities of a combination of such forces are discussed, and a detailed comparison made of territorial defense concepts and forces, as well as civil defense preparations, in four countries—Switzerland and Yugoslavia (which do not participate in NATO's military integration) and Norway and France (which do so to a much lesser extent that the FRG). As long as the Germans and others in NATO believe that a shift toward latent forces endangers the alliance, and as long as U.S. attitudes confirm this belief, the potentialities of such forces will not be fully realized. The study draws on interviews the author conducted with military and civil defense specialists in West Germany, Norway, Sweden, and France."

THE WASTEFUL WAYS OF NATO, by Steven L. Canby, in *Survival*, v. 15. no. 1 (January/

February 1973) 21-26.

"Is NATO using its defence resources in an efficient way? The author, from the RAND Corporation, California, argues that it does not; while the Warsaw Pact has organized its forces for a quick offensive strategy, concentrating on immediate military superiority, NATO's potential, if structured as at present, could only be brought to bear in a protracted conflict. According to the article, reprinted below, NATO should reorganize its forces, relying on larger numbers of smaller divisions and emphasizing its defensive character. The original title of the article which is based on a paper for the Southern California Arms Control and Foreign Policy Seminar is 'NATO Muscle: More Shadow Than Substance'."

WOMEN IN NATO ARMED FORCES, by Nancy L. Goldman, in *Military Review*, v. 54, no. 10 (October 1974) 72-82.

"To meet additional manpower requirements, NATO nations can look to women as volunteers to a greater extent than in prior years since there is more societal acceptance of women's employment in a wider variety of occupations in the 1970s. Most of the Western European NATO countries—with the exception of the Federal Republic of Germany—include women or have plans to include them in their armed services."

2. *Air Defense Aspects*

THE AIR DEFENCE OF EUROPE, by John Marriott, in *NATO's Fifteen Nations*, v. 18, no. 5 (October-November 1973) 37-68.

"NATO's air defences are thus a deterrent and to deter is NATO's major objective. In this survey an attempt has been made to cover the whole aspect of air defence. The NADGE system and the organisation for air defence is explained, the many close range anti-aircraft missiles in development are compared, details of NATO's fighters and missiles are given and there is a brief look at SAM-D, the all purpose ground-to-air missile of the future." Contents: Europe's Air Defence Organization; High and Medium Altitude Ground-To-Air Missiles; Aircraft Used in the Air Defence of Europe; Defence Against Low Level Aircraft; SAM-D The Surface-to-Air Missile of the 1980s.

AIR FORCES OF THE WORLD—PART 1: EUROPEAN NATO MEMBERS, in *Interavia*, v. 28, no. 9 (September 1973) 1003-1007.

A summary of "outlining defence spending and listing equipment inventories of the various nations," including, among others, Denmark and Norway. See also Part 2: Europe's Neutral and Non-Aligned Nations, in Interavia, v. 28, no. 10 (October 1973) 1117-1120, which includes information on Finland.

DEFENSE AGAINST LOW LEVEL AIR ATTACK, by Charles Latour, in *NATO's Fifteen Nations*, v. 19, no. 4 (August-September 1974) 44-51.

"With the improvements that have been effected in modern warning radars, attacking aircraft are now being forced to come in as low as possible to the target so that they are below the main lobes of the surveillance radars. Charles Latour discusses the problems of defence from the ground of these 'hedge hopping' attackers . . . All modern nations are now seriously considering how to improve their defences against low level air attack. In NATO, with the efficient NADGE warning system and the relatively good coverage of the medium and high altitudes by HAWK and NIKE missiles, it has come to be realised that the most likely form of air attack is by low level strike aircraft . . . NATO's close range air defences are still geared to the repulsion of conventional air attack. In the next decade they will have to be designed to repel attacks by unmanned missiles, or other vehicles, travelling at speeds well in excess of those of aircraft, and launched perhaps hundreds of miles away from the target in comparative safety."

EXPENSIVE LUXURY OR PAINFUL NECESSITY? EUROPE'S NEW GENERATION OF COMBAT AIRCRAFT; PART 1:—THE INCREASING THREAT, by R. Meller, in *International Defense Review*, no. 2 (April 1975).

"In the next 10-15 years virtually all the NATO countries in Western Europe, together with France, will introduce third generation jet combat aircraft into service, and the funding required for this could total some $45,000 million. This considerable outlay prompts the question as to whether Europe can support such an expensive re-equipment program, and whether in view of the relaxation of East-West tension there is still a real need for it. The International Defense Review has carried out an in-depth study of this question and has had the opportunity to talk to the Chiefs of Staff of most European NATO air forces and of the US Air Force in Europe. We begin our series in this issue with a detailed presentation of the threat to Europe posed by the Warsaw Pact countries, with emphasis on the threat from the air. In subsequent articles of this series, the assessment of this threat by NATO and the air forces of the European NATO countries will be discussed, together with the current proposals and plans to counter."

NADGE, NATO'S NEW AIR DEFENSE NET, in *Army in Europe*, (September 1973) 2-5.

"It's a $28.6 billion complex that can instantly detect, identify and intercept enemy aircraft and missiles."

NADGE: THE LAST WORD IN COMPUTERIZED AIR DEFENCE, by Elise Nouël, in *NATO Review*, v. 19, nos. 7-8 (July/August 1971) 8-12.

"With an impressive air display of Lightnings, Mirages, Phantoms, F104Gs and other Canadian, Turkish, Greek, Belgian, Danish and Norwegian air force fighters weaving across the sky under the watchful electronic eye of scores of computers and within the 'field of vision' of giant radars, the setting up of the NATO Air Defence Ground Environment is entering its final phase. For more than a year now, all types of fighter aircraft from the countries of the Alliance have been participating, group after group, in the final testing of NADGE. This is the biggest and most complex ground enviroment project of the Alliance and is due to become fully operational in a few months time."

(LI)—NATO AIR DEFENSE: IS NADGE THE ANSWER?, by Maj. John P. Guzalak. Maxwell AFB, Ala., Air Command and Staff College, 1973. 74 p. (Research Study.)

"The NATO Air Defense Ground Environment System (NADGE) is scheduled to be operational late in 1973. This study challenges the very basis of that system. An introductory review of the changing nature of air defense is followed by a discussion of those factors that are unique in the European air defense environment. Against this backdrop, the merits of NADGE are evaluated both as a concept and as an air defense system. Conclusions are reached in each context and recommendations include immediate and future modifications needed to exploit NADGE's present capabilities."

(LI)—NATO AIR DEFENSE: IS THE US FIGHTER CONTRIBUTION APPROPRIATE?, by Lt. Col. Leslie C. Conwell. Maxwell AFB, Ala., Air War College, 1974. 83 p. (Professional Study.)

"An in-depth examination of the NATO air defense system in its early years and an analysis of the reasons for its integration in 1960 provide the background for a review of changes which have occurred since that date. After concluding that the air defense system has developed into an effective force for deterrence and defense, the author then turns to an examination of trends in Europe and America to include a brief threat analysis in an attempt to determine possibilities for the future. It is concluded that with continued modernization and American participation at current levels, the NATO air defense system can continue to satisfactorily meet its roles and missions responsibilities for at least the next decade. Appropriate priorities must be established by American decision-makers to assure continued support. Aside from political and psychological reasons, NATO needs American technology. In a parallel vein, the United States has strong interests in Europe and cannot abandon the alliance due to mutual needs."

THE TACTICAL AIR BALANCE IN EUROPE, by Neville Brown, in *The World Today*, v. 28, no. 9 (September 1972) 385-392.

"In the event of conflict in Europe, NATO's disadvantage on the ground might be offset by the superior quality of its aircraft and ground-to-air weapons."

WORLD MILITARY AVIATION; AIRCRAFT, AIRFORCES AND WEAPONRY, ed. by Nikolaus Krivinyi and others. New York, Arco Publishing Co., 1973. 224 p.

This book is divided into the following chapters: Air Forces (The world's airforces with individual strengths, aircraft types and bases); Aircraft (aircraft dimensions and performance arranged alphabetically within country of manufacture, with 321 three-view drawings); weaponry (missiles, bombs, guns and torpedoes in service with the world's airpowers), Glossary and Abbreviations; Insignia (roundel and fin flash designs, as used by the world's airforces); and Index (index of numerical designations and popular names of aircraft).

3. *Naval and Maritime Aspects*

THE ALLIED COMMAND ATLANTIC—SUBMARINE CHALLENGE, by Comdr. J. O. Naugle, in *NATO's Fifteen Nations*, v. 17, no. 1 (February-March 1972) 62-68.

"The Soviet Union has in recent years developed the capability to interdict NATO sea lanes of communications and challenge the organization's use of ocean areas vital to its security. This expanding military potential has come from many sources over the years but most recently it has appeared in the form of ships.... The Naval Forces of NATO must stand ready to counter the Soviet Bloc threat which is rapidly growing in size and capability. The Allied Command Atlantic (ACLANT) area, generally considered as that ocean area North of the Tropic of Cancer, is where this challenge has most recently been thrust forward, and where it must be met. To do this, a balanced mix of forces, submarine, surface and air is needed. Over the past twenty years an effective organization has been structured to make maximum effective use of these forces. Commander Submarines Allied Command Atlantic (COMSUB ACLANT) enjoys an unusual position in this organization. COMSUBACLANT is one of five major subordinate commanders to the supreme Allied Commander Atlantic (SACLANT). The position is held by Commander Submarine Force, U.S. Atlantic Fleet (COMSUBLANT). This command is a functional command."

THE CHANGING SEASCAPE; ITS IMPLICATIONS FOR THE ALLIANCE, in *NATO Review*, v. 21, no. 5 (1973) 7-9.

"'If the freedom of the high seas were to be denied to us, freedom in our respective countries would wither just as surely as withers a plant to which water is denied,' said NATO Secretary General Mr. Joseph Luns in his opening remarks to the SACLANT Symposium Sea Link I. This symposium was held from 26-28 June in ... the United States Naval Academy, Annapolis ... All participants readily agreed that this indeed was a think exercise because the recent developments in the international military, technological, economic and political fields have led to the urgent need for some new and imaginative thinking. This in no way implies that NATO needs a new strategy. It does mean that, under the existing strategy, the role of NATO's maritime forces, in the light notably of the Soviet naval expansion, is to be reinterpreted."

THE MARITIME EQUATION—SACLANT IN THE 1970s, by Adm. Charles K. Duncan, in *NATO's Fifteen Nations*, v. 17, no. 1 (February-March 1972) 28-35.

"As the members of the North Atlantic Treaty Organization close the chapter on twenty-two years of intimate cooperation, we can look back proudly on solid and concrete accomplishments. Together, we have orchestrated our individual national policies to reinforce the goals of the alliance and have achieved a result which, if we had acted separately would have not been possible. Our alliance has kept the peace we all desire so much; it has been the protective shield that has permitted a generation of allied growth and enrichment. The Allied Command Atlantic has been a significant element in providing the protective maritime structure that, together with Allied Command Europe and the Channel Command, has given muscle to this defensive Alliance ... On a day-to-day basis, SACLANT exercises operational control of the Standing Naval Force Atlantic. It is the only military force available to NATO on a continuing basis ... Supplementing the day-to-day availability of the Standing Naval Force Atlantic are on call forces under the Maritime Contingency Forces Atlantic concept. Under these plans, specially tailored multi-national task forces can be called up to meet various contingencies in the Atlantic area. These forces are, of course, the primary tools that SACLANT has to carry out the NATO strategy of Flexible Response, short of general war."

NATO LIVES OR DIES BY THE SEA; UNHAMPERED USE IS VITAL, by Joseph Palmer, in *NATO's Fifteen Nations*, v. 19, no. 5 (October-November 1974) 20-23 plus.

"The North Atlantic Treaty Organization is a maritime alliance; first, last, and all along the line in between ... NATO is maritime for one simple reason: it is the ocean that binds it together and gives it not only a common purpose but the means of achieving it. And, by the same token, the means whereby may frustrate that achievement ... Let us therefore adopt a practical and realistic point of view from which to inspect just what the Oceans and Seas mean to NATO; the use we make of them, now and in future; the means of ensuring that we can do so. And, if we need an aim, as everyone should, then it is survival."

THE ROLE OF NATO IN THE USE OF THE SEA AND THE SEABED, by Friedhelm Kruger-Sprengel. Washington, Woodrow Wilson International Center for Scholars, October 1972. 45 p.

"Military and security interests have emerged as of utmost importance in determining the future law of the oceans and seabed, with their appropriate regimes. These are now under consideration by the UN Sea-Bed Committee. As a maritime alliance NATO has a special interest in the trend towards limiting the principle of the freedom of the high seas, efforts to achieve complete demilitarization of the sea, and the possible constraint upon free passage for warships in certain straits and waters, such as those in the Baltic Sea. The United States and the Soviet Union, as two great maritime powers, have a coincidence of interests in maintaining the freedom of the high seas and in limiting the extension of territorial waters by coastal states. For NATO the existing rules of international law seem satisfactory, but enlargement of coastal jurisdiction in the Atlantic Ocean could even prove advantageous to the alliance. Bilateral negotiations, with the coastal states involved, over the free transit of international straits would probably be the best diplomatic approach to that vexing question."

TECHNOLOGY AND POLITICAL CHOICE IN FUTURE NATO MARITIME STRATEGY, by John Simpson, in *Orbis*, v. 17, no. 1 (Spring 1973) 258–276.

"In the two decades since the formation of NATO, its attention has been concentrated on the possibility of a Soviet attack on the central land front in Western Europe. With the progress of détente and Ostpolitik, however, the possibility of military aggression on this front seems to have diminished. At the same time, the operational deployment of the Soviet navy has changed from mainly coastal defense to worldwide activity. It is not surprising that some observers view the major area of threat to Western Europe as moving from the central land front to the maritime areas contiguous to NATO states. This shift affects chiefly such states as Norway and Great Britain, which are geographically most vulnerable to maritime activities. And it calls for a review of the functions of NATO maritime forces, together with an analysis of the type of naval forces NATO states should develop."

TIME TO SECURE THE SEAS, by Col. Frank B. Case, in *United States Naval Institute Proceedings*, v. 99, no. 8 (August 1973) 24–31.

"Rapid reinforcement of NATO is the keystone of U.S. strategy for non-nuclear war in Europe. But, as our control of the sea slips away, the concept has become a prescription for disaster."

4. *Exercises and Maneuvers*

EXERCISE STRONG EXPRESS, by John Marriott, in *NATO's Fifteen Nations*, v. 18, no. 1 (February-March 1973) 74–80.

"The largest NATO exercise ever staged took place from September 11th to the 28th last year. The areas involved were the Atlantic, the Channel and Northern Norway and all the NATO nations bordering these areas took part. Code named Strong Express, it was designed to simulate the opening stages of a war. The two sides taking part were designated Blue (NATO) and Orange and an imaginary Blue/Orange border was drawn across northern Norway behind which Orange land forces massed."

SECOND EXERCISE OF MEDITERRANEAN ON-CALL FORCE, in *NATO Review*, v. 19, nos. 7–8 (July/August 1971) 13.

"The second activation of NATO's Naval On-Call Force Mediterranean (NAVOCFORMED) was completed early in June when warships of five nations ended 18 days of exercises at sea including port calls in NATO Mediterranean countries. Five destroyers from NATO Mediterranean nations, the United Kingdom and the United States, participated in gunnery, air defence, anti-submarine and underway replenishment training in the Exercise code-named 'DYNAMIC BOND'."

STRONG EXPRESS, by Peter Jenner, in *NATO's Fifteen Nations*, v. 17, no. 6 (December 1972–January 1973) 90–96.

"Strong Express, involving forces of twelve of the fifteen nations of the Alliance, was one of the most important land, sea and air exercises that NATO has ever held. Some 64,000 men participated, with 300 ships and 700 aircraft. Lasting from 14 to 28 September, the basic scenario envisaged a situation of rising tension which resulted in the political decision to order the re-inforcement of North Norway, a rugged strip of territory that extends for some 420 miles and accounts for one-third of the entire country."

5. *Logistical Aspects (Including Standardization?*

ACLANT MOBILE LOGISTICS A REQUIREMENT FOR STANDARDIZATION, by Rear Adm. Robert W. Timbrell, in *NATO's Fifteen Nations*, v. 17, no. 1 (February-March 1972) 82–84 plus.

"There has also been some international cooperation in particular areas of the logistic field and interest shown in the results of NATO standardization activities. Included within these standardization activities is work concerned with replenishment at sea, a function of mobile logistics. Against this background of increasing interest in logistic affairs, it may be opportune to take a look at the present system of mobile logistics within [Canadian Atlantic Sub-Area] ACLANT. As agreed by NATO nations, logistics is a national responsibility and so it follows that thirteen separate systems exist within NATO."

THE ALLIANCE AND EUROPE: PART III WEAPONS PROCUREMENT IN EUROPE—CAPABILITIES AND CHOICES, by Roger Facer. London, The International Institute for Strategic Studies, 1974. 48 p. (Adelphi Papers 108.)

The Defence-Equipment Market; The Industrial Base of Defense; The Range of Choice; European Collaboration; Appendix—Current European Collaborative Military Projects; and List of Tables.

(LI)—COOPERATIVE RESEARCH, DEVELOPMENT AND PROCUREMENT WITHIN NATO, by Lt. Col. Clovis C. Haddock. Maxwell AFB, Ala., Air War College, 1974. 51 p. (Professional Study.)

"Equipping of forces within NATO is a national responsibility. As a result, many of the nations are going through the same processes to provide different equipment to their individual forces and at the same time committing those forces to operate in wartime as an international force. This paper explores the operational, logistical and economical problems resulting from the present method of provisioning those forces. Past efforts to alleviate those deficiencies are then examined, including joint projects of cooperative research, development and procurement. The conclusion is reached that the deficiency lies in the system used and a case is then presented for a different cooperative approach. This approach involves agreement on weapon specifications to meet a particular military requirement with development done by an individual country."

CURRIE SAYS EXCESSIVE DUPLICATION HARMS NATO; 100 TACTICAL MISSILES IN NATO CITED, in *Defense Space Business Daily*, (23 April 1975) 25.

"The Pentagon's director of research and engineering has told the Congress that excessive duplication of military hardware in NATO and lack of standardization is 'seriously reducing' the overall performance of the alliance and wasting resources. 'This problem' he said, 'has been of serious concern for some time.' Dr. Malcolm Currie told the Senate Armed Services R&D subcommittee that the proliferation of weapon types within NATO includes: 100 separate tactical missile systems, 23 different families of combat aircraft, 36 different fire control radars, 8 different SAM systems, 7 different families of main battle tanks, and over 20 different calibers of weapons of 30 mm or larger."

FOURTH SYMPOSIUM ON NATO CODIFICATION OF EQUIPMENT, LONDON, 15-19 SEPTEMBER 1969, by J. S. Friederich, in *NATO's Fifteen Nations*, v. 15, no. 1 (February-March 1970) 42-47.

"Looking back to the Symposium the codification people will in general feel satisfaction ... Satisfaction that in such a review of their work as the Symposium was, it was revealed that in spite of all kinds of differences in situations, organizations, and ways of thinking, in the 14 NATO-countries participating, results in Materiel Codification were achieved and in the near and far future more results have to and can be produced. As one of the leading officials of NATO said: 'The NCS is playing a key role in the many NATO committees, Groups and Panels, coordinating the varying national interests'."

JANE'S FREIGHT CONTAINERS, ed. by Patrick Finlay. London, Jane's Yearbooks, 1973. 662 p.

Information and photos of ports and inland transport.

MILITARY LOGISTIC SYSTEMS IN NATO: THE GOAL OF INTEGRATION. PART I: ECONOMIC ASPECTS, by Geoffrey Ashcroft. London, The Institute for Strategic Studies, 1969. 35 p. (Adelphi Papers 62.)

The Approach Adopted; The Search for Economy; The Nation Approach; The International Approach to Logistic Economy in Europe; Summary and Conclusions; and Appendices.

MILITARY LOGISTIC SYSTEMS IN NATO: THE GOAL OF INTEGRATION. PART II: MILITARY ASPECTS, by Geoffrey Ashcroft. London, The Institute for Strategic Studies, 1970. 35 p. (Adelphi Papers no. 68.)

SACEUR'S Current Logistic Responsibilities and Activities (SACEUR'S Interest in Logistic Integration and in Standardization, SACEUR and the Infrastructure Programme, the Coordination of Logistic Plans, and the Level of War Reserves); Analysis of Current Approach (Definition of an Integrated System); What Can Be Done? (The AMF, The Leopard, Possible Military Interest in

NAMSO, Joint Training Schemes, War Gaming, and A New Role for Shape).

NATO GLOSSARY OF TERMS AND DEFINITIONS FOR MILITARY USE (ENGLISH AND FRENCH). Brussels, NATO, Military Agency for Standardization, 1974. Various paging. (AAP-6 (L).)

Terms of Reference; Terms and Definitions; Appendices of Terms by Functional Area.

STANDARDIZATION AND THE JOINT DEFENCE, by Gardiner L. Tucker, in *NATO Review*, v. 23, no. 1 (January 1975) 10-14.

"The evolution of NATO strategy in recent years, particularly in light of approaching nuclear parity between the Soviet Union and the United States, has led to a greater emphasis on the role of the Alliance's non-nuclear forces in deterrence or defence. Both Warsaw Pact forces and NATO forces continue to improve but defence budgets in the West are coming under growing economic pressure. In this situation, the allies must devote more attention than ever to improving the effectiveness of their forces through a better use of limited resources. Standardization is an important means to this end."

6. *Budgetary Aspects*

EUROPEAN DEFENSE AND THE EUROGROUP, by Alv Jakob Fostervoll, in *NATO Review*, v. 22, no. 3 (June 1974) 8-11.

"Some two and a half years ago a former chairman of the Eurogroup Defence Ministers—Lord Carrington—recalled how the Eurogroup had developed from a dinner chat to become a regular part of the NATO scene. He also recounted how the Eurogroup came of age, with the announcement of the European Defence Improvement Programme (EDIP) in December 1970. Many things have happened since then in the defence field not the least of these being the move towards détente expressed by the opening of the Conference on Security and Cooperation in Europe (CSCE) and the Mutual Balanced Force Reduction (MBFR) talks, the conclusion of the first phase of the Strategic Arms Limitation Talks (SALT I) and the opening of SALT II. Some things, however, have not changed. The possibility of withdrawals of U.S. troops from Europe remains, and has, to some extent, been given concrete form in the Jackson/Nunn Legislation; the strength of the Warsaw Pact continues to increase yearly; defence budgets in every NATO country are under pressure; and the money available for increasingly expensive equipment goes on being squeezed by rising personnel costs. Indeed the combination of the factors I have mentioned makes cooperation essential if Europe is to maintain and improve its contribution to Alliance defence."

TREATING NATO'S SELF-INFLICTED WOUND, by R. W. Komer. Santa Monica, Calif., Rand Corp., October 1973. 16 p. (P-5092.)

"The advent of nuclear parity makes conventional deterrence and defense much more important than before. Yet inflated manpower and weapon costs risk pricing them out of the market. When America's allies, and increasingly the U.S. itself, shrink from fielding a credible conventional defense, they are victims of a pervasive myth that effective nonnuclear defense against a Warsaw Pact attack is impossible, at least without massive military outlays. But the myth of inevitable Pact superiority is largely a self-inflicted wound. NATO's inferiority springs from its own failure to optimize its defense posture. The solution presented is to restructure NATO's existing force posture, freeing up needed resources by cutting back on marginal activities. emphasizing tradeoffs rather than ad-ons, and reallocating existing budgets rather than buying more forces." (See also under same title in Military Review, v. 54, no. 8 (August 1974) 53-63; and in Foreign Policy, no. 13 (Winter 1973-74) 38-48.)

7. *Weapons and Equipment*

AIRCRAFT, SHIPS, AND WEAPONS IN NATO'S NORTHERN COMMAND, by Charles Latour, in *NATO's Fifteen Nations*, v. 18, no. 1 (February-March 1973) 62-65 plus.

"There are of course many different types of aircraft, ships and weapons in use in the Northern Command. All that has been done here is to pick out some of the more interesting and give a brief description of each."

CONTROLLING QUALITY OF ALLIES DEFENCE EQUIPMENT, by H. Schurkens, in *NATO Review*, v. 20, nos. 3-4 (March/April 1972) 23-25.

"Canada took the initiative and proposed the establishment of a group of experts, which was created in 1965, and forms now, under the name 'Group of Experts on Quality and its Assurance', one of the cadre groups under the Conference of National Armaments Directors . . . The basic framework for its activities are to be found in two detailed Standardization Agreements (STANAGs) produced by the Group itself."

CO-OPERATION ON ARMS PRODUCTION: THE TASK AHEAD, by A. Tyler Port, in *NATO Review*, v. 21, no. 3 (1973) 13-17.

"Taken as a whole, the . . . suggestions encompass a fairly broad range of actions. What precise ingredients are required for a 'new deal' for NATO co-operation in research, development and production of military equipment, is by no means certain. Each element plays a part, and each impacts upon the other. The fact remains, however, that we have not been as successful in encouraging co-operation in the past as we should have been, considering all the work that has been done. We have paid a great deal of lip service to co-operation while going full steam ahead in developing our own unco-ordinated and non-integrated programmes. What is needed is a plan whereby there are only winners—no losers. We need such activities as the CNAD has recently taken. We need such inputs from the NATO Military Authorities as I have mentioned. We need the active participation of Ministers. We need discussion at the top and at the bottom. However, all these actions could produce but another round of frustration and inaction unless there is a real determination to put together what I would call, for lack of a better term, a Common Defence Market incorporating both sides of the Atlantic."

MILITARY APPLICATIONS OF NUCLEAR TECHNOLOGY. HEARINGS BEFORE THE SUBCOMMITTEE ON MILITARY APPLICATIONS OF THE JOINT COMMITTEE ON ATOMIC ENERGY, CONGRESS OF THE UNITED STATES, NINETY-THIRD CONGRESS, FIRST SESSION, MAY 22 AND JUNE 29, 1973, PART 2. Washington, Government Printing Office, 1973. 135 p.

Of special interest in this hearing are those portions dealing with military applications of nuclear technology as they affect NATO and NATO forces.

WEST EUROPEAN COLLABORATION IN WEAPONS PROCUREMENT, by John Simpson and Frank Gregory, in *Orbis*, v. 16, no. 2 (Summer 1972) 435-461.

"The present study will discuss the procedures that have been devised to initiate and manage transnational projects, as well as those international institutions which have been associated with them; will outline the national motivations for collaboration, and attempt to evaluate the nature and potentialities of the current position in the light of an ideal type of West European procurement system. Finally, it will examine the political impact of these developments upon United States/West European relations and analyze their future implications."

8. *Communications*

THE FUTURE OF NATO COMMUNICATIONS, by Comdr. Francesco Amaduzzi, in *NATO Review*, v. 22, no. 1 (1974) 14-18.

"Modern and efficient communications are a vital element in NATO's defensive strength. Not only is it essential for the political authorities of the Alliance to be able to ensure that their decisions reach the military forces in the field, but it is even more important that consultation between the governments of our Alliance and collective decision-making can be carried out effectively. Only thus, in a period of tension between East and West, can Crisis Management, or . . . more accurately described . . .—Crisis Prevention, be exercised by the North Atlantic Council in the interest of peace. It is because NATO must have available to it the most modern communications, combining flexibility, reliability and survivability, that it decided to move into the field of satellite communications."

NATO'S COMMUNICATIONS SATELLITE SYSTEM, by Col. D. R. Valentine, in *NATO's Fifteen Nations*, v. 15, no. 5 (October-November 1970) 61-68.

"Why Satellite communications for NATO? In an area as vast as that protected by the Atlantic Alliance, the transmission of messages over great distances can be subject to a variety of difficulties. Sometimes difficulty is caused by the very number of relay stations which are required to span the great distances. The many commercial communications companies involved, with their differences in engineering standards and practices, further complicate matters. Satellites, on the other hand, can span the entire area of NATO with only one relay—the satellite itself. This then, reduces the possibility of error due to technical reasons and, also, enhances the speed and clarity of all types of communications. With the evergrowing requirement for rapid, reliable, flexible and secure means of communication it became apparent that another means of communication was required by

NATO. This decision, however, did not come easily. The planning for the NATO Satellite Communications System began in 1961 when NATO formed a Working Group. Its task was to study the possible application of satellites to provide another communication link between NATO headquarters, the NATO countries, and the military commanders."

9. *Implications of United States Force Reductions in NATO*

CAN NATO FASHION A NEW STRATEGY?, by R. C. Richardson, in *Orbis*, v. 17, no. 2 (Summer 1973) 415-438.

"Some U.S. force reductions in the NATO area seem likely within the next few years. This is not to argue that they are desirable, only to recognize that the signs point in this direction. The shift in priorities from defense to domestic programs, the unfavorable U.S. trade balance, the détente environment and related force reduction conferences, and a growing public feeling that by now Europe should be able to defend itself will continue to build up pressures for a U.S. withdrawal. The question is less 'if' than 'when.' The present NATO strategy is one of conventional, flexible response. The force levels required to carry it out are at, or below, the level of credibility for this particular strategy. Some claim that so long as these levels are maintained, our NATO commands could do a credible job of defending against most plausible threats. No one claims this to be possible with even less force than is now available. To do so would be to admit that NATO had too many troops for its present strategy—and all responsible NATO leaders argue the contrary. If a force reduction is inevitable, for whatever reason, what happens to the security of Europe? No one proposes to dismantle NATO or abandon any pretense at maintaining as effective defenses as practical, at whatever force levels the member nations agree to support. This being the case, the problem is to devise and 'sell' a new NATO strategy that can be credible and effective at a lower level of force and cost. Is this feasible?"

NATO. This decision, however, did not come easily. The planning for the NATO Satellite Communications [illegible] began in 1967 when NATO formed a Working Group. [illegible] was to study the possible application of satellites to provide mobile communication link between NATO Headquarters, the NATO countries, and the military commanders.

3 [illegible] of NATO.

CAN NATO FASHION A NEW STRATEGY? by R. [illegible], in Orbis, v. 17, no. 2, Summer 1973: 413-[illegible].

"Some U.S. force reductions in the NATO area seem likely within the next few years. This is not to argue that they are desirable, only to recognize that the forces point in this direction. The shift in priorities from defense to domestic programs, the dollar and U.S. trade balance, the détente environment and related force reduction negotiations, and a growing public feeling that a new Europe should be able to defend itself will continue [to] build [illegible] for a U.S. withdrawal. The problem is less if [illegible]. The present NATO strategy is one of conventional flexible response. The force levels [illegible] are at best below the level of readiness [illegible] this particular strategy. Some believe that as long as [illegible] the [illegible] of an NATO command could [illegible] against [illegible] Treaty [illegible] even less force than is now available. To be [illegible] that NATO [illegible] too many troops for its present [illegible]—[illegible] NATO [illegible] the [illegible] is [illegible] able [illegible] NATO or abandon any pretense of maintaining an effective defense as [illegible] whatever force levels the member nations agree to support. [illegible] the problem is to develop a new NATO strategy that can be credible and effective at a lower level of force and [illegible] feasible."

CHAPTER V

DEFENSE AND SECURITY OF WESTERN EUROPE, NATO, AND NATIONAL STRATEGIES WITHIN THE ALLIANCE
(See also Chapter IV and Appendixes)

A. Miscellaneous Aspects

BRITANNICA ATLAS. Chicago, Encyclopeadia Britannica, Inc., 1974. Various paging.

A DICTIONARY OF POLITICS, ed, by Walter Lacqueur and others. rev. ed. New York, The Free Press, 1973. 565 p.

"This dictionary, arranged alphabetically, has assembled over 3,000 entries and covers all the major nations and areas and alliances of the world, leading statesmen and politicians, important political ideas and concepts, and crucial events in world history."

THE EUROPA YEAR BOOK, 1973; A WORLD SURVEY. VOLUME I—PART I—INTERNATIONAL ORGANIZATIONS; PART II—EUROPE. London, Europa Publications Limited, 1973. 1546 p.

The introduction includes a chart providing the following information: area, population, population density, population annual increase, average life expectancy, gross national product, etc. Part I provides detailed information about the following international organizations of which at least some of the Scandinavian countries are members: The United Nations, NATO, Nordic Council. Part II provides the following type of information for all the European countries: Land and the people, recent history, government, defense, economic affairs, transport and communications, social welfare, education, tourism, and statistical surveys of area and population, agriculture, forestry, fishing, mining, industry, finance, external trade, tourism, transport, education, etc. Also provides information on the constitution, government and politics, religion, the press and publishers, etc.

EUROPE AND AMERICA IN THE 1970s: I—BETWEEN DÉTENTE AND CONFRONTATION. London, The Institute for Strategic Studies, 1970. 31 p. (Adelphi Papers 70.)

America and Europe, by Senator Charles McC. Mathias, Jr.; Détente and Security—The Options, by Theodor Sommer; The East—Détente and Confrontation, by Michel Tatu; and Western Europe in the 1970s—Possible Roles, by Anthony Hartley.

EUROPE'S SECURITY IN THE CHANGED WORLD, by Kurt Birrenbach, in *Aussen Politik* (Fall 1973) 285-297.

"From West Germany's viewpoint, the growing détente between the US and the USSR is weakening the Atlantic Alliance and calls for some major readjustments in Europe. The foremost problem . . . is the matter of 'revitalizing' European-American relations, since détente cannot go much further unless West Europe's security is guaranteed, and the US role is essential to that security. Since the Soviet Union is so far superior militarily to West Europe, NATO needs the US as the main element of its defense, for without the weapons and the obligation to use them on the part of the US, none of the Allies can be protected. No amount of economic or political improvement can guarantee peace, . . . nor can the bilateral détente between the two superpowers insure Europe's security. Now is the time, therefore, for Europe to reexamine its requirements for security, as the multilateral efforts toward détente, with Europe's participation, get underway . . ."

THE FORTUNES OF THE WEST: THE FUTURE OF THE ATLANTIC NATIONS, by Theodore Geiger, Bloomington, Indiana University Press, 1973. 304 p.

". . . Geiger analyzes the economic, demographic, social-institutional, and psychocultural influences which have formed Western civilization's 'rationalistic' and 'melioristic' view of society. He believes this spirit of 'redemptive activism' will preserve the best of Western society's technocratic and humane values. In a practical application of his theory on the western will and ability to master nature and improve society, Geiger analyzes how the relevant sociocultural factors within the USSR and the US are likely to affect their foreign policies and external actions in the decades ahead. He discusses probably changes in the world political system that might precipitate a nuclear war between the superpowers. He analyzes the problems and prospects of European unification, as well as the changing economic and political relationships and trends within the Atlantic region as a whole. After warning of the dangers of impersonalized technocratic societies, he projects a change in Western civilization by the year 2000 which may be as profound as the Renaissance and Reformation and the subsequent scientific, industrial, and democratic revolutions . . ."

LIMITS IN THE SEAS. NO. 36—NATIONAL CLAIMS TO MARITIME JURISDICTIONS. Washington, Department of State, Bureau of Intelligence and Research, Office of the Geographer, 1974. 141 p.

Provides this information for the major countries of the world.

NATO STRATEGY UPDATED: A FIRST USE POLICY, by Lt. Col. Joseph Santilli, Jr., in *Military Review*, v. 54, no. 3 (March 1974) 3-20.

"Day by day, the East-West détente grows more believable. The prolonged dearth of crises gives one a curious feeling that the Cold War ended because it never got hot. Revisionists solve the metaphorical dilemma arguing that fear of Soviet aggression in Europe was inspired mostly by the West. Other authorities find scant evidence to conclude the Soviets have abandoned policies aimed at world domination suggesting Cold War temperatures only seem to have normalized because of more subtle Kremlin strategy. Everything has changed, yet nothing has changed. The reality of Soviet goals is obscured by militarism. Soviet bloc force levels and weaponry are inconsistent with efforts to lessen tensions and promote peace. The results of a European security conference and talks on Strategic Arms Limitation and Mutual Balanced Force Reductions are unknowable, but, whether East-West militancy declines or not, a change in relative military power is not likely. During this period—as reassuring and uncertain as any since the Iron Curtain fell—how should Western Europe assure its safety? Since there is no political authority for such a determination, it is more accurate to ask how the North Atlantic alliance plans to defend itself. Should strategies of the North Atlantic Treaty Organization change while disagreement abounds on the nature of the threat? Can NATO strategy be improved in ways that afford a reliable defense at less cost?"

OXFORD WORLD ATLAS. New York, Oxford University Press, Inc., 1973. 190 p.

Ocean Maps (including the Atlantic Ocean); The Physical Environment (including the Arctic Region and all of Europe); The Human Environment (including all of Europe); Topographic Maps (including Scandinavia); Urban Maps; and Thematic Maps.

RECOGNIZING THE CRISIS, by Zbigniew Brzezinski, in *Foreign Policy*, (Winter 1974-1975) 63-74.

". . . The existing international system is in crisis. That system, which came into existence after WWII, was essentially Atlantic-centered but US-protected and -financed. Until now the system has been based on four key and interrelated assumptions: 1. Atlantic cooperation, with European unity as an essential ingredient, and a possible extension of that framework to include Japan. 2. Emergence of a liberal and self-adjusting free trade system, based on stable and fixed monetary rates, and in which the advanced countries would continue to enjoy steady access to relatively inexpensive raw materials and a steady GNP growth rate. 3. Continued exclusion of the Communist world from the system. 4. Prolonged fragmentation of the less-developed countries and their continued dependence on the advanced nations. These basic assumptions . . . , are no longer valid. On the first point, neither European unity not Atlantic cooperation are guaranteed, as domestic demands within the advanced countries prod moves toward nationalism and/or unilateralism. Second, postwar economic assumptions grow weaker as domestic pressures and governmental reactions tend to politicize international economics. In addition, the viability of democratic institutions is increasingly challenged by the concurrent growth in public and personal resource consumption and the decrease in civic commitment and social loyalty. Third, the Communist countries are no longer operating outside of the international system, but are working increasingly within, attempting to benefit from playing off one advanced country against another. Lastly, the less-developed countries are becoming increasingly assertive in the economic realm, a situation which may attempt them to pursue policies of confrontation rather than cooperation with the advanced nations. In view of the current situation, Brzezinski sees the need for a 'major architectural effort rather than an acrobatic foreign policy.' Such a policy, he says, involves cooperation with others, joint planning and consultation, not dictation and overt leadership. The US, particularly, must recognize the depth and extent of the existing crisis and redefine its power in ways that are relevant to the present circumstances . . ."

STATUS OF THE WORLD'S NATIONS. Washington, Department of State, Bureau of Intelligence and Research, September 1973. 20 p. (Geographic Bulletin, Publication 8735.)

Provides nomenclature used by the U.S. Government for the 148 independent nations on the world scene (including the NATO nations). Also included are general data on the capital, area, and population of each nation. This bulletin contains similar data for nonindependent states. Two appendices list the nations which have become independent since World War II. The world map locates all countries described in the text.

STUCK FAST, by John Newhouse, in *Foreign Affairs*, v. 51, no. 2 (January 1973) 353-366.

"Politically, Western Europe is enfeebled if not paralyzed. And the dilemma of the world's most civilized concentration of peoples, deploying more economic power than any region save North America, is more than paradoxical. It is disturbing and potentially troublesome. One wonders if there is still time for Europeans to do anything about it, and, if so, what. Western Europe is caught up in fresh political currents strong enough to restrain any serious efforts by the European Community to enlarge significantly the political influence of the member states and to reduce their dependence on America . . . The NATO flank is also abnormally calm. Reasonably enough, Europeans do not see a unilateral American troop withdrawal around the next bend, and nobody is quarreling about strategy for the moment. The caucus of West European defense ministers known as the Euro-group has acquired experience and some coherence. Of greater importance, relations between the senior political figures in London, Bonn and Paris are good. The mutual suspicion and even antagonism that tormented most relationships of the three predecessor regimes seem to have been largely dissolved. Briefly, West Europeans for the most part appear to be getting on reasonably well with each other, with the Americans and with their neighbors to the East. Yet the implications of what is happening are scarcely encouraging. West Europeans now find themselves either observing or participating in three central processes: negotiations and other contacts between East and West; monetary and trade talks with the Americans and Japanese; and efforts to adapt the European Community to its enlarged membership while establishing, as well as improving, modes of cooperation."

TOWARD A COMMON EUROPEAN ARMAMENTS EFFORT, by Lt. Kenneth C. Stoehrmann, in *Air University Review*, v. 25, no. 2 (January-February 1974) 22-31.

"In the continuing debate over West European security, a major problem concerns the regions ability to defend itself adequately without the active support of the United States. This desire is heavily dependent on many factors, not least of which is the need for a common armaments effort among these nations . . . If Western Europe is to remain independent, she must be willing to defend herself. Even though Europeans 'find it hard to know how they can work together when their ideas about defense, the Alliance and the future of Europe are so fundamentally different,' they must try to solve these problems if they are to succeed. Common weapons development and procurement offer one such area of necessity coupled with practicality that can lead to further West European integration."

UNION OR CONCERT IN EUROPE?, by H. Mendershausen. Santa Monica, Calif. Rand Corp., August 1972. 3 p. (P-4877.)

"In spite of evidence that Western Europe has already found a fairly steady political format, the notion persists that it is on the way to forming a political union. In fact, Western Europe has formed an informal alliance system of autonomous states—a flexible European concert that can join and negotiate with the U.S., the USSR, and Japan as circumstances warrant. The need to believe in eventual union is prompted, in Europe, by the theory that only a union can ensure peace and a yearning by politicians for a great empire, and a justification of the national state. For the people at large, the 'supermarket' matters more than the 'superpower.' In America, it is prompted by a mixture of naivete and political expediency. There are, however, solid reasons and appropriate ways for the U.S. to participate in the European concert of states."

(LI)—US VS ALLIED CONTRIBUTION TO THE SUPPORT OF NATO, by Lt. Col. Niles T. Elwood. Maxwell AFB, Ala., Air War College, 1974. 62 p. (Professional Study.)

"A brief historical background of NATO and the collective efforts involved in its support introduce the report. Statistical comparisons involving gross national products, defense budgets, national budgets, and total and military populations follow. The subjects of infra-structure arrangements and balance of payments are discussed and are followed by a presentation of past and present contributions, trends, and possible problem areas. US and allied efforts to reduce forces and still maintain a credible deterrent are discussed as are the possibilities of unilateral reductions. Options on how future burdens should be borne are presented and evaluated. The report concludes with a review of what the US has done, what it is committed to do, and recommendations on future courses of action. The proven success of NATO is emphasized."

WEST EUROPE, 1973, in *Current History*, (April 1973) 145-185.

"The authors give a wide range of views on the separate policies of the European Community nations, their relations with the superpowers, and their prospects for becoming a united Europe . . ."

WHAT FINLANDISATION MEANS, in *The Economist*, v. 248, no. 6780 (4 August 1973) 15-16.

"Other Europeans will have only themselves to blame if they get into the position that fate has thrust upon the Finns . . . the term 'finlandisation' is misleading and unfair to Finland, in an important respect. Finland has had little choice. Geography and history have so boxed it in that what is remarkable about it is its survival in freedom, not its inhibitions. If other west European countries allow themselves to be 'finlandised,' it will be by their own choice. If they choose to squander their strength and squabble away their cohesion, they may well sink one after another into a state of such feebleness that each in turn could be leant on and manipulated by the Soviet Union. In these circumstances, one can imagine that Russia would be quite happy to see them retain their democratic institutions and would refrain from such crude tactics as making territorial demands. Its priority demands would be the kind it makes on Finland: suppression of direct criticisms of Soviet policies and actions, discouragement of escapers, 'trustful cooperation' and all that, including the making of big deals designed to give Russia more economic leverage. The reduction of western Europe to such a condition would make it much easier for the Soviet rulers to hold down their own empire—and then, of course, in due time they would be tempted to expand it."

B. Defense and Security of Western Europe.

1. *Defense of the Southern Flank*

THE COMPLEX PROBLEMS OF THE SOUTHERN NATO FLANK, by Maj. E. Hinterhoff, in *NATO's Fifteen Nations*, v. 17, no. 2 (April-May 1972) 32-39.

"Although the linguistic purists may insist that the NATO southern flank finds itself along the border between Turkey and Iran, it has been generally understood that the countries of Southern Europe belonging to the Southern Europe Command represent, from the strategic point of view, NATO's right flank. Furthermore, the increasingly dangerous process we have been witnessing during the past few years, namely, the growing Soviet presence in the Mediterranean area, both on sea and in the air, due to growing Soviet penetration into many Arab countries along the North African littoral, using their airfields, must be assessed as a part of a gigantic Soviet maneuvre aiming at outflanking Europe, already in peace-time. Consequently, any examination of the problems facing the countries of the NATO southern flank—and their neighbors—must be made against the background of that growing Soviet presence, its causes and its implications, as they affect every country in that area."

DEFENDING NATO'S SOUTHERN FLANK, by Adm. Richard G. Colbert, in *NATO's Fifteen Nations*, v. 18, no. 4 (August-September 1973) 20-40.

"This article, and the four essays which accompany it, are intended to give the reader a general overview of some of the chief considerations in the defense of NATO's Southern Flank . . . Accordingly, the articles following this one deal with the three main land sub-theaters of the region, with airpower, and with the comparative maritime capabilities of NATO and the Soviet Union in the Mediterranean." Contents: Defense of the Italian Northeastern Theater and Defense of Greece and Turkey.

NATO'S SOUTHERN REGION: PROBLEMS AND PROSPECTS, by Adm. Means Johnston, Jr., in *United States Naval Institute Proceedings*, v. 101, no. 1 (January 1975) 47-51.

"Almost everywhere through this vital region, the advantage lies with the Warsaw Pact forces, not so much because of sheer numbers but, rather, because of qualitative differences . . . The defensive requirements of Southern NATO are complicated by the fact that land fronts to be defended are not only separated but dissimilar. While, on the one hand, mountain ranges guard part of NATO's southern flank, Thrace's flat plains beckon to the Warsaw Pact armored and motorized divisions facing the region. And Turkey's Black Sea beaches must seem especially hospitable to anyone with an amphibious landing capability."

2. *Defense of the Northern Flank*

a. *Miscellaneous Aspects*

[BIBLIOGRAPHY], in TERRITORIAL WATERS IN THE ARCTIC: THE SOVIET POSITION, by S. M. Olenicoff. Santa Monica, Calif., Rand Corp., 1972. pp. 44-52 (R-907-ARPA.)

DEFENCE OF THE NORTHERN EUROPEAN COMMAND; THE WAYS AND THE MEANS, by Col. T. H. Ostendorf, in *NATO's Fifteen Nations*, v. 18, no. 1 (February-March 1973) 50-55 plus.

"The tasks of the Commander-in-Chief Allied Forces Northern Europe (CINCNORTH) are clearly defined, but the forces at his disposal to carry out these tasks are not so easily quantified. This article continues the review of NATO's Northern Flank and will describe CINC-NORTH's tasks, and discuss the forces at his disposal and the way they are exercised to ensure readiness to meet the potential threat . . . CINCNORTH's forces are those of the command's nations—Norway, Denmark and Germany—and those of other NATO member nations whose commitment to collective security has been manifested in obligating considerable striking power in direct defence of Northern Europe. Knitting this collated capability, diverse in strengths, weapons training, even language, into a cohesive force is CINCNORTH's continual concern."

THE DEFENCE OF THE NORTHERN FLANK, by Gen. Walter Walker in *RUSI Journal*, v. 118, no. 3 (September 1973) 21-30.

In discussing the importance of NATO's northern flank, General Walker discusses: The Threat—North Norway; The Threat—Baltic Approaches; Denmark's Defence Proposals; External Reinforcements; Norway and Denmark's Bases Policy; The Soviet Military Build-Up; Norway in NATO but Not in EEC; etc.

THE DEFENSE OF NORTHWEST EUROPE AND THE NORTH SEA, by Maj. Gen. J. L. Moulton, in *United States Naval Institute Proceedings*, v. 97, no. 819 (May 1971) 70-97.

"The defense of Northwest Europe will require powerful armies. But without logistic support, most of which must come through the North Sea, those armies will be as nothing. To assure that such support can pass through the North Sea will be one of the tasks of the North Sea navies . . . Six NATO nations have coastlines on the North Sea, Norway, Denmark, the Federal Republic of Germany, the Netherlands, Belgium, and Britain. As long as the threat of Western escalation to nuclear war remains credible, it is not very likely that any of them could be detached from NATO by brute force. If for any reason Western resort to nuclear weapons became incredible and the danger of conventional attack became immediate, pacifist pressure towards non-resistance might be intensified, but, as was seen after Munich and thirty years later when again a hostile army marched into Czechoslovakia, the display of naked force alerts those who, like so many in the Western democracies, would otherwise prefer to ignore unpleasant possibilities . . . A neutral and weakly armed Scandinavia, unable to expect NATO support and dependent on an isolated Sweden, would find itself under pressure to accept Russian surveillance systems spreading to Spitzbergen, the Faeroes, and Iceland, and might eventually be reduced to the semi-satellite status of Finland. The only stable alternative to the adherence of Scandinavian members to NATO seems, therefore, to be a neutral Scandinavian bloc armed more heavily than Sweden is today and in some way guaranteed by what was left of NATO against isolation and blockade. It could hardly be either as cheap or as effective as the present arrangement."

NATO'S NORTHERN FLANK, in *The Royal Air Forces Quarterly*, v. 10, no. 2 (Summer 1970) 133-143.

"The flanks of NATO have long been accorded less priority than the central region of Europe. There are sound reasons for this: with the Alliance's limited resources it makes obvious sense to concentrate forces in the area where the threat is greatest. However, even if a more uniform allocation of resources were militarily and economically possible, the northern and southern flank countries of NATO could well have political reasons for playing down the East-West military confrontation, as opposed to emphasising it by allowing Allied troops to be permanently stationed on their territory. Thus the defence of NATO's flanks offers both politician and military planner a number of special problems, which are likely to remain with us for several years to come. This article discusses some of these problems as they relate to the northernmost part of NATO's northern flank, that is North Norway."

NATO'S NORTHERN FLANK—VITAL BUT INCREASINGLY VULNERABLE, by Stefan Gesienheyner, in *Air Force Magazine*, v. 54, no. 7 (July 1971) 56-61.

"Also critical to the security of the Western alliance are the approaches from the north, which in tactical terms can be considered equally important. This article . . . draws a gloomy profile of the forces guarding . . . NATO's Northern Flank . . . The broad term, 'northern flank,' applies to the southern littoral of the Baltic Sea, which includes the coastlines of Germany, Denmark, and its Baltic islands; the Norwegian coast from Oslo to the North Cape; and, finally, the approximately 100 miles of land frontier between the USSR and Norway, located far above the Arctic Circle, west of Murmansk. The strategic value of this northern flank rests on two vital anchors. The first is NATO's blocking position in the western Baltic, which serves to contain the Soviet Baltic Sea Fleet. The second is the North Cape region, stretching from Narvik to the Soviet border. NATO forces in that area would counter any Soviet thrust toward the west through northern Norway. They also could threaten Murmansk, the USSR's only year-round, ice-free harbor in the west with free access to the open seas. The Norwegian coastline between these two anchors is of only minor strategic value."

ON NATO'S NORTHERN FLANK, by Capt. Erik B. Johansen, in *Military Review*, v. 51, no. 8 (August 1971) 63-69.

"As in many countries, Denmark's foreign and security policy is largely determined by its geographical situation. In the case of Denmark, it is an offshoot of central Europe, and it commands the exits from the Baltic Sea to the Atlantic Ocean; it is the cork in the Baltic bottle. The Jutland Peninsula borders the Federal Republic of Germany on the south, and contains 2.1 million of Denmark's nearly five million population. Approximately 400 islands of various sizes containing another 2.7 million people are scattered freely in the North Sea, the Skagerrack, the Kattegat, The Sound, and the Baltic. Greenland and the Faroe Islands in the Atlantic are also parts of the country and combined have about 85,000 people. An analysis of the problems of Denmark, with special attention to the specific military and strategic circumstances, may conclude that, because of its geographic position, Danish territory is strategically of such land, sea, and air importance to both East and West that there is no possibility whatsoever of remaining outside a conflict . . . Danish defense strength—that is, the strength of the standing forces—is an important instrument in its foreign relations, even in the absence of conflict. When a conflict arises, the situation can no longer be described by the classical extremes of war and peace because modern practical politics have developed a system representing a continuous number of possibilities between those extremes. This coherence should not be forgotten, and an insight into the position and status of the armed forces of the country in peacetime is, therefore, of great importance."

(*)—PICTURE ATLAS OF THE ARCTIC, by R. Thoren. New York, American Elsevier Publishing Co., 1970. 449 p.

"The author has organized his book by area: the Arctic Ocean, drifting ice stations, Arctic Alaska . . . the Norwegian arctic islands, arctic Scandinavia and the Soviet Arctic. Discussed under each region are such topics as ice conditions, transportation, mineral resources, settlements, physical geography, etc." With bibliography.

(LI)—POLICY AND POSTURE OF NATO ON THE NORTHERN FLANK: AN APPRAISAL, by Comdr. Herman L. Hunt. Newport, R.I., U.S. Naval War College, 1972. (Unpublished Thesis.)

"This is a study of the relationship of Norway and Denmark to NATO, including their military posture and political policies. The historical Soviet interest in Scandinavia has been highlighted in recent years through the increased Soviet military activity on the frontiers of the strategic northern flank of NATO. Even though the northern flank grographically includes all of Scandinavia and Iceland, only Denmark and Norway being members of NATO, are examined. The author finds that the contribution of Denmark and

Norway to the military strength of NATO's northern flank is not as meaningful as is their geographic position. A significant conclusion is that Denmark's and Norway's policies of prohibiting the stationing of foreign troops and nuclear weapons on their territories in peace time increase their vulnerability and that their survival depends to a great extent on the timely arrival of effective reinforcements."

PROBLEMS OF THE DEFENCE OF NATO'S NORTHERN FLANK, by Gen. Walter Walker, in *The Royal United Service Institution Journal*, v. 115, no. 659 (September 1970) 13–23.

A lecture given at the R.U.S.I. on 25 March 1970, in which the Commander-in-Chief, Allied Forces, Northern Europe, said "Today it is my task to introduce a highly intelligent British audience to some of the problems of the defence of Northern European Command, NATO's northern flank . . . I will take you on a 'Cook's Tour' of the Command; show you some of the problems which confront us, and try to explain the strategic importance of NATO's northern flank."

THE PROJECTION OF SOVIET MILITARY POWER IN THE NORTH; MARGINS OF WESTERN SAFETY IN THE NORWEGIAN SEA AND THE NORTH ATLANTIC ARE WEARING THIN, by Eivind Berdal, in *NATO's Fifteen Nations*, v. 19, no. 1 (February–March 1974) 58–64.

"The quantitative and qualitative growth of Soviet military power has been remarkable in recent years, and nowhere in the world has the discrepancy between sheer military might and professed intentions become more glaring than in the North. Governments and public opinion in the three countries of NATO's Northern European Command, Norway, Denmark and Germany, are becoming increasingly aware of this disturbing trend."

THE THREAT TO THE NORTH EUROPEAN COMMAND, by Col. K. A. Kristensen, in *NATO's Fifteen Nations*, v. 18, no. 1 (February–March 1973) 32–39.

"The Northern European Command (NEC), because of its geography, climate and political environment, is a complex military area. This article, before reviewing the potential threat to the NEC, will attempt to describe these features which make the NEC, in a military sense, a unique area in Europe . . . A glance at the map will show that, except at the peripheries of the Command, the NEC is screened from the USSR by two neutral countries, Sweden and Finland. Sweden which shares a common border with Norway over most of its length, follows a policy of non-alignment in peace to permit neutrality in war. Her own armed forces are substantial, however, should her neutrality be challenged. Finland's situation, with her relatively short common border with Norway and her long common border with Russia is very different. The 'Treaty of Friendship, Co-operation and Mutual Assistance' with the Soviet Union restricts her armed forces to a level which could pose little opposition to the Soviets should they wish to make use of Finnish-territory. Thus Finland's situation might be better described as one of enforced neutrality."

b. *Role of Nordic Countries*

NORDIC BALANCE IN THE 1970s, by Col. Albert Leo Romaneski, in *United States Naval Institute Proceedings*, v. 99, no. 8 (August 1973) 32–41.

"'Nordic Balance is a theory of regional equilibrium maintained by the Nordic nations between the major power blocs of NATO vis-à-vis the Warsaw Pact by reasons of geography, political, military, and economic factors, and most importantly, by the roles of the Nordic countries themselves.' . . . Soviet activities in the Mediterranean have focused the attention of the Western Alliance there. The Arab-Israeli dispute has heightened the tension and the danger of a major power confrontation on this southern flank of NATO. By contrast, little or nothing is being written or discussed about the growing Soviet naval threat on NATO's northern flank and more particularly about the Nordic region, largely because few crises have arisen in this area. Nordic balance is a delicate phenomenon which operates only within the limits of relatively low level crises confined primarily to the Nordic area."

THE NORDIC COUNTRIES IN A CHANGING EUROPE, by Egil Ulstein, in *Military Review*, v. 52, no. 9 (September 1972) 50–63.

"This article was condensed from Part III of the original which appeared in the ADELPHI PAPERS, Number 81, published by The International Institute for Strategic Studies (Great Britain), November 1971, under the title, Nordic Security . . . The security problems of the Nordic area are first and foremost functions of the changing international environment. In this respect, the area does not differ from most other parts of the world. It might be held that its problems are of marginal interest in European developments. Equally, one might question whether the area has anything substantial to contribute to West European integration or the liquidation of the legacy of World War II: a Europe split in two with a dividing line along ostensibly ideological frontiers. In some ways, the Nordic countries may be said to straddle the split of Europe. At the same time, their destiny may transcend purely European affairs. Although their security is closely linked with the problems of Central Europe, they might ultimately find themselves pawns in the game of global superpower confrontation. The imponderables of these external factors, which will determine not only the attitude of outside powers to the Nordic area but also its own reactions to them, make it difficult to determine future trends. There is much to be said for the view that, in the Nordic capitals, one awaits the great decisions in Europe, decisions which will be the outcome of events, not in the north, but in Brussels and Berlin. Both the Seidenfaden Report and the trend of informed public debate in the Nordic countries lead to the conclusion that Denmark and Norway can be expected to remain members of the North Atlantic Treaty Organization throughout the 1970s. This view is confirmed by the fact that all the major political parties at present represented in Parliament, both in Denmark and in Norway, support this policy. Public opinion polls over recent years point in the same direction. In this respect, it appears that opinion is influenced by a markedly conservative attitude to matters of national security and would look warily at possible changes in international alignments: 'Better the devil we know . . . '."

NORDIC SECURITY, by Egil Ulstein. London, The International Institute for Strategic Studies, 1971. 34 p. (Adelphi Papers Number Eighty-One.)

"The 'Nordic Area' considered in this paper comprises Denmark, Finland, Iceland, Norway and Sweden. In view of its geographical remoteness from the rest of the area, Iceland's security problems are examined only rather summarily and mainly in the context of the control of the North Atlantic Ocean . . . The Nordic Area can hardly expect to remain unaffected by current developments when these include the search for political solutions to the problems of Central Europe through East-West co-operation and détente, the beginning of a new phase in West European integration with the enlargement of the European Community, the decline in the certainty that the American commitment to Europe can permanently be taken for granted and Soviet naval expansion in the Northern coastal areas. Can these developments be expected fundamentally to influence Nordic co-operation which has an historical background and has expanded remarkably over recent decades? Can they lead to changes in alignments away from the present position where three of the countries, Denmark, Iceland and Norway, are in NATO and two, Finland and Sweden, are neutral? Could former traditions of neutrality and aloofness in international power politics reappear as the memories of World War II fade and the political climate on the world stage changes? This paper attempts to discuss these questions. Contents: The Traditions; The Nordic Balance since the War; and The Nordic Countries in a Changing Europe."

THE NORTH ATLANTIC: THE NORWEGIAN SEA, A SCANDINAVIAN SECURITY PROBLEM, by Capt. Christer Fredholm, in *Naval War College Review*, v. 24, no. 10 (June 1972) 56–64.

"Growing Soviet naval activity in the vital Norwegian Sea and North Atlantic received little notice despite the region's strategic importance and relative vulnerability. Caught in the dilemma occasioned by an expanding Soviet Fleet and a U.S. overseas force reduction, NATO and more particularly small nations like Norway and Denmark which lie within Moscow's sphere of interest may soon face a choice between accommodation to Soviet political goals or precipitating a direct confrontation between the superpowers. A firm commitment in this strategic part of the world by NATO and the United States is the best insurance against such a situation ever becoming reality . . . Iceland would play a vital role in the protection of any allied shipping across the Atlantic. Should NATO find itself in the position of not having access to bases on Iceland, the Soviets would find it far less difficult for their northern fleet units to reach their patrol areas in the Atlantic undetected. Any Soviet occupation of Iceland would breach a vital link in NATO's defense line and greatly facilitate the undetected passage of Soviet submarines into the Atlantic. In terms of air operations, the establishing of a Soviet base on Iceland would be a major strategic disaster for NATO as the Soviet Fleet would then be assured of extended air support in the Atlantic. In essence, an Iceland defended by powerful Soviet fighter and missile units would constitute a gigantic, unsinkable aircraft carrier in an ideal strategic position. The strategic significance of Iceland today cannot be overemphasized. The confined waters in the Greenland-Iceland-Faroes-Scotland region might be likened to a lock, and whoever holds the key controls the North Atlantic. That key is Iceland. A change in the existing situation would result in an entirely new politico-military picture both in Europe and the north."

SCANDINAVIAN SECURITY IN TRANSITION: THE TWO-DIMENSIONAL THREAT, by Nils Orvik, in *Orbis*, v. 16, no. 3 (Fall 1972) 720–742.

"Trends and events on the international scene in 1971–1972 have awakened fresh interest in the old concept of a balance of power. As yet, there is no agreement whether emerging constellations will conform to President Nixon's pentagonal design or appear as modifications of a continued bipolar power structure. What does seem clear is that the postwar pattern of American world dominance, based on strategic superiority, is changing; we have arrived at a crossroad in international affairs where several new directions seem possible. Among the East-West border areas likely to be affected by these new developments is the Nordic region, and particularly the Scandinavian countries, whose security has been closely related to the distribution of power among the major states. Looking at their position on the map and the characteristics of their respective security arrangements, one wonders how possible reshuffles of world power might influence Northern Europe and Scandinavia . . . Comparing the components that formed the security balance twenty-five years ago with those we find today will give some indication of whether there has been an increase or a decrease in the security and stability of the Scandinavian nations."

THE STRATEGIC SIGNIFICANCE OF THE NORTHERN CAP, by B. C. Cuthbertson, in *Royal United Service Institution Journal*, v. 117, no. 666 (June 1972) 45–48.

"The term 'northern cap,' used to describe the northern regions of Fenno-Scandinavia and north-western Russia, first came into common use in the fifties. In its strategical use it includes those parts of Norway, Sweden, Finland and the Soviet Union north of the 66th Parallel and extending from the Norwegian Sea in the west to the White Sea in the east. Also included are the ocean areas and islands (notably the Svalbard archipelago) between the northern coasts of these four countries and the North Pole. The term 'northern cap' should not be confused with the NATO use of the term 'northern flank' which includes the complete NATO front line from northern Germany to North Cape in Finnmark, the northernmost point of mainland Norway . . . The most fundamental change in the strategic significance of the northern cap came with the large expansion of the Soviet Northern Fleet and the general growth of the maritime power of the Soviet Union. The Northern Fleet is today the largest of the four Soviet fleets and contains over 50 per cent of the Soviet submarines. Its operations have gradually expanded westward and now extend to all the Norwegian Sea and into the Atlantic. In case of war or in a crisis situation it seems probable that a Soviet 'forward defensive zone' would be established in the Greenland-Iceland-Faeroe Islands gap covering the access routes to and from the Atlantic. The Norwegian Sea affords the Soviet Union with its most important transit zone for its strategic missile carrying submarines. However, the Soviets have no bases in the area to support operations in the Norwegian Sea. Air cover is severely limited by the increased range of naval operations. There is some dispute about whether there is harbour space not only for the Northern Fleet but also the fishing and merchant fleets that use the ports on the Kola Peninsula. The general consensus is that there is a space problem but how serious it is remains a matter for speculation. More important than the presumed lack of harbour space is that geography seriously restricts operations of the Northern Fleet . . . Strategically, Swedish Lappland has little to offer the Soviets except depth if they controlled north Norway. The Swedes have made it abundantly clear that they would not fight to preserve the territorial integrity of north Norway; their aim would be only to preserve their own neutrality. In the last two decades there has been an increasing effort to provide for the security of north Norway and its flanking waters without being provocative. Geography complicates Norwegian defence planning."

THE WESTERN FRINGE OF SCANDINAVIA; GUARDING THE NORTHERN GATES TO THE ATLANTIC—ALLIED FORCES NORTHERN EUROPE, by Col. L. R. Heyerdahl, in *NATO's Fifteen Nations*, v. 18, no. 1 (February-March 1973) 24–30.

"Denmark, Norway and NATO are mutually dependent on one another. The Northern European Command is the side door through which an enemy of the West could strike at the heart of Allied Command Europe and the sea lines of communication across the Atlantic. By themselves, neither Norway nor Denmark have the forces to enforce neutrality, nor to defend their homeland should an aggressor decide to use this entrance. It is NATO which is the padlock that keeps this door secure. The strategic importance of the NEC to the whole of the defensive alliance that is NATO is thus plain to see."

3. *Defense of Central Europe*

ALLIED LAND FORCES IN NATO'S EUROPEAN CENTRAL REGION, by Gen. Jurgen Bennecke, in *NATO's Fifteen Nations*, v. 17, no. 3 (June–July 1972) 50–56.

"The basic defence policy of the Alliance is to deter war by presenting a united and credible defence capability to the communist block and to provide for the security of NATO people from political blackmail and their territories against military invasion. This policy, approved in January 1950 by the North Atlantic Council, is the foundation of NATO's military planning. The aim of this article is to consider the forces in the Central Region of Europe and in particular the land component."

C. Belgium and West European Defense and Security

THE ROLE OF BELGIUM IN NATO, by Col. G. B. Howard, in *Military Review*, v. 51, no. 7 (July 1971) 17–22.

"Whether Belgium has contributed its fair share to the Atlantic alliance in the first 20 years is a difficult question to answer. Its statistical record is nothing exceptional, scarcely the subject for praise or criticism. On the other hand, it must be given considerable credit for providing the alliance with outstanding leaders and acting rapidly in assuming the role of host country for both the North Atlantic Treaty Organization and Supreme Headquarters, Allied Powers, Europe (SHAPE)."

D. Canada and West European Defense and Security

CANADA AND THE WORLD IN THE SEVENTIES, by Robert Bothwell, in *Current History*, (April 1972) 194–197.

"Canadian foreign policy aims are spelled out in a 1970 White Paper based upon policy studies made by Prime Minister Trudeau . . As an alternative to total dependence on the US, Canada seeks closer ties with West Europe. Because of this, further Canadian withdrawal from Europe is not likely. The government assures its allies that it will observe its obligations under NATO, but it is clear that its political association with NATO is more important than its military commitment . . ."

NATO AND THE FAR NORTH, in *NATO's Fifteen Nations*, v. 15, no. 1 (February–March 1970) 18–19.

"For the countries in the North Atlantic alliance, Canada's northern regions of ice and tundra and Alaska's north slope are bound to have enormous new strategic and economic importance in the 1970's. Defense concepts of the NATO alliance may have to be changed accordingly. The reason is that the Canadian and American Arctic regions are being opened to development on a major scale . . . Over this route will move Alaskan oil to fuel the factories and keep the lights burning in the major cities of North America and Europe. Utilizing the Northwest Passage, tankers will be able to move oil to the refineries of NATO countries in far less time than the tankers now rounding Southern Africa after a long voyage from the Persian Gulf."

NATO'S NAVY, by Joseph Fama. in *Defense & Foreign Affairs Digest*, v. 3, no. 2 (February 1975) 21–24.

A study of Canada's naval commitment to NATO.

E. Denmark and West European Defense and Security

DENMARK AND NATO, by K. B. Andersen, in *The Atlantic Community Quarterly*, v. 11, no. 3 (Fall 1973) 322–326.

"Denmark's foreign policy has, for years, been based on the facts that our country is both Nordic and European, is situated close to the Atlantic, and has a strong wish to participate in the global cooperation in the United Nations and other international organizations. To understand Denmark's policy in relation to NATO it is necessary to have these elements in mind and remember the historical and geographical factors behind its security policy as well as the economic conditions and cultural background of the country. Denmark is relatively poor in natural resources and situated at the crossroads between Scandinavia and the continent of Europe, and between the oceans and the Baltic Sea. Our straits are the only access to the oceans from the Baltic. This geographical situation and the lack of raw materials make us dependent on a large volume of foreign trade and on the maintenance of free communications across the oceans with our trading partners in other continents. Our history, culture, traditions and our basic way of thinking tend to bind us closely to the Western world. All these factors predispose Denmark to seek her security in cooperation with the other Western countries."

DENMARK AND NATO, by K. B. Andersen, in *NATO Review*, v. 21, no. 3 (1973) 3-8.

"Denmark's foreign policy has, for years, been based on the facts that out country is both Nordic and European, is situated close to the Atlantic, and has a strong wish to participate in the global co-operation in the United Nations and other international organizations. To understand Denmark's policy in relation to NATO it is necessary to have these elements in mind and remember the historical and geographical factors behind its security policy as well as the economic conditions and cultural background of the country."

(LI)—DENMARK: THE CORK IN THE BALTIC BOTTLE, by Maj. Robert L. Nesbitt. Maxwell Air Force Base, Ala., Air Command and Staff College, 1973. 51 p. (Research Study.)

"Since the North Atlantic Treaty Organization was established a great deal of change has transpired in European relations. This change has been possible because of the basic stability provided by nuclear bipolarity between the US and USSR. This study examines some of those changes and the effects they are having on Denmark, a NATO ally. Particular attention is paid to the effects of membership in the Common Market, SALT I, and Ostpolitik. From this examination the conclusion is that Europe has changed from a system dominated by military issues to one in which economic matters are paramount. In such a system NATO no longer appears to have a viable role."

THE FAEROES, ISLES OF MAYBE, by Ernle Bradford, in *National Geographic*, v. 138, no. 3 (September 1970) 410-442.

Denmark's Faeroe Islands are made up of 18 islands which are self-governing. The author in text and with numerous color photos provides a survey of the land and the people, including agriculture, fishing, and the other pursuits of life of these Danish citizens whose ancestors were Norwegians.

ON NATO'S NORTHERN FLANK, by Capt. Erik B. Johansen, in *Military Review*, v. 51, no. 8 (August 1971) 63-69.

"As in many countries, Denmark's foreign and security policy is largely determined by its geographical situation. In the case of Denmark, it is an offshoot of central Europe, and it commands the exits from the Baltic Sea to the Atlantic Ocean; it is the cork in the Baltic bottle. The Jutland Peninsula borders the Federal Republic of Germany on the south, and contains 2.1 million of Denmark's nearly five million population. Approximately 400 islands of various sizes containing another 2.7 million people are scattered freely in the North Sea, the Skagerrack, the Kattegat, The Sound, and the Baltic. Greenland and the Faroe Islands in the Atlantic are also parts of the country and combined have about 85,000 people. An analysis of the problems of Denmark, with special attention to the specific military and strategic circumstances, may conclude that, because of its geographic position, Danish territory is strategically of such land, sea, and air importance to both East and West that there is no possibility whatsoever of remaining outside a conflict . . . Danish defense strength—that is, the strength of the standing forces—is an important instrument in its foreign relations, even in the absence of conflict. When a conflict arises, the situation can no longer be described by the classical extremes of war and peace because modern practical politics have developed a system representing a continuous number of possibilities between these extremes. This coherence should not be forgotten, and an insight into the position and status of the armed forces of the country in peacetime is, therefore, of great importance."

F. France and West European Defense and Security

THE DEFENSE OF EUROPE AND SECURITY IN EUROPE, by Michel Debré, in *The Atlantic Community Quarterly*, v. 11, no. 1 (Spring 1973) 93-118.

"The French Defense Minister sees the central problem of our times as resolution of the contradiction between defense, based on fear, and security, based on confidence. Despite the impending conferences on security in Europe and force reductions, and talk of greater European unity, he considers national military strength essential for a very long time."

FRANCE AND EUROPE: A NEW LOOK, by Lawrence Griswold, in *Sea Power*, (April 1974) 21-26.

". . . The February conference of oil-consuming nations held in Washington was, in many respects, a 'showdown' between Paris and Washington: the issue was West Europe's future as an 'Atlantic' or a 'European' socio-political federation, i.e., a Washington-guided NATO or a Paris-guided European Community. Although France's eight European Community associates chose to support US ideas for solidarity among the oil-consumers, it was a somewhat 'hollow' victory for NATO since the participants then proceeded to compete with each other for advantageous oil procurement arrangements. However, the European nations' decision did constitute a setback for the French campaign to establish a national Europe, with Paris as its political capital. This plan for a federation of Europe, says Griswold, faced problems even before the Arab oil embargo as the individual European nations, accepting US détentes with Russia and China, pursued increased trade in an almost 'cut-throat' manner while contending with their grow-internal labor problems. As a result, the countries of Western Europe, beset by domestic ailments, are reluctant to enter into full partnership with similarly-afflicted neighbors . . ."

FRANCE ENSNARED: FRENCH STRATEGIC POLICY AND BLOC POLITICS AFTER 1968, by Edward A. Kolodziej, in *Orbis*, (Winter 1972) 1085-1108.

"Discusses the changed internal and external conditions that prompted a revision of French strategic policy after 1968, and analyzes the chief components of that shift. He maintains that student and worker protests throughout France in May 1968 forced a reordering of governmental priorities. Furthermore, these events triggered an economic and financial crisis that revealed how dependent the ambitious French military program was on the support of its allies. Moreover, the Soviet invasion of Czechoslovakia, in August 1968, underlined how much France depended on the American security guarantee, since Moscow's action diluted the political utility of an independent force de frappe. Kolodziej attempts to show how a reordering of strategic aspirations with political realities began in the final year of the de Gaulle administration and has continued into the Pompidou presidency, culminating in the third military five-year plan under the Fifth Republic passed in 1970. The French security problem is now posed less as a matter of blocking American penetration of Europe and more as a matter of assuring the availability of American military power as a calculated hedge against Soviet expansion . . ."

FRANCE—FOR A EUROPEAN EUROPE, by Maurice Delarue, in *Aussen Politik*, (Second Quarter 1974) 134-145.

". . . The aim of France's foreign policy is to preserve French independence within an independent Europe. France by itself, . . . cannot defend its sovereignty; yet, as part of a European community, it can uphold its right to self-determination. Europe, . . . should be based on the principle of interdependence, 'the essential precondition for an effective exercise of independence.' While US military force is necessary for 'Europe's security, . . . the presence of American troops on the continent forms an 'alibi' for those Europeans who seek to avoid the establishment of a viable and dependent defense posture of their own. Europe, he writes, has both the economic base and technological skill to develop an effective deterrent force . . ."

(LI)—FRANCE, NATO, AND UNITED STATES INTERESTS, by Maj. Kenneth H. Rasmussen. Maxwell AFB, Ala., Air Command and Staff College, 1974. 84 p. (Research Study.)

"The Nixon Doctrine has produced a conflict of United States interests toward Western Europe. The announced goal of increased NATO military strength, with a reduced American presence, has failed as the Europeans refuse to significantly increase the size of their armed forces. This study examines a possible alternative in which the rejoining of French forces into NATO would offset American reductions. The results indicate that the powerful French armed forces are gradually moving toward this goal. Reunification of France and NATO will serve U.S. interests and should be promoted by American foreign policy."

FRANCE, THE THIRD FORCE?, by Lawrence Griswold, in *Sea Power*, (August 1973) 6-12.

". . . Pres. Pompidou of France is continuing to pursue de Gaulle's goal of assuring France's worldwide political and military influence, particularly in those central and north African nations which have achieved independence from France but which maintain sentimental attachments to French culture. Since these countries frequently clear with Paris their decisions on major foreign commercial and political transactions, the French Union seems more a reality today than it was during the Fourth Republic . . . Under Michel Debre, architect of French defense policy since 1958, France has become a much more powerful nation than it has ever been in the past . . . Continuing nuclear tests at the French missile range in the Society Islands have resulted in an improvement in the Mirage IV's nuclear payload and the development of an inter-continental ballistic missile with a range exceeding 3,000 kilometers. The latter will undoubtedly replace the intermediate-range missiles currently deployed in silos in southeast France and on French nuclear submarines. Furthermore, the modern 328,000-man Army maintains a worldwide presence: 58,000 in West Germany, 2,000 in Berlin, 4,000 in continental Africa, 3,000 in Malagasy, Reunion, and Comoro, two battalions in the Pacific islands, and two battalions in the French colony of the Afars and Issas. With new naval vessels emerging from 12 shipyards at a rapid rate, the modernity and numbers of the French Fleet make it at least equal in strength to the British Navy. By developing its Exocet surface-to-surface missile, France was the first nation in the West to match the Russian Styx and remains years ahead of Britain and the US. Most ships on the active list are under 20 years old. The worldwide commitment of the Navy includes the defense of the Channel, Atlantic, and Mediterranean coasts . . ."

FRENCH NUCLEAR DIPLOMACY, by Wilfrid L. Kohl. Princeton, Princeton University Press, 1972. 412 p.

"This analysis of the French development of a force de frappe focuses on the role and impact of nuclear weapons' possession in French politics. In emphasizing the discontinuity between de Gaulle's 'grandiose designs' and the more 'modest' objectives of the Pompidou regime, the author concludes that France's nuclear arsenal will be maintained, not to increase aspirations for an independent role in world politics, but to enhance French status and security in Europe and the Western alliance."

NATIONAL DEFENSE AND EUROPEAN UNIFICATION, by Raymond Aron, in *Revue de défense nationale,* (April 1970) 556–570.

". . . While some Frenchmen may fear the challenge of American supremacy and imperialism to French society, France remains a member of the Atlantic Alliance, its political regime resembles that of other West European countries and the United States, and it still cooperates militarily with the United States and the Atlantic Alliance rather than with the USSR and its allies. France's official military doctrine is not that of an 'all azimuth' defense, despite some speculation in the past. Such a defense might be that of a neutral country. Furthermore, France has not had the funds to build such a defense. In order to be directed to the United States as well as the Soviet Union, the defense would have to be a nuclear deterrent, and France does not now have the resources for this. Even if France does build four nuclear submarines in the 1970s, only two will be operational at any given time—hardly enough to target Leningrad and New York. French governments have probably never seriously considered that relations between France and the United States would deteriorate to the point of a military confrontation. Thus, France's military defense, at least within the next ten years, need hardly include a defense against the United States, or West Europe. France's military defense should be considered within the Atlantic Alliance and a European Community, without jeopardizing its independence. These frameworks are not contradictory or mutually exclusive. European defense cooperation over the next decade could only occur within the framework of the Atlantic Alliance . . . The only event which could change this attitude would be a massive withdrawal of American troops from Europe. If Europeans were obliged to face Soviet power alone, perhaps they would make a greater effort to form a European defense community. At that point they would have to consider whether they could adequately compete in the arms race by building such weapons as MIRVs. However, Europeans still seem content to prosper economically under the shadow of American power, disliking American domination in Europe but unwilling to detach themselves from it."

(LI)—NATO AND FRANCE AFTER DE GAULLE, by Lt. Col. Van Hunn. Maxwell AFB, Ala., Air War College, 1974. 63 p. (Professional Study.)

"Examines some historical aspects that led to the development and maturity of NATO and to the role France played in the Alliance. The paper traces the relationship of the United States with France and particularly with the France of de Gaulle. It describes the current status of NATO without France and looks at some of the other problems plaguing the Alliance. The author concludes that although French territory, resources and support would improve the effectiveness of the organization, it is highly unlikely France will rejoin as a full participating member."

THE NEW FRENCH MAGINOT LINE: A NOTE ON FRENCH STRATEGY, by Roy C. Macridis, in *Journal of Political and Military Sociology*, (Spring 1974) 105-112.

"The present French policy of nuclear 'independence,' . . . is reminiscent of the catastrophic Maginot line posture of the 1930s. In both cases, . . . the nation's preoccupation with deterrence ran contrary to its alliance commitments. The postwar foreign policy of France has been geared to the avoidance of blocs and the reassertion of French influence in Europe and particularly over Germany. To achieve these ends, . . . President De Gaulle created the force de frappe and pulled France out of the military side of NATO . . . De Gaulle's successor, Georges Pompidou, adopted a more realistic stance in international relations, though he questions whether this development marked a significant departure from the Gaullist 'grand design.' The flaw in the Maginot line strategy, according to Macridis, was that military planning and foreign policy were never really coordinated; this same disparity is apparent in French strategic thinking today. The American doctrine of 'flexible response,' he asserts, alarmed the French since they perceived the possibility of a superpower confrontation in Europe over which the Europeans would have no control. Consequently, they formulated their own doctrine of 'massive retaliation,' symbolized by the force de frappe. This French unilateralism, . . . constitutes a considerable risk for the Atlantic alliance . . . The French consider the NATO arrangement as an acceptable 'first line of defense against an aggressor.' The danger, however, lies in French insistence that its nuclear force will be employed by French leaders alone in the event of a direct threat to its national security. Once the 'critical threshold of aggressiveness' is passed, France, according to Macridis, reserves the right to take unilateral action in its defense . . . This strategy is 'contrary to the inherent logic of the alliance' . . ."

THE PARIS VIEW OF BRUSSELS, by Pierre Rocheron, in *Defense & Foreign Affairs Digest*, v. 3, no. 2 (February 1975) 13-15.

"Will France return, after nine years, to formal membership in NATO and the integrated command of the Atlantic Alliance? Very probably not, for reasons which essentially deal with the country's internal politics. However, France is now becoming so close to NATO that the line between official participation and close cooperation will become a matter of mere semantics."

WITNESS TO HISTORY, 1929-1969, by Charles E. Bohlen. New York, Norton, 1973. 562 p.

". . . During his tenure in Paris, [Ambassador] Bohlen was confronted with the imposing figure of de Gaulle at the height of his power. As might be expected, Bohlen has his doubts about Gaullist doctrine: the French leader perceived all international relations in terms of Realpolitik and was shocked by actions dictated by ideological obligations, in particular the 1968 invasion of Czechoslovakia. De Gaulle had little comprehension of the US, regarding it as a polyglot country rather than a pure nation-state. Bohlen also takes de Gaulle to task for his disruption of the Western alliance, which served no practical purpose for France and only benefited the Russians. Bohlen is not optimistic about détente between the US and USSR. He tends to emphasize the ideological element in his analysis of Kremlin policy—the Bolsheviks, as he insists on calling them, still believe they are surrounded by hostile capitalist nations. He sees nascent liberalization within the Soviet Union—in fact, the present leadership seems much more conservative than Khrushchev was . . ."

G. Greece and West European Defense and Security

FOREIGN ASSISTANCE AND RELATED PROGRAMS APPROPRIATIONS. SENATE HEARINGS BEFORE THE COMMITTEE ON APPROPRIATIONS, 93D CONGRESS, SECOND SESSION, FISCAL YEAR 1975. Washington, Government Printing Office, 1974. 1572 p.

Includes among other information, testimony on: Assistance to Greece and Turkey.

GREECE AND US AND NATO MILITARY BASES, by Radovan Pavić, in *Review of International Affairs*, v. 25, no. 587 (20 September 1974) 11-12.

"One of the loudest in the series of reverberations following the outbreak of the Cyprus crisis and fall of the junta has been the announcement that Greece would pull out of the NATO military alliance. The geostrategical location of Greece on the southern flank of NATO puts a special complexion on the naval and airforce bases in this country, its fortifications and right-of-way for the passage of foreign troops... Withdrawal of Greece from the NATO military alliance is obviously a blow to western geostrategy in this area, although Greece is not quite of the same importance as Turkey."

H. Iceland and West European Defense and Security (See also II-F-5)

BASE PACT SET BY U.S. AND ICELAND, by Marilyn Berger, in *Washington Post*, (27 September 1974) 15.

"Iceland agreed yesterday to permit the United States to continue operating a key NATO base at Keflavik that permits surveillance of Soviet submarine routes into the Atlantic. The agreement calls for a token reduction of the 3,300-man American contingent and the separation of military and civilian facilities, which will serve to lower the U.S. profile that had become an irritant in the small island nation.... The United States also agreed to spend $60 million for airport improvements, including new access roads, ramps and taxiways and an additional unspecified sum to build 468 new family units. Iceland will build a new civilian airport separate from the military airport. All American military personnel will be required to reside within a specified defense area. The agreement modifies the 1951 defense agreement under which the United States operated a naval air base which maintains a squadron of F-4's to carry out its primary surveillance mission. Iceland has no armed forces of its own, although it has been a member of NATO since 1949." See also: Iceland Recinds Plan to Close U.S.'Operated Base at Reflavik, in New York Times, (30 August 1974) 3.

(LI)—ICELAND AND NATO: PROBLEMS AND PROSPECTS, by Lt. Comdr. R. Scott McCartney and Lt. Comdr. William L. Triemer. Newport, R.I., U.S. Naval War College, 1972. (Unpublished Group Research Project Report.)

"A study of Iceland's role in NATO, including an analysis of Iceland's strategic importance and a review of the problems which have characterized her involvement in military alliances. The political crisis of 1971 is used as a focus for an analysis of the implications of the loss to NATO of the Iceland Defense Force (IDF). The Icelandic people, their culture and political structures, are examined to determine the roots of the Icelandic attitude towards military alliances. The evolution of Iceland from a policy of neutralism to membership in NATO is traced and the mission and organization of the IDF is described. The paper finds that Iceland's strategic importance, particularly in the ASW realm is increasing but that certain aspects of the IDF mission could be relocated without loss of capability. Continuing political and cultural problems within the Iceland/NATO relationship are forecast, keyed principally to the state of East-West tensions. The study recommends diplomatic and military actions designed to retain certain vital capabilities of the IDF forces while lessening the political and cultural impact of those forces."

ICELAND AND THE MARITIME THREAT TO NATO, by F. P. U. Croker, in *Royal United Service Institution Journal*, v. 117, no. 666 (June 1972) 51-54.

"Although the theory has been advanced that the Red Fleet is intended firstly for the seaward defence of the Soviet Union, there is nothing, in a primarily maritime war, to prevent it being used offensively, almost in its entirety, since Russia and her satellites are economically self-sufficient and hence independent of the seaborne supplies whose protection, in the case of NATO, must absorb so much naval effort. That this is in fact the Soviet intention is proved beyond all doubt by the following extract from the textbook 'Military Strategy' issued under the authority of the veteran Marshal Sokolovsky: 'One of the Navy's main tasks in a future war will be to sever the enemy's ocean and sea transport routes ... Operations against enemy lines of communication should be developed on a large scale from the very beginning of the war ... by destroying convoys and transports at sea.' To implement this policy, one thing only is lacking—an advanced operating base—for the home ports of the Red Fleet are so remote from the vital North Atlantic shipping routes that dependence upon them would entail a very large replenishment at sea effort, itself vulnerable to NATO counter-attack. Nor could land-based maritime air support be effectively provided from the equally distant Warsaw Pact air bases. A glance at the map of Northern Europe suggests that Iceland is the ideal and, indeed, the only feasible site for the advanced base. From this island, all the North Atlantic shipping routes and local areas are within easy reach of the medium-range submarines, surface warships and strike aircraft which the USSR possesses in such abundance; moreover, effective air and sea cover can then be provided for seaborne follow-on supplies from Murmansk—a continuing commitment which could be further eased by the seizure of Northern Norway and its airfields, though this is not mandatory, especially if the Iceland bases can be obtained by peaceful means. The expressed desire of the new leftwing Iceland government to review or terminate its existing military protection agreement with the United States may represent the measure of the success of Soviet diplomatic efforts in this direction, and could result in the loss to NATO of the Keflavik air base. Iceland would then be left internally undefended—a fruit ripe for plucking, since it could be seized by a quite small airborne operation if base rights could not be secured by negotiation."

ICELAND, EUROPE AND NATO, by Ashe Sparring, in *The World Today*, v. 28, no. 9 (September 1972) 393-403.

"The shift in Iceland's foreign policy and her demand for the extension of fishing limits is part of the fight for national and economic survival of a small country of less than a quarter of a million inhabitants . . . From a common-sense standpoint, the security of Iceland (the only unarmed country in the Western world) is based on (1) membership in NATO; (2) her value for NATO; (3) the American presence; and (4) the possibility of moving up reinforcements quickly. This should be thought sufficient protection against any coup-like venture, even though it would be easy enough to land a force secretly on the island, given its long coastline, inland desolation, and small population. On the other hand, if Iceland seeks security in NATO, it is evident that she shares the risks of the other NATO countries . . . History has situated Icelanders on a barren and unfriendly island, which political and technical developments have turned into a cross-roads between Soviet and American security interests. All Iceland can hope for is new techniques and different policies, which would again place the island in a backwater."

ICELAND'S CLOSURE OF U.S. BASE WILL CRIPPLE U.S./NATO DEFENSE, by Col. Robert D. Hainl, Jr., in *Armed Forces Journal*, v. 108, no. 23 (August 1971) 20.

"The announced decision of Iceland's new left-wing government to close out the U.S./NATO base at Keflavik is, in strategic terms, the worst blow sustained by NATO since the defection of Charles de Gaulle and the French armed force . . . Every one of the approximately 175 submarines (roughly half of the Soviet undersea fleet) based at Murmansk has to get by Iceland before it can seriously threaten Europe, the United States, or the Atlantic. Because of this, we and all NATO have counted heavily on Iceland as the cork in the bottle to deny Murmansk subs free access to and free run of the Atlantic."

THE INFLUENCE OF DOMESTIC POLITICS ON THE DEFENSE POLICY OF ICELAND, by Lt. Cmdr. Craig S. Campbell, in *Naval War College Review*, v. 23, no. 4 (December 1970) 76-97.

"Prior to World War II the people of Iceland were, to a great extent, isolated from world affairs. The occupation of their island in 1940 by the British began three decades of controversy in Icelandic politics over the presence of a foreign military force. Today the continued presence of the U.S. Defense Force in Iceland—a key facility for projecting U.S. antisubmarine warfare power in the Atlantic—is directly dependent upon the interaction of this issue with internal domestic politics in Iceland and the quality of the U.S. Armed Forces' community relations program there . . . In this study of the defense policy of Iceland, only selected factors will be considered in the examination and analysis of domestic politics on that policy. These factors are: The physical and political geography, the strategic significance of Iceland and its role in conflicts between other nations. The military and domestic policies and public opinion The intangible known as the national mind and its associated complex of nationalism, neutralism, and xenophobia."

LIVING IN ICELAND; IT'S AS COLD AS YOU MAKE IT, by Andrew Schneider, in *Air Force Times, Family Supplement* (3 November 1971) 10-16 plus.

A review of life at the Iceland Defense Force and NATO Base, including Iceland's outlook towards the military stationed there. "For those Americans stationed at Keflavik who haven't gained that [more accurate] perspective, Iceland can be a depressing experiment. But it is not an irreversible depression. The sadness is not a result of the country, but of a failure to understand it, and this can be the case anywhere."

MILITARY CONSTRUCTION AUTHORIZATION, FISCAL YEAR 1974. HEARINGS BEFORE SUBCOMMITTEE NO. 5 OF THE ARMED SERVICES, HOUSE OF REPRESENTATIVES, NINETY-THIRD CONGRESS, FIRST SESSION ON H.R. 9005. 1973. 691 p. (H.A.S.C. No. 93-18.)

Includes, among others, information on the Naval Air Station at Keflavik, Iceland.

MILITARY CONSTRUCTION APPROPRIATIONS FOR 1974. HEARINGS BEFORE A SUBCOMMITTEE ON APPROPRIATIONS, HOUSE OF REPRESENTATIVES, NINETY-THIRD CONGRESS, FIRST SESSION. Washington, Government Printing Office, 1973. Pts. 3 and 4.

Among other information, includes construction appropriations for particular facilities at the Naval Station in Keflavik, Iceland.

ITALY'S RED BELT, in *Newsweek*, v. 85, no. 9 (3 March 1975) 41.

Map of Italy showing (1) areas of Communist control, and (2) areas of Communist influence.

I. Italy and West European Defense and Security (See Appendixes)

J. Luxembourg and West European Defense and Security (See Appendixes)

K. Netherlands and West European Defense and Security (See Appendixes)

L. Norway and West European Defense and Security (See Appendixes)

M. Portugal and West European Defense and Security (See also Analysts' Note)

THE IBERIAN QUANDARY—SPAIN, PORTUGAL, AND NATO: TURMOIL AND TROUBLE, by Lawrence Griswold, in *Sea Power*, (February 1975) 24–30.

"At the beginning of 1974, Mr. Griswold observes, only the Iberian Peninsula, with 'Strong Men' controlling both Spain and Portugal, seemed politically stable in U.S. eyes, while most of the other governments of western Europe labored under severe economic problems. This situation changed drastically in April 1974 with a military coup in Portugal. To NATO, the event was important, depriving it, for all intents and purposes, of Portuguese ports and harbors, compromising the security of Lajes in the Azores (the only mid-Atlantic naval air base available to U.S. forces), and increasing the threat to the two pro-Western nations of Rhodesia and South Africa. NATO must now look to Spain for a potential base of operations in strategically important Iberia, although Spain was never offered permanent membership in the Alliance and has not enjoyed particularly friendly relations with most of its European members. Spain's present support of NATO stems from the bilateral executive agreement of 1953, negotiated by the U.S., which recognized the strategic necessity for including Spain in any major Atlantic alliance regardless of the other members' prejudices. Under the agreement, the U.S. and Spanish Navies share the extensive facilities of Rota, near Cadiz; and the U.S. Air Force utilizes substantial portions of three airbases at Madrid, Saragossa and Sevilla. Without these bases, says Griswold, the position of the U.S. Sixth Fleet in the Mediterranean and Aegean might be untenable; and, since the Spanish Army now commands the Strait of Gibraltar, a change in Spain's attitude could render the Strait impassable to Western surface ships or even make it a tollgate for western commerce . . ."

PORTUGAL AT THE POLLS, in *Newsweek*, v. 85, no. 18 (5 May 1975) 53.

"One year to the day after the revolution that overturned Portugal's . . . dictatorship, the nation went to the polls. It was the first real election in 49 years . . . The election results were not expected to bring about any softening of the junta's revolutionary line. Indeed, it seemed probable that the military—with the . . . help of the Communists—might now try to dismantle the Parliamentary Parties."

PORTUGAL: SQUEEZING OUT THE MODERATES, in *Time*, v. 105, no. 13 (31 March 1975) 47–49.

"With brisk dispatch, Portugal's leftist-dominated Revolutionary Council moved last week to consolidate its powers. In the aftermath of the previous week's right-wing coup attempt, the all-military 24-member council appeared on television for the first time before being sworn in at ceremonies in the president's office."

PORTUGAL—THE LEFT TIGHTENS UP ITS GRIP, in *Time*, v. 105, no. 12 (24 March 1975) 35–36.

"One thing that emerged clearly from the [recent] coup attempt was that political moderates in Portugal have suffered a set-back. Whether it will prove fatal remains to be seen."

PORTUGAL'S LEFTIST-RUN ELECTION—MEANING TO U.S. AND RUSSIA, in *U.S. News & World Report*, v. 78, no. 17 (28 April 1975) 68–70.

"No matter who gets the votes, pro-Communist military officers will set Portugal's course." This assessment attempts to show where this could all lead.

N. Spain and West European Defense and Security

THE IBERIAN QUANDARY—SPAIN, PORTUGAL, AND NATO: TURMOIL AND TROUBLE, by Lawrence Griswold, in *Sea Power*, (February 1975) 24-30.

"At the beginning of 1974, Mr. Griswold observes, only the Iberian Peninsula, with 'Strong Men' controlling both Spain and Portugal, seemed politically stable in US eyes, while most of the other governments of western Europe labored under severe economic problems. This situation changed drastically in April 1974, with a military coup in Portugal. To NATO, the event was important, depriving it, for all intents and purposes, of Portuguese ports and harbors, compromising the security of Lajes in the Azores (the only mid-Atlantic naval air base available to US forces), and increasing the threat to the two pro-Western nations of Rhodesia and South Africa. NATO must now look to Spain for a potential base of operations in strategically important Iberia, although Spain was never offered permanent membership in the Alliance and has not enjoyed particularly friendly relations with most of its European members. Spain's present support of NATO stems from the bilateral executive agreement of 1953, negotiated by the US, which recognized the strategic necessity for including Spain in any major Atlantic alliance regardless of the other members' prejudices. Under the agreement, the US and Spanish Navies share the extensive facilities of Rota, near Cadiz; and the US Air Force utilizes substantial portions of three airbases at Madrid, Saragossa and Sevilla. Without these bases, says Griswold, the position of the US Sixth Fleet in the Mediterranean and Aegean might be untenable; and, since the Spanish Army now commands the Strait of Gibraltar, a change in Spain's attitude could render the Strait impassable to Western surface ships or even make it a tollgate for western commerce . . ."

NATO AND SPAIN, by Maj. E. Hinterhoff, in *NATO's Fifteen Nations*, v. 15, no. 2 (April-May 1970) 66-70.

"The possibilities and prospects of Spain's membership of NATO and of a degree of interest in such an association."

O. Sweden and the Impact of Its Neutrality on NATO

SWEDISH NEUTRALITY: ITS IMPACT ON NATO, by Lt. Col. Peter J. Gaustad, in *Military Review*, v. 54, no. 4 (April 1974) 46-53.

"Within historical perspectives, the concept of neutrality is relatively recent. Presently accepted laws of neutrality are based upon treaties made during the 17th and 18th Centuries. These concepts are not particularly specific . . . Sweden's very existence as a small but powerful neutral in the critical Baltic area has a definite impact on the credibility and, to a lesser extent, on the viability of the NATO deterrent. Even though the offer to form a Northern Defense Union was rejected by Norway and Denmark, this offer apparently still stands. The Soviets would be delighted to see these two countries split off from NATO, even if the purpose were to form an armed neutral bloc whose existence is dedicated to countering Soviet expansion into Scandinavia . . . The disruptive influences which Swedish neutrality has on NATO result primarily from the apparent attraction Sweden exercises to draw the two Scandinavian members of NATO off to join it in a neutral bloc. While this possibility receives considerable public consideration, it has never been realistically attractive to the two NATO countries. Even though Sweden has not found it in its interests to join NATO, its basic interests are aligned with those of the West. Although NATO cannot count on Sweden's military assistance, there is virtually no possibility it would ever be used against the NATO countries. The Soviets cannot make this assumption. In addition, as German influence in Europe increases, there is the definite possibility that Swedish neutrality will again be slanted toward the German cause and against that of the Soviet Union."

P. Turkey and West European Defense and Security

FOREIGN ASSISTANCE AND RELATED PROGRAMS APPROPRIATIONS. SENATE HEARINGS BEFORE THE COMMITTEE ON APPROPRIATIONS, 93D CONGRESS, SECOND SESSION, FISCAL YEAR 1975. Washington, Government Printing Office, 1974. 1572 p.

Includes among other information, testimony on: Assistance to Greece and Turkey.

TURKEY AT THE CROSSROADS, by Kenneth Mackenzie, in *World Survey*, (May 1974) 16 p.

"Three major factors may influence Turkey's future; . . . the deep-rooted patriotism of the Turks, the present lack of an outstanding leader, and the 'central role' of the army. Among the concerns facing Turkey are its critical geographic location, the huge social and intellectual gulf between the impoverished rural peasants and the wealthy urban businessmen, a rapidly increasing population, economic difficulties aggravated by the rise in oil prices and, last but not least, the ever-troublesome relations with Greece. Mackenzie offers a detailed political history of Turkey since the turn of the century . . . Turkey remains a loyal member of NATO and CENTO . . . but it is now asserting some independence, trying to adopt a 'neutralist' position, as indicated by its resumption of cultivating poppy and its desire to limit the use of US bases in its territory to joint Turkish-US defense . . ."

TURKEY—DIVERSIFICATION OF FOREIGN POLICY, by Udo Steinbach, in *Aussen Politik*, (Winter 1973) 439-449.

"Turkey has long been the accepted bastion of the Western defense system on the Black Sea and the Aegean straits; however, since the late 1960s, according to Dr. Steinbach, Turkey's policy has been evolving from dependence on the West toward a more independent international stance. He cites many reasons for the change, including the general world atmosphere of détente, an internal change signaling a renewed interest in Turkey's non-Western heritage, and anti-Americanism brought on in 1964 by the US denial of support should the Greek-Turkish dispute over Cyprus escalate to involve the USSR. Evidences of its new foreign policy diversification are Turkey's new relations with the USSR, the Balkan countries of East Europe, the Arabic countries in the Middle East, its partners in CENTO, and its desires for bilateral rather than collective alliances and agreements . . ."

TURKEY'S NEW HARD LINE, in *Newsweek*, v. 85, no. 8 (24 February 1975) 36.

The Turks appear to be taking a new "'get tough' attitude resulting from the U.S. Congressional cutoff of aid to Turkey . . . In an interview . . ., Turkish Foreign Minister Melih Esenfel revealed that Turkey is already drawing up plans to close some or all of the U.S. bases on its soil."

THE TURKISH STRAITS AND NATO, by Ferenc A. Vali. Stanford, Calif., Stanford University, Hoover Institution Press, 1972. 348 p.

"An account of the political history of the Bosporus and the Dardanelles, beginning with the Ottoman Empire and continuing through to Turkey's present membership in NATO. The author explains the changing geopolitical importance of the Turkish Straits to various powers, especially the Soviet Union. He provides an extensive appendix of documents relevant to the Straits between 1774 and 1964."

Q. United Kingdom and West European Defense and Security

BRITAIN AND NATO, by James Callahan, in *NATO Review*, v. 22, no. 4 (August 1974) 13-15.

"It was a labour Foreign Minister, Ernest Bevin, who signed the North Atlantic Treaty on behalf of the British Government in 1949. Since that time the British Labour Party has consistently maintained its support for the Treaty and for the aims and ideals to which it gave expression. One of the first acts of the Labour Government which took office in March this year was to reaffirm, in the Government programme presented to Parliament, our commitment to the Alliance. That commitment has been reiterated on many occasions since then. We have made it absolutely clear that NATO is the foundation of our defence and security policies, and that we see no practicable alternative to the protection which the Alliance provides."

BRITAIN RALLIES TO THE AID OF NATO, in *NATO's Fifteen Nations*, v. 18, no. 1 (February-March 1973) 16-20.

"It is many months since so much space has been devoted in the British press to the problems of NATO than in the last few weeks of 1972. The December talks between the NATO Powers suddenly woke up British public opinion, and in addition to the national press publishing sometimes startling details about Russia's three-to-one superiority in several fields of military activity, even Parliament seemed anxious to get as much information as possible from the British Government ... Probably because Britain's leaders speak all too infrequently about defence, their warnings at least make the people sit up and take notice when they are belatedly given. This was particularly the case in December when the British Foreign Minister, Sir Alex Douglas-Home, seemed to seize every opportunity to call attention to the present precarious position of NATO."

(LI)—BRITAIN'S CONTRIBUTION TO NATO: A NEW PERSPECTIVE, by Wing Comdr. Anthony T. Newman. Maxwell AFB, Ala., Air War College, 1972, 41 p. (Professional Study.)

"The emergence of Russia as a sea power is examined, and possible reasons put forward for the Soviet emphasis on naval development. The implications of this to NATO are discussed, with particular regard to the use of sea power as a means of isolating Europe from its sources of strategic materials and its overseas markets, not only in war but in peace. The effect of Soviet naval development on the threat to the NATO flanks is examined. The author suggests ways in which NATO can meet the new challenges and in particular how British defence forces can best help the Alliance in countering the new threat, at the same time enhancing their ability to meet their commitments in the Commonwealth."

BRITAIN'S DEFENCE AXE LOOKS SOMEWHAT BLUNTED; "NATO HAS FIRST CALL ON OUR RESOURCES," in *NATO's Fifteen Nations*, v. 19, no. 3 (June–July 1974) 13–15 plus.

"The attitude of the present British Government is that many of the country's defence commitments are 'a hangover from Empire days.' ... So while maintaining that British defence costs in support of NATO must be reduced to come into line with those of other allies, Britain gives the impression that its own contribution will in future largely be guided by what those allies are prepared to do ... However, the Defence Minister once again assured Parliament—and the British people—that 'NATO will have first call on our resources, because unless we stand hand-in-hand with the United States in Europe, the Warsaw Pact nations, buttressed by the might of the Soviet Union, can militarily and politically dominate our Western European neighbours'."

BRITAIN'S THOUGHTS FOCUSSED INWARDS NOT OUTWARDS, in *NATO's Fifteen Nations*, v. 17, no. 6 (December 1972–January 1973) 12–14 plus.

"Never in Britain has there been such little interest in NATO's progress or problems. This, of course, is due to the fact that the mind of the average Britisher is worrying more about the country's outstanding internal problems ... One encouraging feature of the present position regarding NATO in British minds is the very cool, and almost derisive, way even the Socialists received the proposal from the extreme Left at the annual meeting of the Trade Union Congress that immediate attention should be paid to withdrawing from NATO, or at least making Britain's participation only nominal ... Another proof that British public interest in NATO is not completely dead is the attention paid by several sections of the Press to the recent NATO exercise, reported to be the largest ever staged by the Alliance."

(LI) — CONVENTIONAL REINFORCEMENTS FOR NATO IN THE UK, by Lt. Col. Richard A. Nagel, Jr. Maxwell AFB, Ala., Air War College, 1974. 72 p. (Professional Study.)

"After a procedural introduction, the importance of NATO's ability to defend and reinforce itself conventionally is discussed. The capability of US bases in the UK to receive and employ augmenting forces and the ability of augmenting forces to deploy and be employed is then presented. After a review of the requirement for additional airbase capability and the efforts to meet this need, the assumptions pertinent to the problem are discussed. A discussion of objectives and criteria points to a direction for future actions. Specific alternatives along with relative advantages and risks are discussed as they pertain to an operational concept and a supporting logistics concept. The conclusion drawn from the study is that the USAF cannot and should not attempt to meet unilaterally the initial and long term costs of fixed facilities in Europe solely to support reinforcements for NATO. A policy decision that will provide a concise goal and specific direction to the effort to improve the USAF's capability to reinforce NATO is required."

EUROPEAN DEFENCE — BRITAIN'S CHOICE, by Comdr. David Bolton, in *RUSI Journal*, v. 118, no. 3 (September 1973) 43–48.

"Today, détente is described by a plethora of initials and catch-words. SALT, CSCE, MBFR, Ostpolitik, rapprochement, and even the term détente itself, are all currently in vogue. From the Cold War, through the decade of reappraisal, as the 1960s have been called, we have now entered upon the era of negotiation. Its continuance, as far as the West is concerned, has been validated by the American and West German elections which returned both President Nixon and Chancellor Brandt to power. However, in the euphoria of the apparent ending of strained East-West relations, there is a danger that public opinion in Western Europe will be content to forget the need for effective defensive measures. With the United Kingdom as a new member of the enlarged European Economic Community, it is perhaps an appropriate time to review the present trends which affect European security (and in which the jargon of initials is germane) in an endeavour to determine the options which are open to Britain and which best serve her interests. To give an objective military viewpoint, it is pertinent to look first at the balance of forces in Europe today. Against this background, a review of the United States- involvement in Europe, the development of détente, and an examination of other trends within Western Europe, can better be determined. Thereafter, the strategic options available to Western Europe can be weighed and Britain's choices discussed."

MALTA AND NATO, by John Marriott, in *NATO's Fifteen Nations*, v. 15, no. 5 (October-November 1970) 34-40.

"Before examining the practical value of Malta to NATO," the author reviews "the present situation in the island vis-a-vis Britain."

NATIONAL STRATEGIES WITHIN THE ALLIANCE: GREAT BRITAIN, by Carl. H. Amme, Jr., in *NATO's Fifteen Nations*, v. 17, no. 5 (October-November 1972) 18 plus.

"What emerges as a strategic concept is a conscious synthesis of many pressures and counterpressures that appears to be a logical adaptation of strategy to the realities of the nuclear age, to Britain's reduced world power position, and to the needs of the Atlantic Alliance. The changes in British strategy have been profound . . . It is clear that Britain's commitment to NATO is strong. However, it is perhaps indicative of Britain's distaste for strategic concepts for limited tactical nuclear war that it has opposed the mobile medium-range ballistic missile (MRBM) concept and has declined to incorporate Pershing 'tactical' nuclear missiles into the BAOR. Former Defense Minister Denis Healey rejected 'the American concept of a prolonged defense of West Europe by conventional forces supported by tactical nuclear weapons.' Instead, he suggested that greater nuclear power be given to the NATO commander to indicate that 'any attack could lead to nuclear war and the destruction of the Soviet Union.' (Emphasis added.) Mr. Healey more recently asserted that 'any serious attempt to throw doubt on the continuing validity of deterrence by the threat of nuclear escalation is more likely to feed the latent pressures in Europe for independent national deterrent forces than to encourage European countries to build up their conventional strength'."

ROYAL AIR FORCE, BRITAIN'S DEFENSE OBJECTIVES IN THE 1980s, by Wing Comdr. Duncan Allison, in *Military Review*, (November 1973) 20-30.

". . . Britain's economic and political future lies in the European Economic Community (EEC); its major continuing defense objective in the early 1980s, therefore, is the security of Western Europe through continued support of the Atlantic Alliance. However, the impact of the Common Market membership, the possibility of a partial American withdrawal from the European theater, and the ever-growing cost of equipment, will affect Britain's defense objectives. With the US providing the largest single force commitment to NATO, a partial American withdrawal would leave serious gaps in the already perilously thin conventional wall. At the same time, in the current atmosphere of détente, no European NATO nation would dare increase its defense commitment to fill the gaps. Additionally, the long-established geographic areas of national responsibility in NATO have virtually solidified and restructuring would be costly and time-consuming. Therefore, as the NATO nuclear custodian and the major contributo the thin NATO line, Allison sees America 'hogtied' to Europe if the image of Western solidarity through NATO is to be preserved. Even so, says Allison, America will undoubtedly cut back as much as possible administratively, in view of SAC's potential for fast reaction and in the hope of reducing the long-term German offset burden . . ."

25 YEARS IN NATO, by Col. Norman Dodd, in *Defence*, v. 5, no. 7 (July 1974) 308-310.

"For the lifetime of many of its members the Royal Air Force has played a full part in helping to provide security for the countries of the NATO Alliance. The RAF is truly a NATO air force. Almost all of its combat aircraft are committed to the Alliance either in Germany as part of Second Allied Tactical Air Force, in Britain itself on the bases of Strike Command or in the Mediterranean."

R. United States and West European Defense and Security

1. *Miscellaneous Aspects*

AMERICAN DEFENCE POLICY 1975, by James R. Schlesinger, in *Survival*, v' 17, no. 3 (May/June 1975).

"On 5 February 1975 the US Secretary of Defense, James R. Schlesinger, released his second annual Defense Department report. As in his 1974 report, Schlesinger emphasizes the need to maintain a spectrum of options for American strategic forces, and stresses that important political perceptions flowed from the state of the strategic balance with the Soviet Union. To a greater extent than in his statement last year he also underlines the importance of matching Soviet counterforce capabilities. In assessing the situation in central Europe, Schlesinger argues that NATO has the capability and resources to attain a more equal balance with the Warsaw Pact and, looking at the maritime balance, he appears to scale down the previous year's estimates of Soviet naval power. Excerpts from the first section of the Defense Department Report for Fiscal Year 1976 (and FY 1977) are reprinted . . ."

ATLANTIC DEFENSE AND THE INTEGRATION OF EUROPE, by Otto Pick, in *The Atlantic Community Quarterly*, v. 10, no. 2 (Summer 1972) 174-184.

"Otto Pick accepts the fact that U.S. and European interests are not as congruent as they once were, and will grow somewhat less so as Europe unifies. This is especially true regarding trade and the possibility of a European nuclear force. But given these facts, he argues the importance, greater than ever, of coordination and consultation between the United States and Europe in the defense area."

CHANGING BARGAINING RELATIONS IN THE ATLANTIC ALLAINCE, by P. Y. Hammond. Santa Monica, Calif., Rand Corp., June 1973. 28 p. (P-5033.)

"Discusses the recent assertiveness of U.S. dealings with European allies. Alliance relationhips survived extremely assertive behavior by De Gaulle in the 1960s. NATO's customary relationships date from a time when the U.S. was commonly acknowledged to be in a distinctly advantageous position in both economic and military matters. For 20 years, the European objective has been to keep U.S. troops in Europe, and the U.S. objective has been to share this burden. The allies still spend about the same percentage of GNP for defense and commit about the same forces to NATO emergency plans. Militarily, NATO has been in important ways symbolic rather than realistic. Washington's tough handling of the 1971 monetary crisis, forcing the others to recognize their interest in the U.S. balance of payments, was a marked departure from the friendly U.S. negotiating style. Similarly, the 'Atlantic Charter' proposal of April 1973 links the hitherto separated areas of trade and security. It is unclear, however, whether the Administration has the capacity to effect change in the Alliance. (Based on a lecture at Utah State University.)"

DEPARTMENT OF DEFENSE APPROPRIATIONS FOR 1975. HEARINGS BEFORE A SUBCOMMITTEE OF THE COMMITTEE ON APPROPRIATIONS, HOUSE OF REPRESENTATIVES, NINETY-THIRD CONGRESS, SECOND SESSION; SUBCOMMITTEE ON DEPARTMENT OF DEFENSE, PART I. Washington, Government Printing Office, 1974. 800 p.

Among many others, provides some information on the following: Prepositioning Equipment in Europe; SALT Talks; NATO Obligations; etc.

EUROPE IN THE AGE OF NEGOTIATION, by Pierre Hassner. Washington, The Center for Strategic and International Studies, 1973. 82 p. (The Washington Papers, v. 1, no. 8.)

Part I—Facing West: An Emancipated America? (The New International System and European Security; The Changing Geometry of Power; European Priorities and Arms Control Objectives; The "Struggle for Britain"). Part II—Facing East: A "Normalized" Europe? (The Consecration of Yalta; From Détente Based on Change . . . to Détente Within the Status Quo; Normalization and the Normal; The Uncertainties of Détente; Prospects; A Third Voice). With references.

EUROPEAN-AMERICAN DEFENSE BURDEN-SHARING, by Robert L. Pfaltzgraff, Jr., in *The Atlantic Community Quarterly*, v. 12, no. 2 (Summer 1974) 197-204.

An "exposition of who pays what, how much, and how that corresponds to his share in NATO."

FOREIGN MILITARY SALES AND MILITARY ASSISTANCE FACTS. Washington, Department of Defense, Security Assistance Agency, Agency, April 1974.

Among the various information provided, some of the stastical tables include, among others, the following information: students trained under MAP FY 1950-1973 in Denmark and Norway; U.S. Military sales deliveries to Denmark, Iceland, Norway; U.S. Military assistance program deliveries/expenditures to Denmark and Norway.

(*)—GREAT ISSUES OF INTERNATIONAL POLITICS, ed. by Morton A. Kaplan. 2nd ed. Chicago, Aldine, 1974. 612 p.

"A reorganized and significantly expanded anthology in international relations studies, this edition contains a balanced compilation of thirty-seven articles, two-thirds of which were not in the first edition. New sections of particular interest focus on 'Relations with Europe,' 'The Arms Race and SALT,' and 'The Defense Budget Controversy.' The thirty-one contributors include Richard A. Falk, Stanley Hoffman, William R. Kintner, Donald G. Brennan, Robert E. Hunter and the editor."

SHIFTING MOOD AND SYSTEM; SUBJECTIVE AND OBJECTIVE CHANGES AFFECT US-EC RELATIONS, by Zbigniew K. Brzezinski, in *The Atlantic Community Quarterly*, v. 12, no. 3 (Fall 1974) 319-326.

"It is no longer a world in which it is easy to shape policies pertinent to the American-European relationship, nor is it a world in which it is easy to offer simple and rapidly self-fulfilling prescriptions for East-West relationship. With respect to both, a great deal of patience, prudence and restraint seems very much in order."

SOME EUROPEAN QUESTIONS FOR DR. KISSINGER, by J. Robert Schaetzel, in *Foreign Policy*, no. 13 (Fall 1973) 66-74.

". . . Kissinger's April 23rd talk to the Associated Press editors provoked questions and reactions that persist. These issues include: the linkage among the questions to be dealt with, the description of Europe as a regional bloc, the differences in perspective between Europe and the US, the role of Japan, the ability of the European countries to work out a common approach, and most importantly, whether the US really wants such a common approach . . ."

(LI)—TRAINING AMERICAN PERSONNEL ASSIGNED TO NATO, by Maj. Earl E. Tighe. Maxwell AFB, Ala., Air Command and Staff College, 1974. 41 p. (Research Study.)

"The North Atlantic Treaty Organization (NATO) is important to the security of the United States. This paper briefly reviews the relationship between the United States and its European allies, then focuses on the military people who make the organization function on a day to day basis. Cultural differences between Americans and their allies can easily lead to misunderstanding, yet very few American military personnel receive special training prior to assignment to a NATO headquarters. A training program to correct this deficiency is recommended."

U.S. SECURITY ISSUES IN EUROPE: BURDEN SHARING AND OFFSET, MBFR AND NUCLEAR WEAPONS, SEPTEMBER 1973. A STAFF REPORT PREPARED FOR THE USE OF THE SUBCOMMITTEE ON U.S. SECURITY AGREEMENTS AND COMMITMENTS ABROAD OF THE COMMITTEE ON FOREIGN RELATIONS, UNITED STATES SENATE. Washington, Government Printing Office, 1973. 27 p. (93d Congress, 1st Session, Committee Print.)

2. *The United States and the Atlantic Alliance: Policies and Commitments*

(*)—AMERICAN MILITARY COMMITMENTS ABROAD, by Roland A. Paul. New Brunswick, N.J., Rutgers University Press, 1973. 237 p.

"Mr. Paul, Chief Counsel in 1968-1970 to the Senate Foreign Relations Subcommittee on United States Security Agreements Broad, supplies facts and figures and clarifies the issues relating to U.S. military commitments in Nationalist China, Japan, Okinawa, Laos, the Philippines, South Korea, Thailand, NATO Europe, Greece, Turkey, Spain, Portugal, Ethiopia and Morocco. He reviews the meanings of commitments and identifies eight major treaties and numerous executive agreements, Congressional resolutions and official statements involving different degrees of obligation."

AMERICAN POLICY TOWARD EUROPE: THE NEXT PHASE, by Wilfrid L. Kohl and William Taubman, in *Orbis*, v. 17, no. 1 (Spring 1973) 51–74.

"It is too early to know how the Year of Europe will turn out. But at a time of transition and reassessment in American foreign policy, when there is widespread disagreement about the nature of U.S. involvement in the post-Viet Nam era, it is entirely fitting that Europe should gain increased attention from American policymakers. Of all the regions of the world, Europe presents the clearest case for U.S. involvement. There is broad agreement among American observers on three general objectives: West European integration, Atlantic cooperation, and East–West détente (i.e., relaxation of tensions). But Europe, too, is in transition, undergoing important changes that will determine its evolution for some time to come. There is disagreement on what these changes mean for American interests . . . Increasing economic tensions between the United States and an enlarged European community threaten to undermine fundamental political ties with Europe and to weaken American support for West European unity at precisely the time when a new start is being made. Adhering to the status quo will not do in a time of change. The challenge is to examine the alternatives seriously and to begin to chart a long-term course."

THE ATLANTIC FANTASY: THE U.S., NATO, AND EUROPE, by David Calleo. Baltimore, Johns Hopkins Press (for the Washington Center of Foreign Policy Research School of Advanced International Studies.), 1970. 182 p.

"A . . . critique of American attitudes and policies toward Europe. The author, a political scientist at home on both sides of the Atlantic, writes: 'Europe is not America's front porch, but somebody else's house'."

CONGRESS AND PRESIDENTIAL CONFLICT: FOREIGN POLICY AND NATO, by Stanley L. Harrison, in *NATO's Fifteen Nations*, v. 17, no. 3 (June–July 1972) 83–87.

"Europe has been watching with increasing concern the continuing struggle between the American Congress and the President over the conduct of foreign policy. The stakes are formidable. And issues vital to NATO's future are bound up in the outcome of this clash. Intricacies of the underlying motivations appear arcane to a vast number of Americans; similarly even well-read Europeans may be bewildered at times. Basically, the contest between President and Congress over the proper role of each in the conduct of foreign relations for the Nations is based on the system of government established by the Constitution . . . Strategy and defense policy issues are inextricably linked in NATO to the numbers of Americans available to assist with these alliance tasks. Ideally, military policy pertaining to these and related critical areas should not be affected by politics. But we do not live in an ideal world. Political issues pervade every aspect of domestic and foreign policy for every nation the world over. Hence, a domestic American issue—the traditional struggle between President and Congress for what each claims as its rightful role in foreign policy—will undoubtedly have an impact on the future of NATO. Assuredly, repercussions of this struggle will be felt elsewhere as well. Ignoring the move of events will not help the nations of NATO."

CONGRESSIONAL HEARINGS ON AMERICAN DEFENSE POLICY: 1947–1971: AN ANNOTATED BIBLIOGRAPHY, by Richard Burt and Geoffrey Kemp. Lawrence, Kansas, University Press of Kansas, 1974. 377 p.

"The bibliography focuses on the hearings of the House and Senate Armed Services Committees, which are legally responsible for authorizing defense funds, and on their various specialized subcommittees. In addition, the editors include pertinent hearings conducted in the House Foreign Affairs Committee and the Senate Foreign Relations Committee as well as in the Government Operations Committees of both the House and the Senate, the House Science and Astronautics and Senate Space and Aeronautics Committees, the Joint Atomic Energy Committee and the Joint Economic Committee. Because of the vast nature of the topic, 'American defense policy,' the editors established boundaries from which to produce a practical listing of hearings which bear on the most significant questions of the time period; therefore, they opted not to provide a cumbersome, completely inclusive bibliography. Other committee outputs such as reports, documents and studies were not included in this compilation. In addition, the editors were more selective in including information about periods on which exhaustive research has already been done. The bibliography itself in addition to being an excellent reference tool reveals interesting characteristics of defense thinking during the time; for example a brief perusal of the material included reveals that during the early 1950s manpower and fiscal needs predominated in the defense establishment while strategic issues became dominant in the late 1950s and 1960s."

DEPARTMENT GIVES VIEWS ON U.S. COMMITMENTS TO NATO, by Arthur A. Hartman, in *The Department of State Bulletin*, v. 70, no. 1811 (11 March 1974) 243-247.

"Since the [State Department's] Secretary's speech last April, we have been developing with the nine members of the European Community and with our allies in NATO two declarations designed to establish the framework for our future collaboration—on the one hand with the emerging entity of the Nine and on the other among the 15 members of the Atlantic Alliance. We are also discussing a third declaration that would associate Japan with this undertaking, as well as a bilateral U.S.-Spanish declaration. We are moving forward and hope these important documents will be ready for signature this spring. They will assert the intention of the United States and its partners to continue their close association, taking into account the new factors in their relations."

EXTRACTS FROM PRESIDENT NIXON'S FOREIGN POLICY REPORT TO CONGRESS OF 25 FEBRUARY 1971, in *NATO Review*, v. 19, nos. 5-6 (May/June 1971) 23-29.

". . . In last year's annual report, I noted the variety of views on some central questions of defense policy that had to be faced candidly among the allies: What is a realistic assessment of the military threats to Western Europe? How long could NATO sustain a conventional forward defense against a determined Warsaw Pact attack? How should our tactical nuclear posture in Europe be planned to counter specific military threats? How should our tactical nuclear capabilities be related to our conventional posture? What relative burdens should be borne by the U.S. and its partners in providing the forces and other resources required by our common strategy? Are all NATO's capabilities in Europe sufficient to meet the needs of our strategy? To answer these questions, I proposed that the Alliance conduct a thorough review of its strategy and defense posture in Europe for the coming decade. The United States launched such a review in the National Security Council system, covering all the issues of European security: NATO strategy and forces, mutual force reductions, and our broader effort to enhance security through negotiation. In response to my proposal in last year's report, and at the initiative of Secretary General Brosio, our NATO allies then joined us in a major collective study of the full range of Allied defense problems in the 1970's. The result of our studies in the National Security Council and in NATO was a major achievement. The North Atlantic Council ministerial meeting in December, 1970, which completed the Alliance study, was indeed, as Secretary Rogers called it, 'One of the most important in the history of the Alliance.' We now have the blueprint and substance of a rational defense posture, which provides the framework for resolving the policy questions I raised last year."

FULL COMMITTEE CONSIDERATION OF THE REPORT OF THE AD HOC COMMITTEE ON U.S. MILITARY COMMITMENTS TO EUROPE. Washington, Government Printing Office, 28 March 1974. 37 p. (H.A.S.C. No. 93-42.)

OUR PERMANENT INTERESTS IN EUROPE, by William P. Rogers, in *The Atlantic Community Quarterly*, v. 10, no. 1 (Spring 1972) 21-26.

"Secretary of State William Rogers reiterates in principle and in detail the importance of Europe to American interests. He emphasizes that despite any economic difficulties, the United States has no intention of withdrawing from Europe. He also discusses the prospects of mutual balanced force reductions, a conference on European security and cooperation, and the improvement of relations, especially in regard to trade, with the smaller states of Eastern Europe."

THE UNITED STATES AND THE EUROPEAN COMMUNITY, by James Robert Huntley, in *The Atlantic Community Quarterly*, v. 10, no. 4 (Winter 1972-1973) 527-540.

"James R. Huntley, a well-known American expert in Atlantic affairs, analyzes the relationship between the U.S. and the European Community, looking not only at the present situation but at the past quarter century. He describes the various negative trends which have developed on both sides of the Atlantic in recent years, but makes a convincing case for the need of further, and intensifying, interdependence between the U.S. and the European Community."

THE UNITED STATES AND THE EUROPEAN COMMUNITY, by James Robert Huntley, in *NATO's Fifteen Nations*, v. 17, no. 3 (June–July 1972) 73–74 plus.

"As the states of western Europe grow—fitfully—into some kind of greater union, pursued now for nearly a quarter century, it may be useful for an American to pause anew and ask: Is this something that will help or harm the United States? The question is all the more interesting because rarely, if ever, has one nation looked on so benignly while neighboring states combined into a more powerful political unit. But the relationship between the United States and Europe is itself unique in the world, and fascinating to examine. In so doing, I would like to ask—and try to answer—four questions: 1. Why has America promoted a united Europe? 2. At the present stage in history, are Europe and the United States drawing together—or apart? 3. What are the current issues which dominate the transatlantic dialogue? 4. Does the European Community have an importance which transcends Europe?"

U.S. MILITARY COMMITMENTS TO EUROPE. HEARINGS BEFORE THE AD HOC SUBCOMMITTEE OF THE COMMITTEE ON ARMED SERVICES, HOUSE OF REPRESENTATIVES, NINETY-THIRD CONGRESS, SECOND SESSION, FEBRUARY 15, 26, MARCH 4-6, AND 8, 1974. Washington, Government Printing Office, 1974. 313 p. (H.A.S.C. No. 93–41.)

U.S. MILITARY COMMITMENTS TO EUROPE. REPORT OF THE AD HAC SUBCOMMITTEE OF THE COMMITTEE ON ARMED SERVICES, HOUSE OF REPRESENTATIVES, NINETY-THIRD CONGRESS, SECOND SESSION, 9 APRIL 1974. Washington, Government Printing Office, 1974. 30 p. (Union Calendar No. 449, House Report No. 93-978.)

THE UNITED STATES AND WESTERN EUROPE: PARTNERS OR RIVALS?, by Kurt Birrenbach, in *Orbis*, v. 17, no. 2 (Summer 1973) 405–414.

"The relationship between the members of the European Community and the United States has undergone a change, which urgently calls for a thorough reappraisal. That change has been economic, military and political, but its primary cause has been the change in the relative position of the United States in the world: economically in relation to its NATO partners in the European Community and Japan, militarily and politically in relation to the Soviet Union, and politically in relation to China. This shift in the overall power relationship has altered the constellation of the international system. It has placed the Atlantic Alliance and the Japanese-American Security Treaty into a new frame of reference . . . This development, in conjunction with the policy of East-West détente, has diluted appreciation of the need for political and military interdependence, and hence for an Atlantic community of NATO partners."

WEST EUROPEAN SECURITY TRENDS: IMPLICATIONS FOR THE US MILITARY ROLE. McLean, Va., Research Analysis Corp., June 1970. 123 p. (RAC-R-96.)

"Security trends in Western European nations of the Atlantic Alliance reflect the changing military and political outlooks of these nations vis-a-vis the US. This present dynamic and changing environment within Europe is likely to affect the future position and participation of the role of the US in Europe. The role of NATO will tend to reflect these changes in time. Withal the ranges of options are limited for all parties. Primary concern in Europe centers on (1) NATO strategy and (2) the related question of the nuclear issues. For the US, the significant issues with regard to a continued positive role in Europe emerge as a need for (1) a stable US military presence in Europe within an Alliance context and (2) significant numbers of US divisions present in Europe committed to Europe's defense. Continued and growing instability in Europe is likely to provoke an increased potential for unilateral nuclear weapons, particularly within the Federal Republic of Germany and, given a continued dissatisfaction with NATO strategy, possible bilateral nuclear arrangements within Europe. The requirement incumbent on US planners, then, requires (1) a clear enunciation of the direct linkage between NATO nuclear forces and the US strategic nuclear elements and (2) the implementation of mutually understood and accepted politico-military guidelines for the role of the NATO nuclear weapons as an element of NATO strategy."

3. *Credibility Aspects*

AMERICA AND EUROPE, by Zbigniews Brzezinski, in *Foreign Affairs*, v. 49, no. 1 (October 1970) 11-30.

"For the West Europeans to think in Atlantic terms when Europe was still shattered was a creative leap forward. For Europeans and Japanese to join Americans in defining a common global perspective is the logical next step. Can the United States move in these directions, can it initiate the measures proposed here? Its domestic problems certainly stand in the way, but an even graver impediment is the apparent loss of confidence and of vision among some of its leaders. If the contemporary Soviet leadership can be said to be bureaucratically mediocre and ideologically moribund, much of the American establishment appears to be intellectually paralyzed and politically pusillanimous. Yet the country as a whole is groping for new objectives and for the definition of specific ideals—domestic and foreign—to be attained. To restore Europe is to preserve and to enlarge that part of the world community which has come closest to establishing a humane and just form of social organization. It is with Europe that the United States shares certain concepts of law and personal freedom. Unless America continues actively to promote a broad vision of European restoration America does not have a foreign policy."

BEHIND NATO'S SHINY FACADE—A TROUBLED FUTURE?, by Gen. T. R. Milton, in *Air Force Magazine*, v. 55, no. 8 (August 1972) 49-52.

"While the military alliance in Western Europe is under no imminent threat of collapse, several dark questions have appeared on its horizon. One major concern is the extent of the US's continued commitment. Another is that chronic enigma: Soviet intentions. Will the Soviets' current lullaby of peace and goodwill lure the twenty-year-old Alliance into a dangerous state of euphoria?"

CAN EUROPE'S SECURITY BE "DECOUPLED" FROM AMERICA?, by Andrew J' Pierre, on *Foreign Affairs*, v. 51, no. 4 (July 1973) 761-773.

"A new and contentious concept has seeped into the trans-atlantic dialogue in recent times. It has been suggested that the United States may 'decouple' itself from its strategic commitment to Western Europe in the future, or perhaps is in the process of doing so now. The codification of mutual deterrence in the SALT agreements of a year ago, combined with the earlier loss of U.S. nuclear superiority, is seen as having considerably eroded the remaining credibility of the American nuclear guarantee to Europe. Some go further to find in the agreements an implicit understanding between the two superpowers that neither will henceforth initiate the use of nuclear weapons in any circumstances short of the direct defense of its own territory. And even thoughtful Europeans who still observe the litany of faith in the nuclear guarantee do so with diminished conviction and look for opportunities through cooperative European actions to compensate for a substantial degree of American disengagement."

WHAT FORD WANTS IN EUROPE, in *U.S. News & World Report*, v. 73, no. 22 (2 June 1975) 17-21.

"Shoring up the Atlantic Alliance, searching for peace in Mideast—those are only two of the goals the President is pursuing on a crucial mission."

WHAT HAPPENED TO THE YEAR OF EUROPE?, by Andrew J. Pierre, in *The World Today*, v. 30, no. 3 (March 1974? 110-119.

"The end of 1973 found relations between Europe and America at their lowest ebb since at least the Suez crisis of seventeen years earlier . . . This was to have been the year of redefinition, revitalization, and refurbishing of trans-Atlantic bonds. The Year of Europe and the call for a new Atlantic Charter led instead to misunderstanding and confusion. But the issues which it identified—and helped transform—are too serious and profound to be ignored in a fit of pique or ridicule. They will not go away, although, if left unattended, they could sour and eventually poison European-American relations. We must therefore ask some retrospective questions: What led to the Year of Europe initiative? What went wrong? And what of the future?"

4. *United States and Western Europe: Future Prospects*

AMERICAN FOREIGN POLICY IN THE NIXON ERA, by A. Hartley. London, The International Institute for Strategic Studies, 1975. 35 p. (Adelphi Papers 110.)

The Background of American Foreign Policy; The Intellectual Background; Style and Structure; The New International Conjuncture; The Nixon Doctrine; A 'Five-Power World'; Allies and Opponents; Two Phases of Policy: The United States and Europe; Conclusion; and The Future.

AMERICAN STRATEGY FOR WESTERN EUROPE IN THE 70S, by Capt. Ebbe Mogensen, in *Military Review*, v. 53, no. 8 (August 1973) 3-15.

"An outline for the recommended US strategy for Western Europe in the decade ending 1980 . . . The most serious foreign policy challenges for the United States from now until 1980 will be to avoid staying in Europe too long thus inhibiting development of the 'new partnership' and widening the gap between the American people and Congress and the administration with respect to domestic needs, to avoid reverting to isolationism and losing contact with Europe, to avoid developing a detestation of the 'ungrateful' Europeans, and to avoid upsetting the balance of power by overly rapid change. For the American-European partnership, the period 1973-80 will be an interesting period, presenting tremendous challenges to American diplomats and strategists as they promote the development of the needed cooperation between the Common Market and the United States."

NOW—A TOUGHER U.S.; INTERVIEW WITH JAMES R: SCHLESINGER, SECRETARY OF DEFENSE, in *U.S. News & World Report*, v. 78, no. 21 (26 May 1975) 24-27.

"Impact of Indo-China's fall is reshaping U.S. attitudes. Mideast, Russia, China, Europe all will be affected . . . An assessment of what lies ahead for America."

STRATEGY FOR TOMORROW; AMERICA'S NEED FOR FUTURE SECURITY IN EUROPE, by Stanley L. Harrison, in *Military Review*, v. 52, no. 8 (August 1972) 57-70.

"The time has come for America to come to grips with the hard realities of the nuclear age. For far too long, this Nation has pursued a military posture shackled to past precepts. Today, the United States can no longer afford to continue the luxury of repetitive fallacy; to do so may incur a penalty that the United States—indeed the world—cannot bear. Recognition of reality has not kept pace with recent events, and it is imperative to reconsider some pertinent questions for the present and for the future. We need to take a hard look at out basic security strategy. In order to put words into deeds, we must clearly identify specific areas to be addressed. For purposes of this discussion, it will be useful to limit the focus of examination to the most critical center of US concern, Europe . . . Our NATO allies have every right to insist on US participation in their security. However, they should not be permitted to prescribe a course of action which involves the most catastrophic of risks—even less so if the strategy reduces the willingness of all partners to resist the most likely change. A local deterrent in Europe is required to increase the range of options and to bring policy in line with the strategy it is prepared to implement. A realistic strategy is essential to save the alliance. It is a means by which there emerges the possibility of a conflict which does not inevitably involve catastrophic consequences for the United States or Europe."

AMERICAN ARMS AND A CHANGING EUROPE; DILEMMAS OF DETERRENCE AND DISARMAMENT, by Warner R. Schilling and others. New York, Columbia University Press, 1973. 218 p.

"This book analyzes the problems and choices the United States will face in the decade ahead in the pursuit of three goals: European security, strategic security, and arms control. The major focus of the analysis is on the forms that future European security arrangements may take and how American choices in arms and arms control policy can affect those arrangements. But policies for European security cannot be divorced from those for America's strategic security, and the analysis also considers the changes that may occur in the Soviet-American strategic balance and how they may affect both European security arrangements and the opportunities for strategic arms control. The authors examine the major military, economic, and political trends and developments that may materialize in Europe, the United States, and the Soviet Union over the next decade and how these trends and developments may affect present European security arrangements; identify the pivotal variables that make possible eight different model security arrangements in Europe; and explain how prospective trends and developments could combine to lead to one or another of these eight model forms. The analytical purpose of the book is to delimit the range of possible futures and within that range to identify the main choices the United States will confront over the next decade in its effort to maintain both the European balance of power and the Soviet-American balance of terror. The policy purpose is to prescribe arms and arms control policies that can reduce the political and military costs and risks entailed in the pursuit of these objectives, particularly in an era of détente in Europe and parity in the Soviet-American strategic balance, without jeopardizing either the opportunities for strategic arms control or the effectiveness of the American political and military commitment to the defense of Western Europe. 'American Arms and a Changing Europe' reports the conclusions of a major research project undertaken by the Institute of War and Peace Studies at Columbia University on problems of European security. A number of background papers written for the project, upon which the present volume is partly based, have been published in a companion volume, 'European Security and the Atlantic System'."

UNITED STATES NATIONAL INTERESTS IN A CHANGING WORLD, by Donald E. Nuechterlein. Lexington, University Press of Kentucky, 1973. 203 p.

"Mr. Neuchterlien offers a . . . conceptual framework for the analysis of foreign policy decisions, resting on more precise definitions and distinguishing among the degrees of interest that the United States perceives in the range of foreign policy issues it faces. He also deals with the constitutional problem of checks and balances between the Presidency and Congress in setting the goals of foreign policy, and the influence of private interest groups and the media on the definition of national interest. Underlining the need for constant reassessment of priorities in a rapidly changing international environment, Mr. Nuechterlien illustrates his analysis by drawing on the American experience in foreign affairs since World War II. A case study of the American involvement in Southeast Asia describes how six presidents, beginning with Franklin Roosevelt, viewed United States interests there and the conclusions each drew in terms of policy tools to defend those interests . . . Finally, he assesses what the future vital interests of the United States are likely to be in light of the shifting balance of world power, and the growing importance of international economics."

"WE ARE MOVING INTO A NEW WORLD," in *U.S. News & World Report*, v. 98, no. 25 (23 June 1975) 20-24 plus.

"With events at a critical juncture—in the Mideast, dealing with Russia, China, NATO, the energy crisis—Mr. Kissinger takes a sweeping, analytical look ahead in this interview with editors of the magazine."

WESTERN EUROPE AND AMERICA IN THE SEVENTIES, by Ernst H. van'der Beugel and Max Kohnstamm, in *The Atlantic Community Quarterly*, v. 10, no. 3 (Fall 1972) 295-311.

"Ernst H. van'der Beugel and Max Kohnstamm, leading European academic experts, discuss the major issues likely to confront Western Europe and its allies over the course of the next decade, and the appropriate responses to them. They emphasize in particular the problems of European security and of the international economic order. Basically, they hold that the core of the 'conventional wisdom' of the last twenty-five years, the necessity of Western cooperation, still holds good."

5. *United States Force Structure in NATO*

a. *Miscellaneous Aspects*

FOREIGN ASSISTANCE AND RELATED AGENCIES APPROPRIATIONS FOR 1975. HEARINGS BEFORE A SUBCOMMITTEE ON APPROPRIATIONS, HOUSE OF REPRESENTATIVES, NINETY-THIRD CONGRESS, SECOND SESSION, PART 2. Washington, Government Printing Office, 1974. 1779 p.

Includes, among many others, information pertaining to various administrative aspects of the U.S. Mission to NATO.

NATO: HOW MANY TROOPS ARE ENOUGH?, in *Newsweek*, v. 82, no. 7 (13 August 1973) 36-37.

"Until a few years ago, America's strategic commitment to West Europe was sacrosant. But then along came the trauma of Vietnam, the winds of neo-isolationism and, finally, the Watergate-inspired Congressional challenge to White House foreign policymaking. Today, although the official commitment to the defense of Europe remains as firm as ever, the future of the 305,000 GI's station on the Continent is very much in doubt. The debate on the troop issue lacks the fervor of the bitter clashes over Indochina and it is still largely muffled by the furor over Watergate. Yet beneath the surface, more and more Administration critics have begun to raise questions about just how many soldiers the U.S. should keep on the Continent—or whether the U.S. needs any at all."

THE ROLE AND CAPABILITY OF UNITED STATES GROUND FORCES IN EUROPE, by Gen. Michael S. Davison, in *RUSI Journal*, v. 118, no. 4 (December 1973) 3-9.

"The role of the United States Army in Europe. The foremost factor in that role is America's commitment to the North Atlantic Alliance, a commitment which springs from recognition of a deep and abiding mutuality of interests and which has been solidly affirmed by five successive Presidents. Thus the great bulk (85 per cent) of American soldiers in Europe are here as part of the NATO military structure, which has successfully deterred hostile aggression against the North Atlantic area for over two decades."

U.S. FORCE STRUCTURE IN NATO: AN ALTERNATIVE, by Richard D. Lawrence and Jeffrey Record. Washington, Brookings Institution, 1974. 136 p.

"Another in the . . . series of Brookings staff papers on defense policy. This one argues that the U.S. military posture in Europe is 'dangerously inappropriate,' unsuited for the most likely threat—a short, intense war. The authors make wide-ranging . . . proposals for reorganizing U.S. forces to make them more effective and less costly. Many of these recommendations will be controversial in Western Europe, but they are nevertheless well tuned to the requirements of the future."

U.S. FORCES IN EUROPE. HEARINGS BEFORE THE SUBCOMMITTEE ON ARMS CONTROL, INTERNATIONAL LAW AND ORGANIZATION, OF THE COMMITTEE ON FOREIGN RELATIONS, UNITED STATES SENATE, NINETY-THIRD CONGRESS, FIRST SESSION, JULY 25 AND 27, 1973. Washington, Government Printing Office, 1973. 386 p.

In surveying the problems and prospects of U.S. forces in Europe, this hearing also delves into the various aspects of NATO as well as the Warsaw Pact. Overall this hearing concerns itself with mutual force reductions in Europe.

U.S. FORCES IN EUROPE: HOW MANY? DOING WHAT?, by Alain C. Enthoven, in *Foreign Affairs*, v. 53, no. 3 (April 1975) 513-532.

"Distinguished Senators ask, 'What should we tell our constituents when they ask why we should keep American troops in Europe 30 years after the end of World War II?' The answer remains what it has been throughout that period; because it is in our best interest to keep them there. A free and independent Western Europe aligned with the United States, is vital for our national security and well-being. The U.S.S.R. and its Warsaw Pact allies have large and effective land and air forces in Eastern Europe. If our allies are to be able to preserve their independence, NATO must have in-place forces of equal size and effectiveness, and be able to match the Pact in a mobilization. If the NATO alliance does not provide such forces, a major imbalance in military power will be an intimidating factor that cannot help but influence our allies' freedom and political alignment over the years. American forces are necessary because they help maintain the balance, and also because they demonstrate the seriousness of our commitment . . . While NATO outspends the Pact by roughly a third, and has almost 20 percent more military personnel on active duty, we are not achieving the military effectiveness we need and that we could achieve with the resources we are devoting to the purpose. Making NATO's conventional forces fully effective within existing budgets and manpower ought to be the major goal of the alliance. An important part of this effort, I believe, should be a reassessment of the tactical nuclear weapons now deployed in Europe, leading to an early and sharp reduction in their numbers."

U.S. FORCES IN NATO. HEARINGS BEFORE THE COMMITTEE ON FOREIGN AFFAIRS AND ITS SUBCOMMITTEE ON EUROPE, HOUSE OF REPRESENTATIVES, NINETY-THIRD CONGRESS, FIRST SESSION JUNE 18, 19, 25, 26, JULY 10-12, 17, 1973. Washington Government Printing Office, 1973. 440 p.

The Subcommittee looks at some changes that have taken place in Europe, and their institutional implications, from the viewpoint of the following question: What is the proper force level for the United States in the military alliance of NATO?

U.S. TROOPS IN EUROPE: ISSUES, COSTS, AND CHOICES, by John Newhouse and others. Washington, The Brookings Institution, 1971. 177 p.

"In light of current Congressional efforts to have the number of American military forces in

Europe cut back, made notable by the Mansfield Resolution, this is a timely assessment of the complex economic, military and political factors which require consideration before such a step might be taken. The authors attempt to answer such crucial questions as: Does improvement of the East-West political environment mean that the Soviet threat to Western Europe is diminishing? Is there a stable military balance between NATO and Warsaw Pact forces in Central Europe, and how important to that balance are U.S. forces? What do American forces actually cost, and how could the burden be reduced?"

WHY U.S. FORCES ARE IN EUROPE, by Gen. George Brown, in *Commanders Digest*, v. 17, no. 10 (6 March 1975) 8 p.

The Threat; NATO, Warsaw Pact Comparison; Military Balance by NATO Region; Special Problems; Recent Accomplishments and Planned Improvements; Military Worth and Value of NATO; Atlantic Regional Considerations; Achievements and Shortfalls; and Strategic Problems.

b. *Unilateral Troop Reduction in NATO: Pro and Con*

THE AMERICAN MILITARY PRESENCE IN EUROPE: CURRENT DEBATE IN THE UNITED STATES, by John Yochelson, in *Orbis*, v. 15, no. 3 (Fall 1972) 784-807.

"In two respects Senator Mike Mansfield's unsuccessful attempt in May 1971 to obtain a 50 per cent reduction of U.S. troops in Europe by the end of the year marked a turning point in the American debate concerning NATO . . . The Mansfield phenomenon raises important questions regarding the nature of the American NATO debate—its apparent resistance to long-term policy application, its participants and their objectives, its rhetoric and argumentation, and its likely course in the next several years. The debate is inherently relevant not only because it exposes patterns of competition on a major issue but because it provides insights on the international relations dimension of the U.S. engagement in Europe. Despite the fact that American troop levels are partially a function of intra- and interalliance bargaining as well as of special bilateral relationships, final decisions are invariably made in Washington. This article analyzes the development of the American debate during the Nixon Administration. Part one examines in general terms the scope and structure of the discussion. Part two focuses on objectives, arguments and outcomes in the debates within the executive branch and between it and Congress. The conclusion discusses some of the main factors that will bear upon future decisions."

CONGRESS AND PRESIDENT: NATO TROOP-REDUCTION CONFLICT, by Stanley L. Harrison, in *Military Review*, v. 21, no. 9 (September 1971) 13-24.

"US Forces in Europe will be reduced in number. No one, on either side of the Atlantic, should disillusion himself otherwise. How the US forces will be pared, and when the US presence will shrink on the Continent, are the questions without answer at this time. Settlement of these issues, however, goes straight to the heart of a fundamental controversy involving the Constitution itself. Basically, the conflict involves Congress and the President, but the ramifications inherent in the struggle have considerable impact on the foreign affairs of the Nation and, inevitably, on the role of the North Atlantic Treaty Organization."

(LI)—CONSIDERATIONS FOR THE REDUCTION OF US FORCES IN NATO, by Maj. Louis B. Plants. Maxwell AFB, Ala., Air Command and Staff College, 1974. 54 p. (Research Study.)

"As the United States withdraws its military forces from Southeast Asia, additional discussion and pressure is being applied on the administration to reduce US troop levels in Europe. This study investigates the advantages and disadvantages to the United States and the North Atlantic Treaty Organization (NATO) if US troop reductions are ordered. A comparison and appraisal of NATO and Warsaw Pact forces is provided. The comparison includes reserve strengths, mobilization capabilities, and states of readiness of forces-in-being. Consideration is also given to an analysis of Soviet thinking through a study of Soviet history, doctrine and options."

(LI)—THE FEASIBILITY OF A SUBSTANTIAL UNILATERAL REDUCTION OF UNITED STATES FORCES IN EUROPE, by Maj. Robert G. Morrell. Maxwell AFB, Ala., Air Command and Staff College, 1974. 47 p. (Research Study.)

"The pressure to unilaterally reduce United States troops in Europe is derived from four basic issues: a reduced Soviet threat to Western Europe, the cost of maintaining US troops in Europe, a nuclear 'trip-wire' strategy, and increased burden-sharing by the US allies. This study reviews and analyzes the pros and cons of each of these issues and establishes the probably outcome or impact on the NATO alliance if the US were to implement a substantial reduction of their forces in Europe. Consideration is also given to the actions the United States must take to ensure the continued viability of NATO and to protect the nations of Western Europe."

NATO AND THE AGING PROCESS, by Gen. T. R. Milton, in *Strategic Review*, v. 2, no. 1 (Winter 1974) 39-43.

"The oil crisis highlights the present limits of European unity. NATO countries face other difficulties in the unpopularity of military conscription, the obscuring effect of détente, the pinch of budget restrictions. Some of the NATO powers have reduced their force contributions. The concurrent increases in Soviet and Warsaw Pact forces pose grave questions for NATO defenses just as the United States is debating a possible reduction of its contribution. European members of the alliance point out that NATO is also a defense of the United States and its interests. They are not likely to increase their contributions, will in fact have difficulty holding present levels. Thus an American withdrawal might well cause the collapse of NATO. Substantial reduction of force contributions would have incalculable but potentially disastrous effects on NATO."

NATO'S FUTURE, by Barry Goldwater, in *NATO's Fifteen Nations*, v. 19, no. 1 (February-March 1974) 26-27.

"The future of NATO rests in very large measure on the military plans, determination, and diplomacy of the United States. If the Atlantic Alliance is to hold together, under the strain of uncertain petroleum supplies from the Middle East, a growing Soviet strategic capacity, and the psychological effects of détente between the U.S. and the USSR, we will have to make important moves in all the areas mentioned above. The whole subject of American military strength goes to the heart of the question of NATO's nuclear shield. It involves decisions and plans that may or may not grow out of the SALT III (Strategic Arms Limitations Talks), as well as actions taken by the Congress on questions of weapon systems and defense spending in general. Also involved are troop levels, especially the number maintained by the United States in the NATO organization. On Capitol Hill in Washington, there is heavy agitation for unilateral withdrawal of a large portion of the American troop strength in Europe. Should this pressure prevail, it would demolish the Nixon Administration's attempt to bring about mutual reduction in troop strength between U.S. troops in NATO and Russian troops assigned to the Warsaw Pact Nations."

POLICY, TROOPS, AND THE NATO ALLIANCE. REPORT OF SENATOR SAM NUNN TO THE COMMITTEE ON ARMED SERVICES, UNITED STATES SENATE, APRIL 2, 1974. Washington, Government Printing Office, 1974. 14 p.

"I have been looking into a number of issues surrounding our troop deployments in Europe. This has let me talk with many American and Allied officials, both here and in Europe. The purpose of my inquiries has been to make as assessment and develop some insights into the various issues surrounding the military state of the NATO Alliance. In addition I have been able to get the views of both Allies and U.S. military officers on the conventional balance in Europe."

(LI)—THE POLITICAL AND MILITARY REALITIES OF US MILITARY FORCE REDUCTIONS IN EUROPE, by Lt. Col. Edward B. Robbins. Maxwell AFB, Ala., Air War College, 1972. 61 p. (Professional Study.)

"Remarks on the evolutionary development of the US military presence in Europe introduce the rationale for continuing to maintain American forces on the Continent. The Congressional challenges to the current force levels are described, followed by an analysis of the Soviet military threat. The author then briefly discusses the major proposals which have been suggested as alternatives to maintaining the current number of US troops in Europe. The author concludes that none of these alternatives is entirely satisfactory, and he suggests that force reduction would have an adverse effect on the Atlantic Alliance and the security of the United States. The author advocates an expanded policy making role for Europe in the Alliance, suggesting that an expanded European role may create conditions which will permit the United States to safely reduce its forces in due course."

(LI)—A PROPOSAL FOR A LIMITED WITHDRAWAL OF U.S. GROUND FORCE

TROOPS FROM WEST GERMANY, by Maj. Thomas H. Tait. Maxwell AFB, Ala., Air Command and Staff College, 1970. 77 p. (Research Study no. 1285-70.)

"This study assumes that, due to Congressional pressure, there will be a reduction in United States ground forces in West Germany before the 1972 presidential election. The possible invasion routes to the West that are available to the Warsaw Pact are examined to ascertain where an attack will most likely occur. Based upon this examination, and a comparison of the NATO and Warsaw Pact conventional military strength, this study concludes that a limited withdrawal of United States ground forces, primarily mechanized infantry, can be made from the southern part of West Germany without reducing the combat effectiveness of NATO."

(LI)—TOWARD A REDUCED US PROFILE IN NATO, by Lt. Col. Paul G. Smith. Maxwell AFB, Ala., Air War College, 1972. 76 p. (Professional Study.)

"A discussion of the recent efforts in Congress to reduce the US troop commitment in Europe provides the background for an examination of the major dilemmas is traced to the shifting and confusing policies of the dominant partner, and still sole protector, the United States. A discussion of some practical aspects of the NATO flexible response strategy leads into an analysis of contemporary issues bearing on US force withdrawals. A greater sharing of responsibility with the Europeans would permit a lower US profile in NATO, enhance mutual respect among the partners, and build greater Alliance resolve. Potential areas for personnel reductions are identified, and recommendations are made for achieving a lower US profile in NATO which could benefit NATO in the long run."

c. *Status of United States Air Forces*

(LI)—THE DUAL BASED TACTICAL FIGHTER WING IN NATO, by Lt. Col. Albert S. Borchik, Jr. Maxwell AFB, Ala., Air War College, 1971, 14 p. (Professional Study no. 4078.)

"This study examines the dual base concept as it applies to the tactical fighter wing. The 49th Tactical Fighter Wing was the first tactical fighter wing to implement this concept. Under the dual base concept, the 49th Tactical Fighter Wing is committed to NATO. The major problems and their solutions concerned implementing the dual base posture are discussed. The feasibility of this concept as a United States force posture in NATO commitments is presented. The study concludes that the dual base concept is an effective and responsive force concept. When considering the present NATO strategy of flexible response and the need for the immediate response capability of tactical air, further employment of this concept by tactical air units committed to NATO must be delayed until other country NATO units are ready to assume an in-place immediate response posture."

(LI)—IMPLICATIONS OF PCS VS UNIT ROTATION, by Lt. Col. Stanton G. Lockley. Maxwell AFB, Ala., Air War College, 1972. 49 p. (Professional Study.)

"This study examines the feasibility of providing tactical air forces to the Commander-in-Chief, United States Air Forces in Europe, by the unit rotation concept, as opposed to permanently basing these forces in Europe. It examines both courses of action in relation to the U.S. foreign military commitments, international balance of payments, personnel turbulence, and military effectiveness. The study concludes that the presence of tactical air forces in Europe is a deterrent against conventional as well as nuclear war. Any economic gains dervied from the unit rotation concept would be in the short term only, and the psychological and military issues are the primary considerations. Further, these issues suggest that the tactical air forces in Europe should be assigned on a permanent change of station basis."

(LI)—NATO SUPPORT AND US TACTICAL FIGHTER WITHDRAWAL, by Lt. Col. Robert C. Somers. Maxwell AFB, Ala., Air War College, 1971. 29 p. (Professional Study no. 4453.

"This essay considers some of the problems which are involved in the United States participation in the support of the North Atlantic Treaty Organization. The NATO countries became somewhat complacent during the years of peace. The American commitment became increasingly more expensive. Pressures grew for reduction of forces and expenses. The invasion of Czechoslovakia brought NATO back to reality. Consideration is given to the value of United States tactical fighters in this new era."

(LI)—NATO, THE NIXON DOCTRINE, AND DÉTENTE: A NEW ROLE FOR USAF IN NATO?, by Maj. Michael S. Farman. Maxwell

AFB, Ala., Air Command and Staff College, 1973. 35 p. (Research Study.)

"Since the end of World War II, the United States has provided massive military support to our European NATO allies to insure their political freedom. Recent major diplomatic initiatives by President Nixon and similar acts by NATO and Warsaw Pact members have fostered a state of détente. Therefore, in view of continuing efforts such as the SALT and MBFR negotiations, USAF's participation in NATO warrants reassessment. This study traces NATO's development, USAF's support of the alliance, and the effects of the aforementioned political acts. The study concludes with practical recommendations for USAF mission changes in support of NATO."

(LI)—USAF AND NATO IN THE 70's, by Maj. Hubert R. Hayworth. Maxwell AFB, Ala., Air Command and Staff College, 1973. 54 p. (Research Study.)

"The future role of the United States Air Force (USAF) in the North Atlantic Treaty Organization (NATO) is in question and may be affected by efforts to reduce military expenditures by the US, the power struggle between Congress and the President, Mutual Balanced Force Reductions, and the Conference on European Security. Dual basing, increased force contributions by the West Europeans, a Unified Armed Force of Europe, and a joint nuclear effort by Great Britain and France are examined as alternatives to the present dominant US position in the organization. It is concluded that the USAF nuclear contribution to NATO does not diminish, in fact will probably increase, as more emphasis is placed on a tactical nuclear defense strategy by NATO."

6. *West European Dependence on United States Presence and Power*

AFTER 30 YEARS—WHEN IT COMES TO DEFENSE, IT'S "GI, DON'T GO HOME!", in *U.S. News & World Report*, v. 78, no. 19 (12 May 1975) 79-80.

"It takes little more than a glance at Western Europe's military lineup to understand why U.S. remains the underpinning of Allied defense."

AN ALLIANCE INITIATIVE, by Capt. G. W. Cox, in *United States Naval Institute Proceedings*, v. 100, no. 11 (November 1974) 45-53.

"Weaponry, not words, has made NATO's metaphorical 'Sword and Shield' credible for a quarter-century. But how will future weapons be developed and produced if America can't or won't?"

BONN—WASHINGTON: THE MATURING ALLIANCE, by Klaus Schoenthal in *Aussenpolitik*, no. 1 (1970) 42-52.

"Since the end of World War II, the US and Germany have enjoyed a good relationship, but only in recent years has this association developed into what might be called a mature alliance . . . For example, good relations have not deteriorated over differences in NATO strategy, the stationing of American troops in Europe, and mutual complaints of inadequate consultations. Both governments have broadened their base of decision-making by seeking the advice of non-governmental experts . . . Unilateral withdrawal on the part of the US would only encourage the Europeans to decrease their defense forces, thus making NATO ineffective. Neither would it be sound economics for the US to withdraw its forces. Of the total US defense expenditure of $73 billion in 1967, about $12 billion was NATO-oriented. A withdrawal of one-third of US troops in Europe would save no more than $2 billion annually."

PROSPECTS FOR THE ATLANTIC ALLIANCE, by Maj. Gen. Thomas A. Lane, in *Strategic Review*, v. 3, no. 1 (Winter 1975) 39-45.

"Senator Sam Nunn, a member of the Senate Armed Services Committee, found in a survey of NATO activities a deficiency of long-range policy to guide the participation of the United States. He asked for an evaluation of the prospect of nuclear conflict in Europe, a definition of the duration of the U.S. commitment of military forces to NATO, an appraisal of the prudence of replacing U.S. NATO units with German units, an estimate of the effect of unilateral U.S. withdrawal of NATO forces upon détente and related negotiations, and a judgment about the danger to U.S. troops, families and other citizens of unilateral U.S. withdrawal from NATO. Possible answers are related to the formation of a United Europe to create a third superpower and assure European security. To advance that development, NATO policy and structure should be harmonized with the goal, to include withdrawal of U.S. conventional forces on a five-year schedule and nuclear forces on a ten-year schedule. When Alliance relationships are adjusted to this goal, the transition to the new structure will be made with some Soviet criticism but no interference, and with benefit to all NATO allies. The new structure would restore a logical U.S. strategic posture to be applied also to other areas and other alliances."

WHAT EUROPE WANTS FROM U.S., in *U.S. News & World Report*, v. 74, no. 18 (30 April 1973) 37-39.

Interview with West Germany's Chancellor Willy Brandt. "On the arrival eve of his visit with President Nixon, . . . [he] has a message for Americans: It is 'vitally important' to keep U.S. troops in Europe. Communists . . . are building up militarily in Eastern Europe. Also, from Chancellor Brandt, this reassurance: Anti-Americanism in his country has been exaggerated."

WHAT HAPPENS TO EUROPE IF THE AMERICANS LEAVE? A BRITISH VIEW, by Brig. C. N. Barclay, in *Army*, v. 23, no. 11 (November 1973) 7-11.

"The considered opinion of concerned Europeans is that, eventually, U.S. forces—and our nuclear deterrent—will depart their shores. If this happens, Great Britain and continental Europe can exercise one of several options open to them, or they can do nothing and hope for the best."

7. *Western Europe and the Nixon Doctrine*

EUROPE AND THE NIXON DOCTRINE: A GERMAN POINT OF VIEW, by Werner Kaltefleiter, in *Orbis*, v. 17, no. 1 (Spring 1973) 75-94.

In Washington, the second phase in the implementation of the Nixon Doctrine is generally known as the 'Year of Europe.' Whatever the details of this shift of emphasis in the American world outlook, the United States will be unable to secure its objectives unless it can find partners on the other side of the Atlantic that have the interest, capability and willingness to respond favorably to the U.S. initiative. An analysis of the European scene suggests that U.S. leaders should be prepared for a disappointing response. The situation differs from country to country. As far as the Federal Republic of Germany is concerned, there is little chance that policies designed primarily to strengthen the Atlantic Alliance will be pursued. This reluctance can be attributed to a combination of three factors: (1) the dependence of the Bonn regime on a 'milieu of détente,' largely controlled by Moscow; (2) a revival of a 'national approach' to foreign policy; and (3) a general decrease in the perception of threat from the East and in the Atlantic orientation of the German electorate, together with a revival of radical socialism in the ruling Social Democratic Party. Under these circumstances, if the Western alliance is to be strengthened in accordance with the Nixon Doctrine, a prerequisite in the Federal Republic is the creation of a new domestic consensus for an alliance-oriented foreign policy."

EUROPE AND THE NIXON DOCTRINE: A GERMAN POINT OF VIEW, by Werner Kaltefeiter, in *The Atlantic Community Quarterly*, v. 11, no. 4 (Winter 1973-1974) 456-469.

"The United States will have difficulty in restoring cooperative attitudes in Europe unless it can find partners on the other side of the Atlantic that have interest, capability and willingness to respond favorably to U.S. initiatives. The situation differs from country to country. As far as the Federal Republic of Germany is concerned, the author sees little chance that policies designed primarily to strengthen the Atlantic Alliance will be pursued."

(LI)—"EUROPEANIZATION"; SOME CONSIDERATIONS CONCERNING THE APPLICATION OF THE NIXON DOCTRINE TO NATO, by Col. William G. MacLaren, Jr. Maxwell AFB. Ala., Air War College, 1971. 19 p. (Professional Study no. 4400.)

"Remarks on the content of the Nixon Doctrine introduce a summary of the various applications and implications that have grown out of the Doctrine since it was first announced, including a potential application to the North Atlantic Treaty Organization. The evolution of the current NATO strategy is traced, followed by a comparison of American and European objectives as well as their views of the interrelationship of NATO strategy and force levels. The case for a drawdown of the American force contribution to NATO is introduced as well as a summary of some of the current arguments against drawdown. It is argued that the Nixon Doctrine is applicable to NATO but that force reductions by the United States should be implemented only as a phased and reasoned program carried out over a period of years."

THE NIXON DOCTRINE AND THE NAVY, by Comdr. James A. Barber, Jr., in *Naval War College Review*, v. 23, no. 10 (June 1971) 5-15.

"The Nixon Doctrine is a logical development in contemporary world affairs that reflects the economic recovery of our allies, fissures in the facade of the Communist monolith, and recognition of increased Soviet strategic power. The doctrineés principles of partnership, strength, and willingness to negotiate acknowledge limiting the U.S. role in the world but 'not' withdrawal. When viewed as a whole, the elements of the Nixon Doctrine seem to clearly establish the necessity of a sea-based, blue-water strategy—a lower profile abroad yet with the intention to fulfill commitments by greater reliance upon a mobile sea-based strategy."

THE THRUST OF THE NIXON DOCTRINE, by Col. Richard M. Jennings, in *Military Review*, v. 52, no. 2 (February 1972) 3-9.

"The President outlined the first elements of the Nixon doctrine at Guam in 1969, expanded them in theory and action in 1970, and, in 1971, further updated and clarified the long-range guidelines for US foreign policy. These guidelines, along with his previous statements, frame a doctrine that skillfully adjusts US policy to historical change. However, a challenge remains in carrying it out. The Nixon doctrine recognizes the increased capabilities of Free World nations, the diversity within the Communist camp, and the national interests and domestic mood of Americans. It seeks peace. Yet it recognizes that, realistically, peace and stability are best achieved not by appeasement, but by keeping international forces in equilibrium and moderation. It blends these factors into a flexible foreign policy of neither overcommitment nor isolation. The doctrine is based on partnership and gradual assumption of greater responsibility by US allies and regional and international organizations. One may view it as the relinquishing of US power by degrees. It probably more accurately fosters the redistribution of responsibility among the Free World nations in a way that encourages their initiatives and development. It accepts the idea of an international system of more multipolarity and diversity. It is a policy stressing diplomacy and negotiations between Free World countries and their Communist competitors yet designed to prevent a destabilizing collapse of the balance of power in Europe and Asia."

UNITED STATES NATO STRATEGY, by Maj. Gustav Hogglund, in *Military Review*, v. 54, no. 1 (January 1974) 39-49.

"The Kennedy administration adopted the strategy of flexible response in 1961. It took six years for this concept to become a NATO strategy. Will there be an equivalent lag in implementing the Nixon Doctrine in Europe? Since President Nixon took office in 1969, the emphasis in US national strategy seems to have shifted from the military to the political arm. In 1974, both the number of Americans in uniform and the percentage of the gross national product (GNP) devoted to defense purposes will be the smallest in 24 years. America has urged its allies. to share the burden to help themselves and to maintain higher troop levels."

S. West Germany and West European Defense and Security

1. *Miscellaneous Aspects (Including German View)*

THE FEDERAL REPUBLIC OF GERMANY'S ALLIANCE POLICY, by Hans-Dietrich Genscher, in *NATO Review*, v. 22, no. 6 (December 1974) 3-5.

"For the Federal Republic of Germany there can be no security outside NATO. There can therefore be no doubt of the Federal Government's resolve to render its contribution to the common security of all members of the Alliance . . . To maintain a credible deterrence, the defence capability of the Alliance, and forward defence, the presence of sufficient conventional and also nuclear US forces in Europe is indispensable. In this connection, the Federal Government attaches the greatest importance to the stationing of American troops on its territory. It also appreciates the valuable contribution made by five European allies and Canada in the form of troops based on German territory."

FULL COMMITTEE BRIEFING ON GERMAN OFFSET AGREEMENT. Washington, Government Printing Office, 14 June 1974. 19 p. (H.A.S.C. No. 93-46.)

A briefing on the new offset agreement with the Federal Republic of Germany, together with the procurement plans of our other NATO Allies, to offset the "deficit on military account and substantially cancel out the additional cost of stationing our troops in NATO Europe, as contemplated by our burden-sharing efforts and intended by the Jackson-Nunn Amendment."

A GERMAN VIEW OF WESTERN DEFENCE, by Gen. J. A. Graf Kielmansegg, in *RUSI Journal*, v. 119, no. 1 (March 1974) 11-18.

"In this lecture I have spoken of some facts which in my view form the basis for reshaping the Western defence posture. I have said something about the Soviet danger and the minimum mission which should be given to the armed forces of NATO in Central Europe. Finally I have made a few points about the practical possibility of carrying out the basic mission I defined. The last of these points was a proposal to overcome the weakness of our conventional defence by a new use of certain very small nuclear weapons, based on new thinking, a new policy and new procedures. Perhaps all that was not exactly what you were expecting under the heading 'A German View.' But it is the view of a German who for the last 25 years has worked for the security of Europe. Security means peace."

A GERMAN VIEW OF WESTERN DEFENSE, by Gen. J. A. Graf von Kielmansegg, in *Military Review*, v. 54, no. 11 (November 1974) 43-53.

"The facts presented in this article, in my view, form the basis for reshaping the Western defense posture. I have mentioned the Soviet danger and the minimum mission which should be given to the armed forces of NATO in Central Europe. Finally, I have made a few points about the practical possibility of carrying out the basic mission I defined. The last of these points was a proposal to overcome the weakness of our conventional defense by a new use of certain very small nuclear weapons, based on new thinking, a new policy and new procedures."

NATIONAL STRATEGIES WITHIN THE ALLIANCE: WEST GERMANY, by Carl H. Amme, Jr., in *NATO's Fifteen Nations*, v. 17, no. 4 (August-September 1972) 76 plus.

"The Federal Republic's strategic concept and its policy concerning nuclear weapons are affected by these three goals and interact with them. Under the German strategic concept, tactical nuclear weapons deployed by NATO in West Germany play a key role in ensuring the FRG's security. At the same time the West German option of obtaining a nuclear force—an option which exists, of course, regardless of the provisions of the 1954 WEU agreements—remains an important bargaining factor in an eventual settlement concerning German reunification. West German leaders apparently believe that German renunciation of the Nonproliferation Treaty most likely would be important prerequisites in any reunification scheme. Up to this point, however, West Germany has not made any obvious attempt to acquire an independent nuclear strategic force or independent control over tactical nuclear weapons . . . The official West German attitude appears to be that the present Soviet threat in Europe, while it still exists and should by no means be ignored, is not one of imminent Soviet military invasion in Central Europe. On the other hand, substantive issues have not been resolved. Regardless of whether the nature of the military threat has been altered significantly since the inception of NATO, basic conflicts of interests and real concern exist in both Germany and Russia,"

TACTICAL NUCLEAR DEFENSE—THE WEST GERMAN VIEW, by Charles N. Davidson, in *Parameters*, v. 4, no. 1 (1974) 47-57.

"Discusses the major political considerations affecting NATO's use of tactical nuclear weapons in defense of Western Europe, together with the Federal Republic's view of tactical nuclear defense."

(LI)—WEST GERMANY AND THE NATO STRATEGY OF FLEXIBLE RESPONSE, by Lt. Col. James E. Thompson. Maxwell AFB, Ala., Air Command and Staff College, 1970. 48 p. (Research Study no. 1305-70.)

"The North Atlantic Treaty Organization adopted the strategy of flexible response in 1967. This strategic concept provided NATO with the capability to respond to any Warsaw Pact aggression using one of several available responses. West German authorities have not fully accepted the concept of a conventional response. This study analyzes the conventional option of the flexible response concept to determine what impact it will have on West Germany. The study concludes that a conventional response is compatible with the national interests of West Germany. However, any force reductions will tend to cause the NATO conventional strategy and NATO military posture to be out of balance."

2. *Implications of "Ostpolitic"*

(LI)—THE FUTURE OF EUROPE AND NATO: OSTPOLITIK IMPLICATIONS, by Maj. William C. Barnhart. Maxwell AFB, Ala., Air Command and Staff College, 1973. 39 p. (Research Study.)

"The foreign policy of the Federal Republic of Germany, popularly known as OSTPOLITIK, has contributed significantly to lessening tension between East and West in recent years. This study examines the historical progress and successes of OSTPOLITIK, its relation to internal West German affairs, and its impact on West Germany's position in the North Atlantic Treaty Organization (NATO). Consideration is also given to the role that OSTPOLITIK and its articulators play in the 'Europeanization' of Europe and the future of NATO."

FUTURE WEST GERMAN POLITICO-MILITARY DEVELOPMENTS AND ALTERNATIVE FOREIGN AND DEFENSE POLICY STRATEGIES. McLean, Va., Research Analysis Corp., July 1970. 105 p. (RAC-R-108.)

"This study appraises the changing political and strategic situation of the Federal Republic of Germany between 1966 and 1969, the achievements and failures of the Federal Republic's new Eastern policy (*Ostpolitik*) under the Grand Coalition, and the problems that confront the US in its policy toward Germany within the broader setting of East-West confrontation and partial détente. In anticipation of the Sept. 1969 Federal elections in West Germany, some of the causes and implications of the trend toward independence in West German foreign and defense policy are examined, with the discussion focused on (a) possible implications of this trend for the West German political system, (b) possible alternative strategies in West German foreign and defense policy, and (c) possible implications of these strategies for the future of Europe and NATO and for the US relations with West Germany."

(LI)—OSTPOLITIK: ITS INFLUENCE ON THE MALAISE IN NATO SOLIDARITY, by Lt. Col. Donald J. Cipra. Maxwell AFB, Ala., Air War College, 1974. 56 p. (Professional Study.)

"This study explores the extent of influence West Germany's *Ostpolitik* has had on the North Atlantic Community. The East-West strategic military balance has shifted from American supremacy to near equality, bringing with it the necessity for a new understanding of requirements of common security. *Ostpolitik* and détente have fostered euphoria within NATO, the feeling that because tension has been removed the defense effort can be reduced. But the motives of the Soviets must not be ignored. Their military power continues to grow, their aim seems to be to influence West European policies and to persuade them to make bilateral foreign policy deals with Moscow. Brandt's Ostpolitik has set the stage and could signal the demise of NATO and US presence in Europe. Two conclusions can be drawn as to the Soviet intentions. First, there is no way Moscow will allow the strength of her newly attained equal superpower status with the US to slip behind any group; and second, today's international events confirm the fact that the West will continue to face both political and military probes into its solidarity."

T. The Strategic Importance of Oil (See also I-F-3)

THE DEFENCE OF NORTH SEA OIL AND GAS, by John Marriott, in *NATO's Fifteen Nations*, v. 19, no. 5 (October-November 1974) 73-77 plus.

"Quite apart from our everyday way of life, our heating, our factories and above all our transportation, oil is the one vital commodity without which we in NATO could not possibly resist an enemy attack. Nations of course stockpile oil for use in an emergency, but the stocks are small and must be quickly replenished once the emergency starts. At present NATO relies on oil from overseas, chiefly the Middle East . . . All of which leads to North Sea oil. Here we have a reasonable supply which could in an emergency be used to keep the NATO vehicles in Europe on the move and our factories at work, always assuming that Britain agrees to share the oil with her allies. Let us therefore first of all look at what tapping this vast reservoir under the sea involves . . . If war should come, whatever Britain had said about exporting oil in peace would have to be changed in the interest of survival of NATO as a whole . . . The only organisation large enough to take on the burden is NATO. To provide wartime defences, of course, requires the expenditure of money now, in peace, so it is necessary that Britain should come to some agreement now to share her oil with the NATO countries, or certainly the European ones, in exchange for help in its defence. The whole question is being studied inside NATO, but militarily it is complicated by the fact that the waters in which the oil platforms will stand are controlled by SACLANT, whilst the air space is controlled by SACEUR."

THE GREAT DÉTENTE DISASTER; OIL AND THE DECLINE OF AMERICAN FOREIGN POLICY, by Edward Friedland and others. New York, Basic Books, Inc., 1975. 210 p.

"The current worldwide economic crisis, argues this . . . book, cannot be understood or brought under control without a rethinking of the present course of American foreign policy. Central to this crisis is the recent elevenfold increase in the price of oil; indeed, say the authors, oil may prove to be the catalyst for a large-scale catastrophe. And it is the dangerously personalized foreign policy of reducing tensions with the Soviet Union at all costs which has led to America's failure to deal from strength in the Middle East and has left both our allies and the Third World hostage to OPEC. Despite the fact that the peoples of the West are making an effort to live with the crippling price of oil, the book points out that there will inevitably be a decline in world trade, spreading unemployment, mass starvation in Asia and Africa, and critical economic and political instability among the Western democracies—unless some way is found to break the stranglehold of OPEC. Thus the real challenge to American policy today is not whether we can and ought to play 'policeman to the world' but simply whether we can muster the strength of will needed to protect our own vital interests and those of our allies. Decency as well as self-interest, then, require us to take serious economic, political, and if need be, military measures to reverse our threatened decline."

NORTH SEA OIL: NATO'S REFUGE OR RUIN?, by Lawrence Griswold, in *Air Force Magazine*, v. 58, no. 2 (February 1975) 49-54.

How—"Within the new three years, North Sea oil could relieve NATO nations of dependence on Middle East petroleum."

THE NORTH SEA OIL SCRAMBLE SCORES OF AMERICAN SUPPLIERS ARE COMPETING FOR A WEALTH OF BUSINESS, in *Dun's*, v. 100, no. 6 (December 1972) 109 plus.

"Today, conservative oilmen estimate that the North Sea contains commercial reserves of perhaps over 30 billion barrels, plus another 8.5 billion barrels of sub-commercial oil. By 1980, they see production hitting 3 million-plus barrels a day—a volume that would supply about 15% of Western Europe's oil needs. About one-third of that oil is in Norwegian waters. But the cautious Norsemen have imposed many delays on exploration and development, so the buildup at Stavanger, Norway is consequently modest. In Scotland, though, the government is actively encouraging the establishment of an oil industry, and it is every man for himself. Already, the Moray Firth area has been dubbed "The Texas of the North'."

OCTOBER IN WESTERN EUROPE, by H. Mendershausen. Santa Monica, Calif., Rand Corp., November 1974. 14 p. (P-5318).)

"Reports talks with Western Europe government, NATO, European Commission and oil company personnel and analysts. Despite a pervading sense of foreboding and shaken foundations, disaster had not arrived. Unemployment (6% in the United States) was 3% in Germany, France, and Britain, salaries and pensions are indexed to the cost of living. Energy is freely consumed. International Shell leads a movement to 'nationalize' the daughter companies of transnational corporations—American companies are less forward. Political and financial leaders and managers outdo each other in offering services and assets to the new Arab oil overlords; the most vulnerable countries may be tempted to sacrifice Israel like Czechoslovakia. The clearest repudiation of this view is from FRG Chancellor Helmut Schmidt, who considers Israel an outpost of the Atlantic Alliance. Views of U.S. power are confused and ambivalent—except in France, where anti-Americanism is strong and a spate of books declare the oil crisis a U.S. government plot against Europe."

OIL AND NATIONAL SECURITY, by Barry M. Blechman and Arnold M. Kuzmack, in *Naval War College Review*, (May-June 1974) 8-25.

". . . In the aftermath of the Arab oil boycott, the US ought to re-examine the effect of our increasing need for petroleum imports on the national security . . . By 1985, this country will be obtaining half its oil from foreign sources and will be subject to political and economic contingencies in the producing nations. In a conventional war scenario between NATO and the Warsaw Pact, the USSR would be tempted to disrupt oil supplies from the Middle East to Western Europe and the US . . . Four possible strategies [are] available to the Soviets: 1. destruction of the oilfields which, however, are not especially vulnerable to air attack; 2. occupation of the oilfields, which would probably entail a risky invasion of Iran; 3. bombardment of Western refineries, which is not really feasible because almost half the facilities are situated in the Western Hemisphere; 4. disruption of tanker routes which appears . . . to be the most effective plan. The greatest threat of this sort, Blechman and Kuzmack believe, would be the mining of the Strait of Hormuz at the entrance to the Persian Gulf, since it would block the shipping of 11 to 14 million barrels per day in the 1980s, or roughly one-fourth of the West's demand by that time. But the most plausible menace to national security, in the authors' view, remains a peacetime interdiction of supplies. They point to five possible contingenices: 1. an Arab boycott of only the US, which would have a minimal effect on this country; 2. an Arab boycott of the US tied to a refusal to increase shipments to other Western countries, which would create a marginal shortfall; 3. an Arab boycott of both the US and Western Europe, which would have a major impact on the economies of both the Western and Arab nations; 4. a boycott by all OPEC countries to boost prices, which would be 'extremely serious'; 5. physical disruption due to regional wars or guerrilla sabotage, which would not significantly affect US supplies. Blechman and Kuzmack recommend the stockpiling of oil reserves by the US to deal with these contingencies . . ."

POLITICS, OIL AND THE WESTERN MEDITERRANEAN, by R. M. Burrell and Alvin J. Cottrell. Washington. Center for Strategic and International Studies, 1973. 88 p. (Washington Paper no. 7.)

"Burrell and Cottrell assert that, as the Western nations and Japan increase their dependence on oil imports, the importance of the oil-producing countries in the Middle East and North Africa will intensify. Therefore, the US and its allies should no longer ignore the North African section of the Western Mediterranean (comprised of Libya, Tunisia, Algeria, and Morocco) . . . The authors review the world oil supply and reserve situation, revealing that US reserves are such that its daily production has stabilized at 12 million barrels, even taking into account future production from the Alaskan fields. By 1980 the US will need an additional 14 million barrels a day (b/d), of which at least 7 million will have to come from the Middle Eastern and North African suppliers. West European demands are growing at a much faster rate than those of the US, and by 1980 30 million b/d are likely to be needed. Only 5 million b/d will come from Europe; the rest will have to come from the Middle East and North Africa—if they will sell. Japanese consumption, too, is increasing and by 1980 could reach 13 million b/d, of which 10 million would have to come from the Middle East and North Africa. The importance of North African oil, then, is quite evident. Information regarding USSR oil supplies and demands is at best sketchy, although it is known that at present the USSR is self-sufficient. However, its reserves are located far from industrial areas, and poor Soviet technology and high costs presently prohibit their development. Therefore, the authors maintain, the USSR will attempt to 'stockpile' Middle Eastern oil as a strategic maneuver, thus causing an even higher demand on the world's resources. The authors see little indications that alternate energy sources will be available in the foreseeable future, assuring a seller's market for the world's oil. The North African region is important to the NATO allies for reasons other than oil. The Western Mediterranean area, according to the authors, is now becoming an arena for potential US and USSR conflict, symbolized by the presence of their navies. The US Sixth Fleet, traditionally a symbol of the US commitment to protect the southern flank of NATO, has become a psychologically important security blanket for the nations which border on the Mediterranean. Discussions about reducing the fleet produce panic; therefore, a US naval policy should be pursued to reinforce the 'rapidly deteriorating' Sixth Fleet. The Soviet Navy is increasingly modern and demonstrates the Soviet desire to minimize and ultimately terminate the US monopoly in the area . . ."

WORLD PETROLEUM REPORT '74, v. (1974) 92 p.

An annual review of international oil operations. The first part deals with special reports and area studies, including a world summary and review, and reports on Europe, among many others. The second part is devoted to national studies.

U. The Soviet View of West European Defense, Security, and NATO

EUROPEAN SECURITY AND THE ATLANTIC SYSTEM, ed. by William T. R. Fox and Warner R. Schilling. New York, Columbia University Press, 1973. 276 p.

Review in International Affairs, Moscow, no. 5 (1974) 126–129. "According to the book's compilers, they have attempted to provide a comprehensive forecast of the development of mutual relations within the North Atlantic bloc during the

1970s, bearing in mind the prospects for the setting up of a new security system in Europe and the implementation of measures to limit and reduce armed forces and armaments. This approach should have obliged the authors to give a thorough exposition of the impact on these mutual relations made by the forces and conditions existing both inside and outside the Atlantic community and above all the policies of the socialist countries . . . Their forecast constituted yet another attempt to justify the need to retain the North Atlantic bloc and its military organisation while, at the same time, taking into consideration the influence on their structure exerted by the new tendencies in European relations."

NATO EXACERBATES THE MEDITERRANEAN SITUATION, in *International Affairs, Moscow*, no. 1 (1975) 89–92.

"The Eastern Mediterannean is the area where the vigorous activity of the national liberation movements has scored successes and these movements today question the domination the imperialist multinationals have exercised for years over the national wealth and resources of the Mediterranean countries. The incessant attempts by imperialist powers to contain and hamstring the national liberation forces and to extend in every way their 'military presence' in that area with the help of Israel and NATO countries hamper endeavors to provide conditions for a lasting and stable peace in the Eastern Mediterranean."

THE STRUGGLE FOR EUROPEAN SECURITY AND THE NEW INTRIGUES OF THE ATLANTICISTS, by G. Cogniot, in *International Affairs, Moscow*, no. 3 (1974) 38–35.

"Although the vast majority of the European countries and all realistically-thinking statesmen subscribed to the European Conference, it would be wrong to say nothing of the reactivation of the elements opposed to détente and seeking to hinder the success of that important initiative. Although they have to contend with the new realities of the world today, the imperialist circles are not renouncing their old objectives. Even in this hour of great changes they are hatching out sinister plans and plotting all sorts of intrigues against the forces of peace and progress. NATO remains a threat to world peace. The bosses of the Atlantic bloc continue to urge the further build-up of its strength and the swelling of arms budgets and they continue to organise military exercises in West Germany, the Mediterranean and other areas."

WEST EUROPEAN INTERNATIONAL ORGANISATIONS, by Zbigniew M. Klepacki. Moscow, Progress Publishers, 1973. 487 p.

Review in International Affairs, Moscow, no. 5 (1974) 114–116. "The book by the Polish scholar Z. Klepacki is devoted to studying one of the urgent problems of contemporary international relations, the process of West European integration, and primarily to the activity of international interstate organisations set up in the course of this process. The importance of these organisations in contemporary international relations is indicated by the existence today in Western Europe of about 30 international interstate organisations and of some 400 international nongovernmental agencies. The author deals with various aspects of the activity of a number of West European interstate organisations: the European Council, Organisation for Economic Cooperation and Development (OECD), North Atlantic Treaty Organisation (NATO), Western European Union (WEU), European Economic Community (EEC), European Free Trade Association (EFTA), Euratom, European Coal and Steel Community (ECSC), Benelux Economic Council, Nordic Council, European Defence Community (EDC), European Political Community (EPC), as well as most important West European bodies of technical nature such as European Space Vehicle Launcher Development Organisation (ELDO), and many others. The value of the book lies in that the author thoroughly and systematically surveys each organisation: its origin; aims and purposes; main functions; composition; its various bodies; voting procedures; methods of settling conflicts between its members; legal significance of its decisions; it's sources of financing; general characteristics of its activity in political, economic and military spheres."

CHAPTER VI

EAST-WEST DÉTENTE. PROSPECTS AND LIMITS OF CONCILATION

A. Miscellaneous Aspects

THE BREZHNEV MYSTERY—WHO WILL RUN RUSSIA?, in *U.S. News & World Report* v. 78, no. 6 (10 February 1975) 34-35.

"Will change of command in the Kremlin bring détente to a halt?" An assessment of the outlook.

THE COST OF DETENTE: NO REST FOR THE WARY, by H. A. DeWeerd, in *Army*, v. 24, no. 5 (May 1974) 17-20.

"Seeking peace as an end in itself, the West is clinging to a détente whose advantages have so far accrued to the Soviet Union with a corresponding diminution in the world position of the United States . . . NATO reluctance to assist the United States may have been increased by détente."

(*)—DÉTENTE DIPLOMACY: UNITED STATES AND EUROPEAN SECURITY IN THE 1970's, by Timothy W. Stanley and Darnell M. Whitt. New York, Dunellen, 1970. 170 p. (for the Atlantic Council of the United States.)

"An historical analysis of the main problems confronting the architects of East-West détente in Europe.

DÉTENTE: PROSPECTS FOR INCREASED TRADE WITH WARSAW PACT COUNTRIES. REPORT OF A SPECIAL STUDY MISSION TO THE SOVIET UNION AND EASTERN EUROPE, AUGUST 22 TO SEPTEMBER 8, 1974, COMMITTEE ON FOREIGN AFFAIRS; HOUSE OF REPRESENTATIVES. Washington, Government Printing Office, 1974. 52 p. (93d Congress, 2d Session, Committee Print.)

DÉTENTE WITH THE SOVIET UNION: THE REALITY OF COMPETITION AND THE IMPERATIVE OF COOPERATION, by Henry Kissinger, in *The Department of State Bulletin*, v. 71, no. 1842 (14 October 1974) 505-519.

The Challenge; The Course of Soviet-American Relations (American Goals; The Global Necessities); The Evolution of Détente—The Balance of Risks and Incentives (The Elaboration of Principles; Political Dialogue and Cooperative Agreements; The Economic Component; The Strategic Relationship); An Assessment of Détente; and Agenda for the Future.

THE GREAT DÉTENTE DISASTER; OIL AND THE DECLINE OF AMERICAN FOREIGN POLICY, by Edward Friedland and others. New York, Basic Books, Inc., 1975. 210 p.

"The current worldwide economic crisis, argues this . . . book, cannot be understood or brought under control without a rethinking of the present course of American foreign policy. Central to this crisis is the recent elevenfold increase in the price of oil; indeed, say the authors, oil may prove to be the catalyst for a large-scale catastrophe. And it is the dangerously personalized foreign policy of reducing tensions with the Soviet Union at all costs which has led to America's failure to deal from strength in the Middle East and has left both our Allies and the Third World hostage to OPEC. Despite the fact that the peoples of the West are making an effort to live with the crippling price of oil, the book points out that there will inevitably be a decline in world trade, spreading unemployment, mass starvation in Asia and Africa, and critical economic and political instability among the Western democracies—unless some way is found to break the stranglehold of OPEC. Thus the real challenge to American policy today is not whether we can and ought to play 'policeman to the world' but simply whether we can muster the strength of will needed to protect our own vital interests and those of our allies. Decency as well as self-interest, then, require us to take serious economic, political, and if need be, military measures to reverse our threatened decline."

IS THIS DÉTENTE? by Melvin R. Laird, in *Reader's Digest*, (July 1975).

"Over the past several years, the United States has made major concessions and numerous gestures of good will to induce the Soviet Union to help defuse world powder kegs that could explode into war. We still hope that such efforts will eventually succeed. Certainly, everyone hopes to avoid renewal of Cold War confrontations. But it would be dangerously foolish to confuse hope with reality. Therefore, I am now persuaded that the American people ought to be told some unpleasant facts abouth the true status of détente, so that they can intelligently judge the Kremlin's current intentions. The facts are that, in recent months, the U.S.S.R.—secretly and openly—has repeatedly committed deliberate acts that mock détente and threaten the free world. Let's look at six deeply troubling actions. [Mr. Laird concludes] SALT I prevents us from using defensive weapons within our capability to insure our survival. Now SALT II threatens to undercut the only safeguard the disarmament lobby has consented to grant us—our offensive firepower. If the illusion of détente is allowed to control our policies much longer, we could wind up with no effective defenses at all."

THE NATO ALLIANCE: THE BASIS FOR AN ERA OF NEGOTIATION, by Kenneth Rush, in *The Atlantic Community Quarterly*, v. 11, no. 3 (Fall 1973) 327-334.

"According to the Deputy Secretary of State, the central element of continuity in American relations with Europe are the Atlantic Alliance and NATO—its organizational framework. NATO's two future roles in this new era of East-West negotiations are 'détente management' and the maintenance of a strong defense posture. Only a combination of diplomatic flexibility and a powerful deterrence force will enhance the prospects for successful negotiations on security and force reduction in Europe."

NATO IN THE DEVELOPMENT OF MUTUALLY ACCEPTABLE SECURITY ARRANGEMENTS BETWEEN EAST AND WEST, by Brig. W. F. K. Thompson, in *NATO's Fifteen Nations* v. 15, no. 6 (December 1970-January 1971) 87-90 plus.

"A discussion on the military aspects and possibilities of new systems of European security arising from following a policy of détente. Before attempting to do so, however, is is necessary to define what it is that we in NATO wish to secure, the nature of the threat, and what it is that we, but more importantly the Russians, mean by détente."

A NEW EUROPEAN DEFENSE COMMUNITY, by Francois Duchêne, in *Foreign Affairs*, v. 50, no. 1 (October 1971) 69-82.

"At the moment when East Asis is emerging as the new center of great-power confrontation, the old one, Europe, is showing signs of settling down. Eighteen years of almost glacially imperceptible movement have elapsed between the post-Stalin 'thaw' of 1953 and the wary 'era of negotiations' of 1971. But now the whole constallation of talks between the Soviet Union and its major Western adversaries, around the Strategic Arms Limitation Talks (SALT), the Ostpolitik, Berlin, force reductions and the convocation of a security conference, look like ratifying the stalemate between the two blocs painfully reached in Europe over the years. Since this recognizes in particular the frontiers between the contestants, it amounts not only to a virtual settlement of the cold war but to the nearest approximation one can expect of a peace treaty ending the Second World War. Moreover, this development coincides with another of great importance. The likely enlargement of the European Community from six to ten member countries, including Britain, is bound to open a new phase in the integration of Western Europe. With two such changes, European security in the middle and later 1970s will necessarily be very different from the patterns that have grown familiar during 20 years. On the whole, the natural expectation is a shift away from the quasi-military confrontation of the cold war to civilian and political processes gradually increasing the interdependence of industrial societies with potentially complementary interests. If so, it will probably be the first time that an area vital to the world balance, without being itself a great power, is brought under control not as a victim of rival masters but as a field of cooperation sought keenly by the weaker states. It could be almost the equivalent in nuclear and international terms of the King's Peace which brought the European nation-state out of feudal chaos."

THE SOVIET UNION, 1974, in *Current History*, (October 1974) 146-192.

"The superpowers have sought détente, Alvin Z. Rubinstein suggests, because of the escalating cost of the arms race, a mutual wish to normalize relations in Europe, increasing prominence of China in foreign policy calculations, mounting economic problems which led the Soviets to seek Western technology and credits, and growing US absorption with domestic affairs and weariness of foreign involvements. Although there have been several promising achievements to date, US experts are still uncertain as to whether the USSR views détente as an alternate means of continuing the cold war or as a realistic means of establishing new international relationships. Consequently, US policymakers are divided in their views between those who support immediate expansion of the agreements already achieved, and those who stipulate that the USSR guarantee free emigration of its citizens before the US offers additional economic benefits. At present the benefits of détente for the Soviet Union are more obvious than those for the US . . . According to Lawrence T. Caldwell, a military problem underlies the political and economic problems of US-Soviet relations and related dealings with the European community. The question is US acceptance of strategic parity with the USSR and the effect on the credibility of its deterrent force which now guarantees protection to its European allies. This question affects overlapping sets of negotiations: SALT II, in which the bipolar strategic balance is being negotiated; mutual force reduction (MFR) talks, which concern the balance of conventional forces; and the Conference on Security and Cooperation in Europe (CSCE), which tends to emphasize basic judgments about the political bases of détente. Examining the various aspects of these negotiations, Caldwell concludes the mixture is potentially explosive: the SALT II stalemate threatens to boost the strategic arms race; the determination of strategic parity, combined with conventional disparity, may affect the credibility of overall US protection for its European allies; and the solution of both these issues is complicated by the political dimension of détente as observed in the CSCE... Although the current Soviet leadership has exhibited remarkable cohesiveness, continuity and political 'normalization' during the past 10 years, some chronic problems persist, R. Judson Mitchell says. He questions whether the apparent political stability conceals a real inability to deal effectively with modern social change, and whether the degree of political stability results from essential abandonment of revolutionary goals. Soviet society has lost most of its earlier revolutionary dynamism, Mitchell says, but this has proven advantageous in terms of stabilizing expectations, and promoting social cohesion and Soviet power . . . The Soviet military establishment is undergoing a major transition in terms of technology, theory, expanded capabilities and global political commitments, Timothy J. Colton observes. However, the military establishment's place in the Soviet political system remains remarkably confined and stable. Basic political-military differences seem to center on the urgency of defense as a national concern and the extent to which defense considerations should impede domestic and foreign policy goals . . ."

WHAT IS IT RUSSIA WANTS—DÉTENTE OR A NEW ARMS RACE?, in *U.S. News & World Report*, v. 76, no. 12 (25 March 1974) 40-41.

"It's an anxious eye that U.S. is fastening on Moscow these days. The reasons why—as addressed by top military strategists—are reported by Joseph Froman, an Associate Executive Editor of 'U.S. News & World Report'." Dim Outlook; Behind Russia's Stand; Where U.S. Leads; Key U.S. Programs; U.S. Deal on Arms Limitation.

B. East-West Détente and Its Implications for NATO's Mission and Objectives

THE ATLANTIC ALLIANCE: ITS PRESENT PROBLEMS AND ITS AIMS; LECTURE DELIVERED AT THE NATO DEFENCE COLLEGE ON 4 MARCH 1970, by Nuri Birgi, in *NATO's Fifteen Nations*, v. 15, no. 6 (December 1970-January 1971) 31-33 plus.

"What is the military value and necessity of NATO at present? What is the meaning and aim of détente and how is it possible to reconcile NATO's military character and its continuous attempts to keep the Alliance in good military shape with the attempts to secure détente? Is it necessary and possible to activate the provisions of the North Atlantic Treaty referring to economic, social, cultural and technological co-operation between the members of the Alliance? If so, is NATO fit and equipped for such a task? Is the concept of an Atlantic Community still valid and useful?"

EUROPE AND THE ATLANTIC ALLIANCE

TODAY, by Manlio Brosio, in *The Atlantic Community Quarterly*, v. 10, no. 3 (Fall 1972) 285-294.

"Manlio Brosio, until recently Secretary-General of NATO, takes a hard look at Soviet attitudes after the U.S. Soviet summit conference, at the prospects for a European Security Conference, and at current possibilities for steps in the direction of West European unification. He is concerned that too many people may feel that the Soviet Union has moderated its goals after the summit, and also that some West European leaders may be so beguiled by the idea of pushing the U.S. out of Europe that they indirectly help the Soviets achieve their goals. These are not just idle considerations, as he stresses that the time for some major decisions is rapidly approaching."

THE FUTURE OF THE ATLANTIC ALLIANCE IN THE LIGHT OF PRESENT EUROPEAN DEVELOPMENTS, by Joseph Luns, in *The Atlantic Community Quarterly*, v. 10, no. 2 (Summer 1972) 194-202.

"NATO Secretary-General Joseph Luns reviews the alliance's efforts at achieving détente with the Soviet bloc, emphasizes the importance of keeping up the alliance's forces pending the outcome of such efforts, and makes clear that any special political or defense cooperation within the Common Market must not be at the cost of continued consultation and collaboration with Europe's North American allies."

NATO SOLIDARITY AND UNDIMINISHED DEFENCE BASIS FOR PROGRESS TOWARDS DÉTENTE, by Peter Jenner, in *NATO Review*, v. 21, no. 6 (1973) 3-5.

"Last December's ministerial sessions of the North Atlantic Council and the Defence Planning Committee (DPC) were held at the Brussels headquarters against the background of much public comment about problems in Atlantic relationships, and concern for the consequences for East-West relations of recent events in the Middle East. The communique issued after the Council meeting, on 10 and 11 December, reflected this background. It began by stating that while the ministers were encouraged by the continuing development of bilateral and multilateral East-West contacts, they nonetheless recognized that international peace remains fragile; and they again stressed the importance for the Alliance of maintaining to the full its defensive and deterrent military capacity."

N.A.T.O. UNCERTAINTIES AND PALLIATIVES, by J. H. Trotman, in *Canadian Defence Quarterly*, v. 3, no. 2 (Autumn 1973) 15-20.

"In the circumstances of a Europe with lessening fear of military attack, of apparently increasing coincidence of interests between the superpowers, of security conferences and potentially agreed force reductions, it is a reasonable appreciation that funds for European defence establishments will become increasingly difficult to extract from national treasuries, and support for military activity increasingly hard to justify in politically acceptable terms to national consciences . . . The argument that strength is necessary in order to confront the Soviet Union at a conference table is apparently more appealing than the argument that strength is necessary to confront Russia if no conference table is in prospect. Whether these developments are to be welcomed depends upon a number of factors: first, a view of Soviet general attitudes and policies towards Europe and the confrontation in Europe; secondly, a view of present relative force capabilities; thirdly, the effect of reductions upon NATO doctrine; and, finally and most importantly, upon whether palliatives are available . . . If or when reductions do take place, what palliatives are available that would reduce their impact on doctrine, on deterrence, on credibility, and on NATO's war-fighting capabilities? The emphasis must be on palliatives, for naturally there are not total answers to NATO's problems."

THREATS AND PROMISES OF PEACE: EUROPE AND AMERICA IN THE NEW ERA, by Albert Wohlstetter, in *Orbis*, v. 17, no. 4 (Winter 1974) 1107-1144.

"At the start of 1973 it seemed plain that whether or not we had left behind an era of confrontation, we were surely in a period of negotiation . . . These were only some of the efforts to increase communications with the communist world, and thereby, it was hoped, to relax feelings of antagonism . . . Optimism about peace in Europe derives in part from the feeling that negotiations between NATO countries and Warsaw Pact countries soften Moscow's hostility toward the West, and in part from the knowledge that the Soviet Union's conflict with China keeps her occupied in the East. War, this suggests, has not been abolished, but just redirected. If there is not to be a generation of peace, it is hoped that belligerence might be aimed at someone else. No one seems to rule out confrontation between the two principal communist powers. However derived, this diminished sense of immediate danger in Europe has been a central fact of the alliance for some time."

C. Prospects and Limits of Conciliation (See also VII-D)

CAN RUSSIA BE TRUSTED?, in *U.S. News & World Report*, v. 76, no. 19 (13 May 1974) 38-40 plus.

"Is an end to the Soviet-American arms race in sight? When can the U.S. safely withdraw troops from Europe? To spell out the defense problems this country still faces in a period of détente with Russia, Dr. Schlesinger came to the conference room of 'U.S. News & World Report' for this exclusive interview."

COOPERATION AS A FORM OF CONFLICT, by Franklyn Griffiths, in *The Atlantic Community Quarterly*, v. 12, no. 4 (Winter 1974-1975) 481-499.

"The author examines the main tendencies within the Soviet Union on the question of cooperation with the West—tendencies which have remained for many years, one being dominant now, another later. They are internally inconsistent and should be depicted in terms of conflicting tendencies. The reform tendency offers a basis for East-West cooperation. It seems desirable to withhold trade, credits, technology and capital increasingly until there is a marked reduction in the Soviet strategic and continued build-up and a greater Soviet willingness to negotiate at SALT and MBFR. Similarly, the Western powers should deny Moscow a conclusion to the CSCE until there are Soviet concessions at MBFR."

DÉTENTE AND PEACEFUL COEXISTENCE, in *NATO Review*, v. 19, nos. 7-8 (July/August 1971) 14-16.

"Détente and peaceful coexistence are two essential concepts every human being longs for in this world of tension; arms race and ever spreading local conflicts. However, if one tries to compare what the Soviet leaders and their Warsaw Pact allies understand by these terms, with the Western understanding of détente and peaceful coexistence, it becomes quite clear that East and West are not speaking the same language."

DÉTENTE AND REALITY, by Isaac Don Levine, in *Strategic Review*, v. 2, no. 3 (Summer 1974) 44-50.

"From President Franklin D. Roosevelt to President Richard Nixon, the United States has vigorously pursued a grand design for an era of peace premised on the cooperation of the Soviet government. U.S. hopes have repeatedly been dashed by the hostility of Soviet responses, but the basic design has not been abandoned. SALT I and the October War reveal how far the United States has gone and how costly its pursuit of peace can be. Presidents should forswear summit negotiations and meet there only to sign previously agreed documents. Disarmament should take place where belligerency reigns—in the Middle East and Southeast Asia. Oil wealth should be committed to the development of blighted lands. And cooperation in trade should be extended only to countries in which labor is not enslaved. The principles of freedom should be voiced vigorously in all forums. There can be no true détente except on the basis of common decency."

DÉTENTE IN EUROPE: REAL OR IMAGINARY?, by Josef Korbel. Princeton, Princeton University Press, 1972. 302 p.

"Dr. Korbel discusses in detail the changes in mood, policy and relationships that have ushered in a new era in intra-European relations. He gives major credit for the relaxation of tension to the Soviet bloc countries which have on numerous occasions submitted concrete proposals for the solution of critical problems; points out that this initiative has facilitated rapprochement policies, such as West Germany's Ostpolitik, but has also weakened the political and cultural ties that have bound West Germany to the United States; and concludes that any designs for a stable European détente must be accompanied by a reduction of tensions between the superpowers themselves."

DÉTENTE OR ENTENTE, by Richard Rosecrance, in *Foreign Affairs*, v. 53, no. 3 (April 1975) 464-481.

"The U.S.-Soviet détente is neither fully understood nor certain to endure. The sheer complexity of détente balancing—holding the Soviet Union, China, the Western allies and Japan in a complicated network of associations with the United States which involve conflict as well as cooperation—may not last. Even if it could be sustained, some argue that American interests dictate that it would be dropped or radically modified. To others détente is an attitude, but not a policy. It represents a desirable and overdue recognition of realities in foreign policy—the need to achieve better relations with the Soviet Union and China. But it does not specify where the United States should go from there. Détente without a positive core of policy goals could jeopardize American relations with Japan and Western Europe without gaining any durable benefit from the Soviet Union. The collapse of the Soviet-American trade agreement makes it seem even less likely that the United States can use détente as a means to extract important concessions from the U.S.S.R."

THE DURABILITY OF DÉTENTE, by Maj. Tyrus W. Cobb, in *Military Review*, v. 54, no. 4 (April 1974) 3-15.

"In a rather significant departure from postwar Soviet foreign policy, the USSR has, in recent years, actively sought to normalize relations with the West in order to lay the foundation for a stable and peaceful international order. This policy of 'détente' has become increasingly associated with Communist Party General Secretary Leonid Brezhnev whose efforts toward reaching accommodations with the capitalist countries have been endorsed by the party's Central Committee. Outside the Soviet Union, however, enthusiasm for détente has recently waned, and the viability of Brezhnev's avowed policy of relaxation of tensions has been challenged. As the USSR intensifies its repression of internal dissidents, accelerates the production of advanced military weaponry and technology and continues its campaign to isolate and denigrate the Chinese Communists, some Western observers have been moved to speculate that the shift toward improving relations with the West may be merely a tactical phase rather than a permanent aspect of Soviet foreign policy."

EUROPEAN DEFENSE: THE UNDERLYING TRENDS, by David Bolton, in *RUSI Journal*, v. 119, no. 2 (June 1974) 63-67.

"Certain basic trends which underlie European security were brought into sharp relief by the 1973 Yom Kippur War and its aftermath. The limits of superpower cooperation were more clearly defined when the United States of America brought her forces to an increased state of readiness at the prospect of direct Soviet involvement in the Middle East conflict. Strains within the Atlantic Alliance became apparent as western Europe sought to adopt a more neutralist EEC position and to divorce itself from the USA's overt support of Israel. More significantly, the use of the oil 'weapon' by the Arab States has threatened the already limited cohesion of the Common Market and has further exacerbated European-American relations. For many in western Europe, détente has become synonymous with entente and, with their assumption that our interests are not directly threatened, they believe that expenditure upon defence can be accorded a low priority in the allocation of national resources. When coupled with the sociological bias which is antipathetic to the use of military power, including its political and diplomatic utilisation, then doubt could be cast upon the present military strategy of the Western Alliance. Yet, when the problems of European defence are addressed, and various solutions postulated, only rarely is full account taken of these fundamental trends. Idealised proposals for European defence which run counter to the present trends and do not show how they will be arrested, seem to have only a hypothetical value. It follows that a realistic basis for discussion should include a review of Soviet-American relations, détente in its manifest forms, related sociological trends, developments in the Atlantic Alliance, and their probable combined effects upon the future security of Western Europe."

EUROPEAN SECURITY, in *Survival*, v. 15, no. 5 (September/October 1973) 236-242.

"In the first half of 1973 the stage for multilateral East-West negotiations in Europe was firmly set. Not surprisingly, issues of military security were the slowest to advance, but even preparations for the Conference on Security and Cooperation in Europe which had originally been regarded by the Warsaw Pact countries, who proposed the conference, as a brief diplomatic meeting to agree on the agenda took well over half a year before the 'Recommendations of the Helsinki Consultations' were agreed upon by all 34 delegations. The reason for this was not only the familiar one of a difference of interest and concept between East and West, but also the problem inherent in European détente: the closer the co-operation between East and West, the more the discipline within alliances might be affected and the more societies on either side are exposed to one another. Given the restricted nature of East European political systems, stabilization through agreements between governments might in turn be undermined by destabilization through contact between societies. It is this concern which gives political significance to the repeated assertion that the agreed principles should apply to all states irrespective of their political, economic or social system and to the careful phrasing of the section on cultural exchanges, human contacts and information. A slightly shortened text of the Recommendations is reprinted below. The exploratory East-West talks on a mutual reduction of forces took place simultaneously in Vienna, yielding much vaguer results, except in defining the reduction area more restrictively than NATO had wished by leaving Hungary out and replacing the term 'balanced' for the conditions for reductions by the no less ambiguous term 'undiminished security'. Although negotiations are scheduled to start on 30 October 1973, it seems clear from the Communique, reprinted below, that they will continue to be of an exploratory nature. The Final Communique of the North Atlantic Council of Meeting in Copenhagen sums up the attitude of NATO countries towards these negotiations."

THE FUTURE OF EUROPE: WAYS FORWARD, by Francois Duchêne, in *The World Today*, v. 27, no. 11 (November 1971) 457-462.

"The 'era of negotiations' between the adversaries of the cold war is well under way. Treaties between the German Federal Republic and the Soviet Union and Poland have been signed. Agreement has been reached between the wartime allies on Berlin. The United States and the Soviet Union have jointly announced that they expect to be able to agree on the limitation of their anti-ballistic missile systems. The Soviet Union has taken up suggestions made by NATO that the two cold-war alliances should negotiate mutual and balanced force reduction in Europe. A multilateral conference on Europe will surely follow. Short of the peace treaty which it seems will never consecrate the end of the second World War, these negotiations ratify an East-West agreement to disagree about the post-war dispensation at both the super-Power and European levels. Like all agreements to disagree, this is full of ambiguities. Yet, whatever covert tensions and rivalries subsist, the period of post-war history experienced as cold war centered in Europe is plainly coming to a close. A new phase in Europe, and by extension in world politics, is beginning. In the West, this process is sometimes called 'détente'."

HOW THE U.S.-SOVIET RELATIONSHIP HAS DEVELOPED; CAN THE DÉTENTE POLICY SUCCEED?, by H. George Franks, in *NATO's Fifteen Nations*, v. 20, no. 1 (February-March 1975) 36-38 plus.

"In view of the criticism (and praise) which have followed the tentative agreement reached in Moscow during the visits of President Ford and Secretary of State Kissinger, we feel that a general review of the development of U.S. policy in this sphere and the principles on which it is based, should be carefully studied by all who are interested in the possibility of a more or less lasting peace in general in Europe, and in the prospects for NATO in particular. Accordingly, we summarize here the two voluminous speeches and press statements made by the American leaders in connection with their latest talks with the Soviet Union, including reasonably clear explanations of the present situation and the hopes for the future."

RETHINKING THE DEFENSE OF EUROPE, by Robert Ball, in *Fortune*, v. 78, no. 2 (February 1973) 58-65 plus.

"For more than a generation, the fundament of Europe's security has been the military forces of the North Atlantic Treaty Organization. Now, as cold-war tensions diminish, a major reassessment of European security is being undertaken by East and West. Two conferences beginning this year between the U.S. and its NATO allies on the one hand and the Soviet Union and other Warsaw Pact nations on the other will take up a series of enormously sensitive issues. These include reduction of military forces on both sides of the Iron Curtain, acceptance of the borders set after World War II, and the freer movement of people, trade, and information across those borders. If these talks succeed, the confrontation in Europe can be wound down, with benefit for all. But prudence demands that Western Europe not become dependent on Soviet good will, and the negotiations are fraught with danger. The U.S., in its eagerness to cut defense costs, must avoid relying on token U.S.S.R. concessions to justify a further weakening of NATO's relative strength."

SOVIET-AMERICAN RELATIONS, by Alvin

Z. Rubinstein, in *Current History*, v. 67, no. 398 (October 1974) 145-149 plus.

"It seems difficult to generate a sustained, informative, dispassionate discussion about détente because of the inability or unwillingness of leading spokesmen to separate considerations of its costs and benefits from United States domestic politics and partisan propensities . . . Thus far, the fruits of détente for the Soviet Union are easy to identify; for the United States, the consequences are less obvious."

(*)—THE SUPERPOWERS AND ARMS CONTROL: FROM COLD WAR TO INTERDEPENDENCE, by Walter C. Clemens, Jr. Lexington, Mass., Lexington Books, 1973. 180 p.

"This . . . approach to Soviet-American arms-control negotiations, though somewhat overly systemic, argues persuasively for a gradual and ameliorative approach toward détente through interdependence."

THE USSR AND THE WEST, 1972, by George W. Ball, in *The Atlantic Community Quarterly*, v. 10, no. 2 (Summer 1972) 188-193.

"George Ball, long-time Under Secretary of State in the Kennedy and Johnson Administrations, cautions against undue optimism regarding the aims of, and the constraints on, the Soviet Union in Europe. He warns that the Russians have changed their tactics, realizing that frontal assaults only encourage Western unity, but that their goal of preeminence in Europe remains the same. He is pessimistic about Ostpolitik by West Germany or any one else, and about a European Security Conference, though he looks upon the entry of Great Britain into the Common Market as an important positive portent for the future."

D. Détente and Communism (including Europe's Fear of Communism) (See also Appendixes)

COMMUNISM AND DÉTENTE, in *Journal of International Affairs*, v. 28, no. 2 (October 1974) 133-228.

"During the past several years, détente has been one of the most widely discussed topics in the field of international politics. Most writings concerning this issue have dealt with changing relations among the superpowers and other groups of states. Détente has been discussed in terms of the SALT talks, increasing commercial ties between the Soviet and Western blocs, the development of relations with the People's Republic of China, etc. This issue of the JOURNAL approaches the study of détente from a slightly different direction—that of détente as an influence on the theory and practice of communism. The articles which follow examine various communist parties (and, when necessary, related non-communist groups as well) to determine what effect American-Soviet-Chinese détente has had on their ideology, leadership, domestic posture, and foreign affairs . . . Charles Gati analyzes the effects of détente on Eastern Europe. Reflecting the coincidence of party and state policies in communist-ruled nations, Gati dwells first on improved relations with the West and then on the position of the East European communist states as satellites of the Soviet Union. He points out that on the whole détente has not resulted in a relaxation of Soviet dominance. Rather, controls have if anything been strengthened—events such as the invasion of Czechoslovakia in 1968 are seen as a normal and repeatable expression of Soviet determination not to allow any interference with its hegemony over East Europe."

EUROPE'S PROBLEMS, EUROPE'S CHOICES, by George Kennan, in *Foreign Policy*, (Spring 1974) 3-16.

". . . Analyzes Europe's fears that, in the face of the USSR's increasing strength and the 'undependability' of the US commitment Europe will eventually be forced to subordinate itself to the USSR. He identifies the two key elements of this fear as the credence given to overwhelming Soviet strength and the belief that military strength is concommitant with political subordination. Ignoring a comparison of strategic strength, the intricacies of which Kennan believes 'surpass any layman's facilities for judgment,' the common tendency to overestimate an enemy's strength. Russia, he notes, has always deployed a disproportionate number of troops to what the situation in Europe would demand, which makes for a potentially dangerous confrontation. But he reminds the Europeans of an earlier idea, which they had rejected, of using US troop withdrawals to get the USSR forces removed. In any case, he maintains that Europe's population and industrial resources could support an increase in its forces to match the Soviets, even though the Europeans have until now been unwilling to make the necessary sacrifices and to curb the inflation which has priced Europe out of military competition. Even in the unlikely event that the US withdraws its troops without a concurrent increase in Europe's military capabilities, Europe would not necessarily be forced to become subordinate to the USSR. Many countries weaker than the European group have been able to coexist with the superpowers without subordinating their policies. Indeed, Kennan continues, the spectre of the USSR compelling the NATO countries to do its bidding is 'ludicrous.' The USSR wants no trouble on its Western front, especially in view of the disputes with China on its East. Kennan concludes that Europe's fears are unfounded and its own conception of a gloomy future is a vision *not* forced on it by either the US or the USSR."

E. The United States View of Détente

DÉTENTE: NOW THE QUESTIONS, in *Newsweek*, v. 84, no. 14 (30 September 1974) 39-40.

"Secretary of State Henry Kissinger went before the Senate Foreign Relations Committee last week to discuss—and defend—America's pursuit of warmer relations with the Soviet Union. He contended that 'major progress' has already been made in the quest for détente."

DÉTENTE: THE AMERICAN VIEW, by Henry Kissinger, in *Survival*, v. 17, no. 1 (January/February 1975) 35-42.

"Soviet-American détente cannot be defined in one or two summit meetings or in agreements: it is a process, an evolving relationship. Against the background of mounting criticism of current American détente policy in the United States and growing scepticism whether the efforts of détente policy are justified by its results, the United States Secretary of State, Dr. Henry Kissinger, has defined American détente strategy before the Foreign Relations Committee of the Senate. The text, which has only been slightly shortened, is reprinted . . . [here]."

WITNESS TO HISTORY, 1929-1969, by Charles E. Bohlen. New York, Norton, 1973. 562 p.

". . . During his tenure in Paris, [Ambassador] Bohlen was confronted with the imposing figure of de Gaulle at the height of his power. As might be expected, Bohlen has his doubts about Gaullist doctrine: the French leader perceived all international relations in terms of Realpolitik and was shocked by actions dictated by ideological obligations, in particular the 1968 invasion of Czechoslovakia. De Gaulle had little comprehension of the US, regarding it as a polyglot country rather than a pure nation-state. Bohlen also takes de Gaulle to task for his disruption of the Western alliance, which served no practical purpose for France and only benefited the Russians. Bohlen is not optimistic about détente between the US and USSR. He tends to emphasize the ideological element in his analysis of Kremlin policy—the Bolsheviks, as he insists on calling them, still believe they are surrounded by hostile capitalist nations. He sees no nascent liberalization within the Soviet Union—in fact, the present leadership seems much more conservative than Khrushchev was . . ."

F. The Soviet View of Détente

INTERNATIONAL DÉTENTE AND DISARMAMENT, by V. Israelyan, in *International Affairs, Moscow*, no. 5 (1974) 24-29.

"The favourable changes that have recently taken place in international relations and the growing improvement in the international political atmosphere paved the way for fresh steps aimed at establishing a more stable peace, consolidating the positive changes in world affairs and making them irreversible. The international détente, in particular, helps to create favourable prerequisites for tackling disarmament, one of the key problems of our day. Let us put it bluntly: if the arms race was the ugly offspring of the cold war, détente should naturally lead to disarmament, that is, to stopping the material preparations for war and utilising the resources thus released for economic and social development that would benefit all nations. In his speech at the World Congress of Peace Forces in Moscow, Leonid Brezhnev stated: 'It goes without saying that the further extension of the arms race by the aggressive circles of imperialism, on the one hand, and the relaxation of international tension that has set in, on the other, are two processes running in opposite directions. The two cannot develop endlessly along what might be called parallel lines'."

NATO IN CONDITIONS OF DÉTENTE, by A. Antonov, in *International Affairs, Moscow*, no. 2 (1974) 34-41.

"The USA's policy during the military action in the Middle East in October 1973 extremely sharpened US contradictions with its allies within the military NATO bloc. The press on both sides of the Atlantic was full of exclamations like 'NATO crisis,' 'blow at the alliance,' and 'worst shock ever.' Here are the facts. The USA's West European allies, with the exception of Portugal, publicly dissociated themselves from Washington's pro-Israeli policy . . . The crisis in the relations between the Atlantic partners took such a sharp turn during the Middle East events because this abrupt shift had already been prepared by earlier developments within the bloc. That is why the fresh outburst of differences between the NATO members reflects deep-going processes connected both with an aggravation of inter-imperialist contradictions and the crisis of the imperialist bloc policy in general in the conditions of détente. Divisions within the bloc have become particularly pronounced over the past few years, as international tensions have relaxed. NATO's line of confrontation with the socialist world has become a glaring anachronism, and the West European countries have gained some scope for a more independent policy outside the NATO framework."

SOCIALIST COUNTRIES AND EUROPEAN SECURITY, by A. Chenbarov, in *International Affairs, Moscow*, no. 1 (1975) 8–14.

"Major shifts toward détente and peace in Europe have proved possible in recent years because of the increased influence of socialist countries on the course of international affairs. These shifts were promoted by the growing political realism of the ruling circles of West European countries, who understood the necessity of peaceful cooperation with the socialist states. The steadfast shift in the balance of forces in favour of socialism sets the basis for positive changes in the relationships among European countries. The effectiveness of the socialist countries' impact on the solution of European issues in the spirit of peace has greatly increased, thanks to their growing unity and the cohesion and coordination of their foreign policy moves. This coordination is being carried out mainly within the framework of the Warsaw Treaty Organization. The socialist countries formed a defensive alliance in 1955, countered the imperialist cold war policy with a united front of peaceloving forces, and upheld and consolidated the position of socialism in Europe. The Warsaw Treaty Organisation, established as a counterbalance to the aggressive North Atlantic Alliance, has played its own unique role in developing détente."

USA: DÉTENTE, CRISES AND PROBLEMS, by Mike Davidow, in *International Affairs, Moscow*, no. 4 (1974) 64–71.

"Soviet-US meetings on the summit level, the official acceptance of peaceful coexistence as the principle governing relations between the leading countries of the two world social systems, agreements, extending from limitation on antiballistic defence systems and on strategic arms to working jointly against the two great scourges of mankind, cancer and heart diseases, a several-times increase in trade—these are some of the fruits of the détente for which the Soviet Union long struggled. The significantly improved and normalised US-USSR relations have had a profound impact on world affairs . . . The developing détente in US-USSR relations is equally vital for the American people for normalising conditions on the home front and for the normalisation of international relations as a whole. To strengthen the process of genuine détente on the international scene now is no less urgent task for the USA than the elimination and staving off of the domestic political crisis that is developing at such an uncontrollable tempo. That is why in our days peaceful coexistence between the states of two world social systems and the complete normalisation of relations between the United States and the Soviet Union have become an urgent necessity for the American people."

CHAPTER VII

WEAPONS AND TECHNOLOGY, AND ARMS CONTROL, DISARMAMENT, AND NUCLEAR PROLIFERATION
(See also Appendixes)

A. Weapons and Technology: East and West (Some Aspects)

1. *Miscellaneous Aspects*

THE ALLIANCE AND EUROPE: PART IV MILITARY DOCTRINE AND TECHNOLOGY, by Steven Canby. London, The International Institute for Strategic Studies, 1975. 42 p. (Adelphi Papers 109.)

NATO Strategy (Is a conventional defence desirable and practicable); Soviet Warfighting Concepts (military power from an inferior resource base); Military Doctrine and Technology (how technology has been used and should be used); Design-Conventional Equivalence (restructuring for larger reserves); Deploying for Defensive Superiority (small strongpoints, the checker-board concept—defence by small strongpoints, stand-off technology); New Technology and Lower Defence Costs (artillery, tactical air power); Conclusions.

HIGHLIGHTS OF THE [SECOND] ROYAL NAVY EQUIPMENT EXHIBITION [GREENWICH, ENGLAND, SEPTEMBER 17 to 24], by Charles Latour, in *NATO's Fifteen Nations*, v. 18, no. 6 (December 1973–January 1974) 64 plus.

Minesweeping; Communications; ECM; Underwater Weapons; Navigation; Defence Equipment Company; Radars; Missiles; Helicopters; Boats; Trainers; Plots and Displays; Guns.

INTERNATIONAL R&D TRENDS AND POLICIES: AN ANALYSIS OF IMPLICATIONS FOR THE US. Washington, Aerospace Industries Association of America, 1972. 56 p.

"The USSR, Britain, France, Germany, Sweden, and Japan support active R&D programs which continue to grow in scope and funding. However, the US program is almost stagnant. In terms of expenditure, the American program has more than doubled since 1960, but most of this growth took place before 1968. Expenditures have remained constant since 1968; considering inflation and the higher costs of advanced technology, this constant expenditure represents a declining R&D capability. Since 1966, the growth rate of government R&D funding has dropped from 9% to less than 1%, and increases in non-federal funding have not been able to compensate for the drop in federal money. Other nations are increasing their R&D programs. In France the R&D program grows about 13% per year, while the growth rate is 25% in Japan and 30 to 40% in West Germany. Furthermore, other nations tend to concentrate on economic problems while the US devotes over half of its R&D effort to defense and space . . . One of the problem areas is aerospace. The US currently supplies about 80% of the world's civilian aircraft; the large US market permits longer production runs, lower unit costs, and a wide variety of aircraft. However, West European nations are trying to meet the American challenge through cooperation in R&D and developing new types of Aircraft for which there is no American counterpart. Soviet R&D represents a threat to American technological superiority. The Soviet program has more than doubled since 1960 and is concentrated on defense and space, with perhaps 20% going to civilian problems. The USSR spends $10 to 13 billion more than the US on R&D per year and the growth rate of its program is estimated at 9 to 13% . . . The US needs a technological strategy and policy which define and support national R&D goals. Other free world nations focus on areas offering economic and social benefits; the US might do well to follow their lead in becoming more selective and specialized in its approach to R&D. For example, the US could concentrate on areas in which its trade position is threatened and on new technologies such as pollution control."

MILITARY TECHNOLOGY AND THE EUROPEAN BALANCE, by Trevor Cliffe. London, The International Institute for Strategic Studies, 1972. 58 p. (Adelphi Papers 89.)

Tactical Nuclear Weapons; A New Approach To Tactical Nuclear Weapons; Chemical Weapons; Armoured Warfare; Artillery Weapons; The Automated Battlefield; Air Mobility in the Battlefield; Air Warfare; The Effects of New Technology on Military Capabilities; Technology and Manpower; The Cost Implications of New Technology; A Shopping List; Appendices (Comparative Strengths of NATO and Warsaw Pact Conventional Theatre Forces—Ground and Air, Soviet Military Strategy, Tactical Nuclear Weapons, Main Battle Tanks, Anti-Tank Guided Missiles, Heavy and Medium Lift Helicopters, Tactical Aircraft, Tactical Air Defence Weapons Systems, Tactical Air-to-Surface Missiles, and Unit Costs of Weapons Systems and Other Military Equipment).

NEW EYES AND EARS FOR NATO FORCES, by H. George Franks, in *NATO's Fifteen Nations*, v. 17, no. 4 (August-September 1972) 87-92.

"During the past 20 years almost incredible advances have been made in the development and production of specialized equipment for the world's fighting forces. These in particular have been seen in the fields of radar, weapon control, data handling and air control systems. One firm which has been very prominent . . . in this development has been Philips of Eindhoven. In earlier issues of this magazine surveys have been published showing how Holland is helping to put NATO on wheels as well as keeping the NATO countries up-to-date with their ammunition supplies. In this issue a short survey is given showing how Philips is intensifying NATO's seeing and hearing."

R.U.S.I. AND BRASSEY'S DEFENCE YEARBOOK 1974. New York, Praeger, 1974. 338 p.

". . . Part I studies strategy; Part II (about the same length) delves in somewhat daunting detail into 'modern weapon technology'; . . . a brief Part III lists the more important works on defence published during the year . . ." See also annuals for previous years.

SOME EQUIPMENTS ON DISPLAY AT FARNSBOROUGH, by John Marriott, in *NATO's Fifteen Nations*, v. 19, no. 4 (August-September 1974) 52-59.

Britain's first fully international airshow opened on September 2, 1974. It was the longest airshow staged in the U.K. Civilian aviation products outnumbered those of a military nature. The author reviews some of the "more interesting items" in the following categories: equipments—general, reconnaissance, missiles, electronic warfare, communications, air traffic control system, and air navigation.

SOVIET OBJECTIVE: TECHNOLOGICAL SUPREMACY, by Edgar Ulsamer, in *Air Force Magazine*, v. 57, no. 6 (June 1974) 22-27.

"In addition to four new ICBMs, a new SLBM, and new nuclear-powered submarines, the Soviet Union has under development a dozen new offensive missile systems and is pursuing an ominous, highly sophisticated new technology involving beamed energy weapons. The driving force behind these efforts to outdistance the US in weapons technology is Soviet Defense Minister Marshal Andrei Grechko, who directs the massive campaign to attain the . . . Soviet Objective: Technological Supremacy."

TECHNOLOGY, WESTERN EUROPE'S ALTERNATIVE FUTURES, AND AMERICAN POLICY, by Victor Basiuk, in *Orbis*, v. 15, no. 2 (Summer 1972) 485-506.

"Our era is characterized by an increasingly pervasive impact of technology on society. The swift pace of technological change in this and the following decades will have far-reaching political repercussions. Western Europe, in particular, will be affected by the impact of technology which, if it does not evoke an appropriate response by West European nations, might seriously jeopardize the region's security and its viability as a major political center in the international arena. Western Europe's alternatives in a technology-dominated future and the potential role of the United States in influencing European developments is the subject of this article."

2. *Aircraft*

AIR FORCES OF THE WORLD—PART I: EUROPEAN NATO MEMBERS, in *Interavia*, v. 28, no. 9 (September 1973) 1003-1008.

A guide to what air forces fly what aircraft.

FACETS OF THE FUTURE FIGHTER SPECTRUM, by Eric J. Wootton, in *Interavia*,

v. 29, no. 12 (December 1974) 1192–1194, v. 30, no. 1 (January 1975) 34–38.

Why the Lightweight Fighter?; The Rising Cost of Technology; The Pilot's Viewpoint; Complexity Versus Capability; The Irreplaceable Human Element; Vietnam; Endorsed Agility.

JANE'S ALL THE WORLD'S AIRCRAFT 1974–75, ed. by John W. R. Taylor. London, Jane's Yearbooks, 1974. 830 p.

Provides information on aircraft of most nations of the world, including, among many others the NATO nations as well as the Warsaw Pact Nations. Some information included on air-launched missiles, spaceflight and research rockets, and satellites and spacecraft launched during 1973.

A MODEL FOR EVALUATING VSTOL VERSUS CTOL COMBAT AIRCRAFT SYSTEMS, by S. Horowitz and R. Shishko. Santa Monica, Rand Corp., March 1971. 31 p. (P-4587.)

"A cost-effectiveness study of the use of vertical or short takeoff and landing (VSTOL) aircraft for combat missions VSTOL are compared with conventional (CTOL) aircraft as tactical fighters in a future NATO environment. The conditions under which VSTOL and CTOL aircraft can be considered competitive systems are carefully described. A model yielding the probability of completing successive missions is used as a measure of combat effectiveness. A cost model reflects the resource impact of the same variables or alternatives that affect the measure of effectiveness. This integrated format is a necessary condition for the selection of least-cost designs capable of providing a given level of mission performance."

NATO: TECHNOPOLITICS IN THE AIR, in *Time*, v. 104, no. 13 (23 September 1974) 50 plus.

"Europeans call it the arms deal of the century—and they may well be right. Some time this year, Belgium, Denmark, The Netherlands and Norway—four NATO nations acting as a consortium—will buy more than 350 new jet fighters to replace warplanes bought in the 1960s. France and the U.S. are battling fiercely for this sale because the eventual stakes are enormous. The consortium's purchase, involving an investment of at least $1.7 billion, is only the tip of a lucrative iceberg: a worldwide market for thousands of jets, spare parts and maintenance contracts worth more than $20 billion over the next decade. The NATO consortium has been looking for a supersonic fighter capable of several missions: high-flying interception, close-in ground support and the interdiction of small warships near coasts. Above all, the purchasers want a plane they can afford to buy in quantity."

3. *Electronic Devices*

ELECTRONIC WARFARE, by Charles Latour, in *NATO's Fifteen Nations*, v. 19, no. 2 (April–May 1974) 72–79.

"Electronic Warfare can be defined as the measures taken to disrupt the enemy's sensors, weapons and communications and the measures taken to prevent your own similar devices from being disrupted by the enemy. Modern armed forces have come to rely more and more on electronic means for control, detection and weapon guidance, so much so that if an enemy can prevent them using the means to which they have become accustomed for so long, the result might well be catastrophic. A list of the various types of electronic devices used in modern warfare is shown . . . and from it will be seen that most of modern warfare depends upon two things—an accurate means of locating an enemy who is often unseen, and a method of ensuring that whatever weapon is used finds its target. The most vital factor in all this is radar. If the position of the target is denied to the weapon launcher, he will find it difficult, if not impossible to ensure that his weapon finds its target. Electronic Warfare's (EW) first job therefore is to deny the enemy the position of own forces."

4. *Laser Weapons*

MAJOR HURDLES FOR LASER WEAPONS CITED, by Philip J. Klass, in *Aviation Week and Space Technology*, v. 99, no. 2 (9 July 1973) 38–39 plus.

"Plasma and atmospheric propagation effects that pose major hurdles for projected high-energy laser radiation weapons are described here during the recent Conference on Laser Engineering and Applications. Also reported were several techniques that might ease these problems."

PROGRESS ON LASER WEAPONS FOR TANKS, PLANES, ROCKETS, in *U.S. News & World Report*, v. 75, no. 14 (1 October 1973) 41–42.

"First, it was 'smart' bombs. Next, laser 'ray guns'? Emerging from U.S. research centers are new arms that are reshaping military thinking."

5. *Missiles (Including Surface-to-Surface Artillery)*

MISSILES OF THE WORLD, by Michael J.H. Taylor and John W.R. Taylor. New York, Scribners, 1972. 167 p.

"The authors present a volume containing details, drawings, and photographs (some never before published) of all guided missiles known to be in service or under development throughout the world, including China and Russia. Details contained on each missile are as current and complete as possible. The authors designate each missile by type and operational status and include, as far as possible, the following information on each missile: prime contractor, source of power, guidance and control systems, airframe construction and vital statistics, type of warhead, cruising speed, maximum range, launch weight, and a short history of each weapon's development and use . . ."

SURFACE TO SURFACE ARTILLERY, by John Marriott, in *NATO's Fifteen Nations*, v. 19, no. 6 (December 1974–January 1975) 68–73 plus.

"The object of this article is to discuss the various guns and rockets used in the surface-to-surface role in NATO and the Warsaw Pact, together with the methods of using them. The article is divided into two parts: weapons used on land and weapons used at sea. Guided missiles are not covered, since they form a subject all of their own."

6. *Naval Ships*

JANE'S FIGHTING SHIPS 1974–75, ed. by Capt. John E. Moore. New York, Jane's Yearbooks, 1974. 670 p.

Provides information on fighting ships of most nations of the world, including, among many others, the NATO nations as well as the Warsaw Pact nations.

7. *Nuclear Weapons*

NEW WEAPONS FOR DEFENCE IN EUROPE, by John Marriott, in *NATO's Fifteen Nations*, v. 18, no. 6 (December 1973–January 1974) 54–60 plus.

Tactical Nuclear Weapons; Mini-Nuces; Methods of Delivery; Advantages and Disadvantages; Anti-Tank; Mines; Reconnaissance; Chemical Warfare; Electronic Warfare.

THE RELUCTANT DRAGON: NATO'S FEARS AND THE NEED FOR NEW NUCLEAR WEAPONS, by Floyd Norman, in *Army*, v. 24, no. 2 (February 1974) 16–21.

"A new generation of smaller, precision tactical nuclear weapons could soon be deployed in Europe but many in NATO and Congress believe they might be too efficient, lowering the threshold to nuclear disaster."

8. *Small Arms*

BELGIUM HOLDS NATO ARMY DISPLAY, by G. M. Bailly-Cowell, in *NATO's Fifteen Nations*, v. 19, no. 2 (April–May 1974) 87–88.

"The Belgian Army, at the instigation of NATO's AC/225 Commission III, had staged on 20 March, at the military camp of Bourg-Leopold, 100 km from Brussels and 30 km from the Dutch border, a one day panorama of allied infantry weapons, viewed by approximately one hundred and fifty experts from twelve NATO countries and three non-member states: France, Switzerland and Sweden." Lists weapons displayed giving country origin.

IMPROVEMENTS IN NATO'S CONVENTIONAL WEAPONS 1949/74, by John Marriott, in *NATO's Fifteen Nations*, v. 19, no. 1 (February–March 1974) 28–36.

"In this article John Marriott reviews the changes in conventional weaponry that have taken place in NATO since the alliance was formed."

JANE'S INFANTRY WEAPONS 1975, ed. by Maj. F.W.A. Hobart. London, Jane's Yearbooks, 1974. 860 p.

"This book is the first to cover all infantry weapons likely to be met in use today. It deals with hand-held weapons such as pistols, rifles, submachine guns and machine guns; with grenades and mortars; and with those anti-tank and anti-aircraft weapons used in infantry formations. This book gives detailed specifications and development history of all types of weapon. It does not confine itself to weapons in current production, although naturally more emphasis is given to the latest developments. There is comprehensive coverage of the firearms, grenades and specialised weapons employed by the Soviet Bloc and China as well as the NATO and uncommitted nations. The section on machine guns includes an appreciation of the new Russian GPMG family—the PK, and a description of the first home-produced machine gun from Red China. The information on rifles is presented so as to allow a comparison of American and Russian guns, and there is some discussion of the future programme in the USA. Information is provided on the functioning and characteristics of the Russian infantry anti-tank missiles, with an appreciation of how the Sagger affected the Yom Kippur War."

SMALL ARMS, by Charles Latour, in *NATO's Fifteen Nations*, v. 19, no. 3 (June-July 1974) 62-68 plus.

"There are over 180 small arms manufacturers in the world. America leads the field with 36 manufacturers, closely followed by Germany with 32. Britain has 17 and Russia only known ones. For the purpose of this article 'small arms' has been taken to mean the guns carried by an infantryman and thus comprises Rifles, Sub Machine Guns, Machine Guns and Pistols. With so many weapons available it is not surprising to find little standardisation throughout NATO in their small arms. The only thing that has been standardised is the size of the round." Some of the weapons are described and illustrated.

9. Smart Weapons

'SMART' WEAPONS: A COMING REVOLUTION IN TACTICS, by Col. John T. Burke, in *Bulletin of Atomic Scientists*, v. 23, no. 2 (February 1973) 14-20.

"Many of the tactician's 'if only . . .' dreams suddenly seem capable of realization with ordnance that finds its own way to the target . . . Terminal homing could produce a quantum jump in cost-effective combat power and a major, perhaps revolutionary, change in tactical concepts and organizations . . . With smart weapons, infantry's organic firepower will be enormously increased [and] operations will be much less dependent than now upon artillery and armor support for success . . . Smart weapons are . . . enormously attractive from the political and psychological viewpoint and this alone justifies their development . . . Whether or not we see the potential our opponents surely will. So would any nation with adequate technology but limited resources, desperately seeking a short-cut to combat power."

STRATEGIC SURVEY 1974. London, International Institute for Strategic Studies, 1975.

"New military technologies are reaching a stage of development where they could 'deeply affect' Atlantic alliance politics and superpower arms control arrangements. 'Smart bomb' technology has increased the vulnerability of fixed targets and is blurring the distinction between conventional arms and nuclear weapons. These are among the major assessments."

10. *Tanks and Other Armor*

THE ANTI-TANK PROBLEM, by John Marriott, in *NATO's Fifteen Nations*, v. 17, no. 2 (April-May 1972) 72-82 plus.

"The Warsaw Pact's tank forces outnumber those of NATO by a factor of 3 to 1. The latest count gives the former 21,700 tanks and the latter 7,750. It follows therefore that NATO must expect that the spearhead of any Russian advance, particularly in the central area, will undoubtedly be a massive concentration of armour. NATO's 7,000 old tanks, even if they could all be concentrated in the right area to oppose the attack, would have about as much effect as trying to stop an elephant with a pea shooter. NATO is firmly committed to a policy of flexible response. This means that conventional attack must be met with conventional forces and contained long enough for the politicians to make up their minds as to whether they intend to use nuclear weapons or not. With such a preponderance of armour, it would seem easy for the Soviets to draw off NATO forces by well planned feint attacks. One can well imagine NATO tanks rushing to oppose an apparent attack in one sector, and, when they are all firmly committed, for the Soviets to launch the main attack hundreds of miles away. Whether such a ruse is adopted or not, there seems little doubt that NATO must face the fact that, in the opening stages of a war, Russian armour will penetrate deep into NATO territory unless some new method can be found to mount a far more efficient and mobile antitank defence than is possible at present. When two contestants meet and one is infinitely stronger than the other, the weaker can only hope to win by the use of guile, ruses and surprise. It is the old story of David and Goliath. It is obvious that for NATO to rely on her tanks and her present, pitifully few vehicle and ground mounted anti-tank weapons to stop a Soviet onslaught is just not on. Other means must be found, means which step outside the old concept of anti-tank warfare and which break new bounds. What then are these means?"

DETAILS OF TANKS IN SERVICE IN NATO AND THE WARSAW PACT, in *NATO's Fifteen Nations*, v. 20, no. 1 (February-March 1975) 47-56.

NEW SOVIET WEAPONS UNVEILED IN MIDEAST, by Robert Hotz, in *Aviation Week*, (24 March 1975) 25.

"Soviet Union has developed a new generation of armored weapons designed for swift offensive blitzkrieg-type thrust through battlefields contaminated by nuclear or chemical warfare. This is evident from a detailed examination of a large array of new Soviet-manufactured weapons captured by the Israeli Defense Forces from the Egyptian and Syrian armies during the October 1973, war. The new generation of weapons includes not only a family of armored fighting vehicles but also a wide variety of motorized support vehicles including trench diggers, automatic mine-laying machines, motorized bridging equipment, specially designed missile transporters, mobile missile simulator trainers and a gyro-equipped command vehicle with a moving map display."

TANKS IN TOMORROW'S ARMIES, by Richard M. Ogorkiewicz, in *Military Review*, v. 54, no. 2 (February 1974) 20-26.

"A series of recent events has attracted considerable attention to tanks . . . All these events have aroused serious doubts about the future of tanks. To some extent, these doubts have been eased by the commitment of the US Army to the development of a new battle tank, the XM1. Moreover, the important role played by tanks, despite heavy losses, in the Arab-Israeli War has been widely noted. Notwithstanding, the future of tanks continues to be questioned."

B. Arms Control And Disarmament

1. *Miscellaneous Aspects*

ARMS CONTROL AND DISARMAMENT AGREEMENTS; TEXTS AND HISTORY OF NEGOTIATIONS. Washington, U.S. Arms Control and Disarmament Agency, 1975. 159 p. (Publication 77.)

ARMS CONTROL AND THE MILITARY BALANCE IN EUROPE, by J. I. Coffey, in *Orbis*, v. 17, no. 1 (Spring 1973) 132-154.

"Proposals for arms control in Europe are not new. Ever since the end of World War II there have been a plethora of suggestions for the disengagement of forces, the establishment of denuclearized or demilitarized zones, reductions in troop strength, and cutbacks in levels of weapons. What is perhaps new is that suggestions for arms control which previously received short shrift are now commanding respectful attention—if not yet wholehearted support. The reasons for these changing attitudes vary, both among states and between the North Atlantic Treaty Organization (NATO) and the Warsaw Treaty Organization (WTO). Broadly speaking, NATO members see arms control in Europe as reflecting some degree of progress toward a détente and as facilitating the further improvement of relations between East and West . . . If the United States and the USSR demonstrate their prudence, cement their understandings with improvements in relations, and involve their allies in these measures, a new sense of security may develop, one that will be more meaningful and longer-lasting than any based on the military balance in Europe."

(*)—THE EFFECTS OF DEVELOPMENTS IN THE BIOLOGICAL AND CHEMICAL SCIENCES ON CW DISARMAMENT NEGOTIATIONS. Stockholm, International Peace Research Institute, 1974. 54 p.

"This paper describes some of the recent advances in the chemical and biological sciences and examines the consequences of these advances for the future of chemical warfare. It was written by Professor Vitali Zubov, a SIPRI research fellow who has now returned to the University of Moscow. A summary of a round table discussion on the possible political consequences of recent advances in the biological and chemical sciences, held in Stockholm in July 1973, is included as an appendix."

SOME FUNDAMENTAL PROBLEMS OF ARMS CONTROL AND NATIONAL SECURITY, by Donald G. Brennan, in *Orbis*, v. 15, no. 1 (Summer 1972) 218-231.

"There are two subject areas of basic importance concerning which I should like to raise some fundamental questions. The first subject area is that of American strategic nuclear policy, both unilaterally considered and in relationship to arms control. The second subject area is the relationship of the United States to security in Western Europe. As concerns strategic nuclear policy, much of the community concerned with American foreign policy believes that the 'right' answers are more or less known, at least in the sense of desirable directions for strategic nuclear policy. I believe that the commonly accepted views on desirable directions are wrong, and I shall argue a case for a major change in contemporary thought about strategic nuclear forces. In contrast, there does not appear to be a clear consensus on exactly how the relationship of the United States to the security of Western Europe should evolve during, say, the next decade. I do not myself have clearly defined views on just how that evolution should best proceed, but I should like to raise some fundamental questions concerning that relationship, including some that are rarely, if ever, confronted directly, more in the spirit of experimenting with ways of thinking about and discussing the problems involved than of providing answers that are intended to be definitive."

WORLD ARMAMENTS AND DISARMAMENT: SIPRI YEARBOOK 1974. Stockholm, International Peace Research Institute, 1974. 520 p.

"This fifth account of the major quantitative and qualitative changes that take place in the world's arsenals seems as far away as ever from being able to record any overall downward trend in spending on weapons of destruction. In fact, it points out that although military spending has remained roughly constant since 1968 (after allowing for inflation) at about $200 billion, the trend has been towards a wider distribution. While the large share taken by the USA, USSR, UK and France has declined somewhat, the share of other countries has risen, thus the arms race is increasingly a global phenomenon. But undoubtedly the greatest threat to mankind comes from nuclear weapons, and here, unfortunately, the picture is no brighter. The Yearbook says that in 1973 alone there were 29 nuclear tests. And, despite SALT agreements, the two super-powers continued to make significant advances, both quantitative and qualitative, in their advanced nuclear weapons programmes in 1973. Of course this situation could be significantly changed by progress towards a SALT II agreement."

WORLD MILITARY EXPENDITURES AND ARMS TRADE 1963-1973. Washington, U.S. Arms Control and Disarmament Agency, 1975. 123 p. (Publication 74.)

The information is provided for all the major countries of the world including those of NATO and the Warsaw Pact. Trends in World Military Expenditures; Developed and Developing Worlds; World Arms Trade; Relative Burden. With statistical notes and statistical tables.

2. *Proliferation and Nonproliferation of Nuclear Weapons*

THE CHARADE OF PIECEMEAL ARMS LIMITATION, by Bernard T. Feld, in *Bulletin of the Atomic Scientists*, v. 31, no. 1 (January 1975) 8-16.

"All these recent developments have so eroded confidence in the nuclear Non-Proliferation Treaty (NPT)—already struggling to maintain credibility in the face of the failure of ratification by some of the most important potential nuclear powers—that there is grave question whether the NPT can survive its scheduled review conference to be held in Geneva in May of 1975 ... The strengthening of the NPT—both in the formal sense of the treaty's safeguards against nuclear diversion and in the creation of an international climate that could eliminate national and private incentives for constructing nuclear weapons—should command the highest priority."

NUCLEAR PROLIFERATION PROBLEMS. Cambridge, MIT Press, 1974. 312 p. (for Stockholm International Peace Research Institute.)

Chapter 8, Part IV: European Security and the Non-Proliferation treaty, by J. K. Miettinen.

3. *The Soviet View on Western Ams Control and Disarmament Policies*

NEW SOVIET INITIATIVE ON DISARMAMENT, by V. Israelyan, in *International Affairs, Moscow,* no. 11 (November 1974) 19-25.

"The struggle to end the arms race and achieve disarmament constitutes one of the main lines of the foreign policy activity of the CPSU and the Soviet State. The USSR sought to achieve this aim when it was the only socialist state, against which was ranged the entire capitalist world. This remains the goal of the USSR today, when there exists a radical change in the relationship of forces in the world arena in favour of socialism. The international situation taking shape in the world, the détente, and the normalisation of relations between states belonging to different socio-political systems create favourable conditions for making progress along this path. In turn, the steps taken to limit armaments and achieve disarmament in the past few years, such as the treaty on the non-proliferation of nuclear weapons, the convention on the prohibition of bacteriological weapons and the Soviet-American agreements on limiting strategic armaments help to deepen and extend the international détente. The tasks in the sphere of disarmament formulated in the Peace Programme, as worked out by the 24th Congress of the CPSU, have been embodied in the past few years in the concrete proposals advanced by the Soviet Union on the international scene. They have become the basis of many current negotiations on disarmament."

WESTERN ARMS CONTROL POLICIES IN EUROPE SEEN FROM THE EAST, by W. Multan and A. Towpik, in *Survival*, v. 16, no. 3 (May/June 1974) 127-128.

"Formal negotiations for the mutual reduction of forces and armaments in Eastern Europe have been going on between NATO and Warsaw Pact countries since 31 October 1973. Not surprisingly in these negotiations the motives of the participants are unlikely to be the same, and both East and West are influenced in their own negotiating positions by what they believe to be the other side's opinion. In the following article, based on a paper prepared for a small conference held by the International Institute for Strategic Studies in November 1973, two Polish scholars state what they understand West European motives to be in the sphere of Arms Control. Dr. W. Multan is Scientific Secretary and Dr. A. Towpik Head of the Disarmament and Arms Control Section of the Polish Institute for International Affairs, Warsaw."

C. Mutual and Balanced Force Reductions (MBFR): U.S., NATO, and Eastern Bloc Positions (See also Chapter VI)

1. *Problems, Prospects, Approaches, and Proposals*

BOTH SIDES TABLE PROPOSALS AT MBFR NEGOTIATIONS, in *NATO Review*, v. 23, no. 1 (January 1975) 18-19.

"The mutual and balanced force reduction negotiations (MBFR) went into recess for Christmas with no real progress being reported, but with several proposals having been made by both sides. The Western spokesman, Netherlands Ambassador Willem J. Baron de Vos van Steenwijk, outlined the allied position during an end-of-round press conference in Vienna on 12 December. Given . . . (here) is the text of his opening statement."

(LI)—THE DILEMMA OF MUTUAL AND BALANCED FORCE REDUCTIONS, by Wing Comdr. Douglas H. Major. Maxwell AFB, Ala., Air War College, 1973. 50 p. (Professional Study.)

"A review of the MBFR problems. An attempt was made to evolve the areas most suited to negotiation; but in the absence of significant pointers to any ultimate aims for MBFR, the proposals are general. The paper leans toward naval forces forming the base for reductions."

EUROPE: BALANCING ACT, in *Newsweek*, v. 81, no. 6 (5 February 1973) 50 plus.

"NATO's invitation to the Warsaw Pact to attend a bloc party went out months ago. The time: this week. The place: Geneva. The purpose: to begin exploratory talks on mutual and balanced force reductions (MBFR) in Central Europe. The invitation list was limited to nations with troops stationed in the area, seven from NATO's side and five from the Warsaw Pact. Then, only two weeks before the show was scheduled to begin, the Soviet Union finally sent its formal acceptance—but only on the conditions that the meeting be moved to Vienna and that the session be thrown open to all comers in the European neighborhood. Slightly miffed, NATO gave its answer last week: Vienna was fine, NATO said, but because MBFR promises to be one of the most important and complex meetings on record, let's keep the gathering small and intimate. By late last week, the questions of where, when and who would attend were still unsettled."

MBFR: FORCE LEVELS AND SECURITY REQUIREMENTS, by John Erickson, in *Strategic Review*, v. 1, no. 2 (Summer 1973) 28-43.

"The Conference on Security and Cooperation in Europe, convened in July 1973, culminated a decade of Soviet work to ratify the political status quo in Europe and to soften the NATO anti-Soviet stance. This Soviet interest had not embraced mutual or balanced arms reduction, that aspect of security having been introduced by the U.S. and NATO. The Soviet Union regards its superior military strength and the supporting Brezhnev doctrine as essential to its security, and looks upon the political hostility of the West as the chief threat to peace and security of Europe. The heavy concentration of Soviet forces in Central Europe belies reports of imminent conflict with Red China. Soviet leaders dominate the command structure of the Warsaw Treaty Organization Forces. Soviet armament and doctrine are for aggressive offensive combat. While emphasizing 'peaceful coexistence' and a general military balance, the Soviet Union has built up a formidable superiority in conventional weapons in Europe, which it is unlikely to relinquish in negotiations for balanced force reductions. The Soviet nuclear build-up has neutralized the NATO advantage in U.S. nuclear weapons, leaving NATO in a relatively weak posture. In these circumstances, the

Pentagon estimate that NATO forces could withdraw in an effective delaying action, pending reinforcement, may be optimistic. Unilateral withdrawal of U.S. troops would sorely weaken NATO forces, yet that prospect will enter Soviet calculations against making concessions in the negotiations. Soviet negotiators have eliminated the prospect of 'balanced' force reductions which might consider the Soviet geographic advantage, and have won agreement that cuts will be proportional. NATO negotiators have accepted the exclusion of the Soviet Southern Group of Forces in Hungary from counting in arms-reduction planning. Soviet negotiators have agreed to the date of October 30 for the opening of troop-reduction talks. The prospect is that troop-reduction talks will be extended. Any prospect of reducing the Soviet superiority in conventional arms through these talks is remote. The talks will introduce strains in NATO, at no cost to the Soviet side. It is not the Russians who will be pushed out of Europe."

(*)—MBFR: ITS ORIGINS AND PERSPECTIVES, by James F. Sattler. Paris, Atlantic Treaty Association, 1974. 27 p.

"Dr. Sattler, Research Associate of the US Atlantic Council, has undertaken, on behalf of the ATA, a short study—the main body of the text is only some twelve pages long—on the origins and objectives of MBFR considered from both Soviet and Western viewpoints. Anyone wishing to follow the current negotiations in Vienna will find this a useful guide to what, inevitably, is a complex and slow process. Three appendices give the texts of the communique issued at the completion of the exploratory MBFR talks in June, 1973, opening statements by the American and Soviet representatives in October, 1973, and press briefings by Mr. Quarles van Ufford on behalf of the Western participants in January and April, 1974. The subject can be further brought up to date by a reading of Mr. van Ufford's press briefing of last July, the text of which is to be found in issue No. 5 of the NATO Review."

MBFR: POLITICAL OR TECHNICAL ARMS CONTROL?, by Robin Ranger, in *The World Today*, v. 30, no. 10 (October 1974) 411–418.

"A limited agreement on mutual force reductions, avoiding deadlock over the technical requirements of MBFR, may well prove acceptable to both super-powers as a measure symbolizing their political detente; it would, however, do little to curb their use of military technology. The negotiations between NATO and the Warsaw Pact Organization (WPO) on Mutual and Balanced Force Reductions (MBFR) began in Vienna in October 1973, but there has been relatively little progress towards agreement since the USSR and the US tabled their opening offers. An analysis of these offers shows that in these, as in other arms control negotiations, the Russians were seeking political arms control while the US was seeking technical arms control. Despite the gap between the two super-power positions, their common interest in securing a political agreement preserving the status quo in Europe meant that a limited agreement was possible within the next year, especially given the recent changes in West European governments which made them more favourable to such an agreement."

MUTUAL AND BALANCED FORCE REDUCTIONS IN EUROPE, by Albert Willot, in *NATO Review*, v. 21, no. 1 (1973) 5–9.

"A recent issue of the Chronique de politique Etrangère published by the Royal Institute of International Relations in Brussels contains an interesting study by Mr. Albert Willot entitled 'The problem of Disarmament and its Application in Europe'. One chapter is devoted to mutual and balanced force reductions (MBFR). As the multilateral exploratory talks on MBFR have just opened, his analysis may help readers of the NATO Review to appreciate more clearly the many facets of an issue which bristles with complexities."

MUTUAL AND BALANCED FORCE REDUCTIONS: THE STATE OF A KEY ALLIANCE POLICY, by Roger J. Hill, in *NATO Review*, v. 19, nos. 9–10 (September/October 1971) 17–20.

"Deputy Foreign Ministers and high officials of NATO member countries met at the Brussels headquarters on 5 and 6 October to review recent exploratory contacts on MBFR with the Soviet Union and other interested countries. They also exploratory contacts on MBFR with the Soviet Union and other interested countries. They also consulted on substantive and procedural approaches to MBFR as was foreseen in the communique issued after the Lisbon Ministerial Session of the North Atlantic Council last June. The . . . article traces the origins and developments of MBFR."

MUTUAL AND BALANCED FORCE REDUCTIONS—TOWARD A MODEL. Carlisle Barracks, Army War College, March 1973. 54 p.

"Mutual and balanced force reductions (MBFR) between NATO and the Warsaw Pact have emerged as one of the more important security issues of the 1970's. Exploratory discussions commenced 31 January 1973, and actual negotiations could start in the Fall of 1973. President Nixon has affirmed that the US would not reduce its forces in Europe without reciprocity by the Warsaw Pact. Pact forces outnumber NATO's, better than 2;1 in tanks and aircraft in Central Europe. This imbalance, coupled with a superior Pact mobilization and reinforcement capability and the immutable factors of geography leads to the conclusion that MBFR could be to NATO's disadvantage, unless offset by other comprehensive measures such as constraints and verification. The outline of an illustrative model on 'How to Reduce' is provided—a comprehensive model involving constraints, verification, 50% reductions in US and USSR ground forces, and 10% reductions in the other NATO and PACT nations involved in Central Europe. As a follow-up to a post-MBFR period is the requirement that US and NATO planners need to evaluate the future posture and disposition of residual US ground forces in Europe —toward a reserve role for a highly mobile US Corps."

MUTUAL BALANCED FORCE REDUCTIONS, by Walter C. Clemens, Jr., in *Military Review*, v. 51, no. 10 (October 1971) 3-11.

"Soviet policy toward arms control measures for Europe has shifted dramatically in 1970-71, in tandem with Moscow's attitude toward other possible domains for arms limitation. What is the meaning of these changes? Is the Kremlin groping toward a strategy of interdependence with the West? Or are these changes merely part of a forward strategy carried on with indirect or 'rightist' tactics? Is Moscow interested in a settlement that will accommodate the conflicts and heal the wounds left in the aftermath of World War II? Alternatively, are we witnessing another round in the Soviet Union's historic tendency to fill the vacums susceptible to its power? If we could identify the essential criteria for measuring the willingness of the USSR to move toward a reasonable settlement of European problems—one that took account of Western, as well as Soviet, security concerns—three standards might be noted: A willingness to include the United States and Canada in any European settlement and its planning. A willingness to discuss mutual troop reductions and not just the withdrawal of US troops from Europe. A willingness to regularize the status of West Berlin. Soviet policy on other matters would also be an indicator such as the Kremlin's attitude toward strategic arms aimed at or located in Europe, but these three points are probably the touchstones by which to assess the main thrust of Soviet strategy in the early 1970's."

MUTUALLY BALANCED FORCE REDUCTIONS: THE COMPLEX PROBLEM, by Lt. Edward A. McKenney, in *Naval War College Review*, v. 24, no. 10 (June 1972) 29-41.

"At a time when national leaders have called for an era of negotiation to replace the bitter feelings which grew out of cold war confrontation, the subject of force reduction on the European Continent naturally received renewed attention. The problems associated with moving such proposals from the rhetorical stage to implementation, however, are so complex and interrelated that even the most optimistic of observers see a long and arduous course ahead for these negotiations—despite the advantages ultimate agreement would hold for both sides."

MUTUAL FORCE REDUCTIONS IN EUROPE, by John Yochelson, in *Survival*, v. 15, no. 6 (November/December 1973) 275-283.

"New talks between Warsaw Pact and NATO member states on mutual force reductions in Central Europe have opened in Vienna on 30 October 1973. The following two articles, both excerpts from longer original papers, discuss possible Western aims in the negotiations. John Yochelson, currently with the Center of International Affairs, Harvard University, looks at American options and interests in early 1973; in the meantime the implications of the Watergate affair on the relationship between the US Congress and the Administration, which became clear only after the article was written, may have generated new pressures in favour of Yochelson's 'Quick Fix' option. Johan Holst, the Acting Director of the Norwegian Institute of International Affairs, considers force reductions in the overall setting of European security relations and argues that agreements on the level of forces are less important than agreed restrictions in the use of military force in Europe. The text of his article is an amended version of the original paper 'Force Limitations and European Political Development'."

MUTUAL FORCE REDUCTIONS IN EUROPE: THE POLITICAL ASPECTS, by Christoph Bertram. London, The International Institute for Strategic Studies, 1972. 34 p. (Adelphi Papers 84.)

Genesis, Motives and Pre-Negotiation Positions; MBFR in the East-West Context; MBFR and the Western Alliance; and a Policy for the West.

(LI)—NATO AND THE WARSAW PACT—THE CHALLENGE OF MUTUAL AND BALANCED FORCE REDUCTIONS; by Maj. Allan C. Blaisdell. Maxwell AFB, Ala., Air Command and Staff College, 1972. 63 p. (Research Study.)

"NATO's mutual and balanced force reduction proposal (MBFR) presents the United States with a critical problem: what types of balanced reductions should be affected between NATO and the Warsaw Pact while insuring the Soviet Union does not become the dominant power in Europe through default. This study identifies and analyzes variations of two MBFR alternatives: withdrawal of 'stationed,' troops, and percentage/proportional reductions. The study concludes that no significant reduction in American presence or power in Europe should be affected as such action would be detrimental to the security of both the United States and the free world."

NATO DIVIDED ON ARMS TALKS, by Herbert J. Coleman, in *Aviation Week & Space Technology*, v. 99, no. 2 (12 November 1973) 12-13.

"Communist bloc buoyed by gains in Mideast conflict; negligible European support develops for U.S. policies . . . Negotiations for Mutual and Balanced Force Reductions in Central Europe went into the closed-session stage last week with a badly shaken and divided North Atlantic Treaty Organization sitting across the table from a Soviet-led Warsaw Pact revitalized by political, diplomatic and military gains stemming from the Middle East war. Although spokesmen for both sides emphasized positive aspects of the talks, it was clear that the Soviet Union was pushing for early agreement on specific troop reductions while the West continued to emphasize the complexities of any such reductions. Russia said it would be ready to start cutting back forces in Central Europe in 1975, a date the U.S. declined to acknowledge as meaningful. Divided and leaderless nature of the NATO position could be seen in the . . . events of last week."

NATO FORCES—PROSPECTS FOR MBFR, by Vice Adm. Charles S. Minter, Jr., in *RUSSI Journal*, v. 119, no. 3 (September 1974) 3-8.

"I would like . . . to share some thoughts with you on the complex issue of MBFR. To do so, I propose to discuss the consultative procedures which have evolved within the Alliance for developing MBFR policy; then, to outline some of the goals and principles which the Alliance has established for the MBFR negotiations; next to touch on where the MBFR talks in Vienna stand at present; and, finally, to draw perhaps a few tentative conclusions as to what we can and, equally important, what we cannot expect to come out of the MBFR process. Before tackling this agenda, however, let me begin by spending a few moments on history of MBFR."

NEW APPROACHES TO ARMS REDUCTION IN EUROPE, by J. I. Coffey. London, The International Institute for Strategic Studies, 1974. 28 p. (Adelphi Papers 105.)

Limitations on the Size and Capabilities of Armed Forces (The Establishment of Force Levels, Ceilings on Classes of Weapons, Contraints on Military Budgets, Controls on Research and Development, Evaluation); Restrictions on the Development of Forces (Precluding the Establishment of New Bases, Setting up Restricted Areas, Monitoring Development Restrictions, Acceptability of Restrictions); The Implications for European Security.

PERSPECTIVES OF MBFR IN EUROPE, by Hans-Georg Wieck, in *Aussen Politik*, no. 1, (1972) 36-40.

"In October 1971, Manlio Brosio, former Secretary General of NATO, was asked to explore with the Soviet Union and other East European countries the possibility of negotiations on mutual and balanced force reductions (MBFR) in Europe. Dr. Wieck believes that such a reduction, especially in Central Europe, could be the means of a policy of détente, provided it does not impair the existing balance of forces. Such a process could satisfy security needs, reduce distrust, and free resources for other needs . . . Any agreement on MBFR in Europe will affect Allied strategic concepts, plans, and force structures. Warsaw Pact force capabilities are numerically superior to those of the Alliance in Central Europe . . . Other aspects to consider are whether the stationed forces to be withdrawn will only be redeployed or also disbanded, and whether indigenous forces to be reduced may be converted into mobilizable cadre-strength units . . . Wieck hopes that any MBFR in Europe and, particularly, in Central Europe, will be accompanied by political agreements that will help to ease mutual distrust between East and West and open up additional areas for cooperation. However, all this is good only if the alliance maintains its freedom of action and capability for defense. Finally, Wieck insists upon the interdependence of these questions and those of the future development of NATO and the European Communities. In the interest of all partners, the governments must see that questions which are dealt with in the East-West dialogue must not be allowed to upset or hamper the development of the Alliance and the European Communities."

THE POLITICS OF MBFR, by Cristoph Bertram, in *The World Today*, v. 29, no. 1 (January 1973) 1-7.

"At the end of January 1973, a group of Nato and Warsaw Pact countries will meet in Switzerland for exploratory talks on negotiations for the mutual reduction of forces in Central Europe. After more than four years of communiques, signals, silences, and bilateral explorations, a multilateral East-West meeting will address itself for the first time to a proposal submitted by the Nato Council in June 1968: to reduce the military forces of both Nato and the Warsaw Pact in Europe. The exploratory talks are unlikely to produce more than procedural results: decisions where and when to hold formal negotiations. But it is an appropriate moment to examine what has become of the original political reasons behind the Nato initiative and how they are likely to fare in the future."

SALT AND MBFR: THE NEXT PHASE; REPORT OF A TRILATERAL CONFERENCE, in *Survival*, v. 17, no. 1 (January/February 1975) 14-24.

"From 25 to 29 March 1974 a meeting, sponsored by the International Institute for Strategic Studies (the host), the Japan Institute of International Affairs, and the Brookings Institution, convened at Dunford, England, brought together specialists from Europe, Japan, and the United States, to discuss major problems arising in the negotiations on strategic arms limitation and regional European force reductions. Those attending the meeting took part as individuals. The views expressed should not be attributed to the organizations with which they are associated or the organizations that helped finance the venture. The outcome of these two negotiations could have a significant impact on prospects for stability in inter-allied relations and levels of military expenditures, as well as in super-power relationships. Although strategic arms negotiations are conducted by the United States, their outcome has a direct bearing on the interests of Western Europe and Japan. Although negotiations for balanced force reductions in Europe are conducted by the NATO and Warsaw Pact countries, developments which affect prospects for peace and stability in Europe cannot fail, as has been shown in the past, to have some effect on Asia. In addition, collateral measures being considered in Europe might be applicable in the initial stages of negotiations in Korea should conventional arms control initiatives be undertaken by the two parts of Korea."

2. *United States*

FORCE REDUCTION OPTIONS IN CENTRAL EUROPE, by Gen. James H. Polk, in *Military Review*, v. 53, no. 10 (October 1973) 36-42.

"For some time, it has seemed likely that our European-based forces will be reduced with some functions perhaps being totally eliminated. With the mutual force reduction (MFR) talks about to get underway, that day may be coming closer. It behooves us then to look at the various ways in which this could be accomplished and to understand just how each particular method might affect our defense posture. There are actually about five general ways in which the ground forces can decrease numerical strength. These will be discussed in some detail."

MBFR: THE SEARCH FOR AN AMERICAN APPROACH, by John Yockelson, in *Orbis*, v. 17, no. 1 (Spring 1973) 155-175.

"Talks on mutual and balanced force reductions in Europe, having served Washington as a domestic and diplomatic counter for most of the past five years, no longer remain comfortably distant. Until this year, the prospect of reciprocal troop cuts along the Central Front seemed close enough to be tactically useful yet remote enough not to require troubling choices of priorities, objectives and strategies. The self-proclaimed need to preserve a strong bargaining position for MBFR helped both the Johnson and Nixon administrations to fend off domestic demands for unilateral U.S. reductions. Projected talks served an analogous role for a number of allied governments, promising also to bind the United States into a multilateral process in which West European interests could be taken effectively into account. NATO, with the notable exception of France, used MBFR as a device to parry Warsaw Pact proposals for a European security conference. Western emphasis on force reduction provided a concrete alternative to Eastern agendas emphasizing trade, technological interchange, and non-use of force declarations. Not only did MBFR appear to give substance and practical significance to security negotiations; it also seemed to place the Soviets on the defensive by calling attention to the internal control function of their forces in other Pact countries. The opening of exploratory talks in Vienna in January 1973, however, has marked a new stage by exposing conceptual difficulties and political tensions long recognized but never really faced. How are the diverse military capabilities of participants to be measured? What constitutes balance between which states? How much reduction is to be sought in differing categories of arms? How will nuclear guarantees be affected? How much coordination is possible and desirable within NATO? To what degree do shared superpower interests transcend alliance commitments?"

3. *USSR*

THE SOVIET MILITARY AND FORCE REDUCTIONS, by Capt. John C. Reppert, in *Military Review,* v. 54, no. 10 (October 1974) 24-29.

"More than a year has passed since representatives of the Warsaw Pact and NATO first sat down together at the conference table in Vienna to discuss the possibility of mutual force reductions in Central Europe. While the first concrete agreement on reductions has yet to be reached, a review of the Soviet military press for the past year suggests a clear lack of enthusiasm by the Soviet military leadership toward the talks. Further, the talks have rekindled a number of sensitive problems for the military leadership. The two areas where this has been most acute are the psychological preparedness of Soviet troops and the apparent questioning by some elements of the military concerning their proper role in deciding the military aspects of détente. The first and most obvious aspect of the Soviet military's public reaction to the force reduction talks has been the general lack of enthusiasm toward them."

4. *MBFR Implications for NATO*

(LI)—THE EFFECTS OF MBFR ON NATO STRATEGY, by Maj. Alfred A. Boyd. Maxwell AFB, Ala., Air Command and Staff College, 1974. 54 p. (Research Study.)

"At various times, NATO strategy has relied solely on conventional forces or on nuclear deterrence alone but the present strategy of flexible response depends on both nuclear deterrence and conventional forces. Although NATO forces are numerically inferior to the Warsaw Pact in both troops and equipment, flexible response is a viable strategy since NATO forces are capable of defending Central Europe. The talks on mutual and balanced force reductions will alter the force structures in Central Europe and, depending on the outcome of the talks, the strategy of flexible response may be affected. This study emphasizes the effects on flexible response of numerically equal reductions of troops and equipment by each alliance. Ultimately the size of reductions will determine the precise effect on flexible response; but any such reductions will lessen both nuclear deterrence and conventional capability. If reductions are large enough, conventional capability could be badly eroded and nuclear deterrence could be lost. Under these conditions, flexible response would be unworkable."

SYMMETRICAL FORCE REDUCTIONS VERSUS EUROPEAN COLLECTIVE SECURITY, by Henry M. V. Buntinx, in *NATO's Fifteen Nations,* v. 15, no. 5 (October-November 1970) 29-33.

"As long as Western Europe remains only a loose conglomerate, NATO must not be weakened. In Europe itself only the Soviet Union stands to win from a withdrawal of the USA and from an eventual autonomous but fragmented European balance. Such a Western Europe would soon fall a victim to the 'superior relation of forces of Communism', which means that Moscow would switch over to the underground techniques of subversion. This possibility is a real one, according to the missionary and charismatic impetus inherent in its para-religion. In short, the Communists want a formalistic all-embracing design scheme and the abolition of the alliances, whilst NATO opts for a gradual and pragmatic approach, stage by stage."

(LI)—UNITED STATES NATO STRATEGY

AFTER FORCE REDUCTION, by Lt. Col. Sarkis H. Kavookjian. Maxwell AFB, Ala., Air War College, 1974. 47 p. (Professional Study.)

"The American people, grown weary of United States involvement in world-wide commitments, are seeking to find a lower profile on the world political scene. Specifically, the economic, political, and military factors are exerting tremendous pressures on our commitments to NATO. It seems inevitable that these factors will force the United States into reducing its troops committed to the alliance. The strategy of 'forward defense,' 'dual-basing,' 'flexible response,' and 'mobility of forces,' has successfully deterred a communist invasion of Western Europe. Despite certain economic and political constraints, these concepts are valid today. The Nixon Doctrine has been established as the political and military guideline for conducting foreign policy and seeking to obtain national objectives. The Nixon Doctrine is credible and is supportable by the American people—it should become the new look in the strategy for the defense of Western Europe."

UNITED STATES TROOP LEVELS IN EUROPE; A BALANCE FORCE REDUCTION, by Kenneth Rush, in *Vital Speeches of the Day*, v. 39, no. 20 (1 August 1973) 631-635.

Delivered before the House Committee on Foreign Affairs, and the Sub-Committee on European Affairs, Washington, D.C., July 10, 1973. "We believe that a decision to make unilateral reductions in the number of American troops in Western Europe would be gravely contrary to the vital interests of the United States and its citizens. The friendship and cooperation of Western Europe is essential to the security, economic well-being and peace of mind of every American. Our defense is its defense and its security is essential to our own. That security today depends upon a convincing conventional and nuclear capability to resist pressure, to deter aggression and to defend Western Europe if deterrence fails. Today that dual capability exists, but it hinges upon the presence of substantial US forces in Europe. Our goal is to maintain our present security, but to do so at lower levels of tension and armament. The process of making the transition from security at the present level to security at a lower level will be difficult. But the negotiations to do so are already agreed between the Warsaw Pact and NATO. The substantive phase of the Mutual and Balanced Force Reduction negotiations opens on October 30. These extraordinarily important negotiations cannot succeed nor can they proceed if the United States undercuts them with unilateral troop reductions. Equally important, our efforts with our Allies for more equitable burdensharing trade and monetary arrangements are also underway. Programs to improve NATO's defense and to provide a more cost-conscious and efficient posture are also in train. Nor need we feel compelled by our budget or balance of payments to withdraw our troops from the area where they are most valuable to a distant base in the United States. The improvement in our overall balance of payments that is already beginning to show can be expected greatly to diminish this pressure in the months ahead. It is for these essential reasons that my colleagues and I believe that unilateral troop reductions in Western Europe would be contrary to the interests of the American people and that we ask your continued support for our Atlantic defense policy."

D. Strategic Arms Limitation Talks: East-West Positions on SALT I and II

1. *Miscellaneous Aspects*

ANNALS OF DIPLOMACY; SALT, by John Newhouse, in *New Yorker*, (5 May 1973) 44-50 plus.

"Though the United States and the Soviet Union have been engaged in the talks since November of 1969, and 'SALT' itself is by now among the world's best-known acronyms, the substance of the talks is available only to initiates—the bureaucrats and scientist who are professionally involved. And even many of them are confused; their thinking shifts and oscillates, because the analysis flowing from SALT mocks, if it doesn't overwhelm, tidy, clear-cut points of view. Politicians and editorialists tell us that SALT is the most fateful negotiation in human history, although they are hard pressed to explain exactly what is at issue and why. The arms-limitation agreements reached in Moscow last May—possibly the first in a series—drew a nearly unanimous congressional endorsement, and it is difficult to imagine a SALT agreement's being rejected, any more than the limited-test-ban treaty of 1963 or the nuclear-nonproliferation treaty of 1968 was rejected. Yet the concerned public and its elected representatives can gain much less insight into SALT than they could into these other agreements. SALT, then, is perverse; it enlists our curiosity yet discourages comprehension. Even so, thinking about SALT—understanding what is involved and what is happening—can be rewarding, less because of its self-evident importance than because it is probably the most fascinating episodic negotiation since 1815 and the Congress of Vienna. SALT is likely to go on indefinitely. Thus, even though progress may be slow, and the talks are likely to bog down occasionally, SALT may develop a cumulative impact on world politics comparable to that of the Congress of Vienna, whose achievement was to spare Europe any major bloodletting for a hundred years."

ARMING TO DISARM IN THE AGE OF DÉTENTE, in *Time*, v. 103, no. 6 (11 February 1974) 15-20 plus.

"Is the U.S. falling behind the Soviet Union militarily? Arsenals of experts are likely to be rolled out to argue both sides of the highly complex question. But there is no dispute about the fact that while the U.S. was fighting the expensive and inconclusive Viet Nam War, the Russians were spending lavishly to improve their stores of nuclear and conventional weapons. Their armed forces are now larger than those of the U.S. and, particularly in the case of the Soviet navy, often equipped with newer hardware. More important, the continuing Russian effort, together with the ceilings imposed on U.S. arms levels in the 1972 Strategic Arms Limitations Talks (SALT I) with Moscow, leads analysts to fear that in the mid-1980s the Soviets might finally overtake the U.S. . . . After two summits and SALT I, the nuclear balance is still, looking to the future, weighted to the Soviets' advantage. Schlesinger's task is to provide the muscle and tools to help Kissinger bring the balance back to center in further negotiations."

ARMS CONTROL NEGOTIATIONS: PROGRESS AND PROSPECTS, by Robin Ranger, in *Canadian Defence Quarterly*, v. 4, no. 3 (Winter 1974) 16-25.

1974—A Disappointing Year; Technical vs. Political Arms Control; SALT I to SALT II; MBFR; Undue Pessimism; The U.S. Allies; Divided Opinions; etc. "This survey of the three main areas of arms control negotiations, SALT II, MBFR and CCD, has shown that any agreements to be expected in the foreseeable future will be in the realm of political rather than technical arms control, formally codifying restraint on the political use of specified weapons rather than controlling their development and deployment. Does this mean that arms control is useless? On the contrary, it means that because agreements altering the political intentions, instead of the military capabilities, of the two super-powers are more easily achieved than technical restraint on their strategic competition, political arms control has become the chief means of stabilizing the superpower balance of deterrence."

ASSESSING THE MOSCOW SALT AGREEMENTS, by William R. Kintner and Robert L. Pfaltzgraff, Jr., in *Orbis*, v. 16, no. 2 (Summer 1972) 341-360.

"An ABM Treaty and an Interim Agreement on Offensive Missiles were signed by President Nixon and Secretary Brezhnev on May 26, 1972. Even though great powers have often negotiated and broken international agreements in response to their changing interests, these accords have been hailed, respectively by their supporters and opponents, as the beginning of a new era of peaceful coexistence between the superpowers, and as a mold which would lock the United States into permanent status as a second-rate power. Therefore, it is appropriate to inquire whether the agreements signed by the United States and the Soviet Union in Moscow contribute to international security and the security of the United States, or at least do not detract from existing security. Do they, in fact, restrict the proliferation of nuclear weapons? Do they lead directly to superpower détente or improve the prospects for further agreements between the United States and the Soviet Union? Do they facilitate the reduction of military spending in favor of domestic needs? This article analyzes the outcome of SALT Phase I and seeks tentative answers to such questions."

BAN ALL NUCLEAR TESTING, by William C. Foster, in *The Atlantic Community Quarterly*, v. 9, no. 2 (Summer 1971) 174-183.

"The former head of the Arms Control and Disarmament Agency outlines the intricacies of such negotiations as SALT—but makes a proposal for a possible breakthrough towards control of nuclear weapons."

BEYOND SALT ONE, by Herbert Scoville, Jr., in *Foreign Affairs*, v. 50, no. 3 (April 1972) 488–500.

"Although President Nixon's goal of achieving an initial agreement at the Strategic Arms Limitation Talks (SALT) before the end of 1971 failed to be realized, it still appears likely that at least some limitations will be negotiated by the time that he and Premier Kosygin meet in Moscow in May. After SALT recessed in Vienna the President reported in his state of the world message on February ninth a consensus is developing that there should be a treaty setting comprehensive limitations on anti-ballistic missiles (ABMs) and an interim agreement to freeze certain offensive arms . . . An initial agreement at SALT, even if limited in scope, can mark the beginning of a new era in the nuclear weapons age. Opportunities will be opened up not only for halting the upward march of the arms race, but also for redirecting it downward so that the risks of a nuclear conflagration are reduced and the economic burdens of weapons programs lightened. Many of the new measures proposed will not be arrived at easily. Strong pressures for new weapons programs as hedges against possible treaty violations will have to be resisted vigorously. Complacency after an initial agreement must not be allowed to slow the drive toward further limitations."

MIRV AND THE ARMS RACE: AN INTERPRETATION OF DEFENSE STRATEGY, by Ronald L. Tammen. New York, Praeger, 1973. 162.

"As the last opportunity to limit MIRV is reached in SALT II, the question arises: why was it originally developed? Tammen contradicts the standard view that MIRV was a response to the Soviet ABM as part of the action-reaction phenomenon, arguing . . . that MIRV was developed more in response to internal domestic pressures than to perceived enemy threats."

THE MOSCOW AGREEMENTS AND STRATEGIC ARMS LIMITATION, by Hedley Bull. Canberra, Australian National University Press, 1973. 50 p. (A publication of The Strategic and Defence Studies Centre, no. 15.)

"This paper presents an . . . analysis of the Agreements, which were signed in Moscow in 1972. Professor Bull seeks to estimate the value of the Agreements in relation to the objectives of arms control set out more than a decade ago in his . . . work 'The Control of the Arms Race,' and to assess their significance for the political and strategic relations among the major powers. His findings are based on research and conversations in America, Europe and Japan."

PRESIDENT NIXON AND DR. HENRY KISSINGER DISCUSS SALT AGREEMENTS, in *NATO Review*, v. 20, nos. 7–8 (July/August 1972) 5–12.

"In a special White House briefing for Members of Congress on 15 June, President Nixon said he was totally convinced that the treaty on the limitation of anti-ballistic missile systems, and the interim agreement on the limitation of certain offensive arms are 'in the interest of arms control and world peace'. Both the President's statement and the ensuing briefing by President Adviser Dr. Henry Kissinger, give valuable insights into a number of important aspects of these agreements, as well as the exacting negotiations which preceded them. Excerpts from these two statements are given below. In the Documentation Section of this issue will be found some interpretations of the accords which were drawn up by the two sides."

PROSPECTS FOR STRATEGIC ARMS LIMITATION, in *Survival*, v. 16, no. 2 (March/April 1974) 54–74.

Contents: MIRV Control Is Still Possible; Soviet Interests and MIRV Control; SALT II—A Soviet View; and Reducing the Overkill.

SALT; AN ANALYSIS AND A PROPOSAL, by Henry M. Jackson, in *Vital Speeches* of the Day, v. 40, no. 6 (1 January 1974) 169–172.

"A few weeks ago the Soviet Union proposed a draft treaty at the SALT talks in Geneva. This Soviet proposal, which is so one-sided as to be completely unacceptable to the United States, actually represents a step backwards in the search for a more stable strategic balance and a more peaceful world. With this unfortunate step in the wrong direction, the SALT talks have reached an impasse. I believe, Mr. President, that we ought to make a determined effort to end this impasse by moving from arms control proposals that serve the interests of one side only to a proposal for serious and far-reaching disarmament that would leave both sides in a position of strategic equality. To accomplish this objective I have formulated a specific proposal—one that would mean an immediate reduction in the strategic arsenals of both the

United States and the Soviet Union so that the combined intercontinental strategic forces of the two countries would be reduced by about one-third."

SALT AND MBFR: THE NEXT PHASE; REPORT OF A TRILATERAL CONFERENCE, in *Survival*, v. 17, no. 1 (January/February 1975) 14-24.

"From 25 to 29 March 1974 a meeting, sponsored by the International Institute for Strategic Studies (the host), the Japan Institute of International Affairs, and the Brookings Institution, convened at Dunford, England, brought together specialists from Europe, Japan, and the United States, to discuss major problems arising in the negotiations on strategic arms limitation and regional European force reductions. Those attending the meeting took part as individuals. The views expressed should not be attributed to the organizations with which they are associated or the organizations that helped finance the venture. The outcome of these two negotiations could have a significant impact on prospects for stability in inter-allied relations and levels of military expenditures, as well as in super-power relationships. Although strategic arms negotiations are conducted by the United States, their outcome has a direct bearing on the interests of Western Europe and Japan. Although negotiations for balanced force reductions in Europe are conducted by the NATO and Warsaw Pact countries, developments which affect prospects for peace and stability in Europe cannot fail, as has been shown in the past, to have some effect on Asia. In addition, collateral measures being considered in Europe might be applicable in the initial stages of negotiations in Korea should conventional arms control initiatives be undertaken by the two parts of Korea."

SALT AND THE BLUE-WATER STRATEGY, by Col. Clinton H. Winne, Jr., in *Air University Review*, v. 25, no. 6 (September-October 1974) 25-35.

"Over the past few years, there has been increasing discussion of a so-called 'Blue-Water Strategy.' . . . This article will examine one feature of the proposed strategy—moving our nuclear deterrent to sea—to determine how it is affected by the recently concluded Arms Limitation agreements."

SALT AND THE SOVIET MILITARY, by Raymond L. Garthoff, in *Problems of Communism*, v. 24, no. 1 (January-February 1975) 21-37.

"In November 1969 the USSR and the United States commenced formal talks on the limitation of strategic arms. These talks, commonly known as SALT, led in May 1972 to a treaty between the two powers restricting the deployment of antiballistic missile systems and to an interim agreement on the limitation of strategic offensive arms. During the subsequent phase of the negotiations, popularly called SALT II, the exchanges have focused on further restrictions on strategic offensive weapons systems, and in this connection General Secretary Brezhnev and President Ford reached agreement at Vladivostok in November 1974 on the basis for negotiating during 1975 a 10-year limitation agreement covering such offensive arms. The talks themselves have been private, and the diplomatic record remains closed. But the following article presents observations and reflections on one important aspect of SALT by a direct participant in the negotiations for more than three years, written from his own personal and informed perspective."

SALT FACETS, by Col. Martin J. Slominski, in *Military Review*, v. 54, no. 1 (January 1974) 82-88.

"The Summit Agreements signed by the United States and the USSR in May 1972 represent the beginning of a process that can lead to improvements in the world situation. A large number of agreements were signed. These include protection of the environment; emphasis on medical science and public health; cooperation in space, science, and technology; prevention of incidents at sea; establishment of a Commercial Commission; clarification of basic principles of relations between both countries; a Treaty on the Limitation of Antiballistic Missile Systems; and an Interim Agreement on Certain Measures With Respect to the Limitation of Strategic Offensive Arms. All represent political actions that prelude wider economic and cultural relations and profound effects on military activities. But the Treaty and Interim Agreement are of special interest to us. They are the result of six months of preliminary, extensive technical studies and two and one half years of negotiations. Because they are so important to the survival of the United States, the Treaty and Interim Agreement deserve the scrutiny asked of the Congress and of the Nation by President Nixon. It is our purpose to examine these two agreements from one viewpoint: as seen through the eyes of US and Soviet citizens."

(*)—SALT: IMPLICATIONS FOR ARMS CONTROL IN THE 1970s, ed. by William R. Kintner and Robert L. Pfaltzgraff, Jr. Pittsburgh, University of Pittsburgh Press, 1973. 447 p.

"These fourteen original essays and five reports on symposium discussions deal with many aspects of the complex problem of arms control. Authors and topics included Robert Pfaltzgraff on the rationale for superpower arms control; Thomas W. Wolfe on Soviet interests in SALT; J. I. Coffey on American interests in limitation of strategic armaments; Robert R. Bowie on the bargaining aspects of arms control; Robert A. Scalapino on the American-Soviet-Chinese triangle and implications for arms control; William R. Kintner on arms control for a five-power world; Geoffrey Kemp and Ian Smart on SALT and European nuclear forces; Wynfred Joshua on SALT and the Middle East; James E. Dougherty on SALT and the future of International politics. The editors provide a final paper on 'The Strategic Arms Limitation Agreements of 1972; Implications for International Security'."

SALT I, by Commander Roy L. Beavers, Jr., in *United States Naval Institute Proceedings*, v. 100, no. 855 (May 1974) 204–219.

The Interim Agreement on Offensive Strategic Arms; SALT I and America's Allies; Some Ideological Casualties; Naval Implications; Some Conclusions.

SALT I: A MILITARY EVALUATION, by Maj. G. A. Potter, in *Canadian Defence Quarterly*, v. 3, no. 1 (Summer 1973) 29–30 plus.

"The SALT I agreements open up no real prospect for major reductions in military spending. They limit the quantity of certain weapons, but restrict the quality of none. They provide incentives for both parties to continue, if not increase, major R & D programmes in respect to offensive weapon systems. The conclusion is thus inescapable that SALT I does not represent a real arms control agreement. It does not increase security, does not curb the arms race, and does little to promote international stability and peace. It has certainly failed to meet the U.S. objectives in the talks. What hope there is in something better must now repose in SALT II."

SALT: PROBLEMS AND PROSPECTS, ed. by Morton A. Kaplan. Morristown, General Learning Press, 1973. 251 p.

"... Kaplan and eight contributors discuss the general nature of arms control problems, factors influencing the negotiations and the political context of SALT. These discussions were originally presented as papers during the winter of 1970 and early spring of 1971 at the Arms Control and Foreign Policy Seminar held at the University of Chicago. Despite the fact that, except for Kaplan's, they were prepared before the SALT agreements of 1972, their basic contents generally has not become outdated or overtaken by events. On balance, they are relevant to understanding the current SALT negotiations by helping to clarify the underlying issues and broad concepts to be dealt with by the present and future negotiations ..."

SALT: THE MOSCOW AGREEMENTS AND BEYOND, ed. by Mason Willrich and John B. Rhinelander. New York, Free Press, 1974. 361 p.

"Book on the SALT I accords, in which ten recognized experts explore all facets of SALT: the policy-making process in Washington and Moscow; the perspectives on SALT I as viewed from Europe, China and Japan; the U.S. and U.S.S.R. strategic arsenals and the details of the agreements; and the task ahead in SALT II and beyond. Glossary, bibliography and appendix."

SALT II AND OFFENSIVE FORCE LEVELS, by Richard Burt, in *Orbis*, v. 18, no. 2 (Summer 1974) 465–481.

"One of the most vexing problems facing negotiators at the Strategic Arms Limitation Talks (SALT) is the existence of asymmetries in the U.S. and Soviet offensive strategic nuclear arsenals. A variety of factors—history, bureaucracy, strategy and technology—have caused the two powers to proceed at different rates of force modernization while, at the same time, placing differing emphasis on the various components of their strategic forces ... These asymmetries were dealt with at SALT I by agreeing to a temporary ceiling on offensive strategic missiles (the Interim Agreement) that generally ignored U.S.-Soviet differences in strategic force design and composition. The result is that the guidelines for SALT II agreed upon at the June 14–18, 1973 summit in Washington to (1) achieve permanent ceilings on offensive strategic forces, (2) control qualitative aspects of offensive weaponry, and (3) provide for the eventual reduction of forces, pose difficult challenges for negotiators at the second round of the talks—challenges that negotiators were unable to overcome during the June summit in Moscow . . . At SALT II, an agreement on mutual aggregate ceilings would entail an expansion of the Interim Agreement's 'freedom to mix' sanction, which permits, but does not require, the replacement of older ICBM's with modern SLBM's. A general aggregate ceiling would allow the substitution of forces in one category for those in another, restricted only by a comprehensive mutual ceiling placed on a selected index of offensive power. (Using the measure of launcher numbers, the Interim Agreement permits 'one-way' substitution; under an aggregate ceiling scheme, ICBM's SLBM's and bombers could be freely traded.) Thus, aggregate ceilings would seem to allow each side the opportunity to tailor its strategic inventory to its own technological capability and perceived strategic and geopolitical needs (including third-power threats), while creating an overall situation of offensive parity. In this light, it is worth examining the problem of reaching such an agreement."

SALT II—SOME PRINCIPLES, by Arthur G. B. Metcalf, in *Strategic Review*, v. 1, no. 2 (Summer 1973) 6-17.

"The author discusses the prospects and pitfalls of SALT II negotiations in the post-SALT I environment. His analysis of the realities of strategic arms limitation agreements points out certain guiding principles and suggests a break with past orthodoxies. A critical examination of what constitutes equity and balance in strategic terms is urged as essential to avoidance of irreversible miscalculation in the potentially determinative arena of strategic power."

SALT II: THE SEARCH FOR FOLLOW-ON AGREEMENT, by Joseph Kruzel, in *Orbis*, v. 17, no. 2 (Summer 1973) 334-363.

"During the first six months after SALT II convened in Geneva on November 21, 1972, the two sides devoted themselves largely to exploratory discussions. It became clear during these early talks that some framework was needed to guide the negotiations. Without such a framework, SALT II could easily be reduced to a forum for unproductive exchanges of propaganda. When Secretary Brezhnev visited the United States in June 1973, the two sides agreed that a statement of general principles could give new impetus to the stalled negotiations. Accordingly, the 'Basic Principles of Negotiations on the Further Limitation of Strategic Offensive Arms' were signed on June 21, 1973 with both leaders expressing the hope that these new guidelines would establish a framework making it possible to reach agreement sometime in 1974. The two delegations have since returned to Geneva, and presumably are hard at work on their appointed task of converting the Interim Agreement into a permanent treaty. What should we expect from their deliberations? What are the issues confronting the two sides in SALT II, and what are the prospects for negotiating mutually acceptable solutions to these issues?"

THE SAVOR OF SALT, by J. I. Coffey, in *Bulletin of the Atomic Scientists*, v. 29, no. 5 (May 1973) 9-15.

"The strategic arms limitations agreements should, as Mr. Nixon recommended, be considered on their merits, and the weapons programs recommended by the former Secretary of Defense should be considered on theirs. Attempts to link the two—either by arguing that if we do not proceed with new weapons we will be outclassed five years hence, or that failure to proceed will weaken our international position or our bargaining ability—are perhaps questionable. Moreover, there is little merit to exchanging a quantitative arms race for a qualitative one, especially if there are prospects of controlling both types of races through future negotiations."

A SCENARIO FOR EFFECTIVE SALT NEGOTIATIONS, by Francesco Calogero, in *Bulletin of the Atomic Scientists*, v. 29, no. 6 (June 1973) 16-22.

"'The very fact that (a SALT) agreement has been reached and a treaty signed . . . should be regarded as a major event, possibly signaling the opening of a new phase of history. Therefore now, if ever, is the time when the introduction of novel ideas might not be altogether futile.' One such novel idea which has aroused international interest is to introduce a procedure that would bring about disarmament without requiring any prior specific agreement on the nature and numbers of the weapons to be eliminated. The proposal was presented by Francesco Calogero, assistant professor of physics at the University of Rome, to the 22nd Pugwash Conference on Science and World Affairs at Oxford, England last fall. In this article, Professor Calogero explains in detail how it might work."

SOVIET SEA-BASED FORCES AND SALT, by Richard Burt, in *Survival*, v. 17, no. 1 (January/February 1975) 9-13.

"While the outline of a new Strategic Arms Limitation Talks (SALT) accord worked out at the summit in Vladivostok will supersede the limits on offensive missiles agreed to in the 1972 Interim Agreement (IA), the joint statement released at the talks says that 'relevant provisions' of the IA will be incorporated into the new agreement to be signed in 1975 . . . Because the full meaning of the IA for Soviet SLBM deployment remains to be understood by many in the West and because potential Soviet deployments could generate disagreement in working out the details of a new 10-year SALT package, it appears worthwhile to explore the implications of the IA for existing and future Soviet sea-based force design."

THE SOVIET UNION AND ARMS CONTROL, by Lawrence T. Caldwell, in *Current History*, v. 67, no. 398 (October 1974) 150-154 plus.

"SALT II and MFR agreements should not be sacrificed for elusive, if desirable, goals like the alteration of the political system of the Soviet Union. To accept that goal, perhaps even in terms of 'freer movement of peoples and ideas,' is to regress toward the cold war and toward an incalculably more dangerous world."

SOVIET VIOLATIONS OF THE SALT DEAL. HAVE WE BEEN HAD?, by Tad Szulc, in *New Republic*, (7 June 1975) 3 plus.

"The differences between the United States and the Soviet Union over the implementation of the 1972 nuclear strategic arms' limitation agreements (SALT) are deepening and new ones are emerging around the 'tentative' accord for a second step in SALT that President Ford and Chairman Brezhnev reached in Vladivostok last November. This state of affairs, throwing a pall on the future of détente unless the basic SALT problems are promptly resolved, 'has been generally concealed . . . because of its enormous political sensitivity. That so many of these problems result from ambiguities that the US has accepted in the SALT treaty and the accompanying protocols is also a reflection on the quality of Secretary of State Kissinger's diplomacy. Besides Kissinger, wittingly or not, may have misled the Congress in explaining the 1972 pact.' As far as is known Kissinger and Soviet Foreign Minister Gromyko made virtually no progress in breaking the SALT deadlock when they met in Vienna in May. The standing US-Soviet Consultative Commission on SALT, which was to have resumed its secret discussions in Geneva on June 2, postponed its session for at least a month, possibly pending Kissinger's and Gromyko's scheduled new meeting in July. If they fail to settle the current controversy, not only SALT but détente will be in considerable trouble."

STRATEGIC FORCES: ISSUES FOR THE MID-SEVENTIES, by Alton H. Quanbeck and Barry M. Blechman. Washington, Brookings Institution, 1973. 94 p.

"Despite the SALT I agreements, increased spending on strategic nuclear forces is currently projected. The authors examine the strategic doctrine, military requirements and political needs for such forces, and conclude that cost could be reduced without jeopardizing their retaliatory capability and without adverse international political consequences."

2. *Vladivostok Agreements (Ford-Brezhnev Summit)*

BEYOND VLADIVOSTOK: THE FEASIBILITY AND THE POLITICS OF ARMS REDUCTION, by Luther J. Carter, in *Science Magazine*, (11 April 1975) 16 plus.

"The Vladivostok agreement, which actually would allow the United States and the Soviet Union to add thousands of deliverable weapons to their strategic forces, is perceived by its defenders as one establishing ceilings from which eventual arms reductions could be made. No other claim can be made for it except the speculative one that, without the Vladivostok ceilings, the spiral of arms deployments would know no restraint whatever. Thus, the degree of enthusiasm that can be mustered for this agreement—which will not be ready for signing until the terms of verification have been successfully negotiated in Geneva—depends less on what it would provide than on the possibilities that lie beyond it . . . Two earlier articles (31 January and 21 February) discussed nuclear disarmament and arms control efforts from the early postwar period up through the first two phases of the Strategic Arms Limitation Talks (SALT), culminating in the Moscow agreements of 1972 and the Vladivostok agreement in principle of November 1974. A third article (14 March) reviewed the capabilities of the 'verification' technology for monitoring compliance with arms control accords."

THE "BREAKTHROUGH" ON SALT, in *Time*, v. 104, no. 24 (9 December 1974) 16 plus.

"'We have averted an arms race of unbelievable cost,' declared President Ford. 'A breakthrough,' summed up Secretary of State Henry Kissinger. 'It was something Nixon couldn't do in three years, but Ford did it in three months.' said Presidential Press Secretary Ron Nessen in early exuberance, before apologizing for 'a hasty and oversimplified remark.' Those comments on the preliminary SALT II agreement reached in Vladivostok between Ford and Soviet Party Boss Leonid Brezhnev apparently were the opening statements in another national debate over nuclear weapons. While there seemed to be a growing consensus that the impending deal is better than no agreement at all, it was nevertheless promptly criticized from two contrasting viewpoints: some critics felt that the U.S. was yielding too much, while various arms-control specialists complained that the pact would legitimize both nuclear deployment to date and the further development plans of the two superpowers over the next ten years."

FORD SPELLS OUT THE ARMS AGREEMENT WITH RUSSIA, in *U.S. News & World Report*, v. 77, no. 25 (16 December 1974) 82 plus.

"From the transcript of President Ford's nationally televised news conference on December 2, 1974. Will the new Soviet-American arms accord bring a cut in U.S. defense spending? Does it give the edge to Russia in nuclear weapons?"

HOW U.S. REALLY CAME OUT IN SUMMIT BARGAINING, in *U.S. News & World Report*, v. 77, no. 24 (9 December 1974) 27-28.

"U.S. goal was clear: a deal that would curb a costly arms race and keep Russia from gaining strategic superiority. Experts say the actual results of the Ford-Brezhnev accord could turn up some surprises in months ahead."

NEW PARAMETERS FOR OLD PERILS, by John L. Frisbee, in *Air Force Magazine*, v. 58, no. 1 (January 1975) 2.

"The 'agreement in principle' on strategic arms entered into by President Ford and General Secretary Brezhnev at Vladivostok in late November has been attacked by both doves and hawks. The former—as well as some nondoves such as Sen. Henry Jackson—charge that it sets too high a ceiling on strategic systems; the latter that too much has been given away to the Soviets, particularly in missile throw weight. To some extent we agree with both, but we also feel that the Vladivostok agreement provides an acceptable beginning point at which to revive the stalled SALT II negotiations, provided the necessary and permitted steps are taken to ensure strategic parity."

SETTING A BOUNDARY, in *Newsweek*, v. 84, no. 24 (9 December 1974) 45-46.

"The afterglow of the Vladivostok summit took some of the chill of the Ford White House last week. But the tentative strategic arms limitation agreement that Gerald Ford and Henry Kissinger brought back quickly began to draw as much criticism as acclaim . . . The agreement, nonetheless, underscored the commitment of the Soviet Union and the United States to détente at a time when rising tension in the Middle East was jangling nerves everywhere."

STRATEGIC ARMS LIMITATION (JOINT SOVIET-AMERICAN STATEMENT ON STRATEGIC ARMS LIMITATION, 24 NOVEMBER 1974), in *Survival*, v. 17, no. 1 (January/February 1975) 32-34.

"As a result of their working meeting on 23 and 24 November 1974, the President of the United States and the Secretary General of the Communist Party of the Soviet Union agreed to work for a new agreement on the limitation of strategic weapons. While incorporating 'the relevant provisions' of the Interim Agreement on the Limitation of Offensive Strategic Systems of May 1972, the new agreement's major aspect would be to put a new ceiling on the overall number of strategic delivery vehicles on both sides and a limitation on the number of land- and sea-based missiles that can be equipped with multiple independently targetable re-entry vehicles (MIRV). The overall ceiling for strategic delivery systems has been fixed at 2,400 for each side, and the permitted number of launchers equipped with MIRV at 1,320. This basic understanding will now have to be translated into a workable agreement, and negotiations started in January 1975. The text of the Statement is reprinted . . . [here] together with the relevant parts of the Press statement by the US Secretary of State on 24 November 1974."

THE STRATEGIC ARMS LIMITATION TALKS: A STOCKTAKING, by Kenneth Booth, in *World Survey*, no. 73 (January 1975) 18 p.

"Explains the complicated procedures and results of the Strategic Arms Limitation Talks, including the Ford-Brezhnev agreement in Vladivostok in November 1974."

THE VLADIVOSTOK ACCORD AND AMERICAN TECHNOLOGICAL OPTIONS, by Michael Nacht, in *Survival*, v. 17, no. 3 (May/June 1975).

"Vladivostok is viewed with discomfort precisely because of its failure to deal with the technological issues that are increasingly perceived to be the central focus of the arms competition: the number of MIRV-equipped warheads and their yield/accuracy characteristic, mobile launchers, strategic cruise missiles, and the relative counterforce capabilities of Soviet and American strategic forces. For it is where we are headed rather than where we are that is of greatest concern. It is the activity at the margin, therefore, that deserves our attention."

THE VLADIVOSTOK ACCORD AND SALT II, by Paul H. Nitze, in *The Review of Politics*, v. 37, no. 2 (April 1975) 147-160.

"After the summit meeting in Moscow in June 1974, Dr. Kissinger called for a national debate on the issue of strategic arms and arms control. No such debate has taken place. It has been overtaken by the more immediate issues of inflation, the liquidity of the international banking system, and the extent to which Arab oil profits can be reduced, offset or recycled. But these more immediate issues are, in turn, dependent on what happens in the Middle East with its triple problem of the unresolved Arab-Israeli conflict, the oil weapon, and Soviet ambitions to control the World's economic jugular, the Eastern Mediterranean, the Red Sea and the Persian Gulf. The ability of the United States favorably to influence the resolution of these issues depends upon the strength of its ties with other countries with similar interests and its economic and military potential. Thus, we are once more brought face to face with the interdependence of our economic and our national security policies."

VLADIVOSTOK ARMS RACE, by Doron Bar-Levov, in *Nation Magazine*, (12 April 1975) 15 plus.

"Despite the furor over the arms accord recently concluded between the United States and the Soviet Union, one essential point has been missed. Critics as well as supporters have been arguing about force levels and costs and whether 'we gave away too much to the Russians.' No one, however, seems to have asked the real question: does the United States need strategic arms limitation agreements at all? The answer appears to be no."

E. Conference on Security and Cooperation in Europe As Seen by East and West

AMERICA'S MOVE, by Benjamin S. Rosenthal, in *Foreign Affairs*, v. 51, no. 2 (January 1973) 380-391.

"A European Security Conference (ESC) will almost certainly take place in 1973. It will convene with active, if reluctant, American participation. This unfortunate reluctance is especially pronounced in Washington. The United States now has not only an opportunity but a responsibility to lead the Western nations in a search for a new system in Europe. In view of the inevitability of the conference, it would be especially short-sighted to forsake the dynamic and innovative role we could play. Unhappily, I see no signs, at least from a vantage point on Capitol Hill, that the United States will enter this decisive stage with any policy ideas which might wrest the initiative from the East. The Western impetus for a constructive conference comes almost entirely from some of our NATO allies, whose cautious enthusiasm is under a steady restraint from the Washington flagship of the Atlantic Alliance."

THE CONFERENCE ON SECURITY AND COOPERATION IN EUROPE: A SUCCESSFUL BEGINNING, by L. Vidyasova, in *International Affairs, Moscow*, no. 9 (1973) 11-17.

"The international détente has been gathering momentum and acquiring ever greater scope. The first week of July was marked by yet another international event of primary importance: the first stage of the Conference on Security and Cooperation in Europe took place in Helsinki. At the Finlandia Hall of Congresses, the Foreign Ministers of 33 European countries and the USA and

Canada held an exchange of news on various aspects on the question of consolidating peace and security in Europe as well as in respect to the further work of the Conference. The Ministers adopted the final recommendations including the agenda and assignments for the working bodies of the Conference, the rules of procedure and other regulations concerning the Conference. It was agreed that the second stage of the Conference, in the course of which working committees are to prepare the final documents, will open in Geneva on September 18. The third and culminating stage of the Conference which should adopt decisions will be of particular importance. The Soviet Union and other socialist countries are of the opinion that this stage should be held on a summit level, and are convinced that it could be set for the end of this year."

CONFERENCE ON SECURITY AND COOPERATION IN EUROPE AND NEGOTIATIONS ON MUTUAL AND BALANCED FORCE REDUCTIONS, by Joseph Harned and others, in *The Atlantic Community Quarterly*, v. 11, no. 1 (Spring 1973) 7-54.

"In this issue the Atlantic Community Quarterly presents in full a research paper—in three chapters—prepared by five authors in consultation with an Advisory Committee of the Atlantic Council of the United States. Here are examined in detail the issues for the Conference on Security and Cooperation in Europe: the issues in Mutual and Balanced Force Reductions: and conclusions that might be derived therefrom. Both the Conference on Security and Cooperation in Europe and Negotiations on Mutual and Balanced Force Reductions are expected to begin during the current year in a major shift in emphasis in East-West relations."

(*)—ERA OF NEGOTIATIONS: EUROPEAN SECURITY AND FORCE REDUCTIONS, by Wolfgang Klaiber and others. Lexington, Mass., Lexington Books, 1973. 192 p. (Published by the Atlantic Council of the United States.)

"Members of the Atlantic Council of the United States discuss the relationship between the two major multilateral conferences—the CSCE and the Conference on Mutual and Balanced Force Reductions (MBFR) and the issue of European security during a period of negotiation and détente. In analysing the complex issues involved, the authors consider such questions as whether the conferences will lead to a freezing of the present division of Europe or contribute to better relations between East and West; whether they will lead to better security or only a dangerous illusion of security; and whether they will contribute to more or to less cohesion within the two blocs themselves."

THE EUROPEAN SECURITY CONFERENCE, by Don Cook, in *Atlantic*, (October 1973) 6-12.

"Mr. Cook likens the Conference on Security and Cooperation in Europe, which thirty-five foreign ministers launched in July in Helsinki and are now continuing in Geneva, to the 1815 Congress of Vienna. It too is seeking agreement on a document which will confer multinational 'legitimacy' on the existing political structure of Europe and pledge everyone to its peaceful acceptance. Such 'legitimacy' is not the same as justice, and the Western powers are demanding in return from the communist governments of East Europe more humanitarian behavior toward their own people . . . Although such agreements would not be a panacea, Cook maintains, at least they would introduce a new element into communist behavior and provide some generally accepted standards to which the rest of Europe could hold the communist regimes accountable. This might be a satisfactory return for recognition of the legitimacy of communist control over East Europe and should bring a greater measure of freedom in those countries."

THE FOUNDATIONS OF PEACE AND SECURITY IN EUROPE, by N. Yuriev, in *International Affairs, Moscow*, no. 10 (1973) 15-22.

"The Soviet Union attaches fundamental importance to the success of the Conference on Security and Cooperation in Europe. It considers that the Conference must become an important landmark along Europe's path toward a new historical phase, a phase of development marked by peaceful coexistence and beneficial cooperation. This aim is promoted by the main political task of the Conference—to lay the foundations of enduring security and cooperation in Europe. The Conference agenda, approved at its first stage in Helsinki, makes it possible to raise key questions of safeguarding security on our continent . . . The Soviet draft outlines the basic principles agreed upon by all participants in the multilateral consultations in Helsinki: sovereign equality, refraining from the threat or use of force, inviolability of frontiers, territorial integrity, peaceful settlement of disputes, non-interference in internal affairs, respect for human rights and fundamental freedoms, equal rights and self-determination of peoples, cooperation among states and conscientious observance of commitments under international law."

NATO VIEW OF SECURITY CONFERENCES, by Joseph M. A. H. Luns, in *The Atlantic Community Quarterly*, v. 11, no. 1 (Spring 1973) 55-64.

"NATO Secretary General Luns discusses the proposed Conference on Security and Cooperation in Europe and negotiations regarding Mutual and Balanced Force Reductions. He expresses the firm hope that a period of rapprochement and stability in Europe is ahead of us, but warns that it may not be known for many years whether such hopes are justified."

THE SOVIET UNION AND THE EUROPEAN SECURITY CONFERENCE, by Mojmir Povolny, in *Orbis*, v. 18, no. 1 (Spring 1974) 201-230.

"Since the end of the Second World War the Soviet Union has pursued three main goals in her relations with Western Europe. First, from Potsdam through the fateful year of the Czechoslovak coup d'etat and the Berlin blockade, to Khrushchev's threats to conclude a separate peace treaty with East Germany and his renewed pressure on West Berlin, to the conclusion of the nonaggression pact with the Federal Republic of Germany and proposals for a European security conference, the Soviet regime has sought maintenance of the status quo and Western legitimization of its supremacy in Eastern Europe. Second, the Soviets have never accepted their exclusion from Western Europe. Their early support for, and manipulation of, the West European communist parties and fellow-traveling movements, their diplomacy in Paris, London, and eventually in Bonn, their fight against West European integration, and their promise of a bright and stable future for Western Europe should it open up to the East on their conditions, bear witness to an active Westpolitik in search of the extension of Soviet influence. Third, the Soviets have understood that the American presence in Western Europe has severely circumscribed their freedom of maneuver in pursuit of the first two goals. Consequently, their battle against the Marshall Plan and NATO, the 1954 proposal for a European system of collective security, the persistent pressure for an all-European conference, and all the lesser moves in between have aimed at excluding the United States from playing a role in Europe. In the second half of the 1960's all these threads were woven into the single scheme for a European security conference. The time appeared to be propitious for such a move . . . This essay will argue that in proposing a European security conference the Soviet Union has been promoting a substitute for a peace conference on Germany, the latter, in its traditional form, having been outdated by the course of postwar developments."

THE WARSAW PACT IN THE ERA OF NEGOTIATION, by David Holloway, in *Military Review*, v. 53, no. 7 (July 1973) 49-55.

"It is widely believed that a new stage in the politics of East-West relations has been ushered in by the Four-Power agreement on Berlin, the West German treaties with Poland and the Soviet Union, and the strategic arms limitation agreements. The Conference on European Security and Cooperation for which the Warsaw Pact powers have been pressing since the mid-1960s now seems certain to take place; and it is likely that talks will be held about the reduction of forces in Europe. Whatever procedural arrangements are devised for the Conference and the talks on force reductions, it is clear that a period of protracted and intricate negotiations is beginning in Europe which will place new demands on the Warsaw Pact."

WHO'S AFRAID OF A EUROPEAN SECURITY CONFERENCE?, by Lt. Col. Arthur E. Dewey, in *Military Review*, v. 53, no. 7 (July 1973) 5-16.

"With winds of détente blowing across Europe, there has developed a widely held impression that the proposal for a Conference on Security and Cooperation in Europe (CSCE) was an imaginative Soviet initiative which the West might profitably have thought of first. The 'imaginative initiative' idea appears to be a misconception, and this article will attempt to illustrate why. The article will also analyze several other issues which appear to be central to the CSCE proposal, and which have resulted in confusion and controversy throughout its 19-year history. These include: (1) the timing of such a conference, (2) the risks for the West in going to the conference table, (3) possible opportunities and benefits accruing to the United States and Western European countries through their participation, and (4) and attempt to cast the conference in a realistic perspective."

F. Can the Russians Be Trusted? (The subjects of verification and sincerity of Soviet intentions are covered in various documents cited in Chapters VI, VII, and VIII.)

CHAPTER VIII

*WARSAW TREATY ORGANIZATION: A POLITICO-MILITARY REVIEW AND FORECAST

(See also Appendixes)

A. Miscellaneous Aspects

COMMUNIST EASTERN EUROPE ANALYTICAL SURVEY OF LITERATURE, by Harry Moskowitz and Jack Roberts. Washington, Department of the Army, 1971. 367 p. (DA PAM 550-8.)

"... Provides abstracts of unclassified articles and books on trends and developments in communist East Europe, including its role in the international communist movement, regional problems, strengths and weaknesses of Warsaw Pact members, the invasion of Czechoslovakia, and the internal problems of the separate countries. It also provides descriptions of bibliographies, atlases, yearbooks, and encyclopedias, and includes numerous texts, charts, statistical tables, and maps contributed by several government agencies and research organizations." See also "USSR: Strategic Survey; A Bibliography, 1969 Edition, DA PAM 550-6."

EASTERN EUROPE; A GEOGRAPHY OF THE COMECON COUNTRIES, by Roy E. H. Mellor. New York, Columbia University Press, 1975. 358 p.

Physical Environment and Political Geography; The Demographic and Economic Framework; and Comecon and the National Economies. With illustrations and tables.

NATIONALISM IN EASTERN EUROPE. McLean, Va., Research Analysis Corp., January 1970. (RAC-R-89.)

"This study analyzes the scope and extent of nationalism in Eastern Europe and attempts to determine its impact both on the politics of continental Europe in general and the USSR in particular. US foreign policy implications are also appraised. One principal conclusion is that Eastern European nationalism represents a basic and dynamic political force. Its intensity is in inverse relation to the influence of an outside power (USSR). If colonial control is strong, nationalism weakens, but whenever imperial influences relax, nationalism reasserts itself. A distinction must be drawn between mere anti-Soviet prejudices by the subjugated nations of East Europe and their *true* nationalism, defined here as a long-term historical and ideological force shaping their destinies. Nationalism itself will continue to be relevant in the pro-Soviet countries of Bulgaria, East Germany, Hungary, and Poland, whereas the currently relatively independent countries (Albania, Yugoslavia, and Romania) will become even more independent. US policy for the 1970's will need new principles and guidelines. The slogans of the 1950's or the 1960's will not be sufficient. New cultural and commerical policies must be formulated for a region in which the US has no *direct* military or political interests."

WARSAW PACT: THE BROOD OF THE BEAR, by Lawrence Griswold, in *Sea Power*, (April 1975) 27-32.

"Throughout the Spring of 1975 the Warsaw Pact countries, led by the Russian Army, have conducted a series of military maneuvers designed to 'awe' the NATO Alliance and the Third World nations of Eurasia, Africa and Latin America. However, Mr. Griswold maintains, many sceptics believe the maneuvers were equally intended to impress upon the USSR's own satellite states that the Soviet Union, with the Warsaw Pact, is the greatest military power on earth. Despite Moscow's power, the necessity for such reassurance, he says, indicates the need for a show of force to keep Russia's occasionally rebellious 'slave states' in line. Reviewing the history of the often unstable and quarrelsome Balkan states, Griswold says it was relatively easy for the Soviet military to conquer them and install communist governments after the German surrender at Stalingrad. Similarly, although Western nations objected, the imposition of Soviet influence in the Baltic territories was not difficult. With the exception of occasional 'flare-ups,' no rebellion against communist authority was visible in the Baltic countries until 1969, when Russia initiated its 'rehabilitation of Stalin.' Widespread riots occurred in 1971 and 1972, the result of religious repression, lingering patriotism and inflation due to crop failures. While military action put down these disturbances, the Eastern Baltic remains a potential trouble spot in Soviet eyes. Similar disturbances in the Balkans since 1972 also make the Soviet Union uneasy . . . "

B. The Warsaw Pact: Its Evolution, Achievements, and Prospects (For Text of Warsaw Treaty Organization See Appendix MMM)

THE EASTERN ALLIANCE, by Ugo Mazza, in *Armies and Weapons*, v. 3, no. 12 (15 July-15 September 1974) 48-52.

"The Political Consultative Committee of the Warsaw Pact nations held a meeting in Warsaw last April which was attended by the Party Secretaries and the Prime Ministers of the various nations. Little is known of what happened at the meeting, but the long communique which was issued at the end, apart from mentioning the usual themes of brotherhood and co-operation, confirmed the need to proceed with both the Geneva conference on European security and co-operation and with the Vienna talks on a balanced reduction of forces. According to observers, the Warsaw Pact nations, like their NATO counterparts, are going through a period of 'fatigue,' which has perhaps been brought about by the improved relations between the two blocs and by the diminishing chances of an all-out nuclear war. After all, the situation which led to the creation of the two alliances has considerably altered over 20 years. The Warsaw Pact dates from 14 May 1955, and its was the Eastern Bloc's reply to NATO—as well as being an answer to the entry, and thus the rearmament, of Federal Germany in the Atlantic Alliance."

THE EVOLUTION OF THE WARSAW PACT, by Aurel Brown, in *Canadian Defence Quarterly*, v. 3, no. 3 (Winter 1973/74) 27-36.

Why the Treaty?; Right of Intervention; Overall Structure of the Warsaw Pact; The Organization of the Warsaw Pact High Command; The Place of the Warsaw Pact High Command in the Soviet Defence Ministry; Political Evolution; and Bibliography.

(LI)—THE FUTURE EFFECT OF NATIONALISM ON THE WARSAW PACT: A RUMANIAN CASE STUDY, by Maj. Robert P. Caputo. Maxwell AFB, Ala., Air Command and Staff College, 1973. 113 p. (Research Study.)

"The Rumanian struggle for independent, national Communism since 1945 has irrevocably affected the relationships which have existed between the Soviet Union and the East European Bloc. This study traces the development of both Rumanian-style Communism and the Warsaw Pact to their respective current stages, superimposes the one upon the other, and, finally, injects general East European nationalism. An evaluation of this complex interaction leads to the conclusion that the Warsaw Pact has outlived its usefulness; that the Soviets are becoming increasingly more cognizant of this fact; and that closer East-West European ties will be the inevitable result."

THE FUTURE OF THE WARSAW PACT, by John MacCracken, in *NATO Review*, v. 19, nos. 5-6 (May/June 1971) 11-13.

"NATO celebrated its twentieth birthday two years ago. For the Warsaw Pact, the twentieth anniversary lies four years ahead. In each case, the twenty-year mark has had or will have a certain signifiance, which this article seeks to explore."

(LI)—THE WARSAW PACT—A TWO-EDGED SWORD, by Maj. James B. Fackenthall. Maxwell AFB, Ala., Air Command and Staff College, 1970. 162 p. (Research Study no. 0458-70.)

"This thesis analyzes the evolution of the Warsaw Pact from: its beginning on 14 May 1955 to the present. The background of the area is examined and the reasons for the pact, both expressed and implied, are analyzed. The early crises, Poland and Hungary, are discussed, followed by the early development of the organization, and then a detailed description of the 1968 Czechoslovakian invasion. The results of this action and the changes that have appeared in the pact are then explored. The study then looks at the United States' future policy alternatives in its foreign policy relationships with the pact countries and with its West European neighbors. The author concludes that the United States must be closely attuned to the times in our policy with Europe. The current national desire for less foreign involvement and the intense nationalism in Europe are factors that must be considered. Our policy should be to withdraw only that portion of our troops that still permits us to function as a full NATO partner. In the near future we should encourage, inspire, and teach our European friends how to live and work together. With this policy we may someday have a strong, viable partner and ally in the United States of Europe."

THE WARSAW PACT TODAY, by Malcolm Mackintosh, in *Survival*, v. 16, no. 3 (May/June 1974) 122–126.

In this review of the Warsaw Pact today the author discusses: The Budapest Reforms of 1969; The Warsaw Pact Today; The Future of the Warsaw Pact.

(LI)—THE WARSAW TREATY ORGANIZATION: AN APPRAISAL, by Lt. Col. Donald L. Burt. Maxwell AFB, Ala., Air War College, 1971. 30 p. (Professional Study no. 4087.)

"On May 14, 1955 the Warsaw Treaty was signed by the Soviet Union and seven Eastern European nations as a multilateral military alliance. In early years it was viewed as a continuation of prior arrangements within the Soviet sphere of influence and as a vehicle providing santion for continued Soviet Troop presence in the number states. Initially a political and propaganda answer to the admission of West Germany into NATO, the organization has now changed in character and potential. Military forces have been modernized both qualitatively and quantitatively and the satellite states have been given a greater role in military and political affairs. This has caused NATO to re-appraise the threat posed and to realign NATO strategy accordingly. Several periods of Soviet promotion of relaxation of tension notwithstanding, the Warsaw Treaty Organization remains a Soviet controlled military giant with extensive capability to conduct immediate, unwarned, major operations."

C. Warsaw Pact and USSR's Policy

BEHIND THE IRON CURTAIN, by Aaron D. Thrush, in *Air Force Magazine*, (September 1970) 116–120.

"Since WWII, Soviet political and military strategies have consistently pursued the Marxist-Leninist ideological objective—the world-wide advance of communism—tempered by the preservation of Soviet security. Other factors, however, such as capabilities, opportunities, personalities, internal group interests, and national pride, have also influenced to formulation of these interwoven strategies. Stalin, after WW II, attempted to expand Soviet influence and hegemony wherever prospects seemed favorable, but cautiously retreated from situations that might escalate into nuclear confrontation with America . . . After Stalin's death, Soviet strategists changed the emphasis from economics to armed conflict itself, permitting discussion of nuclear weapons and the decisiveness of an initial nuclear campaign. This, in turn, led to a growing belief that the USSR might not have to fight a major nuclear war unless it chose to do so. Recognizing the importance of nuclear weapons, Khrushchev, in 1956, proclaimed that war was no longer inevitable and that 'peaceful coexistence' might continue until communism finally triumphed . . . In the latter half of the '60s, Khrushchev's successors reduced cutbacks in general purpose forces and began modernizing the Army, Navy and Air Force, combining the 'balanced forces' and nuclear strategies. Such a combination lends itself to support of wars of national liberation while answering the Soviet expectation that, in a general war, the final victory will depend on the use of large-scale frontal ground defenses in the annihilation of the enemy forces and the occupation of the enemy homeland. Furthermore, current Soviet leaders have shown little tendency to shed the Marxist-Leninist ideological objective of furthering world communism."

ROLE OF THE WARSAW PACT IN SOVIET POLICY, by Thomas W. Wolfe. Santa Monica, Calif., Rand Corp., 1973. 19 p. (P04973.)

"Explores prospects for major changes in Soviet policy on the Warsaw Pact. The Pact enables the Soviets to impose their will on Eastern Europe in the name of 'proletarian internationalism' and 'fraternal solidarity.' It also provides bases for 25 to 30 Soviet divisions, tactical air, and missiles, plus joint force exercises and equipment standardization."

D. Warsaw Pact Countries After Czechoslovakia

(LI)—LOOKING AHEAD AT THE WARSAW TREATY ORGANIZATION, by Maj. Franklin D. Johnson. Maxwell AFB, Ala., Air Command

and Staff College, 1973. 62 p. (Research Study.)

"This thesis examines nationalism in Eastern Europe along with the creation and organization of the Warsaw Treaty Organization. It also looks into various changes that have occurred over the years. The study then continues on subsequent to the Czechoslovakian invasion. Results of the Doctrine of Limited Sovereignty are also shown. The remainder of the study looks into what might be expected in the coming years as well as some conclusions drawn by the author."

(*)—THE PEOPLE'S DEMOCRACIES AFTER PRAGUE: SOVIET HEGEMONY, NATIONALISM, REGIONAL INTEGRATION? ed. by Jezy Lukaszewski. Bruges, Belgium, De Tempel, for the College of Europe, 1970. 330 p.

"The papers in this volume were delivered in March 1969 at a symposium organized by the Commission of the European Communities and the Belgian Ministry of National Education and Culture. The contributors and their topics include Michel Tatu on the invasion of Czechoslovakia and the détente in Europe; Heinz Kuby on Eastern Europe in a bipolar world; John Pinder, John M. Montias and Vladislav Pavlat on COMECON and obstacles to the economic integration of Eastern Europe; Ghita Ionescu and Eugen Lemberg on East European nationalism; Werner J. Feld on the utility of the EEC experience for Eastern Europe; and Zbigniew Brzezinski on prospects for the Soviet bloc after Prague."

TRENDS IN WARSAW PACT MILITARY DEVELOPMENTS, in *NATO Review*, v. 21, no. 4 (1973) 8-11.

"Current military trends can best be determined by reviewing developments in recent years. This summer marks the fifth anniversary of the Soviet military invasion of her Czechoslovak ally. That event was a turning point in the development of the Warsaw Pact, both politically and militarily . . . Having reviewed the significant and important growth of the Warsaw Pact armed forces during the last five years, both in a quantitative and qualitative sense, an effort should now be made to explain this growth. What reasons can be offered for expanding still further the already formidable military machine of the Soviet Union and her Warsaw Pact partners?"

(LI)—TWO YEARS LATER—AN EXAMINATION OF THE WARSAW PACT COUNTRIES AFTER CZECHOSLOVAKIA, by Maj. Thomas N. Jones. Maxwell AFB, Ala., Air Command and Staff College, 1971. 60 p. (Research Study no. 1050-71.)

"This thesis examines the effect of the Czechoslovakian invasion of August 1968, on the six East European members of the Warsaw Treaty Organization. Reasons for the creation of the Treaty and the Russian advantages, both military and political, are presented. The events leading up to the invasion and the invasion itself are described, followed by an examination of the aftermath and effect on Czechoslovakia as well as a country-by-country analysis of each remaining satellite. The study concludes that, while liberalization has had quite an effect in a few countries, their necessary dependence on the Russians for economic support will force them to stand behind their commitments."

E. Warsaw Pact, Détente, and European Security

EAST EUROPEAN PERSPECTIVES ON EUROPEAN SECURITY AND COOPERATION, ed. by Robert R. King and Robert W. Dean. New York, Praeger Publishers, 1974. 254 p.

Soviet Policy in Eastern Europe and the Impact of Détente; European Cooperation and Ideological Conflict; Economic Impulses Toward Détente; The Military Dimension; East Germany—The Special Case; Foreign Policy Perspectives and European Security—Poland and Czechoslovakia; Hungary and European Security—Hunting with the Hounds; Rumania—The Difficulty of Maintaining an Autonomous Foreign Policy; Yugoslavia—Ideological Conformity and Political-Military Nonalignment; European Security and the Problem of Balkan Security.

SOVIET AND EAST EUROPEAN FORECASTS OF EUROPEAN SECURITY: PAPERS FROM THE 1972 VARNA CONFERENCE, ed. by Lilita Dzirkals and A. Ross Johnson. Santa Monica, Rand, June 1973. 51 p. (Report R-1272-PR.)

". . . This report is a collection of summaries of Soviet and East European papers on prospective European security arrangements, prepared for the October 1972 Varna Conference of European institutes of international affairs. These papers provide a . . . formulation of public Warsaw Pact and Yugoslav views on present and future military, political, and economic aspects of European security . . ."

THE WARSAW PACT AND EUROPEAN SECURITY AND COOPERATION, by Radovan Vukadinović, in *Review of International Affairs*, v. 25, no. 579 (20 May 1974) 23-25.

"The recent session of the Consultative Political Committee of the Warsaw Pact, which was attended by top party and government officials of seven East European countries, aroused lively interest, because of its timing as well as because of its new decisions . . . As they have already done in many previous declarations, the members of the Warsaw Treaty laid stress on the principles which they consider essential for achieving new international relationships free of tensions, in which states with different socio-political and economic systems can not only exist side by side but also work together successfully . . . After assessing European trends, which were analyzed primarily in the light of the results of Helsinki, Vienna and Geneva, the participants strongly advised that the processes of political détente should be linked with the militarily easing of tensions."

F. Warsaw Pact Armed Forces

1. *Strength and Capabilities*

WARSAW PACT MILITARY POWER, in *NATO Review*, v. 20, nos. 7-8 (July/August 1972) 13-16.

"Throughout this review of the current state of Soviet and Warsaw Pact military strength and capabilities, the obvious question is raised repeatedly: where are they going, and how far? Soviet long-range goals are not known to have changed. How does their military posture support these goals? Is there consistency between the continuing build-up of military power and the concept of 'peaceful coexistence'?"

WARSAW PACT MILITARY STATUS, in *NATO Review*, v. 22, no. 4 (August 1974) 21-22.

"At their meeting in Brussels on 14 June 1974, the NATO Ministers of Defence were given a report on the status of the Warsaw Pact Military strength and capabilities. The main points of the report are given below."

2. *Weapons and Equipment*

AIR FORCES OF THE WORLD—PART 3: SOVIET UNION AND THE WARSAW PACT NATIONS, in *Interavia*, v. 28, no 11 (November 1973) 1232-33.

A continuation of the guide to what air forces fly what aircraft.

DETAILS OF TANKS IN SERVICE IN NATO AND THE WARSAW PACT, in *NATO's Fifteen Nations*, v. 20, no. 1 (February-March 1975) 47-56.

JANE'S ALL THE WORLD'S AIRCRAFT 1974-75, ed. by John W. R. Taylor. London, Jane's Yearbooks, 1974. 830 p.

Provides information on aircraft of most nations of the world, including, among many others the NATO nations as well as the Warsaw Pact Nations. Some information included on air-launched missiles, spaceflight and research rockets, and satellites and spacecraft launched during 1973.

JANE'S FIGHTING SHIPS 1974-75, ed. by Capt. John E. Moore. New York, Jane's Yearbooks, 1974. 670 p.

Provides information on fighting ships of most nations of the world, including among many others, the NATO nations as well as the Warsaw Pact nations.

THE OBSERVER'S SOVIET AIRCRAFT DIRECTORY, comp. by William Green and Gordon Swanborough. London, Frederick Warne & Co. Ltd., 1975. 255 p.

"Provides for the first time a concise yet comprehensive reference to Soviet aircraft development over the past quarter-century. It details the various Soviet systems of designating aircraft and lists the 120-plus reporting names assigned over the past 20 years by the Air Standards Coordinating Committee to Soviet aircraft for use by NATO countries; it illustrates and describes many of the aircraft which competed unsuccessfully with those ordered into production and accordingly assigned western reporting names; it provides detailed information on all aircraft types, both military and civil, known to be currently in service in the Soviet Union, and it includes appendices on the organisation and current status of the Soviet Air Forces and the Soviet national airlines."

SURFACE TO SURFACE ARTILLERY, by John Marriott, in *NATO's Fifteen Nations*, v. 19, no. 6 (December 1974-January 1975) 68-73 plus.

"The object of this article is to discuss the various guns and rockets used in the surface-to-surface role in NATO and the Warsaw Pact, together with the methods of using them. The article is divided into two parts: weapons used on land and weapons used at sea. Guided missiles are not covered, since they form a subject all of their own."

3. *Military Exercises*

WARSAW PACT EXERCISE SHIELD-72, by Graham H. Turbiville, in *Military Review*, v. 53, no. 7 (July 1973) 17-24.

"Shield-72, as with most Pact exercises, was conducted for both political and military reasons. Considering the 1968 events in Czechoslovakia, it is tempting for Western observers to stress the political aspects of the exercise, in which Czechoslovakia was again recognized as a loyal member of the Warsaw Pact alliance, ready to honor its commitment in carrying out the 'unified aims of Socialism.' However, Shield-72 was, first of all, a military exercise conducted by the combined Pact armies to demonstrate their combat readiness and to test contingency plans for the conduct of theater operations. The exercise activity encompassed virtually all types of action expected by Warsaw Pact planners to be encountered in combat operations in Central Europe to include airborne and heliborne operations, river crossings, combined arms offensive operations and ground support/attack missions by tactical aircraft."

G. USSR: New Dimensions in Strategy and Expansion of Military Might (See also Appendix MMM)

1. *Miscellaneous Aspects*

THE COMMUNIST OBJECTIVE, by Foy D. Kohler, in *Ordnance*, (September-October 1971) 118-120.

"Ambassador Kohler traces Soviet ideology from Lenin to the present, maintaining it has undergone no basic change . . . Soviet leaders are also imbued with the traditional Russian attitudes towards vulnerability and the relativity of power: you are stronger if your opponent is weaker (one reason they want the US out of European bases). Despite the great need for capital investment for their underdeveloped lands, the Soviets try to rival us in their military and space efforts. Although their GNP is less than half of ours, they spend 13% of it on military expenditures while we spend 8.7% on ours. One reason for this is the great shock they received when they discovered during the Cuban crisis that bluff is not certain to work in international relations. Kohler relates that in December 1966, when he discussed with Ambassador Dobrynin the possibility of avoiding a new arms spiral with ABMs—which led to the start of the SALT—Dobrynin replied: 'What do you want to do, freeze us into a position of inferiority?' Kohler does not believe that the Soviets' program of the past two years to build up their ICBM level will continue; they had to have as many as possible to continue the SALT with a feeling of equality.

However, he believes they will continue their investment in their naval program, especially submarines, after which they will probably build a bomber force of considerable size, since they are very impressed with our Strategic Air Force."

CONSTRAINTS ON EUROPEAN SECURITY: THE SOVIET FACTOR. McLean, Va., Research Analysis Corp., May 1970. (RAC-R-106.)

"This study examines the Soviet Union's historic and current view of Europe's role in Soviet national security; the postwar Soviet attitude toward NATO, the US, and West Germany; and the postwar Soviet military strategy and posture as determinants shaping the Soviet attitude toward European security arrangements. In the context of the need to take these determinants into account in developing any mutually meaningful arrangements, the study addresses the strategic and political asymmetries between the US and the Soviet role and presence in Europe. It also examines 'the debate' within Soviet politico-military circles in relation to possible fundamental changes in Soviet views and policy toward Europe. Finally, the study addresses the implications of the Soviet attitude and policy toward Europe to date, of the current Soviet military posture and strategy, and of the possible changes in future Soviet policy for prospects of a genuine European security arrangement and US policy in Europe in general and its military presence in particular."

GEOGRAPHY AND SOVIET STRATEGIC THINKING, by Raymond Barrett, in *Military Review*, (January 1970) 17-25.

"Defensive attitudes dominate Soviet military thinking and strategic planning because of the USSR's geographic vulnerability. Long, difficult borders allow the possibility of a land attack from Germany, China, and Japan. In order to protect itself, the USSR established subservient regimes in East Europe. Its domination of East Europe and the protection of its Asian frontiers are guaranteed by large conventional forces. The Warsaw Pact is used to mobilize East European troops while insuring that they serve Russian interests. In addition, the USSR has deployed an ABM system to protect itself against China and other neighboring countries. As a result, the US may be unable to get Soviet agreement to limit ABM constuction. It will also be difficult to achieve agreement on the reduction of conventional forces since the USSR, in view of its geographic situation, may find that such a reduction endangers its strategic posture. Mutual reduction of forces depends largely on the Soviet assessment of the viability of its East European bulwark. However, the invasion of Czechoslovakia and Soviet sensitivity to any change in East Europe indicate that the USSR does not find the situation conducive to a reduction in forces. Soviet control of East Europe and Germany is eroding at a time when the Chinese threat is increasing. As its position deteriorates, the USSR will become increasingly sensitive to potential threats. The USSR may find it necessary to give up opportunities for détente with the US in order to deal with the growing threat to its territorial integrity. The US must follow a careful policy that will encourage gradual changes without simultaneously arousing Soviet sensitivities that can lead to explosive reactions."

THE GLOBAL STRATEGIC PERSPECTIVE FROM MOSCOW, by T. W. Wolfe. Santa Monica, Calif., Rand Corp., March 1973. 17 p. (P–4978.)

"An appraisal of the foreign policy and strategic considerations that help shape the USSR's posture in the seventies and its strategic relationship with the U.S. in the SALT negotiations. The international setting of two rival superpowers in a nuclear age has been replaced by unclarified conditions of global competition and adjustment. The Soviets' recourse to détente and intricate negotiations reflects their intent to take advantage of new opportunities, while consolidating old Soviet positions and easing domestic difficulties. One major consideration is who came out best in the SALT I negotiations. Did the U.S. allay the Soviets' fears of Safeguard, while giving them headroom in ICBMs and SLBMs to develop an even greater threat to the survivability of U.S. forces? Another question is whether, despite the ABM Treaty, the Soviets have fully embraced the American concept of mutual assured destruction. (Prepared for presentation at the National Defence College, Kingston, Ontario, April 3, 1973.)."

THE PEACETIME STRATEGY OF THE SOVIET UNION. London, Institute for the Study of Conflict, 1973. 83 p.

"The basic assumption of this study is that Western societies are vulnerable to Soviet subversion, espionage, and exploitation in a period of détente. It describes the Soviet government as autocratic, revolutionary, using 'peaceful coexistence' for ideological ends, obsessed with security, and having an intricate espionage machinery. The USSR's objectives are to prevail in its rivalry with China, obtain Western technology and a diminution of the arms race, legitimize and consolidate its hold on East Europe, and extend its influence over West Europe. Its methods in accomplishing these objectives are subversion and penetration, encouragement of divisions in the West, and tying the West European economy to the Soviet Union . . ."

SOVIET MILITARY CAPABILITIES IN EUROPE, by John Erickson, in *RUSI*, v. 120, no. 1 (March 1975).

"Recent improvements within Soviet (and non-Soviet Warsaw Pact) forces in the European theatre amount to more than mere tinkering with organisation and weapons. Soviet doctrine, as ever, continues to emphasise the rapid seizure of the initiative from the 'defensive' and high speed penetration into the whole depth of the theatre: while this does imply a 'short war in a nuclear environment', one of the noticeable features over the past year or so has been increased Soviet interest in the possibility of substantial non-nuclear operations even in the initial stage of a major engagement, for which reason the 'attack norms' of a nuclear blitzkrieg have been scaled down to meet the conditions of a conventional phase... Current instruction in the Frunze Academy, in which the first part of the course analyses NATO's capabilities in great detail, followed by the means getting 'in and under' and to great depth with the maximum speed—thus enjoining a Soviet interest in keeping the nuclear threshold quite high. In addition, 'received doctrine' (if I may put it that way) tends to emphasise the need to insure—and that at a high level—against purely local collisions escalating rapidly (a contingency which applies to both halves of Europe and which is perhaps especially relevant within the confines of eastern Europe itself)."

THE SOVIET MILITARY, SOVIET POLICY, AND SOVIET POLITICS, by John Erickson in *Strategic Review* (Fall 1973), 23-36.

"Two recent developments in Soviet military affairs—the new MIRV capability and the unprecedented elevation of Marshal Grechko to the Politburo—spurred Prof. Erickson's analysis of the Soviet military, its perceptions, requirements and constraints. Instead of fearing that 'the Russians are coming,' he believes that they may already have arrived, in the sense that they have achieved certain strategic goals. The Soviet emphasis on military strength does not conflict with its policy of détente, says Erickson, for the Soviets see a rough strategic parity with the US as a prerequisite of détente. Erickson discusses the implications of the increased Soviet military 'presence,' noting that the Soviets view both military strength and détente as essential ingredients to guarantee their security. They define détente, he says, simply as a means of gaining time until they attain military superiority over the US; their military policy is motivated by a desire to retain their world-wide superpower status and to reap the benefits of such status. Another aspect of their military policy is to build the kind of force which will enable them to survive a nuclear war, should deterrence fail; thus, they have a spread of forces designed to cope with both war-waging and war-avoiding. To meet this dual 'job,' they have concentrated on building the largest possible standing force, both strategic and tactical, equipped with the most modern weapon systems. As a result, there has been a constant improvement in the quality of the various components of the entire military system. Regarding the 'strategic balance,' Erickson observes that the Soviets lead in both delivery vehicles and megatons, while they are narrowing the US lead in MIRVs. He characterizes Soviet military strategy and capabilities as having an offensive bias but not truly designed for a first-strike. The buildup reflects the Soviet effort to reinforce its scientific-technological elements and to intensify its R&D programs. At the same time, says Erickson, the Soviets have increased their ground forces in both Europe and Asia, not sacrificing the European front because of the build-up on the Chinese border. The Soviet military command is also undergoing change; in Erickson's view, however, the promotion of Grechko to the politburo reflects Brezhnev's move to secure his own position on détente rather than an indication of vastly greater military influence. Throughout the military command, younger men are replacing the older WW II veterans, with the emphasis on technical training and expertise; the once top-heavy officer system may be shifting to a more balanced one . . ."

THE SOVIET THREAT TO EUROPE, by P. H. Vigor and C. N. Donnelly, in *RUSI*, v. 120, no. 1 (March 1975).

"Any discussion under this general heading must begin by enquiring whether the chief reason for the stationing of large Soviet forces in Central Europe and the creation by the Soviet Union of the Warsaw Pact armies is essentially offensive or defensive. On the one hand it can be argued very persuasively that the whole history of Russia, from the 10th century to the present day, is studded with instances of large-scale invasions of the Russian homeland, some with considerable success; one indeed was so successful that it allowed its perpetrators to conquer Russia completely and rule it for a couple of centuries. Following this line of reasoning, the Russians have every reason to be concerned with the defence of their homeland, and to conclude that their foreign and military policy today is essentially defensive. On the other it can be argued equally well that during this same period, Russia has continually expanded; that one of the major consequences of the seizure of power by the Bolsheviks in 1917 was the intensification of that expansionism by a revolutionary philosophy which aimed to conquer the globe; one which still, 57 years later, confidently looks forward to Communist regimes being installed in all the countries of the world in the not too distant future. From this line of reasoning we might conclude that Soviet foreign and military policy is essentially offensive. Luckily, our present purpose does not require us to decide which of these two answers is correct. It is sufficient to realise that, whether a war between East and West in Europe were to be born of an offensive or a defensive Soviet politico-military policy, or was merely the unhappy offspring of an East-West misunderstanding, the result would be that the Warsaw Pact forces would immediately embark on the offensive and aim to defeat the NATO forces on the field of battle in a short, sharp, decisive campaign. If any should doubt this, they have only to look at Soviet equipment and the reports of Soviet exercises to see that such a war is indeed the only war that the Pact forces are equipped and trained to fight, in addition to Soviet insistence that this is so, which is expressed in their military books and journals. If it is true that current Soviet military doctrine preaches the necessity of fighting a short war, as being the kind of war that the Russians are most likely to win in the context of hostilities in Europe, then the significance of the northern and the southern flanks of NATO becomes of secondary importance in the context of our presentation."

2. *Soviet Naval Buildup: The Growing Challenge in the Strategic Areas of the World*

THE ADRIATIC: SOVIET SEAWAY SOMEDAY?, by Eugene P. Sullivan, in *US Naval Institute Proceedings*, (August 1972) 27-31.

"Maintains that the increase of Soviet naval activity in the Mediterranean has seriously challenged the traditional role of the US Sixth Fleet as protector of NATO's southern flank. Although this situation has prompted some response from NATO, there is a possibility that the situation will deteriorate within the near future because of developments on the Balkan peninsula. According to Sullivan, the greatest weakness of Soviet naval forces in the Mediterranean has been the lack of permanent bases from which to operate. The Soviets have been forced to use permanent bases in the Black Sea or the distant Baltic and Arctic Seas. In time of peace this situation weakens the deterrent effect of the presence of Soviet fleet units, and during a time of war the Soviet Navy would be at a serious disadvantage. As a result, attainment of a direct and unimpeded access to the Mediterranean has been one of the most constant themes of Russian foreign policy. At one time the possibility existed that direct access to the Adriatic could be obtained through the incorporation of Yugoslavia and Albania into the Soviet satellite empire. However, this possibility collapsed when Tito broke with the Soviet Union and led Yugoslavia to national communism. In 1961, Albania also broke with the USSR and has since been allied with China. So far, the Soviet Union has refrained from taking such a serious step as the invasion of these states. Yet, the doctrinal basis for such re-establishment of Soviet power has already been expressed in the Brezhnev Doctrine. This states that one socialist state has a right and an obligation to come to the aid of another when the existence of socialist rule is threatened by hostile forces. Various steps have been taken to provide for the transition of power following Tito's death or retirement, but the success of these measures is still in doubt. Sullivan concludes that the collapse of Yugoslavia will pose new problems for the US in the near future and that the US and its allies may soon have to decide how far they are prepared to go in preserving the barrier between the Russians and the Mediterranean."

BEARS IN THE MED, by Col. Minter L. Wilson, Jr., in *NATO's Fifteen Nations*, v. 17, no. 2 (April-May 1972) 50-56.

"The Russian bear has tried the warm salt water of the Med and finds the temperature to her liking. In the Middle East and across the whole North African littoral, the Soviets are increasingly welcome, much to the concern of NATO and the West. Setbacks such as that suffered in the Sudan notwithstanding, the Soviets are seeking to drive south and seem determined to turn East and West. NATO's leaders have every reason to worry . . . What then is the military significance to NATO of the Soviet move into the Mediterranean?"

THE CORK IN THE BALTIC BOTTLE, by Lawrence Griswold, in *Sea Power*, v. 15, no. 1 (January 1972) 9-13.

"As primary and secondary reservoirs of Russian sea power, the Baltic and Black Seas open to the world's oceans only through bottlenecks controlled by NATO allies. Open in peacetime to all shipping, in a time of acute stress between Warsaw Pact and NATO nations they could, nominally be closed. Turkey's Bosporus is one and the international strait of Orc Sund (Sound), flanked by Sweden at the east and Denmark's Jutland at the west, is the other. Denmark is a NATO ally; Sweden is not. The strength of NATO's control depends on NATO's prestige. At its present low ebb, Moscow's efforts to dominate those bottlenecks by all means short of force are unrelenting. Early last November, en editorial in the official Moscow publication, 'Soviet Diplomatic Lexicon,' by Russian Foreign Minister Andrei Gromyko demanded that all NATO warships be excluded from the Baltic Sea which, it declared, 'must be reserved for the use of nations bordering it.' Excepting Finland, Sweden, eastern Denmark and West Germany, the rest of the Baltic is a Communist lake, although U.S. warships now make occasional 'show the flag' cruises there. Such an editorial demarche, if new, would have stirred considerably more apprehension in western Europe than it did. But it was not a novelty; the same periodical has been issuing the same demand since 1962. What alerted NATO nations this time, however, was the published reply by the new Danish Defense Minister in answer to a question put by a German correspondent. According to this, he stated 'unilaterally' that Denmark would henceforth restrict NATO maneuvers to areas west of the Danish island of Bornholm. Since that would comply with the Russian demand, Denmark's fellow NATO allies were understandably startled. The following day, however, Copenhagen declared that Defense Minister Kjeld Olsen had been 'misquoted' and that Denmark's loyalty to NATO remained unchanged. But a renewed Danish trend to the left might create a different situation. If the misinterpretation did nothing else, it sharpened Western attention to the fact that the international strait of Ore Sund between southern Sweden and northern Denmark was a very narrow bottleneck through which all miaritime traffic, merchant or warship, must pass and, moreover, it is under a form of attack."

NATO'S SOUTHERN FRONT—WHERE SOVIETS SHOW BIG GAINS; INTERVIEW WITH Adm. Means Johnston, Jr., Commander in Chief, Allied Forces Southern Europe, in *U.S. News & World Report*, v. 73, no. 22 (2 June 1975) 22-23.

"Russia's growing naval might in the Mediterranean is worry enough. On top of that—political conflicts harm Allied unity."

NAVAL CHALLENGE IN THE MEDITERRANEAN, in *NATO's Fifteen Nations*, v. 18, no. 4 (August-September 1973) 58-62 plus.

"The emergence of the Soviet Union as a seapower has brought the Warsaw Pact and NATO into competition in the Mediterranean in terms of this historic statement of mission . . . The combatant strength of the Soviet Mediterranean naval force is numerically inferior to the Italian Fleet and the U.S. Sixth Fleet combined. That disparity is even more evident since NATO naval forces in the Mediterranean include not only the U.S. Sixth Fleet and the entire Italian Fleet, but the Greek Navy and elements of the Turkish and British navies as well. Thus on a numerical basis, there is no question that NATO enjoys superiority in the Mediterranean . . . The major difference, and peraps the most significant one, between NATO naval power and Soviet naval power in the Mediterranean rests in the assignment to NATO of STRIKFORSOUTH's carrier task groups. These powerful forces provide tactical naval air power, capable of maintaining local air supremacy in any area of the Mediterranean. Their operations, lacking the presence of substantial air opposition, could be decisive in neutralizing the Soviet naval surface ships in a relatively short period. STRIKFORSOUTH is the major naval combatant force in the Mediterranean and is the core of NATO naval power."

THE PROJECTION OF SOVIET MILITARY POWER IN THE NORTH; MARGINS OF WESTERN SAFETY IN THE NORWEGIAN SEA ON THE NORTH ATLANTIC ARE WEARING THIN, by Bivind Berdal, in *NATO's Fifteen Nations*, v. 19, no. 1 (February-March 1974) 58-64.

"The quantitative and qualitative growth of Soviet military power has been remarkable in recent years, and nowhere in the world has the discrepancy between sheer military might and professed intentions become more glaring than in the North. Governments and public opinion in the three countries of NATO's Northern European Command, Norway, Denmark and Germany, are becoming increasingly aware of this disturbing trend . . . The Director of Research of the Norwegian Institute of Foreign Affairs, Mr. Johan Jorgen Holst, described the Soviet build-up in an article in the following words: 'It is the intention of the Soviets to push their Naval defence line outwards to Iceland and the Faroes. If this is a likely development, then it indicates that the Russians would, to an increasing degree, come to regard the Norwegian Sea as a Soviet lake, behind which, of course, Norway would lie.' This has not come to pass yet: Indigenous forces, combined with powerful NATO reinforcements in emergencies, are there to keep the balance. But a potential 'Mare Sovieticum' must have crossed the mind of the Norwegian Prime Minister Trygve Bratteli when, in a remarkable departure from normal reticence about Soviet Military activity, he told United Press International in an interview in July 1971: 'The Soviet Union has carried out a colossal military build-up on the Northern Flank of NATO, where her military forces are greater than ever before with the possible exception of the Second World War. It is quite clear that the Soviet military build-up, not far from the Norwegian border, is not a bilateral Norwegian-Soviet issue, but part of a global strategy of the Soviet Union. The fact that such great military strength is deployed so near to our country underlines the seriousness of the international strategic situation."

RED STAR RISING AT SEA, by Adm. Sergei

G. Gorshkov. Annapolis, United States Naval Institute, 1974. 150 p.

"The articles that from the core of this book originally appeared in 1972 and 1973 in Morskoi Sbornik, the official journal of the Soviet Navy. The articles were published in translation throughout 1974 in the U.S. Naval Institute Proceedings, with commentaries by American Admirals. The articles were brought together here with those commentaries, a brief biographical account of Admiral Gorshkov, and an introduction and conclusion by the former Chief of Naval Operations, Admiral Elmo R. Zumwalt, Jr., U.S. Navy (Retired)."

SEA POWER IN THE MEDITERRANEAN—THE NEW BALANCE, by Adm. Richard G. Colbert, in *NATO's Fifteen Nations*, v. 17, no. 5 (October-November 1972) 42-48.

"Not so long ago, it used to be that the Mediterranean was an Allied mare nostrum. Its three narrow egresses—Suez, Gibraltar, and the Dardanelles/Bosporus—could be controlled in time of war to ensure the integrity of the entire basin. Not only was the presence of naval opposition non-existent, no such opposition could be deployed to the Mediterranean from elsewhere. Now the situation has completely changed. Admittedly, Gibraltar and the Sea of Marmara would be under NATO control in the event of hostilities, and the Suez is, for the time being, closed. But these choke points have diminished in importance from the defensive point of view in that there are now powerful Russian forces in being continuously on either side of them."

THE SHIFTING BALANCE OF POWER AT SEA, by Adm. R. G. Colbert, in *The Atlantic Community Quarterly*, v. 10, no. 4 (Winter 1972-73) 470-479.

"Admiral Colbert stresses the asymmetries between the NATO and the Soviet naval forces. These include that: NATO operates a multinational cooperative, while the Soviet navy need worry little, about inter-allied coordination, being practically alone on its own side; NATO's naval forces must cover multiple contingencies because of long sea routes, while the Soviets, having internal lines of communication, can specialize in offensive tactics; last but perhaps most important, the Soviet navy is growing rapidly with no sign of a slow-down, while NATO finds it difficult to obtain the funds even to modernize a force which is not growing in size."

SHIFTING STRATEGIC BALANCE IN THE ATLANTIC, by Vice Adm. E. G. N. Mansfield, in *Strategic Review*, v. 2, no. 3 (Summer 1974) 16-21.

"The changing balance of strategic power has been most dramatic at sea. The traditional supremacy of the West has been challenged. NATO powers have reduced their forces substantially to free funds for support of modernization programs. Freedom to use the seas, a vital requirement of the economies and security of NATO nations, is in jeopardy. Soviet inauguration of a prodigious program of building military equipment has supported maritime expansion which now constrains the formerly assured options of NATO. Construction of aircraft carriers and conversion of attack submarines to nuclear power reflect the trend of growth. The new U.S. budget provides for substantial new naval ship construction. It will require strong wills and great determination in the NATO nations to maintain the kind of new ship construction programs required to modernize the fleets and provide the security of shipping lanes vital to Western survival."

THE SILENT THREAT, by Vice Adm. Fred G. Bennett, in *NATO's Fifteen Nations*, v. 17, no. 1 (February-March 1972) 102-108.

"Despite recent significant surface ship improvements, the Soviets continue to develop their submarine fleet as their main naval striking force. There are more than 350 submarines in the Soviet Navy, the vast majority of which operate in waters adjacent to the NATO countries. The Soviet Northern Fleet alone has more submarines than any single NATO navy. In addition, the Soviet submarine force is unrivaled in its diversity, possessing modern nuclear and diesel-powered submarines capable of attacking strategic targets and Western surface ships with missiles as well as torpedoes . . . Because the strategic key to the NATO alliance is maintenance of control over the Atlantic countering the Soviet submarine threat is a major responsibility of the Supreme Allied Commander Atlantic (SACLANT) and his subordinates. There is no single subordinate commander within the NATO organization charged specifically with the conduct of antisubmarine warfare, but rather each area commander is responsible for ASW within his area. However, the Commander

Ocean Area Atlantic is also Commander Antisubmarine Warfare Force, U.S. Atlantic Fleet, in the United States chain of command, and as such has the majority of United States ASW resources in the Atlantic at his disposal. How do NATO naval forces counter the Soviet submarine threat?"

THE SOVIET BUILD-UP IN THE NORTH-EAST ATLANTIC, by Johan Jorgen Holst, in *NATO Review*, v. 19, nos. 9 and 10 (September/October 1971) 21-23.

"The Ministers of Defence attending the NATO Defence Planning Committee at Brussels, last May, noted the continuing build-up of Soviet forces in the North-East Atlantic. They stressed the need for further planning for external reinforcements and others measures to improve the situation on the Northern flank. At a Seminar organised recently in Oslo by the Atlantic Treaty Association, the Research Director of the Norwegian Institute for Foreign Affairs, Mr. Johan Jorgen Holst, gave his views on this subject. We give . . . extracts from his speech."

SOVIET NAVAL POLICY; OBJECTIVES AND CONSTRAINTS, ed. by Michael McGwire and others. New York, Praeger Publichers, 1975. 663 p.

The Context of Soviet Naval Policy; Soviet Policy and the Third World—Case Studies; Some Analytical Material; The Soviet Understanding of Deterrence and Defense; Aspects of Soviet Naval Policy—1960-74.

SOVIET STRATEGIC INTEREST IN THE MARITIME ARCTIC, by Capt. Gerald E. Synhorst, in *United States Naval Institute Proceedings*, v. 99, no. 5 (May 1973) 88-111.

"Some American writers look upon the Arctic Ocean, those waters north of the Arctic Circle, as a buffer between America and the Soviet Union, with both nations having similar minor strategic interests in the Area. In fact, however, control of the Arctic Ocean is central to the Soviet Union's defense network. Soviet strategic and commercial interests in the region are so great as to make U.S. interests there seem minuscule by comparion. Geographically—but, more important, demographically—the Soviet Union is a far more northerly land than the United States; populated Soviet Union is infinitely closer to the Arctic Ocean than is populated America . . . Throughout its length the Soviet Union looks to the north for access to the open sea. The North American continent has had no need to look to the Arctic, and its Arctic coast is far less friendly. America does not have or need a huge Arctic military base like Murmansk. The seasonal shipping along the Arctic Ocean coasts of Alaska and Canada amounts to a mere handful of ships as compared to the hundreds of ships which ply the Northern Sea Route. More important, the Arctic Basin area is so remote and inaccessible from industrial America and Canada that its defense is not vital to the defense of either. Strategically, then, the northern reaches of North America are themselves a buffer for industrial America which lies much farther to the south of the Arctic than does its Soviet counterpart."

THE SOVIET THREAT TO NATO'S NORTHERN FLANK, in *Time*, (18 October 1971) 39.

"On the bleak coast of the Barents Sea, where the Soviet Union shares a common border with Norway near the roof of the world, the Norwegian defense force of 400 men is frequently witness to a disturbing scene. They watch on radar as the Soviets practice assaults on the coast of their Kola Peninsula, some 300 miles away. In the Soviet war games, the attacking force is always victorious and the defenders are always defeated. That spectacle points up a growing Soviet threat to the northern flank of NATO, which extends from Norway's North Cape to West Germany's Baltic coast . . . NATO's northern command is outnumbered by the Soviets four-to-one on the ground, seven-to-one in aircraft and six-to-one in ships in the north. 'The Russians are very busy displaying raw military power on the northern flank,' reports TIME Correspondent John Mulliken, who recently toured the region. 'It is a significant example of how the Soviets intend to use the pressure of their operational armed forces to achieve their political policies in the 1970's and 1980s'."

SOVIET UNION—ALL THE SHIPS AT SEA, in *Time*, v. 105, no. 18 (5 May 1975) 45 plus.

"Around the world last week, ships of the Soviet navy were under full steam . . . At least 200 surface ships and 100 submarines, along with land-based aircraft, were involved in a massive naval exercise . . . The Soviets dubbed the maneuvers 'Spring'; the West called them 'Okean 1975'."

TERRITORIAL WATERS IN THE ARCTIC: THE SOVIET POSITION, by S. M. Olenicoff. Santa Monica, Calif., Rand Corp., July 1972. 52 p. (R-907-ARPA.)

Partial contents: Arctic Basin Territorial Claims; Soviet Reactions to U.S. Activities in the Arctic; The Current Soviet Position on Arctic Waters (The "Soviet Sector" Claim; Territorial Waters in The Soviet Arctic; Internal Waters of the Soviet Arctic; Closed Seas; The Northern Sea Route). With bibliography.

3. *The Role of Nuclear Forces in Current Soviet Strategy*

THE MYTH OF SOVIET NUCLEAR WAR STRATEGY, by Col. Ransom E. Barber, in *Army*, v. 25, no 6 (June 1975) 10-17.

"Major military powers tend to describe their strategy in two different ways, for internal and external consumption. The long-standing Soviet axiom that a big-power war could only be nuclear might be examined in that light, since their force structure suggests other options . . . Evidence shows emphasis on conventional."

THE ROLE OF NUCLEAR FORCES IN CURRENT SOVIET STRETEGY, by Leon Gouré and others. Coral Gables, Fla., University of Miami, Center for Advanced International Studies, 1974. 148 p.

An Overview of Findings and Judgements; Some Basic Considerations; The Utility and Purposes of Soviet Nuclear Forces As Seen from the Kremlin; The Soviet View As to How Much Nuclear Strength Is Enough; Glossaries.

SOVIET NUCLEAR TACTICS, by Martin J. Miller, Jr., in *Ordnance*, (May-June 1970) 624-627.

"The Soviets are well prepared to fight a land nuclear war. Their army is completely equipped with nuclear weapons and delivery systems down to divisional level, and the once dominant role of conventional artillery has largely been replaced with rocket artillery armed with nuclear weapons. They contemplate employing nuclear weapons to support all types of ground operations, and constantly stress the importantance of large operations carried out in the early days of a modern war. They believe that tactical nuclear weapons will be most effective when employed en masse and in support of the main attack forces. To them tactical nuclear weapons are not just quantitatively, but also qualitatively, superior to conventional weapons because of their psychological effects. The Soviets advocate the use of nuclear strikes to contaminate areas with radioactivity so as to deny them to enemy troops. Unlike US doctrine, the Soviet Army does not stress pinpoint accuracy and strict target selection but rather mass barrages intended to smash paths through enemy formations and rear areas for the ground units to exploit. There is little indication that they have seriously considered concepts such as controlled nuclear response. Unlike official NATO strategy, the Soviets make no distinction between tactical and strategic nuclear war, contending that any use of nuclear weapons will lead to all-out nuclear war. According to Western analysts, the Soviet theory of a spontaneous global war is intended to reinforce the credibility of Soviet massive retaliation and to discourage the US and its allies from setting up guidelines for limiting nuclear war."

THE SOVIET THEATER NUCLEAR OFFENSIVE, by Joseph D. Douglass, Jr., Arlington, Va., System Planning Corp., 6 February 1975. 88 p. (Research Note 201.)

"This document presents the initial results of an unclassified examination of translated Soviet documents dealing with tactical nuclear war in Europe. The Soviet image of theater nuclear war is described and analysed." With references.

H. Warsaw Pact Versus NATO: Comparisons and Contrasts

THE ANTI-TANK PROBLEM, by John Marriott, in *NATO's Fifteen Nations*, v. 17, no. 2 (April-May 1972) 72-82 plus.

"The Warsaw Pact's tank forces outnumber those of NATO by a factor of 3 to 1. The latest count gives the former 21,700 tanks and the latter 7,750. It follows therefore that NATO must expect that the spearhead of any Russian advance, particularly in the central area, will undoubtedly be a massive concentration of armour. NATO's 7,000 odd tanks, even if they could all be concentrated in the right area to oppose the attack, would have about as much effect as trying to stop an elephant with a pea shooter. NATO is firmly committed to a policy of flexible response. This means that conventional attack must be met with conventional forces and contained long enough for the politicians to make up their minds as to whether they intend to use nuclear weapons or not. With such a preponderance of armour, it would seem easy for the Soviets to draw off NATO forces by well planned feint attacks. One can well imagine NATO tanks rushing to oppose an apparent attack in one sector, and, when they are all firmly committed, for the Soviets to launch the main attack hundreds of miles away. Whether such a ruse is adopted or not, there seems little doubt that NATO must face the fact that, in the opening stages of a war, Russian armour will penetrate deep into NATO territory unless some new method can be found to mount a far more efficient and mobile antitank defence than is possible at present. When two contestants meet and one is infinitely stronger than the other, the weaker can only hope to win by the use of guile, ruses and surprise. It is the old story of David and Goliath. It is obvious that for NATO to rely on her tanks and her present, pitiully few vehicle and ground mounted anti-tank weapons to stop a Soviet onslaught is just not on. Other means must be found, means which step outside the old concept of anti-tank warfare and which break new bounds. What then are these means?"

ARMS AND STRATEGY: THE WORLD POWER STRUCTURE TODAY, by Lawrence Martin. New York, David McKay, 1973. 320 p.

"Prof. Martin has produced an . . . introduction to strategic, international military affairs . . . He has succeeded in providing a reference book on the world power structure today, or a launching point for those interested in further pursuing the subject of military strategy. In providing a 'succinct guide to all aspects' of the international military scene, Martin deals not only with various weapon systems and the make-up of a nation's military forces, but also includes, in one area, material from a variety of viewpoints on the controversial questions surrounding arms control, trade, and the economics of defense. In the three other broad areas Martin looks at nuclear weapons and total war—examining the state of the art and strategies of not only the superpowers but the lesser and potential nuclear powers, the ranges of limited warfare—from guerrilla to 'tactical nuclear' and the main arenas of world conflict—NATO vs. the Warsaw Pact, the Middle East, Asia, and Southern Africa. He utilizes charts and diagrams to provide additional military and economic details, and provides outlines of major arms limitation treaties and photographs of modern weapon systems."

DEFENSE DILEMMA: INFLATION AND THE SOVIET THREAT, by L. Edgar Prina, in *The National Guardsman*, (February 1975) 2–9.

"Mr. Prina asserts that latest US intelligence reports indicate that Russia has significant new military strengths: increased manpower; new ICBMs equipped with MIRVs (including a mobile land-based, solid-fuel nuclear rocket); a 4,500-mile undersea ballistic missile; a swinging jet bomber (BACKFIRE) and a delta winged bomber; important R&D advances in electronics, lasers, command-and-control; increased tactical airlift capacity; and more effective conventional weapons. Prina also points out that Russia has a comparatively larger defense budget than the US, since its personnel costs are much lower, it is not plagued by inflation, and it is self-sufficient in petroleum. Russia's manpower, with Warsaw Pact support, exceeds that of NATO, and now that Great Britain has announced a 10% decrease in its NATO manpower support, the imbalance is even greater. In addition, he says, the communist bloc has a heavy margin of superiority in tanks and warplanes. If the Congressional advocates of MBFR should succeed, he warns, the NATO alliance could lose its viability. . ."

THE FUTURE OF INTER-BLOC RELATIONS IN EUROPE, ed. by. Louis J. Mensonides and James A. Kuhlman. New York, Praeger, 1974. 217 p.

"Essays which cover a range of topics: an empirical analysis of system change, an aggregate statistical comparison of each bloc, various military, economic and political issues, including analysis of the Warsaw Pact's approach to European security and regional integration in Eastern Europe. The methodology, which includes factor and content analysis, is . . . likely to raise the usual controversy."

HOW MANY DIVISIONS? A NATO-WARSAW PACT ASSESSMENT, by Col. Delbert M. Fowler, in *Military Review*, v. 52, no. 11 (November 1972) 76–88.

"How many divisions should the US Army have? Such a relatively simple question appears at first glance to have some relatively simple answer. But, by now, we should all be prepared to accept the fact that war is but the extension of other forces—political, economic and psychological—and the evidence of their unsuccessful use in pursuit of US foreign policy objectives. We would all likely admit to failure in quantifying the amount of political, economic or psychological force necessary to accomplish a given objective with an opponent; why should it be so easy to calculate the amount of military force required? The difficulty involved in arriving at sound and logical judgments—much less anything approaching a finite unique solution—cannot be exaggerated. For such a critical question, it seems mandatory that solutions, however, one should bear in mind that any military force must be perceived by the enemy as being capable of successfully terminating a conflict if it is to deter that enemy from initiating conflict. In other words, its capabilities must be credible or believable. At the same time, if we are to exact the maximum cooperation from our allies, those same capabilities must be believable to them... The possible scenario of conflict in NATO Europe should be examined for its bearing on how many divisions the Army should have."

THE MILITARY BALANCE 1974-75. London, International Institute for Strategic Studies, 1974. 104 p.

"This annual, quantitative assessment of the military power and defence expenditures of countries throughout the world contains an analytical chapter on the theatre balance between NATO and the Warsaw Pact. Looking at changes which have occurred over a number of years, it is pointed out in this chapter that, in some respects, the balance has shifted slowly in favour of the East. Thus, in 1962, the American land, sea and air forces in Europe totalled 434,000, while now the figure is around 300,000. There were 26 Soviet divisions in Eastern Europe in 1967; now there are 31. But considered qualitatively, it is suggested that NATO has held its own. 'In future, the advent of new weapon systems, particularly precision-guided munitions and anti-tank and air defence missiles, may cut into the Warsaw Pact's advantage in tank and aircraft numbers. The extent to which negotiated force reductions may change the balance also remains to be seen'."

THE MILITARY BALANCE 1974/75, in *Air Force Magazine*, v. 57, no. 12 (December 1974) 41-105.

"As in the past, 'The Balance" is arranged with national entries grouped geographically and with special reference to the principal defense pacts and alignments. Included in the section on the US and USSR is an assessment of the changing strategic nuclear balance between the two superpowers. The section on the European theater balance between NATO and the Warsaw Pact has been expanded and a discussion of Mutual Force Reductions added. Also new this year is an essay on 'Problems of Comparing Defence Expenditures and Gross National Product,' emphasizing the caution with which this particular analytical measure must be applied."

NATO AND THE WARSAW PACT: COMPARISONS AND CONTRASTS, by Walter C. Clemens, Jr., in *Parameters*, v. 4, no. 2 (1974) 13-22.

"A comparison of the Atlantic and Warsaw Treaty Organizations which presents and analyzes Soviet perceptions of the differences between the two alliance systems."

NATO MILITARY POLICY: OBTAINING CONVENTIONAL COMPARABILITY WITH THE WARSAW PACT, by Steven L. Canby. Santa Monica, Rand, June 1973. 94 p. (Report R-1088-ARPA.)

"...NATO can readily attain conventional comparability or parity with the Warsaw Pact forces without an increase in military budget or manpower. He believes many of NATO's deficiencies result from inertia and misunderstanding of the strategic situation in Europe. If these deficiencies can be corrected, he maintains, many of NATO's intra-Alliance and East-West problems will be attenuated. The basic deficiency... is that, because nuclear weapons were relatively cheap and the US enjoyed a technological lead, NATO for too long has emphasized its nuclear 'sword' and neglected its conventional 'shield.' A conventional shield strong enough to thwart or possibly defeat a full-scale Soviet land attack has never been seriously considered because of the presumed expense... Canby goes into considerable detail to show why NATO lacks parity (while spending much more than the Warsaw Pact countries)."

(LI)—NEED FOR AN IMPROVED NON-NUCLEAR FORCE WITHIN NATO, by Maj. Darwin D. Boyd. Maxwell AFB, Ala., Air Command and Staff College, 1971. 66 p. (Research Study no. 0240-71).

"NATO and the Warsaw Pact are direct adversaries in Europe, but it is very doubtful that either side will ever use nuclear weapons. This paper analyzes NATO and the Warsaw Pact to determine if NATO needs to improve its conventional forces to meet the threat of the Warsaw Pact. It concludes that NATO is severely outnumbered in conventional forces and makes some recommendations for bringing NATO up to strength."

NUCLEAR WEAPONS AND FOREIGN

POLICY. HEARINGS BEFORE THE SUBCOMMITTEE ON U.S. SECURITY AGREEMENTS AND COMMITMENTS ABROAD, AND THE SUBCOMMITTEE ON ARMS CONTROL, INTERNATIONAL LAW AND ORGANIZATION OF THE COMMITTEE ON FOREIGN RELATIONS, UNITED STATES SENATE, NINETY-THIRD CONGRESS, SECOND SESSION, MARCH 7, 14, AND APRIL 4, 1974. Washington, Government Printing Office, 1974. 316 p.

U.S. Nuclear Weapons in Europe and U.S.-U.S.S.R. Strategic doctrines and policy.

THE ROLE AND CAPABILITY OF NATO FORCES CENTRAL EUROPE, by Gen. J. Benecke, in *RUSI Journal*, v. 118, no. 2 (June 1973) 17-23.

Warsaw Pact Forces, NATO Forces, Comparison of Forces, Strategic and Operational Concept, Ground and Air Forces, all as related to the role and capability of NATO Forces Central Europe.

SEABORNE AND AIRBORNE MOBILITY IN EUROPE, by Maj. Gen. J. L. Moulton, in *United States Naval Institute Proceedings*, v. 100, no. 855 (May 1974) 122-124.

Warsaw Pact Seaborne and Airborne Capabilities; Western Europe and Strategic Mobility; Allied Command Europe Mobile Force (AMF); The British, the North Sea, and the Northern Flank; The Central Front and the Baltic; Southern Flank and Mediterranean; France; etc.

(*)—SECURITY IN EUROPE, by Robert Hunter. Bloomington, Indiana University Press, 1972. 281 p.

"The author analyzes the growth of the formal European security institutions, first NATO and then the Warsaw Pact, in relation to the onset and progress of the Cold War. He discusses the political role played by each alliance; how the evolution of a strategic doctrine in the West built up tensions with NATO; and how both alliances have fulfilled important non-military needs of the countries involved. The final section of the book assesses the process of détente in Europe and speculates on the outsome of the proposed Security and Cooperation Conference."

SHRINKING DEFENSE RESOURCES IN THE WEST AND THE WORLD BALANCE, by Helmut Schmidt, in *The Atlantic Community Quarterly*, v. 11, no. 4 (Winter 1973-1974) 422-437.

"The Finance Minister of the Federal Republic of Germany analyzes the balance of power and states that it is governed by a wealth of measurable and unmeasurable, objective and subjective factors. These include military, geographic, economic, political and ideological elements. In a scholarly article, he reviews them all as between the East and the West."

U.S. ARMS: ARE OUR DEFENSES DOWN?, in *Newsweek*, v. 85, no. 11 (17 March 1975) 45-48 plus.

An overview of the U.S. military posture, and the role of U.S. Secretary of Defense James R. Schlesinger in strengthening our defenses. Included is an interview with the Secretary in which he was asked whether or not the U.S. is "entering an era of neo-isolationism that will erode its power," among other questions concerning U.S. defense. Also included is a chart on the world strategic balance, including, among others, a comparison between NATO and Warsaw Pact strengths.

THE WARSAW PACT THREAT IN THE 1970's, by Lawrence L. Whetten, in *NATO's Fifteen Nations*, v. 15, no. 5 (October-November 1970) 20-28.

"As public clamour mounts in the West for the withdrawal of troops stationed abroad, and NATO members continue to reduce the proportion of their GNP allocated to defense, and the costs of weapons procurement multiplies rapidly, an assessment is warranted of the military threat posed by the Warsaw Pact as the first step in an assessment of an improvement in East-West relations. The actual strength of the Warsaw Pact is contestable. Few authorities agree on its relative or absolute combat effectiveness or comparative posture to NATO. Most Western observers, however, do agree that marked improvements have been made and that compared to even three years ago its strength has been significantly enhanced. This comparatively stronger posture is due in part to rapid weapons modernization programs and the introduction of energetic training programs, the sharp expansion of the Soviet Navy and its assumption of an offensive role, the enlargement of theater resources resulting from Moscow's attainment of strategic nuclear parity, and the deployment of the Soviet Central Group of Forces into Czechoslovakia. Despite the asymmetrics between NATO and the Pact in mobilization rates, industrail resources, reserves, military geography, weapons effectiveness and rate of fire indices, it is sufficient merely to record the Pact's relative numerical strength over NATO before analyzing improvements in the Pact's posture over the past ten years."

WESTERN TECHNOLOGY AND SOVIET ECONOMIC DEVELOPMENT, 1945 TO 1965, by Antony C. Sutton. Stanford, Hoover Institution Press, 1973. 482 p.

"The theme of this work by an engineer and economist (third of a series covering the period since 1917) is the total dependence of the U.S.S.R. on Western technology, and the refusal of Western governments to recognize this and draw the necessary lessons from it."

---

*For more detailed information see DA PAM 550-8, Communist Eastern Europe, 1971.

[The documents in the following appendixes were the latest ones available at time of preparation. However, subsequent political, and, in some cases, military events have altered some of the data. Therefore, appendixes dealing with Greece, Italy, Portugal, Turkey, etc., should be studied accordingly.]

APPENDIXES

APPENDIX A
ORIGINS OF THE ALLIANCE

[FROM: NATO Facts and Figures. Brussells, The North Atlantic Treaty Organization, Information Service, October 1971.]

ORIGINS OF THE ALLIANCE

In the closing phase of the Second World War, seven weeks after the capitulation of Nazi Germany and six weeks before the Hiroshima bomb, representatives of fifty nations signed the United Nations Charter in San Francisco. The date was June 26, 1945, and the world hoped it had at last learned how to keep the peace. Within four years, ten European countries found themselves faced by a threat the nature of which necessitated some more specific protection than that afforded by the United Nations Charter. Indeed, the latter contained a provision stipulating the right of its members, individually or collectively, to defend themselves against possible armed attack. The Europeans turned to the United States and Canada to underwrite their pledge of mutual security and, on April 4, 1949, the North Atlantic Treaty was signed.

What had happened, in the space of three years and not quite nine months, to convince those twelve countries of the need for a regional defence alliance?

The defeat of the two great military and industrial powers, Germany and Japan, had left an immense vacuum to the east and west of the Soviet Union. Taking advantage of such exceptionally favourable circumstances, the Soviet Union made full use of the combined strength of the Red Army and world Communism to conduct an expansionist policy which was soon to threaten peace and collective security. Even in 1945 the most confirmed optimist could not claim that the international sky was unclouded. The British Prime Minister, Sir Winston Churchill, in his telegram of May 12 addressed to President Truman, expressed his anxiety in the following terms: "What will be the position in a year or two when the British and American armies have melted, and the French have not yet been formed on any major scale, and when Russia may choose to keep 200 or 300 divisions on active service?" and he added: "An iron curtain is drawn down upon their front (Russia). We do not know what is going on behind...". This, it may be noted, was the first occasion on which this subsequently familiar metaphor was used.

Demobilization of Forces

On the morrow of the German surrender, the Western democracies, true to their wartime pledges and to popular demand, began to demobilize. The United States and the United Kingdom quickly withdrew the bulk of their armed forces from Europe. They demobilized most of their troops, with the exception of occupation forces and units committed in other parts of the world. As for the nations of Europe, they addressed themselves to the complex tasks of reconstruction.

The armed strength of the Allied Forces in Europe at the time of the surrender of Germany was about five million men. One year later, following demobilization, their armed strength amounted to no more than 880,000 men. The following table, moreover, shows the exact strengths after demobilization:

	1945	*1946*
United States	3,100,000 men	391,000 men
United Kingdom	1,321,000 „	488,000 „
Canada	299,000 „	0 „

The Soviet Union, on the other hand, continued to keep its armed forces on a wartime footing; in 1945 their strength amounted to more than four million men. It also kept its war industries going at full blast.

On the political side, the Western Powers went to the furthest limits of conciliation. They made every effort to reach agreement with the Soviet Government and to make the United Nations an effective instrument for peace. They met with nothing but obstruction.

Problems of Peace Treaties

At San Francisco in 1945, Poland was not represented at the conference table because the USSR and the Western Powers were unable to agree on the composition of a Polish provisional government.

At the London Conference of Foreign Ministers (September, 1945), Mr. Molotov blocked any discussion of the United Kingdom's proposals for the opening of an impartial enquiry into the situation in Rumania and Bulgaria.

It was only after making concessions that the representatives of the Western Powers were able, in November 1945, to obtain Soviet agreement on a procedure for framing peace treaties with Italy, Finland and Germany's former satellites in the Balkans.

The Peace Conference opened in Paris on July 29, 1946, and the peace treaties with Italy, Finland, Bulgaria, Hungary and Rumania were not signed until February 10, 1947.
In March, 1947, the Foreign Ministers met in Moscow to discuss the drafting of peace treaties with Germany and Austria. They were unable to agree on what Germany's fate should be.
A new Foreign Ministers' Conference was held in London in November, 1947, but it did no more than confirm the impossibility of agreement. Shortly afterwards, the Soviet representatives ceased to take part in the Allied Control Council in Berlin. The Foreign Ministers met once more in Paris in May, 1949, to discuss anew the problem of Germany and Austria and, in 1951, their deputies spent 109 days at the Palais Rose Conference in Paris vainly trying to draw up an agenda for a new meeting at ministerial level.

For all practical purposes, the stalemate at the 1947 Moscow Conference put an end to the co-operation which had developed between the USSR and the Western democratic countries during the war. The signing of the United Nations Charter on June 26, 1945, had raised the hopes of the peoples of the Western countries. But the Soviet Union abused the right of veto at the Security Council.

In the case of Greece, to take an example, where incidents had taken place between her and certain neighbouring states – Albania and Bulgaria – a commission of enquiry was appointed in 1947 by the Security Council of the United Nations. Although the report prepared by this commission established the responsibility of both Albania and Bulgaria, all draft resolutions recommending United Nations action encountered the systematic veto of the Soviet Union.
Since then, the Soviet Union vetoed a decision taken by the Security Council on more than one hundred different occasions.

Soviet Expansion

Soviet territorial expansion under Stalin had already begun during the war by the annexation of Estonia, Latvia and Lithuania, together with certain parts of Finland, Poland, Rumania, North-Eastern Germany and Eastern Czechoslovakia, a total of about 180,000 square miles of territory occupied by more than 23 million inhabitants. It was this that moved Mr. Paul-Henri Spaak, who was at the time the Belgian Prime Minister and Minister of Foreign Affairs, to state in the General Assembly of the United Nations in 1948: "There is but one Great Power that emerged from the war having conquered other territories, and that Power is the USSR".
This territorial expansion continued after the defeat of Germany and was supplemented by a policy of control over the countries of Eastern Europe. The presence of the victorious Soviet armies in the heart of Europe, coupled with Communist infiltration into 'popular front' governments, effectively compelled Albania, Bulgaria, Rumania, Eastern Germany, Poland, Hungary and Czechoslovakia to fall within

the sphere of Soviet domination (an area of about 390,000 square miles and a population of over 90 million non-Russian inhabitants).
Here are the highlights of the 'conquest without war':
In Hungary, from the beginning of 1947, the Communist Party opened a violent campaign against the Smallholders Party, and as a result of its denunciations many arrests were made. The Nagy government had to resign on May 29; new elections did not produce, however, a majority for the Communist Party which was the largest group in Parliament. The Communists quickly formed a new government and formally dissolved the opposition parties on November 21, 1947.

Soviet Political Pressure

In Bulgaria, the operation was carried out along similar lines. Nicolas Petkov, leader of the Agrarian Party and the opposition, was accused of plotting a military coup d'état, sentenced to death on August 16, 1947, and hanged on September 23. On August 26, the Peasant Party was dissolved as 'fascist' and on November 22, the national administration was organized along Soviet lines. On December 11, 1947, Dimitrov, former Secretary of the Comintern, assumed leadership and formed a predominantly Communist cabinet.

In Rumania, after elections which were regarded as invalid by the Anglo-Saxon countries, the members of the opposition were accused of plotting the overthrow of the democratic regime. The Peasant Party was dissolved on October 10, 1947, and its leader, Dr. Maniu, was sentenced to life imprisonment on October 29. Mrs. Anna Pauker, who had served in Moscow during the war as adviser to the Soviet Government on Rumanian affairs, succeeded Mr. Tataresco, and King Michael had to abdicate on January 1, 1948.
In Poland, Mr. Mikolajczyk, head of the Peasant Party, was compelled to leave the country in November, 1947, in the face of constant threats to his life. His party had to relinquish its role as opposition and was finally dissolved on November 21, 1947.
In Czechoslovakia, Soviet interference steadily increased. The Prague government, which had favoured participation in the Marshall Plan, was obliged to revise its views and reverse its decision after a hasty visit by Mr. Gottwald and Mr. Masaryk to Moscow in July, 1947.

In addition, the Communists, by means of a campaign of denunciation, secured the arrest and trial of many members of the democratic party which held an absolute majority. In February 1948, Mr. Zorin, Moscow's special envoy, engineered the resignation of President Benes (May, 1948). A Communist government was then formed.
On March 10, 1948, Mr. Jan Masaryk, Foreign Minister in the Gottwald Government, was found dead on the pavement beneath the windows of his home...
In less than a year, Moscow had thus succeeded in gaining control over the governments in Budapest, Bucharest, Sofia, Warsaw and Prague. The Communist parties

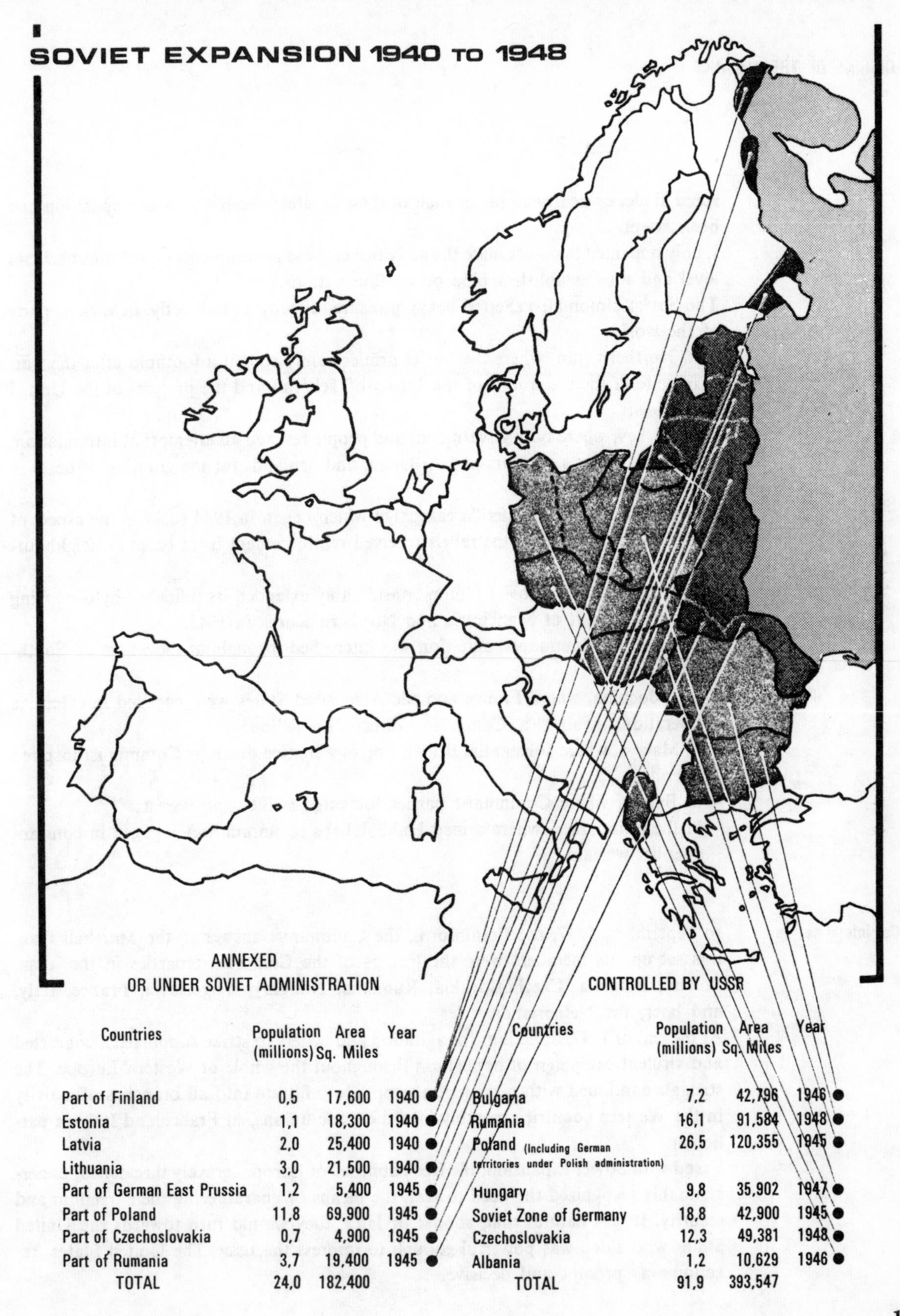

Countries	Population (millions)	Area Sq. Miles	Year
Part of Finland	0,5	17,600	1940
Estonia	1,1	18,300	1940
Latvia	2,0	25,400	1940
Lithuania	3,0	21,500	1940
Part of German East Prussia	1,2	5,400	1945
Part of Poland	11,8	69,900	1945
Part of Czechoslovakia	0,7	4,900	1945
Part of Rumania	3,7	19,400	1945
TOTAL	24,0	182,400	

Countries	Population (millions)	Area Sq. Miles	Year
Bulgaria	7,2	42,796	1946
Rumania	16,1	91,584	1948
Poland (Including German territories under Polish administration)	26,5	120,355	1945
Hungary	9,8	35,902	1947
Soviet Zone of Germany	18,8	42,900	1945
Czechoslovakia	12,3	49,381	1948
Albania	1,2	10,629	1946
TOTAL	91,9	393,547	

ruled alone, or nearly alone, in each of these capitals, from which all opposition had been swept.

It only remained to co-ordinate the activities of these governments on the international level and thus establish a bloc of satellite nations.

The Soviet Union also exerted heavy pressure, directly or indirectly, in various parts of the world:

- in Northern Iran, where the Soviet armies vainly sought a foothold after the war, in spite of the provisions of the Treaty of Teheran and the protests of the United Nations;
- In Turkey, where both government and people resisted all attempts at intimidation, territorial claims on Kars and Ardahan, and demands for the granting of bases in the Straits;
- in Greece, where the guerilla campaign which began in 1944 took on the aspect of real war in 1946, when the rebels received reinforcement from bases in neighbouring states;
- in Asia, where the Soviet Union considerably extended its influence by occupying the greater part of Manchuria and Northern Korea in 1945.

  In addition, Communist agitation was intensified throughout the whole of South-East Asia:
- in Indochina, where France and the Associated States were engaged in extensive operations against a Communist-directed rebellion;
- in Malaya, where substantial British Forces were tied down by Communist-inspired guerillas;
- in Burma, where Communist parties fomented strikes and unrest;
- in the Philippines, where armed Hukbalahaps (Communists) engaged in constant guerilla warfare.

Cominform set up

In September, 1947, the Cominform, the Communist answer to the Marshall Plan, was set up. Its members were the leaders of the Communist parties in the USSR, Poland, Bulgaria, Czechoslovakia, Rumania, Hungary, Yugoslavia, France, Italy, and later, the Netherlands.

At the end of 1947, directions for agitation and orders to strike supported a concerted and virulent campaign of opposition throughout the whole of Western Europe. The struggle continued with persistent attempts to infiltrate into all branches of activity in the Western countries, notably into the trade unions, in France and Italy in particular.

Faced with Soviet expansion, the free countries of Europe, gravely threatened, understandably recognized the need to seek the means of guaranteeing their freedom and security. It was natural that, sooner or later, they should turn towards the United States who alone was powerful enough to impress the USSR. The United States reaction was prompt and decisive.

Truman Doctrine

On March 12, 1947, President Truman told Congress: "It must be the policy of the United States of America to support free peoples who are resisting attempted subjugation by armed minorities, or by outside pressure". Following that statement, which became known as the 'Truman Doctrine' the Congress of the United States authorized the appropriation of $ 400 million for aid to Greece and Turkey up to June, 1948. It was, indeed, on these countries that Soviet pressure had been brought hardest to bear. Congress also authorized the despatch to these countries of American civilian and military missions.

The 'Truman Doctrine' was designed to deal with the specific threat to Greece and Turkey. But the situation in Western Europe generally was no less alarming. In spite of the aid received by the free countries of Europe from the United States to relieve post-war shortages, the mechanism of European economy remained badly jammed and Western Europe would have found itself on the brink of economic collapse. On June 5, 1947, in a speech at Harvard University, the then Secretary of State of the United States, General George C. Marshall, initiated the idea of a Programme for European Recovery. He proposed that the United States should come to the help of Europe and suggested that the European countries should agree on their requirements and draw up a common programme agreed by a number, if not all, of the European nations. He added that this policy was "directed not against any country or doctrine but against hunger, poverty, desperation and chaos".

Marshall Plan

This offer of economic assistance, which, in the next few years, contributed largely to the economic recovery of the Western countries, was also open to the Soviet Union and the countries behind the Iron Curtain. Stalin refused all American aid for the USSR and, despite initial interest on the part of both Czechoslovakia and Poland, forced satellite governments to do likewise. Finally, he set up the Cominform, whose allotted aim was to fight the Marshall Plan as "an instrument of American imperialism".

The world thus found itself split into two blocs. The nature and extent of Soviet intentions were henceforth clearly perceived. As regards the free countries of Europe, the only way they could begin to re-establish a balance of forces was to come together. A number of statesmen, particularly Sir Winston Churchill, the former British Prime Minister, and Mr. Louis St. Laurent, the Canadian Secretary of State for External Affairs, had already contemplated in 1946 the idea of a defensive alliance within the framework of the United Nations.

On January 22, 1948, Mr Ernest Bevin, the United Kingdom Foreign Secretary, suggested a formula for Western Union consisting of a network of bilateral agreements on the lines of the Dunkirk Treaty.

This Treaty had been signed on March 4, 1947 by France and the United Kingdom. It was a "Treaty of alliance and mutual assistance" of 50 years' duration, according to which the two countries would unite in the event of any renewed attempt at aggression by Germany. Under its terms they were also bound, by means of continuing consultation on problems bearing on their economic relations, to take all measures necessary to increase their prosperity and economic stability and thus enable them to make a more effective contribution to the economic and social aims of the United Nations. Although the idea was warmly welcomed it was felt that, as the Dunkirk Treaty had been aimed expressly against a renewed German aggression, it might be preferable to take the Rio Treaty as a model. This Treaty had been signed on September 2, 1947, by the United States and the Latin American countries, with the exception of Nicaragua and Ecuador. It was essentially a collective, defensive alliance against any aggression and provided an example of 'regional grouping' within the framework of the United Nations Charter.

While these problems were under discussion, the Prague coup d'état, in February 1948, drew Czechoslovakia into the Soviet orbit and came as a sharp reminder to the Western Allies that common defensive action was needed.

Brussels Treaty

On March 4, 1948, representatives of Belgium, France, Luxembourg, the Netherlands and the United Kingdom met in Brussels to consider the terms of a treaty of mutual assistance. Their efforts soon met with success. The Brussels Treaty was signed on March 17, 1948 by Belgium, France, Luxembourg, the Netherlands and the United Kingdom. These countries pledged themselves to build up a common defence system and to strengthen their economic and cultural ties.

Article IV of the Brussels Treaty states that should any of the contracting Parties be the object of an "armed aggression in Europe", the other signatories to the Treaty would afford the attacked Party "all the military and other aid and assistance in their power". The Treaty, with a duration of 50 years, provided for the creation of a supreme body in Western Union, known as the Consultative Council, consisting of the five Foreign Ministers. Under it was a Western Defence Committee consisting of the Defence Ministers.

Berlin blockade

The Brussels Treaty was scarcely signed when the Russians started the blockade of West Berlin (June, 1948). It was to last for 323 days and was only countered by the organization of an air-lift by the Western Powers. The Berlin blockade hastened the setting up of Western defence.

On April 30, 1948, the Defence Ministers and Chiefs-of-Staff of the five Brussels Treaty signatory Powers met in London to discuss their countries' military equipment needs, to see how far they could be met from their own production resources, and how much additional aid would have to be requested from the United States. From July, 1948, onwards, United States and Canadian experts attended these meetings as observers.

In September, 1948, a military body was created within the Brussels Treaty known as the Western Union Defence Organization. Field Marshal Montgomery was appointed Chairman of the Commanders-in-Chief Committee and set up his Headquarters at Fontainebleau, France.

Western Union Defence Organization

Commanders-in-Chief were appointed: General de Lattre de Tassigny (France) for the Land Forces; Air Chief Marshal Sir James Robb (United Kingdom) for the Air Forces; Vice Admiral Jaujard (France) for Naval Forces.
The creation of a defence organization by the free countries in Europe could not fail to awaken a response from the United States.
On April 11, 1948, the United States Secretary of State, General George C. Marshall and the Under-Secretary, Mr. Robert M. Lovett, opened preliminary talks with Senators Arthur H. Vandenberg and Tom Connally on the problems of security in the North Atlantic area.

Vandenberg Resolution

On April 28, 1948, the idea of a single mutual defence system, including and superseding the Brussels Treaty, was publicly put forward by Mr. St. Laurent in the Canadian House of Commons. It was warmly welcomed one week later by Mr. Ernest Bevin. But it was essential that the United States should be able, constitutionally, to join the Atlantic Alliance. To this end, in consultation with the State Department, Senator Vandenberg drew up a Resolution which recommended, in particular, "the association of the United States, by constitutional process, with such regional and other collective arrangements as are based on continuous and effective self-help and mutual aid" and its "contribution to the maintenance of peace by making clear its determination to exercise the right of individual or collective self-defence under Article 51 (of the United Nations Charter) should any armed attack occur affecting its national security".
This Resolution, thanks to the timely initiative of Senators Vandenberg and Connally, was adopted on June 11, 1948, by the United States Senate. The road was now clear. Preliminary talks opened in Washington on July 6, 1948, between the State Department and the Ambassadors of Canada and of the Western Union Powers. They ended on September 9, 1948, with a report to governments. This report having been favourably received by governments, the Consultative Council of the Brussels Treaty was able, at the end of October, 1948, to announce complete identity of views on the principle of a defensive pact for the North Atlantic area.
The text of the Treaty was published on March 18, 1949. Even before that, on March 15, 1949, the Brussels Treaty signatory Powers, Canada and the United States, officially invited Denmark, Iceland, Italy, Norway and Portugal to accede to the Treaty.

April 4, 1949
Signature of North Atlantic Treaty

On April 4, 1949, in spite of the pressure brought to bear by the Soviet Union on the Parties to the Treaty (notably a memorandum addressed to the twelve original signatories alleging the hostile nature of their action), the North Atlantic Treaty was signed in Washington.
The Parliaments of the member countries ratified the Treaty within five months thereafter.
Subsequently, three other countries joined the twelve original signatories.
Greece and Turkey were invited to join the Alliance in September, 1951; they formally acceded to the Treaty on February 18, 1952.
The Federal Republic of Germany was invited to accede to the Treaty following the signature of the Paris Agreements in October, 1954, and officially became a member of the North Atlantic Treaty Organization on May 9, 1955.

APPENDIX B

ANALYSIS OF THE NORTH ATLANTIC TREATY

[FROM: NATO Facts and Figures. Brussels, The North Atlantic Treaty Organization, Information Service, October 1971.]

ANALYSIS OF THE NORTH ATLANTIC TREATY

Essentially the North Atlantic Treaty is the framework for wide co-operation among its signatories. More than a military alliance formed to prevent aggression, or to repel it should need arise, it also provides for continuing joint action in the political, economic and social fields.

The signatory countries undertake, in conformity with the provisions of the Charter of the United Nations, to preserve peace and international security and to promote stability and well-being in the North Atlantic area. They also undertake to eliminate incompatibilities in their economic policies and to encourage economic co-operation among themselves.

Thus the Treaty is dual in nature. It proclaims the importance of economic and social progress and, at the same time, reaffirms a security policy based on nations, inherent right to collective self-defence.

The Treaty consists of a preamble and fourteen articles.

The preamble outlines the Treaty's main features. It is a treaty of alliance, within the framework of the United Nations Charter, for the defence of a way of life not only by military means but also through co-operation in political, economic, social and cultural fields.

Article 1 **defines the basic principles to be followed by member countries in the conduct of their international relations in order to avoid endangering peace and world security. It refers expressly to the United Nations Charter and is, indeed, an almost literal repetition of paragraphs 3 and 4 of Article 2 of the Charter.**

Article 2 defines the aims to be followed by the member countries in their international relations and indicates broadly how these aims should be fulfilled. It is inspired by Article 1 of the United Nations Charter, which defines as the aims of the U.N. : preservation of peace, development of friendly relations among nations, achievement of international co-operation in solving international problems of an economic and social character.

Obligations of Signatories

The obligations undertaken by the signatories are as much external (the bringing about of better understanding of the principles upon which Western civilization is founded) as internal (the strengthening of their free institutions and the elimination of disputes or conflicts within the Alliance in the economic and social fields). This article is the clear authority for all co-operation of a non-military character within the Alliance, that is, for co-operation beyond that called for in pursuance of the Treaty's military aims. It underlines the fact that the alliance was brought into being to defend a way of life.

Article 3 deals with ways and means of maintaining and increasing the individual and collective capacity of members to resist armed attack. They must develop this capacity through joint action and through mutual assistance.
From this article stem, among other things, the co-ordination of military instruction and training, joint production programmes for equipment, the infrastructure programme and all the varied forms of military assistance provided by the United States.

Article 4 lays down the obligations incumbent on member countries in the event of a threat to one of them. The only explicitly expressed requirement is that signatories should consult together if the territorial integrity or political independence of any member is endangered.
Such consultation, which may be requested by any member country and not necessarily the one threatened, would in practice take place at a meeting of the North Atlantic Council in Brussels, which can be called at an hour's notice.
It should be remembered, however, that, as stipulated in Article 7 of the Treaty, primary responsibility for the preservation of peace and international security remains with the United Nations Security Council.

Collective Defence

Article 5 contains one of the Treaty's most important provisions: "The Parties agree that an armed attack against one or more of them in Europe or North America shall be considered an attack against them all... " It serves warning on a would-be aggressor that he cannot hope to attain even a limited military objective.
Having stated this principle, the Article goes on to define the obligations of countries in the event of armed attack. They must at once, individually and in concert with

the other members, take such action, including the use of armed force, as each deems necessary.
Each country is free, therefore, to take whatever action it judges necessary. Every armed attack does not of necessity call for an automatic declaration of general war. Moreover, all Parties to the Treaty would not necessarily be required to provide the same type of assistance.
Any such joint action would be justified by the inherent right to self-defence recognized by Article 51 of the United Nations Charter. But the exercise of this right in no way detracts from the responsibility of the Security Council. Article 5 ends with the stipulation that action taken in conformity with its provisions shall be reported to the Security Council and terminated when that body has taken what measures are necessary.

Article 6 defines the area within which the provisions of Article 5 are applicable. This article was amended after the accession of Greece and Turkey.
The definition of a geographical area for the purposes of Article 5 in no way precludes discussion by the Council of events which may occur outside that area. On the contrary. The maintenance of peace and security in any part of the world is dependent upon the international situation as a whole and the Council as a matter of normal practice exchanges information and views on major world events wherever they occur.

Article 7 states the Treaty's compatibility with the United Nations Charter.

In *Article 8* the Parties confirm the compatibility of the Treaty with their other international commitments, and undertake not to enter into any commitments in the future which may conflict with the Treaty.

Creation of the Council

Article 9 calls for the creation of the North Atlantic Council and provides for the setting up of whatever additional bodies may be needed to implement the preceding Articles.
This is the legal basis for the existence of the specialized committees and groups set up by the Council, the International Secretariat which services them, the major and subordinate military commands and the various military and civilian agencies.

Article 10 stipulates that the Parties may, by unanimous decision, invite any other European State in a position to further the principles of the Treaty to accede to it. This was the authority for the invitations to Greece and Turkey in 1951 and the Federal Republic of Germany in 1955.

Article 11 deals with arrangements for ratification of the Treaty and its entry into force.

Articles 12 and 13 provide for the possibility of revisions to the Treaty or withdrawals from it. After the Treaty has been in force for ten years the Parties may agree to revise it. After twenty years any Party may put an end to his own participation, giving one year's notice of denunciation. It follows that, as from August 24. 1969, the 20th anniversary of the Treaty's entry into force, any party may give one year's notice of withdrawal.

Revision of the Treaty

It may be noted that the question of revising the Treaty has never so far been raised, although there have been exercises such as the Three Wise Men's Report in 1956 and the more recent Harmel Report, which have given fresh meaning to some of its provisions. Even the French Government's decision to withdraw from the integrated military commands did not necessitate any alterations to the original Treaty since it proved possible by negotiation to relate this decision to existing arrangements. Since the Treaty is of unlimited duration it will in any case remain in force for as long as it is considered useful irrespective of any decision by any individual member to withdraw.

Finally, *Article 14* deals with arrangements for depositing the Treaty document.

APPENDIX C

EXTRACTS FROM THE BRUSSELS TREATY
17 MARCH 1948

[FROM: NATO Facts and Figures. Brussells, The North Atlantic Treaty Organization, Information Service, October 1971.]

EXTRACTS FROM THE BRUSSELS TREATY[1]

17 March, 1948

The titular heads of the participating States:
Resolved to reaffirm their faith in fundamental human rights, in the dignity and worth of the human person and in the other ideals proclaimed in the Charter of the United Nations; To fortify and preserve the principles of democracy, personal freedom and political liberty, the constitutional traditions and the rule of law, which are their common heritage; To strengthen, with these aims in view, the economic, social and cultural ties by which they are already united; To co-operate loyally and to co-ordinate their efforts to create in Western Europe a firm basis for European economic recovery;
To afford assistance to each other, in accordance with the Charter of the United Nations, in maintaining international peace and security and in resisting any policy of aggression; To take such steps as may be held to be necessary in the event of a renewal by Germany of a policy of aggression; To associate progressively in the pursuance of these aims other States inspired by the same ideals and animated by the like determination;
Desiring for these purposes to conclude a treaty for collaboration in economic, social and cultural matters and for collective self-defence;
Have appointed... their plenipotentiaries... who... have agreed as follows:

ARTICLE I

Convinced of the close community of their interests and of the necessity of uniting in order to promote the economic recovery of Europe, the High Contracting Parties will so organize and co-ordinate their economic activities as to produce the best possible results, by the elimination of conflict in their economic policies, the co-ordination of production and the development of commercial exchanges.
The co-operation provided for in the preceding paragraph, which will be effected through the Consultative Council referred to in Article VII as well as through other bodies, shall not involve any duplication of, or prejudice to, the work of other economic organizations in which the High Contracting Parties are or may be represented but shall on the contrary assist the work of those organizations.

ARTICLE II

The High Contracting Parties will make every effort in common, both by direct consultation and in specialized agencies, to promote the attainment of a higher standard of living by their peoples and to develop on corresponding lines the social and other related services of their countries.
The High Contracting Parties will consult with the object of achieving the earliest possible application of recommendations of immediate practical interest, relating to social matters, adopted with their approval in the specialized agencies.

(1) The Brussels Treaty has been modified by the 'Paris Agreements' (Protocol revising and completing the Brussels Treaty); see page 306.

They will endeavour to conclude as soon as possible conventions with each other in the sphere of social security.

ARTICLE III

The High Contracting Parties will make every effort in common to lead their peoples towards a better understanding of the principles which form the basis of their common civilization and to promote cultural exchanges by conventions between themselves or by other means.

ARTICLE IV

If any of the High Contracting Parties should be the object of an armed attack in Europe, the other High Contracting Parties will, in accordance with the provisions of Article 51 of the Charter of the United Nations, afford the Party so attacked all the military and other aid and assistance in their power.

ARTICLE V

All measures taken as a result of the preceding Article shall be immediately reported to the Security Council. They shall be terminated as soon as the Security Council has taken the measures necessary to maintain or restore international peace and security.
The present Treaty does not prejudice in any way the obligations of the High Contracting Parties under the provisions of the Charter of the United Nations. It shall not be interpreted as affecting in any way the authority and responsibility of the Security Council under the Charter to take at any time such action as it deems necessary in order to maintain or restore international peace and security.

ARTICLE VI

The High Contracting Parties declare, each so far as he is concerned, that none of the international engagements now in force between him and any of the other High Contracting Parties or any third State is in conflict with the provisions of the present Treaty.
None of the High Contracting Parties will conclude any alliance or participate in any coalition directed against any other of the High Contracting Parties.

ARTICLE VII

For the purpose of consulting together on all the questions dealt with in the present Treaty, the High Contracting Parties will create a Consultative Council, which shall be

so organized as to be able to exercise its functions continuously. The Council shall meet at such times as it shall deem fit.
At the request of any of the High Contracting Parties, the Council shall be immediately convened in order to permit the High Contracting Parties to consult with regard to any situation which may constitute a threat to peace, in whatever area this threat should arise; with regard to the attitude to be adopted and the steps to be taken in case of a renewal by Germany of an aggressive policy; or with regard to any situation constituting a danger to economic stability.

ARTICLE VIII

In pursuance of their determination to settle disputes only by peaceful means, the High Contracting Parties will apply to disputes between themselves the following provision:
The High Contracting Parties will, while the present Treaty remains in force, settle all disputes falling within the scope of Article 36, paragraph 2, of the Statute of the International Court of Justice by referring them to the Court...

ARTICLE IX

The High Contracting Parties may, by agreement, invite any other State to accede to the present Treaty on conditions to be agreed between them and the State so invited...

ARTICLE X

The present Treaty... shall enter into force on the date of the deposit of the last instrument of ratification and shall thereafter remain in force for fifty years...
Done at Brussels, this seventeenth day of March, 1948...

APPENDIX D

THE NORTH ATLANTIC TREATY
WASHINGTON, D.C., 4 APRIL 1949

[FROM: NATO Facts and Figures. Brussels, The North Atlantic Treaty Organization, Information Service, October 1971.]

THE NORTH ATLANTIC TREATY

Washington D.C., 4 April, 1949

The Parties to this Treaty reaffirm their faith in the purposes and principles of the Charter of the United Nations and their desire to live in peace with all peoples and all governments.
They are determined to safeguard the freedom, common heritage and civilization of their peoples, founded on the principles of democracy, individual liberty and the rule of law.
They seek to promote stability and well-being in the North Atlantic area.
They are resolved to unite their efforts for collective defence and for the preservation of peace and security.
They therefore agree to this North Atlantic Treaty:

ARTICLE 1

The Parties undertake, as set forth in the Charter of the United Nations, to settle any international dispute in which they may be involved by peaceful means in such a manner that international peace and security and justice are not endangered, and to refrain in their international relations from the threat or use of force in any manner inconsistent with the purposes of the United Nations.

ARTICLE 2

The Parties will contribute toward the further development of peaceful and friendly international relations by strengthening their free institutions, by bringing about a better understanding of the principles upon which these institutions are founded, and by promoting conditions of stability and well-being. They will seek to eliminate conflict in their international economic policies and will encourage economic collaboration between any or all of them.

ARTICLE 3

In order more effectively to achieve the objectives of this Treaty, the Parties, separately and jointly, by means of continuous and effective self-help and mutual aid, will maintain and develop their individual and collective capacity to resist armed attack.

ARTICLE 4

The Parties will consult together whenever, in the opinion of any of them, the territorial integrity, political independence or security of any of the Parties is threatened.

ARTICLE 5

The Parties agree that an armed attack against one or more of them in Europe or North America shall be considered an attack against them all and consequently they agree that, if such an armed attack occurs, each of them, in exercise of the right of individual or collective self-defence recognized by Article 51 of the Charter of the United Nations, will assist the Party or Parties so attacked by taking forthwith, individually and in concert with the other Parties, such action as it deems necessary, including the use of armed force, to restore and maintain the security of the North Atlantic area.

Any such armed attack and all measures taken as a result thereof shall immediately be reported to the Security Council. Such measures shall be terminated when the Security Council has taken the measures necessary to restore and maintain international peace and security.

ARTICLE 6[1]

For the purpose of Article v an armed attack on one or more of the Parties is deemed to include an armed attack on the territory of any of the Parties in Europe or North America, on the Algerian Departments of France [2], on the occupation forces of any Party in Europe, on the islands under the jurisdiction of any Party in the North Atlantic area north of the Tropic of Cancer or on the vessels or aircraft in this area of any of the Parties.

ARTICLE 7

This Treaty does not affect, and shall not be interpreted as affecting, in any way the rights and obligations under the Charter of the Parties which are members of the United Nations, or the primary responsibility of the Security Council for the maintenance of international peace and security.

ARTICLE 8

Each Party declares that none of the international engagements now in force between it and any other of the Parties or any third State is in conflict with the provisions of this Treaty, and undertakes not to enter into any international engagement in conflict with this Treaty.

(1) The definition of the territories to which Article v applies has been revised by Article II of the Protocol to the North Atlantic Treaty on the accession of Greece and Turkey (see p. 000).

(2) On 16th January, 1963, the North Atlantic Council has heard a declaration by the French Representative who recalled that by the vote on self-determination on 1st July, 1962, the Algerian people had pronounced itself in favour of the independence of Algeria in co-operation with France. In consequence, the President of the French Republic had on 3rd July, 1962, formally recognized the independence of Algeria. The result was that the "Algerian departments of France" no longer existed as such, and that at the same time the fact that they were mentioned in the North Atlantic Treaty had no longer any bearing. Following this statement the Council noted that insofar as the former Algerian Departments of France were concerned, the relevant clauses of this Treaty had become inapplicable as from 3rd July, 1962.

ARTICLE 9

The Parties hereby establish a Council, on which each of them shall be represented, to consider matters concerning the implementation of this Treaty. The Council shall be so organized as to be able to meet promptly at any time. The Council shall set up such subsidiary bodies as may be necessary; in particular it shall establish immediately a defence committee which shall recommend measures for the implementation of Articles III and V.

ARTICLE 10

The Parties may, by unanimous agreement, invite any other European State in a position to further the principles of this Treaty and to contribute to the security of the North Atlantic area to accede to this Treaty. Any State so invited may become a Party to the Treaty by depositing its instrument of accession with the Government of the United States of America. The Government of the United States of America will inform each of the Parties of the deposit of each such instrument of accession.

ARTICLE 11

This Treaty shall be ratified and its provisions carried out by the Parties in accordance with their respective constitutional processes. The instruments of ratification shall be deposited as soon as possible with the Government of the United States of America, which will notify all the other signatories of each deposit. The Treaty shall enter into force between the States which have ratified it as soon as the ratifications of the majority of the signatories, including the ratifications of Belgium, Canada, France, Luxembourg, the Netherlands, the United Kingdom and the United States, have been deposited and shall come into effect with respect to other States on the date of the deposit of their ratifications.

ARTICLE 12

After the Treaty has been in force for ten years, or at any time thereafter, the Parties shall, if any of them so requests, consult together for the purpose of reviewing the Treaty, having regard for the factors then affecting peace and security in the North Atlantic area, including the development of universal as well as regional arrangements under the Charter of the United Nations for the maintenance of international peace and security.

ARTICLE 13

After the Treaty has been in force for twenty years, any Party may cease to be a Party one year after its notice of denunciation has been given to the Government of the United States of America, which will inform the Governments of the other Parties of the deposit of each notice of denunciation.

ARTICLE 14

This Treaty, of which the English and French texts are equally authentic, shall be deposited in the archives of the Government of the United States of America. Duly certified copies will be transmitted by that Government to the governments of the other signatories.

APPENDIX E

PROTOCOL TO THE NORTH ATLANTIC TREATY ON THE ACCESSION OF GREECE AND TURKEY LONDON, 22 OCTOBER 1951

[FROM: NATO Facts and Figures. Brussells, The North Atlantic Treaty Organization, Information Service, October 1971.]

PROTOCOL TO THE NORTH ATLANTIC TREATY ON THE ACCESSION OF GREECE AND TURKEY

London, 22 October, 1951

The Parties to the North Atlantic Treaty, signed at Washington on 4 April, 1949,
Being satisfied that the security of the North Atlantic area will be enhanced by the accession of the Kingdom of Greece and the Republic of Turkey to that Treaty,
Agree as follows:

ARTICLE I

Upon the entry into force of this Protocol, the Government of the United States of America shall, on behalf of all the Parties, communicate to the Government of the Kingdom of Greece and the Government of the Republic of Turkey an invitation to accede to the North Atlantic Treaty, as it may be modified by Article II of the present Protocol. Thereafter the Kingdom of Greece and the Republic of Turkey shall each become a Party on the date when it deposits its instruments of accession with the Government of the United States of America in accordance with Article X of the Treaty.

ARTICLE II

If the Republic of Turkey becomes a Party to the North Atlantic Treaty, Article VI of the Treaty shall, as from the date of the deposit by the Government of the Republic of Turkey of its instruments of accession with the Government of the United States of America, be modified to read as follows:
"For the purpose of Article 5, an armed attack on one or more of the Parties is deemed to include an armed attack:
i. on the territory of any of the Parties in Europe or North America, on the Algerian Departments of France, on the territory of Turkey or on the islands under the jurisdiction of any of the Parties in the North Atlantic area north of the Tropic of Cancer;
ii. on the forces, vessels, or aircraft of any of the Parties, when in or over these territories or any other area in Europe in which occupation forces of any of the Parties were stationed on the date when the Treaty entered into force or the Mediterranean Sea or the North Atlantic area north of the Tropic of Cancer."

ARTICLE III

The present Protocol shall enter into force when each of the Parties to the North Atlantic Treaty has notified the Government of the United States of America of its acceptance thereof. The Government of the United States of America shall inform all the Parties to the North Atlantic Treaty of the date of the receipt of each such notification and of the date of the entry into force of the present Protocol.

ARTICLE IV

The present Protocol, of which the English and French texts are equally authentic, shall be deposited in the Archives of the Government of the United States of America. Duly certified copies thereof shall be transmitted by the Government to the governments of all the Parties to the North Atlantic Treaty.

APPENDIX F

PROTOCOL TO THE NORTH ATLANTIC TREATY ON THE ACCESSION OF THE FEDERAL REPUBLIC OF GERMANY PARIS, 23 OCTOBER 1954

[FROM: NATO Facts and Figures. Brussells, The North Atlantic Treaty Organization, Information Service, October 1971.]

PROTOCOL TO THE NORTH ATLANTIC TREATY ON THE ACCESSION OF THE FEDERAL REPUBLIC OF GERMANY

Paris, 23 October, 1954

The Parties to the North Atlantic Treaty signed at Washington on 4 April, 1949,

Being satisfied that the security of the North Atlantic area will be enhanced by the accession of the Federal Republic of Germany to that Treaty, and

Having noted that the Federal Republic of Germany has, by a declaration dated 3 October, 1954, accepted the obligations set forth in Article 2 of the Charter of the United Nations and has undertaken upon its accession to the North Atlantic Treaty to refrain from any action inconsistent with the strictly defensive character of that Treaty, and

Having further noted that all member governments have associated themselves with the declaration also made on 3 October, 1954, by the Governments of the United States of America, the United Kingdom of Great Britain and Northern Ireland and the French Republic in connection with the aforesaid declaration of the Federal Republic of Germany,

Agree as follows:

ARTICLE I

Upon the entry into force of the present Protocol, the Government of the United States of America shall on behalf of all the Parties communicate to the Government of the Federal Republic of Germany an invitation to accede to the North Atlantic Treaty. Thereafter the Federal Republic of Germany shall become a Party to that Treaty on the date when it deposits its instruments of accession with the Government of the United States of America in accordance with Article 10 of the Treaty.

ARTICLE II

The present Protocol shall enter into force, when (a) each of the Parties to the North Atlantic Treaty has notified to the Government of the United States of America its acceptance thereof, (b) all instruments of ratification of the Protocol modifying and completing the Brussels Treaty have been deposited with the Belgian Government, and (c) all instruments of ratification or approval of the Convention on the Presence of Foreign Forces in the Federal Republic of Germany have been deposited with the Government of the Federal Republic of Germany. The Government of the United States of America shall inform the other Parties to the North Atlantic Treaty of the date of the receipt of each notification of acceptance of the present Protocol and of the date of the entry into force of the present Protocol.

ARTICLE III

The present Protocol, of which the English and French texts are equally authentic, shall be deposited in the Archives of The Government of the United States of America. Duly certified copies thereof shall be transmitted by that Government to the governments of the other Parties to the North Atlantic Treaty.

APPENDIX G

THREE-POWER DECLARATION ON BERLIN PARIS, OCTOBER 23, 1954

[FROM: NATO Facts and Figures. Brussells, The North Atlantic Treaty Organization, Information Service, October 1971.]

THREE-POWER DECLARATION ON BERLIN

Paris, October 23, 1954

The following statement was issued on 23 October, 1954, by the Foreign Ministers of the French Republic, the United Kingdom and the United States of America:
"With respect to Berlin, in addition to the Allied security guarantees for the city in the London communiqué of October 3, 1954, the Foreign Ministers of France, the United Kingdom and the United States have noted with deep satisfaction the close and friendly co-operation between the Allied and Berlin authorities. The Three Powers are determined to ensure the greatest possible degree of self-government in Berlin compatible with Berlin's special situation. Accordingly, the three Governments have instructed their representatives in Berlin to consult with the authorities of that city with a view to implementing jointly and to the fullest degree possible the foregoing principles".

APPENDIX H
NATO CIVIL AND MILITARY STRUCTURE (CHART)

[FROM: NATO Facts and Figures. Brussells, The North Atlantic Treaty Organization, Information Service, October 1971.]

CIVIL AND MILITARY STRUCTURE

The fifteen member Governments of the Alliance consult and co-ordinate their policies through the medium of the North Atlantic Council. The Council is thus the highest authority in NATO; it normally meets twice a year at Ministerial level with the fifteen Foreign Ministers present. In permanent session the Council meets at least once a week, often more frequently, at the level of Ambassadors (Permanent Representatives). When integrated defence matters are discussed the fourteen Permanent Representatives (i.e. without France) meet as the Defence Planning Committee (DPC). Similarly twice a year the DPC meets at the level of Defence Ministers. To assist in carrying out their roles, the Council and the DPC have established a number of Committees, the most important of which deal with the subjects shown in the diagram below. These Committees, which cover the whole range of NATO's activities, meet under the Chairmanship of a member of the International Staff. The Secretary General of NATO chairs both the Council and the DPC. He also directs the International Secretariat whose staff is drawn from all fifteen countries.

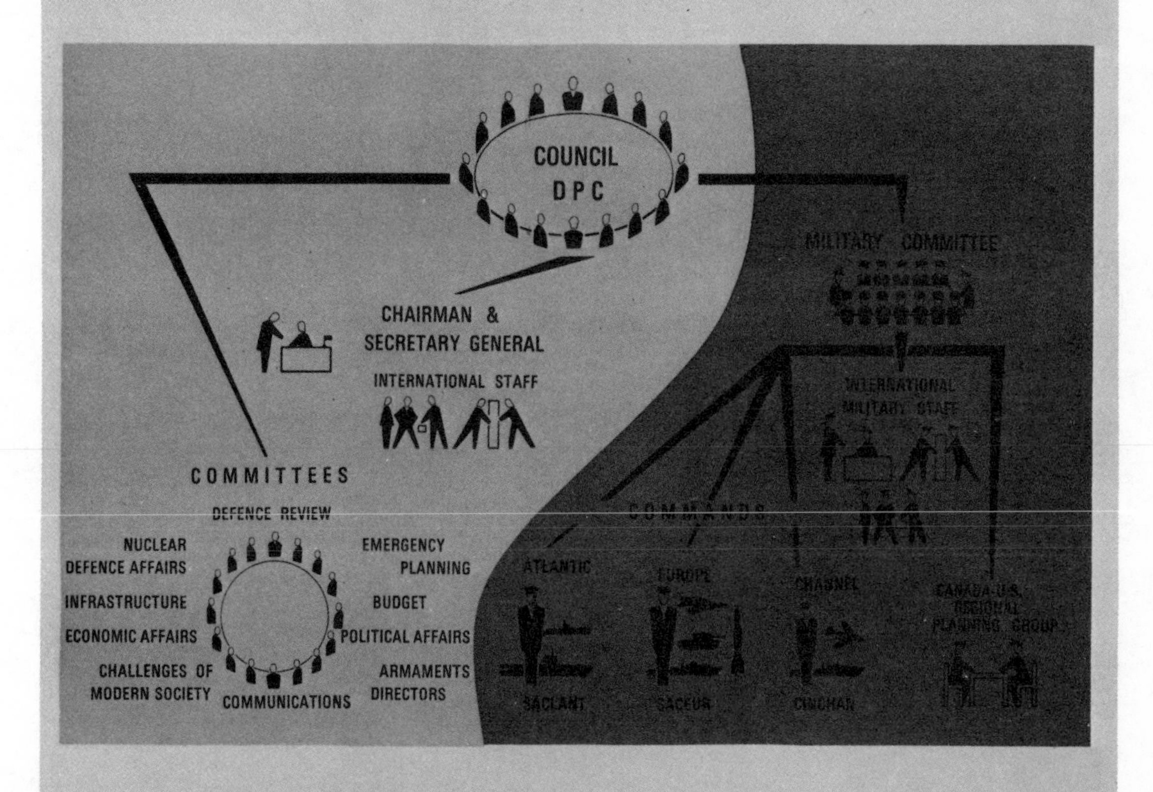

The senior military authority within NATO is the Military Committee which provides military advice to the Council and the DPC. It is composed of the Chiefs-of-Staff of the thirteen member countries participating in NATO's integrated military structure. (France withdrew in 1966. Iceland has no armed forces). Two or three times a year the Military Committee meets at Chiefs-of-Staff level; it meets each week in Permanent Session with national Military Representatives appointed by their Chiefs-of-Staff. The Military Committee is served by an International Military Staff which acts as its executive agency and functions like the civilian Secretariat. The Chairman of the Military Committee is elected by the Chiefs-of-Staff for a period of two to three years and is present at all Council Meetings. The NATO defence area is divided into three major Allied Commands (Atlantic, Europe and Channel) and the Canada-United States Regional Planning Group. Under the general guidance of the Military Committee the major NATO Commanders are responsible for planning the defence of the areas concerned and for conducting NATO's land, sea and air exercises.

APPENDIX I

NATO MILITARY STRUCTURE (CHART)

[FROM: NATO Facts and Figures. Brussells, The North Atlantic Treaty Organization, Information Service, October 1971.]

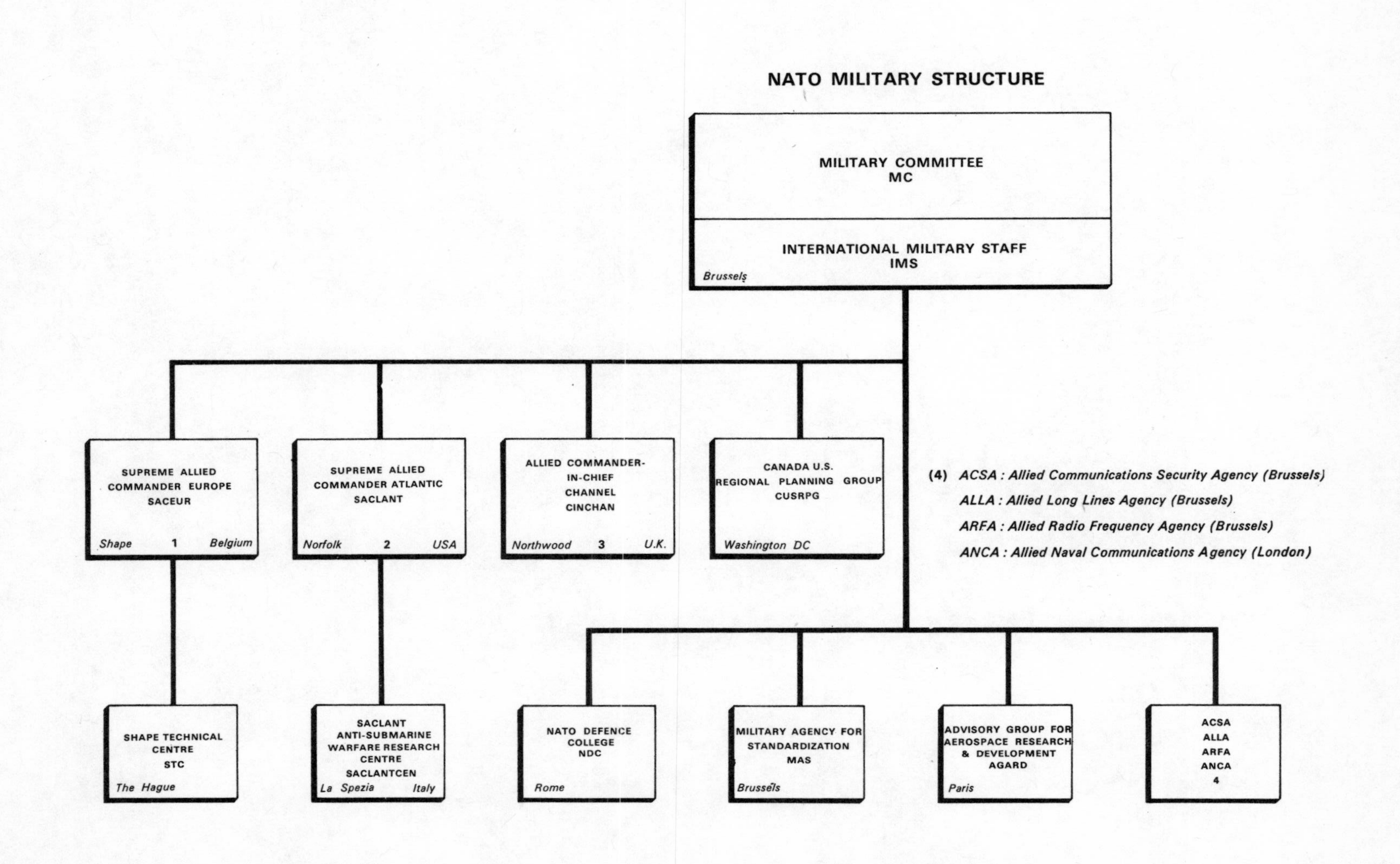

(4) *ACSA : Allied Communications Security Agency (Brussels)*
ALLA : Allied Long Lines Agency (Brussels)
ARFA : Allied Radio Frequency Agency (Brussels)
ANCA : Allied Naval Communications Agency (London)

APPENDIX J

NORTH ATLANTIC COUNCIL DIPLOMATIC WORKSHOP (CHART)

[FROM: NATO Facts and Figures. Brussels, The North Atlantic Treaty Organization, Information Service, October 1971.]

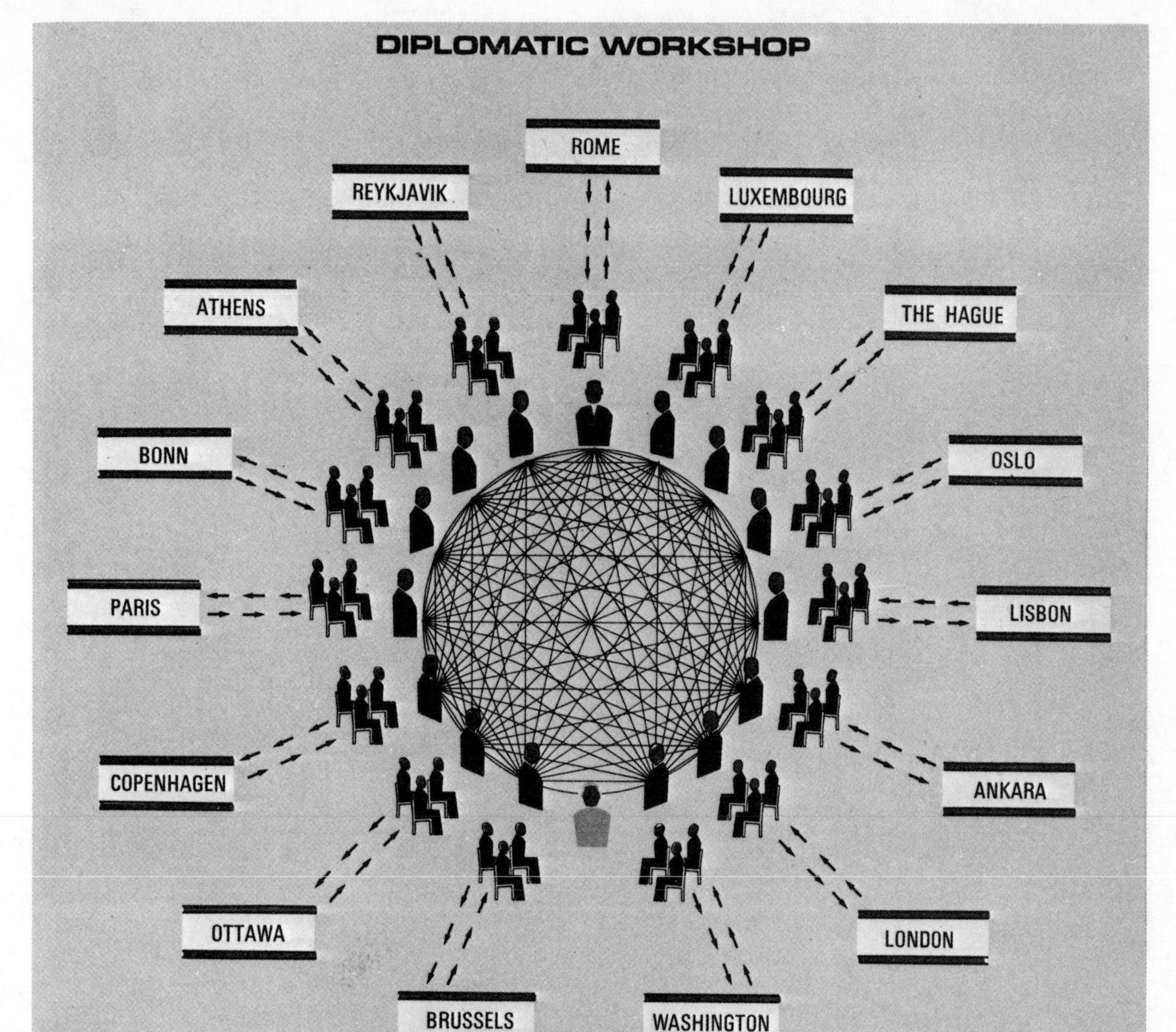

PERMANENT REPRESENTATIVE

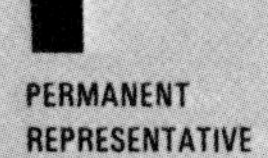

NATIONAL DELEGATION

CHAIRMAN & SECRETARY GENERAL

NATIONAL GOVERNMENT

NORTH ATLANTIC COUNCIL

The North Atlantic Council provides a unique forum for confidential and constant intergovernmental consultation on all topics as well as providing the highest level of decision making machinery within NATO. There is no supranational element in the Organization and all the fifteen sovereign member countries have an equal right to express their views round the Council table. Political consultation ranges over the whole field of foreign affairs and is not limited to NATO's geographical area. The only topics excluded are those relating to the purely internal affairs of member countries. Each national delegation is headed by a Permanent Representative with the rank of Ambassador supported by staffs which vary in size. All act on instructions from their capitals. Thus the Council provides a unique type of " Diplomatic Workshop " under the Chairmanship of the Secretary General. To attain such a high degree of constant consultation between the fifteen by the customary method of bilateral diplomatic exchanges would be quite impracticable - in fact every time the Council meets it provides the equivalent of 105 bilateral exchanges as will be seen from the lines in the diagram above.

APPENDIX K

PRINCIPAL COMMITTEES OF THE NATO COUNCIL (CHART)

[FROM: NATO Facts and Figures. Brussels, The North Atlantic Treaty Organization, Information Service, October 1971.]

PRINCIPAL COMMITTEES OF THE COUNCIL

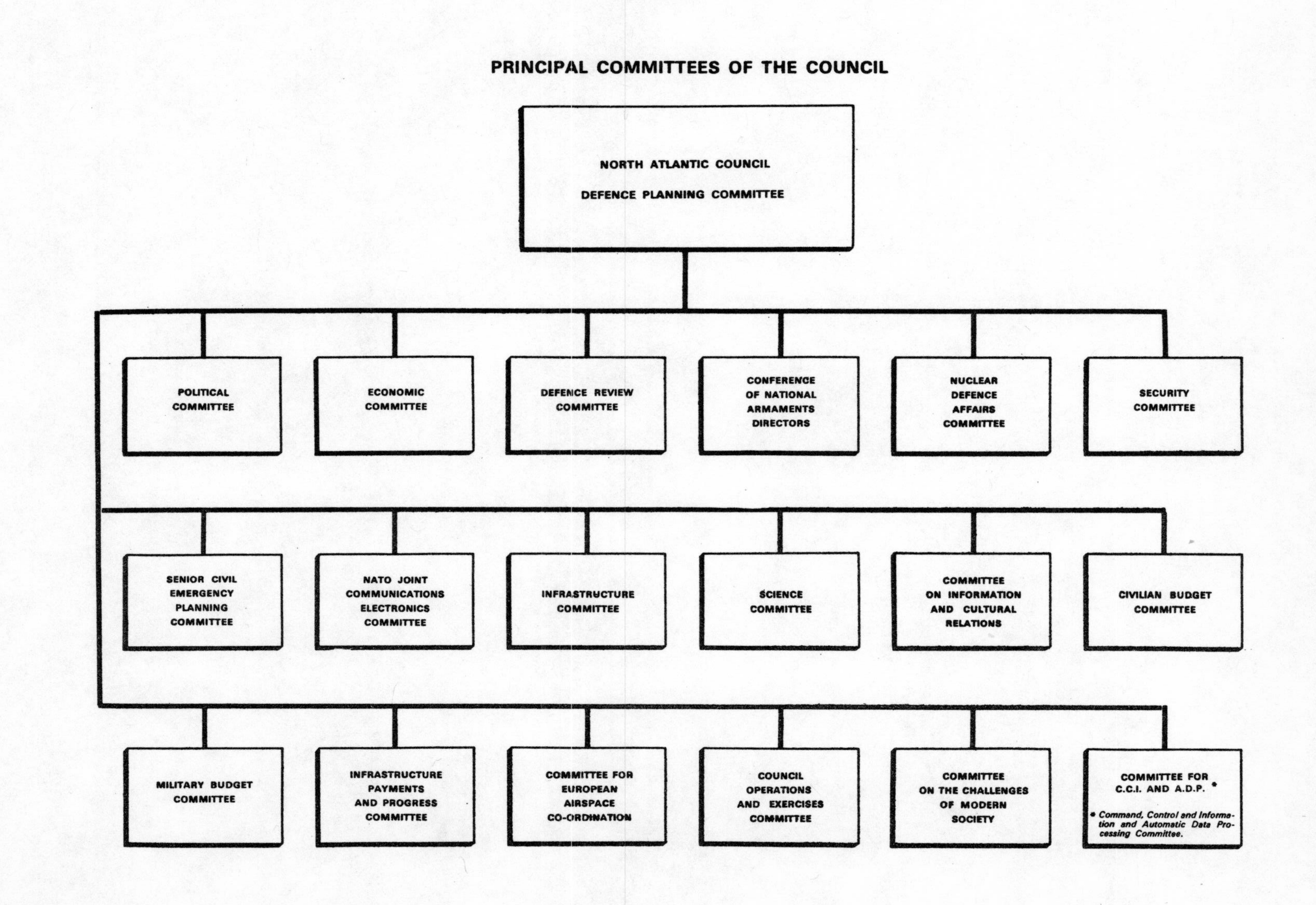

NORTH ATLANTIC COUNCIL
DEFENCE PLANNING COMMITTEE
POLITICAL COMMITTEE
ECONOMIC COMMITTEE
DEFENCE REVIEW COMMITTEE
CONFERENCE OF NATIONAL ARMAMENTS DIRECTORS
NUCLEAR DEFENCE AFFAIRS COMMITTEE
SECURITY COMMITTEE
SENIOR CIVIL EMERGENCY PLANNING COMMITTEE
NATO JOINT COMMUNICATIONS ELECTRONICS COMMITTEE
INFRASTRUCTURE COMMITTEE
SCIENCE COMMITTEE
COMMITTEE ON INFORMATION AND CULTURAL RELATIONS
CIVILIAN BUDGET COMMITTEE
MILITARY BUDGET COMMITTEE
INFRASTRUCTURE PAYMENTS AND PROGRESS COMMITTEE
COMMITTEE FOR EUROPEAN AIRSPACE CO-ORDINATION
COUNCIL OPERATIONS AND EXERCISES COMMITTEE
COMMITTEE ON THE CHALLENGES OF MODERN SOCIETY
COMMITTEE FOR C.C.I. AND A.D.P. *
* Command, Control and Information and Automatic Data Processing Committee.

APPENDIX L

ALLIED COMMAND ATLANTIC (CHART)

[FROM: NATO Facts and Figures. Brussells, The North Atlantic Treaty Organization, Information Service, October 1971.]

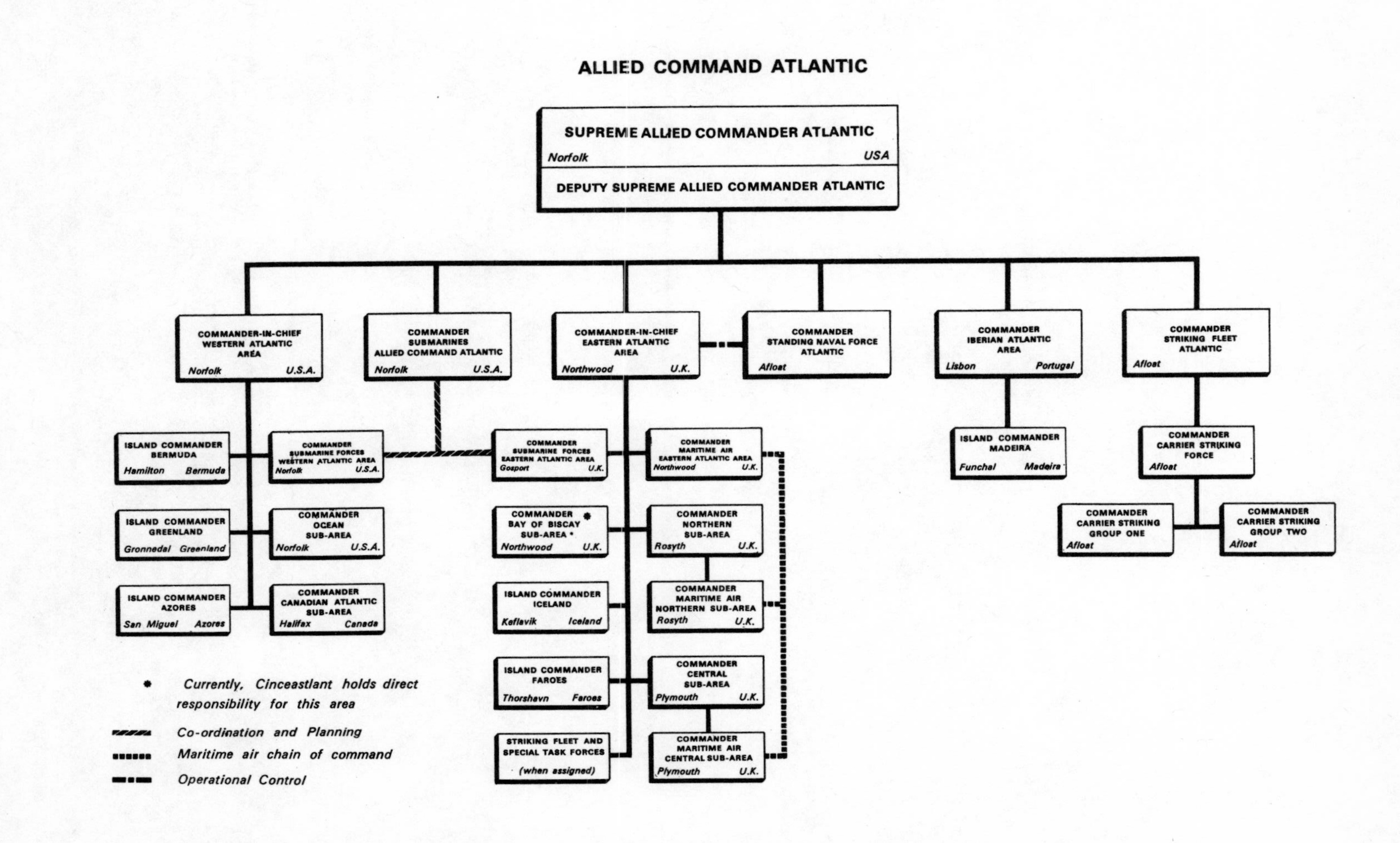
ALLIED COMMAND ATLANTIC
SUPREME ALLIED COMMANDER ATLANTIC
Norfolk USA
DEPUTY SUPREME ALLIED COMMANDER ATLANTIC
COMMANDER-IN-CHIEF WESTERN ATLANTIC AREA
Norfolk U.S.A.
COMMANDER SUBMARINES ALLIED COMMAND ATLANTIC
Norfolk U.S.A.
COMMANDER-IN-CHIEF EASTERN ATLANTIC AREA
Northwood U.K.
COMMANDER STANDING NAVAL FORCE ATLANTIC
Afloat
COMMANDER IBERIAN ATLANTIC AREA
Lisbon Portugal
COMMANDER STRIKING FLEET ATLANTIC
Afloat
ISLAND COMMANDER BERMUDA
Hamilton Bermuda
COMMANDER SUBMARINE FORCES WESTERN ATLANTIC AREA
Norfolk U.S.A.
ISLAND COMMANDER GREENLAND
Gronnedal Greenland
COMMANDER OCEAN SUB-AREA
Norfolk U.S.A.
ISLAND COMMANDER AZORES
San Miguel Azores
COMMANDER CANADIAN ATLANTIC SUB-AREA
Halifax Canada
COMMANDER SUBMARINE FORCES EASTERN ATLANTIC AREA
Gosport U.K.
COMMANDER MARITIME AIR EASTERN ATLANTIC AREA
Northwood U.K.
COMMANDER BAY OF BISCAY SUB-AREA *
Northwood U.K.
COMMANDER NORTHERN SUB-AREA
Rosyth U.K.
ISLAND COMMANDER ICELAND
Keflavik Iceland
COMMANDER MARITIME AIR NORTHERN SUB-AREA
Rosyth U.K.
ISLAND COMMANDER FAROES
Thorshavn Faroes
COMMANDER CENTRAL SUB-AREA
Plymouth U.K.
STRIKING FLEET AND SPECIAL TASK FORCES
(when assigned)
COMMANDER MARITIME AIR CENTRAL SUB-AREA
Plymouth U.K.
ISLAND COMMANDER MADEIRA
Funchal Madeira
COMMANDER CARRIER STRIKING FORCE
Afloat
COMMANDER CARRIER STRIKING GROUP ONE
Afloat
COMMANDER CARRIER STRIKING GROUP TWO
Afloat
* Currently, Cinceastlant holds direct responsibility for this area
Co-ordination and Planning
Maritime air chain of command
Operational Control

APPENDIX M

ALLIED COMMAND CHANNEL (CHART)

[FROM: NATO Facts and Figures. Brussells, The North Atlantic Treaty Organization, Information Service, October 1971.]

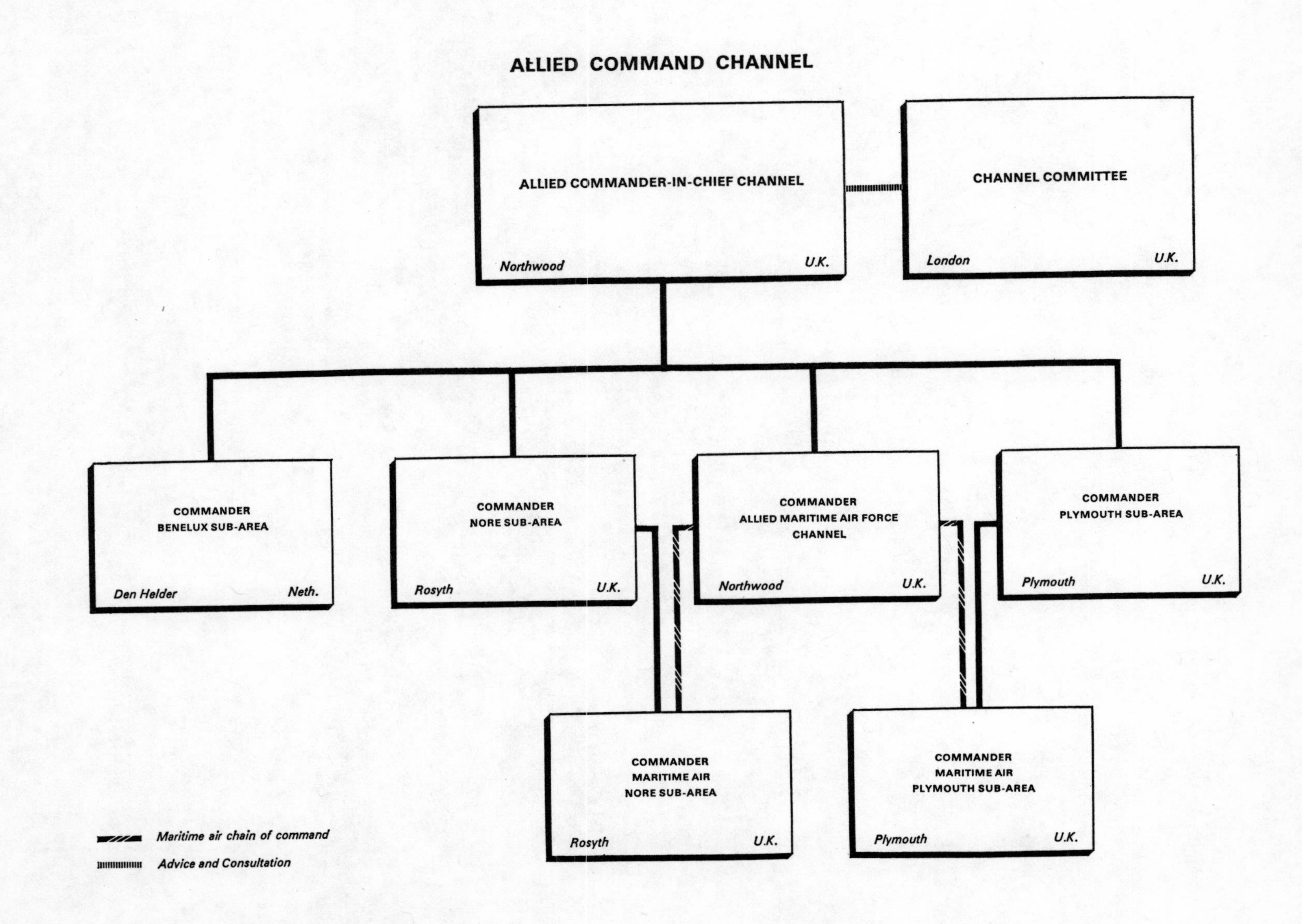
ALLIED COMMAND CHANNEL
ALLIED COMMANDER-IN-CHIEF CHANNEL
Northwood
U.K.
CHANNEL COMMITTEE
London
U.K.
COMMANDER
BENELUX SUB-AREA
Den Helder
Neth.
COMMANDER
NORE SUB-AREA
Rosyth
U.K.
COMMANDER
ALLIED MARITIME AIR FORCE
CHANNEL
Northwood
U.K.
COMMANDER
PLYMOUTH SUB-AREA
Plymouth
U.K.
COMMANDER
MARITIME AIR
NORE SUB-AREA
Rosyth
U.K.
COMMANDER
MARITIME AIR
PLYMOUTH SUB-AREA
Plymouth
U.K.
Maritime air chain of command
Advice and Consultation

APPENDIX N

ALLIED COMMAND EUROPE (CHART)

[FROM: NATO Facts and Figures. Brussels, The North Atlantic Treaty Organization, Information Service, October 1971.]

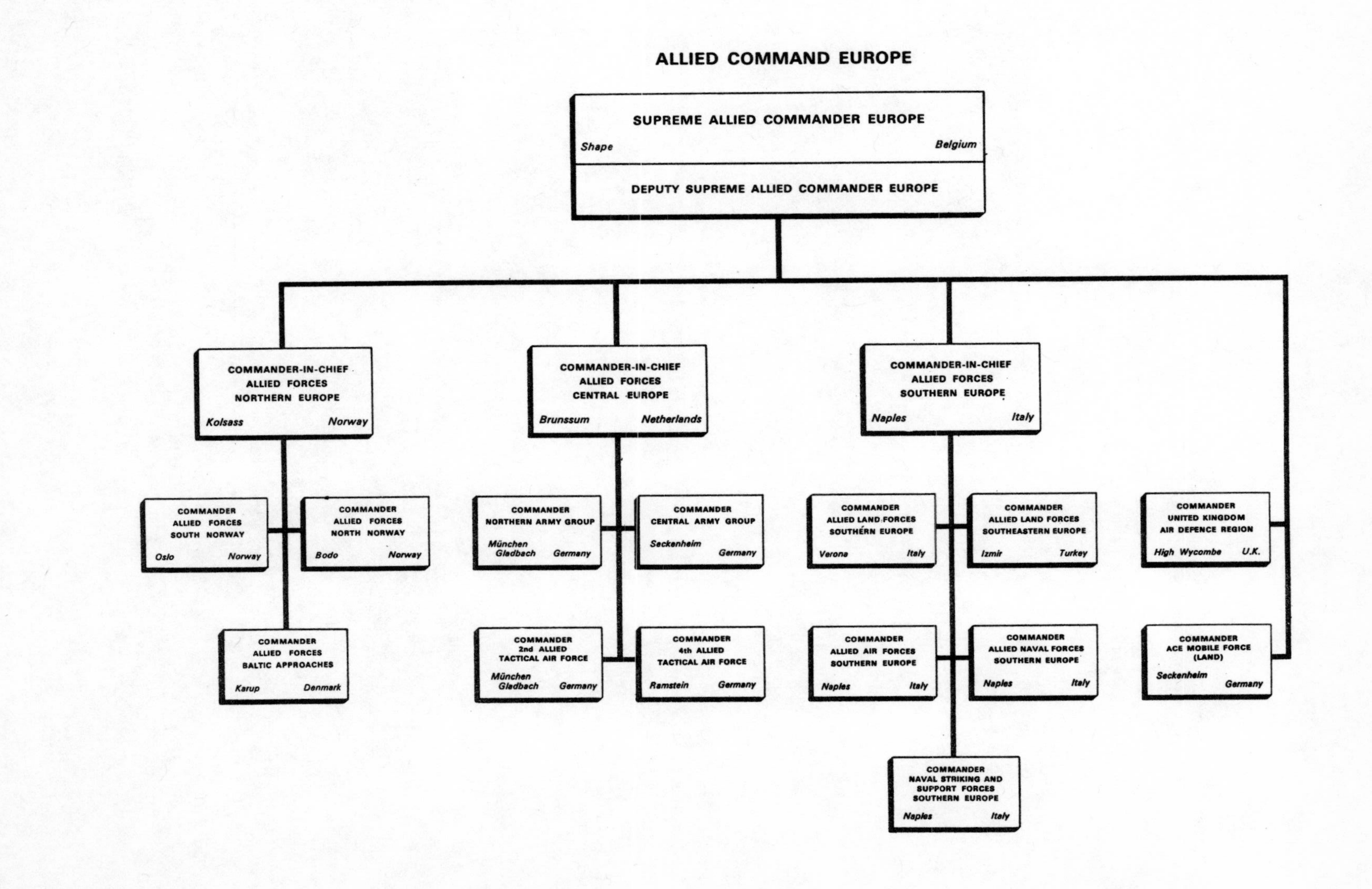
ALLIED COMMAND EUROPE
SUPREME ALLIED COMMANDER EUROPE
Shape Belgium
DEPUTY SUPREME ALLIED COMMANDER EUROPE
COMMANDER-IN-CHIEF ALLIED FORCES NORTHERN EUROPE
Kolsass Norway
COMMANDER ALLIED FORCES SOUTH NORWAY
Oslo Norway
COMMANDER ALLIED FORCES NORTH NORWAY
Bodo Norway
COMMANDER ALLIED FORCES BALTIC APPROACHES
Karup Denmark
COMMANDER-IN-CHIEF ALLIED FORCES CENTRAL EUROPE
Brunssum Netherlands
COMMANDER NORTHERN ARMY GROUP
München Gladbach Germany
COMMANDER CENTRAL ARMY GROUP
Seckenheim Germany
COMMANDER 2nd ALLIED TACTICAL AIR FORCE
München Gladbach Germany
COMMANDER 4th ALLIED TACTICAL AIR FORCE
Ramstein Germany
COMMANDER-IN-CHIEF ALLIED FORCES SOUTHERN EUROPE
Naples Italy
COMMANDER ALLIED LAND FORCES SOUTHERN EUROPE
Verona Italy
COMMANDER ALLIED LAND FORCES SOUTHEASTERN EUROPE
Izmir Turkey
COMMANDER ALLIED AIR FORCES SOUTHERN EUROPE
Naples Italy
COMMANDER ALLIED NAVAL FORCES SOUTHERN EUROPE
Naples Italy
COMMANDER NAVAL STRIKING AND SUPPORT FORCES SOUTHERN EUROPE
Naples Italy
COMMANDER UNITED KINGDOM AIR DEFENCE REGION
High Wycombe U.K.
COMMANDER ACE MOBILE FORCE (LAND)
Seckenheim Germany

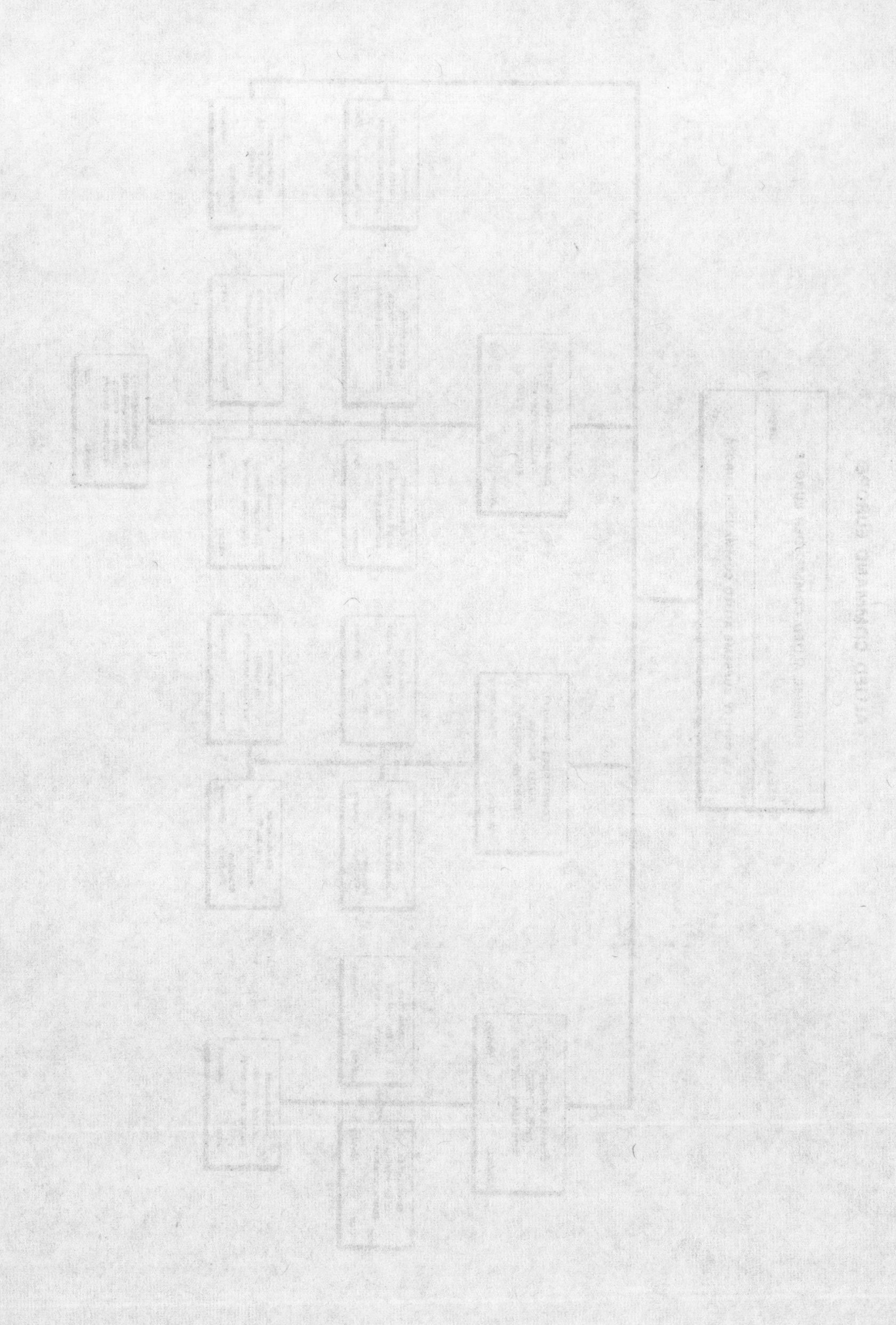

APPENDIX O

NATIONAL VOLUNTARY ORGANIZATIONS BELONGING TO THE ATLANTIC TREATY ASSOCIATION

[FROM: NATO Facts and Figures. Brussells, The North Atlantic Treaty Organization, Information Service, October 1971.]

NATIONAL VOLUNTARY ORGANIZATIONS BELONGING TO THE ATLANTIC TREATY ASSOCIATION

185, rue de la Pompe, Paris XVIème.

BELGIUM:
The Belgian Atlantic Association
12, rue des Taxandres
1040 - Bruxelles

CANADA :
The Atlantic Council of Canada
31, Wellesley Street East,
Toronto 5, Ontario

DENMARK :
Danish Atlantic Association
H.C. Andersens Blvd 11,
1553 Copenhagen V.

FRANCE:
French Association for the
Atlantic Community
185, rue de la Pompe
Paris XVIème

FEDERAL REPUBLIC OF GERMANY:
The German Atlantic Society
Meckenheimer Strasse 62
53 Bonn

GREECE:
Hellenic Atlantic Association
39, avenue Venizelos
Athens

ICELAND:
Association of Western
Co-operation
Box 28
Reykjavik

ITALY:
Italian Atlantic Committee
Piazza di Firenze 27
Rome

LUXEMBOURG:
Luxembourg Atlantic Association
20bis, rue de Louvigny
Luxembourg.

MALTA:
Malta Atlantic Association,
16, Britannia Street,
Valletta

NETHERLANDS:
Netherlands Atlantic Committee
Nassau
Zuilensteinstraat 9
The Hague

NORWAY:
Norwegian Atlantic Committee
Akersgaten 57
Oslo 1

PORTUGAL:
Portuguese Atlantic Committee
Rua Castilho 167
Lisbon

TURKEY:
Turk Atlantik Andlasmasi
Dernegi
Vali Dr. Resit Caddesi N° 35
Çankaya - Ankara

UNITED KINGDOM:
The British Atlantic Committee
Benjamin Franklin House
36, Craven Street
London W.C.2

UNITED STATES:
The Atlantic Council of the United States,
1616 H Street, N.W.
Washington D.C. 20006

APPENDIX P

MILITARY EXPENDITURES, GNP, POPULATION, AND ARMED FORCES, 1963–1973

NATO AND WARSAW PACT

[FROM: World Military Expenditures and Arms Trade, 1963–1973. Washington, U.S. Arms Control and Disarmament Agency, 1975.]

MILITARY EXPENDITURES, GNP, POPULATION, AND ARMED FORCES BY GROUP AND REGION BY YEAR

COUNTRY OR REGION	YEAR	MILITARY EXPENDITURES (MILEX) Current dollars (billions)	MILITARY EXPENDITURES (MILEX) Constant dollars (billions)	GROSS NATIONAL PRODUCT (GNP) Current dollars (billions)	GROSS NATIONAL PRODUCT (GNP) Constant dollars (billions)	MILEX / GNP (%)	PEOPLE (millions)	MILEX per capita (constant dollars)	GNP per capita (constant dollars)	ARMED FORCES (thousands)	MILEX / ARMED FORCES (constant dollars)	ARMED FORCES per 1000 people
NATO TOTAL												
	1963	72.64	103.22	1005.8	1461.6	7.22	495.584	208.27	2949	6067	17013	12.24
	1964	72.63	101.09	1089.8	1545.8	6.66	501.496	201.57	3082	6094	16588	12.15
	1965	73.91	100.47	1180.3	1631.6	6.26	507.476	197.98	3215	5852	17168	11.53
	1966	86.62	113.89	1284.9	1721.3	6.74	512.624	222.17	3358	6321	18018	12.33
	1967	100.09	127.56	1360.4	1770.2	7.36	517.410	246.54	3421	6638	19217	12.83
	1968	104.67	129.36	1462.9	1860.6	7.16	521.808	247.90	3566	6804	19012	13.04
	1969	106.21	125.54	1593.9	1939.8	6.66	526.955	238.24	3681	6706	18721	12.73
	1970	104.37	116.90	1722.4	1977.5	6.06	531.830	219.80	3718	6307	18535	11.86
	1971	105.08	111.61	1897.3	2045.1	5.54	536.957	207.85	3809	6011	18567	11.19
	1972	113.50	113.50	2149.9	2149.9	5.28	541.412	209.64	3971	5704	19899	10.54
	1973	121.38	110.42	2526.3	2275.4	4.80	545.859	202.29	4169	5579	19793	10.22
GROWTH RATE (PCT ANN)			1.1		4.3	-3.3	1.0	.1	3.3	-.5	1.6	-1.5
WARSAW PACT												
	1963	53.80	73.28	373.4	509.5	5 TO 9 (EST) d/	323.578	226.46	1574	4506	16263	13.93
	1964	54.20	72.66	407.7	546.9		327.144	222.11	1672	4500	16147	13.76
	1965	53.46	70.83	440.4	580.3		330.601	214.25	1755	4134	17134	12.50
	1966	55.65	71.81	480.3	616.0		333.858	215.08	1845	4084	17582	12.23
	1967	60.04	74.99	524.7	652.1		336.910	222.58	1935	4311	17395	12.80
	1968	68.99	82.74	576.7	689.1		340.070	243.31	2026	4467	18523	13.14
	1969	73.83	84.20	622.3	709.6		342.936	245.54	2069	4571	18421	13.33
	1970	79.73	86.59	700.5	757.0		345.790	250.42	2189	4594	18849	13.29
	1971	85.74	88.14	767.0	793.3		348.836	252.66	2274	4757	18528	13.64
	1972	93.87	93.87	818.1	818.1		351.779	266.84	2326	4800	19556	13.64
	1973	100.05	94.31	927.0	877.8		354.622	265.94	2475	4860	19405	13.70
GROWTH RATE (PCT ANN)			3.2		5.4		.9	2.2	4.4	1.2	1.9	.3

APPENDIX Q

NORTH AMERICA—Regional Survey

ARMED FORCES AND MILITARY POWER

[Reprinted with permission from: The Almanac of World Military Power, by Col. T. N. Dupuy, U.S. Army, Ret., Col. John A. C. Andrews, U.S. Air Force, Ret., and Grace P. Hayes. 3rd ed. Dunn Loring, Va., T. N. Dupuy Associates, 1974.]

NORTH AMERICA

Regional Survey

MILITARY GEOGRAPHY

The North American continent, here understood to include the United States, Canada, Mexico, and the massive and largely unpopulated island of Greenland, has a total area of about nine million square miles.

Northern North America has generally sparse to moderate population density, moderate birth rates of 17.5 to 27.5 per 1,000, high literacy, and high per capita income, while Mexico shares with the other Latin American countries to the south an extremely high birth rate, relatively low literacy, and low (but growing) per capita income.

The political systems of all North American countries are stable. All are in reality democratic republics, although the Dominion of Canada nominally owes allegiance to the British Crown. The centrally placed United States is bound to each of its contiguous neighbors by a tradition of peaceful relations stretching back at least 50 years, and by mutual assistance defense treaties. The psychological ties with Canada are especially strong.

The continent is crossed by north-south mountain ranges, dividing it into an eastern coastal plain; an eastern mountain region comprising the Laurentian plateau and the Appalachian and Ozark Mountains; the great central plains; and the rugged Cordilleran highlands, which comprise the Rockies and the Pacific coastal ranges, and stretch from Alaska and northern Canada down through Mexico. Mexico falls almost entirely in this mountainous western region and has only very narrow coastal plains. The Great Lakes and St. Lawrence River form the most important inland waterway, stretching across most of the eastern half of the continent between Canada and the United States.

STRATEGIC SIGNIFICANCE

The area is dominated—although not controlled—politically, economically, and militarily by the United States. Eastern North America, including the eastern United States and southeastern Canada, is one of the four leading economic power regions of the world, along with Western Europe, Eastern Europe, and Japan. This power is derived from generally literate, technically skilled populations, wealth in a variety of natural resources, and highly developed methods of economic management. The area's great military strength, including the United States' nuclear-warhead ICBMs, is based on this economic power.

Military invasion from outside the continent has not occurred for more than 100 years.* The central fact of North American military geography for at least two centuries has been the isolation of this land mass, separated from other world powers by the world's two largest oceans. The new significant fact is the revolution in vulnerability that occurred with the development of thermonuclear weapons and ICBM delivery systems. With these weapons in the hands of the United States' chief political power adversary, the Soviet Union, with no tested defense available against them, and with air distance across the North Polar region the significant military distance under current technological circumstances, the United States and its North American allies are in constant danger of devastation by military might—as is their adversary beyond the Pole. The danger of amphibious invasion remains as negligible as ever.

REGIONAL ALLIANCES

The United States and Mexico are both members of the Organization of American States (see Central America and West Indies Regional Survey).

The United States and Canada are members of the North Atlantic Treaty Organization (see Western Europe Regional Survey).

The United States has no formal bilateral treaties with either Mexico or Canada, but bilateral planning agencies exist with both nations, permitting direct military planning for defense of the North American continent (see following articles on Canada and Mexico).

RECENT INTRA-AND EXTRA-REGIONAL CONFLICTS

There have been no international armed conflicts or incidents involving the use of force in North America since 1917, nor have there been any internal conflicts, except in Mexico, shortly after World War I. Both the United States and Canada, however, have been engaged in conflict or crisis operations outside the region. A list of the more important of these since World War II follows:

1948-1949	Berlin Blockade (US)
1950-1953	Korean War (US and Canada)

*The French involvement in Mexico in the 1860s was the last such event; prior to that had been British actions against the United States in 1814.

1954-1965	Assistance to South Vietnam (US)
1955-1965	Formosa Straits crises (US)
1958	Intervention in Lebanon (US)
1961	Bay of Pigs abortive invasion of Cuba (US)
1961-1962	Berlin Crisis (US and Canada)
1962	Cuban Missile Crisis (US)
1965-1973	Indochina War (US)
1965	Intervention in Dominican Republic (US)

APPENDIX R

WESTERN EUROPE—Regional Survey

ARMED FORCES AND MILITARY POWER

[Reprinted with permission from: The Almanac of World Military Power, by Col. T. N. Dupuy, U.S. Army, Ret., Col. John A. C. Andrews, U.S. Air Force, Ret., and Grace P. Hayes. 3rd ed. Dunn Loring, Va., T. N. Dupuy Associates, 1974.]

WESTERN EUROPE

Regional Survey

MILITARY GEOGRAPHY

Western Europe is a mountainous peninsula from which project a number of other peninsulas, and adjacent to which are a number of large and populous islands. This peninsular-insular geography contributed to the development in early history of a number of isolated, self-contained societies, from which emerged the modern nations of Western Europe. The peninsular-insular geography also stimulated the maritime interest which eventually became a prime factor in Europe's world predominance for more than four centuries.

The tides of war have flowed across Europe generally along the routes most feasible for transport and trade: the rivers, the corridors between mountain ranges, and the coastal lowlands. Principal among these routes have been the Danube basin and the North European Plain.

STRATEGIC SIGNIFICANCE

In addition to the influence of geography, a combination of climatological, demographic, and possibly cultural factors led to the dominant importance of Western Europe in world affairs beginning late in the fifteenth century. This predominance has not entirely disappeared even as the loci of world power have shifted east and west in the mid-twentieth century. Save for the United States and Canada, Western Europe still has the largest collection of highly skilled and educated manpower in the world, has the highest overall standard of living in the world outside North America, has the greatest accumulation of economic and financial power outside the United States, and has the greatest combined military potential aside from the United States and the Soviet Union.

NORTH ATLANTIC TREATY ORGANIZATION

Military rivalries among the nations of Western Europe—most notably between France and Germany—that had for centuries led to recurrent wars, have since World War II dwindled or disappeared in the face of common political and economic problems and the hard destructive and geographical realities of modern war. During the years immediately following that war, Soviet truculence posed a serious threat to the postwar recovery of the nations of Western Europe. American economic assistance through the Marshall Plan helped Western Europe avoid the economic chaos that indigenous and Russian Communists apparently expected would result in internal turmoil and revolution. Full economic recovery in these nations was hampered by fears that Soviet Russia, whose armed strength had increased rather than decreased after the war, would take by invasion what its Communist agents had been unable to subvert from within. Although the United States still possessed a monopoly of nuclear weapons, most Western Europeans feared overt Soviet military aggression that could overrun the militarily impotent nations of Western Europe in less than a week. They recognized the weakness of their own defense efforts, and doubted that America would be able to react in time to prevent a sudden Soviet take-over.

This situation led to negotiations that resulted first in the Brussels Treaty of March 17, 1948, to establish the Western European Union (see below), and that culminated in the establishment of the North Atlantic Treaty Organization (NATO) in a treaty signed April 4, 1949, in Washington, effective August 24, by Belgium, Canada, Denmark, France, Iceland, Italy, Luxembourg, the Netherlands, Norway, Portugal, the United Kingdom, and the United States. Greece and Turkey joined later (February 1952), and Western Germany became a member on May 5, 1955.

The members of NATO agreed to settle disputes by peaceful means, to develop their individual and collective capacity to resist armed aggression, to regard an attack on one as an attack on all, and to take necessary action to repel such an attack under Article 51 of the UN Charter.

The political basis for NATO was somewhat altered in the early 1970s by the development of the spirit of detente between East and West, the growing economic strength of the Western European countries, making them less dependent on the United States, political pressures to cut their defense spending, political pressure in the United States to reduce military forces in Europe, and the tension between the Soviet Union and Communist China, which involved large Soviet forces on the Chinese border. Relations between the United States and other NATO nations were strained by the Arab-Israeli War of 1973, when all but Portugal and the Netherlands refused to assist in rushing aid to Israel. In June 1974 the NATO countries reached agreement on a new Declaration on Atlantic Relations that reaffirmed the original objectives of the Treaty, and restored much of the harmonious facade that had been cracked the previous October.

NATO defense areas are divided into three major commands—Europe, Atlantic, and Channel—with a number of subsidiary commands and a US-Canada Regional Planning Group.

Until 1966 the Supreme Headquarters Allied Powers Europe (SHAPE) was located near Paris, but when France withdrew from the NATO Military Committee, SHAPE moved to a new location at Casteau, Belgium, near Mons. NATO headquarters moved from Paris to Brussels at the same time.

The Allied Command Europe (ACE) defends the territory of all continental European members except France and Portugal, and also that of Turkey, Iceland, Canada, and the United States. The Supreme Allied Commander, Europe (SACEUR), heads this command and also serves as Commander-in-Chief, US Forces Europe (CINCUSFE). At present SACEUR is US General Andrew J. Goodpaster; Deputy SACEUR is British General Sir John Mogg. ACE subsidiary commands are Allied Forces Central Europe (AFCENT), with headquarters at Brunssum, Netherlands; Allied Forces Northern Europe (AFNORTH) with headquarters at Kolsaas, Norway; and Allied Forces Southern Europe, headquarters at Naples. There is also a small air-mobile, air-supported ACE Mobile Force (AMF), combat-ready for deployment to points of strain, especially on the northern and southeastern flanks, on short notice.

AFCENT comprises all land and air forces in the Central Europe Sector (West Germany, Netherlands, Belgium, and Luxembourg; since 1966 France has been excluded), and is commanded by a German general. There are 22 divisions assigned by seven countries (forces of the four continental states plus American, British, and Canadian forces) and about 1,600 tactical aircraft in the command (about 350 of the aircraft are US Air Force fighter-bombers). US and German forces have Sergeant and Pershing SSMs at the corps and army level. There are Hawk and Nike SAM battalions in AFCENT. Within AFCENT are the Northern Army Group (NORTHAG) and the Central Army Group (CENTAG). NORTHAG is composed of all the British, Belgian, and Dutch divisions on the Continent, and four German divisions. These forces are supported by the Second Allied Tactical Air Force, composed of British, Belgian, Dutch, and German air units. CENTAG includes all American ground forces, seven German divisions, and a Canadian battle group and is supported by the Fourth Allied Tactical Air Force (American, German, and Canadian units plus the American Army Air Defense Command).

AFNORTH provides for the defense of Norway, Denmark, Schleswig-Holstein, and the Baltic Approaches and is under the command of a British general. It is composed of most of the Danish and Norwegian land, sea, and tactical air forces, one German division (in Schleswig), two German combat air wings, and the German Baltic Fleet.

AFSOUTH defends Italy, Greece, and Turkey, safeguards communications in the Mediterranean, and is responsible for the Turkish territorial waters of the Black Sea. It is under the command of an American admiral. There have been 14 Turkish divisions, nine Greek divisions, and seven Italian divisions in the command, plus the tactical air forces of these countries. The US Sixth Fleet in the Mediterranean, while under national command in peacetime, is NATO-committed for wartime. Ground defense is divided, under the Southern Command at Naples, and the South Eastern Command at Izmir, Turkey. There is an overall air command at Naples, and a single naval command (NAVSOUTH) under an Italian admiral, also at Naples. For several years, strained relations between Greece and Turkey, mainly over Cyprus, have raised questions about the military effectiveness of these commands. In the serious Cyprus crisis of mid-1974 the Greek government announced its decision to withdraw its forces from NATO. With Greek-Turkish relations near a breaking point future collaboration under NATO seemed doubtful.

The Allied Command Atlantic (ACLANT) extends from the North Pole to the Tropic of Cancer, and from the coastal waters of North America to those of Europe and North Africa. The Supreme Allied Commander, Atlantic (SACLANT), has headquarters at Norfolk, Virginia. Under ACLANT are the Western Atlantic, Eastern Atlantic, and Iberian Atlantic Commands, the Striking Force Atlantic (the nucleus of which is the US Second Fleet), the Submarine Command, and STANAVFORLANT (Standing Naval Force Atlantic—a multinational naval squadron).

The Allied Command Channel (ACCHAN) includes the English Channel and the southern portion of the North Sea. Naval forces are those of Britain, Belgium, and the Netherlands. ACCHAN is commanded by a British admiral with headquarters at Northwood, Middlesex.

NATO air defense is to be supported by the NADGE (NATO Air Defense Ground Environment) system. This is essentially a sophisticated, computerized system for tracking aircraft and correlating target information with locations of interceptor aircraft and missiles, using data supplied by numerous ground radar stations.

OTHER ALLIANCES

Western European Union (WEU). The Brussels Treaty of March 17, 1948, established a 50-year alliance for collaboration in economic, social and cultural matters and for collective self-defense among Belgium, France, Luxembourg, the Netherlands, and the United Kingdom. The obvious principal objective was military: mutual security against feared Soviet-Communist aggression. The defense military aspects of the alliance were merged with NATO when that alliance was created one year later. When France rejected the proposed European Defense Community in 1954, the existence of the WEU provided a useful means of integrating West Germany into the Western Alliance, thus facilitating the end of the Allied occupation of West Germany, its rearmament, and its eventual inclusion within NATO. This was accomplished when

West Germany and Italy adhered to the Brussels Treaty on May 6, 1955. After the breakdown of negotiations for Britain's entry into the Common Market, in 1963, the WEU provided a useful vehicle for continuing meetings between the six members of the Common Market and the UK to take stock of the political and economic situation in Europe. France has recently (1973) urged defense consultation within the WEU, a body in which the United States has no part, and the revitalization of the WEU weapons committee as a privileged forum for European cooperation on arms production. There is, however, an apparent movement within the newly elected (1974) French Government toward a cautious reestablishment of at least some military relations with NATO.

European Communities. Pursuant to the Treaty of Rome of March 25, 1957, the European Economic Community (EEC) was established on January 1, 1958, by Belgium, France, West Germany, Italy, Luxembourg, and the Netherlands (the "Inner Six"). The objective was to move gradually toward integrating and strengthening the economies of the members, and ultimately to move toward political unity.

On July 1, 1967, the EEC, generally known as the Common Market, was merged with two other related organizations with the same membership: the European Coal and Steel Community, established on August 10, 1952, pursuant to the Treaty of Paris of April 18, 1951; and the European Atomic Energy Community (Euratom), which was established on January 1, 1958, pursuant to the Treaty of Rome of March 25, 1957.

In 1960 seven European nations–Austria, Denmark, Norway, Portugal, Sweden, Switzerland and Great Britain–became associated in the European Free Trade Association (EFTA). Finland and Iceland subsequently joined. Two of the members, Great Britain and Denmark, together with Ireland, joined the EEC on January 1, 1973. The seven remaining members joined in signing a treaty at Brussels in July 1972, which effectively merged the two economic groups into a single trading bloc by establishing free trade through a gradual reduction of tariff among the 16 signatories.

A long-standing Warsaw Pact proposal for a European Security Conference was accepted by the NATO and uncommitted nations of Europe in late 1972, following signature of a general treaty to normalize relations between East and West Germany. The first formal meeting of this protracted 35-nation conference was held in Helsinki, in July 1973, and has been meeting intermittently in Geneva since September, 1973. The United States and Canada are participating. A variety of issues concerning relations between Eastern and Western Europe has been discussed, paralleling talks between NATO and the Warsaw Pact on the subject of mutual balanced force reduction (MBFR), which began in Vienna in late January 1973. As of mid-1974 the European Security Conference was reported to be deadlocked on all issues, largely, it appears, because of Soviet refusal to adopt an agreement on human rights proposed by the Western European nations.

While the purposes of these communities are primarily economic, and secondarily political, their military implications are great, as they tend to weld the EEC increasingly into what is in effect the third most powerful economic entity in the world.

RECENT INTRA- AND EXTRA-REGIONAL CONFLICTS

There have been no international armed conflicts in Western Europe since World War II. There have been two instances of internal hostilities, and several of the members have been engaged in conflict or crisis operations outside the region. There have been several crises between Western European nations (individually, or as members of the Western Alliance) and members of the Communist bloc, the most serious being those involving the Western Powers and the USSR in Berlin. In the summer of 1974, Turkish forces landed in Cyprus, following a Greek-engineered coup, in order to prevent a possible union of that strife-torn island and Greece. A list of hostilities, or crises involving military operations, in the last ten years follows:

1964	Intervention in East Africa, at local request (UK)
1964	Intervention in Gabon, at local request (France)
1966	Reinforcement of Zambia (UK)
1967	Intervention in Central African Republic, at local request (France)
1967	Military coup in Greece
1968-date	Intervention in Chad, at local request (France)
1968-date	Defense of overseas territories of Mozambique, Angola, and Portuguese Guinea (Portugal)
1969	UK intervention in Anguilla
1970-date	Violence in Northern Ireland
1974	Military coup in Portugal, followed by moves toward independence and peace in Portuguese overseas territories
1974	Coup in Cyprus, followed by Turkish invasion

APPENDIX S

EASTERN EUROPE—Regional Survey

ARMED FORCES AND MILITARY POWER

[Reprinted with permission from: The Almanac of World Military Power, by Col. T. N. Dupuy, U.S. Army, Ret., Col. John A. C. Andrews, U.S. Air Force, Ret., and Grace P. Hayes. 3rd ed. Dunn Loring, Va., T. N. Dupuy Associates, 1974.]

EASTERN EUROPE

Regional Survey

MILITARY GEOGRAPHY

Geographically Eastern Europe includes all of Europe east of a line running generally along the Finnish-Soviet border, the Gulf of Finland and the Baltic Sea, and from the southwest corner of the Baltic Sea to the northeast corner of the Adriatic. Politically it comprises all of the European nations with Communist governments. Since the USSR is both the largest state geographically and the most important politically in this region, the coverage of this chapter also includes all Soviet territory in Asia. The non-Communist nations, Finland, Greece, and Turkey, are included in the chapter on Western Europe.

Within this vast region there are three major sub-regions, each with numerous distinct geographical areas. The sub-regions are: North European and Russian plains; the Carpathian-Balkan mountain complex; and Asiatic Russia.

The plains and steppes of North Europe and Russia are characterized by hot, dry summers, and bitterly cold winters. These extremes are only slightly ameliorated in the south by the tempering effect of the nearby Black Sea. In the center of the sub-region, and throughout its northern extent, there are great swamps, seriously interfering with military movement in summer but easily traversed in winter. There are many broad rivers, creating difficult obstacles, generally to east-west movement. There are extensive forests through much of this region. The road net is relatively limited, compared to Western Europe.

The Carpathian-Balkan region is an essentially mountainous peninsula extending southward from the heart of Europe, and cut by the generally broad and fertile Danube basin and a number of smaller river valleys. Inhospitable terrain, shortages of raw materials (and resultant lack of industrialization) and too-numerous independent nations in a relatively small area, all combine to make this the least-developed region of Europe in economic terms. Despite its general ruggedness, two factors have made this sub-region a traditional highway of war: proximity to the westernmost tip of Asia, in the area of the Turkish Straits; and the traversibility of the river valleys, facilitating commerce and other east and west transit, not only across the Straits, but between Central Europe and South Russia.

Soviet Asia includes practically every type of terrain except tropical: rocky and sandy deserts, steppes, tundra, lofty mountains, great expanses of forests, and a varied assortment of temperate zone farming areas. This tremendous region extends across the entire northern half of Asia; even without European Russia of which it is an extension, it comprises the largest single political territory in the world. It includes the bulk of the Heartland area of Sir Halford J. Mackinder's geopolitical concept of political and spatial relationships.

STRATEGIC SIGNIFICANCE

The first, and possibly most impressive, strategic consideration relating to this region is the geopolitical fact noted above. This region is a combination of Mackinder's Heartland and Eastern Europe, and requires consideration of Mackinder's famous thesis: Who rules East Europe commands the Heartland; who rules the Heartland commands the World Island [Eastern Hemisphere]; who rules the World Island commands the World. Whether or not one agrees with its validity, the idea cannot be ignored.

All except two of the countries of Eastern Europe are solidly within the Soviet orbit, and are members of the Soviet-dominated Warsaw Pact (see below). The two exceptions are Yugoslavia and Albania. The extent of Soviet domination over the other six nations of the region (often referred to as Soviet satellites) varies from country to country. There is no question, however, that such domination exists; this was amply reaffirmed by the 1968 invasion and occupation of Czechoslovakia.

The Soviet satellites of East Central Europe are a strategic protective belt, garrisoned by Soviet and satellite ground forces, within which the Soviet advanced air defense system functions. This belt also encompasses some of the formidable defense obstacles noted above, including the Carpathian Mountains, and the Elbe, Oder, and Vistula Rivers. Moreover, politically this belt helps to insulate Russia's population from Western influence, and at the same time affords an advanced base for penetration of Western Europe by Communist intelligence, subversion and propaganda. It also provides an advance base that would be militarily useful in war. It projects the Soviet military frontier 750 miles westward and 400 miles southward from Russia's pre-World War II border. The Rhine would be the first serious natural obstacle in the path of Soviet armies attacking West Germany.

REGIONAL ALLIANCES

Warsaw Pact. This is an alliance of the Soviet Union and six of the other Communist states of East Europe: East Germany, Poland, Czechoslovakia, Hungary, Romania, and Bulgaria. It was established as a 20-year mutual-defense alliance in May 1955 in a conference called at Warsaw in response to the ratification (March 1955) of West Germany's admittance to the North Atlantic Treaty Organization (NATO). Albania was represented at the conference, and was one of the original Pact members. However, Albania has been excluded from all Warsaw Pact activities since 1962, after that nation aligned itself with Communist China in the Sino-Soviet dispute. Albania formally withdrew from the Pact in September, 1968, after the Soviet invasion of Czechoslovakia.

East Germany also participated in the conference, but was not officially admitted to the Pact until 1958, after it became obvious that Communist-bloc pressures would not reverse the rearmament of West Germany.

The Warsaw Pact established a joint command and defense staff for the combined armed forces of the seven participants. This staff is located in Moscow; the Commander in Chief is a Soviet marshal. Each other member of the alliance provides a General Staff mission, headed by a senior officer. The Pact also maintains permanent military staff missions, composed of Soviet officers only, in the capitals of each of the other member nations. There is also a political Consultative Committee, consisting of the foreign ministers of the participating nations, under the chairmanship of the Soviet Foreign Minister. In the terms of the treaty creating the Pact, armed attack in Europe on a member state will oblige all other members to come to its assistance.

Other Alliances. The USSR has 20-year bilateral treaties of friendship, cooperation, and mutual assistance, renewable on expiration, with each of the other members of the Warsaw Pact. These treaties broaden the terms of assistance in war to specify an attack by any state or combination of states, whether in Europe or not. There are similar bilateral treaties among the other members. Additionally there are status of forces treaties with all Pact countries where Soviet troops are stationed.

In 1949 the USSR established the Council for Mutual Economic Assistance (COMECON, or CEMA). Members were the other members of the Warsaw Pact. Albania left in 1961, and Mongolia joined in 1962. Cuba became the ninth member in 1972. It was originally stated to be a consultative, cooperative body to facilitate through joint action the economic development of all, but the USSR soon assumed dominance in all matters. By 1962 no national mid-range (3- or 5-year) plan, nor its annual fulfillment plan or budget, could be put in effect without USSR approval; items and quantities in international trade were virtually dictated, as were the categories of goods to be produced in each country.

RECENT INTRA- AND EXTRA-REGIONAL CONFLICTS

There have been a few major conflicts or incidents within the region involving the use, or threatened use, of armed forces. In addition to the two Berlin crises noted below, there have been several others of only slightly lesser significance. There have also been two major incidents outside the region in which Soviet armed forces have been directly involved. No attempt is made here to assess the extent to which Soviet influence may have been involved, directly or indirectly, in other incidents or conflicts outside the region.

The major incidents are:

1968	Warsaw Pact (less Romania) occupation of Czechoslovakia
1969	Sino-Soviet border engagements along frontiers with Manchuria and Sinkiang (these were only the most publicized of many border incidents since 1961)
1970	Civil disturbances in northern Poland resulting in major changes in Party and Government leadership

APPENDIX T
COUNTRY DATA CHART

[FROM: Issues: World Data Handbook; Current Information Supplement. Washington, Department of State, Office of Media Services, 1972 (Publication No. 8665).]

APPENDIX U
BELGIUM
ARMED FORCES AND MILITARY POWER

[Reprinted with permission from: The Almanac of World Military Power, by Col. T. N. Dupuy, U.S. Army, Ret., Col. John A. C. Andrews, U.S. Air Force, Ret., and Grace P. Hayes. 3rd ed. Dunn Loring, Va., T. N. Dupuy Associates, 1974.]

BELGIUM

Royaume de Belgique
Koninkrijk Belgie
Kingdom of Belgium

POWER POTENTIAL STATISTICS

Area: 11,784 square miles
Population: 9,727,000
Total Active Armed Forces: 111,000 (includes Gendarmerie; 1.14% population)
Gross National Product: $35.4 billion ($3,639 per capita)
Annual Military Expenditures: $897 million (2.53% GNP)
Steel Production: 14.53 million metric tons
Fuel Production: Coal: 10.5 million metric tons
Gas: 2.97 billion cubic meters
Refined Petroleum Products:* 36.9 million metric tons
Electric Power Output: 35.66 billion kwh
Merchant Fleet: 244 ships; 1.18 million gross tons
Civil Air Fleet: 32 jet, 1 turboprop, 61 piston transports

DEFENSE STRUCTURE

Constitutionally the armed forces are commanded by the King. Overall responsibility for the formulation of defense policy in a parliamentary government is exercised by the Prime Minister and his Cabinet; specific defense decisions are made by the Ministerial Committee of Defense, over which the Prime Minister presides. Implementation of these decisions is the responsibility of the Defense Minister, who is assisted by a military staff system under the direction of the Chief of the General Staff.

*Belgium and Luxembourg.

There are four armed forces—Army, Navy, Air Force and Gendarmerie. There are three elements within the integrated staff echelon of the armed forces: (1) The General Staff, which in turn has two echelons: a conventional, integrated general staff which coordinates the planning of the next echelon of separate Army, Navy, and Air Force general staffs; (2) The Gendarmerie General Staff, responsible for interior order; (3) The Central Administration, to provide administrative support to the operational forces. The operational echelon of the defense establishment includes the principal commands of the four services, the military instruction establishments, and the scientific establishments.

POLITICO-MILITARY POLICY

A traditional policy of neutrality having proved unreliable protection against aggression in two World Wars, since 1945 Belgium has been a leading exponent of collective security. Belgium is a member of the Western European Union established by the Treaty of Brussels in 1948, and was one of the 12 original members of NATO. Belgium's basic defense policy is that of NATO: to prevent war through the deterrent effect of the common efforts of neighbors; if that fails, to defend the common territory by joint military action. The nation's convictions in this regard are demonstrated by the fact that all Belgian armed forces, except those required for internal security, have been fully integrated into NATO forces, and most are deployed in Western Germany under NATO command. Further evidence is the fact that Belgium has provided lodgement for the seat of the NATO Council, and for the principal NATO military headquarters: Allied Command Europe.

Manpower for the armed forces is provided by a combination of long-term enlistment and conscription. Regular enlisted men, with terms of service varying from two to five years, make up about half of the Army, two-thirds of the Navy, and four-fifths of the Air Force. The remainder are conscripts. A new policy announced in 1973 makes it mandatory that Belgian NATO units be all-volunteer. Draftees are to serve six months only, and only on home-guard assignments.

STRATEGIC PROBLEMS

As demonstrated in two World Wars, Belgium is vulnerable to invasion from all directions, with some natural security being provided only by the short seacoast in the northwest and the rugged, forested Ardennes Mountains in the southeast. Some additional defensive capability is provided by lines of the Meuse and Schelde Rivers and many canals, and the potentiality for flooding extensive regions of the western portion of the country. Belgian space is so limited, however, that these natural and man-made obstacles can impose little delay upon the forces of a powerful aggressor. This is adequate reason for Belgium's adherence to the NATO strategic concept.

An internal security problem is created by the ethnic and emotional division of the country between Dutch-speaking Flemings (about 55 percent of the population) and French-speaking Walloons (about 33 percent); (about 11 percent are bilingual). Constitutional reforms in 1971 provided that the ministries be divided equally between the two groups.

The Communist Party is weak and divided, and offers little threat of internal subversion.

MILITARY ASSISTANCE

From 1950 to 1972 Belgium received $1.24 billion in military assistance from the United States. A US Military Assistance and Advisory Group has provided training assistance to the Belgian armed forces in employment of American equipment. Little US military assistance has been received since 1964.

Since 1960 Belgium, at the request of their governments, has provided substantial military assistance to its former colonies: Zaire, Burundi, and Rwanda. While military assistance to Burundi ended in 1973, Belgian military cooperation with Zaire and Rwanda continues, concentrating on military training. This policy is reflected in military assistance expenditures of $7 million for 1974; military missions include 127 Army and six Gendarmerie officers and men for Zaire and 46 Army and six Gendarmerie officers and men for Rwanda; a total of 750 months of military training courses in Belgium for military personnel of Zaire and Rwanda is to be provided; and limited logistical support is to be provided to Rwanda only.

ALLIANCES

Belgium is a member of NATO, of Western European Union, of BENELUX, of the European Common Market, and the UN.

ARMY

Personnel: 71,500

Organization:

1 army corps (assigned to the Central European Command of NATO's Allied Command Europe – ACE)
4 mechanized or armored brigades, forming 2 divisions (assigned to NATO)
1 parachute-commando regiment (one battalion assigned to ACE Mobile Force)
2 SSM battalions (Honest John)
2 SAM battalions (Hawk)
3 helicopter squadrons

1 fixed wing/helicopter mixed squadron
3 infantry battalions for territorial defense (not assigned to NATO)
logistical support units

Major Equipment Inventory:
Leopard and M-47 medium tanks
Scorpion, M-41, AMX-13 light tanks
Striker with Swingfire antitank weapons
M-75, AMX-VTP APCs
105mm, 155mm howitzers
M-109 self-propelled 155mm howitzers
M-44 self-propelled 155mm howitzers
203mm howitzers
M-108 self-propelled 105mm howitzers

On Order:
Scimitar with 30mm Rarden cannon
Samson recovery vehicles
Spartan APC

Reserves: Approximately 120,000 men, organized in two rapidly mobilizable brigades (one mechanized, one motorized), plus independent territorial defense battalions and logistical support units. (About 300,000 additional trained men are available for mobilization.)

NAVY

The Navy is essentially a minesweeping force, earmarked mostly for NATO's Channel Command, partly for coastal minesweeping.

Personnel: 4,500

Major Units:
7 ocean minesweepers/minehunters (MSO)
9 coastal minesweepers/minehunters (MSC)
14 inshore minesweepers (MSI)
2 support and command ships and auxiliaries
6 river patrol boats (PBR)
5 helicopters (S-58 and Alouette III)
10 auxiliaries

Major Naval Base: Ostend

AIR FORCE

All Air Force units except one transport squadron are assigned to NATO Allied Command Europe (ACE).

Personnel: 20,000

Organization:
2 all-weather fighter squadrons (F-104)
5 fighter-bomber squadrons (2 F-104, 3 Mirage 5B)
1 transport wing (1 tactical squadron of C-130, 1 communications squadron of DC-3, DC-6 Pembroke and Falcon 20)
2 SAM wings (8 squadrons; 72 Nike-Hercules; based in West Germany)
1 tactical reconnaissance squadron (Mirage 5 BR)
1 helicopter flight (HSS-1)

Major Aircraft Types:
209 combat aircraft
90 F-104 fighters
59 Mirage 5-BA
24 Mirage 5-BR
16 Mirage 5-BD
20 Mirage 5-BR reconnaissance aircraft
200 other aircraft
12 C-130 transports
2 Falcon 20 transports
4 DC-6 transports
2 C-47 transports
miscellaneous trainer/support aircraft
11 HSS-1 helicopters

Air Bases: Beauvechain, Kleine Brohel, Florennes, Brustem, Koksyde, Bierset

PARAMILITARY

National Gendarmerie: 15,000 men with 30 helicopters and light armored cars FN-4 RM62.

APPENDIX V
BELGIUM
BACKGROUND NOTES

[Washington, Department of State, September 1973 (Publication 8087).]

Belgium

department of state * september 1973

OFFICIAL NAME: Kingdom of Belgium

GEOGRAPHY AND PEOPLE

Belgium is located in Western Europe, bordered by the Netherlands, the Federal Republic of Germany, Luxembourg, France, and the North Sea.

Although generally flat, terrain becomes increasingly hilly and forested in the southeast (Ardennes) region.

Climate is cool, temperate, and rainy; summer temperatures average 60°F. Annual extremes, rarely attained, are 10°F. and 90°F.

Geographically and culturally, Belgium is at the crossroads of Europe, and during the past 2,000 years has witnessed a constant ebb and flow of different races and cultures. Consequently, Belgium is one of Europe's true melting pots with people of Celtic, Roman, German, French, Dutch, Spanish, and Austrian origins.

Today, the Belgians are divided ethnically into the Dutch-speaking Flemings and French-speaking Walloons, with a mixed population in Brussels representing the remainder. Roman Catholicism is the predominant religion.

Population density is the second highest in Europe, after the Netherlands.

PROFILE

Geography

AREA: 11,780 sq. mi. (one-fourth the size of Pennsylvania). CAPITAL: Brussels (pop. 1.1 million). OTHER CITIES: Antwerp (pop. 900,000), Liege (pop. 600,000).

People

POPULATION: 9.7 million. ANNUAL GROWTH RATE: 0.3%. DENSITY: 874 per sq. mi. PRINCIPAL ETHNIC GROUPS: Flemings (51%), Walloons (33%). URBAN: 69%. RELIGION: Roman Catholic, 9.7 million; Jews, 35,000; Protestants, 24,000. LANGUAGES: Dutch, French. LITERACY: 98%. LIFE EXPECTANCY: 74 years.

Government

INDEPENDENCE: 1830. TYPE: Parliamentary democracy under a constitutional monarch.

BRANCHES: *Executive:* King (Chief of State); Prime Minister (Head of Government). *Legislature:* bicameral Parliament (Senate and Chamber of Representatives). *Judiciary:* Court of Cassation.

FLAG: Three vertical bands—black, yellow, and red from left to right.

Economy

GNP: $36 billion (1972). ANNUAL GROWTH RATE: 4%. PER CAPITA: $3,650. PER CAPITA GROWTH RATE: 4.2%.

AGRICULTURE: *Labor,* 6%. *Land,* 53%. *Acres per capita,* 0.4. *Products:* livestock, poultry, sugar beets, potatoes, wheat, barley.

INDUSTRY: *Products:* metal fabrication, coal, textiles, chemicals, and iron and steel industries.

TRADE: *Exports:* $16 billion (1972): manufactures, processed metals. *Partners:* the Netherlands, Federal Republic of Germany, France. *Imports:* $16 billion (1971): raw materials, fuels, machinery, transportation equipment, one-fourth of food supply. *Partners:* Federal Republic of Germany, the Netherlands, France.

OFFICIAL EXCHANGE RATE: about 37 Belgian francs = U.S. $1 (Sept. 1, 1973).

MEMBERSHIP IN INTERNATIONAL ORGANIZATIONS: Common Market, Belgian-Luxembourg Economic Union (BLEU), Benelux Customs Union, NATO, Organization for Economic Cooperation and Development (OECD), U.N.

HISTORY

Belgium derived its name from a Celtic tribe, the Belgae, whom Caesar described as the most courageous tribe of Gaul. However, the Balgae were forced to yield to Roman legions during the fifties B.C. For some 300 years what is now Belgium flourished as a province of Rome.

But Rome's power gradually lessened, and Attila the Hun invaded what is now Germany about A.D. 300 and pushed the Germanic tribes into Belgium. About 100 years later the Franks invaded the south and took possession of Belgium. After coming under the rule of the Dukes of Burgundy and through marriage passing into the possession of the Hapsburgs, Belgium was occupied by the Spanish (1519-1715) and the Austrians (1715-94). During the French Revolution Belgium was invaded and annexed by France in 1794. It was made a part of Holland by the Congress of Vienna in 1815.

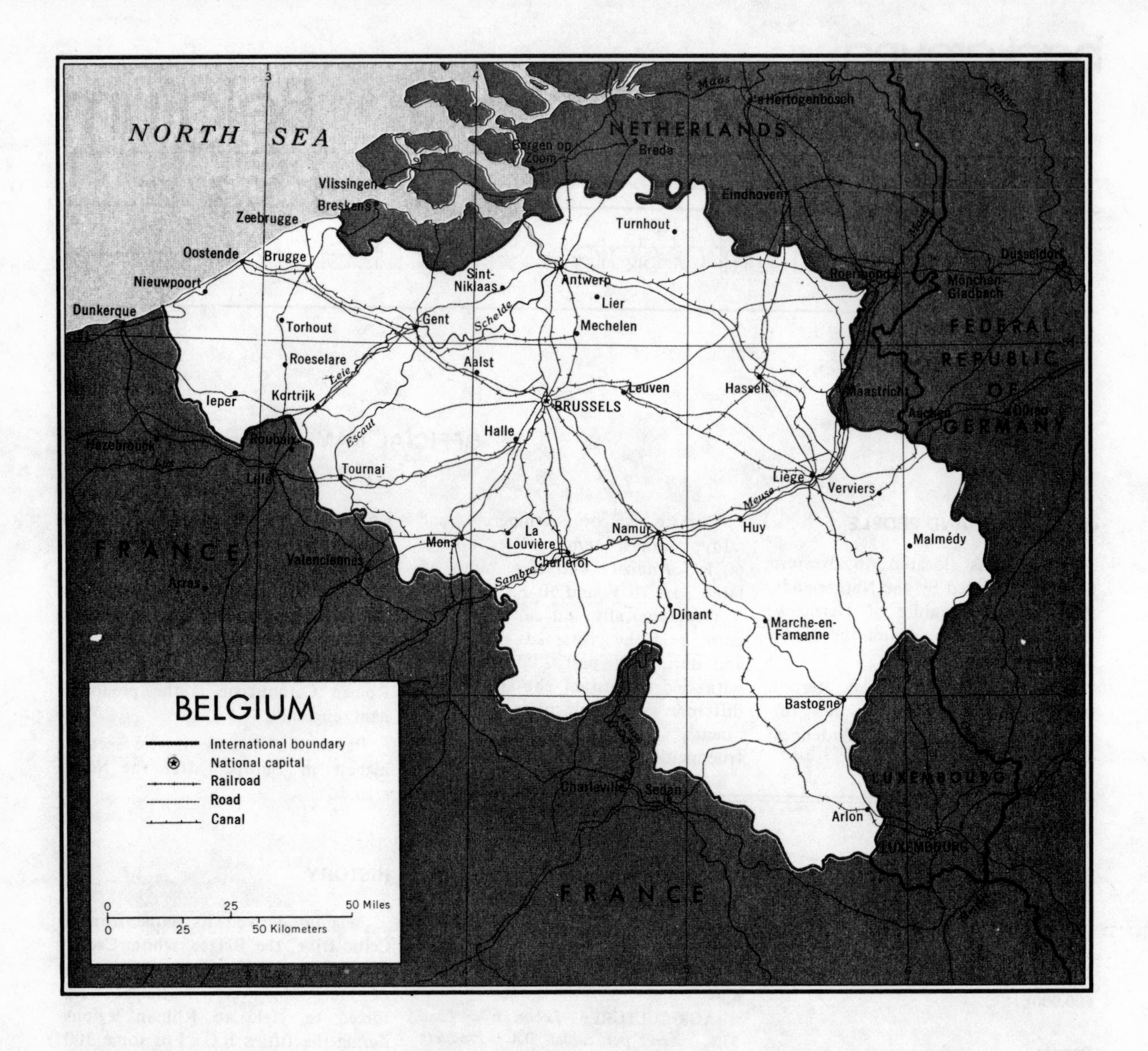

In 1830 Belgium gained its independence as a result of an uprising of the Belgian people. A constitutional monarchy was established in 1831, with the royal family chosen from the House of Saxe-Coburg Gotha. In that same year, Belgium's present Constitution went into effect.

Despite a policy of scrupulous neutrality prior to the two World Wars, Belgium was attacked and occupied by the Germans in 1914 and 1940. This, plus disillusionment over postwar Soviet behavior, had made Belgium one of the foremost advocates of collective security within the framework of European integration and Atlantic partnership.

GOVERNMENT

Belgium is a parliamentary democracy under a constitutional monarch. Although technically the King (Chief of State) is the source of all executive authority, in fact the Council of Ministers (cabinet) is responsible for governmental decisions. The Council of Ministers, led by the Prime Minister (Head of Government), holds office as long as it retains the confidence of the Parliament. Elections are held at least every 4 years by universal suffrage with obligatory voting and a form of proportional representation.

The bicameral Parliament consists of a Senate and a Chamber of Representatives. Of the 178 Senators, 46 are elected by provincial councils, 33 by fellow Senators, and the remainder elected directly. Members of the Chamber of Representatives (212) are elected directly. The Chamber is traditionally the dominant body.

In 1970 the Belgian Constitution was amended to provide for the creation within Parliament of Cultural

Councils comprised of Dutch- and French-speaking members. The amendment granted competence to the councils in certain cultural and linguistic matters and established a system of special majorities of the entire Parliament for enactment of certain measures pertaining to cultural and linguistic questions. Brussels was established as a separate, bilingual area with a Metropolitan Council chosen by proportional representation, but in which parity between Dutch- and French-speaking members is required in its Executive Committee.

The Parliament also was given authority to create regional bodies for Flanders, Wallonia, and Brussels and such powers over social and economic affairs as Parliament wished to delegate to them.

The judiciary is modeled on the French system. The highest court is the Court of Cassation whose Chief Justice is appointed by the King. The courts do not pass on the constitutionality of legislation, but advisory opinions concerning constitutionality of major legislation are given by the Council of State, a special legal group.

Belgium is divided into nine autonomous Provinces. Executive power in each is exercised by a Governor, appointed by the King.

POLITICAL CONDITIONS

All postwar Belgian governments have been formed by one or more of the three major parties–Social Christian, Socialist, and Liberty and Progress. Extremist philosophies are represented by several minor parties. The linguistically oriented parties have gained strength steadily, however.

Political Parties

Traditionally, the Roman Catholic Church has been the basis of unity for the Social Christian Party (SCP), popularly known as the Catholic Party. Long a supporter of the Church's institutions, the Social Christians in recent years have tended more to promote broad principles of Christian humanism without overt reference to ecclesiastical ties. The party, now formally organized into autonomous French-speaking (PSC) and Flemish (CVP) components, draws support for its moderate policies from all classes of society, including the Christian Trade Union Federation (CSC), Belgium's largest labor organization.

While faithful to the tradition of classical Marxist principles, the Socialist Party (PSB) is pragmatic and moderate in outlook. Its followers have concentrated on social welfare and industrial democracy within the framework of Belgium's free enterprise economy. It is closely associated with the General Federation of Belgian Labor (FGTB), the country's second largest trade union organization.

The Party of Liberty and Progress (PLP) is the exponent of free enterprise and individualism. Liberals favor holding down levels of government spending and regulation and encouraging private initiative. The party advocates moderate, gradual social reform. Its main appeal is to the middle class, especially to small businessmen, professionals, and shopkeepers.

The Volksunie, or Flemish Nationalist Party, favors transformation of Belgium into a federal state with autonomous Flemish and Walloon regions. It has shown considerable growth in strength in recent years. The Democratic Front of Francophones (FDF) in Brussels and the Wallon Rally (RW) are militant groups of French-speakers which have joined forces and are now, effectively, one party. They, too, are federalists and seek thereby to block the increasing political strength of the Flemish population, occasioned by the economic and demographic ascendance of Flanders since World War II.

The Communist Party (PCB) is pro-Moscow. Its numerical strength and influence in national affairs are relatively insignificant.

Recent Developments

Belgium is basically a stable political democracy. After the sharp dispute over the Royal Question in 1950, the Social Christian Party emerged as the first single-party government in post-World War II Belgium and held office until 1954. Thereafter coalition governments were formed: Liberal (now PLP)-PSB (1958), PLP-SCP (1961), SCP-PSB (1961 and 1964), and SCP-PLP (1966).

Linguistic rivalries have strongly influenced Belgian politics for over a decade. An SCP-PSB coalition, formed in 1968 under Prime Minister Gaston Eyskens (SCP), succeeded, with PLP help, in adopting the 1970 constitutional revisions. But in the November 1971 elections the linguistic-oriented FDF-RW and Volksunie gained further strength, and linguistic/cultural issues continued to be a problem. The SCP-PSB coalition was reestablished in January 1972 but was unable to resolve outstanding regional and linguistic issues or controversy over increasing subsidies to parochial education; the government fell in November. A tripartite PSB-SCP-PLP coalition, formed in January 1973 under Prime Minister Edmond Leburton (PSB), pledged itself to complete the institutional reforms contemplated by the amended Constitution and to assumption by the State of most parochial school costs. Appropriate cultural and school legislation was adopted in July 1973. The problem of regionalization remains unresolved.

The composition of the present Parliament is:

	Senate	*Chamber*
SCP	61	67
PSB	49	61
PLP	29	34
Volksunie	19	21
FDF-RW	19	24
PCB	1	5
	178	212

ECONOMY

Belgium emerged from World War II with a physical plant more nearly intact than its neighbors. The immediate postwar era saw rapid reconstruction, dismantling of direct controls, trade liberalization, and high growth rates. During the 1950's, however, the pace slackened, and it was not until the Common Market (European Community) was established in 1958 and a sweeping investment incentive program was introduced in 1959 that a new surge in the Belgian economy occurred. Between 1960 and 1964 real growth averaged 4.5 percent and fell slightly to about 3 percent in 1965. A slower rate of progress in 1966 and 1967 reflected a decrease in demand throughout Europe plus inflationary pressures due to full employment. The gross national product (GNP) growth rate accelerated from 1967 through 1970, when it was more than 6 percent. In 1971 and 1972, however, a general economic slowdown in Europe again limited the growth rate in Belgium, where it fell to about 4 percent. GNP in 1972 was about $36 billion (at 43 Belgian francs = U.S.$1), yielding a per capita GNP of about $3,650.

Agriculture plays a relatively minor role in the Belgian economy. It generates roughly 6 percent of the GNP and employs about 6 percent of the active labor force. Livestock and poultry raising are the dominant agricultural activities. Important traditional crops include sugar beets, potatoes, wheat, and barley.

Belgium has a developed processing economy based essentially on the metal fabrication, coal, textile, chemical, and iron and steel industries. At the hub of a major West European crossroads, with a dense concentration of population and industry, Belgium has been an active participant in international trade. Exports totaled $16 billion in 1972. With the exception of coal (which must be subsidized), Belgium does not possess significant natural resources and must import most raw materials, some fuels, machinery, transportation equipment, and one-fourth of its required food supply. In exchange, it employs a highly skilled labor force to export a wide range of manufactures and processed metals. In 1971 imports totaled $16 billion. (The cornerstone of the country's industry remains the iron and steel and metal fabricating industries, which supply some 40 percent of Belgian exports.)

Belgium has found it advantageous to adhere to a generally liberal commercial policy exemplified by its participation in the Common Market (whose members are Belgium's major trading partners), the Belgian-Luxembourg Economic Union (BLEU), and the Benelux Customs Union. The Federal Republic of Germany, France, and the Netherlands are the BLEU's largest individual trading partners.

Foreign investment has found a congenial climate in Belgium due to its central location, high-quality labor, ready access to communications, and a program of financial incentives from the government. These incentives are applied to maximize new direct investment in less prosperous regions—some of which have suffered from the gradual closing of coal mines and the existence of old, less productive industry—and in high technology and labor-intensive industries.

Since 1960 the flow of Belgian financial resources to less-developed countries has been close to a targeted 1 percent of GNP. The government's foreign aid policy has shifted gradually in the past few years from bilateral to multilateral aid. In addition, the government has attempted to diversify its bilateral aid. Formerly, 80 percent or more of bilateral aid went to what are now Zaïre, Rwanda, and Burundi. Recently, Tunisia, Morocco, and a few Asian and South American countries have become beneficiaries. The composition is changing from grants to loans.

FOREIGN RELATIONS

The Belgians are strong supporters of the North Atlantic Treaty Organization (NATO), the European Communities, the Organization for Economic Cooperation and Development (OECD), and the Benelux Customs Union. They have cooperated with the other Benelux nations in efforts to strengthen European unity and to bring the United Kingdom into the European Communities. Further, they actively seek improved East-West relations and strongly support the United Nations. NATO headquarters are located at Brussels.

U.S.-BELGIUM RELATIONS

The excellent relations existing between the United States and Belgium are based on a similarity of outlook and a common dedication to the security of the free world. As President Nixon said upon his arrival at Brussels in February 1969, "The peoples of our two countries have shared many things. We have been allies in war and partners in peace. But even more important, as we look to the future, are the common ideals that inspire us and that have made the friendship of our peoples so warm and so lasting. . ."

An outward-looking nation, Belgium works with the United States bilaterally and in international and regional organizations to further liberal trade, economic and political cooperation, and

Travel Notes

Clothing—**Clothing and shoe needs in Belgium are about the same as for New England, the Middle Atlantic States, and the Pacific Northwest. However, raincoats, umbrellas, and low-heeled, thick-soled walking shoes may be needed more often. Winters generally are less severe than in the U.S. areas mentioned above, and there is much less snow.**

Telecommunications—**Telephone and telegraph services, domestic and international, are efficient. Direct dial service is in use between Brussels and most European capitals. Rates for local telephone service are about the same as in most U.S. cities.**

Transportation—**Streetcars and buses, although somewhat uncomfortable and overcrowded, provide good local transportation. Taxis: Meter starts at 15 BF ($.40) and the rate is 8 BF ($.21) per kilometer.**

Roads are fairly good. Limited access highways link Brussels with Antwerp, Brussels with Ostende, Antwerp with Liege, and Liege with the German border near Aachen. Secondary roads are adequate.

All automobiles driven in Belgium must be covered by unlimited third-party liability insurance against personal or property damage; this insurance must be issued by a company licensed to do business in Belgium.

Community Health—**Belgium requires that at least one pharmacy be open in a given neighborhood at all times. The address of that pharmacy is posted on the door of all pharmacies in the neighborhood, and a list of open pharmacies is also published in newspapers.**

Belgian public health standards are on a par with those in the United States. Brussels has a modern sewage and refuse disposal system and water purification facilities. Water from the tap can be drunk safely.

assistance to the underdeveloped world. Belgium has welcomed many U.S. firms to its territory.

PRINCIPAL GOVERNMENT OFFICIALS

Chief of State–King Baudouin I

Prime Minister–Edmond Leburton (PSB)

Vice Prime Minister and Minister for Budget–Leo Tindemans (SCP)

Vice Prime Minister and Minister of Finance–Willy De Clercq (PLP)

Minister of Foreign Affairs–Renaat Van Elslande (SCP)

Minister of Defense and Coordination for Economic and Social Affairs–Paul Vanden Boeynants (SCP)

Minister of Economic Affairs–Willy Claes (PSB)

Minister of Agriculture–Albert Lavens (SCP)

Minister of Labor–Ernest Glinne (PSB)

Minister of Interior–Edouard Close (PSB)

Minister of Justice–Herman Vanderpoorten (PLP)

Minister of Communications–Edouard Anseele (PSB)

Ambassador to the U.S.–Walter Loridan

Ambassador to the U.N.–Edouard Longerstaey

Belgium maintains an Embassy in the United States at 3330 Garfield Street, N.W., Washington, D.C. 20008.

PRINCIPAL U.S. OFFICIALS

Ambassador–Robert Strausz-Hupé

Deputy Chief of Mission–Louis C. Boochever

Political Counselor–William A. Buell

Economic Counselor–Edwin Crowley

Administrative Counselor–Virgil L. Moore

Public Affairs Counselor (USIS)–Arthur A. Bardos

Defense and Army Attaché–Col. Allen B. Jennings

Air Attaché–Lt. Col. David W. Turner

Naval Attaché–Cmdr. George Culberson

Agricultural Attaché–Quentin R. Bates

Commercial Attaché–Roderick N. Grant

Consular Officer–Cecil St. Clair Richardson

Consul General, Antwerp–Wayne W. Fisher

Labor Attaché–George A. Anderson

The U.S. Embassy in Belgium is located at 27 Blvd. du Regent, Brussels.

READING LIST

These titles are provided as a general indication of the material currently being published on this country; the Department of State does not endorse the specific views in unofficial publications as representing the position of the U.S. Government.

Eyck, F. Gunther. *The Benelux Countries: An Historical Survey.* Princeton: Van Nostrand, 1959.

Huggett, Frank E. *Modern Belgium.* New York: Praeger, 1969.

Mallinson, V. *Belgium.* London: Benn, 1969.

Meeus, Adrien de. *History of the Belgians.* Trans. by G. Gordon. New York: Praeger, 1962.

DEPARTMENT OF STATE PUBLICATION 8087
Revised September 1973

APPENDIX W
BELGIUM
STRENGTH OF THE COMMUNIST PARTY ORGANIZATION—1973

[FROM: World Strength of the Communist Party Organizations—1973. Washington, Department of State, Bureau of Intelligence and Research, 1973.]

BELGIUM

National Political Status: Date of last election - November 7, 1971.

Communist: Communist Party of Belgium (PCB) - 162,463 votes (3.1%), 5 seats (2.4%)

Non-Communist Left: Socialist Party - 1,434,185 votes (27.4%), 61 seats (28.8%)

Center: Social Christian Party - 1,584,269 votes (30.2%), 67 seats (31.6%)

Conservative: Liberal Party - 885,418 votes (16.9%), 34 seats (16.0%)

Other: Volksunie - 584,773 votes, (11.2%), 21 seats (9.9%)
Francophone Linguistic Parties - 591,489 votes (11.3%), 24 seats (11.3%)

Total: 5,242,597 votes, 212 seats

Communist Party Membership: 10,000 (estimate)

Leading Party Figures and Positions:
VAN GEYT, Louis - President
TERFVE, Jean - Vice President (Wallonia)
TURF, Jef - Vice President (Flanders)

Principal Publications:
Le Drapeau Rouge (French)
De Rode Vaan (Flemish)

Areas of Communist Activity: The Communist Party of Belgium (PCB) is of only peripheral importance in Belgian politics. Most of its strength lies in Brussels and Wallonia.

The PCB continued its post-World War II electoral decline when it received only 3.1 percent of the vote in the November 1971 national parliamentary elections (compared to 3.3 percent in 1968 and approximately 13 percent immediately following the war). The continued drop in votes was probably largely due to the growth of linguistic splinter parties, which siphoned off much of the extremist protest vote from the PCB.

Although unsuccessful in 1972 with its approach to the Socialists to form an alternative leftist coalition to then existing center-left coalition government, the PCB leadership has persisted in its pursuit of "unity of popular forces." This theme was highlighted as a major domestic plank at the party's 21st Congress in December 1973.

Within the Communist movement, the PCB has hewed to a pro-Moscow line, but not to the extent of foreclosing the possibility of better relations with the Chinese Communist Party. The party leadership ventured some mild criticism of the Soviet treatment of dissident intellectuals in 1973, following somewhat in the footsteps of the Italian CP, which has often helped to shape the attitude of the PCB in recent years. The party leadership also collaborated closely with its Italian colleagues in laying the groundwork for the conference of West European Communist parties in Brussels in January 1974.

Various other Communist groups remain on the fringes of the Belgian political scene, among them the Marxist-Leninist Communist Party of Belgium (PCBML), a mere shadow of its former self as the first pro-Chinese dissident party in Western Europe; and the small but influential Trotskyist Fourth International led by Ernest Mandel.

In 1973 the PCB publication *Le Drapeau Rouge* converted from a 24-page weekly to an 8-page daily, reflecting the party leadership's concern with promoting greater public awareness of the PCB.

APPENDIX X

CANADA

ARMED FORCES AND MILITARY POWER

[Reprinted with permission from: The Almanac of World Military Power, by Col. T. N. Dupuy, U.S. Army, Ret., Col. John A. C. Andrews, U.S. Air Force, Ret., and Grace P. Hayes. 3rd ed. Dunn Loring, Va., T. N. Dupuy Associates, 1974.]

CANADA

POWER POTENTIAL STATISTICS

Area: 3,851,809 square miles
Population: 22,095,000
Total Active Armed Forces: 83,000 (0.38% population)
Gross National Product: $110 billion ($4,979 per capita)
Annual Military Expenditure: $2.42 billion (2.2% GNP)
Iron and Steel Production: 54.3 million metric tons
Fuel Production: Coal: 14.4 million metric tons
 Crude Oil: 75.5 million metric tons
 Refined Products: 74.9 million metric tons
 Natural Gas: 77.5 billion cubic meters
Electric Power Output: 215.0 billion kwh
Merchant Fleet: 1,228 ships; 2,366,175 gross tons
Civil Air Fleet: 243 jet, 50 turboprop, and 124 piston transports, operated by scheduled carriers. Over 169 other companies operate fleets of all types of aircraft, performing such services as charters and non-scheduled passenger and cargo flights.

DEFENSE STRUCTURE

Canada is the only important nation in the world to have a completely unified defense structure, in which there are no separate or distinct services within the armed forces, but rather (in the words of the legislation by which this was accomplished) "One service called the Canadian Armed Forces." Civilian control over the Canadian Armed Forces is exercised by the Prime Minister and the Cabinet, with the Minister of Defence having direct responsibility. Under him the senior military man of the armed forces is the Chief of the Defence Staff, who in 1964 replaced the former four-man Chiefs of Staff Committee, and who is responsible for administering the armed forces through Canadian Forces Headquarters.

POLITICO-MILITARY POLICY

Canada has, for all practical purposes, linked its security requirements with those of the United States. Thus Canada has become a junior—but important and independent—partner in integrated defense arrangements for the defense of the North American continent. This does not imply that Canada feels obligated to follow the lead of the United States in foreign or military policy. But it does represent Canadian convictions that the principal objectives of the two nations are parallel, and many of their defense problems mutual.

Canada has been one of the leading proponents of the establishment of peacekeeping forces by the UN in instances where internal disorders, or danger of war, pose threats to international peace. Canadian forces have participated in all of the various UN forces and observer groups that have been established by the UN Security Council.

There were three principal reasons why the Canadian government made the policy decision first to integrate, then to unify, its armed forces. The first reason was budgetary; a study of the nation's force structure concluded that there was much unnecessary duplication of functions, personnel, and equipment among the three armed services. Second was the belief that future military requirements upon Canada, either for the defense of North America or for peacekeeping forces, would be in terms of relatively small mission forces including components of two, or of all three, of the conventional services. Third, and aside from the likelihood of requirements for mission forces, was a belief that in modern war all military functions for large forces, as well as small ones, involve joint operations of the conventional services.

In 1968 unification had become a fact, and there is now only one service of the Canadian Armed Forces. All personnel have a common uniform for duty (other than special purpose clothing) and off duty; a common grade structure has been established on a single promotion list.

Manpower for the Canadian Armed Forces is obtained by voluntary enlistment.

STRATEGIC PROBLEMS

Canada's principal strategic problems are geographical. First and most importantly, Canada lies athwart most of the likely paths of Soviet attack on the United States, either by manned aircraft or by ICBM. Second, most of Canada's relatively small population is concentrated in the far southern strip of the nation, close to the American border. Canada does not have the population or other resources to provide adequate defense against Soviet attacks, which would also threaten Canadian population and industrial centers. Thus, it is to Canadian interest to have the assistance of the United States in establishing passive and active defense means along the far-flung northern and northeastern periphery of the continent; it is to American interest to have Canadian cooperation in the Establishment of early warning and interceptor bases along this same periphery, most of which is on Canadian soil.

The great bulk of Canada (second largest nation in the world) in relation to the size of the population, and in relation to its far-northern location, has other strategic implications. It is difficult for Canada to maintain naval forces sufficiently large to provide protection for one seacoast; without American help it is impossible to protect two seacoasts on the opposite shores of a great continent. Similarly, Canada would be indefensible against attack from the south (the experience of the War of 1812 is no longer valid) were it not that both Canada and the United States for more than a century (since the Treaty of Washington, 1871) have acted on the assumption that war between the two nations would be unthinkable, and both are proud that theirs is the longest unfortified frontier in the world.

MILITARY ASSISTANCE

Canada has no foreign assistance program as such, nor is it the recipient of any such programs. However, Canadian military personnel attend service schools and staff colleges in the United States and Great Britain, and students from America, Britain, and other members of NATO attend Canadian military schools.

ALLIANCES

Canada is a member of three overlapping alliances. First, as a member of the Commonwealth, Canada retains close and cordial military ties with the United Kingdom, and with a number of other Commonwealth countries, particularly Australia and New Zealand. The importance of Commonwealth ties has lessened in the years since World War II, however, as Canada has ever more firmly related its defense requirements and arrangements to those of the United States.

Canada was one of the original members of NATO. Until 1969, in addition to one brigade group and six tactical air squadrons stationed in Germany, committed to NATO's Allied Command Europe, approximately half of the remainder of Canada's combat forces was earmarked for NATO in the event of war or grave emergency. However, the land force contingent in Germany has been reduced, but in emergency will be reinforced by airlift from Canada.

Canada's relationship with the United States is perhaps the closest military alliance in the world between fully sovereign nations. This dates back to August 18, 1940, when at Ogdensburg, N.Y., President Franklin D. Roosevelt and Prime Minister William L. Mackenzie King announced the establishment of a Permanent Joint Board of Defense to consider in a broad sense the defense of the north half of the Western Hemisphere. This Ogdensburg Declaration was considered by Canada to be a treaty, although in the United States, for Constitutional reasons, it is classed as an Executive Agreement.

The Permanent Joint Board on Defense, with mixed civilian-military membership representation from both nations, is still the primary instrument for integrating the defense efforts of the two nations. It does not make decisions, but rather prepares recommendations to the two governments. Other bilateral consultative bodies have been established since World War II, including: the Military Cooperation Committee, established in 1946; the Senior Policy Committee on the Canada-United States Defense Production and Development Sharing Program, established in 1958; and the C nada-United States Ministerial Committee on Joint Defense, also established in 1958.

One of the most significant aspects of the alliance is the Defense Development Sharing Program. The origins of this also go back to the period just before American entry into World War II when, on April 20, 1941, President Roosevelt and Prime Minister Mackenzie King agreed at Hyde Park on cooperation in defense production. This close cooperation continued until 1958, when the governments of the two nations agreed upon the virtual integration of their weapons systems design, development, and production procedures, to assure the most complete possible coordination of their defense economies.

The most significant of the various operational military cooperative programs between the two nations is the North American Air Defense Command (NORAD) which was established in 1958 by a 10-year agreement which brought about the virtual integration of the Air Defense Commands of the two nations. In 1968 the agreement was renewed for an additional five years, and in 1973 for two years more.

Canada, while recognizing the necessity for close military, political, and economic ties with the United States, is careful to maintain and proclaim its complete sovereign independence from its giant neighbor. Prime Minister Pierre Elliott Trudeau visited Moscow and signed consultation agreements with the USSR a year before President Nixon's 1972 visit, and Canada also established cordial relations with the People's Republic of China well in advance of US moves.

Canada participated in the three-nation International Commission of Control and Supervision (ICCS) set up to supervise the Vietnam ceasefire in 1973 but withdrew July 31, citing the ICCS's inability to cope with constantly occurring truce violations.

CANADIAN FORCES ORGANIZATION

In subsequent sections, the land, sea and air components are treated separately, for comparative purposes, under the headings of Army, Navy, and Air Force. However, these components are no longer separate services but are unified as one service within the Canadian Armed Forces. These unified forces are organized within functional commands:

Mobile Command: Headquarters: North Bay, Ontario.
Includes ground combat forces and tactical air forces including operational training units.

Air Defense Command: Headquarters: North Bay, Ontario.
Includes air and ground installations required to detect and counter possible air or missile attack on Canada.

Maritime Command: Headquarters: Halifax, Nova Scotia.
Includes bases and naval and air elements required for anti-submarine warfare (ASW) and other naval operations; also maritime transport for Mobile Command

Air Transport Command: Headquarters: Trenton, Ontario.
Includes all air transport functions.

Training Command: Headquarters: Winnipeg, Manitoba.
Provides for all common and basic training requirements and coordination of other training by the various commands.

Materiel Command: Rockcliffe, Ontario.
Responsible for procurement and distribution of weapons and equipment for all commands.

Communications Command: Headquarters: Ottawa.
Manages, operates and maintains strategic communications for the Canadian forces.

ARMY

Personnel: 33,000

Organization:

4 mechanized combat groups (one in West Germany with 2,800 men, and one—Air Mobile—prepared for quick transit to Europe) each group comprised of: 3 infantry battalions, 1 reconnaissance regiment, 1 reduced light artillery battalion (2 batteries)
1 airborne regiment
1 reduced battalion assigned to UNFICYP (Cyprus)
1 supply and logistics contingent in the UN Emergency Force Middle East

Major Equipment Inventory:

248 medium tanks (Centurion; to be replaced with Scorpion APC)
200 light tanks (M-24)
1,000 APCs (M-113)
72 M-109 155mm howitzers
260 105mm howitzers
helicopters (CUH-IN and COH-58A)

Missiles: Blowpipe SAM

Reserves: A total of about 19,000 men are organized for short-notice mobilization.

NAVY

Personnel: 14,000

Organization:

Maritime Command (Halifax, N.S.)
Maritime Forces Atlantic (Halifax)
Maritime Forces Pacific (Esquimalt, B.C.)
Maritime Reserve Forces
Maritime Air Forces

Major Units:

4 submarines (SS)
4 ASW helicopter destroyers with Sea Sparrow SAM, DDH 280 type (DDG)
9 ASW helicopter destroyers (DD)
11 ASW destroyer-escorts (DE)
3 operational support ships (AOR)
6 training vessels
4 oceanographic research vessels (AGS)
4 gate vessels (YNG)
1 diver depot ship
1 hydrofoil ASW, minesweepers, sub-chasers, etc., assigned to the reserve fleet

Major Naval Bases: Halifax, Esquimalt, Hamilton, Greenwood, Summerside, Shearwater, Comox, Patricia Bay

Reserves: There are approximately 2,615 naval reservists.

Maritime Air Forces:

4 maritime patrol squadrons (CL-28)
1 maritime patrol squadron (S-2)
1 ASW squadron (Sea King)
2 utility squadrons (T-33, C-47, UH-1N)
2 training squadrons (S-2, Sea King)

AIR FORCE

Personnel: 36,000

Organization:

3 tactical fighter squadrons (CF-104) Europe

2 tactical fighter squadrons (CF-5) Mobile Command
3 fighter-interceptor squadrons AW (CF-101) Air Defence Command
1 electronic warfare training squadron (CF-100, T-33)
1 fighter-interceptor training squadron (CF-101)
5 operational training squadrons, fighter (1 CF-101, 1 CF-104, 3 CF-5)
3 transport squadrons (1 Boeing 707, 2 C-130)
1 medium range transport squadron (Falcon, Cosmopolitan)
4 transport/rescue squadrons (Buffalo, Twin Otter, Labrador)
3 tactical helicopter squadrons (Iroquois, Kiowa)
28 long range radar squadrons
1 satellite tracking unit

Major Aircraft Types:

235 combat aircraft
  169 fighter-bombers (72 CF-104, 97 CF-5)
  66 CF-101 fighter-interceptors
585 other aircraft
  81 transports (5 Boeing 707, 23 C-130, 7 Falcon, 7 Cosmopolitan, 15 Buffalo, 24 Twin Otter)
  142 helicopters (18 Labradors, 50 Iroquois, 74 Kiowa)
  362 trainers and utility (7 C-47, 25 Musketeers, 84 Tutor, 80 T-33, 6 CF-100, 100 C-45, 25 T-34, 25 Otter, 10 HU-16)

Major Air Bases: Penhold, Sea Island, Moose Jaw, Edmonton Rivers, Cold Lake, Chatham, St. Jean, Lincoln Park, Fort Churchill, Uplands, Trenton, Clinton, Winnipeg, North Bay, St. Hubert, Dawson Creek, Rockcliffe, Halifax, Greenwood, Goose Bay, Gander, Resolute Bay, White Horse.

Reserves: Approximately 800, manning six squadrons with DHC-3 Otters (30 aircraft) for flight training.

PARAMILITARY

The Royal Canadian Mounted Police, approximately 8,000 strong, performs internal security as well as regional police functions, mostly in the lightly inhabited northern territories. The force is equipped with 13 aircraft, approximately 2,000 vehicles, and 24 vessels in the Marine Division of 245 men.

The provinces of Quebec and Ontario have provincial police forces, totaling about 5,000 men. Most of these perform routine regional police functions.

APPENDIX Y
CANADA
BACKGROUND NOTES

[Washington, Department of State, April 1972 (Publication 7769).]

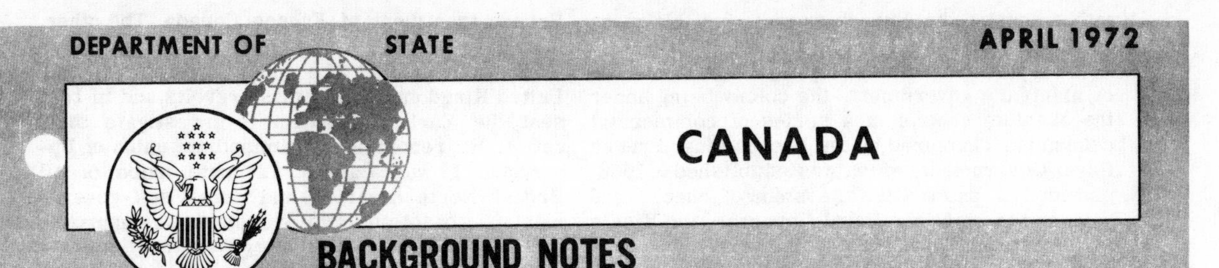

Population: 21.7 million (1971 est.)
Capital: Ottawa

With an area of 3,851,809 square miles, Canada is the second largest country in the world (after the U.S.S.R.). Its territory extends from the United States to the North Pole and includes all the islands in the Arctic Ocean from west of Greenland to Alaska. Its 17,860-mile mainland coastline is one of the longest in the world. Canada shares a 3,986-mile border with the United States, a border that has been unfortified for more than a century.

Almost half of Canada is a plateau of rock. The country's most outstanding physical feature is the Shield, a rugged arc of pre-Cambrian rock extending from Labrador around Hudson Bay to the Arctic islands, which covers most of eastern and central Canada. The northern area of the Shield is a treeless plain that is moss-covered in the summer but whose subsoil is permanently frozen. The Shield is thickly forested in the south. An extension of the Appalachain Mountains breaks up the rumpled contours of the Atlantic coast Provinces.

Prairies extend from the western border of the Shield to the Canadian Rockies. Extending across three Provinces, this rolling lowland is Canada's breadbasket because of its fertile soil and wheat-producing capability. Western Canada, comprising most of British Columbia, is laced with towering mountains. The Yukon and Northwest Territories are similar in topography to the northern area of Canada's Shield.

The climate varies greatly in the many diversified regions—ranging from arctic to mild—but Canada may be described generally as being cool and temperate, with long cold winters.

Canada's flag consists of three vertical bands—a wide, white center band with a narrower red stripe on each side—and a red maple leaf in the center.

THE PEOPLE

More than two-thirds of Canada's estimated 21.7 million people live within 100 miles of the U.S. border, and more than half the total population lives in the southeast near the Great Lakes and the St. Lawrence River. Yet Canadians and Americans are not "just alike" as casual and uninformed observers frequently assume. The Canadian character and outlook have been forged from a distinctive historical and social background which has produced a "Canadian way of life" flourishing in a sovereign nation.

About 44 percent of the population are of British stock and about 30 percent are of French origin. Canada's more than 6 million French-speaking citizens are primarily descendants of colonists who settled the country three centuries ago. The English-speaking population has been built up mostly by immigration from the United Kingdom. The largest influx from the United States occurred during the American Revolution when thousands of "Empire Loyalists" fled to Canada. Those Canadians who are of neither British nor French origin are comprised mostly of Germans, Ukrainians, Scandinavians, Italians, Dutch, and Poles. Indigenous Indians and Eskimos make up only about 1 percent of the population. The population growth rate is only about 1.8 percent annually.

Religion plays an important role in the life of the Canadians with 46 percent of them Roman Catholic. The largest Protestant denomination (about 20 percent of the people) is the United Church of Canada—a union of Methodists, Congregationalists, and Presbyterians. There are also lesser numbers of Anglicans, Presbyterians, Lutherans, Baptists, and Jews. Literacy in Canada is virtually complete.

HISTORY

Canada's early history was dominated by imperial rivalry between Britain and France. John Cabot, a Genoese explorer in the service of Britain, reached Newfoundland in 1497 and took possession of the country in the name of King Henry VII. Jacques Cartier, a French navigator on a similar voyage of exploration in 1534, planted the cross and fleur-de-lis of France on the Gaspé Peninsula.

While the British settled along the coast to the south, the French pushed rapidly into the interior, and Canada's history for more than a century was to be as a French colony. The French explorer, Samuel de Champlain, in 1604 helped establish the first permanent French colony in North America at Port Royal in Acadia—now Annapolis Royal, Nova Scotia. Four years later he founded the settlement of Quebec. The explorations of Cartier and Champlain up the St. Lawrence River and into the Great Lakes set a path whereby the French were to lay claim to the continent.

The political history of early Canada was one of arbitrary government, the colony being under the absolute control of a series of commercial companies chartered by the French king. French Royal Government, which was established in 1663, provided a paternalistic system of checks and balances in which the Royal Governor, the King's Intendant, and the Bishop competed in exercising control.

Meanwhile, explorers, traders, and missionaries, including Marquette, Joliet, and La Salle, extended French influence deep into the New World. Count Frontenac, a forceful Governor of New France, made peace with the Indians. Immigration helped reinforce the French population. In 1670 the British founded the Hudson's Bay Company to compete for the lucrative fur trade.

The war which broke out between Britain and France a few decades later was extended to the New World. The defeat in 1759 of the French Commander, Montcalm, by the British General, Wolfe, resulted in the fall of Quebec. The Treaty of Paris in 1763 ceded Canada to Great Britain.

A decade later the leaders of the American Revolution failed both in their efforts to persuade Canada to join their cause and in their military foray into Quebec. From 1783 to 1787 some 40,000 American colonists loyal to Britain fled to Canada.

The influx of these Empire Loyalists and other immigrants gradually changed the political character of Canada. The Constitutional Act of 1791 divided Canada into two provinces. Upper Canada—chiefly English—consisted of the southern section of what is now Ontario. Lower Canada covered the southern section of Quebec Province. The two provinces had elected legislatures which marked the first important step toward self-government.

This was a period of extensive exploration and accelerated trade. In the 1780's a group of Montreal traders founded the Northwest Company and challenged the virtual monopoly of the Hudson's Bay Company in the fur trade until their amalgamation in 1821. A Scot, Alexander Mackenzie, journeyed to the Arctic Ocean in 1789 and in 1793 reached the Pacific Ocean—the first white man to cross the continent.

War between the United Kingdom and the United States in 1812 again saw an invasion of Canada from the States. The Treaty of Ghent on December 24, 1814, ended the fighting and reestablished the prewar borders; but it did not settle the boundary question or naval disarmament. The latter was resolved in 1817 by the Rush-Bagot Agreement which limited to four each the number of naval vessels the United Kingdom and the United States could keep on the Great Lakes.

Intensive immigration into Canada between 1815 and 1850, largely from famine-beset Ireland, stimulated demands for political reforms. Two abortive revolts took place in 1837. One in Lower Canada, led by Louis Joseph Papineau, sought to redress what was considered unfair British treatment of French Canada. The other, in Upper Canada, was led by William Lyon Mackenzie against the local government. The United Kingdom quelled these revolts and in 1838 sent the Earl of Durham to investigate their cause. He recommended immediate union of Upper and Lower Canada, ultimate union of all British North America, and virtual self-government. Union of the two provinces was approved in 1840, but representative government was not achieved until 1849.

Serious border disputes between the United Kingdom and the United States were settled in the 1840's. Eastern border problems were resolved by the so-called Webster-Ashburton Treaty of 1842. After a period of tension regarding the western border—the famous "fifty-four forty or fight"—the United States agreed to a British offer to accept latitude 49 degrees as the boundary line. The Oregon Settlement was ratified on June 18, 1846.

By 1867 Canada had gained independence through "evolution rather than revolution." However, it was not truly a nation but rather a number of isolated colonies spread across the continent. A movement for political confederation was growing, spurred by several motives: to link the eastern and western provinces; to facilitate the building of a railroad system; and to form a strong union which could prevent encroachment by the United States. The latter was made more urgent by anti-British sentiment during the U.S. Civil War.

The movement culminated in the British North America Act of 1867 which created a union of four Provinces: Quebec, Ontario, Nova Scotia, and New Brunswick. The act provided for a federal union and the parliamentary system then practiced in the colonies. In 1869 Canada purchased "Prince Rupert's Land" from the Hudson's Bay Company and from it created the Provinces of Manitoba (1870), Saskatchewan (1905), and Alberta (1905). British Columbia (1871) entered on the promise of a transcontinental railroad, followed by Prince Edward Island (1873). With the entry of Newfoundland in 1949 as the 10th Province, Canadian confederation was completed.

THE PROVINCES AND TERRITORIES

Newfoundland, Nova Scotia, Prince Edward Island, and New Brunswick (Atlantic Provinces) comprise 5.4 percent of Canada's total area and have a population of about 2 million. The great majority of the people are of British stock, live in small communities, and are engaged in manufacturing, mining, agriculture, fishing, and forestry.

Quebec, the "cradle of Canada" and the center of French tradition, is the largest Province, with about 15 percent of the total area. It has a population of 6 million, more than 80 percent of which are of French origin. The city of Quebec, the provincial capital with 476,000 inhabitants (metropolitan area), retains a distinctively Old World atmosphere. Montreal, with a population of more than 2.7 million (metropolitan area), is Canada's largest city. This Province accounts for about 30 percent of the country's manufacturing sector and is a major producer of hydroelectric power. Its mines produce about 60 percent of the world's asbestos.

Ontario is Canada's most populous Province (7.9 million, or more than one-third of the total) and is the second largest in area (11 percent). Almost 60 percent of the Canadians in this Province are of British origin. The population is concentrated in the southern peninsula around the Great Lakes and the upper St. Lawrence Valley. Ottawa, the nation's capital (population of the metropolitan area: 596,000) and three more of Canada's largest cities are in this region, including Toronto with about 2.6 million inhabitants. Ontario produces half of the country's manufactured goods and is the world's principal source of nickel.

Manitoba, Saskatchewan, and Alberta (Prairie Provinces) occupy about 20 percent of Canada's area. The westward migration in the early 20th century accounts largely for its 3.5 million inhabitants. The Great Central Plains is one of the world's principal wheat-producing regions. These three Provinces also produce almost all of Canada's petroleum and natural gas.

British Columbia is the third largest Province and encompasses the country's entire Pacific coastal area and adjacent islands. More than two-thirds of the population of 2.2 million are of British origin. Lumbering is the leading industry. It ranks third in manufacturing and has great hydroelectric potential.

About 40 percent of Canada's area lies outside the Provinces. This vast northern region is divided into two territories—Yukon (about 207,000 square miles) and the Northwest Territories (about 1,305,000 square miles). The inhabitants number only about 50,000, almost half of them Indians and Eskimos. Since the discovery of gold in the Klondike in 1896, Yukon has produced more than $300 million worth. Yukon is governed from Whitehorse by a Commissioner and a council of seven elected members. The Northwest Territories is governed from Yellowknife by a Commission and a council of nine elected members.

GOVERNMENT

Although the British North America Act of 1867 provides Canada with a form of written constitution, many of the country's legal and parliamentary practices are based on unwritten custom, as is the case in the United Kingdom. On the other hand, the federal structure of the state—the uniting of the 10 Provinces in a Federal Government—resembles the U.S. Federal system. The British North America Act provides for a Federal Government to which are reserved specific powers, such as those relating to defense, trade and commerce, banking and currency, criminal law, postal services, and certain taxes, as well as all powers not expressly granted to the Provinces. The Provinces have authority to administer and legislate on such matters as education, property laws, health, and local affairs generally.

Queen Elizabeth II is Queen of Canada and Chief of State and serves as a symbol of the free association and unity of the equal and sovereign nations of the British Commonwealth. Her personal representative in Canada is the Governor General, whom she appoints on the advice of the Prime Minister of Canada, usually for a 5-year term. The term of the current Governor General has been extended until the spring of 1973.

Parliament consists of the Senate, and the House of Commons. The Senate's 102 members are appointed by the Governor General on the advice of the Prime Minister and hold office until the age of 75. Elections for 264 members of the House are held at least every 5 years but may also occur at any time that the Prime Minister advises the Governor General to dissolve the House.

The executive consists of a Cabinet led by a Prime Minister (Head of Government), who is the leader of the political party in power. The Cabinet remains in power as long as it retains majority support in the House on major issues.

Criminal law, a parliamentary prerogative, is uniform throughout the nation and is based largely on British law. Civil law is based on the Common Law of England except for Quebec, which has retained its own civil code patterned after that of France. Justice is administered by Federal, provincial, and municipal courts.

Government in the Provinces is patterned much along the lines of the Central Government. Each Province is governed by a premier and a single elected legislative chamber. A lieutenant-governor, appointed by the Governor General, represents the Crown.

POLITICAL PARTIES

Canada's Government during this century has been, for the most part, controlled by one or the other of the two major political parties, the Liberals and the Progressive-Conservatives.

As a result of the June 25, 1968, elections, the Liberal Party forms the Government with a majority of 149 seats, having governed from 1963 to 1968 without commanding an absolute majority. The party was out of power from 1957 to 1963, after having dominated Canadian political life for more than 20 years.

The Progressive-Conservative Party governed from 1957 to 1963. It is now the official opposition party with 72 seats, as it was from 1935 to 1957.

The New Democratic Party, formed in 1961 by a merger of the predominantly rural-based Cooperative Commonwealth Federation (CCF) and the Canadian Labour Congress (CLC), elected 25 members to Parliament in the June 1968 elections.

The Social Credit Party originated in the 1930's and split in 1963 when the Quebec-based Ralliement des Creditistes formed its own group. The Creditistes increased their standing in Parliament from nine to 13 seats in the June 1968 election. The national Social Credit Party was reestablished in 1971.

The Communist Party holds no seats in either the Federal or provincial legislatures in Canada. Three parliamentary seats are held by independents and two are vacant.

ECONOMY

Canada's natural wealth is abundant. About 8 percent of the land is farmland, and large areas are covered by valuable forests. With vast resources still untapped, Canada is already one of the most important producers of a wide variety of minerals. It has about a sixth of the world's fresh water and hydroelectric potential several times present levels. The coastal waters and more than 230,000 square miles of lakes provide productive fishing; and wildlife, including fur-bearers, abounds.

Canada is the world's largest producer of newsprint, zinc, silver, nickel, and potash. It ranks second in production of asbestos, gypsum, uranium, titanium, molybdenum, and sulfur; third in cobalt, gold, lead, platinum, and wheat; fourth in magnesium; and fifth in copper.

Manufacturing, now the leading industry of the nation, supports about a third of the population. Canada's manufactures are worth more annually than the wealth produced by its agriculture, fisheries, mines, and electric power combined. The spectacular growth of Canadian manufacturing, particularly during the 1950's and 1960's, has transformed the nation from a rural agrarian society into one primarily industrial and urban in character.

Canada's annual economic growth rate is approximately 5 percent in real terms (1961 prices). In 1971 Canada's gross national product (GNP) grew by 9.1 percent, in current prices, to C $92.1 billion. (Since mid-1970 the Canadian dollar has floated. Recently the Canadian dollar has been approximately equal to the U.S. dollar.) Per capita income was estimated at C $4,249 in 1971.

Forestry

Forests, mostly softwood, cover more than 1.7 million square miles, or more than 45 percent of Canada's land area. About 1 million square miles are estimated to be productive. The forest industry directly or indirectly employs more than 300,000 people, and the sale of forest products abroad represents about 15 percent of Canada's export trade.

Canada's newsprint capacity is nearly three times greater than that of any other country; the industry accounts for about half of world production. Newsprint has been for years one of Canada's principal exports and in 1971 was second to motor vehicles and parts. The United States takes more than three-fourths of the country's newsprint production.

Minerals

Another important set of U.S. imports from Canada are nonferrous metals such as nickel, aluminum, copper, and zinc. Deposits of nickel in Ontario, and asbestos in Ontario, Quebec, and British Columbia, are the world's largest. The Quebec-Labrador region is one of the world's major sources of iron ore. Other important minerals produced include copper, zinc, potash, lead, gold, silver, molybdenum, and platinum. Bauxite is imported to utilize the country's great hydroelectric resources for the production of aluminum, now leading nickel as Canada's principal metal export.

Crude petroleum, natural gas, and iron ore have become highly important to the economy. Crude petroleum is by far the largest single contributor to the value of Canada's mineral output, and the country has proved reserves of more than 10 billion barrels of oil. Oil production in 1971 averaged 1.6 million barrels a day. Recently the vast deposits of Alberta tar sands have undergone commercial development.

Agriculture

Agriculture employs about 7 percent of the working population. Farming is highly mechanized, with a declining number of agricultural workers producing increasing quantities of foodstuffs on larger farms.

Production of wheat in 1971 amounted to 523.7 million bushels. Other leading Canadian agricultural products include feedgrains, oilseeds, and meat and meat products. Canada also produces tobacco, milk and other dairy products, poultry, and fruits and vegetables. In recent years some of these commodities, especially grains, have developed surpluses and required Federal assistance.

Canada is able to export 30-40 percent of its total agricultural production and is one of the world's major food-exporting countries. In 1971 agricultural commodities accounted for about 11 percent of Canada's total exports. Wheat comprises slightly less than half of all agricultural exports, followed by feedgrains, live animals, fish, oilseed, and meat and meat products.

The People's Republic of China and the East European countries take about one-fourth of Canada's agricultural exports. A few years ago their purchases were only a small fraction of today's volume.

Fisheries

Commercial fisheries provide an annual catch of more than 2.5 billion pounds brought in by ocean and inland fleets. The fishing industry provides a livelihood for some 85,000 Canadians, with about 75 percent of the catch being exported.

Transportation and Communications

Much of Canada's production, a third of which is exported, is located inland and must move long distances to market. To meet these needs, a great east-west artery of transportation with radial north-south adjuncts has been developed. Railroads are the backbone of this system. With more than 59,000 railway miles, Canada has more railroad miles per capita than any other country. Of Canada's some 500,000 miles of roads, about 375,000 miles are surfaced, including almost all of the 4,860-mile trans-Canada highway.

Canada's earliest transportation system, the inland waterways, still accounts for a major portion of the nation's commercial traffic. The heart of the system is the St. Lawrence-Great Lakes waterway. It carried more traffic than any other inland waterway in the world even before the opening of the Seaway. A total of 51.8 million tons of cargo moved through the Seaway and the Welland Canal in 1971, including domestic U.S. and Canadian traffic and foreign traffic, by some 5,700 ship transits. Ocean and coastwise ships now penetrate the continent as far inland as ports at the head of Lake Superior.

The "bush pilots," who gave access to the new mining areas of the north in the 1930's and who still play an important role in Canada's transportation complex, pioneered the way for the country's major airlines. Air Canada, owned by the Canadian National Railways, spans the nation and provides service to the United States, the Caribbean, Europe, and Mexico. Canadian Pacific Airlines, which specializes in north-south operations within the country, links Canada with Alaska, Hawaii, and San Francisco, in addition to Asia, Australia, South America, and southern Europe.

In per capita ownership of telephones, only the United States exceeds Canada, which has nearly one phone for every two persons. Telegraph services are operated by the transcontinental railway companies and by the Federal Government to outlying districts.

The Canadian Broadcasting Corp. (CBC) owns and operates two national radio networks (one English, one French) and two television networks, as well as 40 radio stations and 59 television stations. In addition, many privately-owned television stations act as outlets for the CBC network programs.

Some 102 daily newspapers are published in English and about 12 in French; there are approximately 820 weeklies.

Foreign Trade

Canada usually ranks in the top six countries in the world in volume of foreign trade—after the United States, the United Kingdom, the Federal Republic of Germany, France, and Japan. It has alternated with New Zealand in recent years as the nation with the highest per capita trade.

Canada is one of the world's largest importers of steel products, manufactured goods, and fuels. Among the principal imports are industrial machinery, crude petroleum (principally for east coast consumption), automobiles and parts, electrical apparatus, rolling mill products (steel), iron and steel pipes, tractors, and aircraft. In 1971 its total imports were C $15.6 billion, and exports were C $17.7 billion.

The United States and Canada have become the world's greatest trading partners. In 1971 the United States received 68 percent (C $12 billion) of Canada's exports and supplied about 70 percent (C $10.9 billion) of its imports. Twenty-three percent of U.S. exports went to Canada in 1971—more than twice the amount than went to the United States next best trading partner, Japan—and Canada supplied 28 percent of U.S. imports. In 1971 the United Kingdom supplied 5 percent of Canada's imports and ranked second in Canadian import trade, followed by Japan, the Federal Republic of Germany, Venezuela (mostly petroleum and petroleum products), and France. The United Kingdom also ranks second among Canada's export markets, followed by Japan and the Federal Republic of Germany.

On January 16, 1965, President Johnson and Prime Minister Pearson signed the United States-Canada Automotive Products Agreement designed to create a broader market for automotive products by obtaining for both countries and both industries the benefits of specialization and large-scale production. Canada accords duty-free treatment to specified motor vehicles and original equipment parts imported by Canadian manufacturers, and the United States allows duty-free import of specified Canadian motor vehicles and parts of original equipment. Motor vehicles and parts now represent Canada's largest category of exports.

Foreign Investment

Canada's resources are being developed with the help of foreign capital attracted by favorable conditions for investment. Canadians are also capital exporters and in 1969 had a long-term investment abroad of about $10 billion. Nevertheless, Canada is a net importer of long-term capital. Furthermore, the extent of foreign ownership and control of Canadian resources is exceptional. Foreign companies control more than half of Canada's industries.

By far the greatest percentage of the foreign capital has been invested by U.S. citizens, and more than 5,000 subsidiaries of U.S. corporations do business in Canada. The U.S. investments are primarily in the petroleum, rubber, transportation equipment, chemicals, electrical products, machinery, and extractive minerals industries.

FOREIGN RELATIONS

In its early days as a nation Canada's foreign affairs were conducted by the United Kingdom, but by 1909, as Canadian participation increased, it became necessary to create a Department of External Affairs. After World War I Canadian representatives signed the Treaty of Versailles, and the country's first bilateral treaty was signed in 1923 with the United States.

World War II gave considerable impetus to Canadian participation in world affairs. Canada took an active role in the creation of the United Nations, which it has strongly supported. It contributed troops to the U.N. forces in Korea and to the U.N. emergency forces in the Middle East, Congo, Yemen, and Cyprus. Canada is a member of the International Control Commissions in Viet-Nam, Laos, and Cambodia. It has assumed a prominent role in disarmament negotiations.

A member of the North Atlantic Treaty Organization (NATO) since its inception, Canada shares responsibility for the North Atlantic Treaty area. Its mutual aid program has provided NATO allies with about $1.8 billion in military assistance since 1950.

Canada's economic assistance to developing countries has risen to almost $400 million annually. It has been a consistent contributor to the Colombo Plan, which provides financial aid to South and Southeast Asia, and has recently been expanding its assistance to the African Francophone countries.

On June 25, 1970, the Government published a comprehensive foreign policy review which is intended to reflect more closely Canada's national interests. It will give highest priorities to (1) international factors affecting Canada's economic growth, such as export markets, capital flows, currency problems, technological imports, and improved transportation; (2) efforts to resolve race conflicts, raise the living standards of underdeveloped countries through economic and technical aid, and develop international law; (3) programs to enhance the quality of life in Canada through cultural, technological, and scientific exchanges.

Canada has recently made efforts to diversify its foreign relations in the light of its considered need to provide, in the interests of strengthening Canadian independence, some counterweights to what seems to be a pervasive U.S. presence. Recognition of the People's Republic of China in the closing months of 1970, the exchange of visits between Prime Minister Trudeau and Premier Kosygin (U.S.S.R.) in May and October 1971, and the visit of President Tito (Yugoslavia) in November were the major initiatives.

U.S.-CANADIAN RELATIONS

Waters and Fisheries

The St. Lawrence Seaway was inaugurated on April 25, 1959. It is basically an improvement of a water route in use since Canada's earliest days and has opened an important 2,300-mile trade route whereby oceangoing vessels can penetrate into the industrial heart of North America. It was constructed jointly by the United States and Canada at a cost of $471 million, of which Canada paid $341 million. The entire cost is to be repaid from tolls charged to users.

The U.S.-Canadian border is marked by a profusion of streams and other waterways, and it is natural that there should be problems regarding these waters involving navigation, bridge construction, air and water pollution, water use, conservation, and hydroelectric development. The principal instrument for solving such problems is the International Joint Commission, created by the Boundary Waters Treaty of January 11, 1909, and consisting of three members from each country. The commission acts on proposals for use, obstruction, or diversion of boundary waters which would affect the natural level or flow on either side. Increasingly its major work has been to investigate and make recommendations on specific problems, particularly those related to boundary water pollution.

In January 1961 the two Governments signed the Columbia River Treaty whereby Canada undertook to build three dams on the river and receive a lump-sum payment for flood-control benefits from the United States and one-half of the power benefits produced at the U.S. installation as a result of operation of the Canadian dams. The United States agreed to build Libby Dam in Montana, which would provide downstream benefits to Canada. In January 1964 two supplementary agreements were signed providing for clarification of responsibilities under the treaty and for sale in the United States of the Canadian share of power benefits resulting from the Canadian dam construction. An exchange of ratifications by the two Governments at Ottawa on September 16, 1964, put the treaty into effect.

Fisheries have been historically important to the Canadian and United States economies and remain a significant source of income. Fishermen of the two nations have traditionally fished in the same areas, and the countries have cooperated closely in fishery conservation and rational exploitation of fishery resources. Both countries are members of six multilateral fishery commissions and are parties to five bilateral fishery agreements.

In December 1970 Canada proclaimed "fisheries closing lines" designating major areas on its east and west coasts as exclusive Canadian fisheries zones. The areas affected are the Gulf of St. Lawrence and the Bay of Fundy on the Atlantic coast and Queen Charlotte Sound and Dixon Entrance-Hecate Strait on the Pacific. The United States protested this unilateral extension of jurisdiction over areas traditionally regarded as the high seas. Traditional and other U.S. fishing interests were protected, however, by a new bilateral fisheries agreement.

Defense

The U.S. defense arrangements with Canada are more extensive than with any other country; fully a third of the United States major agreements with Canada relate to defense. This cooperation began in 1940 with the establishment of a Permanent Joint Board on Defense, which continues to meet regularly to discuss mutual defense questions, and the Hyde Park Agreement concerning defense procurement which entered into force on April 20, 1941. The principle of defense cooperation embodied in the Hyde Park Agreement was reaffirmed on October 26, 1950, with a "Statement of Principles for Economic Cooperation." This document expressed the agreement of the two Governments to cooperate to the end that their economic efforts "be coordinated for the common defense."

During the ensuing years this principle has been evidenced by extensive reciprocal military purchases. In addition, U.S.-Canadian military forces work together within the framework of the North American Air Defense Command (NORAD), which has been in operation since 1957 at Colorado Springs, Colorado. It exercises operational control over all combat units of the combined national forces made available for air defense. NORAD is headed by a U.S. general with a Canadian general as deputy.

Extensive radar chains stretching across Canada have been constructed. The northernmost of these, the Distant Early Warning (DEW) line, extends from the Alaskan border across the Canadian Arctic to Greenland. It was built by the United States at a cost of some $300 million. The Pinetree line provides not only radar warning of approaching aircraft but also the means to determine their speed and course so that they may be readily intercepted. Its cost of some $250 million was jointly financed. These main warning lines are supplemented by additional land, sea, and air-based radar.

PRINCIPAL GOVERNMENT OFFICIALS

Chief of State—Queen Elizabeth II
Governor General—Roland Michener
Prime Minister—Pierre Elliott Trudeau
Secretary of State for External Affairs—Mitchell Sharp
Ambassador to the U.S.—Marcel Cadieux
Ambassador to the U.N.—Yvon Beaulne

Canada maintains an Embassy in the United States at 1746 Massachusetts Avenue, N.W., Washington, D.C. 20036.

PRINCIPAL U.S. OFFICIALS

Ambassador—Adolph W. Schmidt
Minister—Rufus Z. Smith
Counselor for Political Affairs—Vladimir I. Toumanoff
Counselor for Economic Affairs—Emerson M. Brown

The U.S. Embassy in Canada is located at 100 Wellington Street, Ottawa.

READING LIST

Berton, Pierre. The Last Spike. Toronto: McLelland & Stewart, 1971.

Berton, Pierre. The National Dream. Toronto: McLelland & Stewart, 1970.

The Canada-U.S. Automotive Agreement: An Evaluation. Montreal: Canadian-American Committee.

Canada Year Book. Ottawa: Statistics Canada.

Canadian Annual Review. Toronto: University of Toronto Press.

Clark, Gerald. Canada: The Uneasy Neighbor. New York: McKay, 1965.

Corbett, Edward M. Quebec Confronts Canada. Baltimore: Johns Hopkins University Press, 1967.

Creighton, Donald. The Road to Confederation. Toronto: Macmillan, 1964.

Defense in the 70's. Ottawa: Information Canada, 1971.

Deutch, J. J., and others. The Canadian Economy, rev. ed. New York: St. Martins, 1965.

Dickey, John Sloan, ed. The United States and Canada. Englewood Cliffs, N. J.: Prentice-Hall, 1964.

Foreign Policy for Canadians. Ottawa: Queen's Printer, 1970.

Matthews, Roy A. "A New Atlantic Role for Canada." Foreign Affairs. January 1969.

Merchant, Livingston T., and Heeney, A.D. P. "Canada and the United States—Principles for Partnership." Department of State Bulletin. August 2, 1965.

Merchant, Livingston T., ed. Neighbors Taken for Granted. New York: Praeger, 1966.

Newman, Peter C. Renegade in Power: The Diefenbaker Years. Toronto: McLelland & Stewart, 1963.

Porter, John. The Vertical Mosaic: An Analysis of Social Class and Power in Canada. Toronto: University of Toronto Press, 1965.

A Possible Plan for a Canada-U.S. Free Trade Area. Montreal: Canadian-American Committee, 1965.

Trezise, Philip H. "U.S.-Canadian Economic Relations." United States International Economic Policy in an Interdependent World. 1971.

DEPARTMENT OF STATE PUBLICATION 7769
Revised April 1972

APPENDIX Z

CANADA

STRENGTH OF THE COMMUNIST PARTY ORGANIZATION—1973

[FROM: World Strength of the Communist Party Organizations—1973. Washington, Department of State, Bureau of Intelligence and Research, 1973.]

CANADA

National Political Status: Date of last election - October 30, 1972.

Communist: Communist Party of Canada-Marxist/Leninist (CPC-M/L) 9,339 votes
Communist Party of Canada (CPC) 5,962 votes (0.2%), no seats

Non-Communist Left: New Democratic Party - 1,696,301 votes (17.8%), 31 seats (11.7%)

Center: Liberal Party - 3,679,021 votes (38.5%), 109 seats (41.3%)

Conservative: Progressive Conservative - 3,357,094 votes (35.1%), 107 seats (40.5%)

Other: Social Credit - 708,310 votes (7.4%), 15 seats (5.7%)
Other (Independents) - 98,008 votes (1.0%), 2 seats (0.8%)

Total: 9,554,035 votes, 264 seats

Communist Party Membership:
CPC - 1,500
CPC-M/L - 275 (estimate)

Leading Party Figures and Positions:
KASHTAN, William - General Secretary of the CPC
CRUISE, Robert - National Secretary of the CPC-M/L

Principal Publications:
The Canadian Tribune of Toronto - CPC weekly
The Pacific Tribune of Vancouver - West Coast edition of the *Canadian Tribune*
Combat - official organ of the *Parti Communiste du Quebec*
People's Canada Daily News Release - a publication of the CPC-M/L

Areas of Communist Activity: The overall political strength of the Communists in Canada is minimal; no Communist has sat either in the Canadian Parliament or in a provincial legislature since 1948.

There are now two Communist parties in Canada, the old pro-Soviet Communist Party of Canada (CPC) and the Maoist-oriented Communist Party of Canada-Marxist/Leninist (CPC-M/L). The Communist Party of Canada is primarily an urban organization of industrial workers, white-collar workers, and students and is strongest in Ontario and British Columbia.

The two factions devote as much attention to attacking each other as to mounting campaigns against the overwhelmingly non-Communist majority. In 1973 the CPC presented a few candidates at both Manitoba and Quebec provincial elections but, as usual, did very poorly.

Former National Chairman Tim Buck died in March 1973. He had helped found the CPC in 1921 and had been its leader from 1929 until 1962.

APPENDIX AA
DENMARK
ARMED FORCES AND MILITARY POWER

[Reprinted with permission from: The Almanac of World Military Power, by Col. T. N. Dupuy, U.S. Army, Ret., Col. John A. C. Andrews, U.S. Air Force, Ret., and Grace P. Hayes. 3rd ed. Dunn Loring, Va., T. N. Dupuy Associates, 1974.]

DENMARK
Kongeriget Danmark
Kingdom of Denmark

POWER POTENTIAL STATISTICS

Area: 16,629 square miles (excluding Faroe Islands and Greenland); Greenland, 840,000 square miles
Population: 5,000,000
Total Active Armed Forces: 30,000 (0.60% population)
Gross National Product: $20 billion ($4,000 per capita)
Annual Military Expenditures: $552.9 million (2.76% GNP)
Fuel Production: Crude Oil: 81,307 metric tons
Refined Petroleum Products: 10.3 million metric tons
Electric Power Output: 17.2 billion kwh
Merchant Fleet: 1,264 ships; 4 million gross tons
Civil Air Fleet: 35 jet, 16 turboprop, 9 piston transports (exclusive of Danish-owned portion of SAS)

DEFENSE STRUCTURE

The Monarch (Queen Margrethe II) is nominal commander in chief of the armed forces. Civilian control in the conventional parliamentary government of a constitutional democratic monarchy is exercised by the Defense Minister, responsible to the Prime Minister. Full command of the three services rests in the Chief of Defense, the ranking military officer, who, with his Chief of Defense Staff, the Army, Navy, and Air Force Commanders (with appropriate staff), form an integrated Defense Command. The Defense Minister is advised by a Defense Council of the above officers, plus a Chief of Danish Operational Forces.

POLITICO-MILITARY POLICY

For three-quarters of a century prior to World War II Denmark had adhered to a policy of strict neutrality in European power politics. After having been a victim of German aggression in World War II, Denmark espoused the concept of collective security, and was an original member of NATO.

The armed forces consist mainly of conscripted men, serving 12 months, between the ages of 19 and 25; the annual call-up is about 30,000 men. After active service, they may be recalled for refresher training.

STRATEGIC PROBLEMS

Denmark's position astride the entrance to the Baltic Sea makes it one of the most strategically located nations of the world. Its small size and the lack of natural obstacles (save for relatively narrow channels between the islands) make it vulnerable to invasion from Germany, both overland through Jutland, and by amphibious attack from the coasts of Schleswig-Holstein and Mecklenberg.

Greenland is a special strategic problem. This vast frozen land mass lies athwart possible trajectories of intercontinental missile exchange between the USSR on the one hand, and Canada and the United States on the other. There is a small Greenland Defense Force; Denmark accepts the existence of the US bases in Greenland that are a significant factor in North American defense, despite the fact that in most respects Denmark is one of the most independent of all the European members of NATO.

Denmark is ethnically homogeneous, and there are no significant internal security problems. The Communist Party has an estimated 5,000 members.

MILITARY ASSISTANCE

Denmark received $625 million in military assistance from the United States from 1950 to 1972. The US Military Advisory Group in Denmark numbers about 20.

ALLIANCES

Denmark is a member of the UN, EEC, and NATO. Danish armed forces are earmarked for the Northern European Command, within which the German-Danish Combined Allied Forces Baltic Approaches (COMBALTAP) has been established.

ARMY

Personnel: Standing force 13,000 including a ready supplement of 4,500

Organization:

3 major commands (Western Area Command, Eastern Area Command, Materiel Command)
field army (mobilized)
- 5 armored brigades
- 1 armored reconnaissance battalion
- Defense Forces of Bornholm

local defense (mobilized)
- 21 infantry battalions
- 7 artillery battalions
- 6 engineer companies
- 6 tank destroyer squadrons

Major Equipment Inventory:

- 200 medium tanks (Centurion, M-47, M-48)
- 650 armored personnel carriers (M-113)
- 72 self-propelled howitzers (155mm, M-109)
- 48 light tanks (M-41)
- 276 light and medium artillery pieces

Reserves: 65,000 (includes local defense) plus a volunteer Army Home Guard of approximately 50,000

NAVY

Personnel: 6,000

Organization:

3 major commands (Naval Command, Coastal Defense Command, Naval Materiel Command)

Major Units:

- 2 frigates (PF)
- 3 corvettes (PCE)
- 18 torpedo boats (PT)
- 6 submarines (diesel) (SS)
- 4 minelayers (MMF)
- 3 coastal minelayers (MMC)
- 8 minesweepers (MSC)
- 8 patrol boats (YP)
- 19 auxiliaries
- 8 helicopters (Alouette III)

Major Naval Bases: Copenhagen, Frederikshavn, Korsoer, and shore installations at Stevns and Langeland

Reserves: A volunteer Naval Home Guard of 4,000 operates some small patrol boats.

AIR FORCE

Personnel: 11,000

Organization:

2 major commands (Tactical Air Command, Air Materiel Command)
- 2 SAM battalions (Nike-Hercules and Hawk)
- 2 all-weather fighter interceptor squadrons (F-104)
- 3 fighter-bomber squadrons (F-35, F-100)
- 1 fighter reconnaissance squadron (RF-35)
- 1 transport squadron (C-130, C-54, C-47)
- 1 rescue squadron (S-61 helicopters)

Major Aircraft Types:

116 combat aircraft
- 40 F-104 all-weather fighter interceptors
- 40 F-100 fighter-bombers
- 20 F-35 fighter-bombers
- 16 RF-35 fighter reconnaissance

21 other aircraft
- 5 C-54 (C-130) transports
- 8 C-47 transports
- 8 S-61 helicopters

Major Air Bases: Karup, Aalborg, Skrydstrup, Vandel, Tirstrup, Vaerloese; on Greenland: Thule, Soendre Stroemfjord, Narsarsuak

Reserves: A volunteer air force Home Guard of 8,000

APPENDIX BB
DENMARK
BACKGROUND NOTES

[Washington, Department of State, December 1974 (Publication 8298).]

Denmark

department of state * december 1974

OFFICIAL NAME: Kingdom of Denmark

GEOGRAPHY

Denmark is located strategically at the mouth of the Baltic Sea. It consists of the Jutland Peninsula projecting north from the Federal Republic of Germany and about 500 islands, of which 100 are inhabited. The straits between these islands connect the Baltic and the North Seas.

Denmark proper and the 17 Faeroe Islands (540 square miles) cover an area slightly smaller than Vermont and New Hampshire combined. Greenland, the largest island in the world (857,159 square miles) became an integral part of Denmark under the Constitution of June 5, 1953.

Denmark has a low elevation with a flat or undulating landscape. Nearly the whole area is in productive use. The climate is temperate with mild winters (20°-40°F) and comparatively cool summers (50°-70°F); the prevailing westerly winds are strong.

PEOPLE

The Danes are a homogeneous people of the Gotho-Germanic race, who have inhabited Denmark since prehistoric times. Danish is the principal language. A small German-speaking minority lives in southern Jutland; an Eskimo dialect is spoken in Greenland; and Faeroese is used in the Faeroe Islands. Education is compulsory from age 7 to 16 and is free through the university level.

The Lutheran Church is the established church in Denmark. It is supported by the state and accounts for approximately 97 percent of religious affiliation. Religious freedom exists, and there are several other denominations.

HISTORY

During the Viking period (9th-11th centuries), Denmark was a great power based on the Jutland Peninsula, the island of Zealand, and the southern part of what is now Sweden. In the early 11th century, King Canute united Denmark and England, a union which lasted almost 30 years.

Viking raids brought Denmark into contact with Christianity, and, in the 12th century, crown and church influence increased. By the latter part of the 13th century royal power had waned, and the King was forced by the

PROFILE

Geography

AREA: 16,169 sq. mi. (about half the size of Maine). CAPITAL: Copenhagen (pop. 1.4 million). OTHER CITIES: Aarhus (pop. 190,000), Odense (136,000), Aalborg (124,000).

People

POPULATION: 5.1 million (1974 est.). ANNUAL GROWTH RATE: 0.5% (1974). DENSITY: 296 per sq. mi. ETHNIC GROUPS: Scandinavian, German, Eskimo, Faeroese. RELIGION: Lutheran (approx. 97%). LANGUAGES: Danish, some German, Eskimo dialect, Faeroese. LITERACY: 99%. LIFE EXPECTANCY: 72 yrs.

Government

TYPE: Constitutional monarchy. DATE OF CONSTITUTION: June 5, 1953.

BRANCHES: *Executive*–Queen (Chief of State), Prime Minister (Head of Government); Cabinet. *Legislative*–unicameral *Folketing* (parliament). *Judicial*–Supreme Court (appointed).

POLITICAL PARTIES: Social Democratic, Progress, Moderate Liberal, Radical Liberal, Conservative, Socialist People's, Communist. SUFFRAGE: Universal adult. POLITICAL SUBDIVISIONS: 14 Provinces.

FLAG: The *Dannebrog* (Danish flag) has a white cross on a red field. It is among the oldest flags in continuous use.

Economy

GROSS NATIONAL PRODUCT (GNP): $26.8 billion (1973). ANNUAL GROWTH RATE: 3% (1973). PER CAPITA INCOME: $5,400.

AGRICULTURE: *Land* 75%. *Labor* 7.5%. *Products*–meat, fish, dairy products, fur.

INDUSTRY: *Labor* 37.2%. *Products*–industrial and construction equipment, furniture, textiles.

NATURAL RESOURCES: Some low-grade iron ore.

TRADE: *Exports*–$6 billion (1973): farm products, including canned goods (30%), manufactured goods (65%), fish, furs. *Imports*–$7.5 billion (1973): industrial raw materials, fuels, machinery and equipment, consumer goods. *Partners*–Sweden, U.K., F.R.G. (each 15-17%); U.S. (7%); Communist bloc (6%).

OFFICIAL EXCHANGE RATE: Approx. 6 kroner=US$1.

MEMBERSHIP IN INTERNATIONAL ORGANIZATIONS: U.N. and many of its specialized agencies, North Atlantic Treaty Organization (NATO), Nordic Council, European Communities (EC).

nobles to grant a constitution, Denmark's "Magna Carta." The struggle between the crown and the nobility continued in the 14th century, but Queen Margaret succeeded in uniting Denmark, Norway, Sweden, Finland, the Faeroe Islands, Iceland, and Greenland under the Danish crown. This union lasted until 1814 although Sweden and Finland seceded in 1520.

The Reformation was introduced in Denmark in 1536. Denmark's provinces in southern Sweden were lost in 1658, and Norway was transferred from the Danish to the Swedish crown in 1814, following the defeat of Napoleon with whom Denmark was allied. The Danish liberal movement gained momentum in the 1830's, and in 1849 Denmark became a constitutional monarchy. After the war against Prussia and Austria in 1864, Denmark was forced to cede Schleswig-Holstein to Prussia and adopt a policy of neutrality. In the latter part of the 19th century Denmark inaugurated important social reforms laying the basis for the present welfare state.

Denmark maintained its neutrality in World War I. Despite a declaration of neutrality at the beginning of World War II, it was invaded by the Nazis in 1940 and occupied until its liberation by the British in May 1945. Denmark became a charter member of the United Nations and was one of the original signers of the North Atlantic Treaty. On January 1, 1973, Denmark joined the European Communities (EC).

GOVERNMENT

Denmark is a limited, or constitutional, monarchy. Queen Margrethe II has largely ceremonial functions; probably her most significant independent power lies in her right to appoint the Prime Minister and Cabinet Ministers, who are responsible for administration of the government. But she must consult with parliamentary leaders to determine the public will, since the Cabinet may be dismissed by a vote of no confidence in the *Folketing* (parliament). Cabinet members may be recruited outside of the ranks of the *Folketing*, but this is not customary.

According to the Constitution of 1953, the unicameral *Folketing* consists of not more than 179 members, of whom two must be elected from the Faeroe Islands and two from Greenland. Elections are held at least every 4 years, but the Prime Minister can dissolve the *Folketing* at any time and call for new elections.

The judicial branch consists of about 100 local courts, two high courts, several special courts (arbitration, maritime, etc.), and a Supreme Court of 15 judges appointed by the Queen.

Directly below the national level, Denmark is divided into 14 Provinces *(Amter)*. Each Province is made up of a varying number of rural municipalities of which there are 275 in all. The chief official of the Province, the County Mayor *(Amtsborgmester)*, is elected to the county council from among its members, according to the municipal reform of 1970.

The Faeroe Islands are partially self-governing, and the Queen is represented by a High Commissioner. In Greenland she is represented by a Governor.

Principal Government Officials

Monarch—Queen Margrethe II
Prime Minister—Poul Hartling
Foreign Minister—Ove Guldberg
Finance Minister—Anders Andersen
Economics and Commerce Minister—Poul Nyboe-Andersen
Defense Minister—Erling Bröndum
Agriculture and Fisheries Minister—Niels Anker Kofoed
Labor and Housing Minister—Johan Philipsen
Environment and Greenland Minister—Holger Hansen

Ambassador to the U.S.—Eyvind Bartels
Ambassador-designate to the U.N.—Henning Hjorth Nielsen

Denmark maintains an Embassy in the United States at 3200 Whitehaven Street, NW., Washington, D.C. 20008. There are also Consulates General at Chicago, Los Angeles, New York, and San Francisco.

READING LIST

These titles are provided as a general indication of the material currently being published on this country. The Department of State does not endorse the specific views in unofficial publications as representing the position of the U.S. Government.

Anderson, Stanley V. *The Nordic Council: A Study of Scandinavian Regionalism.* Seattle: University of Washington Press, 1967.

Bjornsen, Mette, and Ludvig Bramsen. *Facts About Denmark*, 15th ed. Copenhagen: Politikens Forlag, 1966.

Department of State. "NATO and the Defense of Europe." No. 2 in *Issues in United States Foreign Policy* series. Pub. 8476. Washington, D.C.: U.S. Government Printing Office, revised 1970.

Lauring, Palle. *A History of the Kingdom of Denmark.* Copenhagen: Host, 1960.

Lauwerys, J. A. *Scandinavian Democracy.* Copenhagen: A/S J. H. Schultz, Universitets-Bogtrykkeri, 1958.

O'Dell, Andrew C. *The Scandinavian World.* London: Longmans, Green, 1957.

Royal Danish Ministry of Foreign Affairs. *Denmark.* Copenhagen: A/S H. P. Hansens-Bogtrykkeri, 1970.

Simpson, Colin. *The Viking Circle: Denmark, Greenland, Norway, Sweden, Finland, Iceland.* New York: Fielding, 1968.

POLITICAL CONDITIONS

Political life in Denmark is carried on in an orderly and democratic fashion. Political changes occur gradually, and political methods and attitudes are generally moderate. Compromise is an essential element in Danish political life, as no single party since 1945 has been able to command a majority in the *Folketing.*

The elections of December 4, 1973, resulted in a minority Liberal government. In order to remain in power, the Liberals, who have only 22 seats in the

TRAVEL NOTES

Climate and Clothing—Winters are warmer and summers are cooler than in New England. Woolen clothing is worn most of the year.

Customs and Currency—A valid American passport is the only document needed for entry into Denmark. A visa is not required, nor is any vaccination certificate.

There are no currency restrictions. The Danish monetary system consists of kroner and øre. Coins are issued in 5, 10, and 25 øre pieces and in 1 and 5 kroner pieces. Notes are in 10, 50, 100, and 500 kroner denominations.

The Danish National Bank issues currency, supervises its circulation, and handles discount and clearing operations for commercial banks. Several American banks now have sections in Copenhagen.

Health—Competent specialists practice in all fields. Professional standards are like those in the U.S., and most doctors speak English.

Sanitary conditions in Denmark are above average. Danish law is strict about commercial processing, cooking, handling, and serving of food. No special health risks exist in Denmark, and no special inoculations are required.

Hotels—Copenhagen has many good hotels. Prices are fairly high, and it is advisable to book in advance for the April-October season.

Transportation—Direct flights are available between Copenhagen and major U.S. cities, and many international carriers serve Copenhagen's Kastrup International Airport, providing worldwide connections.

Rail and air services connect all major European centers. Daily rail service leaves for London, Paris, and the Scandinavian capitals. Ferries travel to Oslo, Stockholm, Helsinki, and points in England and Germany.

Copenhagen's bus, suburban train, and taxi service is good, and rates are reasonable.

Telecommunications—Local telephone service is good. Worldwide telephone and telegraph service is available at reasonable rates.

Folketing, have had to depend on shifting majorities, including usually the other non-Socialist parties, plus either the Social Democrats or the Progress Party. Consequently, the Liberal government is relatively weak and prone to periodic crises.

The former government was Social-Democratic, depending on support from the Socialist People's Party, one Greenlander, and one Faeroese.

Party strengths in parliament following the 1973 election are as follows:

	1973	*1971*
Social Democrats	46	70
Progress Party	28	0
Liberals	22	30
Radicals	20	27
Conservatives	16	31
Center Democrats	14	0
Socialist People's Party	11	17
Christian Party	7	0
Communist Party	6	0
Justice Party	5	0
Greenland	2	2
Faeroes	2	2

ECONOMY

Since World War II the Danish economy has been characterized by a high level of economic activity, a rapidly expanding industrial sector, continued heavy dependence on foreign trade (involving more than one-fourth of GNP), and recurrent balance of payments problems.

Gross national product (GNP) in 1973 increased about 3 percent over 1972. Since 1960 unemployment has been below 2 percent, but some rise has been registered in 1974.

Because of favorable terms of trade and idle capacity, the postwar economic boom did not generate major inflationary pressures until 1961, when prices and wages began to climb steeply and growing deficits on the current balance of payments developed. Stern fiscal measures temporarily halted this development in 1963 but also curtailed overall economic growth. With resumption of economic activity and growth in the following years, inflation again set in.

From 1963 to 1973 Denmark's consumer prices have risen more than 86 percent (75 percent without sales taxes), although import prices rose only 55 percent. During the same period, hourly wages in manufacturing more than tripled, and unit labor costs, despite productivity gains, rose at an annual average of about 3.5 percent.

Rising costs of administration and ambitious public programs have weakened fiscal restraint, and strong monetary measures have been necessary. Quantitative restrictions have been imposed on bank credits, and Denmark's interest level has reached a record high of about 16 percent.

The rising cost level has made Denmark increasingly susceptible to international competition and economic fluctuations. Shrinkage in major Danish export markets affected the economy in 1966-67 and again in 1970-71, and the government's efforts to control the economy have not prevented stop-go effects.

Since 1963 economic growth has averaged 4.5 percent annually, but with fluctuations from 0.5 to 8.9 percent. The growth rate has not been sufficient to finance rising domestic demand, particularly in the public sector and in residential construction. Foreign exchange reserves have been preserved only through liberal capital imports.

Eighty-six percent of Denmark's farmland is cultivated, largely for animal feed. Ninety percent of farmers' gross income derives from animal production, the chief products being butter, cheese, bacon, beef, veal, poultry, and eggs. The export market for these agricultural products is divided principally between the United Kingdom and the Federal Republic of Germany.

Denmark is poorly endowed with fuel resources. The only ferrous mineral is a low-grade iron ore found in southern Jutland. Denmark is entirely dependent on imports for its supply of nonferrous metals.

Rapid industrialization is gradually reducing the significance of agricultural production and exports; Denmark continously has a large import surplus, only in part covered by shipping and tourist earnings. (About 400,000 U.S. tourists visit Denmark annually.)

Denmark supports the economic and political integration of Western Europe to improve economic prospects in a politically stable Europe. Denmark became a member of the European Communities (EC) January 1, 1973. Together with the United Kingdom and Ireland, Denmark signed the accession treaty in January 1972. It was ratified by referendum in October 1972.

Denmark has abolished literally all quantitative import restrictions for nonagricultural commodities and is an active supporter of the liberal trade policies in the General Agreement on Tariffs and Trade (GATT) and other international organizations. The price review authority and monopolistic agreements registration requirements are administered leniently by the Monopoly Review Board. Agricultural subsidies were introduced in 1961 for the first time on a major scale, partly as direct subsidies and partly as fixed home market prices on food products. Since Denmark became a member of the EC these subsidies are being replaced by the EC common agricultural policy system of subsidies.

Approximately 225 U.S. firms have offices, affiliates, or subsidiaries at Copenhagen. There is no American Chamber of Commerce, but an American Club draws members from the American business community and Danes interested in trade with the United States.

FOREIGN RELATIONS

Danish foreign policy is founded upon four major pillars: the United Nations, the North Atlantic Treaty, Nordic cooperation, and the European Communities (EC).

Denmark places great emphasis on its role in the United Nations and strongly supports U.N. programs. While seeking peaceful resolution of international problems, Danish security is based on membership in NATO.

As a member of the Nordic Council, Denmark has strong economic, political, and social ties with the Nordic countries–Iceland, Norway, Finland, and Sweden. Accession to the EC in 1973, however, has reconfirmed its economic ties to the Continent and Great Britain. As the only Nordic country in the Community, Denmark aspires to be a bridgebuilder between the two regions.

U.S.-DENMARK RELATIONS

U.S. relations with Denmark, a European friend of long standing, are close and cooperative. In the NATO context, the Danish defense effort is important to the United States and the alliance. U.S. bases in Greenland continue to be of great value to Western defense.

Principal U.S. Officials

Ambassador–Philip Kingsland Crowe
Deputy Chief of Mission–Thomas J. Dunnigan
Economic Counselor–Paul K. Stahnke
Political Counselor–Charles E. Rushing
Defense and Naval Attaché–Capt. Sheldon O. Schwartz
Army Attaché–Col. George McIlwain
Air Attaché–Col. Frederic S. Ross
Counselor for Public Affairs (USIS)–Peter J. Heller

The U.S. Embassy in Denmark is located at Dag Hammarskjolds Alle 24, DK 2100, Copenhagen.

DEPARTMENT OF STATE PUBLICATION 8298
Revised December 1974

APPENDIX CC

DENMARK

STRENGTH OF THE COMMUNIST PARTY ORGANIZATION—1973

[FROM: World Strength of the Communist Party Organizations—1973. Washington, Department of State, Bureau of Intelligence and Research, 1973.]

DENMARK

National Political Status: Date of last election - December 4, 1973.

Communist: Danish Communist Party (DKP) - 110,809 votes (3.6%),
6 seats (3.4%)

Socialist People's Party support of the former Social Democratic government of Anker Jørgensen. As the Communist organ, *Land og Folk*, declared, "The Social Democrats/SF majority did not listen to the workers and failed to use its influence to put through their demands."

The DKP's electoral program featured a new tax program which would benefit lower income groups; a call for abolition of the sales tax on food; cheaper rents; and a stop to unnecessary government spending on the military. In addition, the DKP's continued opposition to Danish membership in the EC and, in the midst of Denmark's severe energy crisis, its vigorous campaign against international monopolies, particularly the large oil companies, proved popular in some segments of Danish society.

The dissatisfaction which helped boost Communist representation, however, also was a boon to those on the right, most particularly the Progressive Party, the creation of Danish lawyer Mogens Glistrup, which captured 28 seats in the *Folketing* in its first electoral attempt. Party theoretician Ib Nørlund commented on this development:

> "The support rendered to him [Glistrup] is explained primarily by the protest of the petty-bourgeois segments of society against the economic and political situation that has developed. At the same time that support creates the soil for the increased activity of the most reactionary forces." ("Class Battles in Denmark," Moscow, *Rabochiy Klass i Sovremennyy Mir*, No. 5, 1973, pp. 35-41.)

Following the DKP's electoral success, Party Chairman Jespersen described his program:

> "We are optimistic, despite the wave of reaction that is also flooding in over the country. Our party has a policy as well as methods for developing its policy that can make us a good support for all leftist movements among the Danish people in order to break up the planned assault of right-wing forces on the people's standard of living, halt EC integration and harmonization and one-sidedness, settle accounts with some of the militarists, and take new steps toward disarmament." (*Land og Folk*, December 8-9, 1973, p. 8.)

Within the international Communist movement, the DKP maintained its traditional loyalty to Moscow, praising the Brezhnev visits to the United States, France, and West Germany as illustrative of the success of the Soviet peace program. DKP leaders attended the September 27-28 Stockholm meeting of several West European Communist parties and joined in the call for a future conference of all the Communist parties in the capitalist countries of Europe. The party urged that the European Conference on Security and Cooperation (CSCE) be carried forward so that Europe may become a "zone for peace." It called for Denmark to leave NATO and strongly condemned the overthrow of the Allende regime in Chile.

APPENDIX DD

FEDERAL REPUBLIC OF GERMANY

ARMED FORCES AND MILITARY POWER

[Reprinted with permission from: The Almanac of World Military Power, by Col. T. N. Dupuy, U.S. Army, Ret., Col. John A. C. Andrews, U.S. Air Force, Ret., and Grace P. Hayes. 3rd ed. Dunn Loring, Va., T. N. Dupuy Associates, 1974.]

(WEST) GERMANY

Bundesrepublik Deutschland
Federal Republic of Germany

POWER POTENTIAL STATISTICS

Area: 95,974 square miles (includes West Berlin)
Population: 61,700,000 (includes West Berlin)
Total Active Armed Forces: 500,500 (including security and border forces: 0.81% population)
Gross National Product: $243 billion ($3,938 per capita)
Annual Military Expenditures: $9.0 billion (3.7% GNP)
Steel and Iron Production: 70.6 million metric tons
Fuel Production: Coal: 255.2 million metric tons
Crude Oil: 7.1 million metric tons
Refined Petroleum Products: 104.5 million metric tons
Gas: 34.22 billion cubic meters
Electric Power Output: 259.6 billion kwh
Merchant Fleet: 2,826 ships; 8.7 million gross tons
Civil Air Fleet: 121 jet, 3 turboprop, 61 piston transports

DEFENSE STRUCTURE

The President of the Federal Republic as chief of state is the titular head of the armed forces of West Germany; actual control is exercised by the Chancellor (Prime Minister) through the Minister of Defense in typical parliamentary governmental fashion. Under existing law the Minister of Defense is commander in chief of the armed forces in peacetime, the Chancellor in wartime. Parliamentary authority is exercised by a Defense Committee with power to investigate any aspect of military affairs.

There is no overall military command structure in the West German armed forces. The rearmament of West Germany was begun while the nation was still nominally occupied by the Western Allies of World War II. The purpose was to integrate West German forces into the NATO defense structure so that they could participate in the defense of their own country as a part of Western Europe. This philosophy is still the basis of West Germany's defense policy, partly to continue to reassure its allies, and partly as a key element of the determination of modern West Germany to maintain unquestioned civilian control over the armed forces. Thus the West German armed forces can operate effectively only as elements of an integrated, international, NATO army. There is no national General Staff, although a General Staff Corps provides officers for operational headquarters; the senior military officer in the West German defense structure is the Inspector General; there is no West German operational command larger than an army corps or air wing (although German officers can, and do, serve as army and regional commanders and staff officers in the international command structure of NATO's Allied Command Europe).

There are three territorial defense commands–Schleswig-Holstein, North, and South–and six military regions under these commands. The Territorial Defense Organization is under army command but staffed by all three services.

POLITICO-MILITARY POLICY

One of the most important features of the deliberate and carefully structured renunciation of traditional German militarism is the effort to make the armed forces truly democratic without seriously impairing military efficiency. In a series of laws beginning with the initial authorization of German armed forces in 1955, the West German Bundestag (Parliament) has included measures to assure the maintenance of civilian control and to guarantee the rights of all citizens who are members of the armed forces.

The present German military policy of eschewing nationalistic, aggressive military operations, and of participating in war only as an integral element of an international army is a dramatic reversal of one of the most consistent national policies in history.

Something over half of the manpower of the armed forces (*Bundeswehr*) is obtained through conscription under the compulsory Military Service Law of 1956. The present term of service is 15 months.

STRATEGIC PROBLEMS

The strategic situation that contributed to the development of Germany's former aggressive politico-military policies has not changed fundamentally. Germany's southern frontier is secured by the Alps. In all other directions, however, its frontiers are vulnerable. Its participation in NATO has safeguarded the western frontier, and has provided some protection for the north (although the military weakness of NATO allies Denmark and Norway, combined with Soviet Baltic strength, perpetuates that vulnerability to some extent). Traditional German vulnerability to attack from the east across the North European Plain is exacerbated by the continuing division of Germany, with East Germany and Czechoslovakia occupied by very powerful Soviet forces; this division also has formed West Germany geographically into an elongated shape, north and south, with a narrow waist that permits the peacetime concentration of Soviet armored spearheads less than 100 miles east of the Rhine River. Thus NATO's problem for the defense of Western Europe is essentially how to stop a westward thrust by Soviet forces before they can reach the Rhine; West Germany's problem, within this, is how to contribute effectively to this defense without assuring the devastation of its national territory.

The country's strategic position is affected by the initiatives of former Chancellor Willy Brandt in seeking and obtaining treaties with the USSR and Poland in 1970. In the August treaty with the USSR, both nations mutually renounced the threat or use of force, and affirmed the permanence of the existing boundary between East and West Germany, and the Oder-Neisse boundary of Poland. The Polish treaty affirms recognition of the Oder-Neisse line as permanent and inviolable by either party, and otherwise parallels the USSR treaty.

Simultaneously with these negotiations, the four occupying powers of Berlin (France, the United Kingdom, the United States, and the USSR) held meetings concerning access to Berlin from the West, and the problems of transit between East and West Berlin. One of the provisions of the resulting agreement, signed in September 1971, was that details of German intra-city and intra-Germany transit would be settled between the two Germanies. In December 1972 the two German states signed a treaty normalizing relations. It provided for an exchange of diplomatic representatives. Although West Germany hoped this might lead to reunification East Germany made plain its intention that it would not.

The potential threat to West Germany through the Baltic has led not only to the establishment of special military arrangements with Denmark, through NATO (see NATO and Denmark), but also to the revival of a small but efficient West German Navy. Although there was no naval tradition in Germany prior to the establishment of the German Empire in 1871, the outstanding performance of the German Navy in two world wars has created a rich naval heritage. The size of ships is limited by the Paris Agreements of 1954. In September 1973 West Germany was authorized by the Council of Western European Union to build conventionally-powered submarines up to 1,800 tons (almost twice the earlier limit), to permit greater responsibility for surveillance of the North Sea and the Atlantic Ocean.

West Germany is a homogeneous nation, without any significant minorities that might assist a hostile invader. There is, however, evidence of some perpetuation in a small minority of the German people of the ultranationalistic, reactionary philosophy which brought Hitler to power. How significant this is, and whether, in a period of turmoil, crisis, or economic hardship, the majority of the people might be vulnerable to such a philosophy, or to the opposed philosophy of Communism, is difficult to estimate.

MILITARY ASSISTANCE

Between 1954 and 1965 Germany received $900.8 million in military assistance from the United States, plus more than $200 million in excess military stocks. Germany's economic recovery has rendered further military assistance unnecessary.

West Germany has offered assistance to a number of African countries on both a sales and a grant basis. This has included aircraft and pilot training, patrol craft and naval training, police training and equipment, and military transport.

ALLIANCES

West Germany is a member of three overlapping alliances: the 15-member NATO alliance, the Western European Union (with Britain, France, and Benelux), and a bilateral alliance with the United States. Within these alliances West Germany has undertaken several collaborative projects. The continuing presence of forces of the United States, Britain, Canada, France, and Belgium on German soil, as part of the NATO shield forces, has created an acute shortage of training facilities in Germany. The West German government has reached agreements with Portugal and France whereby the Bundeswehr can send contingents to train on the territory of those NATO partners. Also, joint research and development has been done with NATO allies. Military aircraft have been jointly produced by West Germany and France, and a number of military items have been designed and produced in cooperation with the United States. West Germany was admitted to the United Nations in 1973.

ARMY

Personnel: 327,000 (292,000 for NATO forces; 35,000 in a Territorial Force which is held for rear-area duties, and not assigned to NATO)

Organization:

- 3 army corps
- 12 armored brigades
- 1 armored regiment
- 13 armored infantry brigades
- 3 infantry brigades
- 2 mountain brigades
- 3 airborne brigades
- 15 SSM battalions (Honest John and Sergeant)

Major Equipment Inventory:

- 1,050 medium tanks (M-48A2)
- 2,250 medium tanks (Leopard)
- 250 105mm howitzers
- 75 155mm howitzers
- 432 155mm self-propelled howitzers
- 150 175mm self-propelled guns
- 75 203mm self-propelled howitzers
- 209 multiple rocket launchers
- 500 40mm self-propelled AA guns
- 1,600 APCs (Marder)
- 1,770 APCs (HS-30)
- 3,140 APCs (M-113)
- 1,086 tank destroyers (90mm Kanonpanzer or SS-11 mounted on APCs)
- 150+ light aircraft (mostly Do-27; some OV-10)
- 460 helicopters (UH-1, Alouette II, CH-53, Bell 47)
- 100 SSM Sergeant, Honest John

Reserves: There are approximately 1.8 million Bundeswehr reservists, including all men who have actually served in the Bundeswehr. Of these, 540,000 are available for immediate mobilization. Enlisted reservists are subject to recall up to the age of 45 in peacetime and up to 60 in wartime. Officers and non-commissioned officers are subject to recall at any time up to age 60; those who have been members of the professional regular cadre of the Bundeswehr can be called back up to age 65, regardless of rank. There is a regular reserve training program, part obligatory and part voluntary, which has been only partially implemented to date due to shortages of facilities.

NAVY

Personnel: 35,900 (including 6,000 Naval Air Arm)

Major Units:

- 3 guided missile destroyers with Tartar SAM (DDG)
- 8 destroyers (DD)
- 6 fast frigates (DE)
- 11 coastal submarines (SSC)
- 6 patrol escorts (PF)
- 13 escorts (PCE)
- 28 fast minesweepers (MSC)
- 24 coastal minesweepers (MSC)
- 20 inshore minesweepers (MSI)
- 38 fast torpedo boats (PT)
- 1 landing ship medium (LSM)
- 16 landing craft mechanized (LCM)
- 22 landing craft utility (LCU)
- 83 auxiliaries
- 1 training ship (light cruiser-type)
- 84 F-104/TF-104 (four fighter-bomber/reconnaissance squadrons)
- 20 BR 1150 Atlantique (2 maritime patrol squadrons)
- 23 helicopters (S-58 for search and rescue; being replaced by 22 SH-3)
- 20 Do-28 liaison aircraft

Under Construction:

- 4 guided missile destroyer escorts (DEG)
- 10 guided missile patrol craft (PTFG)
- 20 fast patrol craft (PG)

Reserves: 36,000 for direct mobilization

AIR FORCE

Personnel: 104,000

Organization:

- 2 tactical air divisions (each with ground attack, reconnaissance, and guided missile wings)
- 2 air defense divisions
- 1 air transport command (2 groups)
- 4 fighter/interceptor squadrons (F-104)
- 10 fighter-bomber close-support squadrons (F-104)

10 light ground attack squadrons (2 normally used for training; G-91)
4 fighter reconnaissance squadrons (RF-4)
6 transport squadrons (Transall)
24 SAM batteries (Nike-Hercules; 9 launchers each)
36 SAM batteries (Hawk; 6 launchers each)
2 SSM wings (Pershing; 36 launchers each)
4 helicopter squadrons (UH-1; Alouette II, H-13)

Major Aircraft Types:

661 combat aircraft
- 80 RF-4 reconnaissance aircraft
- 252 F-104 interceptors, fighter-bombers
- 119 TF-104 fighter trainers (with full combat capability)
- 210 G-91 light ground attack aircraft (delivery of 175 F-4F fighter-bombers to begin in 1974)

1,539 other aircraft
- 110 Transall transports
- 4 Boeing 707-320 transports
- 175 miscellaneous transports (C-140, C-47, DC-6, Pembroke, Heron, T-43)
- 1,000 miscellaneous trainer/support aircraft (Do-27, Do-28, L-4, P-149, T-37, T-38)
- 250 helicopters (UH-1, H-13, Alouette II)

Reserves: 87,000 for direct mobilization

PARAMILITARY

In addition to the Territorial Force, and reservists for that force, there are approximately 18,500 Border Police (equipped with Saladin armored cars and nine patrol boats) and 15,000 internal security forces.

APPENDIX EE
FEDERAL REPUBLIC OF GERMANY
BACKGROUND NOTES

[Washington, Department of State, November 1974 (Publication 7834).]

Germany, Federal Republic of

department of state • november 1974

OFFICIAL NAME: Federal Republic of Germany

GEOGRAPHY

The Federal Republic of Germany (F.R.G.) is a large and strategically located country in central Europe. Its neighbors to the west are France, Luxembourg, Belgium, and the Netherlands. It is bounded on the east by Czechoslovakia and the German Democratic Republic, on the south by Austria and Switzerland, and on the north by Denmark and the North Sea.

The country is generally flat in the north and hilly in the central and western areas, rising in the south to more than 4,000 feet above sea level in the Black Forest. The highest elevation is the Zugspitze in the Bavarian Alps at 9,719 feet above sea level.

The main commercial harbor of Germany is Hamburg, located in the north at the mouth of the Elbe River. The principal rivers are the Rhine, Ems, Weser, and Elbe, all of which flow to the North Sea, and the Danube, which flows southeast to the Black Sea. The largest lake is Lake Constance on the Swiss border.

Summer temperatures average about 65°F. and winter temperatures about 30°F., dropping at times to below zero. Annual rainfall, occurring mostly in summer, ranges from 20 inches in the northern lowlands to 79 inches or more in the German Alps.

PEOPLE

The population of the Federal Republic is primarily German. A small minority of Danes live along the Danish border. Over 2 million foreign workers, mainly from Greece, Turkey, Italy, and Yugoslavia, also live in the F.R.G.

Northern Germany and Berlin are predominately Protestant, and Bavaria and the Rhineland are largely Catholic.

Compulsory elementary education is in effect throughout the country. The F.R.G. has 29 universities, the oldest of which is the University of Heidelberg founded in 1386.

PROFILE

Geography

AREA: 95,930 sq. mi. (about the size of Wyoming). CAPITAL: Bonn (pop. 300,000). OTHER CITIES: West Berlin (pop. 2.1 million), Hamburg (pop. 1.9 million), Munich (pop. 1.3 million), Frankfurt am Main (pop. 690,000).

People

POPULATION: 61.2 million (1974 est.). ANNUAL GROWTH RATE: 0.5% (1974). DENSITY: 627 per sq. mi. ETHNIC GROUPS: German 99%, other 1%. RELIGION: Protestant 49%, Roman Catholic 44.6%, other 6.5%. LANGUAGE: German. LITERACY: 99%. LIFE EXPECTANCY: women 73.4 yrs., men 67.2 yrs.

Government

TYPE: Federal republic. INDEPENDENCE: 1954 (London-Paris Agreements gave F.R.G. full sovereignty). DATE OF OCCUPATION STATUTE: September 21, 1949, granted full self-government.

BRANCHES: *Executive*–President (titular Head of State), Chancellor (executive Head of Government). *Legislative*–bicameral Parliament. *Judicial*–Independent, Federal Constitutional Court.

POLITICAL PARTIES: Christian Democratic Union/Christian Social Union (CDU/CSU); Social Democratic Party (SPD); Free Democratic Party (FDP); National Democratic Party (NPD); Communist Party (DKP). SUFFRAGE: Universal over 18. POLITICAL SUBDIVISIONS: 10 *Lander* (states). The Western sectors of Berlin are governed by the U.S., the U.K., and France which together with the U.S.S.R. have special rights and responsibilities in Berlin.

FLAG: Three horizontal bands, black, red, and gold, from top to bottom.

Economy

GROSS NATIONAL PRODUCT (GNP): $357 billion (1973). ANNUAL GROWTH RATE: 11.9% (5.3% at constant prices). PER CAPITA GROWTH RATE: 11.3% (current prices).

AGRICULTURE: *Land* 56%, forested 29%. *Labor* 8.4%. *Products*–grains, potatoes, sugar beets.

INDUSTRY: *Labor* 36.3%. *Products*–iron, steel, coal, cement, chemicals, machinery, ships, vehicles.

NATURAL RESOURCES: Iron, coal, and potash.

TRADE: *Exports*–$68.6 billion (f.o.b., 1973): chemicals, motor vehicles, iron and steel products. *Partners*–EEC countries, U.S., Latin America, Communist countries. *Imports*–$55.9 billion (c.i.f., 1973): raw materials, fuels, machinery. *Partners*–EEC countries, U.S., Latin America, Communist countries.

OFFICIAL EXCHANGE RATE: Fluctuating around DM2.60=US$1.

ECONOMIC AID RECEIVED: *Total*–None since Marshall Plan.

MEMBERSHIP IN INTERNATIONAL ORGANIZATIONS: U.N. and affiliated agencies, Council of Europe, European Communities (EC), Western European Union (WEU), Organization for Economic Cooperation and Development (OECD), European Atomic Energy Community (EURATOM), International Atomic Energy Agency (IAEA).

HISTORY

Upon the unconditional surrender of Germany to the Allies on May 8, 1945, the United States, the United Kingdom, and the U.S.S.R. occupied the country and assumed responsibility for its government. Under the terms of international agreements the three Commanders in Chief exercised supreme authority in their respective occupation zones and, sitting as the Allied Control Council (ACC), acted jointly by unanimous decision on questions affecting Germany as a whole. At Potsdam in August 1945, the United States, the United Kingdom, and the Soviet Union agreed to a broad program of decentralization which would treat the country as a single economic unit with certain central administrative departments. (Subsequently, France became a member of the ACC and was given a separate zone of occupation.) These plans for a common allied policy and for the treatment of Germany as a single economic unit failed, primarily because of ever-increasing differences with the Soviet Union. In 1948 the Soviets withdrew from the four-power governing bodies of Germany and Berlin and instituted the Berlin blockade.

The year 1948 marked a turning point in the postwar history of Germany. In order to create a nucleus for a future German Government, the United States and the United Kingdom expanded the size and powers of the German Economic Council, established a year earlier in their two zones. This move was an effort to cope with the enormous economic problems which had grown out of the war as well as a response to the Allies' inability to achieve any forward economic movement on a countrywide basis. France then joined its Western Allies in a program for the future development of the three Western zones. The program provided for a constituent assembly in the West German territory, an occupation statute governing relations between the Allies and the German authorities, and the economic merger of the French with the British and U.S. zones.

On September 21, 1949, the occupation statute came into force, granting, with certain exceptions, full powers of self-government to the new West German state. One day earlier, under a coalition led by Chancellor Konrad Adenauer, the new Government of the German Federal Republic came into being. During the following years progress continued toward fuller sovereignty and association with European neighbors and the Atlantic community. The London and Paris agreements of 1954 gave the German Federal Republic full sovereignty, opening the way for its membership in the North Atlantic Treaty Organization (NATO) and the Western European Union (WEU). The three Western Allies reserved only powers affecting the operation and security of their forces, for Berlin and Germany as a whole.

In July 1955 the F.R.G. began to rearm. It now has a force of approximately 460,000, all under NATO command. The F.R.G. makes the largest European contribution of military strength to NATO.

The German Parliament has adopted extraordinary measures to assure civilian political control over the military and to prevent the reestablishment of militarism. At the same time, the F.R.G. is keenly interested in disarmament.

Allied military forces retained in the F.R.G. are under the command of NATO's joint defense forces and are no longer occupation troops. Special agreements have been negotiated with the F.R.G. on the status of these forces.

GOVERNMENT

The F.R.G. government is parliamentary in form and is based on a democratic constitution (Basic Law) emphasizing the protection of individual liberty and divided power in a Federal structure. The Republic consists of 10 states, or *Lander.* (Provisions of the Basic Law of the F.R.G. and the Berlin Constitution to the effect that Berlin is a *Land* of the F.R.G. were suspended by the Allied authorities at the time these documents were submitted to those authorities for approval.)

The President and Chancellor (Prime Minister) head the executive branch of the Federal Government. The Cabinet, consisting of the Chancellor and the Federal Ministers, is usually referred to as the Government.

The President (Chief of State) is the symbol of authority but exercises little real power. His duties are largely ceremonial. The real powers are exercised by the Chancellor (Head of Government), who directs the administrative structure and guides the legislative leadership. Although he is responsible to the *Bundestag,* the Chancellor cannot be removed from office during his 4-year incumbency unless the *Bundestag* has already agreed on a successor.

The *Bundestag* (lower chamber), elected for a term of 4 years, represents the people of the F.R.G. as a

READING LIST

These titles are provided as a general indication of the material currently being published on this country. The Department of State does not endorse the specific views in unofficial publications as representing the position of the U.S. Government.

Brandt, Willy. *A Peace Policy for Europe.* trans. Joel Carmichael. Holt, Rhinehart and Winston.

Grosser, Alfred. *Germany in Our Time.* New York: Praeger, 1971.

Hohn, H. *The Mind of Germany.* New York: Scribners, 1960.

Leonhardt, Rudolf Walter. *This Germany, the Story Since the Third Reich.* Greenwich, Conn.: N. Y. Graphic Society, 1964.

Merkl, Peter H. *Germany, Yesterday and Tomorrow.* New York: Oxford University Press, 1965.

Michelin Tourist Service. *Germany: West Germany and Berlin.* 2nd English edition. London: Dickens, 1974.

Pinson, Koppel S. *Modern Germany, Its History and Civilization.* 2nd ed. New York: Macmillan, 1966.

Stern, Fritz. *Essays on the Political Culture of Modern Germany.* Knopf, 1972.

U.S. Senate, Committee on Foreign Relations, *Documents on Germany, 1944-1970.* Washington D.C.: U.S. Government Printing Office, 1971.

TRAVEL NOTES

Climate and Clothing–Germany is located in the temperate zone and is subject to frequent changes in weather. The same type of clothing may be worn as in the northeastern United States. Lightweight summer clothing is seldom needed.

Telecommunications–Telephone and telegraph services, domestic and international, are efficient. Telegraph and cable services are available to all countries.

Transportation–Frankfurt's international airport is a center of European air traffic. Most airlines operate services to and within the F.R.G. There are a number of international express trains.

An extensive network of roads makes Germany an ideal place for motoring. Express highways (*Autobahnen*) connect most major cities. Third party liability insurance is mandatory and must be obtained from a company in Germany.

Mass transportation facilities (trains, streetcars, subways) are crowded but efficient. Taxi service is available in all cities.

Health–Community sanitation and cleanliness are comparable to those found in American cities. Drinking water, dairy products, and other food products are under strict government control and generally meet or exceed U.S. standards of sanitation.

whole and is the principal parliamentary chamber. It consists of 496 deputies (plus 22 representatives from Berlin, who have no vote in plenary sessions except on procedural matters).

The *Bundesrat* (upper chamber), or federal council, consists of 41 members who are delegates of the 10 *Lander,* and four representatives of the Berlin government who have non-voting status.

The legislature has powers of exclusive jurisdiction and concurrent jurisdiction (with the *Lander*) in fields specifically enumerated by the constitution. The *Bundestag* bears the major responsibility in the legislative process. The role of the *Bundesrat* is limited except in matters concerning *Lander* interests where it can exercise substantial veto powers.

The F.R.G. has an independent judiciary consisting of a Federal Constitutional Court, a Federal High Court of Justice, and high Federal courts in the spheres of ordinary administrative, financial, labor, and social jurisdiction. The highest court is the Federal Constitutional Court, which consists of 24 members serving in two panels of 12 each. The principal functions of the court are to insure uniform interpretation of constitutional provisions and to protect the fundamental rights of the individual as defined in the Basic Law.

Principal Government Officials

Chancellor–Helmut Schmidt (SPD)
Vice Chancellor, Foreign Minister–Hans-Dietrich Genscher (FDP)
Minister of Defense–Georg Leber (SPD)
Minister for Economic Cooperation–Egon Bahr (SPD)
Minister of Economics–Hans Friderichs (FDP)
Minister for Education and Science–Helmut Rohde (SPD)
Minister of Finance–Hans Apel (SPD)
Minister for Food, Agriculture and Forestry–Josef Ertl (FDP)
Minister for Inner-German Relations–Egon Franke (SPD)
Minister of the Interior–Werner Maihofer (FDP)

The F.R.G. maintains an Embassy at 4645 Reservoir Road, NW., Washington, D.C., 20007.

POLITICAL CONDITIONS

Since the establishment of the F.R.G. in 1949 political life has been marked by remarkable stability with orderly succession of governments. The Adenauer era (1949-63) was followed by a brief period under Ludwig Erhard (1963-66) who in turn was replaced by Kurt Georg Kiesinger and the grand coalition (1966-69). These were all Christian Democratic (CDU/CSU) governments, either alone or in coalition with the Free Democratic Party (FDP) or the Social Democratic Party (SPD). In the 1969 election the SPD reversed the trend, gaining enough votes to form a coalition government with the FDP headed by Chancellor Willy Brandt, leaving the CDU/CSU in the opposition.

Chancellor Brandt, in his first address to the *Bundestag* in October 1969, outlined a program of broad social and economic reforms which would be the main thrust of his administration's activity. He declared that the Government would follow a foreign policy of continuity firmly rooted in the Atlantic alliance but seeking to improve relations with Eastern Europe and the German Democratic Republic–G.D.R.–(East Germany). In a key statement he declared: "International recognition of the G.D.R. by the Federal Republic is out of the question. Even if there exist two states in Germany, they are not foreign countries to each other; their relations with each other can only be of a special nature."

The F.R.G. commenced this Eastern Policy *(Ostpolitik)* by negotiating non-aggression treaties with Czechoslovakia, Bulgaria, and Hungary. The F.R.G.'s relation with the German Democratic Republic posed particularly difficult questions. While anxious to relieve serious hardships for divided families and to reduce friction with the G.D.R., the F.R.G. was also intent on retaining its concept of "two German states in one German nation." This requirement made its negotiations with the G.D.R. on a number of subjects prolonged and difficult. Nevertheless, the two German states concluded a number of agreements, including one providing for the exchange of Permanent Representatives, who took their posts in 1974. Both the F.R.G. and the G.D.R. were admitted to the United Nations on September 18, 1973.

In November 1972, a series of party crossovers resulting from disagreements over *Ostpolitik* led to the F.R.G.'s first special federal elections. The SPD/FDP coalition emerged from these elections with a stable parliamentary majority, the SPD increasing its seats in the *Bundestag* from 224 to 230 and the FDP from 30 to 42. The representation of the opposition CDU/CSU coalition dropped from 242 to 224 seats. Brandt remained the head of the coalition government until May 1974 when he resigned as Chancellor in the aftermath of the arrest of a senior member of his staff, Gunter Guillaume, who was accused of being an officer in the G.D.R. intelligence service. The SPD selected Finance Minister Helmut Schmidt to form a new government. He was confirmed by the *Bundestag* in which he received the unanimous support of the SPD and FDP members. Hans-Dietrich Genscher, a leading FDP official who had served as Interior Minister under Brandt, became the new Vice Chancellor and Foreign Minister, replacing his fellow FDP leader Walter Scheel who was elected to the Federal Presidency by a similar vote.

In his first speech to the *Bundestag* on May 17, Chancellor Schmidt described the principal themes of his administration as "continuity and concentration." A strong supporter of both the European Community and the Atlantic alliance, Schmidt expressed his commitment to "the political unification of Europe in partnership with the U.S.A." The theme of "concentration" is considered to reflect Schmidt's emphasis on economic matters and his desire to exercise close control over the Federal budget. He is known to be particularly concerned over the economic dislocations facing the industrialized nations as a result of the steep increase in oil prices and other inflationary pressures.

The annoying but numerically unimportant political extremism of left and right poses no threat to internal security in a Germany enjoying economic health and political stability.

On the left, the main party is the German Communist Party (DKP), which is basically Moscow-oriented. It is the successor to the Communist Party of Germany (DPK) which was declared unconstitutional in 1956. A July 1974 poll indicated that the DKP was supported by only 1.5 percent of the national electorate, far short of the 5 percent minimum required for representation in the *Bundestag*. The DKP has also failed to win representation in the *Land* legislatures, where a 5 percent minimum is similarly required.

The principal party on the right is the National Democratic Party (NPD), a strongly nationalistic group whose popularity has declined in recent years to the point where, like the DKP, it is represented in neither the *Bundestag* nor the *Land* legislatures. NPD support in Federal elections, for example, declined from a 1969 high of 4.3 percent to 0.6 percent in 1972.

The Government follows closely the activities of both of these parties. If they demonstrate themselves to be totalitarian in nature, or to be attempting to subvert the democratic order guaranteed under the Basic Law, they can be declared unconstitutional by the courts.

An important aspect of postwar German politics has been the emergence of a moderate Christian party, the Christian Democratic Union, operating together with its Bavarian sister party, the Christian Social Union. The two are often referred to as a single unit (CDU/CSU), although each maintains an individual party structure. The CDU/CSU is a loosely organized framework containing Catholics, Protestants, provincialists, and members of all economic classes. Its strength derives from a generally conservative policy with broad appeal to the electorate. Until the 1969 election the CDU/CSU had participated, either alone or as the dominant coalition partner, in every Federal Government. It is now the opposition party.

The Social Democratic Party (SPD) is the second major party in the F.R.G. and, since the 1969 election, the senior partner in the SPD/FDP governing coalition. It originally advocated Marxist principles, but in recent years it has increasingly moderated its traditional doctrines. In 1959 it abandoned the concept of a class party and assumed for the first time a distinctly pro-NATO viewpoint. It has played down nationalization of industry and economic planning but continues to lay major stress on social welfare programs. In foreign policy it stresses German ties with the Atlantic alliance but seeks accommodation with Eastern Europe, including the G.D.R. Ex-Chancellor Willy Brandt remains the Party Chairman. The SPD has acquired a powerful base in the bigger cities and industrialized *Lander*.

The FDP is composed mainly of middle- and upper-class Protestants who consider themselves "independents." The FDP has been moving leftward in its orientation. The party favors a more active Eastern policy, especially in economic matters and in dealing with East Germany. The Free Democrats have frequently been torn by internal dissension which in 1955 led to a serious split in the party. In the 1961 election the FDP considerably strengthened its position, only to lose a number of seats in 1965. The FDP received only 5.8 percent of the national vote in the 1969 elections but strengthened its position with an impressive 8.4 percent showing in 1972. It remains the coalition partner of the SPD.

The most recent Federal elections, the seventh in the postwar period, were held on November 19, 1972, with a voter turnout of 91.2 percent.

ECONOMY

The F.R.G. is a highly developed, prosperous, industrial nation which ranks among the world's most important economic powers. It has enjoyed almost unbroken economic expansion since the currency reform of 1948. The very significant annual economic growth of the F.R.G. has shown signs of slowing down somewhat in 1974. Nevertheless, its gross national product (GNP) grew by 11.9 percent in 1973 to U.S. $365 billion (in current prices), third highest in the world. Per capita GNP in 1973 was about $5,612. The F.R.G. recorded exports of $68.6 billion (f.o.b.) and imports of $55.9 billion (c.i.f.) in 1973 and retained its position as the world's second most important trading nation after the United States. The F.R.G.'s monetary unit, the Deutsche Mark, one of the strongest currencies in the world, fluctuates at around 1 DM=US$.39. It is backed by large reserves of gold and foreign exchange which at the end of 1973 totaled $34.02 billion.

The F.R.G.'s economy operates for the most part on a free-market basis. Competition and free enterprise are fostered as a matter of government policy. There is, however, extensive emphasis on social security, and the state participates in the ownership and management of a significant segment of the economy, including such public services as railroad, airline, and telephone systems.

Before the 1966-67 recession, German officials were wary of taking direct expansive government action to promote the economy. Public policy was based on the principle of the so-called market economy which included a minimum of state intervention. The Economic Stability and Growth Law (1967) altered this policy by transferring from the legislative to the executive branch certain powers over taxation and Federal borrowing in order to permit the Government to react quickly to economic change. It also provided for better coordination between policies of the individual *Lander* and the Federation. As another step toward coordinating its economic policies, the Government has initiated a medium-term fiscal plan which attempts to project public revenues and expenditures over a longer period.

The F.R.G. is one of the leading members of the European Communities (the European Coal and Steel Community, the European Economic Community, and the European Atomic Energy Community), and its commercial policy is more and more determined by agreements among members of the Communities. The Government has followed a liberal policy toward U.S. investment: at the end of 1971 U.S. private investment amounted to about $5.2 billion. About two-thirds of U.S. capital is invested in manufacturing (the largest share is in the automobile industry), and another 25 percent is in petroleum.

The United States, France, and the Netherlands are the F.R.G.'s major trading partners. The United States had sales of about $4.6 billion in 1973. In that year the F.R.G. exported goods valued at about $5.7 billion to the United States. Main exports to the United States include motor vehicles, machinery, rolling mill products, chemicals, and electrical equipment. U.S. sales to the F.R.G. are concentrated in chemicals, machinery, soybeans, defense items, electrical equipment, edible fats and oils, aircraft, tobacco, and grains.

FOREIGN RELATIONS

The F.R.G.'s foreign policy has placed particular emphasis on West European integration, Franco-German reconciliation, maintaining good relations with the United States, and improving relations with Eastern Europe.

The F.R.G. has taken part in all of the common postwar efforts aimed at closer political, economic, and defense cooperation among the countries of Western Europe. It is a charter member of the European Coal and Steel Community formed in 1952, and it joined the Brussels treaty members in 1954 in the formation of the Western European Union, which placed certain controls on German rearmament. At the same time the F.R.G. also renounced the manufacture of atomic, bacteriological, and chemical warfare weapons. The Brandt government signed the Nuclear Nonproliferation Treaty. The Biological Warfare Convention was signed on April 10, 1972.

The F.R.G. became a member of NATO in 1955. In 1957 it signed the treaties of Rome, thereby becoming a member of the European Economic Community (Common Market) and the European Atomic Energy Community (EURATOM), both of which were established in 1958. In January 1963 the F.R.G. signed a treaty with France for political, military, and cultural cooperation. The F.R.G. became a member of the United Nations in 1973.

Relations With Soviet Bloc

Since World War II Germany's Eastern problems have been particularly complex. In 1955 it establshed diplomatic relations with the U.S.S.R. By 1958 the U.S.S.R. had repatriated thousands of prisoners of war and German civilians, and the F.R.G. and the Soviet Union had reached limited trade and consular agreements. A series of Soviet-engineered Berlin crises and a steady campaign of vilification from the Soviet side to discredit the F.R.G. Government and divide it from its Western Allies kept relations strained.

Soviet pressure on Berlin took a new form in November 1958 with a Russian threat to sign a separate peace treaty with East Germany and end the basis for the Allied occupation of Berlin. At the foreign ministers' conference at Geneva in 1959, the British, French, and U.S. proposed solving the Berlin problem by establishing a unified German state on the basis of free elections within a framework of measures guaranteeing European security. This proposal was rejected by the U.S.S.R. which insisted on the conclusion of peace treaties with "both German states." The Soviets also advocated, as the only acceptable method of achieving reunification, direct negotiations between West and East Germany under conditions which could lead to the merging of the two. These conditions included the dissolution of German ties to the West and the extension of Communist influence throughout Germany. Western efforts to induce the Soviet Union to modify these unacceptable proposals were unsuccessful at Geneva and later during Premier Khrushchev's visit to the United States. Preparations to discuss German reunification and Berlin at a summit in May 1960 were likewise unavailing because the conference failed to materialize.

A state of uneasy equilibrium existed until January 1961. A June meeting between President Kennedy and Premier Khrushchev resulted primarily in a Sovet ultimatum that the U.S.S.R. would sign a peace treaty with the East German regime before the end of the year. Again no basis for negotiation had been found. The Soviets did not, however, carry out their threat to sign a separate peace treaty.

A major development occurred on August 13, 1961, when the East Germans began building a wall through the center of Berlin effectively dividing the city and putting an end to any significant flow of refugees from East Germany through Berlin to the West. The wall became the symbol of the East's political debility and Germany's division. It has prevented East Germans from visiting West Berlin. However, since the implementation of the

Quadripartite Agreement on Berlin, West Berliners have been able to visit East Berlin and East Germany on a regular basis.

The F.R.G.'s Eastern Policy seeks to improve the situation in Germany (which the wall has exacerbated), reduce tensions in central Europe, and promote the normalization of relations between the F.R.G. and its East European neighbors. This policy originated in the 1950's and 1960's when the F.R.G. sought first to establish trade pacts, and later diplomatic relations, with East European countries. Agreements, including the so-called "Berlin clause" providing for the inclusion of West Berlin, were signed with Poland, Hungary, Bulgaria, and Romania. Diplomatic relations were established with Romania and reestablished with Yugoslavia. The F.R.G. also signed agreements with Czechoslovakia, renouncing the use of force, and with the G.D.R. establishing relations.

This policy of reconciliation with Eastern Europe was intensified by Chancellor Brandt's government when it assumed power in October 1969. Brandt met twice with G.D.R. Prime Minister Willi Stoph in early 1970 in an effort to establish Brandt's concept of a special relationship between the two German states within one German nation.

The F.R.G. also negotiated treaties with the Soviet Union and Poland in 1970, accepting the present European borders as inviolable and undertaking to settle disputes by peaceful means. During these negotiations the F.R.G. consulted its Western allies. Four Power rights and responsibilities for Berlin and Germany as a whole were not affected by these bilateral agreements. The two treaties were submitted to the German Parliament in December 1971 and ratified in May 1972; they were signed into law by President Gustav Heinemann on May 23, 1972.

Concurrently, the Ambassadors of the United Kingdom, France, the U.S.S.R., and the United States began negotiations in Berlin in March 1970 with the goal of reaching a new agreement on Berlin. In September 1971, they signed the first phase of a quadripartite agreement which empowered German authorities in East and West to negotiate further agreements and arrangements on civilian travel in and around Berlin. These intra-German agreements and arrangements were signed in December 1971. The Final Quadripartite Protocol, encompassing and putting into effect the quadripartite and the intra-German sections, was signed by the four Foreign Ministers on June 3, 1972, in Berlin.

BERLIN

Berlin is located 110 miles inside the G.D.R. and is entirely surrounded by its territory. Although the city is not a part of the F.R.G. and is not governed by it, the strong ties which have developed between the city and the F.R.G. over the years have been maintained.

Many people in Germany, West and East, look upon Berlin as the German capital and believe that it will ultimately be restored to its former position whenever Germany is reunified. The German Democratic Republic claims Berlin as its capital, and its principal government offices are located in the city's Eastern sector. In spite of the Wall which has physically divided the city since 1961, West Berlin remains a vital urban center and a magnetic attraction and source of hope to the people of East Germany.

Berlin's Special Status

Following World War II Berlin was not included in any of the other zones of occupation but was made a separate area under quadripartite control. Berlin was the seat of the Allied Control Authority, which was to govern Germany as a whole and which was also to be the seat of the eventual central German Government. In 1948, however, the Soviets repudiated their wartime agreements and refused to participate any longer in the quadripartite administration of Germany. At the same time they refused to continue to cooperate in the joint administration of Berlin, drove the Government elected by the people of Berlin out of its seat in the Soviet sector, and installed a Communist regime in its place.

Berlin today remains a quadripartite responsibility, although the Allied authority (the Berlin *Kommandatura*) can exercise effective authority only in the three Western sectors of Berlin. West Berlin (U.S., U.K., and French sectors) has a population of 2 million and covers an area of 186 square miles. East Berlin (Soviet sector) has a population of 1.1 million and an area of 155 square miles. The infamous 28-mile-long Berlin Wall, constructed by the G.D.R., divides the two halves of the city. Access through the Wall is restricted to eight crossing points.

To a degree compatible with the special status of the city, the Western Allies have turned over control and management of city affairs to the Berlin *Senat* (Executive) and House of Representatives, governing bodies established by constitutional process and chosen on the basis of free elections. The Allies and the German authorities in the F.R.G. and West Berlin do not recognize the Communist city regime in East Berlin.

F.R.G.-West Berlin Ties Fostered

To reduce the psychological and practical effects of Berlin's isolation, a close relationship has been developed between the Government of West Berlin and that of the F.R.G. For example, representatives of the city participate in the F.R.G. Parliament, although as non-voting members; appropriate West German agencies, such as the Supreme Administrative Court, have their permanent seats in West Berlin; and the Governing Mayor of Berlin takes his turn as President of the *Bundesrat*. These ties between the F.R.G. and West Berlin were reaffirmed in the Quadripartite Agreement on Berlin concluded in 1972. In addition, the Allies carefully consult with the F.R.G. and Berlin Governments on foreign policy questions involving reunification and the status of Berlin.

The Quadripartite Agreement on Berlin has contributed to many practical improvements in easing the everyday life of Berliners and offers hope for a brighter future for the city. It provides for unhindered civilian access to Berlin, greater freedom of movement between the Eastern and Western sectors of the city, and it contains a Soviet acknowledgement of the ties which have grown between West Berlin and the F.R.G., including the latter's right to represent Berlin abroad.

Major events such as fairs and festivals have been sponsored in West Berlin, and investment in commerce and industry have been encouraged by special concessionary tax legislation. The result of such efforts, combined with effective city administration and the Berliners' natural energy and spirit, have been encouraging. Berlin's morale has been sustained, and its industrial production has considerably surpassed the prewar level.

Nonetheless, West Berlin would have great difficulty maintaining a high standard of living without continued external aid. Industrial production also must be expanded further to compensate for the loss of prewar activities and governmental services which were performed for the German nation as a whole or for the surrounding area. Aid to Berlin comes largely from the F.R.G. where Berlin's significance is underscored to encourage the development of commercial interests in the productive capabilities of the city.

German Democratic Republic

At the December 1972 NATO ministerial meetings in Brussels, it was agreed that individual members of the Alliance would be free to establish relations with the G.D.R. after the signing of the Basic Treaty between the G.D.R. and the F.R.G. That treaty was signed December 21, 1972. The United States established diplomatic relations with the G.D.R. on September 4, 1974.

For additional information on the G.D.R., see *Background Notes* (Department of State pub. 7957).

U.S.-F.R.G. RELATIONS

Following the signature of an agreement between the Soviet Union and the G.D.R. on June 12, 1964, the United States, United Kingdom, and France, in consultation with the F.R.G., issued a tripartite declaration on June 26, 1964. This declaration outlined their basic policies toward Germany as a whole and Berlin in particular and emphasized the following points:

1. Any agreement on the subject of Germany, including Berlin, between the U.S.S.R. and the G.D.R., cannot affect Soviet obligations or responsibilities under previous agreements or arrangements with the Allies. The Allies will continue to hold the U.S.S.R. responsible for the fulfillment of its obligations.

2. The city of "Greater Berlin" was placed under four-power administration. No unilateral initiatives by the U.S.S.R. to block the quadripartite administration will modify this legal situation. In accordance with an agreement of October 23, 1954, the Allies authorized the establishment of close ties between Berlin and the F.R.G. to insure representation of Berlin and its people outside the city.

3. The final frontiers of Germany must await a peace settlement for the whole of Germany.

4. On October 3, 1954, the F.R.G. Government renounced the use of force to achieve reunification or modification of present boundaries, and this remains its policy.

5. The safeguarding of peace and security requires the application in the whole of Germany of self-determination. The exercise of self-determination, leading to German reunification in peace and freedom, remains the fundamental objective of the Allies.

6. The Allies remain ready to take advantage of any opportunity which would peacefully re-establish German unity in freedom.

These basic Western policies are echoed repeatedly in U.S. policy statements. For example, in his foreign policy report to the Congress of February 9, 1972, President Nixon stated that if a relaxation of tension was to cor about in the 1970's it would be testea in new efforts to address the central question of the division of Germany and Berlin. In the foreign policy report of the Secretary of State (March 8, 1972) the Berlin agreement is listed as one of the principal developments involving the concerns of U.S. foreign policy. "The U.S. objective in Germany," the report states, "remains the preservation and consolidation of our vital close relationship with the Federal Republic, as friends and tradir partners, but particularly as allies shai ing common institutions and having similar outlooks. U.S. policies were shaped by the awareness that the security and prosperity of each depends to a major degree on that of the other. A parallel long-term U.S. objective, one fully shared by the Federal Republic, has been to safeguard the freedom, access, welfare, and security of the Western sectors of Berlin."

Principal U.S. Officials

Ambassador; Chief, U.S. Mission, Berlin—Martin J. Hillenbrand

Deputy Chief of Mission; Minister—Frank E. Cash, Jr.

Counselor for Political Affairs—Francis J. Meehan

Counselor for Economic Affairs and Minister—Edwin C. Crowley

Counselor for Public Affairs (USIS)—McKinney H. Russell, Sr.

Counselor for Administration—Earl Bellinger

Chief, Military Assistance Advisory Group—Maj. Gen. Wagstaff

The U.S. Embassy in the F.R.G. i located at 5400 Mehlemer Ave., Bad Godesberg, Bonn. There is also a Mission in Berlin and Consulates General at Bremen, Dusseldorf, Frankfurt, Hamburg, Munich, and Stuttgart.

DEPARTMENT OF STATE PUBLICATION 7834, Revised November 1974

APPENDIX FF

FEDERAL REPUBLIC OF GERMANY

STRENGTH OF THE COMMUNIST PARTY ORGANIZATION—1973

[FROM: World Strength of the Communist Party Organizations—1973. Washington, Department of State, Bureau of Intelligence and Research, 1973.]

FEDERAL REPUBLIC OF GERMANY

National Political Status: Date of last election - November 19, 1972.

Communist: German Communist Party (DKP) - 113,891 votes (0.3%), no seats

Center-Left: Social Democratic Party - 17,175,169 votes (45.9%), 230 seats (46.4%)

Free Democratic Party - 3,129,982 votes (8.4%), 41 seats (8.3%)

Center-Right: Christian Democratic/Christian Social Union - 16,806,020 votes (44.9%), 225 seats (45.4%)

Conservative: National Democratic Party - 207,465 votes (0.6%), no seats

Other: 27,223 votes (0.1%), no seats

Total: 37,459,750 votes, 496 seats

Communist Party Membership: 35,000 (estimate)

Leading Party Figures and Positions:
MIES, Herbert - Chairman
GAUTIER, Hermann - Deputy Chairman

Principal Publication:
Unsere Zeit - weekly newspaper

Areas of Communist Activity: In the November 1972 *Bundestag* (lower house) election, the German Communist Party (DKP) received only .3 percent of the total vote, far from the statutory 5 percent minimum required for representation. Its percentage was only half that won in the 1969 *Bundestag* election by the Action for Democratic Progress (ADF), a far-left electoral alliance in which the DKP had participated. In terms of actual votes, the DKP in 1972 received 83,679 fewer votes than the ADF received in 1969.

The DKP's vote was only .1 percent above the alltime low (1957) registered in a *Bundestag* election by a Communist party or its fronts since the founding of the Federal Republic in 1949. The highest vote percentage received by the DKP in a single *Land* (state) in 1972 was .7 percent in Bremen, where the party had received 3.1 percent in the last local election (1971).

The DKP's poor showing emphasizes the West German electorate's continued rejection of a party that is so patently manipulated by the Socialist Unity Party of East Germany and by the Communist Party of the Soviet Union. Despite an active election campaign and some headway in organizing groups in industrial plants and in issuing plant newspapers, the DKP is of little importance on the domestic political scene.

At its November 1973 Party Congress, the DKP retired 64-year-old Party Chairman Kurt Bachmann and replaced him with 44-year-old Herbert Mies, former Deputy Chairman and seasoned party functionary. Otherwise, there is little change in the party. By now it has fully succeeded in absorbing the veterans of the old Communist Party of Germany (KPD), which was banned as unconstitutional in 1956 by the Federal Constitutional Court.

The DKP continues to regard the F.R.G.'s large industrial enterprises as the focal point for its political activity and recruitment. By involving itself in the bread-and-butter issues of concern to workers, the party leadership not only seeks to appear as the most devoted defender of workers' interests but also hopes to promote thereby the sort of unity of action which will bring it into closer contact with Social Democratic, Christian-oriented, and nonpolitical groups at the factory level. While these attempts at rapprochement are uniformly rebuffed at the official level by the other parties, they achieve occasional breakthroughs lower down the line.

In January 1972 Interior Minister Hans-Dietrich Genscher, in a report released to the public, concluded that both the DKP and the right-radical National Democratic Party (NPD) "clearly have goals that are unconstitutional." In a statement to the *Bundestag*, Genscher added that he did not intend to seek the dissolution of the parties by court order. The extremely weak showing by both parties in the 1972 election presumably reinforces that decision.

Although there is organizational chaos among the radical groups to the left of the DKP, the party was considerably disturbed over the formation of a new Communist Party of Germany (KPD) in May 1972. This party is completely separate from the old, illegal KPD and profoundly critical of it and the DKP. As a radical Marxist-Leninist and Maoist group, its choice of the old party initials, however, caused DKP leaders to fear that it would both alienate potential adherents and confuse the public.

The new KPD also is in competition with the Maoist Marxist-Leninist Party of Germany, which has existed since 1967. In addition, there are a number of independent "Red Cells," especially in the universities. The number of activists in these organizations, which have existed for some time, remains quite small.

APPENDIX GG

FRANCE

ARMED FORCES AND MILITARY POWER

[Reprinted with permission from: The Almanac of World Military Power, by Col. T. N. Dupuy, U.S. Army, Ret., Col. John A. C. Andrews, U.S. Air Force, Ret., and Grace P. Hayes. 3rd ed. Dunn Loring, Va., T. N. Dupuy Associates, 1974.]

FRANCE

La Republique Francaise
French Republic

POWER POTENTIAL STATISTICS

Area: 212,918 square miles (including Corsica)
Population: 52,300,000
Total Active Armed Forces: 573,500 (includes 70,000 Gendarmerie; 1.10% population)
Gross National Product: $217 billion ($4,149 per capita)
Annual Military Expenditures: $9.1 billion (4.2% GNP)
Steel and Iron Production: 41.2 million metric tons
Fuel Production: Coal: 33.0 million metric tons
Natural Gas: 7.2 billion cubic meters
Refined Petroleum Products: 122.2 million metric tons
Electric Power Output: 147.8 billion kwh
Merchant Fleet: 1,399 ships; 7.01 million gross tons
Civil Air Fleet: 67 jet, 59 turboprop, 33 piston transports

DEFENSE STRUCTURE

The President of France is the commander in chief of the armed forces. He also presides over the Council of Ministers, the High Defense Council, and the Defense Committee. The Council of Ministers defines defense policy as part of the general national policy. The High Defense Council is the decision-making body for general defense policies within the framework established by the Council of Ministers, and includes the Premier, the Ministers of Foreign Affairs, National Defense, Interior, and Finance, and the General Secretary for National Defense. The High Defense Council advises the Council of Ministers.

The Premier is responsible for overall defense management,

the coordination of defense activities, and the implementation of the decisions of the Council of Ministers and the Defense Council. The Minister of National Defense, who functions as the executive of the Premier, has authority over the three integrated services and is responsible for their preparedness. He is assisted by the Chief of Staff of the Armed Forces and the general staffs of the three services. The French armed forces are organized on the basis of three task-oriented operational systems (the Nuclear Strategic Force, the Forces of Maneuver, and the Territorial Defense Force), each including elements of all three services.

POLITICO-MILITARY POLICY

The structure and missions of the French armed forces reflect the government's basic conviction that for reasons of national security and national prestige France should remain responsible for its own defense, and that it should retain a substantial degree of independence of the two superpowers. The French government also believes that with its own nuclear force France contributes to a more stable international environment. Because of its diminished confidence in the US commitment to invoke its deterrent on behalf of a European ally, France believes that it has to possess its own nuclear forces to deter attack by another power. The French feel, therefore, that their nuclear capability complements the US nuclear deterrent. France hopes that eventually a European security system will evolve, built around the French nuclear force.

The Strategic Force forms France's major deterrent and is capable of attack over intercontinental range. It is projected in three generations. The first generation is fully operational and consists of Mirage IV bombers armed with 100 kiloton nuclear bombs. The second generation, consisting of intermediate range ground-to-ground solid fuel ballistic nuclear missiles stationed in southern France, has recently become fully operational. Four nuclear-powered submarines with Polaris-type missiles will complete the third generation, to become fully operational by 1976. In 1973 the government announced construction in southeastern France of sites for an additional group of intermediate range ballistic missiles equipped with thermonuclear warheads of almost megaton strength. The Strategic Force operates directly under the President.

The Forces of Maneuver have as their mission the containment of a nuclear or conventional attack inside or outside Europe. They include the bulk of the Army, the Navy, and the tactical Air Force units.

The Territorial Defense Forces (DOT) are responsible both for the defense of national territory and for internal security. An Alpine brigade, which is entrusted with the protection of the strategic missile silos in southeastern France, 25 other Army battalions, and gendarmerie units, constitute the core of the DOT. Light air force squadrons support the DOT.

France's independent defense policy in 1966 led to French withdrawal from NATO's military structure, even though it remained a member of the North Atlantic Alliance. France has also retained its membership in the Western European Union. Two French mechanized divisions continue to be stationed in Western Germany under a bilateral arrangement; one independent brigade remains in West Berlin. France also retains nominal membership in SEATO. Despite France's withdrawal from ACE, it cooperated in Mediterranean naval exercises in 1970, and has never left NATO's air defense communications system. As a result of the 1974 elections, France seems to be moving cautiously toward reestablishing closer ties with NATO.

Because of France's determination to establish its own nuclear capability, it refused to sign the Limited Test Ban Treaty. France has continued nuclear and thermonuclear tests at its Pacific test range near Tahiti, despite a call from the International Court of Justice in mid-1973 to stop them.

Economic, military and cultural treaties with former French colonies in Africa maintain France's influence there.

Universal military service in principle, but modified by exception of certain classifications, provides the majority of the armed forces. Active service lasts 12 months and is followed by three and one-half years of availability, with another 12 years of reserve service.

STRATEGIC PROBLEMS

The country's geographic situation gives it a marked contrast of defensive strength and vulnerabilities. The Pyrenees and the Southern Alps, combined with the existence of a determinedly neutral Switzerland, provide protection from land attack on the southern and southeastern frontiers. Although the Rhine from Switzerland to north of Strasbourg is a difficult obstacle, it is not impassable. From the Rhine to the North Sea the northern border is rugged in places and subject to inundation in a few, but is nevertheless demonstrably passable to troops. The ocean borders—Channel, Atlantic and Mediterranean—while they strengthen France's economic position in seaborne trade, are not invulnerable to modern amphibious assault. French realization of this geographic situation goes far to explain the incompleteness of France's separation from the North Atlantic Alliance, despite its insistence both on political independence and on rejection of NATO military command.

The internal political situation is traditionally fraught with dissension among a multiplicity of contending parties. As a result of the 1974 elections no single party has a majority in the National Assembly, but control is exercised by a centrist coalition. However the Communist Party and the Federation of the Left hold nearly a fifth of the seats. In times of international crisis, minor parties have in the past rallied to the national cause but the Communist Party of 400,000 members (the second largest in the West) has the capability of weakening the national effort in the fields of politics, economics, and defense.

In January 1974 the government banned four separatist movements: two rival Breton groups, the Liberation Front of Brittany (FLB-ARB) and the left-wing Liberation Front of Brittany for National Liberation and Socialism (FLB-LNS); the Corsican Peasant Front for Liberation (FPCL); and Basque Enbata. These groups were believed to have foreign support.

Agreement was reached with Spain in January 1974 on the limits of each country's claims to the continental shelf in the Bay of Biscay.

MILITARY ASSISTANCE

The United States provided France with $4.153 billion in military aid from 1950 to 1966, plus $96.6 million in excess military stocks. France has various kinds of multilateral and bilateral defense accords with most of its former African colonies and territories. These arrangements usually call for military aid in the form of equipment and training. Under some of the agreements, the African government can call upon French military intervention in case of an internal or external threat.

French naval, army, and air units participate in joint exercises with indigenous troops in Africa. Some 3,000 French officers and NCOs are serving on secondment or on contract with African armed forces.

The French armament industry has become a major pillar of the French economy, and France now sells arms worldwide.

ALLIANCES

France is a member of the UN, the Western European Union, NATO (limited), SEATO, and the European Common Market. It also has bilateral treaties with most of its former colonies.

ARMY

Personnel: 331,000

Organization:
- 1 Army consisting of 2 Army Corps (5 mechanized divisions, 2 in Germany) plus supporting elements
- 2 Alpine brigades
- 1 parachute division (2 paratroop brigades)
- 1 independent brigade (in Berlin)
- 1 air portable motorized brigade
- 2 motorized infantry regiments
- 2 armored car regiments
- 1 parachute battalion
- 19 infantry battalions (with 120mm mortars)
- 3 regiments SAM (Hawk)

Deployment: France remains responsible for the protection and security of its overseas departments and territories, which have been organized into five defense zones; the Antilles and Guiana zone in the Caribbean (one battalion); the Indian Ocean zone with Headquarters in La Reunion Island (two regiments); the Pacific Ocean zone (divided into two zones, New Caledonia and Polynesia, two battalions); and French Territory of the Afars and Issas (two battalions). Additional units are stationed in independent Africa: Senegal, Chad, Ivory Coast.

Major Equipment Inventory:
- 800 AMX-30 medium tanks
- 800 AMX-13 light tanks (with 90mm guns and 4 SS-11 antitank missiles)
- EBR heavy armored cars
- AML light armored cars
- 500 APCs (AMX-VTT)
- AMX 105mm and 155mm self-propelled howitzers
- AMX twin 30mm self-propelled AA guns
- 155mm field artillery
- 40 fixed wing aircraft
- 550 helicopters (including 130 SA.330 Puma)

Missiles: SSM: Pluton; SAM: Hawk, Crotale, Roland; ATM: Nord SS-11, Entac, Nord/Bolkow Hot, Milan.

Reserves: There are approximately 450,000 trained reservists available for mobilization, organized in 70 infantry battalions and seven armored car regiments. They comprise 27 mobilized infantry regiments.

NAVY

Personnel: 68,500 (includes a Naval Air Force of 11,500 and some 2,500 Marines)

Major Units:
- 2 light aircraft carriers (CVL)
- 1 ASW helicopter carrier (24 helicopters: CVS)
- 1 helicopter carrier (training/Marine Commando: CLG)
- 2 nuclear-powered ballistic missile submarines (SSBN)
- 19 diesel submarines (SS)
- 1 antiaircraft cruiser (CLAA)
- 2 assault landing ships (LSD)
- 2 guided missile frigates (DLG)

5 guided missile destroyers (DDG)
12 destroyers (ASW, radar picket, and command; DD, DER)
27 destroyer escorts (DE)
13 ocean minesweepers (MSO)
62 coastal minesweepers (MSC)
15 inshore minesweepers (MSI)
5 minehunters
15 coastal escorts (PCE)
4 patrol boats (PC)
9 survey ships (AGS)
180 support ships and service craft
4 experimental ships

Entering service or nearing completion: 3 guided missile frigates (C67 type) and 2 nuclear powered ballistic missile submarines (SSBN)

Naval Air Force:

Organization:

2 fighter-bomber squadrons (Etendard IV-M)
2 interceptor squadrons (F-8E Crusader)
1 reconnaissance squadron (Etendard IV-P)
3 ASW squadrons (Alize)
5 maritime reconnaissance squadrons (Neptune and Atlantique)
6 helicopter squadrons (Super Frelon, SH-34, Alouette II and III)

Major Aircraft Types:

246 combat aircraft:
- 90 Etendard IV-M and IV-P fighter-bomber and reconnaissance aircraft
- 37 F-8E Crusader interceptors
- 58 Alize ASW aircraft
- 26 P-2E/H Neptune maritime reconnaissance aircraft
- 35 BR 1150 Atlantique maritime reconnaissance aircraft

300+ other aircraft:
- 17 Super Frelon helicopters
- 43 SH-34 helicopters
- 38 Alouette II and III helicopters
- 67 miscellaneous transports
- 135+ trainer/support aircraft

Missiles: long-range SSM: MSBS; anti-surface: MM38 Exocet; surface to air: Masurca and Tartar; surface to sea; Malafon; air to air: Sidewinder and Matra D530; air to surface: Nord AS20, Nord AS37 Martel and Nord S210

Major Naval Bases: Brest, Toulon, Cherbourg, Lorient

Major Naval Air Bases: Lann Bihoue, Nimes Garons, Landivisiau, Hyeres

Reserves: About 90,000 trained reservists

AIR FORCE

Personnel: 104,000

Organization:

Strategic Air Command (CFAS): subject to President's command
- 1 IRBM group (2 squadrons of 9 missiles each)
- 3 strategic bomber wings (3 squadrons per wing; Mirage IV-A)
- 3 tanker squadrons (1 per bomber wing; KC 135 F)

Tactical Air Command (FATAC)
- 2 tactical air commands
- 2 light bomber squadrons (Vautour 2B)
- 16 fighter-bomber squadrons (1 Mirage III-B, 8 Mirage III-E, 2 Jaguar, 3 F-100 D, 2 Mirage V)
- 3 tactical reconnaissance squadrons (Mirage III-R and III-RD)

Air Defense Command (CAFDA): coordinated by the automatic STRIDA II air defense system
- 3 interceptor squadrons (Mirage III-C)
- 2 all-weather interceptor squadrons (Vautour 2N) converting to F-1
- 5 fighter squadrons (Mystere IV-A, Super Mystere B2)

Military Air Transport Command (COTAM)
- 1 squadron DC-6 and BR-765 Sahara transports
- 4 squadrons Nord 2501 Noratlas transports
- 1 squadron STOL BR 941 S
- 3 squadrons C.160 Transall
- 2 mixed squadrons
- 4 helicopter squadrons (H-34, Alouette II)

Air Force Schools Command (CEAA)
Air Communications Service (CTAA)

Overseas Deployment: 1 squadron of F-100, 1 squadron of A-1Ds and 1 mixed transport squadron of H-34 and Alouette II helicopters and Noratlas transports in French Territory of Afars and Issas

Major Aircraft Types:

600+ combat aircraft
- 60+ Mirage IV-A strategic bombers
- 24 Vautour 2B light bombers
- 95 Mirage III-C light bombers

160 Mirage III-B, E, and V fighter-bombers
20 Mirage IV-A fighter-bombers
60 F-100 D Fighter-bombers
15 F-100 F fighter-bombers
60 Mirage III-R reconnaissance aircraft
28 Vautour 2 N all-weather interceptors
47 Super-Mystere B 2 fighter-bombers
20 A-1D/E fighter-bombers
15 Jaguar fighter-bombers

1,960 other aircraft
10 KC-135 F tankers
6 DC-6 transports
4 DC-8 transports
160 Noratlas transports
52 Transall C-160 F transports
123 miscellaneous transports
170 helicopters (H-34, Alouette II and III)
1,435 miscellaneous trainers/support aircraft

Missiles: AAM: Matra R-511 and R-530; ASM: Matra Martel, Nord AS-12, AS-20, AS-30, and AS-33; SAM: Crotale; SSM: SSBS (IRBM)

Major Air Bases: LeBourget, Metz, Bordeaux, Aix, Bretigny, Tours, Chartres, Orange, Strasbourg, Cognac, Pau, Reims, Toulouse, Dijon, Nimes, Villacoublay, Limoges, Cambrai, Etampes, Creil

PARAMILITARY

The Gendarmerie of some 70,000 men plus 85,000 more in reserve is administered by the Ministry of the Armed Forces and can augment the regular forces. There is also a Republican Security Force (*Compagnies Republicaines de Securite*) of 17,000 men, under the Ministry of the Interior.

APPENDIX HH

FRANCE

BACKGROUND NOTES

[Washington, Department of State, May 1973 (Publication 8209).]

FRANCE

BACKGROUND NOTES

PROFILE

GEOGRAPHY

AREA: 212,650 square miles; CAPITAL: Paris (pop. 8 million). OTHER CITIES: Marseille (1 million); Lille (1 million).

PEOPLE

POPULATION: 51.7 million (1972 est.); ANNUAL GROWTH RATE: 1%; DENSITY: 240 per sq. mile. ETHNIC GROUPS: Principally Celtic and Latin with large Teutonic minority. RELIGION: Roman Catholic. LANGUAGE: French. LITERACY RATE: 96.5%.

GOVERNMENT

TYPE: Republic. CONSTITUTION: September 28, 1958. CHIEF OF STATE: President (elected to 7-year term). HEAD OF GOVERNMENT: Prime Minister (appointed by President). LEGISLATURE: National Congress—Senate (281 members elected to 9-year terms); National Assembly—(490 members elected to 5-year terms). JUDICIARY: Court of Appeals; Council of State (administrative courts). FIRST-LEVEL ADMINISTRATIVE DIVISIONS: 95 metropolitan departments, 4 overseas departments, 5 overseas territories, Paris.

ECONOMY:

GNP: $197 billion (1971); GROWTH RATE: 5%; PER CAPITA: $3800; PER CAPITA GROWTH RATE: 4%.

TRADE: Exports: $25.7 billion (1972, FOB); agricultural products: $5.1 billion; motor vehicles: $3.1 billion; non-electric machinery: $3.0 billion. Partners: Enlarged European Economic Community (EEC): $14.4 billion, of which Federal Republic of Germany $5.4 billion; Franc Area Countries: $2.3 billion; United States: $1.4 billion. Imports: $26.5 billion (1972, CIF); agricultural products: $4.2 billion; non-electric machinery: $3.6 billion; mineral fuels: $3.5 billion. Partners: EC: $14.8 billion of which Federal Republic of Germany $5.9 billion; U.S.: $2.2 billion; Franc Area Countries: $1.7 billion.

AGRICULTURE: Arable/cultivated/pasture: 66%; principal products: cereals, feed grains, sugar beets, wine grapes, dairy products, livestock and meat, fruits, and vegetables. Labor: 12%.

INDUSTRIES: Products: Aircraft, automobiles, food processing, iron and steel, machinery and equipment, textiles and clothing, chemicals. Labor: 40%.

NATURAL RESOURCES: Iron ore, soft coal, bauxite, hydroelectric power, potash, natural gas.

OFFICIAL EXCHANGE RATE: 4.5 francs=$1 (4/72).

MEMBERSHIP IN INTERNATIONAL ORGANIZATIONS: U.N. and specialized agencies; SEATO; WEU; OECD; European Community Council of Europe; EURATOM; NATO.

GEOGRAPHY

Largest of the West European nations, mainland France has an area of about 213,000 square miles, roughly four-fifths the size of Texas. Combining natural wealth with a central geographic location, France has a wide variety of landscape, two-thirds of which is flat or gently rolling and the remainder mountainous. A broad plain covers most of northern and western France from the Belgian border in the northeast to Bayonne in the southwest, with upland areas in Normandy, Brittany, and the east. This large plain is bounded on the south by the steeply rising ridges of the Pyrenees; on the southeast by the mountainous plateau of the Massif Central; and on the east by the rugged Alps, the low ridges of the Jura, and the rounded summits of the densely-forested Vosges. The principal rivers are the Rhone and the Durance in the south, the Loire and the Garonne in the west, and the Seine in the north. The Rhine River forms part of France's eastern border with the Federal Republic of Germany.

The climate of France is varied with generally cool winters and mild summers in the west and the north. Southern France has a relative Mediterranean climate of hot summers and mild winters.

For centuries the French cultural influence has been strong in many parts of the world. Outstanding figures in government, science, philosophy, literature, theater, and art have made lasting impressions in their fields. Western political and legal systems bear the imprint of forms developed in France.

The French flag, adopted early in the French Revolution, consists of three vertical stripes of blue, white, and red.

THE PEOPLE

Since prehistoric times France has been a crossroads of trade, travel, and invasion. Thus the French people comprise large elements of all three basic European stocks—Nordic, Alpine, and

Mediterranean. However, because of extensive mixture, these basic types may be referred to in only the broadest sense.

Most immigrants have been from neighboring countries with similar ethnic stocks; nearly 600,000 residents from East European Slavic countries—notably Poland, Czechoslovakia, and Yugoslavia. Approximately half a million North Africans reside in France.

The population grew slowly during the century before 1945, but the rapid rate of growth since 1945 has caused a net increase considerably greater than that of the previous 100 years.

Language

French, a Romance language of the Indo-European family, evolved from the vulgar Latin spoken in the north of France, the Langue d'Oil. In 1539 French replaced Latin as the official language of the kingdom, and by the first half of the following century French philosophers and scientists were causing the language to be learned and read throughout Europe. Cardinal Richelieu founded the French Academy in 1635. Its purpose, then and now, was to form rules for the French language and to purify and standardize it. By the 18th century French writings in all fields of literature acquired a European reputation as models of clarity, order, precision of language, and strict logic. The growing political influence of France furthered the prestige of the language, and in 1714, with the Treaty of Rastatt, French supplanted Latin as the diplomatic language of the Western World.

Religion

Religion in France, as elsewhere in Western Europe, profoundly influenced the molding of the national culture from the late Roman occupation to the Renaissance. Philosophy, architecture, sculpture, painting, and music of that period clearly reflect the influence of Christianity. With the coming of the modern age, however, such influence was challenged by rational free inquiry in philosophy—and hence in other disciplines. By the 20th century, religion was no longer a major force in the society, but the legacy of the Christian ethic has tempered national values in France much as in other Western countries.

Approximately 83 percent of the population have been baptized in the Roman Catholic Church. The most devoutly Catholic regions are the Brittany peninsula and surrounding area in the west; Alsace, Lorraine, and surrounding area in the east; and a fairly large section of south-central France, starting at the city of Lyon.

Protestantism at the time of the Reformation was a major force in France, producing in Jean Calvin one of the most influential early reformers and commanding the allegiance of fully one-half of the French nobility by the mid-16th century. Although delivered from persecution after the Revolution of 1789 and accorded comparable legal status with the Catholics as a state-supported religion, the Portestants have never recovered their former numerical strength. There are now about 800,000 Protestants in France, or less than 2 percent of the population. There are about 300,000 Jews in France today, less than 1 percent of the population. The Muslim population, also less than 1 percent of the total population in France, increased in the 1960's to about 400,000 due to immigration from North Africa, especially Algeria.

HISTORY

Paris, the capital of France, celebrated its "2,000th anniversary" in 1951. The early history of the Gauls, Charlemagne, etc., is a long and colorful story. Modern France emerged after the Renaissance as one of the principal leaders of the general movement away from feudalism and into the era of the nation-state. Its monarchs surrounded themselves with capable ministers, and French armies achieved a degree of discipline and professionalism far beyond anything known up to that day. But the ambitious projects of the monarchs, culminating in the series of ruinous wars waged by Louis XIV at the beginning of the 18th century, led to chronic financial problems for the Government. This, along with the complicated system of special privileges granted the nobility and other favored groups, was one of the principal causes of the French Revolution of 1789-94.

Following the example of the American Colonies, the French Revolution established a republican form of government in France. But in the ensuing century France reverted to a form of monarchy on four occasions—the Empire of Napoleon, the Restoration of Louis XVIII, the reign of Louis-Philippe, and the Second Empire of Napoleon III. Following the Franco-Prussian War (1870), the Third Republic was established and lasted until the military defeat of 1940.

France began to align itself with the United Kingdom after the turn of the century, and the two became allies in 1914. The First World War was a ruinous one for France in terms of its losses of manpower and materiel. In the 1920's France began to rebuild its army (then the largest in Europe) and to establish an elaborate system of frontier defenses (the Maginot Line) and alliances to offset resurgent German strength. The inadequacy of French military strategy and tactics was demonstrated by its defeat in 1940. France emerged from the Second World War in 1944, after 5 years of strife and occupation, in a state of virtual exhaustion and with a whole series of new problems.

After the fall of the provisional government initially led by Gen. Charles de Gaulle, the Fourth Republic was established under a new constitution with a parliamentary form of government controlled by a series of coalitions. The weakness of this system was that the balance of power in the National Assembly frequently rested on the support of a small political party or even on a single influential deputy. Toward the end of the

Fourth Republic the heterogeneous nature of the coalitions and the difficulty of agreeing on measures dealing with the Algerian problem (see section on "Africa and the Middle East") caused successive cabinet crises and changes of government. The structure finally collapsed on May 13, 1958, over the Algerian question. A threatened coup d'etat led Parliament to call on Gen. de Gaulle to head the Government and prevent incipient civil war. De Gaulle became Prime Minister in June 1958 and was elected President in December.

Following Gen. de Gaulle's election to the presidency, Michel Debré was appointed Prime Minister. Debré served in that post until April 1962, when he was succeeded by Georges Pompidou. In October 1962 the Pompidou government lost a vote of confidence on the procedures to be used to amend the Constitution to provide for direct election of the President. President de Gaulle dissolved the Assembly, and in the ensuing elections a Gaullist majority was elected.

On December 5, 1965, for the first time in this century, the French people went to the polls to elect a President by direct ballot. In the first round of the election Gen. de Gaulle failed to receive the full 50 percent required for victory, but in the runoff on December 19, Gen. de Gaulle defeated Francois Mitterrand with 55 percent of the vote. In the parliamentary elections of March 5 and 13, 1967, Gaullist candidates retained a slender majority in the National Assembly.

Student dissatisfaction and protest triggered major disturbances and nationwide strikes in May 1968. Students took over university buildings and battled police in Paris and other large cities, while workers occupied factories virtually throughout the country. President de Gaulle's announcement of a referendum on a vaguely defined program of reforms had little effect in stemming the tide of discontent. The economy was grinding to a halt and France seemed on the brink of chaos. President de Gaulle dissolved the National Assembly, called for national elections, and announced his intention to pursue a policy of sweeping reform based on the principle of "participation." The subsequent campaign diverted discontent into political channels; striking workers gradually returned to their jobs; and the voters, fearing disorder and a possible Communist takeover, swept an overwhelming Gaullist majority into the National Assembly. Maurice Couve de Murville was named to replace Georges Pompidou as Prime Minister in a reshuffled cabinet on July 12, 1968.

In April 1969 Gen. de Gaulle's government conducted a national referendum on the creation of 21 regions with limited political powers. Also proposed was the transformation of the Senate into a consultative body representing economic and social interest groups. President de Gaulle threatened to resign if the proposed reforms were not approved by the voters. On April 27 the Government's proposals were defeated (48 percent in favor, 52 percent opposed), and Gen. de Gaulle resigned.

A number of candidates presented themselves in the ensuing election for a new President: Georges Pompidou, who was supported not only by the Gaullists but also by their Independent Republican allies and some Centrists; Senate President and Centrist candidate Alain Poher; Gaston Defferre for the Socialists; and Jacques Duclos for the Communists. In the first round of voting Pompidou led Poher, with Duclos running a surprisingly strong third (21 percent of the votes), but no candidate received a majority. In the runoff election between Pompidou and Poher on June 15, Pompidou was elected with a 58 percent majority of the votes. Installed as President on June 29, 1969, Pompidou appointed Jacques Chaban-Delmas as Prime Minister of a Cabinet which included Centrists and Independent Republicans as well as Gaullists. The theme of the new Government was announced as "continuity and openness."

Chaban-Delmas was replaced by Pierre Messmer on July 6, 1972. Messmer was reappointed Prime Minister after the national legislative elections of March 4 and 11, 1973. The next major elections will be for the President of the Republic and are scheduled to occur in 1976.

GOVERNMENT

The Constitution for the Fifth Republic was approved by public referendum on September 28, 1958. It greatly strengthened the authority of the executive in relation to Parliament. Under the Constitution the President of the Republic is elected directly by the voters for a 7-year term. He assures, by his arbitration, the regular functioning of the public powers as well as the continuity of the state. He names the Prime Minister, presides over the Cabinet, commands the armed forces, and concludes treaties. He may submit questions to a national referendum and can dissolve the National Assembly. In certain defined emergency situations, he may assume full powers. The President of the Republic is thus the dominant element of the constitutional system.

The Constitution provides for a bicameral Parliament consisting of a National Assembly and a Senate. The Assembly is elected directly; Senators are chosen by an electoral college. Parliament meets in regular session twice annually for a maximum of 3 months on each occasion. Although parliamentary powers are diminished from those existing under the Fourth Republic, the National Assembly can still overthrow the Government at any time if an absolute majority of the total membership of the Assembly votes a censure motion. The National Assembly is the senior legislative body. The Senate's legislative powers are limited, as the National Assembly has the last word in the event of a disagreement between the two houses. The Government has a strong influence in shaping the agenda of Parliament.

The Government can also link its life to any legislative text, and, unless a motion of censure is introduced and voted, the text is considered adopted without a vote.

The National Assembly is made up of 490 deputies elected for 5 years by direct vote. All seats are voted upon in each election. The Senate has 281 seats. Senators are elected by indirect vote for 9-year terms, and one-third of the Senate is renewed every 3 years.

The most distinctive feature of the French judicial system is that it is divided into two categories: a regular court system and a court system which deals specifically with legal problems of the French administration and its relation to the French citizen. The Court of Cassation is the supreme court of appeals in the regular court system; at the pinnacle of the administrative courts is the powerful Council of State.

For administrative purposes, metropolitan France is divided into 95 Departments. Each Department is headed by a Prefect who is appointed by the Central Government.

POLITICAL CONDITIONS

In the National Assembly elections of March 4 and 11, 1973, the three parties supporting the Government lost slightly over 100 seats but, nonetheless, emerged with an absolute majority of 268 seats (out of 490). The Gaullist party, the Union of Democrats for the Republic, won 183 seats, and their allies, the Independent Republicans and the Center Union won respectively 55 and 30 seats. The United Left, consisting of the Socialist and Communist parties plus a splinter party called the Left Radicals, won 175 seats. A center group, the Reformers, won 34 seats. The remaining 13 seats are held by Independents.

The French Communist Party, with 73 seats in the National Assembly, continues to be an important element in French political life. It is one of the best organized political groups in France, claiming 400,000 members. Moreover, it receives a substantial portion of the national vote (traditionally about 20 to 25 percent; in the March 1973 elections the Government won 21.3% on the first round of voting).

ECONOMY

France is unique among the major industrial countries of Western Europe in that it combines an important agricultural sector with substantial indigenous resources of primary raw materials, a well-diversified, modern industrial plant, and a capable labor force. Government ownership of industry is important, about 30 percent of all industrial output being produced in nationalized enterprises. As in all member countries of the European Economic Community—EEC (Common Market), the French economy is in the process of adapting to the Common Market environment. In 1971 France's economy, with a gross national product (GNP) of U.S. $197 billion, ranked fifth in the world after the United States, the Soviet Union, Japan, and the Federal Republic of Germany. The 1971 per capita GNP was $3,800.

Agriculture

A generally mild climate, fertile agricultural land, the application of modern technology, and high prices under the EEC's Common Agricultural Policy have combined to make the country an overabundant producer of many temperate zone foodstuffs. French agriculture produces growing surpluses of soft wheat, dairy products, and many fruits and vegetables, which are absorbed only in part by the other Common Market countries. The principal deficiencies in agricultural production are fats and oils; hard wheats; long-grain rice; citrus and other tropical products; and natural textile fibers, such as cotton and wool, most of which must be imported.

Industrial Resources

The French are amply provided with such raw materials and resources as iron ore, soft coal, bauxite, uranium, and hydroelectric power. A major supplier of metals and minerals in Europe, France is one of the world's leading producers of iron ore, bauxite, and coal. In addition, it has large deposits of antimony, magnesium, pyrites, tungsten, and certain radioactive minerals and is self-sufficient in salt, potash, fluorspar, and sulfur.

On the other hand, French iron ore has a low iron content, and local production has declined somewhat in recent years in favor of high-grade African imports. Similarly, French coal production has declined because of competition from fuel oil and to a lesser extent from less expensive coal imports. Except for bauxite, foreign sources supply virtually all of the nonferrous ores and concentrates, notably those for copper, lead, tin, and zinc. The country has a very limited domestic reserve of crude petroleum and high-grade coking coal and must rely heavily on imports. French production of natural gas is increasing moderately due to recent discoveries, but the country's rapidly growing demand will be filled more and more by natural gas imports from Algeria and the Netherlands.

Industry

Historically one of the leading manufacturing nations, France is active in all major branches of industry. French metallurgical industries are important suppliers of ferroalloys and steel products. The aluminum and chemical industries rank among the largest in the world, and the mechanical and electrical industries rival those of the other advanced industrial countries. In 1969 the French automobile industry produced more than 2 million vehicles. Research and development in the electrical, electronic, telecommunications, aeronautical, and space industries have contributed to a high level of technology. Military applications of atomic energy and certain civilian applications have achieved a degree of sophistication in design and performance surpassed in the West only by the United States and the United Kingdom. France has joined with the United Kingdom to develop and manufacture the Concorde supersonic commercial jet transport. The prototypes of this model first flew in early 1969. France launched its first earth satellite in 1965 and is pursuing an active space research program which includes an equatorial launch site in French Guiana.

Economic Growth and Policy

To meet growing inflationary and other economic problems, the French Government in 1958 devalued the franc and adopted a highly successful stabilization program. In the 10-year period 1959-69 the French economy grew in real terms at an average annual rate of 5.9 percent while retail prices rose an average rate of only 3.4 percent annually.

The high growth rate of the 1960's was interrupted in 1968 when the May-June strikes and demonstrations disrupted the economy and drastically reduced production. The growth rate for that year was only 4.2 percent. However, the strike settlement injected a high level of additional demand into the economy while at the same time handicapping French exports.

In 1969 industrial production quickly recovered and early in the year it rose to record highs. Inflationary pressures, however, began to build up during the first half of 1969 while at the same time capital flight in the face of continuing uncertainties regarding the Government's ability to maintain the parity of the franc began to plague the external finance position. To meet this deteriorating situation the Government on August 10, 1969, devalued the franc and announced a series of austerity measures designed to reduce inflation and restore equilibrium in the nation's foreign trade accounts.

Since 1969, although inflation has continued as a significant problem, France has been one of the star economic performers in the developed world. The French economy now seems well on the way to meeting many of the targets set forth in the Sixth Economic Plan covering the years 1971-75. These include a 6 percent growth rate, rapid industrialization, and strong export growth.

Trade

France is the second largest trading nation in Western Europe (after West Germany). Three-fourths of total French exports consist of manufactured goods. With the expansion of agricultural production, exports of foodstuffs and beverages are becoming increasingly important. Manufactured goods account for two-thirds of French imports, and agricultural products, crude materials, and fuels for the remainder.

Since the establishment of the European Economic Community (EEC), French trade with member countries has expanded rapidly. Trade with members of the enlarged EEC presently accounts for 56 percent of the total. In the past, trade with Communist nations has been relatively unimportant, but the French are actively seeking to expand it, with apparent success. In 1972 France's imports amounted to about $26.5 billion, while its exports totaled approximately $25.5 billion. Traditionally one of France's major trading partners, the United States in 1972 bought about $1.46 billion of French exports. The value of U.S. exports to France that year was $2.2 billion.

Balance of Payments

Between 1958 and 1967, France enjoyed a healthy balance-of-payments position. Widespread labor strikes and social unrest during May-June 1968 led, however, to balance-of-payments difficulties. Net gold and foreign exchange reserves fell from $6.9 billion in April 1968 to $1.3 billion in August 1969. At that time, the franc was devalued by 12.5 percent, and a series of remedial measures was adopted.

The French external position has been strong since 1970 with the balance on current and long-term capital transactions (basic balance) close to equilibrium. In 1973 a small basic surplus is expected. In addition, in 1972 net reserves reached record levels over $10 billion.

French Debts to the United States

France holds to the view generally prevailing among European countries (except Finland) that have large World War I obligations to the United States: They have never denied the juridical validity of the debts but assert that the payment of these debts is dependent on resumption of World War I reparations payments by Germany, interrupted by the Hoover Moratorium of 1932. As of July 1972 the unpaid World War I indebtedness, both principal due and accrued interest, of the Government of France was about $6.1 billion.

With regard to its $2.4 billion post-World War II debts to the United States, France has not only been servicing these debts regularly but has paid more than $880 million in advance of due dates. As of July 1972, France's remaining post-World War II obligations to the United States amounted to about $226 million.

FOREIGN RELATIONS

France, a charter member of the United Nations, occupies one of the permanent seats in the Security Council and is a member of numerous specialized agencies such as the United Nations Educational, Scientific and Cultural Organization (UNESCO); the International Labor Organization (ILO); and the World Health Organization (WHO).

Asia

France continues to be a member of the Southeast Asia Treaty Organization (SEATO), although it has not been represented at the organization's ministerial meetings since 1967.

The French Asian and African colonial empire has virtually disappeared, but France has been strengthened rather than weakened by the transformation of its former colonies into independent states. The maintenance of the empire involved France in a series of costly colonial wars between 1946 and 1962. The first of these, the Indochinese war, ended in 1954 when France, under Prime Minister Mendes-France, signed the Geneva accords granting full independence to Viet-Nam, Laos, and Cambodia.

France recognized the People's Republic of China (P.R.C.) on January 27, 1964, and exchanged ambassadors with Peking.

Since 1968 France has played an important role in the Vietnam peace settlement, first as host for the peace talks and, subsequently, as host for the International Conference on Vietnam. Following the signing of the Vietnam agreement on January 27, 1973, Paris has been the site of meetings between the United States and North Vietnam within the framework of the Joint Economic Commission, and the site of bilateral talks between representatives of the two South Vietnamese parties to the conflict.

Africa and the Middle East

The Algerian conflict, which erupted in 1954, turned out to be the most difficult colonial war to resolve. Although the military challenge presented by the Algerian Front of National Liberation was eventually met, the war provoked a fundamental emotional and eventually political issue within France. Algeria had been one of France's oldest possessions and more than 1 million Europeans, most of them French citizens, lived there. When Gen. de Gaulle assumed power in 1958, he pursued a liberal policy which resulted in 1962 in a negotiated settlement between the French Government and the Algerian nationalists. Following a referendum, an independent Algerian state emerged in July 1962.

With the Algerian war settled, France was able to quickly reestablish and steadily expand its relations with the Arab states, notwithstanding its close relationship with Israel. Since the Arab-Israel war of June 1967 the resulting Arab alienation from the United Kingdom and the United States, coupled with France's pro-Arab posture, has enhanced France's standing among Arab countries. In April 1969, growing out of a French initiative, representatives of France, the United States, the United Kingdom, and the Soviet Union began four-power talks at New York in order to find means of achieving a peaceful solution of the Middle East conflict under the terms of U.N. Resolution 242 of November 1967.

France granted partial autonomy to its former colonies in sub-Saharan Africa in 1956 and complete internal autonomy in the fall of 1958 by means of a referendum after Gen. de Gaulle's return to power. By 1962 all of its former African possessions, with the exception of the French Territory of Afars and Issas (formerly French Somaliland), had chosen full independence. France's aid program influence in Africa remains strong, and most of its former African territories have maintained very close military, economic, financial, and cultural ties with France.

In 1969, in response to a request by the Republic of Chad under the Franco-Chadian military agreement, France sent a military force to that country to help combat outbreaks of insurrection there. The forces were withdrawn in June 1972.

Europe

France has participated in the general postwar recovery of Europe. The French Government favors cooperation among the West European nations and between Eastern and Western Europe. It maintains that West European countries should increase their ties and contacts with the Soviet Union and Eastern Europe with a view to lessening tension, increasing confidence and cooperation, and encouraging individual countries to loosen their bloc ties. At the end of his official visit to the Soviet Union October 6-13, 1970, President Pompidou signed a French-Soviet protocol calling for expanded political consultations, meetings of their Foreign Ministers biannually, and immediate consultations in case of a threat to peace. In previous years France and the Soviet Union have concluded agreements providing for cooperation in space exploration, science, and technology, and for greater trade between the two countries, as well as a consular convention. At the same time, the French have expanded their contacts with the East European countries through ministerial visits and conclusion of cultural, commercial, and technical agreements.

France also recognized the importance of Franco-German collaboration by concluding a Treaty of Cooperation with the Federal Republic of Germany in 1963. The treaty provides for close cooperation and consultation in the fields of foreign, defense, cultural, and scientific affairs, including biannual meetings between the heads of the two countries.

France plays a key role in important European regional organizations. It is a member of the Western European Union. It was an original sponsor of the European Coal and Steel Community and supported the subsequent steps which led to the conclusion of the Treaty of Rome in March 1957 whereby the European Economic Community (Common Market) was established. Implementation of the provisions of the Treaty of Rome has been a major factor among the economic and social forces changing the traditional forms of French life. In 1969 France dropped its long-standing political veto of British entry into the Common Market. By a referendum in April of 1972, the French people formally approved the enlargement of the European Community.

Although France continues to adhere to the North Atlantic Treaty and thus remains a member of the North Atlantic Council, it has withdrawn from the military structure of the North Atlantic Treaty Organization (NATO). Consequently, France no longer supplies forces to the NATO commands or participates in many activities of the alliance.

Other Areas

There are French Overseas Departments and Territories in the Caribbean (Martinique, Guadeloupe, and French Guiana), off the Atlantic coast of Canada (St. Pierre and Miquelon), in the Gulf of Aden (Territory of Afars and Issas), the Pacific Ocean (French Polynesia, New Caledonia, and the islands of Wallis and Futuna), the Indian Ocean (Réunion and the Comoro Islands), and islands in the southern Indian Ocean and the French-claimed segment of Antarctica.

DEFENSE

France maintains an important military establishment with a budget of more than $5 billion, or approximately 17 percent of its national budget. These forces consist of five army divisions, a navy of about 75 warships, and a modest but well-equipped air force. French military planning and resources since 1958 have been increasingly based on the creation of an independent nuclear strike force with associated air defense forces. This force is now operational in the form of the Mirage IV strategic bomber and intermediate range ballistic missiles with nuclear warheads, deployed from submarines and land silos. As part of this program the French are carrying out a program of nuclear tests at their Pacific test range near Tahiti. As a consequence of its determination to develop and maintain its own independent nuclear force, France has not signed the limited test ban treaty. The French Government has stated its willingness to participate in nuclear disarmament if disarmament can be agreed to by all other nuclear powers.

France has not signed the nonproliferation treaty but has agreed to be bound by its terms.

U. S. -FRENCH RELATIONS

Few modern nations have enjoyed a longer history of friendship and cooperation than the United States and France. This relationship began during the American Revolutionary War when France sent significant military assistance to the forces of Gen. George Washington. The friendship continued in the early days of U.S. independence with the negotiation in 1778 of a Treaty of Amity and Commerce between the two countries and has existed through two world wars in the 20th century.

Following World War II, France received massive financial aid under the Marshall Plan, which helped make possible the rapid reconstruction of its land and economy. In addition, from 1945 to 1964, the United States supplied France with substantial military assistance, part of which (prior to 1954) went to assist France in its war with Indochina.

In its basic policy lines, the present French Government has preserved its ties with its traditional allies, including the United States. It also lays great stress on French independence of action, as shown by its policies on such issues as NATO, the Middle East, and Southeast Asia, and by its refusal to sign the limited test ban treaty and the nuclear nonproliferation treaty.

An improvement in U.S.-French relations began with President Nixon's visit to France in February 1969. President Pompidou's state visit to the United States in February-March 1970 kept up the momentum and allowed the two Chief Executives to develop a personal friendship and understanding. A meeting between President Nixon and President Pompidou in the Azores in December 1971 further strengthened the relationship. Both Governments, as a matter of policy, are making a sustained effort to build a closer, more communicative relationship.

There has also been a significant increase in practical bilateral cooperation, notably in the scientific and technological fields. There is an active program of exchanges of individual leaders and groups from government, political groups, and different private fields. In addition, through an expansion of mutual efforts by their respective enforcement agencies, the United States and France have achieved close cooperation in the fight against illegal narcotics production and trafficking.

It is the policy of the United States to emphasize in its relations with France the fundamental mutual interests which the two nations have long shared. Specifically, they are pledged to the mutual defense of the West through the North Atlantic Treaty, to which France remains a party. And both nations continue to appreciate a common cultural heritage to which France has made an inestimable contribution.

PRINCIPAL GOVERNMENT OFFICIALS

President—Georges Pompidou
Prime Minister—Pierre Messmer
President of the National Assembly—Edgar Faure
President of the Senate—Alain Poher
Ambassador to the U.S.—Jacques Kosciusko-Morizet
Ambassador to the U.N.—Louis de Guiringaud

Ministers

Justice—Jean Taittinger
Foreign Affairs—Michel Jobert
Interior—Raymond Marcellin
Defense—Robert Galley
Finance—Valéry Giscard d'Estaing
National Education—Joseph Fontanet
Equipment and Housing—Olivier Guichard
Administrative Reform—Alain Peyrefitte
Environment—Robert Poujade
Cultural Affairs—Maurice Druon
Agriculture—Jacques Chirac
Industry—Jean Charbonnel
Commerce—Jean Royer
Parliamentary Relations—Joseph Comiti
Labor—Georges Gorse
Health—Michel Poniatowski
Transportation—Yves Guena
Information—Philippe Malaud
Posts and Telecommunications—Hubert Germain
Overseas Territories—Bernard Stasi
Veterans Affairs—Andre Bord

The French Republic maintains an Embassy in the United States at 2535 Belmont Road, N.W., Washington, D.C. 20008. It also maintains Consulates General at Boston, Chicago, Detroit, Houston, Los Angeles, New Orleans, New York, San Francisco, and San Juan.

PRINCIPAL U. S. OFFICIALS

Ambassador—John N. Irwin II
Deputy Chief of Mission—Galen L. Stone
Minister-Counselor for Economic Affairs—Chris G. Petrow
Counselor for Political Affairs—H. Allen Holmes
Consul General—David A. Betts
Counselor for Public Affairs (USIS)—Burnett F. Anderson
Counselor for Commercial Affairs—Borrie I. Hyman
Counselor for Administrative Affairs—Peter J. Skoufis
Defense and Army Attaché—Brig. Gen. John W. Donaldson
Naval Attaché—Captain Peter P. Cummins
Air Attache—Brig. Gen. Georges R. Guay
Consul General, Marseille—Philip H. Chadbourn, Jr.
Consul, Bordeaux—William D. Boggs
Consul, Lyon—Peter Tarnoff
Consul, Nice—A. Joseph Williams
Consul, Strasbourg—Ronald Woods

The U.S. Embassy in France is located at 2 Avenue Gabriel, Paris 8 (telephone: ANJ-7460) or ANJ-7400).

READING LIST

Ardagh, John. The New French Revolution; a Social and Economic Survey of France, 1945-1968. New York, Harper and Row, 1968. 501 pp.

Aron, Raymond. France, Steadfast and Changing; the Fourth to the Fifth Republic. Translated from the French. Cambridge, Harvard University Press, 1960. 201 pp.

Blondel, Jean and E. Drexel Godfrey, Jr. The Government of France. 3d ed. New York, Thomas Y. Cromwell, 1968. 230 pp.

Brinton, Clarence Crane. The Americans and the French. Cambridge, Harvard University Press, 1968. 305 pp.

Cartier-Bresson, Henri. Cartier-Bresson's France. Text by Francois Nourissier translated from the French. New York, The Viking Press, 1971. 287 pp.

Earle, Edward M., ed. Modern France; Problems of the Third and Fourth Republics. Princeton, Princeton University Press, 1951. 522 pp.

Gagnon, Paul A. France Since 1789. New York, Harper and Row, 1964. 560 pp.

Gaulle, Charles de. Complete War Memoirs. Translated from the French. New York, Simon and Schuster, 1964. 3 volumes: V.1. Call to Honor, 1940-42. V.2. Unity, 1942-43. V.3. Salvation, 1944-46.

Gaulle, Charles de. Memoirs of Hope. Translated from the French. New York, Simon and Schuster, 1972.

Gramont, Sanche de. The French: Portrait of a People. New York, Putnam, 1969. 479 pp.

Guerard, Albert Leon. France, a Short History. New York, Norton, 1946. 274 pp.

Hartley, Anthony. Gaullism; the Rise and Fall of a Political Movement. New York, Outerbridge and Dienstfrey, for sale by Dutton, 1971. 373 pp.

Hoffmann, Stanley and others. In Search of France. Cambridge, Harvard University Press, 1963. 443 pp.

Knapton, Ernest. France; an Interpretative History. New York, Schribners, 1971. 616 pp.

Kulski, W. W. De Gaulle and the World; the Foreign Policy of the Fifth French Republic. Syracuse, N.Y., Syracuse University Press, 1966. 428 pp.

Luethy, Herbert. France Against Herself: A Perceptive Study of France's Past, Her Politics, and Her Unending Crises. Translated from the German. New York, Praeger, 1955. 476 pp.

Maurois, Andre. History of France. Translated from the French. New York, Farrar, Straus and Cudahy, Inc., 1957. 598 pp.

Nourissier, Francois. The French. Translated from the French. New York, Alfred A. Knopf, 1968. 310 pp.

Ouston, Philip. France in the Twentieth Century. New York, Praeger, 1972. 290 pp.

Pickles, Dorothy Maud. The Fifth French Republic; Institutions and Politics. 3rd ed. New York, Praeger, 1966. 261 pp.

Ritchie, R. L. France: A Companion to French Studies. 5th ed. rev. London, Methuen, 1965. 505 pp.

Serfaty, Simon. France, De Gaulle and Europe; the Policy of the Fourth and Fifth Republics Toward the Continent. Baltimore, Johns Hopkins Press, 1968. 177 pp.

Siegfried, Andre. France; a Study in Nationality. Translated from the French. New Haven, Yale University Press, 1930. 122 pp.

Tannenbaum, Edward R. The New France. Chicago, Chicago University Press, 1961. 252 pp.

Thompson, I. B. Modern France; a Social and Economic Geography. Totowa, N.J., Littlefield, 1971. 465 pp., maps.

Wahl, Nicholas. The Fifth Republic: France's New Political System. New York, Random House, 1959.

Williams, Philip M. and others. French Politicians and Elections, 1951-1969. New York, Cambridge University Press, 1971. 312 pp.

Williams, Philip M. and M. Harrison. Politics and Society in De Gaulle's Republic. London, Longmans, 1971. 403 pp.

Wright, Gordon. France in Modern Times: 1760 to the Present. Chicago, Rand McNally, 1960. 621 pp.

Wylie, Laurence W. Village in the Vaucluse. 2d ed. Cambridge, Harvard University Press, 1964. 350 pp.

DEPARTMENT OF STATE PUBLICATION 8209
Revised May 1973

APPENDIX II

FRANCE

STRENGTH OF THE COMMUNIST PARTY ORGANIZATION—1973

[FROM: World Strength of the Communist Party Organizations—1973. Washington, Department of State, Bureau of Intelligence and Research, 1973.]

FRANCE

National Political Status: Date of last election - March 5 and 12, 1973.

Communist: Communist Party of France (PCF) - 5,156,619 votes (21.26%), 73 seats (14.89%)

Non-Communist Left: Socialist Party - 4,579,888 votes (18.88%), 89 seats (18.16%)

Left Radical - 359,715 votes (1.48%), 12 seats (2.45%)

Center: Reform Group - 3,015,472 votes (12.43%), 28 seats (5.72%)
Center Union - 901,136 votes (3.71%), 23 seats (4.70%)

Conservative: Union of Democrats for the Republic - 5,788,796 votes (23.86%), 186 seats (37.95%)

Independent Republicans - 1,674,972 votes (6.91%), 54 seats (11.02%)

Others: Diverse majority - 972,623 votes (4.01%), 12 seats (2.45%)
Extreme left - 810,645 votes (3.34%), 13 seats (2.66%)
Diverse right - 684,580 votes (2.82%), no seats
Diverse left - 314,604 votes (1.30%), no seats

Total: 24,259,050 votes, 490 seats

Communist Party Membership: 400,000-425,000 (claimed); 260,000-295,000 (estimated)

Leading Party Figures and Positions:
MARCHAIS, Georges - Secretary-General
SEGUY, Georges - Head of the CGT and Politburo member

Principal Publications:
l'Humanite - daily newspaper
Cahiers du Communisme - monthly theoretical journal

Areas of Communist Activity: The results of the March 1973 parliamentary elections vindicated the policy of the French Communist Party (PCF) of seeking patiently to parlay its temporary electoral alliances with the non-Communist left into a lasting relationship which could end the party's long political isolation.

Numerically speaking, the Communists and the non-Communist left only wiped out their defeat of 1968. But the political context of the 1973 contest probably was much more important to the PCF leadership: the election came in the wake of the joint program that Socialists and Communists had concluded in June 1972, and thereby signaled the viability of the "popular unity" for which the PCF had worked for almost a decade.

While the election failed to bring about the long-heralded leftist alternative to Gaullist domination, the PCF throughout the year bent every effort to shore up and expand its newly won position by taking advantage of domestic and international trends that seemed less resistant to its comeback. At the same time, the PCF leadership had to contend with certain risks entailed by the party's policy of domestication and accommodation with its non-Communist partners.

Traditionally, Communist-Socialist collaboration, beyond limited electoral support, had foundered on the rocks of deeply ingrained ideological differences and the constant fear on the part of the Socialists that Communist electoral strength would mean Communist domination of the Socialist Party. Conversely, the PCF had always suspected the Socialists of merely using Communist votes to get elected, not to share government power with the PCF. By drawing the Socialists into a common governmental program, the PCF sought to forestall such a gambit, not without running the risk, however, that such a program would be drained of revolutionary content and would reduce the PCF to a reformist party.

Another problem for the PCF arose in the last weeks before the election when it appeared that the revamped and also renamed Socialist Party--its predecessor, SFIO, had become defunct--might actually gain more votes than the Communists, for the first time in the post-World War II period. For the Communists, such an outcome not only would have strengthened unduly the hand of the Socialists in any future collaboration, but also it would have tarnished the image of the PCF as "the first party of the left." Actually, the Communists retained their preeminence although the Socialists proportionately benefited more from the unity pact.

The PCF's preoccupation with its domestic role subjected the party's traditional loyalty to the Soviet Union to repeated strains as it dealt warily with such sensitive issues as Jewish emigration and the treatment of dissenters in the Soviet Union. When the leader of the Socialist Party, Francois Mitterrand, became embroiled in an argument with the Soviets over their emigration policy, *l'Humanite* printed an attack on him by the Soviet Ambassador, without any comment. When the former editor of the defunct PCF literary magazine, *Les Lettres Francaises*, attacked the Soviets for their treatment of Solzhenitsyn and the party for its questionable attitude on literary and political freedom, the PCF leadership was in a quandary. Anxious not to appear as endorsing suppression of artistic freedom, party leaders nevertheless felt compelled to censure any expression of what they regarded as "anti-Soviet attitudes."

In spite of these obstacles and difficulties, the PCF, under its present leadership, no longer is "a stranded whale" on the French political scene. The party enjoys significant support among urban industrial and white-collar workers, particularly in the Paris region and the industrialized north. It also has a sizable following among farmers and farm workers in the economically depressed areas of central France and the Mediterranean coast, and some support among the middle classes, particularly teachers and the technical intelligentsia.

The country's largest trade union federation, the *Confederation Generale du Travail* (CGT), is controlled by the party. The party also directs a number of front organizations--e.g., among students, women, and young people--but many of them are little more than paper organizations.

Concomitant with its efforts to enter the political mainstream domestically, the PCF also has sought to mend its fences on the West European scene. While still observing customary etiquette toward Moscow--Secretary-General Georges Marchais concluded his November trip there with the time-honored obeisance to "proletarian internationalism"--there are signs that the party now is somewhat more prone to favor its own interests over those of the Soviets in certain situations. By distancing itself more explicitly from the notion of a single Socialist model of general applicability, the PCF is challenging Soviet claims to that effect. Also, there is some indication that Moscow was not entirely happy with the Communist-Socialist unity program of 1972, e.g., Politburo member Mikhail Suslov's cavalier treatment of it at the 20th PCF Congress in December 1972.

Finally, the gradual rapprochement between the PCF and the Italian Communist Party has seen the French Communists increasingly giving way to the more flexible policy of the Italian Communists on European integration. Not only has there been a growing exchange of visits between the two parties, capped by Marchais' trip to Italy in the spring of 1973, but the PCF also has somewhat modified its former rigid hostility toward the EC. When Marchais spoke in Bologna of a "joint struggle within the EC," French Communist parliamentarians had just joined other Communist representatives from Italy and Denmark in the European Assembly for the first time.

In the trade union field, the CGT showed greater interest in participating in the emerging new West European trade union confederation and less concern for the Soviet idea of a pan-European labor federation. The PCF also joined the Italian Communists in preparations for a meeting of West European parties.

On other international issues, the PCF denounced the ouster of the Allende government in Chile, but not without first hearing a rather critical appraisal of its failure to stop extreme leftist excesses by a senior PCF leader who had visited the area shortly before September 1973.

With Marchais now formally replacing the head of the PCF, the ailing Waldeck Rochet, the party not only has been engaged in trimming its ideological sails to conform to domestic exigencies but also has sought to spruce up its stodgy appearance. At its December 1972 Congress, the PCF placed great emphasis on youth: the average delegate's age was 33, and many young faces made their first appearance on the Central Committee.

Whether all these efforts have contributed to a massive increase in membership is doubtful. While the party's organizational secretary announced a membership of 410,000 in November--not much of an increase since the 1970 claim of 400,000--actual membership probably is well below this figure. The PCF only announces occasionally how many membership cards were requested by lower organizational units; it keeps silent on those who drop out.

The PCF continues to dismiss in anger, and to oppose in practice, its ideological opponents on the extreme left as "only a few hundred renegades, adventurers, or petty bourgeois who have no influence at all on the working class." In this respect, the PCF probably is largely correct. From the very outset of the formal establishment of the pro-Chinese, French Communist dissident organizations, the excesses of the Chinese cultural revolution helped ease the PCF's problem on this score, with the result that these French Communists outside the party continue to fare very poorly. Indeed, the "grouplets" in which such Communists are organized are split among themselves.

However, the extreme left dealt a blow to the PCF at the university level when in 1971 the Trotskyites gained control of France's largest student organization, the *Union Nationale des Etudiants Francais* (UNEF), and caused a split when the Communists organized themselves under the rival banner of UNEF-*Renouveau*. The latter claims to have 30,000 members while UNEF claims 19,000.

APPENDIX JJ

GREECE

ARMED FORCES AND MILITARY POWER

SEE PAGE 142

[Reprinted with permission from: The Almanac of World Military Power, by Col. T. N. Dupuy, U.S. Army, Ret., Col. John A. C. Andrews, U.S. Air Force, Ret., and Grace P. Hayes. 3rd ed. Dunn Loring, Va., T. N. Dupuy Associates, 1974.]

GREECE

Hellenic Republic

POWER POTENTIAL STATISTICS

Area: 50,944 square miles
Population: 9,100,000
Total Active Armed Forces: 184,000 (includes 25,000 Gendarmerie; 2.05% population)
Gross National Product: $12.8 billion ($1,407 per capita)
Annual Military Expenditures: $608 million (4.75% GNP)
Refined Petroleum Products: 6.8 million metric tons
Electric Power Output: 10.6 billion kwh
Merchant Fleet: 2,056 ships; 13.1 million gross tons
Civil Air Fleet: 12 jet, 9 turboprop, 13 piston transports

DEFENSE STRUCTURE

The government of Greece was controlled by military officers from 1967 to 1974. Elections in early 1974 confirmed General Phaedon Gezikis as president of an unpopular government. A number of plots and attempted coups resulted in forced retirement of many officers, both senior and junior, in the armed forces, leaving Greece's military organization weak. The government's debilities became apparent during the Cyprus crisis in July 1974, and Gezikis called on Constantine Karamanlis (Greece's most effective statesman since World War II, who had resigned and gone into voluntary exile in 1963, in protest against the turbulent political proclivity) to return and form a civilian government. Gezikis remained as President, but Karamanlis moved toward restoration of democratic government and replacement of junta military appointees.

The three services are integrated under the Ministry of National Defense. Under the Defense Minister is a Commander in Chief, Armed Forces, who heads a staff composed of the Chiefs of Staff of the Army, the Navy, and the Air Force.

POLITICO-MILITARY POLICY

During much of the century-and-a-half existence of the modern Greek state, its military policy has reflected traditional hostility to Turkey, the former occupying power, despite the fact that Greece and Turkey have been allies in NATO. Discovery of oil off the island of Thasos, at the northern end of the Aegean Sea, in early 1974 exacerbated a long-standing rivalry over maritime sovereignty in that area. Tensions between the two nations were already high when the coup d'etat in Cyprus, supported if not engineered by the Greek military junta, brought them to the brink of war in July 1974. With almost 40,000 Turkish troops ashore on the island, the Greek government realized the futility of sending units to attempt to resist them.

In January 1973 US and Greek representatives signed an agreement granting the United States home port facilities for the Sixth Fleet in the Athens area, but the installation was subsequently postponed indefinitely by the Greek government. Karamanlis announced the withdrawal of Greek units from NATO during the crisis in 1974. What effect this would have on US NATO force bases in Greece was not clear.

The armed forces are supported by conscription, with all able-bodied men between the ages of 21 and 50 being liable to

24 months' service. In the Navy, which has many volunteers, conscript service is 18 months. The annual call-up is about 50,000.

STRATEGIC PROBLEMS

Greece commands a significant geographic position from which to control the eastern basin of the Mediterranean, and consequently the maritime communications to and from the Black Sea and the Middle East. It was because of this that foreign armies invaded Greece in two world wars, and NATO now considers Greece a fundamental link in its defenses of southeastern Europe.

Although the long northern frontier of Greece is largely mountainous, the corridors and natural communications lines are generally perpendicular to the frontier, and thus the mountains do not form an effective barrier to invasion. This is compounded by the narrowness of northeastern Greece. The vulnerability of this frontier was not only amply demonstrated in World Wars I and II; it was successfully exploited by Greece's northern communist neighbors during the Greek Civil War of 1945-1949.

The emotional and political involvement of Greece in the bitter dispute between Greek and Turkish Cypriots brought Greece and Turkey to the threshold of war twice (1963 and 1964) before the military coup in Cyprus in July 1974 resulted in Turkish invasion of the island and caused a military and political crisis in Greece. Weakened by the upheavals and forced retirements of military leaders in recent years, Greece refrained from a military response and sought a solution through the UN, NATO, and meetings of the foreign ministers of Great Britain, Turkey and Greece in Geneva, Switzerland.

MILITARY ASSISTANCE

The original stimulus to the American foreign aid program was provided when the United States decided, in 1947, to replace faltering British military and economic assistance to Greece. This resulted in the Truman Doctrine, followed by the Marshall Plan, and the subsequent US worldwide military assistance programs to underdeveloped Free World nations threatened by Communism. Greece has received a total of $1.7 billion in military assistance since 1950, in addition to about $200 million immediate assistance (mostly economic) provided under the Truman Doctrine in the two previous years. US military assistance to Greece was briefly suspended after the 1967 coup d'etat, but has been resumed.

Under the terms of the Zurich-London Agreements of 1959 Greece is committed to assist (in concert with Turkey) in the establishment and training of the armed forces and internal security forces of Cyprus. This agreement was never fully implemented, and was completely ended by the mid-1974 events in Cyprus.

ALLIANCES

Greece is a member of NATO. It is also a member of the 20-year Balkan Alliance of 1954 with Yugoslavia and Turkey.

ARMY

Personnel: 118,000

Organization:
- 3 corps (2 on northern frontier assigned to NATO)
- 11 infantry divisions (8 under strength)
- 1 armored division
- 1 commando brigade (marines)
- 2 SSM battalions (Honest John)
- 1 SAM battalion (Hawk)

Major Equipment Inventory:
- 250 medium tanks (M-47)
- 270 medium tanks (M-48)
- 50 medium tanks (AMX-30)
- light tanks (M-24 and M-41)
- APCs (M-2, M-59, and M-113)
- 105mm, 155mm and 175mm self-propelled guns
- 105mm, 155mm, and 203mm self-propelled howitzers
- armored cars (M-8 and M-20)
- scout cars (M-3)
- Hawk SAMs
- Honest John SSMs
- 40mm, 75mm, and 90mm AA guns
- 20 light aircraft, helicopters

Reserves: About 350,000 reservists available for mobilization

NAVY

Personnel: 18,000

Major Units:
- 9 destroyers (DD)
- 4 destroyer escorts (DE)
- 7 diesel submarines (SS)
- 2 minelayers (MMC)
- 5 minesweepers (MSO)
- 3 submarine chasers (PC)
- 15 coastal minesweepers (MSC)
- 4 fast patrol boats with Exocet SSM (PTFG)
- 14 torpedo boats (PT)
- 1 landing ship dock (LSD)
- 8 landing ships tank (LST)

6 landing ships medium (LSM)
8 landing craft (LCU/LCT)
13 landing craft mechanized (LCM)
34 landing craft vehicle-personnel (LCVP)
17 auxiliaries

Major Naval Bases: Piraeus, Salonika, Valos, Mitilini

Reserves: About 50,000 trained reservists

AIR FORCE

The 28th (Hellenic) Tactical Air Force is made up of 7 combat squadrons, and 1 transport squadron and has been assigned to NATO's Sixth Allied Tactical Air Force.

Personnel: 23,000

Organization:
- 6 fighter-bomber squadrons (F-104 and F-84F)
- 4 day interceptor squadrons (F-5)
- 1 all-weather interceptor squadron (F-102)
- 2 reconnaissance squadrons (RF-84F and RF-5)
- 3 transport squadrons (Noratlas, C-47, C-119, Do-28)
- 2 helicopter squadrons (Alouette II, Bell 47, AB-204, H-19)
- 1 ASW/search and rescue squadron (under Navy control; HU-16)
- 1 SAM wing (1 battalion each of Nike-Ajax and Nike-Hercules)

Major Aircraft Types:
- 240 combat aircraft
  - 108 fighter-bombers (36 F-104, 72 F-84F)
  - 18 F-102A all-weather fighter interceptors
  - 72 F-5A fighter-interceptors
  - 30 fighter reconnaissance aircraft (15 RF-5, 15 RF-84F)
  - 12 HU-16 ASW/rescue aircraft
- 244 other aircraft
  - 108 transports (27 C-47, 40 Noratlas, 31 Do-28, 10 C-119)
  - 36 helicopters (12 Bell 47, 6 AB-204, 10 H-19, 8 Alouette II)
  - 100 trainer/support aircraft
  - 38 F-4 fighters on order to be delivered starting in March 1974

Reserves: About 30,000 trained reservists

PARAMILITARY

There is a National Gendarmerie of 25,000 men for internal security. In addition the National Guard of 50,000 organized March 30, 1970, has the duty of ensuring internal order a safeguarding the country from Communist, anarchist, or a other form of hostile action. It is manned by reservists from three services between the ages of 19 and 50, and is also op to volunteers up to age 60; it is organized on a regional ba all its members serving a minimum of six months and train on Sundays and holidays.

APPENDIX KK

GREECE

BACKGROUND NOTES

SEE PAGE 142

[Washington, Department of State, November 1973 (Publication 8198).]

Greece

department of state * november 1973

OFFICIAL NAME: Hellenic Republic

GEOGRAPHY

The Greek mainland is situated in southeastern Europe on the southern tip of the Balkan Peninsula. Many islands, such as Crete, Corfu, and the Dodecanese, are included within its boundaries. The mainland is bounded on the north by Bulgaria, Yugoslavia, and Albania; on the east by Turkey and the Aegean Sea; and on the west by the Mediterranean and Ionian Seas.

The country is predominantly mountainous. Much of the land is dry and rocky; only about 25 percent is arable. Greece has mild, wet winters and hot, dry summers. The climate varies considerably between the southern and northern parts of the country, but the temperature is rarely extreme.

PROFILE

Geography

AREA: 51,182 sq. mi., including islands (about the size of Alabama). CAPITAL: Athens (pop. 2.5 million). OTHER CITIES: Thessaloniki (pop. 550,000), Patras (pop. 110,000), Iraklion (pop. 77,000), Volos (pop. 51,000), Larissa (pop. 72,000), Kavalla (pop. 46,000), Chania (pop. 40,000), Kalamata (pop. 40,000), and Serres (pop. 40,000).

People

POPULATION: 8.8 million (1971 census). ANNUAL GROWTH RATE: 0.4%. DENSITY: 172 per sq. mi. ETHNIC GROUPS: Greek, Muslim. RELIGION: Greek Orthodox (98%). LANGUAGE: Greek (Demotic Greek; Katharevousa). LITERACY: 85%. LIFE EXPECTANCY: 74 years.

Government

TYPE: Presidential Parliamentary Republic. INDEPENDENCE: 1833. DATE OF CONSTITUTION: 1968, revised 1973.

BRANCHES: *Executive:* President (Chief of State), Prime Minister (Head of Government). *Legislative:* In abeyance since 1967; new unicameral parliament to be elected in 1974. *Judicial:* Council of State.

ADMINISTRATIVE SUBDIVISIONS: 52 Prefectures.

FLAG: White cross superimposed on a blue background in the upper left corner. Remainder of flag consists of five blue and four white horizontal stripes.

Economy

GROSS NATIONAL PRODUCT: $12.6 billion (1972). ANNUAL GROWTH RATE: 10% PER CAPITA INCOME: $1,400. PER CAPITA GROWTH RATE: 6.7%.

AGRICULTURE: *Labor:* 41%. *Land:* 67%. *Acres per capita:* 2.4. *Crops:* Tobacco, cotton, wheat, raisins, currants, fresh fruit, olive oil, and olives.

INDUSTRY: *Labor:* 25%. *Products:* Chemicals, petroleum and aluminum refining, mining, and textile manufactures.

TRADE: *Exports* $835.5 million (1972): tobacco, cotton, wheat, raisins, currants, textiles and cotton, aluminum and metal products, fresh fruit, olive oil, olives. *Partners:* Western Europe (54.1%), U.S. (19.5%), Soviet Bloc (13.6%). *Imports* $2.4 billion: meat and meat products, consumer goods, raw materials, heavy machinery, electronic equipment, motor vehicles, and chemicals. *Partners:* U.S. (11.4%), Western Europe (64.6%), Soviet Bloc (6.8%).

OFFICIAL EXCHANGE RATE: 27 drachmas = 1 U.S. dollar.

MEMBERSHIP IN INTERNATIONAL ORGANIZATIONS: European Economic Community (EEC), North Atlantic Treaty Organization (NATO), United Nations.

ECONOMIC AID RECEIVED: *Total U.S. only:* $3.9 billion (1946-72).

PEOPLE

Traditionally a highly mobile society, the Greeks have over the past two decades become increasingly urbanized. The 1961 census showed an urban population of 43 percent against a rural and semi-urban population of 57 percent. By 1971 the urban population had grown to 53 percent. The greater Athens area alone accounts for almost 30 percent of the country's population.

There is only one numerically significant minority. In Greece, the Muslim population, concentrated in Thrace, was recognized by the exchange of populations provisions of the Treaty of Lausanne in 1923, and constitutes about one percent of the total population. Other bilingual groups make up another one percent of the population. The Greek Orthodox Church, to which 98 percent of the Greeks belong, is the established religion. The Church is self-governing under the spiritual guidance of the ecumenical Patriarch, resident in Istanbul, Turkey. During the centuries of Ottoman domination, the Greek Church played a key role in preserving the language, values, and national identity of the Greeks and served as an important rallying point in the struggle for independence. The Church is under the protection and partial control of

the state, which pays the clergy's salaries.

The Greek language has an unbroken history of 3,000 years, preserving many features of the classical language in the idiom spoken today. Modern Greek has taken two principal forms. Demotic Greek, the "popular" tongue–informal, relatively simple, and susceptible to external influences–has generally been the language of modern literature and the vehicle of contemporary speech. Katharevousa, the language of official intercourse and of university instruction, was devised in the 19th century to purify Greek and return the language to a form nearer to the structure of the ancient Attic dialect from which it had developed.

The current population of Greece is about 8.8 million or about 172 persons per square mile. The metropolitan area of greater Athens (including the port city of Piraeus) is estimated at 2.5 million.

HISTORY

Greece came into existence as a modern state following a War of Independence from the Ottoman Empire (1821-30). Under the tutelage of the United Kingdom, France, and Russia, a monarchy was established in 1833 with Otto of Bavaria ascending the throne. Otto was deposed 30 years later, and the great powers selected as his successor a member of the Danish house of Glucksberg who became George I of the Hellenes. The Greece of 1830 was 18,346 square miles in area with a northern boundary extending from the Gulf of Volos on the east to the Gulf of Arta on the west. Since then, Greece has almost tripled in size: the Ionian Islands were added in 1864; Thessaly and part of Epirus in 1881; Macedonia, Crete and the Aegean Islands in 1913; Western Thrace in 1918; and the Dodecanese Islands in 1947.

The struggle for power between monarchists and republicans, a continuing feature of Greek politics, was particularly sharp in the period between the two World Wars. Greece was proclaimed a republic in 1925, but King George II was returned to the throne in 1935. The monarchy was reconfirmed in a plebiscite in 1946.

Greece entered World War II on the side of the Allies on October 28, 1940, when the country was invaded by Italy. That date is celebrated in Greece in memory of the one word, "Ochi" (no), which constituted the Greek reply to a number of demands made by Mussolini. Despite the Italian superiority of numbers and equipment, the determined Greeks drove the invaders back into Albania. Hitler was then forced to divert German forces to Greece to protect his southern flank. The German attack began on April 5, 1941, and by the end of May Greece had fallen. But Greek resistance had cost Germany precious weeks and delayed the invasion of Russia.

Following the war, the Communists made two attempts to take over Greece. During the winter of 1944-45 the first effort failed in the face of Greek determination assisted by British forces. The second Communist insurgency began in the spring of 1946 and received substantial assistance from the neighboring Soviet satellites but was defeated in the summer of 1949 with extensive U.S. economic and military aid (the first implementation of the Truman doctrine). The Communist Party of Greece (KKE) was outlawed in December 1947 and remains proscribed although it developed a legal political front in the United Democratic Left Party (EDA). From 1952 to late 1963, Greece was governed by conservative parties, the Greek Rally of Marshal Papagos, and its successor the National Radical Union (ERE) of Constantine Karamanlis. In the fall of 1963 the Center Union Party (EK) came to power and governed until July 1965. It was followed by a succession of conservative governments or coalitions until 1967.

On April 21, 1967, a group of middle-grade military officers took control of the government. Martial law was declared, key articles of the Constitution were suspended, Parliament was dissolved, and political activities were forbidden. However, the military leaders retained the constitutional monarchy as the basic structure of government. On December 13, 1967, King Constantine attempted and failed to overthrow the coup government. Following the King's flight to Rome, the military regime appointed a regent in his place.

A new Constitution was accepted by a large majority vote in a national referendum in September 1968 and became effective in part in November.

On June 1, 1973, Prime Minister Papadopoulos declared the abolition of the Greek monarchy following an abortive coup that was said to have been undertaken by elements of the Greek Navy on behalf of King Constantine. Simultaneously, Georgios Papadopoulos assumed the position of President of a provisional government. On July 29 a plebiscite was held on proposed changes in the 1968 Constitution and the unopposed candidacy of Papadopoulos to become first President of the "Hellenic Republic." Official results of the referendum showed 77 percent of the valid votes cast in favor of the revised Constitution and the presidency of Papadopoulos. In his August 19 inaugural address, President Papadopoulos announced that politically inspired crimes that had taken place in Greece since the 1967 coup would be amnestied. He also lifted martial law (in effect in Athens) and declared that parliamentary elections would be held in 1974.

GOVERNMENT AND POLITICAL CONDITIONS

The Government of Greece is described in the revised Constitution as a "presidential parliamentary republic." Broad executive power is vested in the presidency. The President directly appoints the Prime Minister and the Ministers and Under Secretaries of Defense, Foreign Affairs, and Public Order and has executive, legislative, and considerable budgetary responsibility in these three areas of national life. The President appoints and dismisses the remaining Cabinet members on the recommendation of the Prime Minister. The President may declare a "state of seige" for a period up to 3 months without consulting Parliament. If the President does not agree with legislation passed by Parliament, he has recourse to national referendum. He is also the head of the Greek Armed Forces; he appoints the Chief of the Hellenic Armed Forces and the three service chiefs. The Constitution provides for a Vice President to assist the President and assume his duties in case of his absence, resignation, or death. The Constitution limits the President of the Hellenic Republic to a single 7-year term.

The revised Constitution calls for a Parliament composed of 200 members, 20 of whom are selected by the President. The elected deputies are chosen by direct, secret, and universal ballot. With the exception of some unalterable provisions, Parliament may revise the Constitution. The President, however, may submit any constitutional amendment to plebiscite. The government must enjoy the confidence of Parliament.

Greece is divided into 52 prefectures (Nomi), each headed by a perfect (Nomarch) appointed by the Minister of Interior. Since 1971, in an attempt to decentralize administration, the prefectures have been grouped into seven districts under Governors who are concurrently Under Secretaries of the Ministry of Interior.

Principal Government Officials

President–Georgios Papadopoulos
Vice President–Odysseus Angelis
Prime Minister–Spyros Markezinis
Deputy Prime Minister–Charilaos Mitrelias
Minister of Agriculture–Yeorgios Koutsoumaris
Minister of Commerce–Nicholaos Grigoriades
Minister of Coordination–Thanos Kapsalis
Minister of Culture and Science–Constantine Panayiotakis
Minister of Education and Religion–Panayotis Sifnaios
Minister of Energy–Apostolos Papageorgiou
Minister of Finance–Ioannis Koulis
Minister of Foreign Affairs–Christos Xanthopoulos Palamas

Minister of Industry–Nicholaos Momferatos
Minister of the Interior–Ioannis Agathangelou
Minister of Justice–Constantine Christopoulos
Minister of Labor–George Alexiadis
Minister of Merchant Marine–Alexandros Constantine Voultzos
Minister of National Defense–Nicholaos Efessios
Minister of Public Order–Panayiotis Therapos
Minister of Public Works–Constantine Papadimitriou
Minister of Social Services–Charalambos Panayiotopoulos
Minister of Transport and Communications–Orestes Yakas
Ambassador to the United States–John Sorokos
Ambassador to the United Nations–Constantine Panayotakos

Greece maintains an Embassy in the United States at 2221 Massachusetts Avenue, N.W., Washington, D.C. 20008. There are also Consulates General at San Francisco, Chicago and New York, and Consulates at New Orleans and Boston.

ECONOMY

Over the past several years, Greece's gross national product (GNP) has shown a real growth rate of more than 8 percent annually, and preliminary data indicates that this rate was more than 10 percent in 1972. In current prices the Greek GNP in 1972 was $12.6 billion, or $1,400 per capita. Greece's official foreign reserves more than trebled between 1970-72 to a total of over $1 billion.

The rapid growth of the Greek economy during the past decade was attended by significant changes in the structure of production. During this period, manufacturing expanded even more rapidly than the economy as a whole, growing from 17 percent of the gross domestic product (GDP) in 1960 to 24 percent in 1972. In 1972 agriculture accounted for 16 percent of the GDP. The distribution of Greece's labor force of 3.3 million has also reflected the changing pattern of production: whereas agriculture employed 54 percent and industry only 19 percent of the Greek labor force in 1961, these sectors accounted for 41 percent and 24 percent, respectively, in 1972. Emigration of Greek workers, primarily to Western Europe, has been in decline in recent years, reflecting favorable demand conditions in Greece's domestic labor market.

Greece's growing industrial sector accounted for 38 percent of total exports in 1972 (23 percent in 1968), while agricultural exports decreased their share to 49 percent (65 percent in 1968). The Greek balance of trade has suffered a chronic and widening deficit which is partially met by large and increasing invisible receipts from tourism, shipping, and workers' remittances. Foreign borrowing, including suppliers' credits, fills the remaining gap in the balance of payments.

Greece's primary exports are tobacco, fresh and prepared fruits, cotton, textiles, and aluminum and metal products. The country's most important imports include meat and live animals, heavy machinery, and manufactured consumer goods. The bulk of Greek trade is with members of the Common Market and the United States, but a substantial share (13.6 percent) of Greek exports went to the Soviet Union and other East European countries in 1972; these countries accounted for 6.8 percent of Greek imports in 1972.

Trade between the United States and Greece is consistent with Greece's worldwide trade pattern. Major Greek imports from the United States include heavy machinery and consumer goods while significant U.S. imports of Greek goods include tobacco, foodstuffs, aluminum, and petroleum products. Greek imports from the United States comprised 11.4 percent of the total in 1972, and exports to the United States were 19.5 percent of total Greek exports that year. Greece traditionally runs a trade deficit with the United States, and in 1972 the

TRAVEL NOTES

Passage–Nationals of most countries may enter Greece with a valid passport for identification; no Greek visa is required for those holding regular passports, and they may remain in Greece for 2 months without documentation. Those wishing to extend their stay must submit an application 20 days before the expiration of the 2-month period.

The following international certificates of inoculation are required: Smallpox for travelers coming from Asia and Africa, except Egypt and Turkey; yellow fever for travelers arriving from a few areas, including U.S. official travelers; and cholera for travelers coming from infected areas.

Customs–The following items may be imported by nonofficial visitors duty free: (1) 200 cigarettes or 50 cigars; (2) personal clothing; and (3) such items as airguns, radios, cameras, typewriters, and $150 worth of gifts.

Transportation–Main streets in Athens and the main highways in Greece are macadam, and off the main arteries roads are rough and ungraded. A few roads in the more remote areas are still essentially wagon roads or mule tracks. The border between Greece and Yugoslavia is open to private automobiles and the road to Belgrade is good.

Except for rush hours, the Greek bus system provides adequate and cheap local transportation. Taxis are plentiful, and rates are reasonable.

An international drivers license is required for tourist driving in Greece. The international car insurance card is valid in Greece if Greece is listed on the card.

Communication–a shortage of trunklines for telephones continues to exist in Greece. Telephone service within the city is satisfactory. Trunkline long-distance calls may be made to the U.S.; connections are available 24 hours a day via London and Paris and are usually satisfactory. Automatic direct dialing to the U.S. and Canada is available at $2.25 a minute.

Health–The existence of TB and intestinal parasites constitutes a certain health hazard, and Americans should use common sense in selecting places to eat.

Care should be observed in drinking water in rural areas; bottled soda or beer are recommended alternatives. Milk from local sources should not be used unless boiled.

Athens Time–Two hours ahead of Greenwich mean time.

ratio of imports over exports was almost 2:1. However, invisible receipts from the United States more than offset the trade deficit resulting in a bilateral balance on current account that is favorable to Greece.

On October 19, 1973, the Greek drachma was revalued by 10 percent against all foreign currencies.

Economic Development

Though remarkable gains in economic recovery have been made from the destruction of World War II and its aftermath, Greek economic progress must continue in anticipation of Greece's becoming a full member of the Common Market in 1984.

The Five-Year Plan for 1968-72 was primarily concerned with modernizing the Greek economy by means of structural adjustments which emphasized improved productivity in the industrial sector and coordination of public and private investment. Generally, the quantitative goals of the Plan were met or exceeded except for the targets set for price stability, agricultural income, and the international merchandise trade.

The principles of the 1973-77 Five-Year Plan represent a continuation of the program of the previous 5-year period. The Plan calls for an annual real growth rate of 8 percent and the continued encouragement of private and public investment. In particular, merchant shipping, secondary production, tourism, and agriculture are to be emphasized. Other goals incorporated into the Plan include a general rise in the standard of living and an increase and expansion of social services.

U.S. Assistance

U.S. military and economic aid to Greece from 1946 to 1972 amounted to more than $3.9 billion. These funds helped Greece to recover from almost 10 years of war and occupation and to establish the base for sustained economic growth. Grant economic aid to Greece was discontinued at the end of FY 1962. Since then Greece has received some further economic assistance in the form of Export-Import Bank loans and sales of U.S. surplus agricultural commodities. Military assistance to Greece, beginning in 1947, continued under arrangements growing out of the North Atlantic Treaty Organization (NATO) in which Greece became a member in 1952. The Greek Government decided to forego further U.S. grant military assistance as of January 1, 1973, but is continuing to make use of foreign military sales credits. Through FY 1973, grant military assistance to Greece totaled $1.6 billion, and foreign military sales credits were about $150 million.

European Economic Community (EEC)

The agreement providing for association of Greece with the European Economic Community (the "Common Market") was signed on July 9, 1961, and went into effect in November 1962. In addition to providing Greece with a 5-year credit of $125 million by the European Investment Bank, the agreement calls for the formation of a customs union between Greece and the Common Market. During this period Greek products are admitted to the EEC at steadily reduced tariff rates as Greece gradually reduces its tariffs on manufactured goods imported from the Common Market, so that in 1984 Greek and EEC tariffs on such goods will be in complete alignment.

Because of political developments in Greece, $55 million of the European Investment Bank credit of $125 million have been frozen. Although the EEC appears to have met all the requirements of the association agreement, some special exemptions granted to Greek agricultural products have lapsed.

Association with the EEC has provided stimulus to the Greek economy by offering foreign investors access to

The Acropolis

the Common Market and by challenging Greek agriculture and industry to reach a level of technological development necessary to compete in West European markets within the 22-year transition period.

Defense Burden

Greece now spends about 25 percent of its regular budget (about 5 percent of its GNP) on defense. Greek authorities have pointed out that this is a greater burden than is borne by many other NATO members and that Greece also has more men under arms in ratio to total population than most of the other members of the Alliance.

FOREIGN RELATIONS

Communist Countries

Diplomatic relations with Bulgaria, severed for 25 years, were fully restored in 1965 with significant economic and cultural agreements. Bulgaria formally renounced its claim on Greek Thrace and Macedonia, which had been an obstacle to Greek-Bulgarian cooperation in the Balkans since World War I.

Greece restored contact with Albania in May 1971 and established diplomatic relations with the German Democratic Republic 2 years later, so that Greece now maintains diplomatic relations with all the Communist states in Europe.

Relations with the People's Republic of China were established in 1972.

Greece has increased its level of trade with the Communist countries, as well as improved its political relations with them. Trade relations are carried out through clearing accounts under bilateral agreements.

The Soviet Union and other Communist countries continue to attempt to weaken Greek ties with the West. Propaganda from these countries, particularly through a clandestine radio (Voice of Truth), has been aimed especially at NATO and has sought to undermine Greek confidence in the United States and their other Western allies.

Middle East Policy

Greece has a special interest in the Middle East arising from still sizable

READING LIST

These titles are provided as a general indication of the material currently being published on this country; the Department of State does not endorse the specific views in unofficial publications as representing the position of the U.S. Government.

Campbell, John, and Philip Sherrard. *Modern Greece*. London: Benn, 1968.

Carey, Andrew and Jane. *The Web of Modern Greek Politics*. New York: Columbia University Press, 1968.

Couloumbis, Theodore A. *Greek Political Reaction to American and NATO Influences*. New Haven: Yale University Press, 1966.

Durrell, Lawrence. *Prospero's Cell and Reflections on a Marine Venus.*

Fermor, Patrick Lee. *Roumeli*. London: Murray, 1966; *Mani*. London: Murray.

Hamilton, Edith. *The Greek Way to Western Civilization*. New York: Mentor, 1948.

Holden, David. *Greece Without Columns*. London: Faber, 1972.

Kousoulas, Dimitrios G. *Revolution and Defeat, the Story of the Greek Communist Party*. London: Oxford Univ. Press, 1965.

Kubly, Herbert. *Gods and Heroes*. New York: Doubleday, 1971.

Lancaster, Osborne. *Classical Landscape with Figures*. London: Thames, 1954.

Legg, Keith R. *Politics in Modern Greece*. Stanford University Press, 1969.

McNeill, William H. *Greece, American Aid in Action 1947-56*. New York: the 20th Century Fund, 1957.

Miller, Henry. *The Colossus of Maroussi*. London: Secker and Warburg, 1941.

O'Ballance, Edgar. *The Greek Civil War, 1944-1949*. New York: Praeger, 1966.

Sanders, Irwin T. *Rainbow in the Rock*. Cambridge: Harvard University Press, 1962.

Stockton, Bayard. *Phoenix with a Bayonet*. Ann Arbor: Georgetown Publications, 1971.

Vasiliev, A. A. *History of the Byzantine Empire*. Madison: University of Wisconsin Press, 1956.

Wolff, Robert Lee. *The Balkans in Our Time*. Cambridge: Harvard University Press, 1956.

Woodhouse, C. M. *The Greek War of Independence*. London: Hutchison's University Library, 1952.

Woodhouse, C. M. *The Story of Modern Greece*. London: Faber and Faber, 1968.

Xydis, Steven G. *Greece and the Great Powers, 1944-1947*. Thessaloniki: Inst. Balkan Studies, 1963.

Young, Stephen. *Greek Passion*. London: Dent & Sons, 1969.

The following publications are available from the Superintendent of Documents, U.S. Government Printing Office, Washington, D.C. 20402:

Department of Commerce. *Basic Data on the Economy of Greece*. OBR-72-014. May 1972.

Department of Commerce. *Foreign Trade Regulations of Greece*. OBR-69-25. June 1969.

Department of Commerce. *Selling in Greece*. OBR-73-30. July 1973.

Department of Commerce. *Market Factors in Greece*. OBR-72-044. August 1972.

Department of State. "NATO and the Defense of Europe." No. 2 in *Issues in United States Foreign Policy* Series. Publication 8476. 1970.

Area Handbook for Greece. Foreign Area Studies. American University, 1970.

Greece, Spain and the Southern NATO Strategy. Hearings before the Subcommittee on Europe, of the Committee on Foreign Affairs, House of Representatives, 1971.

Political and Strategic Implications of Homeporting in Greece. Joint Hearings before the Subcommittee on Europe and the Subcommittee on the Near East and the Committee on Foreign Affairs, House of Representatives, 1972.

Greek communities in some Arab states and the influence of the Eastern Orthodox Church in the area. It has attempted quietly to improve on its good relations and to use its influence to promote understanding with other countries in the Middle East. Greece maintains cordial relations with the Arab states as well as with Israel.

Relations between Greece and Turkey, both members of NATO, deteriorated in 1955, 1963, and in late 1967 because of the Cyprus question. United Nations efforts, with which the United States has been associated, have encouraged the continuance of intercommunal talks designed to seek solutions to the problems between the Greek and Turkish segments of the island's population. The association of Greece and Turkey with the intercommunal talks and an awareness in both countries of their common interest in a just settlement has led to markedly improved relations between them.

Europe

Greece's relations with some of its European treaty partners have suffered since the coup of 1967. Disapproval toward developments in the Greek domestic political situation led to the withdrawal of Greece from the Council of Europe in December 1969.

North Atlantic Treaty Organization

The United States led the way to Greek membership in NATO in 1952. Since then, participation in the Alliance has remained one of the keystones of Greek foreign policy. All Greek governments since 1952, recognizing the relationship between Greek interests and the purposes of the Alliance, have maintained a firm commitment to NATO. Greece obtains important security benefits from its participation in NATO, and NATO enjoys access to facilities in Greece which are important to the deterrent posture of the Alliance.

U.S. POLICY

The United States wishes to maintain the strong bonds of friendship that have historically existed between the two countries and to preserve the important mutual security relationship that has developed between Greece and the United States. We have always recognized that long-term stability in Greece and, therefore, the long-term protection of our mutual security interests are best served by a political system that provides governments that enjoy broad popular support. For this reason, we have consistently encouraged the Greek Government to restore representative rule.

The U.S. military assistance program for Greece was designed to enable Greece to carry out its NATO defense obligations. A reduction of the program with a gradual shift from grant aid to foreign military sales credits has corresponded to the ability of Greece's growing economy to finance larger portions of the country's defense requirements.

In January 1973 a technical agreement was signed between the Greek and U.S. Navies permitting the homeporting of an element of the Sixth Fleet in the Athens area. Six U.S. destroyers have been homeported in Greece, and dependents of their crews are now residing in Athens. About 2,000 Navy men and 1,200 dependents are involved, bringing the number of U.S. Government employees and dependents in Greece to about 11,000. Of the total more than 90 percent are U.S. military personnel and their families.

U.S. military personnel, except for the Joint U.S. Military Aid Group, Greece (JUSMAGG), are subject to Greek civil and military jurisdiction. Under a Status of Forces Agreement of September 1956, Greece waives primary right to criminal jurisdiction except in those cases which it considers of "particular importance."

Principal U.S. Officials

Ambassador–Henry J. Tasca
Deputy Chief of Mission–Robert M. Brandin
Counselor for Political Affairs–Elizabeth Ann Brown
Counselor for Economic Affairs–L. Milner Dunn
Counselor for Administrative Affairs–Zachary P. Geaneas
Consul General–Charles S. Kennedy, Jr.
Public Affairs Officer–Edward Alexander
Cultural Affairs Officer–Leo LeClair
Commander, Military Aid Mission Staff–Major General Charles W. Ryder
Defense Attaché–Colonel James R. French
Army Attaché–Colonel S. P. Rogers
Navy Attaché–Captain George F. Smith
Consul General at Thessaloniki–Edward T. Brennan

The U.S. Embassy in Greece is located at 91 Queen Sophia Avenue, Athens. The Consulate General is at 59 King Constantine Street, Thessaloniki.

DEPARTMENT OF STATE PUBLICATION 8198
Revised November 1973

APPENDIX LL

GREECE

STRENGTH OF THE COMMUNIST PARTY ORGANIZATION—1973

SEE PAGE 142

[FROM: World Strength of the Communist Party Organizations—1973. Washington, Department of State, Bureau of Intelligence and Research, 1973.]

GREECE

National Political Status: A series of developments changed Greece's political status twice in 1973. Greece became a republic on June 1, 1973, when Prime Minister George Papadopoulos abolished the monarchy and declared himself President. Papadopoulos, who had headed the government since the April 1967 coup, had also been serving as regent in the absence of exiled King Constantine. A plebiscite on July 29 ratified the constitutional changes establishing the republic and soon thereafter Papadopoulos appointed a Prime Minister to prepare the country for parliamentary elections in 1974. (Parliament had been suspended since the *coup d'etat* of April 21, 1967.)

When students and workers began to riot, however, the army intervened, not only to suppress the rioters but also to conduct a coup on November 25. Army officers under Brig. Gen. Dimitrios Ioannides ousted Papadopoulos and installed Gen. Faidon Gizikes as President with a civilian cabinet headed by Adamandios Androutsopoulos. Elections, however, have been postponed indefinitely.

Communist Party Membership: 28,000 (estimate)

Leading Party Figures and Positions:

FLORAKIS, Harilaos - Secretary-General of Moscow-supported faction of the Greek Communist Party (KKE)

DRAKOPOULOS, Kharalambos)
PARTSALIDES, Dimitrios) leaders of the dissident Communist faction

Principal Publications:

Rizopastis - journal published abroad and periodically circulated in Greece clandestinely

Avghi - EDA (United Democratic Left) paper, now underground, formerly published by Dimitrios Partsalides, leader of Communist opposition faction

Areas of Communist Activity: Since the April 1967 *coup d'etat* all political parties have been dissolved. The EDA, which served as a legal political front for the Greek Communists for nearly 18 years, survived underground in 1973, but remained in a relatively weak, disorganized state. It continued active and vocal among Greek émigrés abroad, particularly in the main metropolitan centers of Europe where it has many small groups which enjoy the financial support of the Soviet Union and of the Communist parties of Eastern Europe.

In Greece, Communists attempt to exploit social inequalities, unequal distribution of national income, the alleged loss of national freedom within the NATO framework, and, often in cooperation with democratic political forces, the absence of free political expression. Communists cooperated in the student demonstrations of November 1973, and Communist-inspired slogans were much in evidence, but their participation fell short of dominating the demonstrations.

Personal and doctrinal differences led to a split in the Greek Communist Party (KKE) in February 1968, with Moscow backing the old-line KKE, and another faction attempting to form a Communist party independent of Soviet control. In December 1972 the long-time head of the Moscow-backed KKE, Konstantinos Koligiannis, was replaced by Harilaos Florakis in an apparent move to improve chances for unification. This leadership change had at least the tacit support of Moscow; the CPSU has long shown concern over the divisions in the Greek CP and has taken a hand in previous efforts at reconciliation. The removal of Koligiannis has not thus far bridged the differences.

The split at home is mirrored in the Greek Communist groups abroad; they suffered a serious setback in 1972 when Mikis Theodorakis publicly broke with the party. Theodorakis, best known as a Greek composer, had also been one of the most illustrious members of the KKE.

Deprived of EDA, their recognized political front, both factions of the KKE endeavored to create new front organizations based on interest groups. Several of these fronts are organized into the Patriotic Anti-Dictatorship Front (PAM), which is also split into Moscow-backed and dissident factions. In addition, there are a number of relatively small radical leftist groups that do not adhere to either of the KKE factions.

APPENDIX MM
ICELAND
ARMED FORCES AND MILITARY POWER

[Reprinted with permission from: The Almanac of World Military Power, by Col. T. N. Dupuy, U.S. Army, Ret., Col. John A. C. Andrews, U.S. Air Force, Ret., and Grace P. Hayes. 3rd ed. Dunn Loring, Va., T. N. Dupuy Associates, 1974.]

ICELAND

Lydveldid Island
Republic of Iceland

POWER POTENTIAL STATISTICS

Area: 39,768 square miles
Population: 213,000
Total Active Armed Forces: None
Gross National Product: $977.6 million ($4,684 per capita)
Electric Power Output: 1.6 billion kwh
Merchant Fleet: 288 ships; 125,912 gross tons
Civil Air Fleet: 7 jet, 4 turboprop, 4 piston transports

POLITICO-MILITARY POLICIES AND POSTURE

A member of NATO, Iceland maintains no military forces, although there is an internal security police force of about 500 men, and a Coast Guard of five ships and 120 men. Iceland provides its NATO allies with air and radar base sites on its territory; there are 3,300 US Air Force and Navy personnel in Iceland, stationed at the NATO air base of Keflavik. In March 1974 Iceland proposed their removal by mid-1976. The Icelandic government extended its coastal limits for fishing from 12 miles to 50 on September 1, 1972, evoking sharp protests from the governments of Great Britain and West Germany. A "cod war" developed in 1973 as fishermen from both countries ignored the limits. Great Britain responded to harassment by Icelandic patrol craft by sending an unarmed sea-going tug to the area. After several reported incidents between British trawlers and Icelandic gunboats, Britain sent three frigates to the area in May 1973. Incidents continued, and attempts at negotiation through the UN and NATO accomplished little. In October, following an ultimatum by Iceland, Great Britain agreed to withdraw its warships beyond the 50-mile zone and an agreement was reached limiting the catch and the number of ships that could fish in areas close to Iceland, pending resolution of the dispute by the International Court of Justice. In mid-1974 that court reached a decision favoring Britain, but Iceland has threatened not to comply.

Iceland is a member of the UN and the Council of Europe.

APPENDIX NN
ICELAND
BACKGROUND NOTES

[Washington, Department of State, April 1974 (Publication 8227).]

background notes

Iceland

department of state * april 1974

OFFICIAL NAME: Republic of Iceland

GEOGRAPHY

Iceland is an island in the North Atlantic Ocean east of Greenland and immediately south of the Arctic Circle. It is approximately 2,600 air miles from New York and 520 miles from Scotland.

Almost 75 percent of Iceland's land area, which is of recent volcanic origin, consists of glaciers, lakes, a mountainous lava desert (highest elevation 6,590 feet above sea level), and other wasteland, with the remainder used for cultivation or grazing. The inhabited areas are on the coast, particularly in the southwest.

Due to the moderating influence of the Gulf Stream, the climate is characterized by damp, cool summers (Reykjavík: July average 52° F.) and relatively mild but extremely windy winters (Reykjavík: January average 30° F.).

PEOPLE

Most Icelanders are descendants of Norwegian settlers and Celts from the British Isles. The population today is remarkably homogeneous, and 85 percent of Icelanders live in urban areas. The Icelandic language is closest of the Nordic languages to the Old Norse language and has remained relatively unchanged since the 12th century. Iceland is the most literate nation in the world with literacy estimated at 99.9 percent.

About 98 percent of the population belongs to the state church, the Evangelical Lutheran Church. However, there is complete religious liberty; and other Protestant and Roman Catholic congregations are present.

HISTORY

Iceland was settled in the late 9th and early 10th centuries principally by Norwegians. In 930 the ruling chiefs of Iceland established a republican constitution and an assembly called the *Althing*—the oldest parliament in the world. Iceland remained independent until 1262 when the Norwegian King succeeded in extending his sovereignty to Iceland. It passed to Denmark late in the 14th century when Norway and Denmark were united under the Danish crown.

Early in the 19th century national consciousness revived in Iceland. The *Althing* had been abolished in 1800, but in 1843 it was reestablished as a

PROFILE

Geography

AREA: 39,709 sq. mi. (about the size of Kentucky). CAPITAL: Reykjavík (pop. 90,000). OTHER CITIES: Akureyri, Hafnarfjordur.

People

POPULATION: 213,000 (1973 est.). ANNUAL GROWTH RATE: 1.9%. DENSITY: 4 per sq. mi. LANGUAGE: Icelandic. LITERACY: 99.9%. RELIGION: Evangelical Lutheran. LIFE EXPECTANCY: 73 yrs.

Government

TYPE: Constitutional republic. DATE OF CONSTITUTION: 1874. INDEPENDENCE: Home rule—1903; Independent republic—1944.

POLITICAL SUBDIVISIONS: 16 Provinces.

BRANCHES: *Executive*—President (Chief of State), Prime Minister (Head of Government), Cabinet (6 Ministers). *Legislative*—bicameral parliament. *Judicial*—Supreme Court, District Courts, Special Courts.

POLITICAL PARTIES: Independence, Social Democratic, Progressive, Organization of Liberals and Leftists, People's Alliance.

SUFFRAGE: Universal adult (over 20).

FLAG: Red cross edged in white on a field of blue.

ECONOMY

GROSS NATIONAL PRODUCT (GNP): $997.6 million (1973 projected). GROWTH RATE: 4-5%. PER CAPITA INCOME: $4,697 (1973 projected).

AGRICULTURE: *Labor*—11%. *Products*—livestock, hay, fodder.

INDUSTRY: *Labor*—14%. *Products*—fishing.

NATURAL RESOURCES: Diatomite, fish, hydroelectric power.

TRADE: *Exports*—$289.3 million (1973): fish. *Partners*—U.S. 30%, U.K. and F.R.G. 24%. *Imports*—$353.9 million (1973): petroleum products, machinery, transportation equipment, fishing vessels and gear. *Partners*—Norway, F.R.G., Denmark.

OFFICIAL EXCHANGE RATE: Icelandic kronur 83.60 = US$1.

MEMBERSHIP IN INTERNATIONAL ORGANIZATIONS: Nordic Council, Council of Europe, U.N. and its specialized agencies, General Agreement on Tariffs and Trade (GATT).

consultative assembly. In 1874 the *Althing* obtained limited legislative authority, and a constitution was granted to Iceland. The constitution was revised in 1903 when home rule was granted, and the Danish Minister for Icelandic Affairs was made responsible to the *Althing.* An agreement was reached with Denmark in 1918 recognizing Iceland as a sovereign state united with Denmark under a common king. Iceland was granted its own flag, but Denmark retained control of Iceland's foreign affairs and defense.

The German occupation of Denmark in 1940 severed communications between Iceland and Denmark. In May 1940 Iceland was occupied by British military forces. In July 1941 responsibility for the defense of Iceland passed to the United States under the U.S.-Icelandic Defense Agreement. Following a plebiscite, the country was formally established as an independent republic on June 17, 1944. In October 1946 the Icelandic and U.S. Governments agreed to terminate U.S. responsibility for the defense of Iceland, but the United States retained certain rights at Keflavík. In 1949 Iceland became a charter member of the North Atlantic Treaty Organization (NATO). After the outbreak of hostilities in Korea in 1950 and pursuant to the request of NATO military authorities, the United States and Iceland agreed that the United States should be responsible for the defense of Iceland. This agreement, signed on May 5, 1951, is the authority for the U.S. military presence in Iceland. Iceland is the only NATO country with no military forces of its own.

GOVERNMENT

The government is a constitutional republic consisting of executive, legislative, and judicial branches.

The President (Chief of State) is elected to a 4-year term. His powers are limited. The Prime Minister (Head of Government) and the Cabinet exercise most executive functions.

The *Althing* (parliament) is composed of 60 members, normally elected every 4 years. After elections, the *Althing* divides itself into Upper (20 members) and Lower (40 members) Houses, but the two houses often meet together. Suffrage for presidential and parliamentary elections is universal (at age 20), and the electoral system combines direct and proportional representation.

The judiciary consists of the Supreme Court, District Courts, and various special courts. The Constitution protects the judiciary from infringements by the other two branches.

Principal Government Officials

President—Kristjan Eldjarn

Prime Minister; Minister of Justice and Ecclesiastical Affairs—Olafur Johannesson (Progressive)

Foreign Minister—Einar Agustsson (Progressive)

Minister of Finance and Agriculture—Halldor Sigurdsson (Progressive)

Minister of Education and Health and Social Security—Magnus Kjartansson (Labor Alliance)

Minister of Commerce and Fisheries—Ludvik Josefsson (Labor Alliance)

Ambassador to the U.S.—Haraldur Kroyer

Ambassador to the U.N.—Ingvi Ingvarsson

Iceland maintains an Embassy in the United States at 2022 Connecticut Ave., N.W., Washington, D.C. 20008.

POLITICAL CONDITIONS

Parliamentary elections were held on June 13, 1971. A loss of four seats caused the downfall of the coalition government of the *Independence* (conservative) and *Social Democratic* (moderate Socialist) *Parties* which had governed Iceland since 1959. A new government consisting of the former opposition parties was formed on July 14, 1971, after difficult negotiations. It is composed of the *Progressive Party* (supported by farmer, labor, and cooperative society groups), the *People's Alliance* (Communist-dominated), and the *Organization of Liberals and Leftists* (OLL), a non-Communist leftist party established in 1969. The election result reflected a shift of Social Democratic voters to the OLL and was a personal triumph for the party's founder, Hannibal Valdimarsson. The relative strengths of the other three political parties were changed little. In the last presidential election, June 1972, Dr. Kristjan Eldjarn was reelected unopposed.

REPRESENTATION IN THE ALTHING

	Elections		
	1963	1967	1971
Progressive	19	18	17
People's Alliance	9	10	10
Organization of Liberals and Leftists	–	–	5
Independence	24	23	22
Social Democratic	8	9	6

Icelanders depend heavily on fishing for their economic survival and have become increasingly alarmed by the depletion of fish stocks, allegedly caused by foreign vessels overfishing in waters close to Iceland. The present government, reflecting the will of the vast majority of Icelanders, extended the country's fisheries jurisdiction from 12 to 50 nautical miles from the coastlines on September 1, 1972. The government has also committed itself to improved wages and working conditions

READING LIST

Davis, Morris. *Iceland Extends Its Fisheries Limits.* Oslo: Universitetsforlaget, 1963.

Department of State. "NATO and the Defense of Europe." No. 2 in the *Issues in United States Foreign Policy* series. Pub. 8476. Discussion Guide, Pub. 8487. Washington, D.C.: U.S. Government Printing Office, 1969.

Gislason, Gylfi Th. *The Problem of Being an Icelander—Past, Present, and Future.* Translated by P. K. Karlsson. Reykjavik: Almenna bokafelagio, 1973.

Griffiths, John C. *Modern Iceland.* New York: Praeger, 1969.

Gröndal, Benedikt. *Iceland: From Neutrality to NATO Membership.* Oslo: Universitetsforlaget, 1971.

Johnson, Skuli, ed. *Iceland's Thousand Years.* Winnipeg, 1945.

and to more effective industrial development planning.

ECONOMY

The fishing industry is Iceland's primary national resource and in most years has made possible a high standard of living. About 14 percent of the population depend on fishing and fish processing for a livelihood, 11 percent on agriculture, and almost 30 percent on manufacturing and construction. Processed fish and fish products comprise more than 70 percent of Iceland's exports, and the United States is the predominant overseas market.

In 1973, 27 percent of Iceland's exports went to the United States. The United Kingdom and the Federal Republic of Germany were the next most important customers and together accounted for 24 percent of Iceland's exports. The other European Free Trade Association (EFTA) and European Economic Community (EEC) countries and the Soviet Union were smaller but significant purchasers of Icelandic goods.

Principal imported items are petroleum products, machinery, transportation equipment, and fishing vessels and gear. During the last few years the U.S. share of Iceland's imports has ranged from 7 to 15 percent. The principal products of U.S. origin sold to Iceland have been nonelectrical machinery, tobacco, grains and cereals, and transportation equipment. Trade with the U.S.S.R. and Eastern Europe in 1973 accounted for 8.6 percent of Iceland's exports and 8.9 percent of its imports.

Iceland has few proven mineral resources, although deposits of diatomite (skeletal algae) are being developed and perlite (volcanic glass) explored. The hydroelectric power potential is abundant and is being harnessed gradually. The Alusuisso aluminum smelter near Reykjavík has an annual capacity of 77,000 tons. Extraction of chemicals from seawater and the generation of power from geothermal sources are being studied for possible development. A ferro alloy plant is also under consideration for completion in 1976.

The Icelandic economy has undergone a tremendous expansion and experienced far-reaching changes since World War II. The gross national product (GNP) rose by an annual average of about 4.5 percent in real terms during the decade 1961-70. Iceland's per capita income is higher than the average for all of Europe.

There are no railroads in Iceland. Organized roadbuilding did not begin until about 1900. The present national road system connecting most of the population centers is largely in the coastal areas and consists of about 6,000 miles of dirt and gravel roads, and some 60 miles of hard surface road. There are regular air and sea services between Reykjavík and the other main urban centers. In addition, Iceland is connected with Europe and North America by regularly scheduled airlines.

Iceland became a full EFTA member on March 1, 1970 and entered into a free-trade agreement with the EEC in 1973.

FOREIGN RELATIONS

Iceland wishes to maintain and strengthen its economic and political independence and a balanced foreign trade without becoming unduly involved in controversies among other nations. While Iceland maintains diplomatic and commercial relations with the leading nations of the East and West, its ties with the other Nordic nations and with the United States are especially close. Iceland plans to continue its active participation in NATO under existing world conditions, although the People's Alliance Party opposes NATO membership.

U.S.-ICELAND RELATIONS

U.S. policy is aimed at maintaining the present cordial, cooperative relations with Iceland, both as a NATO ally and as a friend interested in the commonly shared objectives of establishing world peace and freedom and encouraging worldwide economic and social development.

In 1953 and 1956 the question of whether U.S. defense forces stationed at Keflavík under NATO auspices should be requested to withdraw from Iceland was among the principal issues in public debate. The present government raised this matter again in 1973 and negotiations regarding the future of the Defense Force were in progress in March 1974.

Principal U.S. Officials

Ambassador–Frederick Irving
Deputy Chief of Mission–Doyle V. Martin
Political Officer–Joseph Becelia
Economic Officer–Dennis C. Goodman
Administrative Officer–Stefan C. Nadzo
Commander, Iceland Defense Force–Rear Adm. Samuel M. Cooley, Jr., USN

The U.S. Embassy in Iceland is located at Laufasvegur 21, Reykjavík.

Travel Notes

Clothing–**The climate in Iceland is similar to that on the northwest coast of the United States. Wool or other warm clothing is worn year-round.**

Telecommunications–**Telephone and telegraph service is state-owned and is available to all parts of Iceland and principal points throughout the world.**

Transportation–**Iceland has no railroads or streetcars. Local taxi and bus services are safe and efficient, but taxi fares are higher than on the U.S. east coast. Most roads outside the immediate vicinity of Reykjavík are dirt or gravel and are only poor to fair quality. One can rent cars or four-wheel-drive vehicles.**

Community Health–**There are no endemic health problems in Iceland. Adequate medical facilities are found in the major cities.**

DEPARTMENT OF STATE PUBLICATION 8227
Revised April 1974

APPENDIX OO

ICELAND

STRENGTH OF THE COMMUNIST PARTY ORGANIZATION—1973

[FROM: World Strength of the Communist Party Organizations—1973. Washington, Department of State, Bureau of Intelligence and Research, 1973.]

ICELAND

National Political Status: Date of last election - June 13, 1971.

Communist: People's Alliance (PA) - 18,055 votes (17.47%), 10 seats (16.7%)

Non-Communist Left: Organization of Liberals and Leftists - 9,445 votes (9.14%), 5 seats (8.3%)
Social Democratic Party - 11,020 votes (10.67%), 6 seats (10.0%)

Non-Socialist Parties: Progressive Party - 26,641 votes (25.78%), 17 seats (28.3%)
Independence Party - 38,169 votes (36.94%), 22 seats (36.7%)

Total: 103,330 votes, 60 seats

Communist Party Membership: 2,000-2,500 (estimate)

Leading Party Figures and Positions:
ARNALDS, Ragnar - Chairman
JOSEFSSON, Ludvik - Member of Political Committee and Cabinet Minister
KJARTANSSON, Magnus - Member of Political Committee and Cabinet Minister

Principal Publications:
Thjodviljinn - daily newspaper
Ny Utsyn - biweekly journal

Areas of Communist Activity: During 1973 the Communist-dominated People's Alliance (*Altydubandalagid, PA*)--a disparate amalgam of laborers, radical students, disgruntled Social Democrats, ardent nationalists, and Marxist ideologues--remained small in membership but large in influence. Members number an estimated 2,000-2,500 in a total population of 207,300.

The PA is one of the few Communist parties in the world to participate in a democratically elected government. It has polled between 12 percent and 20 percent of Iceland's popular vote since World War II. It received 17.1 percent of the vote at the last national election, held in June 1971, and won 10 of the 60 seats in the *Althing* (Parliament). Together with the Progressive Party (PP) and the Organization of Liberals and Leftists (OLL), the PA formed a center-left coalition which has been in power since July 14, 1971. Two Communists--Ludvik Josefsson and Magnus Kjartansson--played key roles in Prime Minister Olafur Johannesson's seven-man cabinet.

The settlement of the Icelandic-U.K. fishing dispute in November 1973 deprived the People's Alliance of one of its most popular stands--the aggressive defense of the preservation of Icelandic fishing rights. During the dispute with Britain, which resulted from an extension of Iceland's fishing limits from 12 to 50 miles, the PA adopted the motto, "We shall not negotiate with the British, we shall defeat them." In September, when tensions were at their highest following an incident at sea which led indirectly to the death of an Icelandic seaman, the Board of the People's Alliance adopted a resolution which urged the Icelandic Government to demand, *inter alia*, the recall of the British Ambassador in Reykjavik, the closing down of the Icelandic mission to NATO, and an end to Icelandic participation in that organization.

The PA continued to play upon traditional Icelandic isolationism and xenophobia by espousing the ouster of the U.S.-manned Icelandic Defense Force (IDF). In June the Johannesson government invoked Article VII of the 1951 Defense Agreement and set in motion negotiations with the United States concerning the future of the IDF. As 1973 drew to a close without settlement of the issue, the People's Alliance spokesman on defense matters, Minister of Industries Magnus Kjartansson, urged the government to make a decision "on an important part of the coalition agreement which has not been handled decisively until now, i.e., the departure of the Defense Force from Keflavik." Kjartansson supported a plan by which the government "should develop a position on the Base collectively, and present this position to the United States side as an ultimatum which, if not approved, would lead to a unilateral termination of the defense agreement" (*Thjodviljinn*, December 22, 1973). The PA consistently uses this tactic.

Domestically, the PA urged basic changes in the country's economic system--with particular emphasis on tax reform and guaranteed full employment On the labor front, PA member Snorri Jonsson became Chairman of the Icelandic Federation of Labor, and the PA continued to play an important role in many unions.

Internationally, the PA espoused a neutral stance in the Sino-Soviet dispute and maintained an attitude of aloofness regarding activities and issues in the world Communist movement. The PA maintains no relations with the CPSU, and Chairman Ragnar Arnalds stated in an interview that his party was more in tune with Scandinavian Social Democratic parties than with Communists in those countries (*Die Welt*, December 27, 1973).

APPENDIX PP

ITALY

ARMED FORCES AND MILITARY POWER

SEE PAGE 142

[Reprinted with permission from: The Almanac of World Military Power, by Col. T. N. Dupuy, U.S. Army, Ret., Col. John A. C. Andrews, U.S. Air Force, Ret., and Grace P. Hayes. 3rd ed. Dunn Loring, Va., T. N. Dupuy Associates, 1974.]

ITALY

Repubblica Italiana
Italian Republic

POWER POTENTIAL STATISTICS

Area: 116,315 square miles
Population: 54,600,000
Total Active Armed Forces: 503,000 (includes 86,000 Carabinieri; 0.92% population)
Gross National Product: $136.6 billion ($2,502 per capita)
Annual Military Expenditures: $3.87 billion (2.83% GNP)
Steel and Iron Production: 26.2 million metric tons
Fuel Production: Coal: 1.6 million metric tons
Crude Oil: 1.15 million metric tons
Refined Petroleum Products: 129.5 million metric tons
Electric Power Output: 126 billion kwh
Merchant Fleet: 1,690 ships; 8.14 million gross tons
Civil Air Fleet: 94 jet, 23 turboprop, 5 piston transports

DEFENSE STRUCTURE

Italy has a parliamentary republican government; the President is the nominal commander of the armed forces. Actual civilian control of the armed forces is exercised by the Cabinet, through the Minister of Defense, who in turn is advised by a Defense Committee, consisting of the Chief of the Defense Staff, the Secretary of State for Defense, and the chiefs of staff of the three services.

POLITICO-MILITARY POLICY

Since its emergence as a great power in the late nineteenth century, Italy has been a member of one of the major European military alliances, but prior to World War II Italian policy was largely opportunistic, with no fixed ideological or regional orientation or commitment. Since World War II, despite the strong political trend toward socialism, and the influence of the most powerful communist party in Western Europe, Italy has aligned itself consistently with the Western European democratic powers, and was a charter member of NATO.

The armed forces of Italy are raised and maintained through conscription. For the Army and the Air Force the term of conscript service is 15 months; for the Navy it is 24 months.

STRATEGIC PROBLEMS

Italy's relatively large population is densely concentrated in the narrow coastal lowlands and river valleys of this mountainous peninsula. Thus its population and industrial centers are particularly vulnerable to air attack, and the homeland of the originator of the concept of modern strategic air bombardment (Giulio Douhet) is perhaps more susceptible to this controversial form of warfare than any other major power.

As demonstrated in World War II, Italy's elongated coast line is vulnerable to hostile amphibious operations. This vulnerability is to some extent offset by the mountain barrier of the Alps in the north, and the central spine of the Apennines, which create effective obstacles to military movement in all directions in the Italian peninsula.

There are three principal and traditional overland invasion routes across the Alpine barrier: from France along the Mediterranean coast and across the Maritime Alps; from Germany and Austria through the Brenner Pass; and from Yugoslavia through the Ljubljana Gap and the Julian Alps. There are a number of other passes which have been successfully exploited by the innumerable invasion forces that have been attracted to Italy through the course of history.

There is an irredentist dispute with Yugoslavia involving the Istrian Peninsula and the major Italian city of Trieste and the Yugoslav city of Rijeka (Fiume), where a mixed population (including about 200,000 Slavs) inhabiting a strategic invasion route region has prompted dispute and hostility in the past, and creates serious defense and internal security problems for Italy.

Italy's greatest internal security problem is the very large Communist Party, comprising approximately 25 percent of the electorate. Italy and its NATO allies are forced to conclude that a substantial number of these would provide direct or indirect support to a communist bloc enemy in the event of hostilities.

MILITARY ASSISTANCE

A bilateral military assistance alliance with the United States has greatly facilitated the equipping of the relatively large Italian armed forces. US military assistance totalled nearly $2.3 billion from 1950 to 1967. There is a US Military Advisory Group of about 35 still in Italy. Partly as a result of the off-shore procurement policies of the United States, and partly through Italian and joint allied research and development projects, Italian industry has been greatly benefitted, and has become a major supplier of American and Italian-designed weapons within the NATO alliance.

ALLIANCES

Italy is a UN member and is one of the four major contributors of military forces to the NATO alliance; Italian forces form essentially the entire force structure of Allied Forces, Southern Europe. Within the NATO alliance the United States maintains in Italy a small combat force headquarters, and the necessary logistical support elements: the South European Task Force, or SETAF. The principal mission of SETAF is to provide nuclear artillery and missile support to Allied Forces, Southern Europe, in Italy. In 1973 the United States opened a submarine base on La Maddalena Island, north of Sardinia.

ARMY

Personnel: 306,500

Organization:

- 2 armored divisions* and 1 independent calvalry brigade* with M-47, M-60 and Leopard tanks
- 5 infantry divisions*
- 4 independent infantry brigades
- 5 alpine brigades
- 1 parachute brigade
- 1 amphibious regiment
- 1 SSM brigade* (including 4 battalions with Honest John)
- 4 SAM battalions* with Hawk

*Assigned to NATO

Major Equipment Inventory:

- 1,200 medium tanks (800 M-47, 200 M-60, 200 Leopard)
- 3,300 M-113 APCs
- self-propelled guns (M-7 65mm, M-109 155mm, M-36 170mm, M-107 175mm, M-55 203mm)
- howitzers (105mm, 120mm, 155mm, 105mm pack)
- antitank guided missiles (Mosquito, Cobra, SS-11)
- SSM (Honest John)
- SAM (Hawk)

On order: TOW, 26 CH-47

Army Aviation:

- 220 aircraft (60 L-21, 60 L-19, 100 SM-1019 fixed wing)
- 260 helicopters (50 AB-47, 50 AB-204, 50 AB-205, 84 AB-206, 26 CH-47C)

Reserves: About 700,000 trained reservists are available to bring active units to full combat strength, to create new units, or to act as replacements.

NAVY

Personnel: 41,000 (including Air Arm and Marines)

Major Units:

- 9 submarines (SS)
- 3 GM cruisers with Terrier SAM and ASW helicopters (one with ASROC ASW missiles; CLG)
- 3 GM destroyers with Tartar SAM (DDG)
- 5 destroyers (DD)
- 10 destroyer escorts (DE)
- 8 coastal escorts (PF)
- 9 fast patrol boats (PT)
- 5 motor gunboats (PG)
- 4 ocean minesweepers (MSO)
- 37 coastal minesweepers (MSC)
- 20 inshore minesweepers (MSI)
- 2 amphibious transport ships (AKA)
- 2 landing ships tank (LST)

· 1 marine infantry battalion

Naval Aviation:

2 squadrons with 30 S-2 aircraft
1 squadron with 18 Atlantic
60 ASW helicopters (24 AB-204 and 12 A-106 embarked; 24 SH-3D shore based)

Principal Naval Bases: Spezia, Naples, Taranto, Ancona, Brindisi, Genoa, Leghorn, Augusta, Venice

Reserves: 140,000 men available for rapid mobilization.

AIR FORCE

Personnel: 69,500

Organization:

6 air regions: headquarters at Rome, Milan, Bari, Padua, Sicily, Sardinia
2 fighter-bomber squadrons* (F-104G)
2 fighter-bomber squadrons* (F-104S)
2 fighter-bomber squadrons* (G-91Y)
3 light-attack/reconnaissance squadrons* (G-91R)
1 AWX fighter-interceptor squadron* (F-86K)
5 AWX fighter-interceptor squadrons* (F-104S)
3 fighter-reconnaissance squadrons (RF-104G, RF-84F)
3 transport squadrons* (C-119, C-130E; C-119 to be replaced by FIAT G-222)
2 transport squadrons (PD-808, Convair 440, DC-6)
2 SAR squadrons (HU-16, AB-204 helicopters)
12 Nike-Hercules SAM groups*

Major Aircraft Types:

366 combat aircraft
- 150 fighter-bombers (F-104, G-91)
- 54 G-91 light attack/reconnaissance aircraft
- 90 F-104 AWX fighter-interceptors
- 18 F-86K AWX fighter-interceptors
- 54 fighter reconnaissance aircraft (RF-104, RF-84F)

742 other aircraft
- 106 transports (34 C-130, 40 C-119, 32 G-222)
- 38 liaison/transports (PD-808, Convair 440, DC-6, P-166)
- 440 miscellaneous trainers/support (MB-326, G-91, TF-104, P-148, P-166)
- 158 helicopters (60 AB-204, 90 AB-205, 2 AB-206, 6 AB-47)

*Assigned to NATO

On Order: 20 Agusta S-61B to replace HU-16; 40 F-104

Principal Air Bases: Vigna de Valle, Cageari, Taranto, Milan, Augusta, Grottaligia, Amendola, Alghero, Grossetto, Brindisi, Bari, Ciampino, Licce, Latina, Liriate, Foggia, Raisi, Genoa, Cameri, Pisa, Catania, Albenga

PARAMILITARY

There is an 86,000-man *Carabinieri*. This superbly trained force performs internal security, frontier guard, and military police duties. Because of the insurgency potential in Italy, the *Carabinieri* should not be considered as normally available to reinforce the Army; however, as demonstrated in World War II, the combat potentialities of this corps are probably superior to any comparable number of Army infantry troops. There are 30,000 other security personnel.

APPENDIX QQ
ITALY
BACKGROUND NOTES
SEE PAGE 142

[Washington, Department of State, April 1973 (Publication 7861).]

DEPARTMENT OF STATE

APRIL 1973

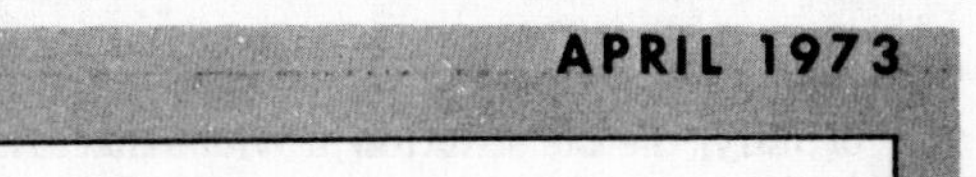

ITALY

BACKGROUND NOTES

Population: 54.5 million (1972 est.)
Capital: Rome

Flag: Three vertical bands—green, white, and red. A variation of the French revolutionary flag, it flew over Italy during the Napoleonic period and was later adopted by the country. The colors symbolize democracy, independence, and unity.

GEOGRAPHY

Italy is a 700-mile-long peninsula extending into the heart of the Mediterranean Sea. With an area of 116,303 square miles, it is nearly the size of Georgia and Florida combined. On the west and south it includes the large islands of Sardinia and Sicily, Pantelleria, and the Eolian (Lipari) group. Throughout history, Italy's position on the main routes between Europe, Africa, and the Near and Far East has given it great political, economic, and strategic importance. The peninsula is 43 miles from Albania, and Sicily is 90 miles from mainland Africa.

Except for the Po Valley area in the north, the heel of "the boot" in the south, and small coastal areas, Italy is rugged and mountainous. The climate is generally mild and "Mediterranean," but there are wide variations. Sicily and the south are comparable to southern California, though warmer on the average, whereas the Alps and Dolomites in the north have a climate similar to that of our Mountain States.

PEOPLE

With a population of about 54.5 million, Italy has the fifth highest density in Europe—some 469 persons per square mile—after Malta (2,657), Belgium (822), Netherlands (819), and West Germany (636). The 0.6 rate of population growth—about 300,000 annually—is somewhat lower than in the United States. Minority groups are small, the largest being the German-speaking people of Bolzano Province and the Slovenes around Trieste. In addition, there are ancient communities of Albanian, Greek, Ladino, and French origin. About 99 percent of Italians are nominally Catholic. There are some 200,000 Protestants, about 35,000 Jews, and a very small number of Greek Orthodox. Literacy is estimated at 93 percent.

HISTORY

Modern Italian history dates from 1870 with the unification of the entire peninsula under King Victor Emmanuel II of the House of Savoy. From 1870 until 1922 Italy was a constitutional monarchy with a parliament elected under limited suffrage. During World War I, Italy denounced its standing alliance with Germany and Austria-Hungary and in 1915 entered the war on the side of the Allies. Under the post-World War I settlement, Italy received some former Austrian territory, along the northeast frontier. In 1922 Benito Mussolini came to power and in the course of the next few years eliminated the old political parties, curtailed personal liberties, and installed a Fascist dictatorship, the Corporate State. The King, with little or no power, remained titular Head of State.

World War II found Italy allied with Germany; it declared war on the United Kingdom and France in 1940. Following the Allied invasion of Sicily in 1943, Italy became a co-belligerent of the Allies against Germany. There was a noteworthy resistance movement by the people especially in central and northern Italy against the remaining Germans, who were finally driven out in April 1945. The monarchy ended in a plebiscite in 1946, and a Constituent Assembly was elected to draw up the plans for the present Republic.

Under the 1947 Peace Treaty, minor adjustments were made in Italy's frontier with France, the eastern border area was transferred to Yugoslavia, and the area around the city of Trieste was designated as a Free Territory. In 1954 the Free Territory, which had remained under the administration of U.S.-British forces (Zone A, including the city of Trieste) and of Yugoslav forces (Zone B), was divided between Italy and Yugoslavia substantially along the zonal boundary. Under the Peace Treaty, Italy also gave up its overseas territories and certain Mediterranean islands.

The position of the Catholic Church in Italy since the end of its temporal powers in 1870 has been governed by a series of accords with the Italian Government, the most recent being the Lateran Pacts of 1929. Under these pacts, which were confirmed by the present Constitution, the Vatican City State is recognized by Italy as an independent sovereign state. Although Roman Catholicism is the official religion of the Republic of Italy, the Constitution provides that all religious faiths are equally free before the law.

GOVERNMENT

Italy has been a democratic republic since June 2, 1946, when the monarchy was abolished by popular referendum. The Constitution, which was promulgated on January 1, 1948, established a bicameral Parliament, a separate judiciary, and an executive branch composed of a Council of Ministers (cabinet) and headed by the President of the Council (or Prime Minister). The Cabinet, which in practice is composed of members of Parliament, must retain the confidence of both houses. The President of the Republic, who is Chief of State, is elected for 7 years by Parliament sitting jointly with a small number of regional delegates. He nominates the Prime Minister, who chooses the other ministers.

Except for a few Senators, both houses of Parliament—the Chamber of Deputies (630 members) and the Senate (323 members)—are popularly and directly elected by proportional representation. In addition to 315 elected members, the Senate includes 3 ex-Presidents and five other persons appointed for life according to special provisions of the Constitution. Both houses are elected for a maximum of 5 years, but either may be dissolved before the expiration of its normal term. Legislative bills may originate in either house and must be passed by a majority in both.

The Italian judicial system is essentially based on Roman law as modified in the Napoleonic Code and subsequent statutes. There is only partial judicial review of legislation in the American sense. A constitutional Court, whose function it is to pass on the constitutionality of laws, is a post-World War II innovation. Its powers, volume, and frequency of decisions, however, are not as extensive as those of the Supreme Court of the United States.

The Italian State is highly centralized. The chief executive of each of the 93 Provinces (the Prefect) is appointed by, and answerable to, the Central Government. In addition to the Provinces, the Constitution provides for 20 regions with limited governing powers. Five regions with special statutes—Sardinia, Sicily, Trentino-Alto Adige, Valle d'Aosta, and Friuli-Venezia Giulia—have long been functioning. The other 15 regions, however, were not established and did not vote for their first regional "Councils" (parliaments) until 1970. The establishment of regional governments throughout Italy may, in time, bring about some decentralization of the national governmental machinery which, in the view of many, has become too unwieldly to cope with the rapid socioeconomic evolution of the country.

POLITICAL CONDITIONS

With the mergers in 1972 of the Proletarian Specialists with the Communist Party and of the Monarchists with the Neo-Fascist Social Movement, there are now seven major political parties and a number of minor ones. The major parties, in the order of their approximate strength in the last general elections (1972), are:

The Christian Democratic Party (DC), the descendant of the Popular Party of the pre-Fascist area, it has been the core of all postwar governments. It represents a wide range of interests and views which sometimes makes it difficult to reach agreement on specific issues. The DC polled 38.8 percent of the popular vote in 1972. Party Secretary: Arnaldo Forlani. Official newspaper: Il Popolo.

The Italian Communist Party (PCI), the largest Communist Party in Western Europe, has generally supported the policies of the Soviet Union in foreign affairs and reform of the state in domestic affairs. The PCI obtained 27.2 percent of the popular vote in 1972. Secretary General: Enrico Berlinguer. Newspaper: L'Unita.

The Italian Socialist Party (PSI), reemerged in 1969 from a 2-1/2 year merger with the Italian Social Democrats. The two groups had originally split in 1947 over the issue of Socialist alliance with the Communists, a policy pursued by the Socialists until the Hungarian revolt in 1956. The PSI polled 9.6 percent of the vote in 1972. Party Secretary: Giacomo Mancini. Newspaper: Avanti!

The Italian Social Movement (MSI), on the extreme right,. is considered to be imbued with the traditions of fascism. The MSI, together with the now defunct Monarchist Party (PDIUM), polled 8.7 percent of the popular vote in 1972. Political Secretary: Giorgio Almirante. Newspaper: Il Secolo.

The Italian Social Democratic Party (PSDI) resumed its former identity following its second secession from the PSI in 1969. The PSDI polled 5.1 percent of the vote in 1972. Party Secretary: Flavio Orlandi. Newspaper: Umanita.

The Italian Liberal Party (PLI) is right-center and strongly pro-NATO. In the last elections it won 3.9 percent of the popular vote. Secretary General: Agostino Bignardi. Newspaper: La Tribuna.

The Italian Republican Party (PRI) is a small party with a long historical tradition of support for republican institutions. The PRI polled 2.9 percent of the vote in 1972. Party Secretary: Ugo La Malfa. Newspaper: La Voce Repubblicana.

Postwar Coalitions

Despite the frequency of government crisis (the present government of Premier Giulio Andreotti is the 34th of the postwar period) the Italian political situation has been relatively stable, principally because of the long continuity in power of the ruling Christian Democratic Party. The Christian Democrats have governed—either alone or in coalition with smaller democratic parties—uninterruptedly since 1945, and three of their leaders (the late Premier Alcide De Gasperi, and former Premiers Amintore Fanfani and Aldo Moro) have dominated the Italian political scene for most of that time.

PARLIAMENTARY STRENGTH OF ITALIAN POLITICAL PARTIES

Chamber of Deputies

	% of Popular Vote					Seats*				
	1953	1958	1963	1968	1972	1953	1958	1963	1968	1972
MSI (Neo-Facists)	5.8	4.8	5.1	4.5	8.7****	29	24	27	24	56
PDIUM (Monarchists)	6.9	4.8	1.7	1.3		40	25	8	6	
PLI (Liberals)	3.0	3.5	7.0	5.8	3.9	13	18	39	31	20
DC (Christian Democrats)	40.2	42.3	38.2	39.1	38.8	263	273	260	266	267
PRI (Republicans)	1.6	1.4	1.4	2.0	2.9	5	6	6	9	15
PSDI (Social Democrats)	4.5	4.5	6.1	14.5**	5.1	19	22	33	91	29
PSI (Socialists)	12.7	14.2	13.8		9.6	75	84	87		61
PSIUP (Proletarian Socialists)	-	-	-	4.5	1.9	-	-	-	23	0
PCI (Communists)	22.6	22.7	25.3	26.9	27.2	143	141	166	177	179
Miscellaneous	2.7	1.8	1.5	1.4	1.9	3	3	4	3	3

Senate

	% of Popular Vote					Seats*				
	1953	1958	1963	1968	1972	1953	1958	1963	1968	1972
MSI	6.1	5.3	5.9	4.6	9.2****	9	8	15	11	26
PDIUM	7.0	5.4	1.8	1.0		16	7	2	2	
PLI	2.9	3.9	7.5	6.8	4.4	4	4	19	16	8
DC	39.7	41.2	36.9	38.4	38.1	114	123	132	135	135
PRI	0.9	1.4	1.0	2.2	3.0	2	0	0	2	5
PSDI	1.1	4.5	6.3	15.2**	5.4	4	5	14	46	11
PSI	12.9	14.4	14.0		10.7	31	35	44		33
PSIUP	-	-	-	30.0	28.4***	-	-	-	14	94
PCI	21.2	22.3	25.5			54	60	85	87	
Miscellaneous	1.7	1.6	1.1	.2	.8	3	4	4	2	3

* The Chamber had 630 seats in 1972, 1968 and 1963, 596 in 1958, and 590 in 1953; the Senate had respectively 315 (plus 8 Senators for life), 246, and 237.

** In 1968 the PSI and PSDI (then united) ran joint lists in both the Chamber and Senate contests.

*** The PCI and the PSIUP ran joint lists in the Senate election in both 1968 and 1972 and the PSIUP merged with the PCI after the 1972 elections.

**** The PDIUM merged with the MSI prior to the 1972 elections.

From 1947 to the end of the 1950's, the Christian Democrats ruled in a series of "center" coalition alignments with the Social Democrats, Republicans, and Liberals. In the 1960's, in an effort to expand the "democratic area" and promote reform legislation, the Christian Democrats pursued a "center-left" policy which involved the inclusion of the Socialists in, and the exclusion of the Liberals from the national government. Political and programmatic divisions within the center-left alignment in the late 1960's culminated in 1972 in the dissolution of Parliament and early elections. The persistence of these divisions after the elections, especially between the Christian Democrats and the Socialists led to the formation of Premier Andreotti's "center" coalition government in which the Liberals replaced the Socialists.

The present cabinet, which has a narrow majority in Parliament, comprises, in addition to Premier Andreotti, 16 Christian Democrats, 5 Social Democrats, and 4 Liberals. The Republicans lend their parliamentary support, but do not participate in the government.

Communism

The Italian Communist Party is the largest nonruling Communist Party in the world, and is the second largest party in Italy, after the ruling Christian Democrats. Although its membership has shrunk considerably over the years (from a high of some 2.5 million in the mid-50's to a little over 1.5 million today), Communist electoral strength has steadily increased in each succeeding national election to 27.2 percent of the total vote in 1972. Except for the immediate post-World War II period, the Communists have been barred from participation in the national government. Nevertheless, Communist adherence to "constitutional legality" and its pursuit of power "within the system" continue to fuel a divisive debate among democratic forces over the issue of the proper relationship between the government and the Communist opposition. The debate centers on the degree of "democratization" which the Communists may be undergoing, and hence on the possibility of their eventual acceptability in the governing process. The overwhelming majority of the democratic forces remain highly skeptical over the degree of Communist "democratization" and do not favor or anticipate a Communist role in the national Government in the foreseeable future.

ECONOMY

Italy has a total gross national product (GNP) of approximately $115 billion and a per capita GNP of about $2100. The gross national product grew at an impressive yearly average of better than 6 percent in real terms from 1954 to 1963, a rate exceeded only by Japan and the Federal Republic of Germany among the industrial nations of the free world. High and expanding levels of investment, particularly in industrial equipment and in construction and low labor costs, sparked the high growth rate, particularly in the late 50's and early 60's. Following a short-lived recessionary dip in 1964 and early 1965, economic growth resumed at a steady pace beginning in mid-1965. In the period 1966-1969, the growth target of 5 percent per year of Italy's first 5-year "economic plan" was consistently exceeded, averaging more than 5.5 percent annually. Relative price and interest rate stability were a hallmark of these years in Italy.

The delayed effects of the prolonged series of strikes in the industrial sector during the so-called "hot autumn of 1969"—which continued well into early 1970, and which resulted in sharply higher labor costs and lower productivity—were eventually felt throughout the economy beginning in late 1970. By 1971 the country was faced with one of its most serious postwar recessions. Real growth for 1971 was an insignificant 1.4 percent, the lowest in postwar Italy. In the same year, industrial production, which had been Italy's strongest suit during most of the 1960's, was minus 2.7 percent compared with that of 1970. Consumer prices, which had been relatively stable during most of the 1960's, jumped sharply in both 1970 and 1971 (nearly 5 percent each year). Although statistics are not yet available, economic trends in 1972 continued to be dominated by inadequate growth and cost-push inflation. At the outset of 1973, however, there is some optimism that a gradual upswing is underway. Despite its current stagnation, Italy remains the seventh ranking industrial power in the world.

Italy has essentially a private enterprise economy. Although the Government has a controlling interest in a number of large industrial and commercial enterprises, these enterprises are operated along conventional business lines. As is true in many foreign countries, the electricity, transportation system, telephone and telegraph, and the radio and television systems are state-owned.

By comparison with most other European countries, Italy is poorly endowed by nature. Much of the country is unsuited for farming because of mountainous terrain or unfavorable climate. There are no significant deposits of coal or iron ore. The deposits of most other minerals required by a modern industrial nation and the reserves of crude petroleum are dispersed and of poor quality. Natural gas reserves, mainly in the Po Valley, were discovered after 1945 and constitute the country's most important mineral resources, but these reserves are being depleted rapidly. Thus, most of the raw materials required in manufacturing are imported. Other factors adversely affecting the Italian economy are the low level of productivity in agriculture and some industrial sectors and the need to upgrade labor skills. Also, the peninsula south of Rome and the islands lag behind the rise in living standards of the north, despite substantial agricultural and industrial investments in the past 20 years. Only recently has the rate of growth in the south begun to catch up with that in the north, but it will take considerable time to close the gap.

More than 40 percent of the GNP comes from industry and construction. Principal industrial products are chemicals and petrochemicals, transportation equipment, capital equipment, food and beverages, and consumer goods. Agriculture, forestry, and fishing are the third most important sector of origin of the GNP. The importance of agriculture has declined from 20 percent of the GNP in 1958 to only 10.2 percent in 1971 as a result of the rapid increase in industrial activity and the movement of labor from rural to urban areas. Major agricultural products are wheat, rice, grapes, olives, and citrus fruits. In 1971 the most important sector of the origin of GNP was provided by services which accounted for 49 percent of the total.

Foreign Trade and International Reserves

One of the major factors in Italy's economic growth over the years has been the sharply increasing volume of its foreign trade. Italian exports in 1971 increased by 14.7 percent to more than $15 billion and imports by 7 percent to nearly $16 billions. Italy traditionally imports more than it exports. Deficient in certain foodstuffs and in most raw materials, it has been forced to increase its imports of these commodities as demand has expanded in step with rising living standards, changing consumption patterns (e.g., increasing meat consumption), and rising industrial production. This trade deficit in foodstuffs and raw materials normally is more than offset by large receipts from invisibles (tourism, emigrant remittances, transportation, etc.). Italy's overall balance of payments in 1972 showed a deficit of about $900 million, following surpluses in 1971 and 1970 of $783 million and $350 million, and a large deficit (almost $1.4 billion) in 1969. On a worldwide basis, Italy's largest import items, by value, are crude oil, corn, meats, wool, cotton, coal, scrap iron, and steel. Its principal exports are automobiles; machinery; typewriters; fresh fruits and vegetables; and woolen textiles, shoes, and other consumer goods.

Italy's closest trade ties are with the other eight countries of the enlarged European Community (EC) which in 1971 provided markets for 49.4 percent of Italy's total exports and were the source of 46.9 percent of Italy's total imports. Italy's three largest trading partners in 1971 were in descending order of magnitude: the Federal Republic of Germany (22.8 percent of Italy's exports and 20.2 percent of imports); France (13.5 percent of exports and 14.1 percent of imports); and the United States (9.8 percent of exports and 9.0 percent of imports). As in previous years, only a modest amount of Italy's trade in 1971 (5.7 percent of total exports and 6.1 percent of imports) was with Communist countries of Eastern Europe. Trade with the Communist countries of Asia and with Cuba was negligible.

Official reserves at the end of 1972 stood at $6.1 billion. Approximately $3.1 billion in reserves was in the form of gold, $2.2 billion in foreign exchange, and the remainder in Special Drawing Rights and the IMF reserve position.

Labor

Of the labor force of almost 20 million people, nearly 44 percent are in industry and 36.7 percent in services or other activities, while only 19.6 percent are engaged in agriculture. This reflects a major shift from agriculture, which occupied about half the labor force before the war.

Chronic unemployment, formerly one of Italy's principal problems, has virtually disappeared. Skilled labor is short in many categories, although concealed unemployment, inefficient use of manpower, and underemployment continue to exist, particularly in the south.

About a quarter of the labor force is unionized. The Communist-dominated CGIL controls 45 percent of organized labor, the Christian Democratic-oriented CISL 40 percent, and the Social Democratic-oriented UIL about 5 percent.

FOREIGN RELATIONS

Italy has achieved its basic postwar objective of equality and partnership in the community of democratic nations. It was admitted to the United Nations in 1955. It is a member and strong supporter of the North Atlantic Treaty Organization (NATO), the Organization for Economic Cooperation and Development (OECD), General Agreement on Tariffs and Trade (GATT), and the various organizations of the European Community (the European Coal and Steel Community, the European Atomic Energy Community, and the European Economic Community). Italy is also active in the Western European Union and the Council of Europe.

U.S. POLICY

The United States enjoys warm and friendly relations with Italy as attested by two visits to Rome by President Nixon during his first administration and the visit of Prime Minister Colombo to Washington in February 1971. The two nations are NATO allies, and they cooperate in the United Nations, various regional organizations, and bilaterally in the interests of peace, the freedom of all nations, and mutual defense. There are no outstanding bilateral problems of basic importance between the two nations.

PRINCIPAL GOVERNMENT OFFICIALS

President of the Republic—Giovanni Leone
Prime Minister—Giulio Andreotti (DC)
Deputy Prime Minister and Defense Minister—Mario Tanassi (PSDI)
Minister of Foreign Affairs—Giuseppe Medici (DC)
Minister of Interior—Mariano Rumor (DC)
Minister of Justice—Guido Gonella (DC)

Minister of Budget and Economic Planning—Paolo Emilio Taviani (DC)
Minister of Finance—Athos Valsecchi (DC)
Minister of Treasury—Giovanni Malagodi (PLI)
Governor of the Bank of Italy—Guido Carli
Ambassador to the United States—Egidio Ortona
Ambassador to the United Nations—Piero Vinci

Italy maintains an Embassy in the United States at 1601 Fuller Street, N.W., Washington, D.C. 20009.

PRINCIPAL U.S. OFFICIALS

Ambassador—John Volpe
Deputy Chief of Mission—Robert Beaudry
Minister-Counselor for Economic and Commercial Affairs—Michael Ely
Counselor for Political Affairs—William J. Barnsdale
Counselor for Public Affairs (USIS)—Alexander A. Klieforth
Counselor for Commercial Affairs—Harry Keikenen
Agricultural Attaché—Radboud Beukenkamp
Treasury Attaché—Donald Templeman
Chief of Military Assistance Advisory Group—Maj. Gen. John B. Kidd
Defense and Naval Attaché—Capt. George W. Cogswell
Air Attaché—Col. Joseph R. Castelli
Army Attaché—Lt. Col. Patrick A. Vitello (acting)

Consular Posts

Consul, Florence—Robert Gordon
Consul General, Genoa—
Consul General, Milan—John Davis
Consul General, Naples—Daniel Horowitz
Consul General, Palermo—Alfred Vigderman
Consul, Trieste—Theodore Russell
Consul, Turin—C. Melvin Sonne, Jr.

The United States maintains an Embassy in Italy at Via Veneto 119, Rome.

READING LIST

These titles are provided as a general indication of the material currently being published on this country; the Department of State does not endorse the specific views in unofficial publications as representing the position of the U.S. Government.

Battaglia, Roberto. The Story of the Italian Resistance. London: Odham Press, Ltd., 1957.
Carlye, Margaret. The Awakening of Southern Italy. London: Oxford University Press, 1962.
Jemolo, A. O. Church and State in Italy 1850-1950. Oxford: Basil Blackwell, 1960.
Kogan, Norman. The Politics of Italian Foreign Policy. New York: Frederick A. Praeger, 1963.
Mammarella, Giuseppe. Italy After Fascism. Montreal: Casalini, Ltd., 1964.
Olschki, Leonardo. The Genius of Italy. New York: Cornell University Press, 1954.
Smith, Denis Mack. Italy, A Modern History. Ann Arbor: University of Michigan Press, 1959.
Trevelyan, J. O. A Short History of the Italian People. London: Allen and Unwin, Ltd., 1956.
Walker, D. S. A Geography of Italy. London: Methuen & Co., Ltd., 1958.

DEPARTMENT OF STATE PUBLICATION 7861
Revised April 1973

APPENDIX RR

ITALY

STRENGTH OF THE COMMUNIST PARTY ORGANIZATION—1973

SEE PAGE 142

[FROM: World Strength of the Communist Party Organizations—1973. Washington, Department of State, Bureau of Intelligence and Research, 1973.]

ITALY

National Political Status: Date of last election - May 7, 1972. Data below are for the Chamber of Deputies (lower house) election.

Communist: Italian Communist Party (PCI) - 9,085,927 votes (27.2%), 179 seats (28.4%)

Non-Communist Left: Italian Socialist Party of Proletarian Unity - 648,368 votes (1.9%), no seats

Italian Socialist Party - 3,209,503 votes (9.6%), 61 seats (9.7%)

Center: Italian Social Democratic Party - 1,716,197 votes (5.1%), 29 seats (4.6%)

Italian Republican Party - 973,681 votes (2.9%), 14 seats (2.2%)

Christian Democratic Party - 12,943,675 votes (38.8%), 267 seats (42.4%)

Italian Liberal Party - 1,300,074 votes (3.9%), 21 seats (3.3%)

Conservative: National Right (Neo-Fascist/Monarchists) - 2,894,789 votes (8.7%), 56 seats (8.9%)

Other: 606,483 votes (1.8%), 3 seats (0.5%)

Total: 33,378,697 votes, 630 seats

Communist Party Membership: 1,617,100 (claimed). Youth membership in FCGI (Federation of Italian Communist Youth) - 110,785 (claimed).

Leading Party Figures and Positions:

LONGO, Luigi - President
BERLINGUER, Enrico - Secretary-General
AMENDOLA, Giorgio - senior party leader
LAMA, Luciano - Secretary-General of the Italian General Confederation of Labor (CGIL)
TORTORELLA, Aldo - Editor of party's daily, *l'Unita*

Principal Publications:

l'Unita - daily paper
Rinascita - weekly theoretical journal

Areas of Communist Activity: The Italian Communist Party (PCI) was active in 1973 in both domestic and international affairs. Domestically, it strongly opposed the Andreotti center government, which fell in June, and then offered a "softer" opposition to the Rumor center-left government that followed. Internationally, 1973 was a year of European involvement for the PCI: the party took the lead in organizing the Communist parties of Western Europe for a congress to be held in January 1974 and in an attempt to move the European leftist parties closer to effective participation in the European Community.

Communist Political Muscle. The PCI continues to be the largest non-ruling Communist party in the world, and the second largest political party in Italy, after the ruling Christian Democrats. The Communists claimed a membership of 1,617,091 in 1972, 32,432 more than in 1971. They also claimed 110,735 members in the party Youth Federation (FCGI).

The PCI's preeminence in and dominance over both the country's largest trade union--the 3 million-strong Italian General Confederation of Labor (CGIL)--and the largest cooperative organization--the National League of Cooperatives, which has a claimed membership of some 3.5 million and a business turnover estimated in the hundreds of millions of U.S. dollars--remained unchallenged in 1973. Finally, the Communists appear to have improved slightly the already sizable control they have, alone or in alliances with other left-wing parties, over local administrations, i.e., more than 1,000 of Italy's 8,000 municipalities, 12 of the 93 provinces, and 3 of the 20 regions.

Party Domestic Strategy. As 1973 opened, Italy was governed by Premier Giulio Andreotti's center-right government, which the Communists vigorously opposed as anachronistic and as a dangerous opening to a seemingly reinvigorated right-wing. The party hoped to topple it and see a move back toward the left with the Socialists replacing the Liberal Party in the government. The PCI goal, besides a government with a more leftist composure, was the beginning of a direct dialogue with the dominant Christian Democratic Party in order to increase PCI input into the government's program, eventually leading to its participation in the government. The PCI constantly stressed that this was the only way to restore stability and efficiency in Italy.

When Mariano Rumor's center-left government replaced Andreotti's center-right experiment in July, it was greeted favorably by the PCI, which announced that the party would act as "an opposition of a different type." Instead of implacable resistance to all governmental projects, the Communists pledged to judge the government's performance on its merits and support reforms when they felt them to be right.

While this type of soft opposition had been offered during the formation period of the original center-left coalition in the early sixties, the offer was fully implemented this time. As a result of the PCI's behavior and a general desire for action in the populace, Rumor was given an initial breathing space during which he moved some emergency measures through Parliament which were designed to attack the economic problems of stagflation. Communist muscle was especially evident in the trade union field, where it assured labor acquiescence in the government's austerity measures.

Having cited the political importance of the move back to the center-left and the need to help that coalition through a difficult economic situation so as to ensure the continuation of the new direction, Secretary-General Enrico Berlinguer took the party's thinking a stage further in October when he proposed a "historic compromise"--i.e., a sort of political dialogue between his party and the ruling Christian Democrats. In a series of articles analyzing the Chilean coup, which had jolted the party, Berlinguer discarded any hope for the emergence of a popular front or "union of the left" in Italy. He argued that, even if such a coalition of leftist groups won an absolute majority in Parliament, it could not govern well.

In order to obtain "progressive social transformation without social division and frontal battles," Berlinguer stated that it would be necessary to gain the support and consent of the middle class. In party political terms, this would be a power-sharing arrangement between the Christian Democrats and the Communists, with the probable inclusion of the Socialists. His proposal was an updating of the old Italian Communist historical dream of uniting the Communist and Catholic forces in wielding national power, a policy pursued, off and on, ever since the foundation of the post-World War II Italian Republic.

Berlinguer's proposal was quite explicitly an offer to the whole Christian Democratic Party, however, not just to progressive Catholics. The offer excited much debate in the PCI even though it was refused for the time being by the Christian Democrats and denounced by other parties. At present, the proposed "historic compromise" is just another indication of slowly evolving changes in Communist political strategy. Berlinguer probably prefers slow progress toward his goals so as to be in a position to bring the party along.

International Strategy. While these important domestic innovations had historical precedents, the PCI made some novel moves in 1973 in expanding its contacts with other Communist parties and in developing a European strategy. The party stated that it favored a European political union and a European Parliament elected by universal suffrage, with full power to deal with international economic and political crises. Berlinguer visited many capitals in 1973 to preach the PCI sermon on the need for unity among all leftist EC forces to "democratize" the Common Market.

In February, he visited London, where he stated that his party "intends to engage itself even more actively in order to contribute to the development of cooperation between left-wing and democratic workers' forces in Western Europe." To prove his point, he conferred with British Labor Party officials as well as his hosts, the British Communist Party. He also called for a Europe which was neither anti-Soviet nor anti-American, an important change from the party's anti-NATO and anti-U.S. slogans of yesteryear.

In March, Berlinguer went to Moscow to explain his point of view on the role of the Communist parties in Western Europe and on the need to work with Social Democrats. The meeting had a stormy aftermath in a polemic which developed between *Pravda* and *l'Unita* over the failure of *Pravda* to print a key point in the joint communique which stressed the autonomy of each individual Communist party.

In May, French Communist leader Georges Marchais went to Italy for a visit which may have marked the beginning of the realization of a new strategy for the European Communist parties. The PCF accepted the PCI concept of a democratic European Constituent Assembly and the union of all left-wing social and political forces in a drive to "democratize" Europe. In the same month Berlinguer consulted with the French Socialist leader Francois Mitterrand.

In the second half of 1973, Berlinguer concentrated on a push for a conference of European Communist parties. A series of meetings beginning in Stockholm on September 27 and 28 crowned the efforts of the PCI behind-the-scenes campaign. At the Stockholm meeting, representatives of 17 West European parties agreed to hold a West European Communist Summit in January 1974. In a sense it could be regarded as a preparatory step along the way to a possible World Communist Party Congress.

In the months following the Stockholm meeting, Berlinguer capped his international forays with visits to Bulgaria, Poland, and East Germany. These visits probably were a continuation of his efforts to prepare for a World Communist Party Congress as well as an explanation of the PCI's position on this subject.

Local Elections. Partial local elections, involving some 10 percent of the national electorate, were held November 18-19. The Communists gained in comparison with their performance in previous local elections in the same districts, but did not do as well as in the parliamentary elections of 1972. It is normal for both the PCI and the Christian Democrats to score better in national elections. The Socialists made about a 3 percent gain over 1972 as they picked up the majority of the voters who voted for the defunct Socialist Proletarian Unity Party in the previous election. The failure of the PCI to absorb all of these voters resulted in overall losses for the entire far left.

Other Communist Groups. Splinter Communist groups, most of them born of the Sino-Soviet split in the mid- and late sixties, continued to exist, but all of them remained weak numerically and insignificant politically. The best known, in addition to the former Communist leftwingers of the so-called Manifesto group, are the *Partito Communista d'Italia, Marxista-Leninista* (Communist Party of Italy, Marxist-Leninist), and the ultra-leftist *Lotta Continua* (Continuous Struggle). Some of them, the Manifesto group in particular, ran slates of candidates in the May 1972 parliamentary elections. They failed to win any seats, but they undoubtedly drained away a few hundred thousand votes which otherwise would have gone to the PCI.

NOTE: The Communist Party of San Marino, while nominally independent, is an offshoot of the PCI.

APPENDIX SS
LUXEMBOURG
ARMED FORCES AND MILITARY POWER

[Reprinted with permission from: The Almanac of World Military Power, by Col. T. N. Dupuy, U.S. Army, Ret., Col. John A. C. Andrews, U.S. Air Force, Ret., and Grace P. Hayes. 3rd ed. Dunn Loring, Va., T. N. Dupuy Associates, 1974.]

LUXEMBOURG

Grand Duche de Luxembourg
Grand Duchy of Luxembourg

POWER POTENTIAL STATISTICS

Area: 999 square miles
Population: 400,000

Total Active Armed Forces: 900 (including Gendarmerie; 0.23% population)
Gross National Product: $1.2 billion ($3,000 per capita)
Annual Military Expenditures: $10.8 million (0.90% GNP)
Iron and Steel Production: 9.8 million metric tons (largest per-capita production in the world)
Electric Power Output: 2.4 billion kwh
Civil Air Fleet: 4 jet, 3 turboprop transports

POLITICO-MILITARY POLICIES AND POSTURE

The government of Luxembourg abandoned its traditionally neutral policy at the close of World War II, and has since been an enthusiastic partner in all Western European mutual security agreements as a member of the Benelux bloc. A member of NATO, Luxembourg maintains only a nominal armed force, composed of one light infantry battalion of 550 men. US military assistance to Luxembourg since 1950 has totalled slightly more than $8 million, most of which was provided in the early 1950s. Military service is voluntary; enlistment is for three years. The Gendarmerie is 350 strong.

APPENDIX TT
LUXEMBOURG
BACKGROUND NOTES

[Washington, Department of State, July 1973 (Publication 7856).]

DEPARTMENT OF STATE JULY 1973

LUXEMBOURG

BACKGROUND NOTES

PROFILE

Geography

AREA: 999 square miles (slightly smaller than Rhode Island). CAPITAL: Luxembourg (population 76,000). OTHER CITIES: Esch-sur-Alzette (pop. 28,000), the center of the steel and mining district southwest of the capital; Differdange (pop. 18,000).

People

POPULATION: 339,848 (1970 census).

ANNUAL GROWTH RATE: 0.8%. DENSITY: 329 per square mile. URBAN: 67%. ETHNIC GROUPS: Blend of French and German, Italian, others from Mediterranean countries.

RELIGION: Roman Catholic (97%). LANGUAGES: French, German, Luxembourgish (a Germanic tongue). LITERACY: 98%. LIFE EXPECTANCY: 73 years.

Government

INDEPENDENCE: 1867. TYPE: Constitutional Monarchy. DATE OF CONSTITUTION: 1868.

FLAG: Three horizontal stripes—red, white, and blue from top to bottom (colors date from 1235).

BRANCHES: Executive—Grand Duke (Chief of State); Prime Minister (Head of Government). Legislature—Bicameral Parliament: Chamber of Deputies (56 members, 5-year term); Council of State (members appointed by Grand Duke). Judiciary—Superior Court.

ADMINISTRATIVE DIVISIONS: 126 Communes.

Economy

GNP: $1.3 billion (1972). ANNUAL GROWTH RATE: 3.3%. PER CAPITA: $3,500. PER CAPITA GROWTH RATE: 3.5%.

AGRICULTURE: Labor—10%. Land—52%. Acres per capita—1. Crops—livestock, products of small farming, grapes (vineyards).

INDUSTRY: Labor—50%. Products—rubber, chemicals, fertilizers.

TRADE: Exports—$1.1 billion (1972). Imports—$1.1 billion. Partners—U.S., Federal Republic of Germany, Belgium, France.

MEMBERSHIP IN INTERNATIONAL ORGANIZATIONS: NATO, U.N., Organization for Economic Cooperation and Development (OECD), Benelux Economic Union, European Communities.

GEOGRAPHY

The Grand Duchy of Luxembourg is located in Western Europe, bordered on the south by France, on the east and north by the Federal Republic of Germany, and on the west and north by Belgium.

A hilly, wooded country, Luxembourg has a climate much like that of the U.S. Pacific Northwest—cool, temperate, and rainy. Summer temperatures average 60° F., and winters are mild with an average low of 29°F.

HISTORY

In 1815, after 400 years of domination by various European nations, Luxembourg was made a Grand Duchy by the Congress of Vienna. It was granted political autonomy in 1839 under King William I of the Netherlands, who was also the Grand Duke of Luxembourg.

By the Treaty of London in 1867, Luxembourg was recognized as an independent state and guaranteed its perpetual neutrality. After being overrun by Germany in both World Wars, Luxembourg formally abandoned neutrality in 1949 by becoming a charter member of the North Atlantic Treaty Organization (NATO).

The present sovereign, Grand Duke Jean, succeeded his mother, Grand Duchess Charlotte, on November 12, 1964, when she voluntarily abdicated after a 45-year reign.

GOVERNMENT

Luxembourg has a parliamentary form of government with a constitutional monarchy. Under the Constitution of 1868, as amended, the Grand Duke is the Chief of State. Executive power is exercised by the Grand Duke and the Council of Government (cabinet), which consists of a President of the Government (Prime Minister) and at least three other Ministers. The Prime Minister is the leader of the political party or coalition of parties which has the most seats in the parliament.

Legislative power is vested in the Chamber of Deputies, elected directly by universal adult suffrage to a term of 5 years. A second body in the parliament is the Council of State, largely composed of elder statesmen and appointed by the Grand Duke. It exercises some of the functions of an upper house but can be overridden by the Chamber of Deputies.

The law is codified, as in France and Belgium, and is a composite of local practice, legal tradition, and foreign systems (French, Belgian, and German). The apex of the judicial system is the Superior Court whose judges are appointed by the Grand Duke.

For administrative purposes, Luxembourg is divided into 126 Communes, each of which is administered by an elected council. This system, modeled on that of Belgium, accords a large degree of independence to the Commune in matters of local interest.

POLITICAL CONDITIONS

Luxembourg has a firmly based tradition of social and political stability. The three major political parties—Christian Social, Socialist, and Democratic—agree on basic constitutional and political principles. Thus, the coalition governments—a coalition being virtually inevitable because of proportional representation voting—have tended to be quite stable.

Traditionally the strongest political group, the Christian Social (Catholic) Party, enjoys a widely based popular following among farmers, conservative groups, and Catholic labor circles. It is relatively "internationalist" in outlook and has strongly supported NATO.

In its present period of opposition following its participation in government, the Socialist Party split in January 1971 into a moderate and a more left grouping which continues to bear the name of the old party. The moderate element styles itself the Social Democratic Party and opposes cooperation with the Communist Party at any level of government.

The Democratic (Liberal) Party is mildly anticlerical and moderately conservative. While it favors progressive social legislation, it advocates a minimum of governmental activity in the national economy. Supporters are drawn largely from the professions, merchants, artisans, and the urban middle classes. It is strongly pro-NATO.

Virtually assured of some parliamentary seats by Luxembourg's proportional representation voting system, the Communist Party is currently represented by six deputies—five from the industrial south around Esch-sur-Alzette and one from the Luxembourg city area.

Prime Minister Pierre Werner's current Christian Social-Democratic coalition was formed in January 1969, following a general election held the previous month. The previous Christian Social-Socialist government had fallen at the end of October 1968 due to its inability to meet Socialist demands for increased salary and pension benefits. The largest gains in the subsequent election were scored by the moderately conservative Democratic Party, as the Luxembourg electorate seemed to shift slightly to the right. The next parliamentary elections will be held in June 1974.

The present composition of the Chamber of Deputies is: Christian Social (21). Socialist (12), Democratic (11), Social Democrat (6), and Communist (6).

ECONOMY

Highly industrialized Luxembourg has a standard of living which is well above the West European average. Its estimated 1972 gross national product (GNP) of about U.S.$1.3 billion amounted to $3,500 per capita, the highest of those members of the European Communities (Common Market). Luxembourg's overall growth rate was 3.5 percent in constant prices, in 1972.

Although Luxembourg has been successful in diversifying its economy away from exclusive reliance on iron and steel, this industry still represents the most important economic pursuit in the Grand Duchy and accounts for about 50 percent of Luxembourg's industrial production. The 1972 steel output was about 5.4 million tons, or about 1 percent of world production. Its per capita production of more than 16 tons is the highest in the world. Almost half of the iron ore consumed is mined domestically, while the rest comes from France. All coal is imported, primarily from the Federal Republic of Germany.

Luxembourg has a growing number of medium and light industries which have been encouraged as part of an effort to broaden the country's industrial base. These new industries contribute about half as much to the GNP as the steel industry. The most significant of these are rubber, chemicals, and fertilizers. Almost 50 percent of the total labor force is employed in industry, with about 42 percent engaged in services.

Agriculture absorbs about 10 percent of the labor force, mostly in livestock raising and small mixed farming. The vineyards of the Moselle Valley provide excellent dry white wines which are beginning to be exported in commercial quantities to the United States.

There are 20 U.S. firms with manufacturing facilities in Luxembourg that employ about 5,000 workers. The three largest of these are Goodyear (almost half the total U.S. investment), DuPont, and Monsanto. Total U.S. investment in Luxembourg is approximately $300 million.

Luxembourg's total exports during 1972 were estimated at $1.1 billion. Of that total, $40 million in steel and a small quantity of plastics were exported to the United States. Estimated 1972 imports totaled $1.1 billion, $21 million of which came from the United States in the form of rubber tires, industrial chemicals, machines and electrical products, and processed foods. Besides the United States other major trading partners include the Federal Republic of Germany, Belgium, and France.

Since the early 1960's Luxembourg has been one of the fastest growing financial centers in the world. There are more than 60 banks, 17 of which are owned partially or completely by U.S. interests. Luxembourg is also the center for trading in multinational company securities. Finally, favorable tax treatment offered by the Government has attracted many holding companies.

FOREIGN RELATIONS

Luxembourg participates in many international and regional organizations, including NATO, the United Nations and several of its specialized agencies, and the Organization for Economic Cooperation and Development (OECD). One of the forerunners of the movement toward European unity, Luxembourg joined Belgium in 1921 to form the Belgian-Luxembourg Economic Union (BLEU). In 1944 Belgium, the Netherlands, and Luxembourg decided to unite their economies. A customs union was inaugurated on January 1, 1948, and the Benelux Economic Union became effective on November 1, 1960. Luxembourg is an active member of the European Communities (European Economic Community, European Coal and Steel Community, and European Atomic Energy Community). The Council of the European Communities meets on occasion at Luxembourg, and various organs of the communities are located there.

U. S.-LUXEMBOURG RELATIONS

U.S.-Luxembourg relations traditionally have been warm and close. Luxembourg was liberated by American forces in both World Wars, and more than 5,000 American soldiers who died in World War II, including Gen. George S. Patton, are buried at Hamm, outside Luxembourg city.

In 1948 the United States, Belgium, and Luxembourg signed an agreement to finance a cultural and educational program, and the Fulbright-Hays Program was implemented in Luxembourg. Fulbright exchanges have promoted and increased mutual understanding between the United States and Luxembourg. Good cultural contacts have also been established through the American Field Services and the Experiment in International Living.

PRINCIPAL GOVERNMENT OFFICIALS

Chief of State—Grand Duke Jean
President, Chamber of Deputies—Pierre Grégoire
President of the Government (Prime Minister); Minister of State; Finance—Pierre Werner (Christian Socialist)
Vice President of the Government; Minister of the Interior, Justice, and Public Force (Defense)— Eugene Schaus (Democrat)
Minister of Foreign Affairs—Gaston Thorn (Democrat)
Minister of Public Works; Family, Social Housing and Social Solidarity; Viticulture—Jean-Pierre Buchler (Christian Socialist)
Minister of National Education and Youth—Jean DuPong (Christian Socialist)
Minister of National Economy, Energy, Transportation, Tourism, and of the Middle Classes—Marcel Mart (Democrat)
Minister of Agriculture and Public Health—Camille Ney (Christian Socialist)
Secretary of State for Interior—Emile Krieps (Democrat)
Secretary of State for Labor, Cultural Affairs, and Church Affairs—Jacques Santer (Christian Socialist)
Ambassador to the U.S.—Jean Wagner
Ambassador to the U.N.—Jean Rettel

Luxembourg maintains an Embassy in the United States at 2210 Massachusetts Avenue, N.W., Washington, D.C. 20008.

PRINCIPAL U. S. OFFICIALS

Ambassador—Ruth Lewis Farkas
Counselor of Embassy—Peter Tarnoff
Political Officer—Mark Wyatt
Economic Officer—Warren A. Lavorel
Consular Officer—John A. Hollingsworth
Defense Attaché (resident at Brussels, Belgium)—Col. Allen B. Jennings, USA

The U.S. Embassy in Luxembourg is located at 22 Boulevard Emmanuel Servais, Luxembourg.

READING LIST

Cooper-Prichard. A. H. History of the Grand Duchy of Luxembourg. Luxembourg: P. Linden, 1950.

Department of State. "The European Communities." No. 5 in the International Organizations series. Pub. 8410. Washington, D.C.: U.S. Government Printing Office, 1969.

Department of State, "NATO and the Defense of Europe." No. 2 in the Issues in United States Foreign Policy series. Pub. 8476. Washington, D.C.: U.S. Government Printing Office, 1969.

Department of State. "The Organization for Economic Cooperation and Development." No. 4 in the International Organizations series. Pub. 8460. Washington, D.C.: U.S. Government Printing Office, 1969.

Eyck, F. Gunther. The Benelux Countries: An Historical Survey. Princeton: Van Nostrand, 1959.

Gade, John A. Luxembourg in the Middle Ages. Leiden, Netherlands: E.J. Brill, 1951.

Taylor-Whitehead, W. J. Luxembourg, Land Of Legends. London: Constable, 1951.

DEPARTMENT OF STATE PUBLICATION 7856, Revised July 1973

APPENDIX UU

LUXEMBOURG

STRENGTH OF THE COMMUNIST PARTY ORGANIZATION—1973

[FROM: World Strength of the Communist Party Organizations—1973. Washington, Department of State, Bureau of Intelligence and Research, 1973.]

LUXEMBOURG

National Political Status: Date of last election - December 15, 1968.

Communist: Communist Party of Luxembourg (CPL) - 402,610 votes (15.5%), 6 seats (10.7%)

Non-Communist Left: Socialist Party - 837,555 votes (32.2%), 18 seats (32.1%)

Center: Christian Socialist Party - 915,944 votes (35.2%), 21 seats (37.5%)

Conservative: Democratic Party (includes former Independent Popular Movement) - 430,262 votes (16.5%), 11 seats (19.6%)

Other: National Solidarity Party - 16,485 votes (.6%), no seats

Total: 2,602,856 votes,[1] 56 seats

Communist Party Membership: 500 (estimate)

Leading Party Figures and Positions:
URBANY, Dominic - Chairman
USELDINGER, Arthur - Central Committee executive member

Principal Publication:
Die Zeitung vum Letzeburger Vollek - party organ

Areas of Communist Activity: No parliamentary elections have been held in Luxembourg since December 1968, when the Communist Party of Luxembourg (CPL) increased its representation in the 56-member Parliament from 5 to 6.

Elections are scheduled for May 1974. The party's perennial top leaders, President Dominic Urbany and Esch Mayor Arthur Useldinger--reelected at the party's 21st Congress in March 1973--are ill, and the CPL may face some competition from active left-wing extremist movements, the Trotskyite Communist Revolutionary League and the Maoist Communist League of Luxembourg.

The CPL continues to give unconditional support to the Soviet Union. It is opposed to the Common Market in a country which the polls show to be the most favorable in the EC to European integration, and it praises Arab militants, considered by many voters as responsible for inflation and petroleum shortages.

The Luxembourg Socialist Workers Party, the left wing of the split Socialist Party, has recently turned down an offer from the CPL to furnish financial support, establish joint lists, and issue a common governmental program.

1/ The total vote greatly exceeds the number of voters because each voter has as many votes as there are seats to be filled in his district's delegation.

Totals: 2,[illegible] votes, 56 seats

[illegible], [illegible] - Central Committee [illegible]

APPENDIX VV
NETHERLANDS
ARMED FORCES AND MILITARY POWER

[Reprinted with permission from: The Almanac of World Military Power, by Col. T. N. Dupuy, U.S. Army, Ret., Col. John A. C. Andrews, U.S. Air Force, Ret., and Grace P. Hayes. 3rd ed. Dunn Loring, Va., T. N. Dupuy Associates, 1974.]

NETHERLANDS

Koninkrijk der Nederlanden
Kingdom of the Netherlands

POWER POTENTIAL STATISTICS

Area: 14,140 square miles
Population: 13,400,000
Total Active Armed Forces: 113,500 (0.84% population)
Gross National Product: $57.2 billion ($4,269 per capita)
Annual Military Expenditures: $1.04 billion (1.8% GNP)
Steel Production: 5.6 million metric tons
Iron Production: 4.2 million metric tons
Fuel Production: Coal: 2.8 million metric tons
Crude Oil: 1.6 million metric tons
Refined Petroleum Products: 118.6 million metric tons
Gas: 58.4 billion cubic meters
Electric Power Output: 49.6 billion kwh
Merchant Fleet: 786 ships; 3.3 million gross tons
Civil Air Fleet: 93 jet, 15 turboprop, 278 piston transports

DEFENSE STRUCTURE

The Queen is nominal commander in chief of the armed forces. The Council of Ministers is responsible to the Prime Minister for the preparation and implementation of all defense plans. The Minister of Defense, as member of the Council and assisted by his three service Secretaries of State, is responsible for military preparedness and the organization of the armed forces. A Military Committee, consisting of the three chiefs of staff and a chairman (general or admiral), advises the civilian authorities. Command authority is vested in the individual chiefs of staff, who are directly accountable to the government.

POLITICO-MILITARY POLICY

The Netherlands is a charter member of the North Atlantic Treaty Alliance, and its commitment to NATO is reflected in the missions of the armed forces. Most of the Dutch Army is assigned to the Northern Army Group of NATO's AFCENT Command. Only a few ground units are retained for the territorial defense of the country. The Dutch Air Force is largely integrated into NATO's Second Allied Tactical Air Force. The bulk of the Dutch Navy is divided between two NATO commitments: the Eastern Atlantic Command (part of ACLANT) and the Channel Command (ACCHAN)

The Dutch armed forces are also responsible for the defense of the overseas territories in the West Indies.

Universal military service provides the bulk of the manpower for the armed forces (*Krijgsmacht*). Some 50,000 men annually are called to the colors for a term of 16 to 21 months, depending on the branch of service.

STRATEGIC PROBLEMS

The location of the country and the lack of territorial and air-space depth render the Dutch dependent on the NATO Alliance for their security.

MILITARY ASSISTANCE

The Netherlands received $1.23 billion in military aid from the United States from 1950 through 1967.

ALLIANCES

The Netherlands is a member of the UN, NATO, Western European Union, Benelux, and the European Economic Community.

ARMY

Personnel: 73,000
Organization:

1 corps (assigned to NATO)
2 armored brigades
4 armored infantry brigades
2 SSM battalions (Honest John) units for territorial defense
1 infantry battalion in Surinam

Major Equipment Inventory:

900 medium tanks (500 Centurion, 400 Leopard)
120 light tanks/tank destroyers (AMX-13 with 105mm gun)
2,000 APCs (AMX-VTT, M-113, DAF-YP-408, M-106, M-577; includes reserves)
260 self-propelled guns/howitzers (203mm M-110, 175mm M-107, 105mm and 155mm AMX-105 and M-109)
SSM launchers (Honest John)
140 light aircraft/helicopters (including 3 squadrons of observation aircraft helicopters)

Reserve: Approximately 40,000 men are immediately available for mobilization into one infantry division plus combat and service support corps troops earmarked for NATO. Privates are subject to recall up to the age of 35; NCOs up to the age of 40; and officers can be recalled up to 45 years. Trained reservists total about 350,000.

NAVY

Personnel: 19,000 (including 2,900 Marines and 2,000 Naval Air Force)

Major Units:

1 guided missile light cruiser (CLG)
6 diesel submarines (SS)
12 destroyers (DD)
6 frigates (DE; armed with Seacat SAMs)
3 patrol escorts (PC)
5 submarine chasers (SC)
32 coastal minesweepers (MSC)
3 coastal minehunters (MHC)
16 inshore minesweepers (MSI)
3 command support ships
40 auxiliaries
1 reconnaissance squadron (BR1150 Atlantique and P-2 Neptune)
3 ASW squadrons (S-2 Trackers; 1 squadron in Surinam)
4 helicopter squadrons (H-34, AB204)

Major Aircraft Types:

9 BR1150 Atlantique reconnaissance aircraft (replacing Neptunes)
15 P-2 Neptune reconnaissance aircraft
43 S-2 Tracker ASW aircraft

8 H-34 helicopters
12 Westland Wasp helicopters (carried on DEs)
7 AB204 helicopters

Missiles: SAM: Terrier and Seacat; ASM: Nord AS-12

Major Naval Bases: Valkenburg, Vlissengen, Den Helder

Reserves: About 10,000 reservists (including naval air and Marine personnel)

AIR FORCE

All Air Force units are assigned to NATO

Personnel: 21,500

Organization:

- 2 interceptor squadrons (F-104)
- 5 fighter-bomber squadrons (F-104, F-5)
- 1 reconnaissance squadron (RF-104)
- 1 transport squadron (Fokker F-27)
- 3 light aircraft squadrons (including helicopters; under Army command; Alouette III, L-21, Beaver)
- 20 SAM squadrons (12 Hawk, 8 Nike-Hercules)

Major Aircraft Types:

- 174 combat aircraft
  - 72 F-104 interceptors/fighter-bombers
  - 18 RF-104 fighter reconnaissance aircraft
  - 54 F-5 fighter-bombers
  - 30 F-5 fighter trainers
- 154 other aircraft
  - 12 F-27 transports
  - 70 miscellaneous trainer/support aircraft (L-21, Beaver, C-45, S-11)
  - 72 helicopters (Alouette III)

Major Air Bases: Bilze-Rijen, Deelen, Twenthe, Bolkel, Eindhoven, Soesterberg.

Reserves: About 20,000 trained reservists

PARAMILITARY

The State Police Corps, numbering 4,600, includes water, mounted, and motor police and is under the Ministry of Justice. The Royal Marechaussee (Gendarmerie) number about 3,200 men.

APPENDIX WW
NETHERLANDS
BACKGROUND NOTES

[Washington, Department of State, September 1973 (Publication 7967).]

Netherlands

department of state * september 1973

OFFICIAL NAME: Kingdom of the Netherlands

GEOGRAPHY

The Netherlands is bordered on the north and west by the North Sea, on the south by Belgium, and on the east by the Federal Republic of Germany. The country is low and flat except in the southeast, where some hills rise to 300 feet above sea level. Much of the remaining area is below sea level, making the famous Dutch dikes a requisite to use of the land. Continuing reclamation of land from the sea *(polders)* provides fertile land for this densely populated country.

The warmest period falls between June and September, the other 8 months being cool or cold. Despite an occasional warm spell in summer, temperatures rarely exceed 75°F. Winter is long, often dreary, and the damp cold is penetrating.

PEOPLE

The Dutch are primarily of Germanic stock with some Gallo-Celtic mixture. They have clung tenaciously to their small homeland against the constant threat of destruction by the North Sea and the recurrent danger of extinction at the hands of the great European powers.

Religion strongly influences Dutch history, institutions, and attitudes and is closely related to social and political life. The right of every individual to profess his religion is guaranteed by the Constitution. Although church and state are separate, a few historical ties remain—e.g., the Royal Family belongs to the Dutch Reformed Church (Protestant). According to the latest available figures 40.4 percent of the Dutch are Roman Catholic, 28.3 percent are Protestant Reformed, 9.3 percent are Protestant Calvinist, 3.6 percent are other denominations (mainly Protestant), and 18.4 percent have no religious affiliation.

HISTORY

Julius Caesar found the Netherlands inhabited by Germanic tribes, one of which, the Batavi, did not submit to Rome until 13 B.C. and then only as an ally. A part of Charlemagne's empire in the 8th century A.D., the area later passed into the hands of the House of Burgundy and the Austrian

PROFILE

Geography

AREA: 12,617 sq. mi. (about one-third the size of Indiana). CAPITAL: Amsterdam (pop. 985,000). SEAT OF GOVERNMENT: The Hague (pop. 715,000). OTHER CITIES: Rotterdam (pop. 900,000) and Utrecht (pop. 275,000). Terrain mostly low and flat; one-third below sea level, one-fifth reclaimed from the sea through use of dikes.

People

POPULATION: 13.3 million (1972 est.). ANNUAL GROWTH RATE: 1%. DENSITY: 1,046 per sq. mi. URBAN: 71%. ETHNIC GROUPS: Dutch.

RELIGION: Dutch Reformed Church (Protestant), Roman Catholic, Protestant Calvinist. LANGUAGE: Dutch. LITERACY: 98%. LIFE EXPECTANCY: 76 years.

Government

TYPE: Constitutional monarchy. DATE OF CONSTITUTION: 1954, Statute of the Realm.

FLAG: Three horizontal stripes—red, white, and blue from top to bottom.

BRANCHES: *Executive:* Queen (Chief of State), Prime Minister (Head of Government). *Legislature:* bicameral Parliament (States General): First Chamber (75 members elected for a term of 6 years), Second Chamber (150 members elected for a term of 4 years). *Judiciary:* Supreme Court.

Economy

GNP: $51 billion (1972). ANNUAL GROWTH RATE: 4% (1972). PER CAPITA: $3,853. PER CAPITA GROWTH RATE: 3.7%.

AGRICULTURE: *Labor,* 8%. *Land,* 56%. *Acres per capita,* 0.4. *Crops:* wheat, barley, sugar beets, fruits, potatoes, oats, flax.

INDUSTRY: *Products:* metal fabrication, textiles, chemicals, electronics.

TRADE (1970): *Exports*—$11.8 million: foodstuffs, machinery, transportation equipment, consumer goods, chemicals, petroleum products, textiles. *Imports*—$13.4 million: machinery, transportation equipment, crude petroleum, animal feed, chemicals, raw cotton, base metals and ores, wood pulp. *Partners*—Federal Republic of Germany, Belgium, France, U.S.

MEMBERSHIP IN INTERNATIONAL ORGANIZATIONS: Benelux Economic Union, European Communities, Organization for Economic Cooperation and Development (OECD), United Nations.

Hapsburgs. Falling under harsh Spanish rule in the 16th century, the Dutch revolted in 1568, led by William of Orange. By virtue of the Union of Utrecht in 1579 the seven northern Dutch Provinces became the Republic of the United Netherlands.

During the 17th century, considered its "Golden Era," the Netherlands became a great sea and colonial power. Its importance declined, however, during the 18th-century wars with Spain and France; in 1795 French troops ousted William V.

Following Napoleon's defeat in 1813 the Netherlands and Belgium became the "Kingdom of the United Netherlands" under William I, son of William V, the *Stadtholder* under the Dutch Republic, and head of the House of Orange. The Belgians withdrew from the union in 1830 to form their own Kingdom. William I abdicated in favor of William II in 1840; the latter was largely responsible for promulgation of a liberal constitution in 1848.

The Netherlands prospered during the long reign of William III (1849-90). At the time of his death, his daughter, Wilhelmina, was 10 years old. Her mother, Queen Emma, reigned as regent until 1898 when Wilhelmina reached the age of 18 and succeeded to the throne.

Although the Netherlands was neutral during World War I and again proclaimed neutrality at the start of World War II, German troops overran the country in May 1940. Queen Wilhelmina and Crown Princess Juliana fled to London, where a government-in-exile was established. The German Army in the Netherlands capitulated May 5, 1945. The Queen and Crown Princess returned to the Netherlands shortly thereafter. Queen Juliana succeeded to the throne in 1948 upon her mother's abdication.

Indonesia gained its independence from the Netherlands in 1949. West New Guinea was placed under the administrative control of the United Nations in 1962 and from 1963 was administratively controlled by Indonesia. In 1969 an "Act of Free Choice" confirmed the Indonesian claim to the territory. Surinam and the six islands of the Netherlands Antilles (Aruba, Curacao, Bonaire, Saba, Sint Eustatius, and a part of Sint Maarten) are integral parts of the Netherlands realm but are increasingly autonomous. (For more information, see *Background Notes* on Surinam, Department of State pub. 8268, and Netherlands Antilles, Department of State pub. 8223.)

The Netherlands is still often referred to as Holland, which was the largest Dutch province and incorporated the country's three largest and most prosperous cities: Amsterdam, The Hague, and Rotterdam. The original province is now two Provinces—Noord-Holland and Zuid-Holland.

GOVERNMENT

The present Constitution, known formally as the Statute of the Realm, was adopted in 1954. Under it the government is based on the principles of ministerial responsibility and parliamentary government common to most constitutional monarchies in Western Europe. It is composed of three basic institutions: (1) the Crown (Monarch, Council of Ministers, and Council of State); (2) the States General (parliament); and (3) the Courts.

Monarch

Although her functions are largely ceremonial, the Queen has certain influence deriving from: (a) the traditional veneration for the House of Orange; (b) the personal qualities of Queen Juliana and Queen Wilhelmina; and (c) the political party system, which makes it difficult to obtain a parliamentary majority, thereby enabling the Queen to influence the choice of Ministers through her designation of the individual charged with forming a coalition Council of Ministers.

Council of Ministers (Cabinet)

Ministers have two general functions. With the exception of the Ministers without portfolio, they head ministries or departments. Collectively the Ministers form the Council of Ministers, which formulates and carries out government policies and can initiate legislation. The Ministers collectively and individually are responsible to the States General.

Council of State

An advisory body to the Crown, the Council of State consists of members of the Royal Family and Crown-appointed members generally having political, commercial, diplomatic, or military experience. It is consulted on legislative proposals only after the Council of Ministers has approved the consultation.

States General (Parliament)

The States General consists of the First Chamber (upper house) and the Second Chamber (lower house), which meet separately except for ceremonial occasions. In addition to their legislative authority, both chambers exercise a check on the Council of Ministers through questioning and investigation. The Second Chamber, however, is far more important, for it alone has the right to initiate legislation and amend bills submitted by the Council of Ministers. The First Chamber has 75 members elected for a term of 6 years by the 11 provincial legislatures. One-half of its membership is renewed every 3 years. The Second Chamber has 150 members directly elected on the basis of proportional representation for a term of 4 years, if the session goes to full term. It can be dissolved at any time by a ministerial vote of no-confidence.

Courts

The judiciary is composed of 62 cantonal courts, 19 district courts, five courts of appeal, and a Supreme Court. All judicial appointments are made by the Queen. There are 24 Justices on the Supreme Court. Judges are technically appointed for life but generally retire at the age of 60.

Administrative Divisions

The first-level administrative divisions are the 11 Provinces, each governed by a provincial executive council elected by the inhabitants on the basis of proportional representation. The Queen's Commissioner, the chief executive officer of each Province, is appointed by the Monarch.

POLITICAL CONDITIONS

Political life in the Netherlands is in transition. The stability which characterized a succession of coalition governments has diminished in recent years. Instead, there has been political polarization and decreased support for religious-based parties and social institutions. Despite these recent changes, the major parties accept the monarchy, the parliamentary framework, and political tolerance.

From the end of World War II until December 1958, the Netherlands was governed by a series of coalitions built on a Labor-Catholic base. Thereafter—until 1973—governments were formed primarily from Catholics, Liberals, and two major Protestant parties, leaving the Labor Party in opposition except from April 1965 to October 1966. The government formed in 1971 based on this coalition, with the addition of the Democratic Socialists '70 (DS'70) Party fell after a Cabinet crisis in July 1972. Following the parliamentary elections for the Second Chamber in November 1972, it took nearly 6 months to form a new government. This was unprecedented in Dutch constitutional history. The present government under Labor Prime Minister Johannes den Uyl is based on a coalition of the so-called "progressive" parties (Labor, Radicals, and D'66), the Catholic People's Party, and the Anti-Revolutionary (Protestant) Party.

Four principal groups—Catholics, Labor, Protestants, and Liberals—form the historical basis for the five main political parties in the country. These parties, however, have evolved to cut across social and economic lines and now hold generally moderate policy positions. In the foreign policy field they support the North Atlantic Treaty Organization (NATO) and West European integration. The more extreme philosophies of the right and left are represented by smaller minor parties.

The high degree of consensus among the principal parties contrasts with increasing tensions within them. Political renewal, a movement for institutional and doctrinal reform and for greater popular participation, has special appeal for younger elements—especially in the Catholic and Labor Parties, the two largest. Most of the major parties have political renewal groupings who cooperate across party lines. While the Netherlands may be evolving toward a fundamental political realignment, this will require formal restructuring which will be bitterly opposed by significant elements within all of the political groupings.

The next parliamentary elections for the Second Chamber are scheduled for the fall of 1976.

Labor Party (PvdA)

The Labor Party, largest in the Second Chamber and the nation, is the principal partner in the current coalition. The Labor Party has been exploring cooperative arrangements with the D'66 Party and the Political Party of the Radicals (PPR) in an effort to create a new Progressive People's Party. Though these three parties presented a common program in the last parliamentary election, enthusiasm for a new Progressive People's Party has waned considerably, especially in D '66 which lost some seats in the November 1972 elections and among the Radicals who object to what they term the Labor Party's "doctrinal socialism."

Catholic People's Party (KVP)

As the second largest party both in the Second Chamber and in the coalition, the KVP is the main defender of the small- and medium-size businessmen and farmers of the Catholic faith who provide the party's basic electoral strength. The party supports free enterprise and holds to the principle that government activity should supplement but not supplant communal action by citizens. This philosophy, however, has not prevented the KVP from supporting many of the social programs now in force in the Netherlands. The KVP has lost strength during the last few years and is working toward a cooperative arrangement with the two other major religious (both Protestant) parties—the Anti-Revolutionary Party (ARP) and the Christian Historical Union (CHU). However, this effort to form a Christian Democratic Party, first launched in 1966, faces serious opposition, especially from within the two Protestant parties.

Liberal Party (VVD)

The VVD made an especially spectacular showing in the latest parliamentary election, going from 16 to 22 seats. The VVD has become popularly identified as the party of the urban upper and middle classes. It strongly supports free enterprise against government controls. However, the VVD supports public control as opposed to the denomination system in fields such as education.

Anti-Revolutionary Party (ARP)
Christian Historical Union (CHU)

These two major Protestant parties advocate the application of Christian doctrine in politics. The main differences between them are organizational and tactical. Both generally support the present welfare state and equality of denominational education. The CHU is more loosely organized, generally considered more conservative than the ARP, and includes perhaps more members of the upper-middle class and fewer workers. The CHU, which elected not to participate in the current coalition, lost some seats in the last election while the ARP, whose election list was headed by the then Prime Minister, gained one seat.

Political Party of the Radicals (PPR)

Formed in March 1968, this party was originally composed of left-wing Catholics who objected to their party's decision to participate in a coalition with the Liberals rather than the Labor Party. It is now a completely secular political group. The Radicals, appealing primarily to younger voters, made an impressive showing in the November 1972 parliamentary elections and increased their representation in the Second Chamber from two to seven seats. The PPR, which inclines to be suspicious of doctrinal socialism, supports radical restructuring of current society. It is opposed to the use or even threat of use of nuclear weapons and is a strong proponent of increased Dutch assistance to the developing countries.

Democrats '66 (D'66)

Formed in October 1966, this party made a dramatic entrance into Dutch transit trade is included, or about $900 million if only Dutch imports for domestic consumption are considered. U.S. direct investments in the Netherlands have a total book value (end 1971) of about $1.7 billion and Dutch investments in the United States exceed $2.2 billion.

FOREIGN RELATIONS

Prior to World War II the Netherlands adhered strictly to a policy of neutrality. Wartime occupation and disillusionment over postwar Soviet behavior brought about a radical change in this position, however, and the Netherlands has become one of the foremost proponents of Atlantic partnership and European integration.

The Netherlands is a strong supporter of the North Atlantic Treaty Organization (NATO) and a unified Europe including the United Kingdom. It is also an energetic member of the European Communities (European Economic Community, European Atomic Energy Community, and the European Coal and Steel Community), the Organization for Economic Cooperation and Development (OECD), and the Benelux Economic Union.

Further, in continuation of its tradition of international activity in the political and economic fields, it provides important support for the Western position in the United Nations and maintains an impressive program of foreign aid.

The major part of its foreign aid is bilateral in nature and devoted to 12 countries, among them Indonesia, India, Pakistan, Tanzania, and Colombia and to the other parts of the Realm, Surinam and the Netherlands Antilles. The Netherlands also contributes significantly through multilateral channels such as the Asian Development Bank and the UNDP.

From 1950 to 1973 the Netherlands had relations with all Communist countries except North Korea and North Viet-Nam. In 1973 the Netherlands recognized North Viet-Nam.

U.S.–NETHERLANDS RELATIONS

The excellent relations existing between the United States and the Netherlands are based on close historical ties and a common dedication to the security of the Western world. These relations are facilitated by the remarkable level of English language comprehension in the Netherlands–estimated at 70 percent nationwide and as high as 90 percent in Amsterdam, the capital. An outward-looking nation, the Netherlands works with the United States, bilaterally and in the United Nations and other international and regional organizations, to further free trade, economic cooperation, and assistance to the developing countries.

PRINCIPAL GOVERNMENT OFFICIALS

Monarch–Queen Juliana

Council of Ministers

Labor Party

Johannes den Uyl–Prime Minister and Minister of General Affairs

Max van der Stoel–Minister of Foreign Affairs

Henricus Vredeling–Minister of Defense

W. Duisenberg–Minister of Finance

Jan P. Pronk–Minister Without Portfolio for Development Assistance

Irene Vorrink–Minister of Health and Environment

J. A. van Kemenade–Minister of Education

Catholic People's Party

Andreas A. M. van Agt–First Deputy Prime Minister and Minister of Justice

Rudolph F. M. Lubbers–Minister of Economic Affairs

T. Brouwer–Minister of Agriculture and Fisheries

Theodorus Westerterp–Minister of Traffic and Waterways

Anti-Revolutionary Party

W. F. de Gaay Fortman–Minister of Interior Affairs

Jacobus Boersma–Minister of Social Affairs

Political Party of the Radicals

Henri Willem van Doorn–Minister of Culture, Recreation and Social Work

Ferdinand H. P. Trip–Minister Without Portfolio for Scientific Affairs

Democrats '66

J. P. A. Gruijters–Minister of Housing and Physical Planning

Ambassador to the U.S.–Baron Rijnhard von Lynden

Ambassador to the U.N.–Robbert Fack

The Netherlands maintains an Embassy in the United States at 4200 Linnean Avenue, N.W., Washington,

Travel Notes

Climate–**The warmest period falls between June and September, the other 8 months being cool or cold. Temperatures rarely exceed 75°F. Winters are long and wet.**

Transportation–**Good public transportation is available in the cities by bus and streetcar, which serve principal sections of the city as well as the suburbs. Most Dutch cities are connected by rail and almost all regions in the Netherlands are accessible by good public transportation. Excellent transportation to other principal cities in Europe is also available.**

The Netherlands is a standard right-hand-drive country.

Telephone–**Facilities are good for local and long distance use. Local calls are about 2¢ each; a 3-minute call to the U.S. is about $12.**

Mail–**Deliveries to and from the U.S. are frequent and reliable. Transit time varies from 2 to 6 days (airmail) and 3 to 6 weeks (surface) from major U.S. east coast cities.**

Radio & TV–**Radio reception is good; programs from a number of neighboring countries can be heard. TV is on from 7 to 11 nightly, 7 days a week. Two channels are available.**

Health and Sanitation–**Medical facilities are good in the Netherlands. Community sanitation is comparable to standards maintained in U.S. urban areas. Public eating places, butcher shops, dairies, etc., are inspected regularly.**

Currency–**Official currency unit is the Netherlands guilder (Fl.); foreign exchange control regulations place no limit on the amount of foreign currency or negotiable instruments which may be imported.**

Weights and Measures–**The Netherlands uses the metric system.**

transit trade is included, or about $900 million if only Dutch imports for domestic consumption are considered. U.S. direct investments in the Netherlands have a total book value (end 1971) of about $1.7 billion and Dutch investments in the United States exceed $2.2 billion.

FOREIGN RELATIONS

Prior to World War II the Netherlands adhered strictly to a policy of neutrality. Wartime occupation and disillusionment over postwar Soviet behavior brought about a radical change in this position, however, and the Netherlands has become one of the foremost proponents of Atlantic partnership and European integration.

The Netherlands is a strong supporter of the North Atlantic Treaty Organization (NATO) and a unified Europe including the United Kingdom. It is also an energetic member of the European Communities (European Economic Community, European Atomic Energy Community, and the European Coal and Steel Community), the Organization for Economic Cooperation and Development (OECD), and the Benelux Economic Union.

Further, in continuation of its tradition of international activity in the political and economic fields, it provides important support for the Western position in the United Nations and maintains an impressive program of foreign aid.

The major part of its foreign aid is bilateral in nature and devoted to 12 countries, among them Indonesia, India, Pakistan, Tanzania, and Colombia and to the other parts of the Realm, Surinam and the Netherlands Antilles. The Netherlands also contributes significantly through multilateral channels such as the Asian Development Bank and the UNDP.

From 1950 to 1973 the Netherlands had relations with all Communist countries except North Korea and North Viet-Nam. In 1973 the Netherlands recognized North Viet-Nam.

U.S.–NETHERLANDS RELATIONS

The excellent relations existing between the United States and the Netherlands are based on close historical ties and a common dedication to the security of the Western world. These relations are facilitated by the remarkable level of English language comprehension in the Netherlands–estimated at 70 percent nationwide and as high as 90 percent in Amsterdam, the capital. An outward-looking nation, the Netherlands works with the United States, bilaterally and in the United Nations and other international and regional organizations, to further free trade, economic cooperation, and assistance to the developing countries.

PRINCIPAL GOVERNMENT OFFICIALS

Monarch–Queen Juliana

Council of Ministers

Labor Party

Johannes den Uyl–Prime Minister and Minister of General Affairs

Max van der Stoel–Minister of Foreign Affairs

Henricus Vredeling–Minister of Defense

W. Duisenberg–Minister of Finance

Jan P. Pronk–Minister Without Portfolio for Development Assistance

Irene Vorrink–Minister of Health and Environment

J. A. van Kemenade–Minister of Education

Catholic People's Party

Andreas A. M. van Agt–First Deputy Prime Minister and Minister of Justice

Rudolph F. M. Lubbers–Minister of Economic Affairs

T. Brouwer–Minister of Agriculture and Fisheries

Theodorus Westerterp–Minister of Traffic and Waterways

Anti-Revolutionary Party

W. F. de Gaay Fortman–Minister of Interior Affairs

Jacobus Boersma–Minister of Social Affairs

Political Party of the Radicals

Henri Willem van Doorn–Minister of Culture, Recreation and Social Work

Ferdinand H. P. Trip–Minister Without Portfolio for Scientific Affairs

Democrats '66

J. P. A. Gruijters–Minister of Housing and Physical Planning

Ambassador to the U.S.–Baron Rijnhard von Lynden

Ambassador to the U.N.–Robbert Fack

The Netherlands maintains an Embassy in the United States at 4200 Linnean Avenue, N.W., Washington,

Travel Notes

Climate–The warmest period falls between June and September, the other 8 months being cool or cold. Temperatures rarely exceed 75°F. Winters are long and wet.

Transportation–Good public transportation is available in the cities by bus and streetcar, which serve principal sections of the city as well as the suburbs. Most Dutch cities are connected by rail and almost all regions in the Netherlands are accessible by good public transportation. Excellent transportation to other principal cities in Europe is also available.

The Netherlands is a standard right-hand-drive country.

Telephone–Facilities are good for local and long distance use. Local calls are about 2¢ each; a 3-minute call to the U.S. is about $12.

Mail–Deliveries to and from the U.S. are frequent and reliable. Transit time varies from 2 to 6 days (airmail) and 3 to 6 weeks (surface) from major U.S. east coast cities.

Radio & TV–Radio reception is good; programs from a number of neighboring countries can be heard. TV is on from 7 to 11 nightly, 7 days a week. Two channels are available.

Health and Sanitation–Medical facilities are good in the Netherlands. Community sanitation is comparable to standards maintained in U.S. urban areas. Public eating places, butcher shops, dairies, etc., are inspected regularly.

Currency–Official currency unit is the Netherlands guilder (Fl.); foreign exchange control regulations place no limit on the amount of foreign currency or negotiable instruments which may be imported.

Weights and Measures–The Netherlands uses the metric system.

D.C. 20008. There are also Consulates General at Los Angeles, San Francisco, New Orleans, New York City, and Houston.

PRINCIPAL U.S. OFFICIALS

Ambassador–Vacant
Chargé d'Affaires–Charles R. Tanguy
Political Counselor–Robert L. Burns
Economic/Commercial Counselor–John Q. Blodgett
Commercial Counselor–Harold C. Voorhees
Public Affairs Counselor–R. Dabney Chapman
Defense and Naval Attaché–Capt. John P. Sundberg
Army Attaché–Col. Lucien E. Rising
Air Attaché–Col. Andrew M. Riddle
Agricultural Attaché–Jerome M. Kuhl
Chief, MAAG–Capt. Emil Saroch, Jr.
Consul General, Amsterdam–Eugene M. Braderman
Consul General, Rotterdam–Elden B. Erickson

The U.S. Embassy in the Netherlands is located at 102 Lange Voorhout, The Hague. Consulates General are at Museumplein 19, Amsterdam, and Vlasmarkt 1, Rotterdam.

READING LIST

These titles are provided as a general indication of the material currently being published on this country; the Department of State does not endorse the specific views in unofficial publications as representing the position of the U.S. Government.

Bailey, Anthony. *The Light in Holland.* New York: Knopf, 1970.

Barnouw, Adriaan J. *The Making of Modern Holland.* New York: Norton, 1944.

Barnouw, Adriaan J. *Pageant of Netherlands History.* London: Columbia University Press, 1952.

Blok, Petrus Johannes. *History of the Peoples of the Netherlands,* 5 vols. New York, 1898-1912.

Edmundson, George. *History of Holland.* Cambridge: Cambridge University Press, 1922.

Eyck, F. Gunther. *The Benelux Countries: An Historical Survey.* Princeton: Van Nostrand, 1959.

Goudsblom, Johan. *Dutch Society.* New York, 1967.

Huggett, Frank E. *The Modern Netherlands.* New York: Praeger, 1971.

Landheer, Bartholomew, ed. *The Netherlands.* Berkeley: University of California Press, 1943.

Lyphart, A. *The Politics of Accommodation–Pluralism and Democracy in the Netherlands.* Berkeley: University of California Press, 1968.

Maass, Walter B. *The Netherlands At War: 1940-1945.* New York: Abelard-Schuman, 1970.

Meade, James E. *Negotiations for Benelux: An Annotated Chronicle.* Princeton, 1957.

Raalte, E. van. *The Parliament of the Kingdom of the Netherlands.* London: Hansard Society for Parliamentary Government, 1959.

Schoffer, I.A. *A Short History of the Netherlands.* Amsterdam, 1956.

Van Campen, S.I.P. *The Quest for Security.* The Hague: M. Nijhoff, 1958.

Van den Bosch, A. *Dutch Foreign Policy Since 1815: A Study in Small Power Politics.* The Hague: M. Nijhoff, 1959.

Vlêkke, Bernard H. M. *Evolution of the Dutch Nation.* New York: Roy, 1945.

DEPARTMENT OF STATE PUBLICATION 7967
Revised September 1973

APPENDIX XX

THE NETHERLANDS

STRENGTH OF THE COMMUNIST PARTY ORGANIZATION—1973

[FROM: World Strength of the Communist Party Organizations—1973. Washington, Department of State, Bureau of Intelligence and Research, 1973.]

THE NETHERLANDS

National Political Status: Date of last election - November 29, 1972.

Communist: Communist Party of the Netherlands (CPN) - 329,973 votes (4.5%), 7 seats (4.7%)

Non-Communist Left: Labor Party - 2,021,473 votes (27.4%), 43 seats (28.7%)
Radical Party - 354,356 votes (4.8%), 7 seats (4.7%)
Democrat Socialists '70 - 304,625 votes (4.1%), 6 seats (4.0%)
Democrats '66 - 306,787 votes (4.2%), 6 seats (4.0%)

Center: Catholic Party - 1,304,974 votes (17.7%), 27 seats (18.0%)
Anti-Revolutionary Party - 653,237 votes (8.8%), 14 seats (9.3%)
Christian Historical Union - 354,291 votes (4.8%), 7 seats (4.7%)

Conservative: Liberal Party - 1,067,325 votes (14.4%), 22 seats (14.7%)

Other: 693,802 votes (9.4%), 11 seats (7.3%)

Total: 7,390,843 votes, 150 seats

Communist Party Membership: 8,800 (estimate)

Leading Party Figures and Positions:
DE GROOT, Paul - Former Chairman
HOECKSTRA, Henk - Chairman
WOLFF, J. F. - Editor of *De Waarheid*

Principal Publication:
De Waarheid - party newspaper

Areas of Communist Activity: In 1971 and 1972, in each of two successive elections for the Second Chamber (lower house), the Communist Party of the Netherlands (CPN) won one additional seat, bringing its total to seven (out of 150). Despite this increase, the party continues to remain outside the parliamentary mainstream.

The CPN is isolated both domestically, where it is considered to be a band of aging men, and internationally, where it comes under strong attack from the CPSU for its insistence on autonomy and freedom from interference. There has been some recent evidence that the CPN is attempting to break from its isolation and reestablish contact with European Communist parties. It was represented by two observers at a meeting of West European Communist parties in Stockholm in 1973.

Besides the CPN, there are a few minuscule Peking-oriented Communist splinter groups in the Netherlands which have no influence either within or outside the CPN.

APPENDIX YY
NORWAY
ARMED FORCES AND MILITARY POWER

[Reprinted with permission from: The Almanac of World Military Power, by Col. T. N. Dupuy, U.S. Army, Ret., Col. John A. C. Andrews, U.S. Air Force, Ret., and Grace P. Hayes. 3rd ed. Dunn Loring, Va., T. N. Dupuy Associates, 1974.]

NORWAY

Kongeriket Norge
Kingdom of Norway

POWER POTENTIAL STATISTICS

Area: 149,150 square miles
Population: 4,000,000
Total Active Armed Forces: 35,900 (0.90% population)
Gross National Product: $16.8 billion ($4,200 per capita)
Annual Military Expenditures: $604.8 million (3.6% GNP)
Iron and Steel Production: 2.1 million metric tons
Aluminum Production: 529,000 metric tons
Fuel Production: Coal: 446,000 metric tons
  Crude Oil: 1.6 million metric tons
  Refined Petroleum Products: 6.3 million metric tons
  Manufactured Gas: 29.8 million cubic meters
Electric Power Output: 62.7 billion kwh
Merchant Fleet: 2,814 ships; 21.7 million gross tons
Civil Air Fleet: 10 jet, 8 turboprop, 15 piston transports (exclusive of the Norwegian-owned portion of SAS)

DEFENSE STRUCTURE

Norway is a constitutional monarchy; the King is the nominal commander in chief of the armed forces. Control is exercised, however, by the parliamentary Cabinet, with the Minister of Defense responsible for administering the three independent military services.

POLITICO-MILITARY POLICY

Before World War II Norway adhered to the traditional Scandinavian policy of neutrality. The experience of that war convinced Norwegians that neutrality will not deter an aggressor, and that Norwegian defense policy must be built upon a mutual security alliance, since Norway cannot possibly muster the military strength to defend itself against a major aggressor. Thus Norway has been a wholehearted participant in the NATO alliance but, to avoid offense to its Soviet neighbor (Norway is the only NATO country, except Turkey, with a mutual frontier with Russia), it has consistently refused to allow allied troop units, or bases, or stored nuclear weapons, on Norwegian soil.

NATO maintains a regional headquarters, that of Commander in Chief North (CINCNORTH) at Kolsaas near Oslo. Officers of various NATO nations are represented on the staff. NATO units visit Norway to participate in maneuvers.

Norway has a battalion in the UN force on Cyprus, and furnished a unit for the UN Emergency Force in the Gaza Strip until evacuated in June 1967.

Norway's armed forces are maintained by conscription, with an annual call-up of more than 20,000 young men.

Service is for 12 months in the Army, and 15 months in the Navy and Air Force. Most of the Norwegian armed forces are earmarked for AFNORTH (Allied Forces Northern Europe).

STRATEGIC PROBLEMS

Norway's extreme length (its eastern boundary is over 1,600 miles long), the rugged nature of the interior of the country (particularly in the north), and the near total absence of a ground communications network in the north, pose almost insuperable defense problems, particularly near the Soviet border.

Introduction of Soviet submarines into the numerous ice-free fjords would facilitate interdiction of North Atlantic sea lanes, and thus the loss of even northern Norway would represent a severe setback to NATO. In addition to the coastal invasion route from Kerkenes near the Soviet-Norwegian border, a serious threat is posed by the Finnish wedge, a salient of Finland with a good road which stretches close to the coast in the strategic Bardufoss-Tromso-Harstad area. A Soviet offensive on this axis could quickly seize northern Norway.

Problems of defense are compounded by the Arctic climate, and by a deeply indented, sparsely inhabited coastline more than 2,000 miles long, very vulnerable to surprise amphibious attack. The nature of these defense problems was thoroughly demonstrated during World War II.

Near the Soviet Union on the strategic polar route from the US, the archipelago of Spitsbergen (Svalbard) was awarded to Norway in 1920 by an international treaty, which also prohibited establishment of naval or military bases. There are a number of active coal mines on the islands, worked by some 700 Norwegians and 2,000 Russians. Beginning in 1944 Russia sought revision of the treaty to include joint Soviet-Norwegian defense measures. Norway has refused to consider this without the concurrence of all treaty signatories, which has not been forthcoming.

It is believed that there are also extensive oil and gas deposits in the continental shelf of the Barents Sea between Spitsbergen and the Soviet Union. Norway and the USSR have overlapping claims to this area, and negotiations on these claims were to be held between the two governments in the fall of 1974.

MILITARY ASSISTANCE

Since 1950 Norway has received $908.2 million in American military aid. The US Military Advisory Group in Norway numbers about 30.

ALLIANCES

Norway is a member of the NATO alliance. Otherwise it has maintained a strict neutrality in international relations and, as noted above, has to some extent limited its involvement in NATO. Norway is a member of the UN.

ARMY

Personnel: 18,000

Organization:

5 regional commands divided into land defense districts
2 regimental combat teams (one in north, one in south)
4 tank companies

Major Equipment Inventory:

80 medium tanks (M-48)
78 medium tanks (Leopard)
47 light tanks (M-24)
armored cars (M-8)
30 artillery pieces (including M-109 155mm SP howitzers)
APCs (M-113 and BV-202)
40mm AA
34 light aircraft (L-4, 0-1)
10 helicopters

Reserve: About 160,000 men who will be organized into 11 RCTs, supporting units, and territorial defense forces.

NAVY

Personnel: 8,500 (including 800 coast artillerymen)

Major Units:

5 destroyer escorts (DE)
15 coastal submarines (SS)
5 coastal minelayers (MMC)
10 coastal minesweepers (MSC)
2 patrol escorts/submarine chasers (PCE)
20 gunboats/fast patrol boats (PG/PBF; refitting with Penguin SSM)
26 torpedo boats (PT, six with Penguin SSM)
7 landing craft (LCT)
14 auxiliaries
coast defense artillery battalions

Main Naval Bases: Haakonsvern, Harstad, Tromso, Trondheim, Bergen

Reserves: 18,000 trained reservists

AIR FORCE

Personnel: 9,400

Organization:

- 2 fighter-interceptor squadrons (F-104)
- 5 fighter-bomber squadrons (F-5)
- 1 reconnaissance squadron (RF-5)
- 2 maritime patrol squadrons (P-3 and HU-16)
- 1 transport squadron (C-130)
- 2 helicopter squadrons (UH-1, Bell 47, Sea King)
- 4 SAM battalions (Nike-Hercules)

Major Aircraft Types:

- 141 combat aircraft
  - 38 F-104 interceptors
  - 80 F-5 fighter-bombers
  - 16 RF-5 fighter reconnaissance aircraft
  - 5 P-3 maritime patrol aircraft
  - 2 HU-16 maritime patrol aircraft
- 128 other aircraft
  - 6 C-130 transports
  - 4 Twin Otter light transports
  - 2 Falcon 20 light transports
  - 22 miscellaneous transports
  - 3 PBY patrol/fishing protection aircraft
  - 49 miscellaneous trainer/support aircraft (25 Safir, 20 L-18, 4 Twin Otter)
  - 44 helicopters (UH-1, Bell 47, Sea King)

Reserves: 19,000 trained reservists. Twelve light antiaircraft defense battalions.

Major Air Bases: Stavanger, Bodo, Bardufoss, Andoya (Lofoten Islands)

PARAMILITARY

There is a highly organized Home Guard consisting of 75,000 individuals. Most of them are in Army units, linked to the nation's territorial defense area commands. There are also a few Navy and Air Force Home Guard units. All these are organized in small groups and platoons with specific defense missions in their home localities. Weapons are kept at home, and a relatively high state of readiness is maintained by periodic drills and alerts.

APPENDIX ZZ
NORWAY
BACKGROUND NOTES

[Washington, Department of State, June 1974 (Publication 8228).]

Norway

department of state * june 1974

OFFICIAL NAME: Kingdom of Norway

GEOGRAPHY AND PEOPLE

Norway is located in northwestern Europe on the Scandinavian Peninsula and is bounded by a 2,125-mile-long coastline along the North and Norwegian Seas and the Arctic Ocean. On the east it has common frontiers with Sweden, Finland, and the Soviet Union.

Norway's terrain is comprised mainly of high plateaus and rugged mountains. The highlands are broken by fertile valleys and dotted with lakes. About 25 percent of the land is forested; only 3 percent is arable.

The climate is strongly influenced by the Gulf Stream, resulting in relatively mild winters for the latitude, particularly along the coast. However, interior winter temperatures are extremely cold. Rainfall is generally at a maximum during the fall-winter period. Spring and summer are moderately warm, with maximum temperatures reaching the low 70's and, rarely, the low 80's.

Except for Iceland, Norway has the lowest mean population density in Europe. Sixty-five percent of the people live in the South and along the coast.

Most Norwegians are of Germanic descent, whose ancestors mixed with the original inhabitants and with the Finns and Lapps. The Lapps still live in the north, some of whom follow their traditional reindeer culture.

Complete religious freedom exists. Education is free through the university level and is compulsory from ages 7 to 16.

PROFILE

Geography

AREA: 150,000 sq. mi., including the island territories of Spitzbergen and Jan Mayen (slightly larger than New Mexico). CAPITAL: Oslo (pop. 477,500). OTHER CITIES: Bergen (pop. 212,000), Trondheim (pop. 129,200).

People

POPULATION: 3.96 million (1973 est.). ANNUAL GROWTH RATE: 0.7% (1973). DENSITY: 31 per sq. mi. ETHNIC GROUPS: Germanic (Nordic, Alpine, Baltic) and a racial-cultural minority of 20,000 Lapps. RELIGION: Evangelical Lutheran (state church–96%). LANGUAGES: Norwegian (official), Lappish dialect. LITERACY: 100%. LIFE EXPECTANCY: men–71 yrs.; women–77 yrs.

Government

TYPE: Hereditary constitutional monarchy. INDEPENDENCE: 1905. DATE OF CONSTITUTION: May 17, 1814.

BRANCHES: *Executive*–King (Chief of State), Prime Minister (Head of Government), Council of Ministers (cabinet). *Legislative*–modified unicameral Parliament (Storting). *Judicial*–Supreme Court, appellate courts, city and county courts.

POLITICAL PARTIES: Labor Party, Conservative Party, Center Party, Christian People's Party, Liberal Party, Socialist Electoral League, Anders Lange Party, New People's Party. SUFFRAGE: Universal over 20 yrs. POLITICAL SUBDIVISIONS: 19 Fylker (counties).

FLAG: White cross with blue inner cross on red field. The white cross and red field are derived from the Danish flag; the blue cross was added to symbolize Norway's independence.

Economy

GROSS NATIONAL PRODUCT (GNP): $18.4 billion (1973 est.). ANNUAL GROWTH RATE: 4.3%. PER CAPITA INCOME: $4,649. PER CAPITA GROWTH RATE: 3.7%.

AGRICULTURE: *Land* 3% under cultivation. *Labor* 10%. *Products*–dairy products, livestock, wool, furs, potatoes, wheat, barley, berries.

INDUSTRY: *Labor* 40%. *Products*–fish, timber and forest products, aluminum, zinc, nickel, fertilizer, nitrogen, iron, hydroelectric power, pulp and paper, transport equipment.

NATURAL RESOURCES: Fish, timber, hydroelectric power, ores, oil, gas.

TRADE: *Exports*–$4.53 billion (1973 est.), metals, chemicals, iron and steel, paper. *Partners*–Sweden, Federal Republic of Germany (F.R.G.), United Kingdom (U.K.), United States (7.2%, 1972). *Imports*–$6 billion (1973 est.), ships, nonelectrical machinery, crude oil, clothing, textiles, foodstuffs. *Partners*–Sweden, F.R.G., U.K., United States (6.2%, 1972).

OFFICIAL EXCHANGE RATE: 5.70 Norwegian kroner=US$1 (March 5, 1974).

MEMBERSHIP IN INTERNATIONAL ORGANIZATIONS: U.N. and several of its specialized agencies, North Atlantic Treaty Organization (NATO), Organization for Economic Cooperation and Development (OECD), Nordic Council.

HISTORY

The Viking period was one of national unification and expansion. The Norwegian royal line died out in 1319, and Norway entered a period of "union" with Denmark and for a time also with Sweden. By 1536 Norway

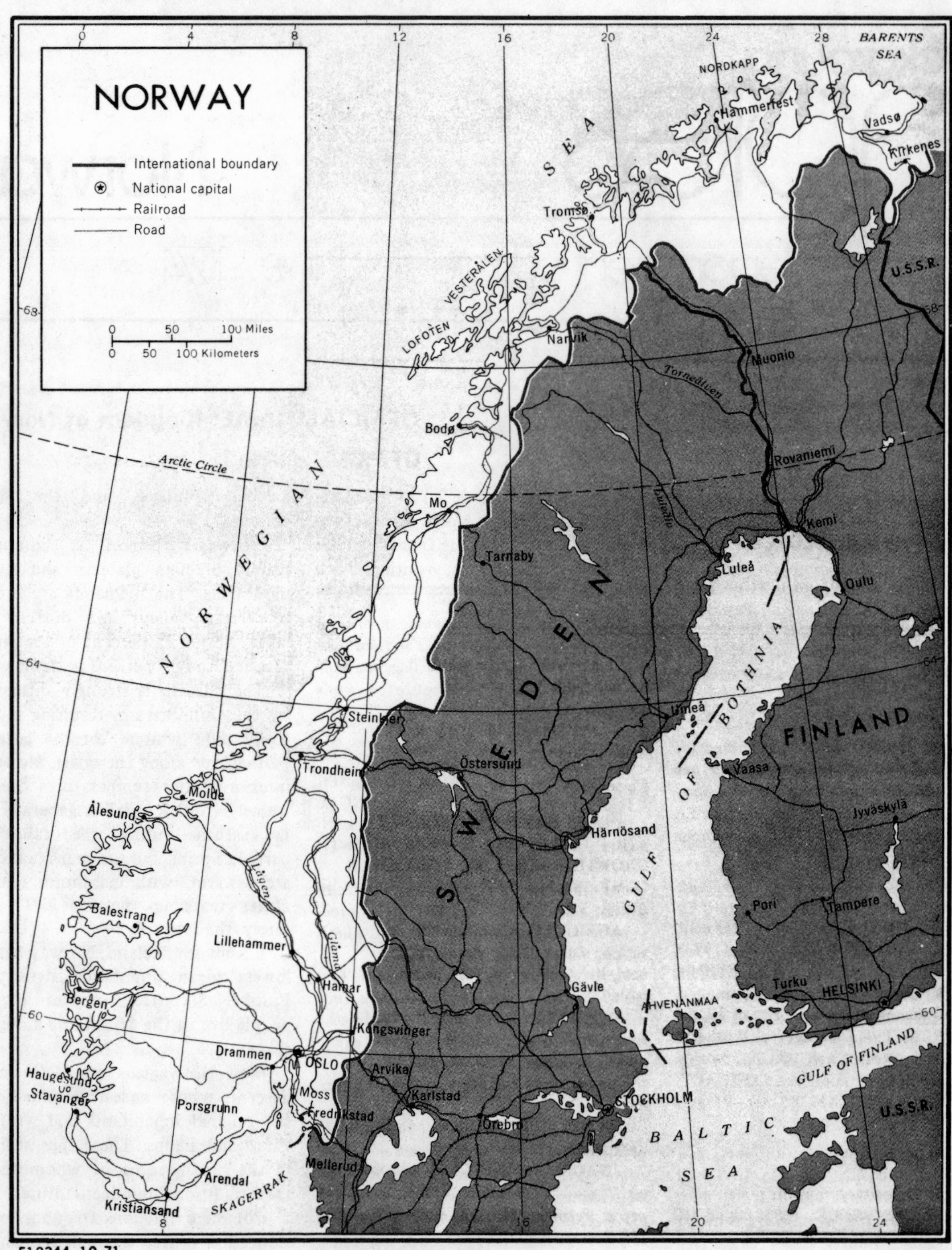

had become part of the Danish Kingdom. In 1814, as a result of the Napoleonic wars, Norway was separated from Denmark and joined with Sweden under the Swedish crown. An abortive movement for independence, which included the adoption of the Constitution of 1814, was put down by the Swedes, and the union persisted until 1905 when Norwegian independence was recognized by Sweden.

The Norwegian Government offered the throne of Norway to Danish Prince Carl in 1905. After a plebiscite that approved the establishment of a monarchy, the Parliament unanimously elected him King. He took the name of Haakon VII, harking back to the kings of independent Norway during the Middle Ages and before union with Denmark. He reigned until his death in 1957, when he was succeeded by his son, Olav V. Olav's 37-year-old son, Harald, is Crown Prince and heir apparent.

Norway remained a nonbelligerent during World Wai I, but as a result of the German invasion and occupation during World War II Norwegians generally became skeptical of the concept of neutrality and turned instead to collective security. Norway was one of the original signers of the North Atlantic Treaty in 1949. In a 1972 national referendum, Norwegian voters rejected membership for their country in the European Common Market. Nonetheless, Norway continues to play an active, important role in the economic and political affairs of Western Europe and remains a strong supporter of NATO.

GOVERNMENT

The functions of the King (Chief of State) are mainly ceremonial, although he has influence as the symbol of national unity. While the present Constitution grants important executive powers to the King, these are almost always exercised by the Council of Ministers in the name of the King (King in Council). The Council of Ministers (cabinet) consists of the Prime Minister (Head of Government), chosen by the political parties that enjoy the confidence of Parliament and other ministers.

The 155 members of the Storting (Parliament) are elected from 19 electoral districts (Fylker) for 4-year terms according to a complicated list system of proportional representation. After the Storting is elected, it divides into two chambers, the Odelsting and the Lagting, which meet separately or jointly depending on the legislative issue under consideration.

The judicial structure is similar to that in the United States, and, aside from the special High Court of the Realm which hears impeachment cases, the regular courts include a Supreme Court (17 permanent judges and a president), courts of appeal, city and county courts, and conciliation councils. Judges attached to regular courts are appointed by the King in Council after nomination by the Ministry of Justice.

Norway is divided into 19 provinces or counties (Fylker) plus the city of Oslo. Each province is headed by a governor appointed by the King in Council, but only one governor represents both Oslo and the adjacent Province of Akershus.

Principal Government Officials

King–Olav V
Prime Minister–Trygve Bratteli
Foreign Minister–Knut Frydenlund
Defense Minister–Alv Jakob Fostervoll
Commerce Minister–Jens Evensen
Ambassador to the U.S.–Søren Christian Sommerfelt
Ambassador to the U.N.–Ole Aalgaard

Norway maintains an Embassy in the United States at 3401 Massachusetts Avenue, NW., Washington, D.C. 20007.

POLITICAL CONDITIONS

With the exception of a brief period in 1963 and two longer interludes since (1965–71 and 1972–73), Norway has been governed by Labor Party governments since 1935. The Labor Party lost its majority in the Storting in the 1961 elections and thereafter, when in power, it has ruled as a minority government dependent upon votes from one or more opposition parties to obtain a majority. Where this additional support comes from depends largely upon the particular issue under consideration. Generally speaking, the Labor Party can count on support for its defense and foreign policies from more conservative elements of the opposition while socialists and other groups to the left of the Labor Party tend to support government proposals for social legislation and industrial reform.

The September 1973 elections again produced a minority Labor government headed by Prime Minister Trygve Bratteli. Prior to this, the most recent Labor government, also led by Bratteli, took power in March of 1971. Bratteli resigned in September 1972 when Norwegian voters rejected Common Market membership, which the Labor Party leadership had strongly supported.

The Labor Party won only 62 seats in the 1973 elections, 12 fewer than in the 1969 elections. Although far short of a majority (78 seats), Labor remains the dominant party and was able to form a new minority government. The 1973 elections were characterized by a splintering of the traditional parties. On the extreme right wing, the Anders Lange Party, opposed to high taxes and government interference, won 5 percent of the vote and four seats. On the far left, three smaller parties, including the Communists, united to form the Socialist Electoral League, which won 11 percent of the votes plus 16 seats in the Storting.

Despite the changes in party representation, no radical departures are expected in the main lines of Norwegian foreign or domestic policies which enjoy broad popular support.

Party Representation in the Storting

	1965	1969	1973
Labor Party	68	74	62
Socialist Electoral League	2	0	16
Conservative Party	31	29	29
Center Party	18	20	21
Christian Peoples' Party	13	14	20
Anders Lange Party	0	0	4
Liberal Party	18	13	2
New Peoples' Party	0	0	1

ECONOMY

The Norwegians have developed a progressive, prosperous, and increasingly diversified economy, as evidenced by their major industries:

TRAVEL NOTES

Health–**Norwegian public health standards are on a par with those in the United States. Tap water is safe to drink. Medical facilities are of a high standard.**

Telecommunications–**Telephone and telegraph services, domestic and international, are efficient and available to most parts of Norway and the world.**

Transportation–**Bus and taxi service is readily available in most cities of Norway, and reliable tram service is also found in Oslo. Oslo is served by daily flights to the major cities of Europe and to the United States. Norway has efficient railroad, coastal steamer, and ferry services. Roads in Norway, except for the main highways, can be narrow and often are not paved.**

offshore oil and gas exploration and exploitation, shipbuilding, metals, pulp and paper products, chemicals, and to a lesser extent, fishing and forestry. Norway's merchant fleet is the world's fourth largest and the country's largest foreign exchange earner. Recent discoveries of large offshore oil and gas reserves and the abundance of hydroelectric power will facilitate Norway's economic expansion, despite the country's lack of other major natural resources.

Norway has enjoyed unprecedented economic expansion since 1960. At the same time, the economy has expanded under conditions of full resource utilization with consequent pressure on prices. Despite a certain tightening of economic policy, mainly through monetary measures, inflation remains Norway's most difficult economic problem.

The problems connected with the split between the European Economic Community (EEC), or Common Market, and the declining European Free Trade Association (EFTA) have been hard on Norway. While the Common Market has been taking a growing share of Norway's exports in recent years, tariffs and other Common Market trade barriers have tended to harm such important export industries as fisheries, aluminum, pulp and paper. Although the Norwegians rejected membership in the European Economic Community in 1972 in a national referendum, a free trade agreement for manufactured products, effective July 1973, was subsequently negotiated with the EEC.

Insufficient time has elapsed to assess adequately the effects of the economic realignment in Europe on the various sectors of the Norwegian economy.

Since the total of Norway's exports and services, including shipping, is equivalent to about 40 percent of its GNP, the economy is heavily influenced by levels of world trade. Norway has been a net capital importer in the postwar period and as a result has been able to balance recurrent trade deficits in its GNP as well as increase its foreign exchange holdings. In 1968 and 1969 Norway recorded surpluses in its balance of payments for the first time in several years, but this was a temporary situation and mainly the result of reduced net imports of ships. In 1972, Norway's trade deficit amounted to $75 million and climbed to $450 million in 1973. However, the exploitation and eventual export of the country's offshore oil and gas should insure a surplus in Norway's balance of trade during the late 1970's. Norway is strongly dedicated to freedom of international competition in trade and transportation and reacts quickly to any developments it believes would threaten this freedom. The United States ranks fourth among Norway's trading partners.

READING LIST

Connery, Donald S. *The Scandinavians*. New York: Simon and Schuster, 1966.

Derry, T.K. *A Short History of Norway*. London: Allen and Unwin, 1968.

Popperwell, R.G. *Norway–Land and People*, "Nations of the Modern World" series. London: Benn, 1972.

Udgaard, Nils M., *Great Power Politics and Norwegian Foreign Policy*. Oslo: University Forlaget, 1973.

FOREIGN RELATIONS

Norway fully believes in international cooperation and the peaceful settlement of international conflicts, while recognizing the need for maintaining a strong national defense posture through collective security. Accordingly, the traditional cornerstones of Norwegian policy are support for the United Nations and its specialized agencies and active membership in NATO. Also, Norway pursues a broad policy of economic, social, and cultural cooperation with the other Nordic countries (Denmark, Sweden, Finland, and Iceland) through the Nordic Council.

In addition to strengthening traditional ties with developed countries, Norway seeks to build friendly relations with developing countries and has undertaken important humanitarian and development aid efforts with selected African and Asian nations. Norwegian policy is also dedicated to elimination of colonialism, encouragement of democracy, and protection of human rights throughout the world.

U.S.-NORWAY RELATIONS

The United States and Norway enjoy a long tradition of friendly association, bonded by common Western institutions and values and cemented by the presence in the United States of millions of Americans of Norwegian ancestry. Another indication of the continuing strong ties between the two countries is reflected in the latest statistics on the number of Americans residing in Norway. According to the Norwegian State Alien Control, 9,588 American citizens presently reside in Norway. This figure represents the second largest foreign community in the country. U.S. policy seeks to continue this close relationship and to help the Norwegians maintain a free, friendly, and prosperous Norway.

Principal U.S. Officials

Ambassador–Thomas R. Byrne

Counselor of Embassy–Thompson R. Buchanan

Public Affairs Officer (USIS)–Robert C. Voth

Chief, Political Section–William H. Mansfield

Chief, Economic Section–John C. Griffith

The U.S. Embassy in Norway is located at Drammensveien 18, Oslo.

DEPARTMENT OF STATE PUBLICATION 8228
Revised June 1974

APPENDIX AAA

NORWAY

STRENGTH OF THE COMMUNIST PARTY ORGANIZATION—1973

[FROM: World Strength of the Communist Party Organizations—1973. Washington, Department of State, Bureau of Intelligence and Research, 1973.]

NORWAY

National Political Status: Date of last election - September 9-10, 1973.

Communist: Communist and electoral allies[1] - 238,744 votes (10.1%), 16 seats (10.3%)

Red Alliance - 8,835 votes (0.4%), no seats

Non-Communist Left: Norwegian Labor Party - 1,004,311 votes (42.3%), 62 seats (40.0%)

Center: Liberals - 48,551 votes (2.0%), 2 seats (1.3%)
New People's Party[2] - 73,247 votes (3.1%), 1 seat (0.6%)

Center Party - 145,149 votes (6.1%), 21 seats (13.5%)
Christian People's Party - 252,475 votes (10.6%), 20 seats (12.9%)
Non-Socialist joint lists[1] - 126,824 votes (5.3%)

Conservative: Conservative Party - 369,492 votes (15.6%), 29 seats (18.7%)

Party for Reduction of Taxes - 106,034 votes (4.5%), 4 seats (2.7%)

Total: 2,373,662 votes, 155 seats

Communist Party Membership: 2,500 (estimate)

Leading Party Figures and Positions:

LARSEN, Reidar T. - Chairman
OVESEN, Georg - Leader of NKP youth group
HARBU, Kolbjorn - NKP secretary for trade union work

(All three are members of the 32-member National Board reconstituted in November 1973 from the previous Central Board as the governing body of the NKP.)

1/ The Norwegian Communist Party (NKP) running on its own in 1969 won 22,250 or 1 percent of the votes cast. The Socialist People's Party, a left offshoot of the Labor Party, polled 75,505 votes, or 3.5 percent. In 1973 the two formed a "Socialist Electoral Alliance," which also included dissident Laborites who bolted the Labor Party in 1972 over the issue of Norwegian adherence to the European Community. It is impossible to apportion the Alliance's votes among its constituent parties and groups. Of the 16 seats that the Alliance won, 9 are held by members of the Socialist People's Party, 6 by spokesmen for the 1972 Labor dissidents, and one by the chairman of the NKP.

2/ The New People's Party is an offshoot of the Liberal Party, which, like Labor, split over the EC affiliation issue.

Principal Publications:

Friheten (Freedom) - organ of the NKP (published weekly)
Kommunistisk Ungdom (Communist Youth, KU) - bulletin issued by KU
Klassekampen (Class Struggle) - Maoist publication

Areas of Communist Activity: The Norwegian Communist Party (*Norges Kommunistiske Parti, NKP*) celebrated its 50th birthday at its November 1973 congress. More important, this congress marked the party's emergence from political isolation.

Briefly significant in the immediate post-World War II period, NKP membership and influence had been dwindling since 1948. It elected no members of parliament and no national trade union officials in the 1950's and attracted only 1 percent of Norwegian voters in the 1969 election. Internally, the party, as recently as 1971, was wracked by dissension. It also was caught between the governing Labor Party and its allied trade union federation (LO), which had the overwhelming support of the working class, and the emerging Socialist People's Party (SF), which, along with several small far left groups, had more appeal to young radicals than did the discredited Moscow-linked NKP.

The burgeoning debate in 1972 over Norway's adherence to the European Community opened the way for the NKP's return to the political scene. Always opposed to Norway's entry, the NKP formed part of the narrow majority which rejected EC affiliation in the September 1972 referendum. In this endeavor the party joined the SF, which split off from the Labor Party in 1961; another secession movement of left-Laborites; some traditionalist politicians; and a number of small rural and fishing interests, local business, and trades people who felt themselves competitively threatened by the EC link. Their success not only brought the government down, but also enabled the Communists to start moving toward an electoral alliance with the SF and other dissident Laborites.

Subsequently, the left joined forces in an alliance in April 1973, in time to permit the construction of joint electoral lists for the September election. Their effort succeeded, and NKP Chairman Reidar Larsen, who headed the joint list in one electoral district, won a seat in parliament. The Socialist Electoral Alliance (SEA) itself received 11.2 percent of the vote in the same election and won 16 seats in parliament.

1/ Seats of parliamentarians elected on these lists are ascribed to the parties to which they have adhered in parliament.

This chain of development also seems to have effected a change of attitude in the more dynamic but erratic SF. Originally hostile to the NKP, the SF's fraternal delegate at the NKP's November 1973 congress announced his party's willingness to work toward fuller cooperation with the Communists at local political and trade union levels, and even held out the prospect of an ultimate merger with them. Similar sentiments were voiced by the spokesmen of the smaller groups in the SEA who also attended the NKP congress.

This cautious approach of all forces to the left of the Labor Party accorded with the objectives of the NKP. Reelected NKP chairman Larsen noted that meaningful coordination or unity on the left can only follow complete ideological and programmatic agreement. Surprisingly, Larsen extended this unity concept to include Maoist and Trotskyite groups who had futilely run their own slates in the 1973 elections. Not without some piquancy, one of the key left extremist groups formerly was the SF's Youth Group, which had stated that it wanted to be part of a larger Communist movement with the NKP, once the latter rid itself of its "slavish adherence" to Moscow. Meanwhile, The NKP served notice on the minority Labor government of Prime Minister Trygve Bratelli, which had resumed office in late 1973, that its parliamentary support was conditional upon the government's repealing a value-added tax.

The apparent change in the domestic fortunes of the NKP have further solidified the party's neutral stance in the Sino-Soviet dispute as well as its cautious criticism of Soviet policy regarding the treatment of Soviet dissident intellectuals. In this respect, the NKP has echoed the views of other West European Communist parties, notably the Italian CP. The NKP also has supported preparations for a conference of West European Communist parties.

APPENDIX BBB

PORTUGAL

ARMED FORCES AND MILITARY POWER

SEE PAGE 142

[Reprinted with permission from: The Almanac of World Military Power, by Col. T. N. Dupuy, U.S. Army, Ret., Col. John A. C. Andrews, U.S. Air Force, Ret., and Grace P. Hayes. 3rd ed. Dunn Loring, Va., T. N. Dupuy Associates, 1974.]

PORTUGAL

Republica Portuguesa
Portuguese Republic

POWER POTENTIAL STATISTICS

Area: 35,553 square miles (including the Azores and Madeira)
Population: 9,200,000
Total Active Armed Forces: 217,000 (2.36% population)
Gross National Product: $10.5 billion ($1,141 per capita)
Annual Military Expenditure: $524 million (4.99% GNP)
Fuel Production: Coal: 253,000 metric tons
Refined Petroleum Products: 4.4 million metric tons
Electric Power Output: 7.9 billion kwh
Merchant Fleet: 384 ships; 925,793 gross tons
Civil Air Fleet: 18 jet, 2 turboprop, 14 piston transports

DEFENSE STRUCTURE

In April 1974 forty years of civilian dictatorship in Portugal came to an end when the Armed Forces Movement seized the government and installed a seven-man "junta of national salvation." The new President, General Antonio de Spinola, moved immediately to change established orders and procedures throughout the country. The new President is in fact, as well as nominally, the commander in chief of the armed forces, exercising close central direction over the three partly integrated military services.

The Portuguese armed forces are organized within two major joint commands: the Home Command, which includes Continental Portugal, Madeira, and the Azores; and the Overseas Command, which includes all other overseas provinces.

POLITICO-MILITARY POLICY

Portugal has traditionally relied upon its remoteness from the center of Europe, as well as its long-standing alliance with Great Britain (since 1381; now largely nominal) for external security. It is also greatly influenced by events in Spain, its larger neighbor. Thus, the conservative, highly centralized regime of former Prime Minister Salazar (ideologically pro-Franco) remained neutral in World War II but (under some pressures from Britain and the US) nevertheless provided air base rights to the Allies. After World War II the strongly anti-communist Salazar regime brought Portugal into NATO as a charter member.

The armed forces are maintained by conscription; until recently the terms of service have been 24 months for the Army, 36 months for the Air Force, and 48 months for the Navy. In mid-1967, however, due to the pressure of guerrilla warfare in the African colonies, the maximum term for all services was increased to 48 months. Before the Spinola coup many young men emigrated to escape conscription. Another result of the overseas hostilities has been to accept more women volunteers for non-combat military service, in order to make more men available for troop duty.

STRATEGIC PROBLEMS

Portugal determinedly opposed the anticolonial tide of international affairs after World War II. As a result, there has been considerable nationalistic unrest, including extensive guerrilla conflict, in most of Portugal's remaining overseas territories: Angola, Mozambique, Portuguese Guinea, and the islands of Sao Tome and Principe in the African region; Macao (on the Chinese coast near Hong Kong) and Timor (in Indonesia) in the Far East. In 1961 Portugal lost its three small Indian provinces to Indian occupation. Problems of nationalism do not affect two of Portugal's Atlantic island possessions: the Azores and Madeira. The Cape Verde Islands, however, have close ties with Portuguese Guinea. Spinola announced in July 1974 his government's plan to grant independence to the three African colonies promptly, the first probably being Portuguese Guinea, or Guinea-Bissau.

The sudden liberalization of the Portuguese government under Spinola, after so many years of repression, encouraged excesses of liberalism which for a while came closely to anarchy. Spinola and the armed forces have been quietly but firmly re-establishing controls, while endeavoring to avoid the dictatorial measures of the former government. The poverty of Portugal will make it difficult to achieve stability and security without inhibiting the new-found democratic liberties of the Portuguese people.

MILITARY ASSISTANCE

Portugal has received $327.2 million in military aid from the United States since 1950. The present US Military Advisory Group in Portugal numbers about 20.

ALLIANCES

Portugal is a member of the UN and the NATO Alliance. It also has bilateral treaties with the United Kingdom, with the United States, and with Spain. The treaty with the United States provides base rights in the Azores. The Iberian Defense Alliance with Spain provides a convenient NATO link with the Franco government.

ARMY

Personnel: 179,000

Organization:

7 regional commands
2 infantry divisions (under strength; one subordinated to NATO, the other to joint Iberian defense)
21 infantry regiments
13 independent infantry battalions
13 independent infantry companies
7 battalions of cacadores
7 artillery regiments (5 light, 2 medium)
6 artillery groups
5 independent artillery batteries
1 coast artillery regiment
1 antiaircraft artillery regiment
2 independent AA battalions
3 independent AA and coastal batteries
4 cavalry regiments
1 cavalry group
5 independent cavalry batteries
1 MP regiment
2 tank regiments

1 engineer regiment
3 engineer battalions
1 signal regiment
3 signal battalions
1 railway battalion
logistic units

Major Equipment Inventory:
medium tanks (M-47 and M-4)
light tanks (M-41)
armored cars (Humber Mk IV and EBR-75)
scout cars (AML-60)
200 light artillery pieces (mostly 140mm howitzers)

Reserve Forces: There are at least 550,000 trained reserves, available to bring the existing units up to strength, and to create new units in the event of national mobilization.

NAVY

Personnel: 19,500 (including 3,400 in the Marines)

Major Units:
8 frigates (DE)
4 diesel submarines (SS)
9 coastal minesweepers (MSC)
6 submarine chasers/corvettes (SC)
29 coastal patrol vessels (PG)
25 patrol launches (YP)
6 landing craft (LCT)
58 landing craft (LCU, LCM)
12 auxiliaries

Major Naval Base: Lisbon

Reserves: 12,000 reservists (including Marines)

AIR FORCE

Personnel: 18,500 (including 4,000 paratroops)

Organization:
2 light bomber squadrons (B-26 and PV-2)
1 fighter-interceptor squadron (F-86)
2 fighter-bomber squadrons (G-91)
6 COIN flights (T-6)
1 maritime patrol squadron (P-2)
1 transport group (C-47, C-45, DC-6, Noratlas)
1 paratroop regiment

Major Aircraft Types:
133 combat aircraft
6 B-26 light bombers
10 PV-2 light bombers
25 F-86 fighter-interceptors
30 G-91 fighter-bombers
50 T-6 armed trainers
12 P-2 maritime patrol aircraft
306 other aircraft
65 transports (20 Noratlas, 20 C-47, 10 DC-6, 15 C-45)
70 Do-27 light transports
78 trainers (13 T-33, 25 T-37, 40 T-6)
93 helicopters (2 Alouette II, 80 Alouette III, 11 Puma)

Major Air Bases: Montijo, Tanoas, Sintra, Porto, Ota, Alverca, Jacinto

Reserves: Approximately 30,000 reservists, including parachute troops.

PARAMILITARY

There are 9,700 active duty personnel in the National Republic Guard for internal security.

APPENDIX CCC

REPUBLIC OF PORTUGAL

BACKGROUND NOTES

SEE PAGE 142

[Washington, Department of State, November 1972 (Publication 8074).]

REPUBLIC OF PORTUGAL

BACKGROUND NOTES

Population: 24.7 million* (1972 est.)
Capital: Lisbon

Metropolitan Portugal is composed of the southwestern one-sixth of the Iberian Peninsula on the West European mainland and the Azores and Madeira Islands in the Atlantic Ocean. It has an area of about 35,510 square miles (including 1,198 square miles for the Azores and Madeira Islands), approximately the size of Indiana. In addition, Portuguese territory includes the Overseas Provinces of Angola, Mozambique, and Portuguese Guinea on the African Continent; the Cape Verde Islands in the Atlantic Ocean; Macao on the southern coast of mainland China; Timor in the Indian Ocean north of Australia; and the São Tomé and Príncipe Islands in the Gulf of Guinea west of Gabon. The total area of the Overseas Provinces is 805,326 square miles.** (The Portuguese Indian provinces of Goa, Diu, and Damao were taken over by India in 1961.)

Mainland Portugal is divided into two distinct topographical regions by the Tagus River which flows into the Atlantic Ocean near Lisbon. The northern part of mainland Portugal is mountainous, receives considerable rain, and has a moderate climate. To the south are rolling plains with less rainfall and a climate in the interior which resembles that of North Africa.

Approximately one-third of Portugal's flag is green (along the staff); the remainder is red. Centered on the dividing line is the national coat of arms.

THE PEOPLE

Metropolitan Portugal has a 1972 population estimated at 8.7 million and the Overseas Provinces have a total population of about 16 million. There are approximately 245 persons per square mile in metropolitan Portugal. The two largest cities are Lisbon, with an estimated 1 million inhabitants, and Oporto, with 310,000 inhabitants.

Portugal was the only country in Europe to suffer a significant population decline (about 2 percent) since 1960, reflecting large-scale emigration. The loss in population makes difficult the prediction of future trends in population growth. A constant population is assumed between 1970 and 1975 (natural increase offset by emigration) and after that a growth rate of 0.8 percent (the 1970 reported rate of natural increase).

*Includes the population of Portugal's Overseas Provinces.
**For additional information, see the Background Notes on Angola (pub. 7962), Macao (pub. 8352), Mozambique (pub. 7965), and Portuguese Guinea (pub. 7966).

During the past 3,000 years the Portuguese have experienced considerable mixture with other peoples, notably Iberian, Celtic, Germanic, Roman, Arabic, and African. These ethnic groups have been assimilated, and metropolitan Portugal's population is relatively homogeneous. There are no significant minorities.

Roman Catholicism is the established religion and has traditionally been a stabilizing influence on the society. Portuguese is the official language. Metropolitan Portugal has a low literacy rate (about 65 percent) compared to the rest of Europe.

HISTORY

Portugal is one of the oldest states in Europe, tracing its modern history to 1140. Prior to that time much of Portugal was inhabited by Celtiberic people and ruled by the Romans, Visigoths, and finally the Moors.

Beginning in 997 A.D., however, a series of revolts by Galician, Leonese, and Castilian kings led to the establishment of the County of Portugal which incorporated the area between Galicia in Spain and the Mondego River. Between 1130-39 Afonso Henriques, the son of the first Count of Portugal, fought four wars with the King of Leon-Castile, succeeded in establishing the independence of Portugal in 1140, and became its first king. He then turned his attention to the Moors and by 1147 had captured Lisbon, thus freeing the future capital and establishing the base for the great explorations of the 15th and 16th centuries. By 1250 all of Portugal had been liberated from Moorish rule.

The actual beginning of Portuguese exploration is difficult to pinpoint, but by 1336 Portuguese explorers had reached the Canary Islands. Following the inspiration of Prince Henry the Navigator (1394-1460), such explorers as Vasco da Gama, Bartolomeu Dias, and Pedro Alvares Cabral roamed the globe from Brazil to India and Japan, bringing knowledge and wealth to the Portuguese kingdom. The epic Portuguese poet, Luis Vaz de Camões (1524-80), author of the "Lusiadas," took part in the colonization of India. The anniversary of his death, June 10, is observed as the Portuguese National Day.

Monarchal problems led in 1580 to the succession of Philip II of Spain to the Portuguese throne. In 1640 Spanish rule was ended by a revolt, and the House of Braganza was established as the Portuguese ruling family. The 18th century was dominated by the Marques de Pombal who served as first minister to King José and directed the recovery from the disastrous Lisbon earthquake in 1755. Other important events were the

Peninsular War (1808) and the independence of Brazil (1822).

In 1910 dissatisfaction with the monarchy led to its overthrow and the establishment of a Republic. The Republic, however, was dominated by political rivalries which fostered instability; in 1926 Gen. Carmona, after a brief rule by a military junta, took over the presidency. To assist in overcoming the financial chaos which had developed, Dr. Antonio de Oliveira Salazar, a university professor, was named Finance Minister in 1928. In 1932 he became Prime Minister, a position he held until incapacitating illness necessitated his replacement on September 29, 1968, by Dr. Marcello Caetano.

GOVERNMENT & POLITICAL CONDITIONS

According to the Constitution of March 19, 1933, Portugal is a Republic organized on corporative principles. The President (Chief of State) is elected for a 7-year term by an Electoral College composed of members of the Legislature, representatives of metropolitan and overseas municipalities, and representatives of the legislative and governors' councils of the Overseas Provinces. The President appoints the Prime Minister (Head of Government) who presides over a 10-member Council of Ministers (cabinet).

Portugal's bicameral Legislature is composed of a National Assembly and Corporative Chamber. The 130 Deputies in the National Assembly are elected to 4-year terms. The Corporative Chamber is an advisory body whose members are elected by the various economic, administrative, and cultural organizations comprising the Portuguese corporative system, or are appointed by the Government. The size of the Corporative Chamber is not fixed by the Constitution. There were 217 members in mid-1972.

Portuguese jurisprudence has been influenced heavily by the French model. The Supreme Tribunal of Justice is the highest court in Portugal and consists of a President of the Supreme Tribunal and 15 judges.

For administrative purposes, metropolitan Portugal is divided into 18 Districts, each headed by a Governor who is appointed by the Minister of Interior. Regional governmental affairs are under the direct aegis of the Central Government.

Adm. Americo Thomaz was elected President in 1958, defeating his opponent, the late Gen. Humberto Delgado. In 1959 the Constitution was amended to provide for a change from a direct popular vote to an electoral college system for the election of the President. President Thomaz was the only candidate in the 1965 and 1972 presidential elections. He was inaugurated for his third 7-year term on August 9, 1972.

During the 40-year rule of Dr. Salazar, a highly centralized government was developed in Portugal. That situation has continued under Dr. Caetano, a leading figure in developing the Portuguese Corporate State. Only one political organization, the National Popular Action (ANP), has legal status. The ANP is headed by Prime Minister Caetano and holds all of the seats in the Portuguese National Assembly. Rival political movements are permitted to organize and conduct campaigns in the month preceding elections for the Assembly. The next elections for the National Assembly are scheduled to be held in October 1973.

ECONOMY

Although metropolitan Portugal's per capita gross national product (GNP) is still the lowest in Western Europe (U.S. $828 in 1971), the Portuguese economy has experienced healthy growth in recent years. Since 1960 the percentage of the labor force engaged in agriculture has fallen from 42 to 32 percent and now contributes only 15 percent to the country's GNP. Industrial employment, on the other hand, rose during the same period from 21 to 34 percent of the labor force and contributes 44 percent to the GNP. In 1971 the GNP totaled $6.9 billion, a real increase of 4.9 percent over that of the previous year.

Portugal's major agricultural products are wine grapes, tomatoes, olives, and citrus fruits. The small but expanding industrial sector produces tomato paste, canned seafood, olive oil, textiles, automobiles, electronic equipment, steel, pulp and paper, and refined petroleum and petrochemical products. Portugal's expanding ship repair and ship building facilities promise to make the country a European leader in this sector.

The volume of foreign trade increased from U.S. $873 million in 1960 to $2.5 billion in 1970. In 1971 metropolitan Portugal's imports totaled $1.7 billion and its exports amounted to $1 billion. The major trading partners are the countries of Western Europe. Imports from the United States were $142 million—the leading products being aircraft, agricultural products (wheat, corn, and soybeans), electronic equipment, and machinery. Exports to the United States totaled $112 million—the principal commodities being tomato concentrate, table wines, and textiles. Despite Portugal's foreign trade deficit, the Escudo Monetary Zone (Portugal and its Overseas Provinces) normally records a surplus in its balance of payments, resulting from remittances from Portuguese workers abroad and earnings from tourism (some $800 million in 1971, approximately 80 percent of the value of total merchandise exports).

Portugal is a member of the Organization for Economic Cooperation and Development (OECD), as well as the European Free Trade Association (EFTA). In 1972 Portugal negotiated an agreement with the European Communities (EC) which provides for the creation of a free trade area in industrial products.

Portugal's declared policy is to work toward the economic integration of the Escudo Monetary Zone. It levies no duties on imports from its Overseas Provinces and maintains no restrictions on payments to them. The Overseas Provinces, on the other hand, are permitted to charge duty on imports from Portugal and to maintain certain controls over transfers of capital to the metropole. The duties levied by the Provinces on imports from metropolitan Portugal are at a preferential rate, in most cases 50 percent of the normal duty.

FOREIGN RELATIONS

Portugal has been a member of the North Atlantic Treaty Organization (NATO) since its founding in 1949 and of the United Nations since 1955.

Portugal's principal foreign policy concern has been the question of its African Overseas Provinces. In recent years U.S.-Portuguese relations have been affected by problems connected with Portuguese Africa. Violence broke out in 1961 in Angola, in 1962 in Portuguese Guinea, and in 1964 in Mozambique when African nationalists based in neighboring countries launched independence movements involving guerrilla warfare. The independent African states at the United Nations have kept the question of the Portuguese territories on the U.N.'s agenda and have sought majority support for resolutions critical of Portuguese policy and of Portugal's NATO allies. In turn, the Portuguese Government (1) emphasizes the goal of creating a multiracial, pluricontinental society, (2) considers the relations of the Overseas Provinces to the metropole to be a domestic matter outside the competence of the United Nations, and (3) points out that Portugal is the victim of external aggression, actively supported by the Communist states.

U.S. POLICY

Portugal receives both economic and military aid from the United States. Since 1953, the United States has authorized almost U.S. $130 million in economic aid. Most of it has been under the Public Law 480 (Food for Peace) program credits and long-term Export-Import Bank loans. In U.S. fiscal year 1970 total official aid authorized by the United States to Portugal was $5.6 million. Although U.S. aid has diminished considerably from the levels of the early 1960's, the United States made new aid commitments in December 1971 as part of an agreement extending U.S. military base rights in the Azores until 1974. The United States agreed to sell $30 million of surplus agricultural commodities (PL 480), to provide a $1 million grant for educational development, $5 million in non-military excess equipment, and to loan an oceanographic ship to Portugal for research purposes.

The primary objectives of the United States with respect to Portugal are as follows:

(1) Maintenance of a friendly, cooperative relationship consistent with mutual international undertakings;

(2) Portuguese understanding of the U.S. position on various world issues;

(3) Continuation of U.S.-Portuguese military cooperation envisaged by the NATO treaty and the 1951 defense agreement by which the United States has the use of defense facilities in the Azores Islands; and

(4) Progress toward a peaceful and equitable solution of problems arising in Portugal's African Overseas Provinces, based on self-determination—whether the choice is independence or continued association with Portugal.

The United States has supported resolutions in the United Nations aimed at encouraging this objective and has opposed those which it considered extreme and not conducive to a peaceful and equitable solution to the problem.

The United States recognizes Portugal's role in Africa, especially in promoting racial equality, and believes that it is important that Portugal continue to contribute to stability and progress on that continent.

PRINCIPAL GOVERNMENT OFFICIALS

President—Americo Deus Rodriques THOMAZ
Prime Minister—Marcello CAETANO
Minister of Foreign Affairs—Rui PATRICIO
Ambassador to the U.S.—Joao Hall THEMIDO
Ambassador to the U.N.—António PATRICIO

Portugal maintains an Embassy in the United States at 2125 Kalorama Road, N.W., Washington, D.C. 20008.

PRINCIPAL U.S. OFFICIALS

Ambassador—Ridgway B. Knight
Deputy Chief of Mission—Richard St. F. Post
Public Affairs Officer—James D. Conley
Consul, Oporto—Rush W. Taylor, Jr.
Consul, Ponta Delgada—Hyman Bloom

The U.S. Embassy in Portugal is located at Avenida Duque de Loule No. 39, Lisbon.

READING LIST

Abshire, David M., and Michael A. Samuels, eds. Portuguese Africa: A Handbook. New York: Praeger, 1969.

dos Passos, John. The Portugal Story: Three Centuries of Exploration and Discovery. New York: Doubleday, 1969.

LaFay, Howard. "Portugal at the Crossroads." National Geographic. October 1965.

Livermore, H. V. A New History of Portugal. Cambridge: Cambridge University Press, 1966.

Smith, Robert C. The Art of Portugal: 1500-1800. Meredith, 1968.

DEPARTMENT OF STATE PUBLICATION 8074, Revised November 1972

APPENDIX DDD

PORTUGAL

STRENGTH OF THE COMMUNIST PARTY ORGANIZATION—1973

SEE PAGE 142

[FROM: World Strength of the Communist Party Organizations—1973. Washington, Department of State, Bureau of Intelligence and Research, 1973.]

PORTUGAL

National Political Status: Date of last parliamentary election - October 28, 1973.

Only one formal political entity, the National Popular Action (ANP), formerly known as the National Union, has continuing legal status in Portugal. During electoral periods, persons not affiliated with this entity may be allowed to form candidate slates and thereby run as "opposition" candidates. After a shrill campaign in 1973, however, the ANP had the electoral field all to itself when the left-wing coalition, the Democratic Electoral Commission (CDE), withdrew all its candidates three days prior to the election, claiming that the campaign had been a great victory for the CDE in "informing the people" and strengthening the "democratic movement" while condemning the electoral system. Of metropolitan Portugal's 2,096,020 registered voters, 65 percent went to the polls on October 28 and ratified the ANP's clean sweep.

Prime Minister Marcello Caetano, appointed in September 1968, faces little threat from liberal and leftist opposition groups. Some internal political pressures come from the more conservative elements within the establishment who resist changes in the old Oliveira Salazar system of government.

Communist Party Membership: Less than 1,000 in Portugal (estimate)

Leading Party Figure and Position:
CUNHAL, Alvaro - Secretary-General (in exile)

Principal Publication:
Avante - monthly journal

Areas of Communist Activity: The illegal Portuguese Communist Party (*Partido Comunista Portugues, PCP*) operates as an underground and exile organization. Within Portugal, the PCP is hampered by constant police surveillance and arrests. The party nevertheless has had some success in maintaining an underground organization, recruiting new members, disseminating propaganda, and penetrating non-Communist opposition groups.

In mid-1972, Portugal's traditional social democratic-type Socialists reached agreement with the PCP to form a coalition for the electoral campaign. As the Communists in the coalition came to control it, however, the moderate Socialists became increasingly restive and finally pulled out altogether in July 1973. The PCP, the remaining Socialists, and a handful of others who were left to carry on then formed the CDE. The CDE campaigned, among other things, for an end to the "colonial war" in Africa and "foreign domination" at home and price stabilization, accompanied by pay hikes. Some CDE candidates also called for Portugal to quit NATO and to renounce its agreement with the EC. The campaign ended prematurely when the CDE denounced the elections and withdrew all its candidates three days before election day.

Communist membership within Portugal consists mainly of urban workers (concentrated in and around the industrial areas of Lisbon and Oporto), a small number of farm laborers, and some students and young intellectuals. PCP members also active in expatriate intellectual circles and in the Portuguese African possessions. The PCP has gained some strength from among the thousands of workers who have migrated (mostly illegally) to the other West European countries, where they have been targets of Communist propaganda.

In Portugal, Communist propaganda is distributed clandestinely in the form of leaflets, pamphlets dealing with special subjects, and even a number of fairly regular periodicals. This domestic propaganda is supplemented by broadcasts in Portuguese from Radio Moscow and from the party's clandestine "Radio Free Portugal," which broadcasts from Bucharest.

Over the years the PCP has been pro-Moscow. A pro-Peking Communist faction, the *Frente de Accao Popular* (Popular Action Front, FAP), is now believed to be moribund. During 1973, the PCP continued to support the Communist Party of the Soviet Union. The party viewed the Conference on Security and Cooperation in Europe (CSCE) as a victory for the Soviet Union in its search for detente and peaceful coexistence and saw the conference as increasing the international isolation of Portugal's "fascist, colonialist regime."

Domestically, the PCP has become increasingly concerned with the competition it has been receiving from rival leftist organizations. It has strongly condemned and ridiculed the claims of the Patriotic Front for National Liberation (FPLN), a dissident left Communist group with headquarters in Algiers. The FPLN has claimed that many of the bombings and other acts of sabotage committed in Portugal in recent years were conducted by its own "Revolutionary Brigades." While criticizing the FPLN and the "Revolutionary Brigades," the PCP has taken an altogether different line vis-a-vis another underground organization, the Armed Revolutionary Action (ARA).

It is believed that there is at least some linkage between the PCP and the ARA. According to the PCP, the ARA is a real revolutionary organization which "modestly contributes with its actions to the general struggle of the Portuguese People" and which recognizes the PCP as "the most firm, consequential, and outstanding revolutionary force in the present spectrum of the Portuguese political forces." In 1973 the PCP lauded the actions of ARA and supported violence as a "tool of the people's struggle." The party continued, however, that this violence must not "assume the nature of terrorist actions."

Because of "increasingly widespread opposition" to the regime, the PCP saw opportunities opening up for "legal and semi-legal political actions." In July 1973, the Central Committee of the PCP called for a "great political mass campaign" whose objectives would be an end to repression, democratic liberties for all, amnesty for those who have opposed the regime, pay increases, redistribution of the tax burden, and an end to the domination of the monopolies and of submission to imperialism.

APPENDIX EEE

TURKEY

ARMED FORCES AND MILITARY POWER

SEE PAGE 142

[Reprinted with permission from: The Almanac of World Military Power, by Col. T. N. Dupuy, U.S. Army, Ret., Col. John A. C. Andrews, U.S. Air Force, Ret., and Grace P. Hayes. 3rd ed. Dunn Loring, Va., T. N. Dupuy Associates, 1974.]

TURKEY

Turkiye Cumhuriyeti
Turkish Republic

POWER POTENTIAL STATISTICS

Area: 301,380 square miles
Population: 38,600,000
Total Active Armed Forces: 563,500 (includes gendarmerie; 1.46% population)
Gross National Product: $15.08 billion ($391 per capita)
Annual Military Expenditures: $802 million (5.32% GNP)
Iron and Steel Production: 2.0 million metric tons
Fuel Production: Coal: 13.8 million metric tons
Crude Oil: 3.4 million metric tons
Refined Petroleum Products: 11 million metric tons
Electric Power Output: 9.7 billion kwh
Merchant Fleet: 328 ships; 713,767 gross tons
Civil Air Fleet: 16 jet, 7 turboprop transports

DEFENSE STRUCTURE

The President of the Republic of Turkey constitutionally exercises power as a strong executive; he is the actual as well as nominal commander in chief of the armed forces. This responsibility is exercised through the Prime Minister and the Minister of National Defense. The Army is the predominant element of the partially integrated armed forces. The Chief of the General Staff is also Commander-in-Chief of the armed forces.

POLITICO-MILITARY POLICIES

For several centuries Russia has been the principal traditional enemy of Turkey. After the republic was established, following World War I, Turkey followed an essentially neutral policy, in which an important element was rapprochement with Soviet Russia. Soviet domination of the Balkans after World War II brought renewed Russian pressure to obtain control over the Turkish Straits. Despite occasional gestures of friendship on both sides, security from the threat of Russia has been the principal element of Turkish foreign and military policy since 1945. Turkish appeals for support in opposing Russian threats stimulated the enunciation of the Truman Doctrine in 1947, and the beginning of a bilateral alliance with the United States. This same Turkish policy caused Turkey to contribute a highly effective brigade to the UN forces during the Korean conflict and to join the NATO alliance in 1952 and the Baghdad Pact (later the CENTO alliance) in 1955. Recently Turkey has taken steps to normalize its relations with the Soviet Union, without weakening its membership in NATO. In 1973, during the Arab-Israeli confrontation, Turkey made clear both that NATO bases might not be used to ship war material to Israel, and that any Soviet airlift to Arab nations might not traverse Turkish air space.

In 1971, Turkey established diplomatic relations with the People's Republic of China.

The Turkish armed forces are raised by conscription. The term of service is 20 months for all services. The quality of the armed forces is greatly enhanced by a proud national military tradition, and by the toughness, frugality, courage, loyalty, and self-reliance of the Turkish peasants, who make up the bulk of the rank and file. Since World War II, about 30 percent of the annual budget has been for defense.

STRATEGIC PROBLEMS

Turkey's location between the Mediterranean and Black Seas, and between Europe and Asia, is one of the most significant in the world militarily and strategically. Turkey has been the principal obstacle to Imperial and Soviet Russian expansion into the Mediterranean and also to Soviet movement into the oil-rich Middle East. By its participation in the NATO and CENTO alliances, and because of the effectiveness and reliability of the Turkish armed forces, Turkey has become one of the key elements of the chain of mutual security alliances that has manifested misgivings at Communist expansionism since 1947.

The security of the Straits (Bosporus, Sea of Marmara, and Dardanelles) is perhaps the greatest Turkish strategic problem. For 200 years the right of foreign warships to go through them has been the subject of controversy–and of agreements. The Montreux Convention of 1936 allowed Turkey to fortify the Straits, and provided for free passage in peacetime of warships under a certain size, and for closing the Straits in wartime to belligerents so long as Turkey should remain neutral. A related problem is the defense of the small and isolated region in Europe north and west of the Straits. The defense of Turkey's eastern frontiers with the USSR and Iran is facilitated by extremely rugged mountains. A security weakness in this area, however, is the presence of two ethnic minorities: the Kurds and the Armenians.

Turkey's interest in preventing the absorption of Cyprus by Greece is mainly nationalist and emotional, in support of the Turkish Cypriot minority. There is, however, an important strategic aspect of this interest. Despite their joint participation in the NATO alliance, Greek-Turkish enmity has deep and lasting roots, and Cyprus in Greek hands would place Turkey at a significant strategic disadvantage. Thus in 1974, when the status quo in Cyprus was violently upset, an estimated 40,000 Turkish troops were landed on the island. (See Cyprus and Greece.)

Except for the small Armenian and Kurdish minorities mentioned above, and an equally insignificant Greek minority in western Anatolia and European Turkey, the population is quite homogeneous. Communism has had little impact upon the predominantly Moslem people, and despite the low standard of living of most Turks, is not likely to. Leftist disaffection is apparent among university students and intellectuals, however, and has resulted in many riots, bombings, kidnappings and murders. This unrest, partly directed against the presence of American NATO personnel, has created some governmental instability, and in 1971 eleven provinces were put under modified military law.

MILITARY ASSISTANCE

Largely because of Turkey's strategic location, and its military reliability, the United States has provided it with more than $5.0 billion in foreign aid since 1950; of this more than half has been direct military assistance. There has also been military assistance from West Germany.

ALLIANCES

As noted above, Turkey is a member of the UN and both NATO and CENTO. It is a member, along with Pakistan and Iran, of the Regional Cooperation for Development, established in 1964. It also has extensive bilateral arrangements with the United States.

Izmir is a major NATO base and headquarters area, and the main location of a number of US installations in Turkey. Although the number of US military personnel in Turkey is being drastically reduced, partly because the presence of these affluent soldiers and their dependents has caused considerable unrest, there are still about 6,000 US military personnel stationed in Turkey. There are extensive US and NATO radar and other surveillance installations. At least 200 US military aircraft and some Greek combat air units, part of NATO's 6th Allied Tactical Air Force, are also based in Turkey. Izmir is also a major base for the US Sixth Fleet.

ARMY

(Except for some fortress and territorial formations, all units are assigned to NATO.)

Personnel: 400,000

Organization: 3 armies: one in European Turkey, protecting the northern approach to the Straits; one in western Anatolia, concentrated near the Asiatic side of the Straits; and one in eastern Anatolia, concentrated near the Soviet frontier.

- 6 army corps; two for each army
- 1 armored division (M-48 tanks)
- 1 mechanized infantry division
- 12 infantry divisions
- 4 armored cavalry brigades
- 4 armored brigades (M-48 tanks)
- 3 mechanized infantry brigades
- 2 parachute battalions
- 2 SSM battalions (Honest John)

Major Equipment Inventory:

- 1,500 medium tanks (M-47 and M-48)
- light tanks (M-24 and M-41)
- tank destroyers (M-36)
- armored cars (M-8)
- 500+APCs (M-113 and M-59)
- 105mm and 155mm self-propelled guns
- 105mm, 155mm, and 203mm howitzers
- 40mm, 75mm, and 90mm AA artillery pieces
- SS-11 ATGW
- SSM Honest John launchers
- 40 light aircraft (Do-27, Do-28, Beaver)
- 20 helicopters (AB-206, Bell 47, CH-47)

Reserves: There are over 800,000 trained reservists.

NAVY

(All combat units are assigned to NATO)

Personnel: 38,500 (including 3 battalions of Marines)

Major Units:

- 15 destroyers (1 used as training ship; DD)
- 16 submarines (4 more on order; SS)
- 2 frigates (DE)
- 16 coastal minesweepers (MSC)
- 4 inshore minesweepers (MSI)
- 3 fleet minelayers (2 converted LST; MMF)
- 6 coastal minelayers (MMC)
- 11 torpedo boats (PT)
- 4 patrol gunboats (PGM)
- 38 patrol boats and motor launches (YP and smaller classes)
- 24 landing craft (4 LCU, 2 LCM, 18 LCVP)
- 39 auxiliaries
- 3 helicopters (AB-205; ASW)

Reserves: There are 70,000 trained reserves

AIR FORCE

(All formations are assigned to 6 ATAF, NATO)

Personnel: 50,000

Organization:

- 2 tactical air forces
  - 2 fighter-interceptor squadrons AW (F-102)
  - 2 fighter-interceptor squadrons (F-5)
  - 5 fighter-bomber squadrons (F-100)
  - 2 fighter-bomber squadrons (F-104)
  - 2 fighter-bomber squadrons (F-5)
  - 3 fighter reconnaissance squadrons (RF-84F, RF-5)
  - 4 transport squadrons (C-45, C-47, C-54, C-130, Viscount, Transall)
  - 1 helicopter squadron (UH-1, H-19)
  - 2 SAM battalions (Nike-Hercules; 6 batteries)

Major Aircraft Types:

- 349 combat aircraft
  - 130 F-5 interceptor/fighter-bombers
  - 38 F-104 fighter-bombers
  - 100 F-100 fighter-bombers
  - 36 F-102 AW fighter-interceptors
  - 30 RF-84 fighter reconnaissance aircraft

15 RF-5 fighter-reconnaissance aircraft

224 other aircraft

- 12 C-47 transports
- 6 C-45 transports
- 3 C-54 transports
- 10 C-130 transports
- 20 Transall transports
- 23 helicopters (UH-1, H-19)
- 150 trainer/support aircraft (including T-33, TF-102, TF-104, T-37, T-41, T-42, T-34, T-11, F-100F, and F-5)

On Order: 40 F-4, 42 F-5 Tiger II

Major Air Bases: Izmir, Adana, Bandirma, Diyarbakir, Esluboga, Sivas, Etimesgut, Eskisehir, Yesilkoy, Merzifon, Balikesir.

Reserves: There are 80,000 trained reserves

PARAMILITARY

75,000 National Gendarmerie (3 mobile brigades)
20,000 National Guard

APPENDIX FFF
REPUBLIC OF TURKEY
BACKGROUND NOTES

SEE PAGE 142

[Washington, Department of State, December 1971 (Publication 7850).]

DEPARTMENT OF STATE NOVEMBER 1971

REPUBLIC OF TURKEY

BACKGROUND NOTES

Population: 36.3 million (1971 est.)
Capital: Ankara

Turkey lies partially in Europe and partially in Asia, sharing common borders with Greece and Bulgaria on the northwest, the U.S.S.R. and Iran on the east, and Iraq and Syria on the south. Of its total area of 296,184 square miles (approximately the size of Texas and Louisiana combined) about 97 percent is in Asia Minor. The Bosphorus, the Sea of Marmara, and the Dardanelles, known collectively as the Turkish Straits, connect the Black and the Mediterranean Seas.

The coastal areas enjoy sufficient rainfall to support considerable vegetation. A wide variety of crops, ranging from tea in the northeast to tobacco in the west and cotton in the south, is grown on those relatively narrow coastal plains. The coastal regions, particularly in the south and west, enjoy mild winters. Inland, wheat is the principal crop grown on much of the rolling terrain of the western regions of the Anatolian Plateau. This plateau generally becomes more mountainous and less productive the farther east one goes. Winters are quite severe in eastern Turkey, but only moderately so in the western Anatolian Plateau. To the southeast, the terrain has a mean elevation of 3,000 feet above sea level and is treeless, sparsely populated, and crisscrossed by mountain chains. The Tigris and Euphrates Rivers rise in eastern Turkey and flow southward to the Persian Gulf through Iraq and Syria. The largest all-Turkish river is the Kizil Irmak, which flows northward east of Ankara to the Black Sea.

Turkey's flag carries a white crescent and a white star on a red field. On conquering Constantinople in 1453, the Ottoman Turks adopted the city's ancient symbol, the crescent, as their own. The flag's crescent frames Al Tarek, the Koran's morning star.

THE PEOPLE

Turkey's population is about 36.3 million, representing a density of approximately 123 persons per square mile. The annual rate of population increase is estimated at 2.6 percent. Approximately 65 percent of the populace are villagers, and the population is more dense along the coastal regions and in the western half of the country than it is in the east and southeast. The largest city is Istanbul with a population of about 2.3 million. Ankara, the capital, has about 1 million inhabitants. These urban areas, as is the case with most Turkish cities, have experienced tremendous growth since 1950 as a result of the movement of villagers to the cities. Neatly whitewashed squatter dwellings can be seen around the city peripheries, posing a constant challenge to the abilities of the municipalities to provide essential services.

Ninety-eight percent of the Turks are Moslem, belonging principally to the Sunni sect, but the state recognizes no established religion and is secular in form. There is no legal discrimination against the non-Islamic minorities, which consist mainly of small groups of Greeks, Armenians, and Jews.

The Kurds, who number about 3 million, constitute an ethnic and linguistic minority, although not a religious one. They live in poor, remote sections of the east and southeast, areas which have not kept pace with the economic and social development of most of Turkey. The state of martial law, which was declared in 11 of 67 Provinces for several months in April 1971, encompassed two Provinces where Kurdish separatist activity was felt by the Government of Turkey to be a problem.

In addition to Turkish and Kurdish, Arabic and English are also spoken. About 55 percent of the people are literate.

HISTORY

The Republic of Turkey was founded by Mustafa Kemal (later named Ataturk) in 1923 after the collapse of the 600-year-old Ottoman Empire. The Empire, which at the peak of its influence controlled vast stretches of North Africa, southeastern Europe, and western Asia, had failed to keep pace with the social and technological developments of Europe in the 19th century. The rise of nationalism was a centrifugal force which impelled several nations of the Empire to seek their independence, leading to its progressive fragmentation. This process reached its culmination in the disastrous Ottoman participation as one of Germany's allies in World War I. Defeated, shorn of much of its former territory, partially occupied by forces of the victorious European states, the Ottoman structure was repudiated by Turkish nationalists who rallied under the leadership of Ataturk. After a bitter war against invading Greek forces, the nationalists expelled them from Anatolia. The sultanate and caliphate, the temporal and religious ruling institutions of the old Empire, were abolished, and Turkey became a Republic.

The new Republic turned its back on the imperial ambitions and traditions of the Empire and concentrated on modernizing and Westernizing the ethnically Turkish core of the old Empire—

Anatolia and Thrace. The series of social, political, linguistic, and economic reforms and attitudes introduced by Ataturk before his death in 1938 forms the ideological basis of modern Turkey. Referred to as Ataturkism, its meaning, continued validity, and applicability are the subject of frequent discussion and debate in Turkey's political life.

Turkey was not a participant in World War II until shortly before its end, but this brief belligerency facilitated its status as a charter member of the United Nations. The difficulties faced by Greece in quelling a Communist rebellion and demands by the Soviet Union, shortly after the end of World War II, for Turkey's cession of some of its eastern territory and for military bases in the Turkish Straits, led in 1947 to the declaration of the Truman Doctrine. Large-scale U.S. military and economic aid began at this time. Turkey's contribution of a highly effective brigade to the U.N. forces during the Korean conflict was tangible evidence of its determination to help prevent Communist aggression, and recognition of this led to Turkey's entry into the North Atlantic Treaty Organization (NATO) in 1952.

The one-party rule (Republican People's Party) established by Ataturk in 1923 lasted until the 1950 elections, when the Democrat Party came to power. From 1950 until May 26, 1960, the Democrat Party ruled, with Celal Bayar as President of the Republic and Adnan Menderes as Prime Minister. Economic difficulties and internal political tensions culminated in a military coup d'état on May 27, 1960. The Committee of National Union (CNU) governed while a new constitution was written, a referendum was held to approve it, and elections carried out. A return to civilian government came with the convening of the Grand National Assembly on October 25, 1961.

GOVERNMENT

Turkey is a parliamentary Republic operating under a Constitution approved by a national referendum on July 9, 1961, and put into full operation on October 25, 1961.

The President, who may not succeed himself, is chosen by the Grand National Assembly (GNA) from among its members for a 7-year term and is Chief of State. He promulgates the laws enacted by the GNA or, within 10 days, returns the law with the reasons for his veto. Laws vetoed by the President may be reenacted by the GNA; presidential promulgation is then required within 10 days. The President designates a Prime Minister, usually the leader of the political party or coalition of parties which can command a majority of votes in the National Assembly. As Head of Government the Prime Minister supervises the implementation of the Government's general policies. Working with him is the Council of Ministers (cabinet) whose members are selected by the Prime Minister from the GNA or from among private citizens qualified to be elected to the GNA.

The Grand National Assembly is a bicameral parliament composed of the National Assembly and the Senate of the Republic. The 450 National Assembly members are directly elected to 4-year terms on the basis of universal adult suffrage. The Senate is composed of 150 members popularly elected to 6-year terms, 20 lifetime members from the former CNU, 15 members designated by the President, and former Presidents of the Republic. The GNA has the usual parliamentary powers of enacting, amending, and repealing laws. Bills are first debated in the National Assembly, and a mixed committee decides questions on which the two houses cannot agree. The power of interpellation is vested exclusively in the National Assembly.

The Court of Cassation sits at the apex of Turkey's regular judicial system and serves as a court of last instance in most cases. The Council of State has a similar function in the administrative court system. The Constitutional Court, added to the judicial system by the 1961 Constitution, reviews, on appeal, the constitutionality of laws and, when necessary, hears cases against the President and other senior officials.

For administrative purposes Turkey is divided into 67 Provinces, each headed by a Provincial Governor appointed by the Central Government.

POLITICAL CONDITIONS

The body politic of Turkey is divided into a majority, which is conservative and frequently traditional in outlook, and a minority, which seeks more rapid pursuit of the secular, Westernizing, statist philosophy propounded by Ataturk. This fundamental dichotomy underlies the party structure within which a large populist party and a somewhat smaller elitist party have been most prominent since 1950 and helps to explain the recurrent political difficulties which Turkey has experienced since 1950.

Until a severe illness incapacitated President Cemal Gursel, Gen. Cevdet Sunay was Chief of the Turkish General Staff. Gen. Sunay was appointed a Senator in order to make him eligible for the presidency and was elected to that office in March 1966 for a 7-year term. Gursel died the following September.

In the elections of October 1961 no party won a dominant position. A period of coalition governments ensued until the elections of October 1965, at which time the populist Justice Party came to power alone. It ruled until the elections of October 1969, when it was returned to power with a reduced percentage of the popular vote but with a sizable majority of National Assembly seats. Disruptions of public order began in 1968 and progressively increased over the next 3 years as extremists of the left, an aberration of the elitist trend in Turkish politics, took to the streets in opposition to the populist government. A countermovement of extremists on the right emerged in opposition to the leftists; clashes between the two became more frequent, and more than a score of student-aged youths had lost their lives by early 1971.

In March 1971 the apparent inability of the Justice Party government to bring a halt to the continuing incidents of violence in Turkey's large cities and the dissatisfaction of the Turkish military at the failure of the Justice Party government to pursue reforms with the speed and vigor deemed by the military as necessary, led to a political crisis. The senior military officers called for the replacement of the Justice Party government by one which could attain these objectives.

A new Prime Minister, Nihat Erim, was designated by the President in March 1971 to establish a reform, nonparty government composed of independents and members of the GNA from the three largest political parties in Turkey. Prime Minister Erim reorganized the Council of Ministers in December 1971 to give greater representation to the political parties, but he did not alter the basic orientation of the Government.

Prime Minister Erim is a former member of the Republican People's Party, the second largest party in Turkey, while the majority in the Grand National Assembly is from the Justice Party, the largest party. The nonpartisan nature of the Council of Ministers and the introduction of martial law in April 1971 in 11 Provinces, have altered for the time being the role of the political parties in Turkey. However, the normal role of the parties is expected to be restored in October 1973, when the next general elections for all National Assembly and two-thirds of the Senate seats are scheduled to take place.

Political Parties

Turkey has two major parties, two other with sufficient strength to form parliamentary groups, and several minor political parties.

The Justice Party (JP), founded in 1961 and currently headed by former Prime Minister Suleyman Demirel, inherited much of the political support enjoyed by the Democrat Party, which was overthrown in the 1960 coup, and may be described as a populist party. The JP places greater emphasis on private capital participation in the development process than does the principal opposition party. It has considerable support from among Turkey's rural majority, as well as from business and artisan groups.

After brief participation in the first postcoup coalition, the JP was the principal opposition party until February 1965, when it formed a new coalition with several minor parties. In the October 1965 elections, it came to power with 53 percent of the popular vote. Although its popular vote declined to 46.5 percent in the October 1969 elections, the altered proportional representation system enabled it to retain a majority in the GNA. A challenge to Suleyman Demirel's leadership of the JP resulted in a schism in the ranks of the JP in February 1970, leading to resignation of the JP government. The same Council of Ministers was reconstituted and received a vote of confidence on March 15, 1970, but with the virtual elimination of the JP's majority and with the estrangement and disciplining of the dissident element.

The JP strength was further reduced when a group of dissident Deputies, led by Ferruh Bozbeyli, former Speaker of the National Assembly, formed the Democrat Party in December 1970. This party is generally viewed as a rallying point for the more conservative former JP members, and it now constitutes the third largest party in the GNA.

The Republican People's Party (RPP) is headed by Ismet Inonu, a colleague of Ataturk. This party was founded by Ataturk in 1923 and was in power from then until 1950. It was the dominant party in coalition governments from November 1961 until February 1965. It received 37 percent of the votes in the 1961 elections, dropped to 29 percent in the elections of 1965, and received only 27.5 percent of the votes in the 1969 elections. Following the March 12, 1971, resignation of the JP government, Nihat Erim, a long-time member of the party, resigned from the RPP in order to qualify as the nonpartisan head of a nonparty Government. These events and the RPP decision to support the new Government led to the resignation of party Secretary General Bulent Ecevit, who had provided much of the day-to-day leadership of the RPP.

The RPP has basically adhered to the paternalistic approach to Turkey's economy which Ataturk originated, but since 1965 it has advocated an even greater role for the state through its espousal of a "left-of-center" philosophy. This party commands a high degree of support from among the urban population, civil servants, military officers, and others who regard it as the repository of Ataturk's traditions.

The party with the fourth largest representation in the Grand National Assembly is the National Reliance Party, led by Turhan Feyzioglu. A centrist grouping which broke with the RPP in 1967, the Reliance Party won 8 percent of the vote and 15 National Assembly seats in the 1969 elections, a sufficient number to make it a recognized parliamentary group. None of the other minor parties won enough seats to secure this recognition. They were: the New Turkey Party, the Nation Party, the National Movement Party, the Unity Party, and the Turkish Labor Party, which was experiencing a period of internal realignment after the 1969 elections.

In July 1971 the Turkish Labor Party, the only noteworthy Socialist party in the country, was banned by a ruling of the Constitutional Court. It had received less than 3 percent of the popular vote in general elections. The other minor parties generally range from the center to the right of the political spectrum, an orientation less important on occasion than the ethnic, sectarian, or regional identifications of certain of these groupings.

Another political group, the National Order Party, was organized by a group of conservatives following the 1969 elections. This conservative, religious party was banned in May 1971 following the Constitutional Court ruling that it had been attempting to make use of religion for political purposes.

All parties recognize the importance of economic development, although they differ on the best means for its achievement. The nation is united on the need to achieve a settlement of the Cyprus dispute acceptable to the Turkish community on the island, as well as on the necessity to use whatever measures might be required to forestall an imposed, unacceptable solution. Turkey's participation in NATO is supported by all parties, except the now-banned Turkish Labor Party.

As of May 1971 the political parties held the following number of seats in the Senate and National Assembly:

	Senate	National Assembly
Justice Party	89	224
Republican People's Party	34	141
Democrat Party	7	41
National Reliance Party	10	14
Nation Party	-	4
Unity Party	-	2
Turkish Labor Party	1	1
New Turkey Party	-	1
National Movement	1	1
Independents	6	15
(Vacant)	2	6
Total	150	450

ECONOMY

Turkey's economy is still predominantly agricultural (mainly cotton, tobacco, and grains) with about two-thirds of the labor force engaged in farming and related occupations. It is a mixed economy with government-owned or controlled enterprises which account for about half of the aggregate industrial output of the public and private sectors.

The 1960's were the longest period of sustained and rapid economic growth in Turkey's history. This compares favorably with the 1950's which witnessed serious inflation and a series of balance-of-payments crises. At the end of 1969 inflation and balance-of-payments problems returned to plague the Turkish economy. To curb these the Government undertook, in August 1970, a major economic stabilization and reform program which included a 40 percent devaluation of the Turkish lira to 15 per U.S. dollar. Currency gains from the devaluation have been used to strengthen considerably Turkey's official reserves. Export expansion was also accorded high priority in the new program in order to earn the foreign exchange necessary to import the capital investment items and raw materials required to sustain a high rate of growth. In 1970 gross national product (GNP), totaling about U.S. $8 billion (at 15 Turkish lira per dollar) grew by 5.6 percent, compared with an average of 6.6 percent during the mid- and late 1960's. The decline in the rate of expansion was mainly a result of industrial growth slowing to 3 percent in 1970 (compared to 10 percent in 1969), creating a shortfall from the projected growth rate of 7 percent for the second 5-year plan (1968-72). A target rate of 8 percent reportedly is being adopted for the third 5-year plan (1973-77).

Turkey continues to be dependent in part on external assistance for economic development and to help meet its debt obligations. A consortium of 14 donor countries (including the United States) and the International Bank for Reconstruction and Development (IBRD) was organized in 1962 under the Organization for Economic Cooperation and Development (OECD) to consider Turkey's problems and to extend financial and technical assistance. The consortium provided about $2.3 billion from 1963 through 1970 in financial assistance and debt relief. The International Monetary Fund (IMF) and the European Monetary Agreement, a lending agency composed of a number of European countries, also have assisted Turkey with standby arrangements and short-term credits.

Turkey signed an agreement of association with the European Communities (the European Economic Community, the European Coal and Steel Community, and the European Atomic Energy Community) in 1963. In mid-1971 Turkey entered the second, or "transitional," stage of its association with the European Economic Community (Common Market), which will provide free entry of Turkish industrial exports to the Common Market, improved access for agricultural goods, and up to $195 million in credit for investment in industrial projects. In turn, Turkey's tariffs will be progressively reduced or curtailed for the Common Market's products over a 30-year period.

Turkey, with an annual per capita income of about $240 at the new exchange rate, is attempting to narrow the considerable gap between its economy and the thriving economies of Western Europe. Economic development with financial stability is a major domestic policy of the country. Turkey's central economic problem is the need for increased foreign exchange earnings to match the growing cost of the imports required for development. In addition, much of the industrial sector is still devoted to assembly rather than basic manufacture and is dependent on high-cost imports. Turkey is in the process of stimulating the expansion of the export sector of the economy. It is also recognized that high-cost, protective industry must undergo major adjustment if it is to be competitive as Turkey moves toward full membership in the European Communities. At the present time Turkey's primary industries are iron and steel manufacturing and coal mining.

Turkey's imports are mainly machinery and raw materials, and its main exports are cotton and tobacco. Imports in 1970 amounted to about $948 million while exports were approximately $588 million. Major trading partners are the members of the European Communities and the United

States. In 1970 Turkey's imports from the United States totaled $194 million and its exports to the United States were $56 million.

FOREIGN RELATIONS

Turkey is a member of the North Atlantic Treaty Organization (NATO), which it joined in 1952 and which is still its major foreign alliance. The Turks have a traditional suspicion of Russians and hence of international communism. There are few Communists in Turkey—the Communist Party is officially banned. Turkey is also an important regional member of the Central Treaty Organization (CENTO), which has its headquarters at Ankara. In the United Nations Turkey has been an effective proponent of collective security within the U.N. framework, and it participates in a number of U.N. specialized agencies.

Turkey, lying in the historic path of Russian expansion to the Mediterranean, has expended since World War II about 30 percent of its annual budget for defense. It jealously guards its frontiers and places special emphasis on modernization of its armed forces. Use of the Turkish Straits is regulated by the Montreux Convention of 1936, the provisions of which are implemented and enforced by Turkey, as established by the convention. The prominence of Turkey's security problems has resulted in its international alliances and has contributed to its eagerness to fulfill its NATO military commitments; increasing Soviet naval activity in the eastern Mediterranean underscores the continuing importance of the southeastern flank of NATO.

During the past few years Turkey has taken steps to normalize its daily relations with the Soviet Union without in any way weakening Turkey's continuing full membership in NATO. In August 1971 Turkey and the People's Republic of China established diplomatic relations. The Republic of China (Taiwan) then suspended relations with Turkey.

U. S.-TURKEY RELATIONS

Turkish-American friendship dates to the late 18th century and was first officially sealed in a treaty of 1830. During World War II there was a flow of some lend-lease materials to Turkey, but the present close relationship really began with the agreement of July 12, 1947, which implemented the Truman Doctrine. Since then the United States and Turkey have worked together with exceptional cooperation to achieve their joint aims and establish a strong, healthy relationship. The United States is trying to assist Turkey in moving toward greater economic and military self-reliance. As part of the cooperative efforts toward that end, the United States has lent and granted Turkey more than $2.6 billion in economic and $3.1 billion in military assistance. In fiscal year 1971 U.S. development assistance of $40 million was provided.

Several thousand U.S. military personnel, along with several thousand dependents, are stationed in Turkey under the provisions of the North Atlantic Treaty. They man several communications/electronics facilities, a major air base at Incirlik near Adana, and a number of smaller facilities scattered throughout the country. Two NATO headquarters near Izmir also have sizable U. S. contingents.

Turkey is one of seven countries permitted to export opium, in accordance with international agreements, to meet the world's legitimate medical requirements for opium-based drugs such as morphine and codeine. (India is the world's largest legal exporter; Turkey ranks second with approximately 20 percent of the market.) Opium-poppy cultivation has existed in Turkey for centuries, and it is an important part of the livelihood for thousands of Turkish villagers in the western Anatolian Plateau. In addition to the cash return for the opium gum, the byproducts of poppy production are important to the farmer as the seeds are used for oil and flavoring and the stalks used for fuel and fodder.

In the past a significant portion of the opium has been diverted at the farm from legal production and smuggled out of Turkey to France and other countries where it was processed into heroin. While precise estimates are not possible, it is believed that opium diverted from Turkish poppy fields is the largest single source for heroin entering the United States.

In recent years the impact of drug abuse, particularly of heroin, in the United States has led to U.S. efforts to obtain the cooperation of other countries in suppressing trafficking in narcotic substances. The United States has given priority attention to curtailing supplies of illicit opium, which is the raw material from which heroin is produced. Despite efforts to curb the illicit traffic in opium, the Government of Turkey has not been successful in eliminating it. Therefore, on June 30, 1971, Prime Minister Erim announced that further opium-poppy cultivation in Turkey would be banned effective after the 1972 harvest. (According to Turkish law, farmers must be given 1 year's notice before prohibition can take place.) President Nixon characterized this decision as a courageous and statesmanlike act.

The Turkish Government is planning to assist the families that will be affected by the opium ban and will undertake programs to develop alternative sources of income for them. In order to help Turkey's transition from opium-poppy cultivation to other crops, or other types of activity, the United States has agreed to provide financial and technical assistance to help the Turkish Government during the transition period. This assistance will be in the form of compensation for the loss of foreign exchange earnings previously accruing from legitimate opium sales and to help establish alternative economic activities in the former poppy-growing areas.

PRINCIPAL GOVERNMENT OFFICIALS

President—Cevdet Sunay
Prime Minister—Nihat Erim
Minister of Foreign Affairs—Haluk Bayulken
Minister of National Defense—Ferit Melen
Minister of Interior—Ferit Kubat
Minister of Finance—Sait Naci Ergin
Minister of Justice—Suat Bilge
President, Republican Senate—Tekin Ariburun
President, National Assembly—Sabit Osman Avci
Chief, Turkish General Staff—Gen. Memduh Tagmac
Ambassador to the U.S.—Melih Esenbel
Ambassador to the U.N.—

Turkey maintains an Embassy in the United States at 1606 23d Street, N.W., Washington, D.C. 20008. There are also Consulates General at Chicago, Los Angeles, and New York.

PRINCIPAL U. S. OFFICIALS

Ambassador—William J. Handley
Deputy Chief of Mission—David C. Cuthell
Director, U.S. AID Mission—Joseph Toner
Chief, Joint U.S. Military Mission—Maj. Gen. Edward Scherrer, USA
Counselor for Political Affairs—Morris Draper
Counselor for Economic Affairs—Robert Brungart
Counselor for Mutual Security Affairs—Richard Boehm
Counselor for Administrative Affairs—Neil Muhonen
Public Affairs Officer (USIS)—Raymond E. Benson
Army Attaché—Col. Benjamin F. Gibbons
Navy Attaché—Capt. Frank K. Boushee
Defense and Air Attaché—Col. William M. Long
Consul General, Istanbul—James W. Spain
Consul General, Ismir—Thomas D. McKiernan
Consul, Adana—William H. Hallman

The U.S. Embassy in Turkey is located at 110 Ataturk Boulevard, Ankara.

READING LIST

American University. Area Handbook for Turkey. Washington, D.C.: U.S. Government Printing Office, 1970.

Davison, Roderic. Turkey. New York: Prentice-Hall, 1968.

Department of State. "The Central Treaty Organization." No. 1 in the International Organizations Series. Pub. 8418. Washington, D.C.: U.S. Government Printing Office, 1970.

Department of State. "The European Communities." No. 5 in the International Organizations Series. Pub. 8410. Washington, D.C.: U.S. Government Printing Office, 1969.

Department of State. "NATO and the Defense of Europe." No. 2 in Issues in United States Foreign Policy series. Pub. 8476. Washington, D.C.: U.S. Government Printing Office, 1969.

Dodd, C. H. Politics and Government in Turkey. Berkeley: University of California Press, 1969.

Eren, Nuri. Turkey Today and Tomorrow: An Experiment in Westernization. New York: Praeger, 1963.

Karpat, Kemal. Turkey's Politics. Princeton: Princeton University Press, 1959.

Kinross, Lord. Ataturk. London: Weidenfeld and Nicholson, 1964.

Kinross, Lord. Within the Taurus. London: Murray, 1954.

Lewis, Bernard. The Emergence of Modern Turkey. London: Oxford University Press, 1961.

Lewis, Geoffrey L. Turkey. New York: Praeger, 1956.

Makal, Mahmut. A Village in Anatolia. London: Valentine, Mitchell, 1954.

Muller, Herbert J. The Loom of History. New York: Harper, 1958.

Stewart, Desmond S. Turkey. New York: Time-Life Books, 1969.

Thomas, Lewis, and Frey, Richard. United States, Turkey and Iran. Cambridge: Harvard University Press, 1951.

Yalman, Ahmet Emin. Turkey in My Time. Norman: University of Oklahoma Press, 1956.

DEPARTMENT OF STATE PUBLICATION 7850
Revised December 1971

APPENDIX GGG

TURKEY

STRENGTH OF THE COMMUNIST PARTY ORGANIZATION—1973

SEE PAGE 142

[FROM: World Strength of the Communist Party Organizations—1973. Washington, Department of State, Bureau of Intelligence and Research, 1973.]

TURKEY

National Political Status: The 1961 Turkish Constitution provides for a bicameral Grand National Assembly consisting of a National Assembly of 450 deputies and a Senate with 150 elected and 33 non-elected senators. The Deputies are elected every four years, while one-third of the Senate is elected every two years.

Elections were held on October 14, 1973, for the National Assembly and for one-third of the Senate. The left-of-center Republican People's Party unexpectedly won a plurality, handing the Justice Party its first major setback since it won a majority in 1965. Another surprise was the relatively strong showing of the newly formed National Salvation Party (NSP). Organized in the summer of 1973, the NSP appeals to traditional Islamic and nationalist sentiment.

Date of last parliamentary elections - October 14, 1973. The following data show election results for 52 Senate seats. The percentages apply to total elected seats (150).

Communist: none

Moderate Left: Republican People's Party - 25 new, 16 old = 41 seats (27.3%)

Center: Republican Reliance Party - 1 new, 9 old = 10 seats (6.7%)

Moderate Conservative: Justice Party - 22 new, 58 old = 80 seats (53.3%)
Democratic Party - 0 new, 6 old = 6 seats (4.0%)

Conservative: National Salvation - 3 new, 0 old = 3 seats (2.0%)

Other: Independents - 1 new, 9 old = 10 seats (6.7%)
Presidential Appointees - 15 seats
Lifetime Senators - 20 seats

Total: 185 seats

The following data give the results of the National Assembly election.

Communist: none

Moderate Left: Republican People's Party - 3,482,438 votes (33.3%), 185 seats (41.1%)

Center: Republican Reliance Party - 565,841 votes (5.6%), 13 seats (2.9%)

Moderate Conservative: Justice Party - 3,082,773 votes (29.6%), 149 seats (33.1%)
Democratic Party - 1,229,573 votes (11.9%), 45 seats (10.0%)

Conservative: National Salvation Party - 1,248,675 votes (12.0%), 48 seats (10.7%)
Nationalist Action Party - 364,838 votes (3.6%), 3 seats (.7%)

Other: Turkish Unity Party[1] - 112,280 votes (1.0%), 1 seat (.2%)
Independents - 319,751 votes (3.0%), 6 seats (1.3%)

Total: 10,465,910 votes, 450 seats

Communist Party Membership: 1,000-1,500 (estimate)

Leading Party Figure and Position:
DEMIR, Yakub (also known as Zeki BASTIMER) - A Turkish political émigré, long resident in Eastern Europe; spokesman for the "Communist Party of Turkey" at international party gatherings

Principal Publications: Occasional clandestinely circulated pamphlets

Areas of Communist Activity: The Communist Party has been illegal within Turkey since 1925. Small groups of Turkish Communists in exile maintain the shadow of a party abroad, carrying on propaganda activities, primarily Turkish language broadcasts over *Bizim Radyo* out of East Germany. This station transmits to Turkey as well as to several hun-

1/ The TUP is primarily an Alevi (Shiite) Moslem party.

dred thousand Turkish workers in West Germany and other West European countries. *Bizim Radyo* has an outlook which is on the whole more ideological and critical than that of official Soviet media and also is bitterly anti-NATO and anti-American.

The radical left within Turkey consists of small but vociferous groups, some of which cooperated within the Turkish Labor Party (TLP) from 1962 until its dissolution in 1971. From its founding the TLP looked to urban intellectuals, students, workers, and some groups of eastern Kurdish peasants for its main support. When it won 3 percent of the vote in 1965, largely among these groups, its future looked promising though not spectacular. Its share of the vote dropped slightly, however, in 1969.

Even prior to its proscription, the TLP, consistently pro-Soviet and anti-American, but representing a variety of Marxist, Maoist, and other Socialist ideologies, had been beset by factionalism. Moreover, as more and more radical groups arose in 1970-71 advocating violence, the TLP became increasingly isolated from its student and intellectual base of support. Clashes among its leading personalities further weakened the party. Having nowhere else to turn, many TLP supporters probably voted for the RPP in the October 1973 elections.

In the years 1970-72 several radical leftist groups, generally made up of college students and exemplified by the Dev Genc group, perpetrated a series of increasingly violent acts which culminated in the kidnap-murder of the Israeli Consul General in Istanbul in May 1971 and the murder of three NATO technicians in the spring of 1972--all with the avowed purpose of bringing down the government and radically altering the structure of Turkish society. Widespread arrests under the martial law regime, which was originally proclaimed in April 1971 and finally lifted in September 1973, served to disperse, force into exile, or drive underground much of what remains of these groups. They are thought, nonetheless, still to constitute a serious potential for trouble to the Turkish Government.

APPENDIX HHH
UNITED KINGDOM
ARMED FORCES AND MILITARY POWER

[Reprinted with permission from: The Almanac of World Military Power, by Col. T. N. Dupuy, U.S. Army, Ret., Col. John A. C. Andrews, U.S. Air Force, Ret., and Grace P. Hayes. 3rd ed. Dunn Loring, Va., T. N. Dupuy Associates, 1974.]

UNITED KINGDOM OF GREAT BRITAIN AND NORTHERN IRELAND

POWER POTENTIAL STATISTICS

Area: 94,216 square miles
Population: 57,000,000
Total Active Armed Forces: 370,000 (including 9,900 non-British; 0.65% population)
Gross National Product: $151.6 billion ($2,161 per capita)
Annual Military Expenditures: $8.1 billion (5.34% GNP)
Steel and Iron Production: 40 million metric tons
Fuel Production: Coal: 149.7 million metric tons
Gas (manufactured): 20.5 billion cubic meters
Gas (natural): 19 billion cubic meters
Electric Power Output: 254 billion kwh
Merchant Fleet: 3,785 ships; 27.3 million gross tons
Civil Air Fleet: 246 jet, 83 turboprop, 108 piston transports

DEFENSE STRUCTURE

The Sovereign is the nominal commander in chief of all the armed forces. Actual control is exercised by the Prime Minister and the Cabinet, through the Secretary of State for Defence. Within the Cabinet all defense matters are considered by the Defence and Overseas Policy Committee, which includes the Prime Minister, the Secretary of State for Defence, the Foreign Secretary, the Home Secretary, the Chancellor of the Exchequer, and such others as are appointed by the Prime Minister; the Secretary of State for Defence is responsible to Parliament for carrying out the decisions of this Committee and for administering the Ministry of Defence. His principal assistant in carrying out these tasks is a civil servant, the Permanent Under-Secretary of State for Defence.

Within the Ministry of Defence are the three Service Departments, each headed by an Under-Secretary of State (one each for Navy, Army, and Air Force), although each department retains its individual identity (Admiralty Board, Army Board, and Air Force Board). Directly under the Secretary of State for Defence, and next to him in rank within the Ministry, are two Defence Ministers, one for Administration, the other for Equipment. There is a military Defence Staff, coordinating planning and operations for all of the services; each of the services retains its traditional General Staff (or equivalent); overall defense military planning is directed by the Chiefs of Staff Committee, under the chairmanship of the Chief of the Defence Staff, and with the three service staff chiefs as members. Under the Secretary of State is a Defence Council (of which he is chairman), responsible for exercising the powers of command and administrative control over the largely integrated services. Members of this Council are: Secretary of State, the two Defence Ministers, the three Service Parliamentary Under-Secretaries of State, the Chief of the Defence Staff, the chiefs of the three service staffs, the Chief Scientist, and the Permanent Under-Secretary of State for Defence.

A substantial degree of military integration has been achieved through centralized operational directives to overseas commands, and through assignment of multi-service logistical responsibilities to various functional agencies of the three services; for instance, the Navy is responsible for procurement of petrol, oil, and lubricants (POL).

POLITICO-MILITARY POLICY

In the years since World War II it has been necessary for Britain to make a painful transition whereby policies are necessarily related to the facts of diminished power and wealth, and the consequent situation of diminished influence in world affairs. Nevertheless, residual reservoirs of power are substantial, and Britain is still unquestionably first among the handful of major powers of secondary rank. Its position as leader of the Commonwealth reinforces that status.

Traditionally the most important of Britain's politico-military objectives were: to command the seas surrounding the British Isles; to maintain the European balance of power; to keep open the shipping lanes to Britain to provide food for the people and raw materials for the industry; to protect overseas possessions and to encourage them (since

1783) to become self-governing and economically and militarily self-reliant partners within a world-wide British system (formerly called an Empire, more recently a Commonwealth).

Among the most important traditional military policies supporting these objectives were: to undertake whatever military operations were necessary to prevent any major European power from controlling the Low Countries; to maintain a fleet at least as large and as powerful as the combined naval forces of the next two most powerful European maritime nations; to dominate the Mediterranean and the Middle East littoral; to avoid major land force involvement in a European war, but rather to encourage Continental allies to bear the brunt of land operations while Britain bore the major burden of naval and amphibious operations; to maintain major forces overseas, particularly in Asia and the Indian Ocean; to secure and protect overseas possessions and all sources of valuable materials.

It is probable that all of the cited objectives are still valid, within a more limited frame of reference. None of the major traditional policies listed above are fully applicable today, mostly because of Britain's diminished capabilities and resources, and its consequent reduced influence as a world power. Thus its need to protect Britain through seapower requires emphasis on retaining a formal or informal alliance with the United States; its reduced ability to influence Continental affairs, on the other hand, requires more direct involvement on the Continent and provision to Continental allies of substantial evidence of willingness to participate militarily, politically, and economically as an equal partner.

Slowly but inexorably the policies for dominating the Mediterranean, the Middle East, the Indian Ocean, and the rimlands of Southern Asia have been abandoned in the years since World War II. The last vestiges of these policies were the retention of control of the Persian Gulf, maintenance of major military forces at the principal exits from the Indian Ocean (Aden and Singapore), and the retention of other bases in the Indian Ocean. By 1974 even these vestiges of far-flung power east of Suez had been abandoned.

The British withdrawal from Aden was complete in 1968, and the Headquarters Far East Command at Singapore was closed November 1, 1971. It was succeeded by Headquarters ANZUK Force (Australian, New Zealand, United Kingdom). Malaysian and Singapore forces fill out this Five-Power command. The UK furnishes an infantry battalion group on station at Singapore, as well as Nimrod maritime patrol bombers and ASW helicopters. Patrolling the Indian Ocean and Mozambique Channel and the South China Sea are Royal Navy frigates. The RAF maintains staging posts at Masirah and Gan, and the Navy has a base at Hong Kong. The Army has five infantry battalions (three of them Gurkhas) and an artillery regiment there.

Britain relies upon voluntary enlistment to maintain its armed forces. To gain flexibility and attract recruits, volunteers are offered options of early release, on 18 months' notice, provided they serve at least three years, though long-term service is still encouraged.

STRATEGIC PROBLEMS

Britain's greatest strategic problem is its lack of sufficient raw materials to feed the population and to feed the vital industries. It can obtain these raw materials only by sea, and thus is vulnerable to any hostile capability to interfere with its overseas lanes of trade. It is this potential vulnerability that has been the principal determinant of British objectives and British policies since the end of the 16th Century. Next in importance among Britain's strategic problems is its proximity to the continent of Europe, and its vulnerability to attack across the narrow waters of the English Channel and North Sea, and the even narrower waters of the Strait of Dover (22 miles across). This has been the basis of traditional British sensitivity to the possibility that a hostile power could establish dangerous bases in the Low Countries.

Another strategic vulnerability is the concentration of a large population, and of an extensive industrial complex, in a limited area. This vulnerability, which was serious in World War II, has become critical in the era of nuclear-armed missiles. This has convinced the British government and people—despite the changing political complexion of the leadership—that Britain must maintain an effective and convincing deterrent to possible aggression.

Britain has tiny groups seeking independence within both Scotland and Wales, and a comparable, but much more difficult, problem in Northern Ireland. Dealing with the Welsh and Scottish separatists is essentially a police problem, and does not pose any substantial security threat to the United Kingdom. In Northern Ireland, however, approximately one-third of the population of about 1.5 million are Irish Catholics, with strong religious, cultural, and emotional ties with the people of Eire. More than half of the remainder are Scots-Irish in origin and strongly Protestant, anti-Eire, and anti-Catholic in attitude. Feelings run high between these two groups, and are exacerbated by the activities of a group of terrorists—claiming to be members of the outlawed Irish Republic Army, disavowed by the government of Eire—who are seeking to bring about the union of Northern Ireland with Eire by employing urban guerrilla tactics of murder, arson, and bombing. In an effort to control the situation, Britain has employed at times as many as 17 major units of all services on internal security duty in Northern Ireland. The Ulster Defense Regiment, specially created for such duty, is at a strength of about 6,000. Naval units patrol off-shore to intercept arms runners. In 1974 strife between Catholics and Protestants in Ulster continued, acts of violence on both sides increased, and a British attempt to establish a new, joint government failed.

One strategic security problem is the preservation of control over certain overseas territories where British rights or sovereignty are challenged. Most important among these is Gibraltar, which Spain seeks to regain, demanding that Britain renounce the rights gained by the Treaty of Utrecht in 1713. Of less significance are Belize, where British rights are disputed by neighboring Guatemala, and the Falkland Islands, claimed by Argentina.

In 1973 Britain and Iceland became involved in a "Cod War" over fishing rights off Iceland's coasts. After numerous incidents between fishing trawlers and Icelandic gunboats, the British government sent three frigates to the area. Temporary agreement was finally reached in October, limiting catches, numbers of boats and areas in which they might fish. The issue is not resolved, however, since Iceland apparently intends to defy a ruling in favor of Britain by the International Court of Justice.

MILITARY ASSISTANCE

In the sense that it relies to a considerable degree upon the United States for the production of all or parts of many of the most expensive weapons systems, Britain has been the recipient of US military assistance. For the most part, however, American aid has taken the form of making available weapons and equipment for purchase by Britain. A small Military Advisory Group (currently one civilian employee) has been stationed in Britain, and since 1950 a total value of $1.0345 billion (virtually none since 1963) has been provided to Britain by the United States.

Over the years since World War II Britain has provided to other nations far more military aid than it has received from the United States. Most of this assistance has been given to other Commonwealth nations, and mainly to those that have received their independence since 1945.

ALLIANCES

The United Kingdom, a UN member with a permanent seat on the Security Council, is a participant in seven major alliances, and a number of lesser or subsidiary bilateral alliances.

First, Britain is the leading member of the Commonwealth of Nations. The Sovereign of Great Britain is accepted by all members of this free association of independent states as the Head of the Commonwealth. There is no other tangible link, and the objectives of the members are rarely in full accord with each other. The purposes of the alliance are vague, but generally are economic in practical effect. Nevertheless, there are implied political and military commitments, more demanding upon Britain and the other English-speaking members, perhaps, than on the others. The members of the Commonwealth are: United Kingdom, Canada, Australia, New Zealand, India, Sri Lanka, Ghana, Nigeria, Cyprus, Sierra Leone, Jamaica, Trinidad and Tobago, Uganda, Kenya, Malaysia, Tanzania, Malawi, Malta, Zambia, Gambia, Singapore, Guyana, Botswana, Lesotho, Barbados, Mauritius, Bahamas, Bangladesh, Swaziland, Tonga, Western Samoa, and Fiji. The UK hasseparate defense agreements or understandings with most of these, and provides most with various forms of military assistance.

The United Kingdom is also a member of the three major regional alliances established between 1950 and 1954 to deter threatened Communist aggression in Europe and Asia: NATO, CENTO, and SEATO. Related to NATO is the earlier Western European Union (WEU) which was established by the Brussels Treaty between Britain, France and the Benelux countries in 1948, and has been enlarged by the addition of Italy and West Germany.

Britain in 1971 joined with Malaysia, Singapore, Australia, and New Zealand in the so-called Five-Power Pact for the defense of British Commonwealth interests in Southeast Asia (see Malaysia).

Britain's principal alliance is that with the United States. A special relationship between these two nations has existed since Prime Minister Winston Churchill and President Franklin D. Roosevelt met aboard warships in Argentia Bay, off Newfoundland, in August 1941. Rarely, if ever, have two major powers established so close and cordial a wartime alliance as that which existed between them in World War II. The peacetime relationship that followed is equally unprecedented. America's ties with Canada are perhaps closer than those with the United Kingdom, but the Canadian alliance is one for the defense of the homelands of the participants, one being a major partner and the other a relatively minor one. In the continuing Anglo-American alliance the UK is, perforce, now a junior partner, but nonetheless still a major power, with worldwide interests, influence, and commitments. This alliance between the two major English-speaking nations is perhaps the most powerful force for peace in the world today.

The UK joined the European Common Market on January 1, 1973, without relinquishing its membership in the European Free Trade Association (EFTA), a step which followed the trend of its foreign trade and was widely considered to augur further changes in foreign policy.

ARMY

Personnel: 176,000 (including 8,200 enlisted abroad, and 5,600 women)

Organization:
Within the United Kingdom:
United Kingdom Land Forces (Headquarters, Wilton)
Strategic Command
Southern Command
Northern Command
Western Command

Scottish District (Headquarters, Edinburgh)
Northern Ireland District (Headquarters Lisburn)–Ulster Defense Regiment of 6,000 men (plus other units rotated through Northern Ireland during the continuing disturbances there)

Overseas:
- Near East Land Forces (part of Near East Command; Headquarters, Cyprus)
- Forces in Far East (now under five-power control, see above)
- British Army of the Rhine (BAOR; Headquarters: Munchen-Gladbach)

Operational Units:
- 12 infantry brigades
- 49 infantry battalions (6 Gurkhas, equalling 1 brigade)
- 1 parachute brigade
- 1 Special Air Service regiment (air-mobile commandos)
- 12 armored regiments
- 5 armored car regiments
- 27 artillery regiments (3 with Honest John SSMs and 203mm howitzers)
- 14 engineer regiments
- 10 signal regiments

Deployment:
- 18 battalions in UK commands (forces in Northern Ireland comprise three brigade headquarters, one armored reconnaissance regiment, one field squadron of Royal Engineers, 17 major units–five of which are redeployed from BAOR). In the latter part of 1971 a battalion of Gurkhas was deployed to the UK.
- Strategic Command (three infantry brigades–air portable–and one parachute force of two battalions forming one division, stationed in Strategic Command area; one SAS regiment)
- British Army of the Rhine (BAOR) (54,900 men, assigned to NATO)
  - 3 divisions (one corps) plus two artillery brigades
  - 5 armored brigades
  - 1 mechanized brigade
  - 2 armored car regiments

Far East
- 1 battalion group at Singapore (under ANZUK, Five-Power Pact)
- 5 infantry battalions (including 3 Gurkha) in Hong Kong
- 1 artillery regiment in Hong Kong
- 1 battalion (Gurkha) in Brunei
- 1 Marine Commando Brigade afloat (1,650 Marines, 200 soldiers, 50 sailors)

Mediterranean
- 2 infantry battalions on Cyprus (including 1 in UNFICYP)
- 1 armored car squadron
- 1 battalion at Gibraltar
- 2 air portable reconnaissance squadrons (UNFICYP)

Other Detachments
- 1 brigade in Berlin Garrison (3,200)
- 1 infantry battalion (less one company) in Belize

Major Equipment Inventory:
- about 1,000 Chieftain heavy tanks and Centurion medium tanks (latter being phased out)
- armored cars (Saladin and Ferret)
- scout cars (Ferret)
- APCs (Saracen and Trojan)
- Honest John SSM (2 batteries per regiment in three BAOR regiments)
- 175mm/203mm self-propelled guns/howitzers (with nuclear capability)
- 5.5 inch howitzers
- 155mm self-propelled howitzers (M-109 and M-44)
- 105mm self-propelled howitzers (Abbot)
- Vigilant and Swingfire antitank guided weapons
- 200 light aircraft
- 190 helicopters

Reserves: The Territorial and Army Volunteer Reserve (volunteer militia) numbers 56,400. Its mission is UK home defense and preservation of law and order in emergency. The Regular Army Reserve of 120,000 comprises men with specific mobilization assignments in war or in situations short of war. An additional 180,000 men, without specific mobilization assignments, belong to the Army General Reserve.

NAVY

Personnel: 83,100 (including 8,000 Royal Marines, Fleet Air Arm, and 3,400 women)

Organization:
- Commander in Chief, Fleet (Headquarters, Northwood)
- Naval Home Commands
- Fleet Air Arm
- Royal Marines (four 800-man Commandos with a

brigade headquarters; the balance of the force serving on various duties afloat and ashore)

Major Units:

Operational Fleet:
- 1 aircraft carrier (CVA)
- 2 guided missile cruisers (CLG; Seacat SAM helicopters)
- 2 Commando carriers (LPH)
- 2 amphibious assault ships (LPD)
- 8 guided missile frigates (guided missile destroyers, DLG)
- 3 radar picket destroyers (antiaircraft frigates, DDR)
- 45 escort ships (26 general purpose frigates, 19 ASW frigates, DE)
- 4 radar picket escort ships (aircraft direction frigates; DER)
- 3 fleet ballistic missile submarines (SSBN), 48 Polaris A-3 missiles
- 8 fleet nuclear submarines (SSN; 3 more under construction; a further one ordered)
- 16 diesel submarines (SS)
- 42 coastal and inshore minesweepers (36 MSC and 6 MSI)
- 226 auxiliaries
- 24 attack aircraft (Buccaneer Mk.2) being transferred to RAF
- 72 All-weather fighters (Phantom FG.1 and Sea Vixen Mk.2)
- 120 helicopters (14 squadrons Wessex, Sea King, Wasp, and Whirlwind)
- 40 miscellaneous trainer/support aircraft

Reserve Fleet or Refitting:
- 10 escort ships (9 general purpose and 1 ASW frigate, DE)
- 1 Polaris submarine (SSBN)
- 6 diesel submarines (SS)
- guided missile destroyers (DLG)
- ,7 submarines (SS)
- 2 coastal minesweepers (MSC)
- 2 fleet maintenance ships

Major Naval Bases: Portsmouth, Devonport, Chatham, Rosyth, Portland, Gibraltar, Hong Kong.

Reserves: Royal Navy and Marine regular reserves number 26,300, and Volunteer Reserve and Auxiliary forces account for an additional 8,400.

AIR FORCE

Personnel: 110,900 (including 6,000 women)

Organization:

Strike Command: Headquarters: High Wycombe
- 4 medium bomber squadrons (Vulcan Mk-2)
- 3 tanker squadrons (Victor Mk-1)
- 1 strategic reconnaissance squadron (Victor Mk-2)
- 1 photo-reconnaissance squadron (Canberra PR-7)
- 1 electronic reconnaissance squadron (Canberra, Nimrod)
- 3 maritime strike/attack squadrons (Buccaneer Mk-2)
- 6 interceptor squadrons (5 Lightning, 1 Phantom)
- 4 patrol bomber squadrons (Nimrod Mk-1)
- SAM squadrons (Bloodhound Mk-1)
- 10 strategic transport squadrons (2 Britannia, 1 VC-10, 1 Belfast, 1 Comet, 5 Hercules)
- 6 ground attack squadrons (1 Harrier, 2 Hunter, 3 Phantom)
- 3 helicopter squadrons (1 Wessex, 2 Puma)
- 1 light transport squadron (Andover)

Training Command: Headquarters: Brampton
- 17 training/support squadrons

RAF Germany (2nd Allied Tactical Air Force): Headquarters: Rheindahlen
- 2 fighter-interceptor squadrons (Lightning)
- 7 reconnaissance/attack squadrons (3 Harrier, 4 Phantom)
- 2 attack squadrons (Buccaneer)
- SAMs (Bloodhound)
- 1 helicopter squadron (Wessex)

Near East (Air Force) Command: Headquarters: Cyprus
- 1 interceptor squadron (Lightning)
- 2 medium bomber squadrons (Vulcan assigned to CENTO)
- 2 reconnaissance squadrons (Canberra based on Malta)
- SAMs (Bloodhound)
- 1 helicopter squadron (Whirlwind)
- 1 squadron (Hunter) based on Gibraltar
- 1 maritime patrol/ASW squadron (Nimrod) based on Malta
- 1 transport squadron (Hercules, Argosy)

RAF in Far East (under ANZUK, Five-Power Pact force)
- 1 patrol bomber squadron (Nimrod) based in Singapore
- 2 helicopter squadrons, 1 in Singapore, 1 in Hong Kong

Royal Air Force Regiment (Mission: ground defense of airfields, and manning of SAMs)
- 12 squadrons (deployed in UK and overseas)

SAM batteries (Tigercat, Bloodhound, Rapier)

Major Aircraft Types:

618 combat aircraft
- 118 Phantom fighter/attack aircraft
- 90 Harrier V/STOL attack/reconnaissance aircraft
- 100 Lightning interceptors (Firestreak Redtop AAM)
- 100 Buccaneer attack aircraft
- 35 Hunter fighter-bombers
- 12 Victor Mk-2 medium bombers (reconnaissance)
- 41 Nimrod maritime patrol aircraft
- 50 Vulcan Mk-2 medium bombers
- 20 Canberra light bombers
- 12 Shackleton patrol bombers
- 40 Canberra photo reconnaissance aircraft

929 other aircraft
- 38 Victor Mk-1 tankers
- 51 strategic transports (Belfast, Britannia, Comet, VC-10, Hercules)
- 91 light transports (HS-125, Andover, Bassett, Pembroke)
- 115 helicopters (Whirlwind, Wessex, Sioux, Puma)
- 565 trainers (170 Chipmunk, 195 Jet Provost, 54 Varsity, 65 Gnat, 40 Bulldog, 19 Dominie, 22 Hunter)
- 45 miscellaneous support aircraft
- 24 helicopters (8 Sioux, 16 Whirlwind)

Major Air Bases: Stanmore, W. Raynham, Wattisham, Conningsby, Oldham, Brampton, Linton-on-Ouse, White Waltham, Waterbeach, Bassingbourne, Binbrook, Coltishall, Chivenor, Finningley, Thorney Island, Gaydon, Stradishall, Syerston, Leeming, Oakington, Aclington, Waddington, Cottesmore, Scampton, St. Mawgan, Wyton, Marham, Wittering, Kinloss, Ballykelly, Lindholm, Church Fenton, Lynham, Odiham, Bawtry, Topcliffe, St. Anthan, Benson, Mancy, Shawbury, Boscombe, High Wycombe, Upavon, Brize Norton, Colerne, Abingdon, Fairford, Pitreavie

Reserves: There are approximately 33,000 regular RAF reservists plus several hundred Volunteer Reserve and Auxiliary Force members.

APPENDIX III
UNITED KINGDOM
BACKGROUND NOTES

[Washington, Department of State, January 1973 (Publication 8099).]

UNITED KINGDOM

BACKGROUND NOTES

Population: 55.3 million (1971 est.)
Capital: London

The United Kingdom of Great Britain (England, Scotland, Wales) and Northern Ireland lies off the northwest coast of the European Continent, separated from it by the English Channel, the Strait of Dover, and the North Sea. At the closest point England is only 22 miles from France. London is in the southeastern part of England. Together with its many islands, the United Kingdom occupies a land area of 93,025 square miles, slightly smaller than Oregon.

England has generally rolling land. Its largest city is London with a population of about 7.4 million. Scotland lies north of England. Its Lowlands, about 60 miles wide, divide the farming region of the southern Uplands from the granite Highlands of the north. Edinburgh (449,000) is Scotland's capital; Glasgow is its largest city (898,000) and one of the greatest industrial centers of the United Kingdom. Wales borders England to the west and is almost entirely mountainous; its largest city is Cardiff (278,000 inhabitants). Northern Ireland occupies the northeast corner of Ireland across the North Channel from Scotland and is primarily an agricultural region. Its capital and largest city, Belfast, has an estimated population of 359,000.

Owing to prevailing southwesterly winds, the climate of the United Kingdom is temperate and equable. Temperatures range from a mean of about 40°F. in winter to about 60°F. in summer. Average annual rainfall in the United Kingdom is 35-40 inches, distributed relatively evenly throughout the year, and fogs are frequent.

Flags: The red, white, and blue British Union Jack combines crosses of the patron saints of England (Saint George), Scotland (Saint Andrew), and Ireland (Saint Patrick). The red ensign, with Union Jack in the upper left corner, flies above merchant ships commanded by civilians; the blue above those under Royal Navy command; the white above warships.

PEOPLE

The U.K. population was estimated at 55.3 million in 1971, about 2.8 million more than in 1961 and a sevenfold increase since 1700. Its population is the third highest in Europe (after the U.S.S.R. and the Federal Republic of Germany). The United Kingdom's population density, one of the highest in the world, is 603 persons per square mile. Almost one-third of the total population resides in England's prosperous and fertile southeastern corner, with population declining in the more rugged areas to the north and west. The population of the United Kingdom as a whole is predominantly urban and suburban.

The contemporary Briton is descended mainly from the varied racial stocks which settled there before the end of the 11th century. As an island lying close to the European Continent, Great Britain has been subject to many invasions and migrations, especially from Scandinavia and the continent, including Roman occupation for several centuries. Under the Normans, Scandinavian Vikings who had settled in northern France, the pre-Celtic, Celtic, Roman, Anglo-Saxon, and Norse influences were blended into the Briton of today. While the Celtic languages still persist in Northern Ireland, Wales, and Scotland to a small degree, the predominant language has long been English, a blend of Anglo-Saxon and Norman-French.

The high literacy rate in the United Kingdom (99 percent) is attributable to the introduction of public primary and secondary education in 1870 and 1900 respectively. In 1971 there were about 10.8 million students in attendance at educational institutions, the great majority of which are publicly financed in whole or in part.

The Church of England (Episcopal) with 27 million baptized members is the established church, but religious freedom is guaranteed to all. A number of other churches, including the Roman Catholic and the Church of Scotland (Presbyterian), have substantial numbers of adherents.

HISTORY

The Roman invasion of 55 B.C. and subsequent incorporation into the Roman Empire stimulated the development of Britain and brought it into an active relationship with the rest of Europe. After the Romans' departure, the country remained prey to other invasions until the Norman conquest of 1066. Norman rule effectively assured Britain's safety from further invasion and stimulated the development of institutions, both new and indigenous, which have since distinguished British life. A central administration, the development of a separate but established church, common law, and representative government, for example, gradually evolved after 1066.

Union

In its earliest history, Wales was an independent kingdom which for centuries repeatedly thwarted invasion attempts from England. The English conquest succeeded in 1282 under Edward

I, and the Statute of Rhuddlan established English rule 2 years later. To appease the Welsh, Edward's son (later Edward II), who had been born in Wales, was made Prince of Wales in 1301. The tradition of bestowing this title on the eldest son of the British Monarch remains today. An act of 1536 completed the political and administrative union between England and Wales.

Scotland was also an independent kingdom which resisted English invasion attempts. England and Scotland united under one crown in 1603, when James VI of Scotland succeeded his cousin Elizabeth I as James I of England. In the ensuing 100 years strong religious and political differences continued to divide the kingdoms. Finally in 1707 England and Scotland agreed to union under the name of Great Britain. It was at this time that the Union Jack became the national flag.

The Anglo-Norman invasion of Ireland in 1170 was the beginning of centuries of strife. Successive English kings sought to impose their will on the Irish, whose cause was finally defeated in 1602 after which Ireland was subjected, with varying degrees of success, to control and regulation by Britain. The legislative union of Great Britain and Ireland was completed on January 1, 1801, under the name of the United Kingdom. However, armed struggle for political independence continued sporadically into the 20th century. The Anglo-Irish treaty of 1921 established the Irish Free State (see Background Notes on Ireland, pub. 7974). The six northern and predominantly Protestant Irish counties remained part of the United Kingdom.

British Expansion

Begun initially in support of William the Conqueror's (c. 1028-1087) holdings in France, a policy of active involvement in European affairs was embarked on which endured for several hundred years. By the end of the 14th century, foreign trade, originally based on wool exports to Europe, had emerged as a cornerstone of national policy. The foundations of sea power—to protect Britain's trade and open up new routes—were gradually laid. Defeat of the Spanish Armada in 1588 firmly established Britain as a major sea power. Thereafter, its interests outside Europe grew steadily.

Attracted by the spice trade, British mercantile interests spread first to the Far East. In search of an alternate route to the Spice Islands, John Cabot reached the American Continent in 1498. Sir Walter Raleigh organized the first, short-lived British colony in Virginia in 1584, and permanent British settlement followed. During the ensuing two centuries, alternately in contest and concord with its European neighbors, Britain extended its influence abroad and consolidated its political development at home. The territorial foundation of the 20th century British Empire, with the principal exceptions of parts of Africa and India, had already been laid by the time of the Boston Tea Party in 1773.

Great Britain's industrial revolution— developed with impressive force at the very time it lost the American colonies—greatly strenthened its ability to oppose Napoleonic France. By the conclusion of the Napoleonic wars in 1815, the United Kingdom had no peer in Europe, and its navy ruled the seas. The peace in Europe that followed allowed the British once again to focus their interests on more remote parts of the world, sometimes at the expense of European rivals. During this period, the British Empire reached its zenith. British colonies, skillfully managed, contributed to the United Kingdom's extraordinary economic growth and strengthened its voice in world affairs. Paradoxically, the United Kingdom became more imperial as it continued to strengthen and broaden its democratic institutions.

Twentieth Century

By the time of Queen Victoria's death in 1901, however, the tide had turned. Other nations, including the United States and Germany, had benefited from their own industrial development. The United Kingdom's comparative economic advantage had lessened, and the ambitions of its rivals had grown. The First World War drastically depleted British resources and consequently undermined its ability to maintain the dominant role of the previous century. As the United Kingdom's independent power base weakened, it began to move toward the close ties with the United States characteristic of current policy.

British control over the Empire loosened during the interwar period. Ireland, with the exception of Ulster, broke away from the United Kingdom in 1921. Nationalism became stronger in other parts of the Empire, particularly in India and Egypt. In 1926 the United Kingdom granted Australia, Canada, and New Zealand complete autonomy within the Empire. As such, they became charter members of the British Commonwealth of Nations, an informal but closely knit association destined to succeed the Empire. Throughout the interwar period, moreover, the British economy continued to lose ground to competitors.

World War II sealed the fate of the British Empire. Unable to maintain control, the United Kingdom began the process of dismantling the Empire in 1947. Most of the viable colonial units have now been granted independence in an orderly and generous manner. Southern Rhodesia, however, unilaterally declared itself independent in November 1965 in opposition to British attempts to foster a government representing blacks as well as whites.

GOVERNMENT

The unwritten British Constitution is based partly on statute, partly on common law, and partly on the "traditional rights of Englishmen." Constitutional changes may come about formally through new Acts of Parliament, or informally through the acceptance of new traditions and usage, or by new judicial pre' dents. Although Parliament has the theoretical power to make or unmake any law, in practice the weight of 700 years of tradition restrains arbit ·ary actions.

Executive government rests nominally with the Monarch (Chief of State). In actual practice it is exercised by a committee of Ministers (Cabinet) who traditionally are selected from among the members of the House of Commons and, to a lesser extent, the House of Lords. The Prime Minister (Head of Government) is the leader of the majority party in the Commons, and his government is dependent on its support.

The Parliament of the United Kingdom represents the entire country and can legislate for the whole or for any constituent part or combination of parts. The life of a Parliament is fixed by law at 5 years, although the Prime Minister may dissolve it and call a general election at any time if his policies are severely criticized. The locus of legislative power is the 630-man House of Commons, which has sole jurisdiction over finance. The House of Lords, although shorn of most of its powers, can still review, amend, or delay for a limited time any legislation except money bills. Only a fraction of the some 900 members attend regularly, but the House of Lords has greater lesiure than does the House of Commons to debate public issues—one of its more important functions.

The judiciary is independent of the legislative and executive branches of government, but it cannot review the constitutionality of legislation.

The separate identity of each of the Kingdom's constituent parts is taken into account. Welsh affairs, for example, are adminstered at the national level by a Cabinet Minister (the Secretary of State for Wales), with the advice of a broadly representative Council for Wales. At the local level, the Welsh-speaking minority in Wales are permitted their own schools. Scotland continues, as before the union, to enjoy a different system of law (Roman-Dutch), education, local government, judiciary, and national church (the disestablished Presbyterian Church of Scotland). In addition, most domestic matters are handled by separate government departments grouped under the Secretary of State for Scotland, who is also a Cabinet member. Until March 1972 Northern Ireland had its own Parliament and Prime Minister, although the British Government retained ultimate responsibility. As a result of civil strife over the past several years, however, the Northern Ireland Parliament was suspended for one year. The shape of the new institutions which will replace it has not yet been decided. Northern Ireland continues to be represented by 12 members in the U.K.'s House of Commons.

POLITICAL PARTIES

The Conservative Party is led by Prime Minister Edward Heath. It was returned to power in the general election of June 1970, winning 330 of the 630 seats in the House of Commons. The party was supported by most farmers, about two-thirds of the middle and white-collar classes, and almost one-third of the working class. The party derived its strength from the generally conservative nature of British society and from a successful effort to convince the electorate that it would move with the times.

In foreign policy, the Conservatives are strongly committed to the NATO alliance. They successfully pursued the British application to join the European Communities and Britain became a member on January 1, 1973. The United Kingdom has continued to play an important role in U.N. affairs consistent with its status as a permanent member of the Security Council, its Commonwealth ties, and global interests.

In domestic policy, the Conservatives in their two years as Government have embarked on a program attempting to achieve rapid economic growth, a reduction in unemployment and curbing the rate of inflation. This has been coupled with an effort to rationalize legislation in such areas as taxation, housing, immigration, and industrial relations.

The Labor Party won 288 of the 630 seats in the House of Commons in the election of 1970. It is led by Harold Wilson, who was Prime Minister from 1964 to 1970. Ideologically, the party is an amalgam of social democrats and radical socialists. Organizationally, it is heavily dependent on British trade unions, which provide the bulk of its financial support.

The Liberal Party occupies a place in the center of the political spectrum between the two major parties. In the June 1970 election it drew 7.5 percent of the votes cast but won only six seats. In 1972 it picked up two additional seats in by-elections, one at the expense of each major party.

Minor parties and independents hold six seats in the Commons. The Communist Party is numerically and political insignificant and holds no seats in Parliament.

ECONOMY *

The United Kingdom is one of the world's foremost industrial and trading nations. Because of its economic importance the United Kingdom has had a major impact on the development of the international trading and monetary systems as they are known today. The United Kingdom has few natural resources, and its soil is capable of yielding only about half of its total food requirements; hence, it is one of the world's leading importers of primary products and an important exporter of manufactured goods. The pound sterling is still an important trading currency.

Since World War II, the British economy has grown substantially, although at an uneven rate. The United Kingdom's gross national product (GNP) in 1971 was U.S. $115 billion, compared with $89.2 billion in 1962.

*There have been many changes in the U.K. exchange rate: from $2.40 to $2.60 in 1971 and through the first half of 1972 to as low as $2.32 since the floating of the pound (£) in June 1972. These changes make exact comparisons in terms of U.S. dollars difficult and imprecise. In this section, conversions have been made at the rate in effect at the time.

Despite this expansion and the accompanying rise in the British standard of living (per capita GNP is currently a little over $2,000, compared with $1,672 in 1962, an increase of 20 percent in real terms), the economy has not grown as rapidly as those of many other Western European countries. Per capita GNP is less than half that of the United States. At the present time, the United Kingdom ranks fifteenth in the world in per capita GNP. It was second in 1938, fifth in 1950, and seventh in 1960.

Agriculture and Industry

Although the United Kingdom is highly industrialized and dependent on foreign sources for almost half of its food supply, agriculture remains one of its largest and most important sectors of economic activity. Highly mechanized, British agriculture contributed 3.0 percent to the GNP while employing 2.9 percent of the total labor force. The Government is seeking to increase farm size, which averages about 70 acres, by merging farms and easing small, uneconomic producers out of agriculture.

British industry is a mixture of public and privately owned firms. Several important British industries are under public ownership—steel, railroads, coal mining, certain utilities, and a large part of civil aviation. In 1971, the private sector accounted for 54 percent of capital investment (compared with 61 percent in 1961), 27 percent came from central and local government, and 19 percent was provided by public corporations. The share of manufacturing industry in total capital expenditure was 22 percent in 1971. Private British industry is characterized by a large number of comparatively small firms, but there is a growing trend toward larger industrial units.

The rate of economic expansion is uneven between areas within the United Kingdom, and the Government has taken important measures aimed at promoting more balanced economic development. Large parts of the United Kingdom have been designated as development areas; investment grants and a wide range of financial and other inducements are available to businesses deciding to locate or expand their operations in these areas.

The United Kingdom issued its first licenses for the exploration of oil and gas resources under the western half of the North Sea in 1964. Since then, discoveries of gas and oil have clearly established the North Sea as a major source of energy for Britain and the Continent. By the 1980's, North Sea oil and gas may be providing 50 percent of Britain's energy requirements. Of the remainder, depending on investment decisions made in the 1970's, 10 percent of Britain's requirements may be met by nuclear power, while the rest of her requirements may be about equally divided between imported oil and domestic resources of coal.

Government agencies primarily responsible for economic policy are the Treasury, the Department of Trade and Industry, the Department of Environment, and the Department of Employment and Productivity. The National Economic Development Organization and a number of subsidiary economic development committees in the major industrial sectors serve as a link between industry and Government in encouraging more efficient use of labor. The Confederation of British Industry (CBI) is the central body representing British industry. It serves as an important channel between Government and industry.

Labor

In mid-1971, the United Kingdom had about 25.5 million workers, some 46 percent of the total population. Approximately 43 percent (around 11 million) of the labor force belong to the country's 481 unions. More than 70 percent of all trade unionists are in the 19 largest unions while more than half are in the nine unions with a membership of over 250,000. Nearly 10 million workers are members of the 137 organizations affiliated with the Trades Union Congress (TUC), a federation of constituent unions which celebrated its centenary in 1968.

The general unemployment rate in Britain as a whole in the last 25 years has been among the lowest in the world, usually between 1 and 2 percent of the working population. In 1966, however, it rose markedly to about 2.2 percent, and in the next five years steadily increased. It has been in excess of 3.0 percent since January 1971. It has been consistently higher in those parts of the country which have the greatest dependence on shipbuilding, coal mining, and certain branches of the heavy engineering and metal manufacturing industries (notably parts of Scotland, Wales, northeast England and Merseyside).

The British labor scene since 1969 has been marked by a rapid increase in wages and prices and by deteriorating industrial relations. The Government sought to control this situation by passage of two highly controversial pieces of legislation. In August 1971 the Conservative Government's Industrial Relations Bill was enacted—the first industrial relations reform legislation in over 50 years. In particular the Act set up a National Industrial Relations Court (to deal with complaints from employers and employees and Government applications for "cooling off" periods and strike ballots), and a Register of Trade Unions and Employers Associations. The TUC has adopted a policy of non-cooperation with the Act, instructing affiliated unions not to register, which has resulted in a further deterioration of industrial relations in Britain. In 1971 the number of working days lost due to strikes was the highest since the General Strike year of 1926.

Upon assuming power in 1970 the Conservative Government rejected the idea of statutory wage and price controls, but was forced to abandon this policy by late 1972 following its failure to agree on a voluntary system of controls with the TUC and the employers. A counter-inflation bill was enacted in November 1972 freezing wages and prices for ninety days to be followed by "second stage" legislation to combat inflation.

Budget

The comparative Central Government budget figures for the 1971-72 and 1972-73 fiscal years are as follows:

	1971-72 (£ Billions)	1972-73 (£ Billions)
Revenues	16.9	16.8
Expenditures	15.5	16.6
Surplus	1.4	.2

The 1971 and 1972 budgets provided for far-reaching changes in the structure of personal taxation and in taxes on expenditure. The old system of income tax and surtax was replaced by a single graduated personal tax. As of April 1973, the selective employment tax (SET) and the purchase tax will be abolished and a value-added tax (VAT) will be instituted. Various tax cuts and depreciation allowances were introduced by the Government in July 1971 and 1972 to strengthen the economy by stimulating consumer demand and industrial investment.

Foreign Investment

The United Kingdom, perhaps more than any other European country, has welcomed foreign direct investment, particularly from companies which promise to contribute to the expansion of British exports, introduce new techniques, or increase employment in areas of high unemployment. In 1971 more than 1,600 U.S. companies had subsidiaries in the United Kingdom with a book value at year end of nearly $8 billion. The United Kingdom has received about 10 percent of total U.S. foreign direct investment and, next to Canada, is the largest single recipient of such investment.

Balance of Payments

Since 1945 the United Kingdom has been plagued with recurring balance-of-payments problems. The inability of the country to earn sufficient foreign exchange to cover its import needs and foreign economic and military expenditures forced several devaluations of the pound sterling. The first devaluation in 1949 cut the par value of the pound from $4.03 to $2.80. The second devaluation, in November 1967, further reduced the pound's value to $2.40. In December 1971 the U.K. agreed, in the context of the Smithsonian agreement, to revalue the pound to the level of $2.60. After several months, this rate came under heavy pressure and in June 1972 the U.K. Government decided to let the pound float. The rate subsequently fell back to $2.40 and in January 1973 stood at about $2.35. The U.K. Government hopes to fix a new parity as soon as possible in 1973. There are many factors which have contributed to U.K. post World War II balance-of-payments problems. Some of these factors have been:

(1) The decline in the U.K.'s share of exports of manufactures among the leading free world industrial countries (from 18.2 percent in 1958 to 10.8 percent in 1971);

(2) The loss of British overseas investment during World War II and British industry's efforts to expand its foreign investments; and

(3) The high cost of fulfilling overseas defense and aid commitments of a major world power (although these costs have been declining over recent years).

In 1969, the British balance of payments finally began to respond to the 1967 devaluation and a current account surplus of £443 million ($1.06 billion) was registered. This surplus rose to £952 million ($2.3 billion) in 1971. Invisible earnings have continued to grow and have been responsible for much of the current account surplus. In 1972 the current account was £ 50 million in deficit and is expected to be in deficit once again in 1973, due to large deficits on the visible trade account. Inflation in the United Kingdom and rising demand for imports are the main reasons for the turnaround in the current account. The further devaluation of the pound in the latter half of 1972 (about 10 per cent) should eventually help to bring this account back into a more favorable position, as U.K. exports will be cheaper and foreign imports more expensive.

Foreign Trade

The United Kingdom is one of the world's foremost trading nations, partly because it has few raw materials in relation of the size of its population and industry, and partly because of its important roles as international banker and investor. Throughout its history the United Kingdom has not, except for rare periods, realized a sufficiently high level of merchandise exports to cover the cost of essential imports. It has had to earn large amounts of foreign exchange through "invisible" exports (e.g. by providing shipping, banking, and insurance services to the rest of the world). Although relatively small in area and accounting for less than 2 percent of the world's population, the United Kingdom is the world's third largest trading nation, and shared over 7 percent of international trade in 1970.

There has been a distinct shift in the composition of the United Kingdom's exports and imports since World War II. In 1971 imports amounted to $25.6 billion consisting primarily of petroleum, machinery, chemicals, meat, and nonferrous metals. The U.S. share of these imports was 11.1 percent in 1971. While foodstuffs and raw materials are still important import items, the relative importance of manufactured goods has increased significantly in recent years. Exports, a total of $23.9 billion in 1971, consisted primarily of machinery and transportation equipment, chemicals, textiles, and precious and semi-precious stones. The U.S. share of these exports was 11.7 percent in 1971.

There has also been a marked change in the geographic distribution of British trade. In recent years there has been a pronounced growth of trade between the United Kingdom and Western Europe and North America, and a relative decline in trade between the United Kingdom and the Commonwealth countries. The United States is the United Kingdom's principal trading partner. The leading importers of British goods after the United States in 1971 were West Germany, Ireland, the Netherlands, Sweden, and Australia. The leading exporters to the United Kingdom after the United States in 1971 were Canada, West Germany, the Netherlands, Sweden, France, and Ireland. As a result of British membership in the European Communities, the importance of British trade with the other eight members is likely to increase.

Foreign Assistance

The United Kingdom's aid program to developing countries includes loans and grants, technical assistance, budgetary support, and contributions to international agencies which provide financial aid and technical assistance.

Although the British aid program is global in character, approximately 90 percent goes to Commonwealth countries. The total net financial flows from Britain to developing countries during 1971 was £ 652.5 million, representing 1.15 percent of GNP.

The bulk of Britain's bilateral aid went to Commonwealth countries who received £ 218.0 million. Of this amount, £93.3 million went to Commonwealth countries in Asia, £65 million to those in Africa, and £24.5 million to the Caribbean. India was the largest recipient with £62.1 million. Other leading recipients were Malawi (£10.1 million), Kenya (£9.8 million), Malta (£9.4 million), Pakistan (£8.3 million), Singapore (£7.7 million), and Nigeria (£7.1 million).

The British aid program is administered by the Overseas Development Administration (ODA), a self-contained wing of the Foreign and Commonwealth Office, headed by a Minister for Overseas Development.

International Economic Relations

International trade accounts for about 16 percent (almost four times that of the United States) of the U. K.'s gross national product. In addition, the United Kingdom must sustain adequate foreign exchange earnings on visible and invisible exports in order to pay for its imports and to help finance government and private investment abroad. Hence, successive British Governments have been firmly committed to a liberal trade policy and to increasing world liquidity. The United Kingdom plays an important role in the General Agreement on Tariffs and Trade (GATT) and other economic international organizations.

As of January 1, 1973, the United Kingdom became a member of the European Communities (EC) after having its application blocked in 1963 and 1967. Prior to EC membership, the United Kingdom had been a member of the European Free Trade Association (EFTA). Although the U.K. trade with its EFTA partners grew rapidly in recent years, trade with the original six EC members (France, Germany, Italy, Belgium, The Netherlands, and Luxembourg) is now larger and growing faster. The United Kingdom in 1971 sent 21 percent of its exports to the Common Market as compared to 14 percent in 1958.

FOREIGN RELATIONS

The United Kingdom remains a major world power even though it has given up its Empire. It has reduced its military commitments in the Middle East and southern Asia but retains substantial economic and political interests in all quarters of the world. It is a charter member of the United Nations (with a permanent seat on the Security Council), and belongs to most of its specialized agencies. The United Kingdom has played a major role in such collective security arrangements as the North Atlantic Treaty Organization (NATO), the Southeast Asian Treaty Organization (SEATO), and the Central Treaty Organization (CENTO).

The United Kingdom recognized the new Government of the People's Republic of China (P.R.C.) in 1949, and has maintained diplomatic relations with Peking since that time. Relations, which at times have been strained, improved markedly in 1972 when Ambassadors were first exchanged. The United Kingdom supported the P.R.C.'s entry into the United Nations and seeks gradually to improve bilateral relations and to encourage responsible P.R.C. participation in international affairs.

The U.K.'s entry into the European Communities is a move with major consequences for Europe and U.S.-European relations. It will inevitably bring in its wake greater British involvement in Europe and a reordering of British foreign policy priorities in favor of the European connection.

The Commonwealth of Nations*

Almost all of the former British colonies have become independent members of the Commonwealth, a tribute to its latter-day enlightenment as a colonizer. While increasingly weakened by economic and political nationalism and most recently by Southern Rhodesia's unilateral declaration of independence (see Background Note on Southern Rhodesia, pub. 8104), the Commonwealth offers the United Kingdom an important entree and a voice in many less-developed countries. Moreover, it helps to preserve in those countries

---

*Members are: United Kingdom, Australia, Bangladesh, Barbados, Botswana, Canada, Ceylon, Cyprus, Fiji, The Gambia, Ghana, Guyana, India, Jamaica, Kenya, Lesotho, Malawi, Malaysia, Malta, Mauritius, New Zealand, Nigeria, Pakistan, Sierra Leone, Singapore, Swaziland, Tanzania, Tonga, Trinidad and Tobago, Uganda, Western Samoa, and Zambia. Nauru and the Associated States of the eastern Caribbean are associated with the Commonwealth but are not full members in every respect.

many British institutions, such as parliamentary democracy. The United Kingdom maintains a military presence in Southeast Asia as part of a joint Commonwealth force.

United States

The United Kingdom places primary emphasis in its foreign policy on the maintenance of a close relationship with the United States. U.S.-U.K. cooperation reflects the common language, ideals, and democratic practices of the two countries, as well as the historical circumstances which have given the United Kingdom and the United States similar interests and objectives. The relationship was strengthened by the United Kingdom's alliance with the United States during both World Wars and the Korean conflict. After World War II it took on renewed meaning in opposition to the threat of forceful Soviet expansion.

The United Kingdom and the United States continually consult on foreign policy issues and problems ranging all over the globe. It supports the major foreign and security policy objectives of the United States and remains one of the United States' most valued allies.

The United Kingdom has cooperated with the United States in attempts to accelerate the growth of less developed countries through national and international channels.

Defense and Disarmament

The United Kingdom is determined to deter any military threat from the Soviet Union but at the same time desires to work for relaxation of tensions between East and West. Within the limitations of its economic resources, it has, therefore, given strong and active support to NATO as a means of defense and an instrument of détente. The United Kingdom has been especially anxious to achieve progress on arms control and disarmament and consequently has taken a leading role in the Conference of the Committee on Disarmament (formerly the Eighteen Nation Disarmament Conference) at Geneva. It has adhered to the Nuclear Nonproliferation and Limited Test Ban Treaties.

It has strongly supported the United States in negotiating strategic arms limitations with the Soviets, but remains a cautious advocate of Mutual and Balanced Force Reductions in Europe.

PRINCIPAL GOVERNMENT OFFICIALS

Queen Elizabeth II
Prime Minister—Edward Heath
Secretary of State for Foreign and Commonwealth Affairs—Sir Alec Douglas-Home
Chancellor of the Exchequer—Anthony Barber
Secretary of State for Defense—Lord Carrington
Ambassador to the U.S.—The Earl of Cromer
Ambassador to the U.N.—Sir Colin Crowe

The United Kingdom maintains an Embassy in the United States at 3100 Massachusetts Avenue, N.W., Washington, D.C. 20008. There are also Consulates General at Atlanta, Chicago, Los Angeles, St. Louis, New York, San Francisco, and Philadelphia and Consulates at Miami, Honolulu, Boston, and Minneapolis.

PRINCIPAL U.S. OFFICIALS

Ambassador—Walter H. Annenberg
Deputy Chief of Mission—Earl D. Sohm
Minister for Economic Affairs—Robert A. Brand
Counselor for Political Affairs—William J. Galloway
Counselor for Consular Affairs—Jack Herfurt
Counselor for Administration—William D. Calderhead
Counselor for Public Affairs—William Weld

The U.S. Embassy in the United Kingdom is located at 24/31 Grosvenor Square, W. 1, London. There are also Consulates General at Belfast, Northern Ireland; Edinburgh, Scotland; and Liverpool, England.

Reading List

Brittan, Samuel. Steering the Economy—The Role of the Treasury. London: Secker and Warburg, 1969.

Calleo, David P. Britain's Future. New York: Horizon Press, 1969.

Caves, Richard E., and others. Britain's Economic Prospects. Washington, D.C.: Brookings Institution, 1968.

Department of State. Commonwealth of Nations. Pub. 8398. Washington, D.C.: U.S. Government Printing Office, 1968.

Department of State. "NATO and the Defense of Europe." No. 2 in the Issues in United States Foreign Policy series. Pub. 8476. Washington, D.C.: U.S. Government Printing Office, 1969.

Hugo, Grant. Britain in Tomorrow's World. London: Chatto & Windus, 1969.

McKenzie, R. T. British Political Parties. New York: Praeger, 1964.

Pfaltzgraff, Robert L., Jr. Britain Faces Europe. Philadelphia: University of Pennsylvania Press, 1969.

Sampson, Anthony. The New Anatomy of Britain. New York: Stein and Day, 1972.

DEPARTMENT OF STATE PUBLICATION 8099, Revised January 1973

Belligerent Disarmament

Butler, David. Electoral Change in Britain. New York: Harcourt Press, 1969.

APPENDIX JJJ

UNITED KINGDOM

STRENGTH OF THE COMMUNIST PARTY ORGANIZATION—1973

[FROM: World Strength of the Communist Party Organizations—1973. Washington, Department of State, Bureau of Intelligence and Research, 1973.]

UNITED KINGDOM

National Political Status: Date of last election - June 18, 1970. (As a result of by-elections, membership in the House of Commons on December 31, 1973, was: Conservative, 323; Labor, 287; Liberals, 11; others, 8. There was one vacancy.)

Communist: Communist Party of Great Britain (CPGB) - 37,996 votes (0.1%), no seats

Non-Communist Left: Labor Party - 12,141,676 votes (43.0%), 288 seats (45.7%)

Center: Liberal Party - 2,109,218 votes (7.4%), 6 seats (1.0%)

Conservative: Conservative Party - 13,106,965 votes (46.4%), 330 seats (52.4%)

Other: 862,477 votes (3.1%), 6 seats (1.0%)

Total: 28,258,332 votes, 630 seats

Communist Party Membership: In June 1973 the CPGB claimed a membership of 29,943, alleging that this was an increase of 1,140 over a 2-year period. In November 1973 an official speaking at the party congress stated that the Young Communist League had 2,890 members, a decrease of 300 over the same 2-year period.

Leading Party Figures and Positions:
SWAN, Irene - Chairman
GOLLAN, John - General Secretary
FALBER, Reuben - Asst. General Secretary
RAMELSON, Bert - Industrial Organizer
McLENNAN, Gordon - National Organizer
McGAHEY, Mick - Vice President of National Union of Mineworkers

(All of the above except Irene Swan are members of the 13-man Political Committee of the party, and all except McGahey are fulltime party functionaries.)

Principal Publication: *Morning Star* "incorporating the *Daily Worker*." Press run of 45,000, but actual circulation, which is below 45,000, is said to have increased by 2 percent in 1973.

Areas of Communist Activity: The British Communist Party emerged in 1973 as the most important of the smaller Communist parties in Western Europe, if not in the non-Communist world. Minuscule membership gains, barely offsetting deaths and lapsed memberships, and the party's continued failure to participate significantly in parliamentary by-election campaigns, were more than compensated for by the deepening of the left-right schism in the British trade union movement and the Labor Party; the success of overtly Communist and other "militant" candidates for trade union office; and finally, in late 1973, the crucial role which these developments had in exacerbating the coal miners' and locomotive drivers' strikes during Britain's energy crisis.

At its 33d national congress, in November 1973, the CPGB welcomed this leftward drift, which had accelerated since the previous autumn at the annual conferences (September and October) of the Trades Union Congress and the Labor Party. In the unions the most significant expression of this trend was a hardening of trade union opposition to cooperation in the wage restraint policies of the Conservative government's anti-inflation program, thereby increasing the likelihood of major strike actions.

Politically, the trade unions furnished the overwhelming majority of the votes cast at the Labor Party conference for an open-ended program of nationalization should a Labor government be elected and an all but unqualified demand for British withdrawal from the European Community. While both trade union leaders and Labor Party parliamentarians who opposed the left drift had no choice but to accept nominally the "left's" conference victories, they continued to hold majorities on the General Council of the TUC and the "Shadow Cabinet" of the Labor Party.

Consequently, the Communists, while hailing the fruits of "left unity," proclaimed a continuing battle against the "moderates," at their November congress. To this end the CPGB had already selected 32 candidates to stand for parliament in the general election which must be held by mid-1975, and which at the end of 1973 seemed likely to take place in the first half of 1974. The party was anxious to win a few parliamentary seats in its own right. But its woeful performance in the four by-elections of November 1973, when it fielded one candidate who obtained only 128 votes, suggested that the party would be fortunate if it won a seat. Despite the Communists yearning for a recognized place in political life, their principal activity during 1974 will continue to take place in the industrial relations arena.

In that area the CPGB can benefit from the widespread conviction in the working class that the Conservative government has failed to control prices and profits while looking upon wage limitations to blunt the edge of inflation at the workers' expense. Much resentment exists in trade union ranks against the government's 1971 Industrial Relations Act, which even moderate trade union leaders denounced roundly as fines were levied against the treasuries of unions which breached or endeavored to ignore the Act. To exploit this mood the Communists, through their organizational and propaganda mechanisms, have coupled the work-place activity of their rank-and-file shop stewards with the official union wage drives that were in several major instances promoted by Communist fulltime trade union officials.

During 1973 Communists won election to such important posts as national vice president of the National Union of Mineworkers (NUM), an additional seat on the closely divided executive of the locomotive drivers' union, and a number of contests in midlands districts of the Amalgamated Union of Engineering Workers (AUEW). Of equal significance were the victories scored by Communist-supported "left Labor" men in the NUM, the AUEW, and a number of other unions at both national and district levels. Few such candidates were defeated in 1973 union elections, a record somewhat better than that of Communist candidates. One such victory delivered the crucial vote of the Yorkshire miners to the "left coalition" in the NUM.

A few of the "left Labor" candidates were ex-Communists who had broken with the party more on local than national issues. Most of these individuals espouse a left Socialist, fundamentalist outlook. In nearly every case the party played an important part in organizing their campaigns. It also has continued to publicize the activity and stands of such powerful non-Communist national trade union leaders as Jack Jones of the Transport and General Workers Union and Hugh Scanlon of the AUEW.

At the same time, the CPGB has continued to sponsor the Liaison Committee for the Defense of Trade Unions, whose national secretary is a party member. This Committee, and shop steward movements of various unions which are loosely affiliated to it, was active in generating the AEUW wage claim in the last quarter of 1973 which culminated in an official AEUW decision to launch an overtime ban and other work restrictions on the morrow of the end of a government-decreed 3-day working week. The action subsequently received the endorsement of the Transport and General Workers' Union. This development confronted the government with the prospect of seeing the nation's most important manufacturing industry crippled before Britain could recover from the devastating effects of the energy-related strikes which began in late 1973.

These activities demonstrate how the Communists and the "left" generally have evolved some new industrial strategies in the period since the 1970 electoral defeat of the Wilson Labor government. For one, the party has shown a new willingness to assist non-Communist leftists to gain important trade union posts, without requiring them to adhere rigidly to the party's political line. Two, the current strategy has developed the technique of overtime bans and "working-to-rule" to cut back work while processing a wage claim, without resort to formal strike ballots and the payment of strike benefits.

In several industrial constituencies, the party, through its trade union officials, has in fact restrained rank-and-file groups and "militant" trade union officers from slipping into formal strike action. Thus the party is able to continue to appeal to "militants" without incurring the stigma of irresponsibility. There is ample indication of rank-and-file support for these strategems which is not always forthcoming for official strike action because of the cost of such action to unions and members as well as to industry.

While a majority of the CPGB's 42-member Executive Committee are trade unionists (for the most part conveners of shop stewards, not fulltime trade union officials), 8 of the 13-member Political Committee which runs the party are fulltime party functionaries. Women (such as Party Chairman Irene Swan) and representatives of ethnic minorities are on the Executive Committee but not on the Political Committee. A few veteran shop floor leaders, however, are on the important Political Committee. A case in point is the newest recruit to top party leadership--Mick McGahey, Vice President of the NUM, President of its Scottish Area, and President of the Scottish Committee of the CPGB. At the party's 1973 conference McGahey, in fact, outpolled the Gollan-Falber-Ramelson-McLennan leadership clique by 25 or more votes in the balloting for the Executive Committee.

In late 1973 McGahey was participating with the NUM's "moderate" president and its "militant" general secretary in all critical miners' negotiations with government bodies, an unprecedented role for an NUM vice president. It is also unprecedented for miners' national officers to hold party political posts as prominent as McGahey's, though two party members, Arthur Horner and Will Paynter, have in the past been general secretaries of the NUM. Their image was of militants who were "trade unionists first, Communists second," but McGahey seemed to be cast for a dual industrial-political leadership role. In official statements at the end of 1973, he and the party described their position as being one of seeking to destroy the government's industrial relations and economic policies by industrial action, thereby forcing the government to resign and call a general election.

The other important area of party activity is the youth and student field. Party recruitment among young people has been singularly unsuccessful, with the Young Communist League actually losing members, and only a third of those members paying dues, according to one party conference delegate. Nonetheless, the party seemed to have curbed the far left (Trotskyite, Maoist, and Anarchist) drive which several years ago threatened to displace both democratic and Communist leadership groups in the important National Union of Students (NUS). In some cases the party organized joint electoral slates with Labor Party-oriented students, "moderates" as well as "militants," against the "far left" revolutionary groups after initially politicizing the NUS in collaboration with the "far left."

At the end of 1973 there was an uneasy balance between Communist, revolutionary, and democratic groups in the NUS, with the Communists successfully pursuing their policy of identifying the NUS with trade union struggles. On the other hand, fearing a rebuff, the party followers in the NUS have supported but not pushed a move to affiliate the NUS with the Moscow-controlled International Union of Students.

Continued credibility in the student organizing field, where ideological competition, primarily from an amalgam of revolutionary but libertarian groups and individuals, is keener than in trade union work, requires the CPGB to appear to keep its distance from the least attractive features of Soviet Russian communism. At the 1973 congress, a motion calling on the party to "move back into the main stream of the world Communist movement" (i.e., to accept uncritically all nuances of Russian policy) was roundly defeated after having been characterized as "totally irrelevant" to the situation facing the movement by *Morning Star* editor George Mathews on behalf of the Executive Committee.

Early in 1973, a fraternal delegation to the Soviet Union issued a joint communique with the CPSU which was highly laudatory of Soviet and East European Communist accomplishments, but avoided all of the issues which might compromise either party. At the November congress the executive managed to discourage attempts to discuss relations with other Communist parties, but in September the party, through Tony Chater, head of its press and publicity department, denounced "the statements made by the scientist Dr. Sakharov and the novelist Solzhenitsyn to launch a new campaign of anti-Soviet hostility," albeit adding that it is "also essential for socialist states not to use administrative measures to suppress dissent and inhibit the development of socialist democracy." The CPGB also has refrained from disciplining one of its members, the British-born mother of an imprisoned dissident Czech Communist, who has organized a campaign on behalf of Czech political prisoners.

In assuming a more critical stance toward the Soviet Union, the current CPGB leadership is influenced by the losses it incurred almost 20 years ago, when the party suffered heavily among intellectuals in the trade unions because of its slavish endorsement of the Soviet suppression of the Hungarian revolution. Subsequent developments in the world Communist movement, particularly the Sino-Soviet dispute, only have strengthened the CPGB's resolve to pay greater heed to its domestic image. As a result, the CPGB dissociated itself sharply from the Soviet invasion of Czechoslovakia and has refrained from going all the way with Soviet denunciations of the Chinese leadership, partly because the party recognizes that among young British leftists China has greater appeal today than does the ideologically stagnant Soviet Union.

As the last party congress shows, the CPGB, in essence, has come to adopt a domestic and foreign policy line which, similar to that of the Italian and Spanish Communist parties, seeks to give greater weight to its own needs than to maintaining its previous virtual subordination to Moscow's wishes.

APPENDIX KKK
UNITED STATES
ARMED FORCES AND MILITARY POWER

[Reprinted with permission from: The Almanac of World Military Power, by Col. T. N. Dupuy, U.S. Army, Ret., Col. John A. C. Andrews, U.S. Air Force, Ret., and Grace P. Hayes. 3rd ed. Dunn Loring, Va., T. N. Dupuy Associates, 1974.]

UNITED STATES

POWER POTENTIAL STATISTICS

Area: 3,615,210 square miles (50 states, including interior waterways and bodies of water)
Population: 211,600,000
Total Active Armed Forces: 2,201,539 (1.32% population)
Gross National Product: $1,304.5 billion ($6,165 per capita)
Annual Military Expenditure: $87.1 billion (6.68% GNP)
Iron and Steel Production: 84.3 million metric tons
Fuel Production: Coal: 495.1 metric tons
Crude Oil: 465.8 million metric tons
Refined Products: 557.2 million metric tons
Natural Gas: 636.9 billion cubic meters
Electric Power Output: 1,718 billion kwh
Merchant Fleet: 3,327 ships; 16.27 million gross tons
Civil Air Fleet: 2,192 jet, 431 turboprop, and 955 piston transports operated by scheduled carriers. Over 2,000 other companies perform such services as charters and non-scheduled passenger and cargo flights, operating fleets of all types of aircraft.

DEFENSE STRUCTURE

Under the US Constitution, responsibility and authority for national defense are divided between the Executive and Legislative branches of government. The President is Commander in Chief of the Armed Forces in peace and war; he is responsible for the formulation and execution of defense policy and for the administration of the defense establishment. His administrative defense responsibilities are carried out by the Department of Defense, whose top officials he appoints; these officials also assist him in policy making. The Congress has broad military powers that are largely limited to the making or withholding of appropriations. Since World War II, there has been a considerable and continuing increase in the practical powers of the Executive Branch over military policy and posture, with a corresponding decrease in Congressional power. Two factors have, in recent years, intensified the struggle over defense power between the President and Congress, with Congress attempting to regain its virtually abandoned prerogatives: (1) the long and frustrating Vietnam War, initiated and conducted by successive presidents and their Defense Department officials; (2) the fears of a strong and irresponsible Presidency engendered by the Watergate affair, and the opportunity it offered Congressmen to place pressure on the President. In June 1973 Congress forced a compromise with the President providing that bombing in Cambodia could continue until August 15, provided that it stopped permanently on that date. Later in 1973 a War Powers Act, passed over the President's veto, required that any future emergency war action taken by a President would have to cease after 30 days if it had not been approved by Congress.

Under the 1947 National Security Act, as amended, the Department of Defense (DOD) is a unified instrument for policy and action under the direction of the Secretary of Defense. The three autonomous military departments (Army, Navy, and Air Force, with the Marine Corps within the Navy Department), and their civilian secretaries, are subject to centralized authority of the Secretary of Defense. For instance, supply purchases for all services are made by one Defense Supply Agency; military intelligence reports and interpretation are handled in Washington by one Defense Intelligence Agency; The Readiness Command is a mission-centered headquarters to be made up of both Army and Air Force elements. Weapons development for all services is under the DOD Director of Research and Engineering.

POLITICO-MILITARY POLICY

At the conclusion of World War II, collective security and preparedness had replaced isolation and disarmament as the US national security principles for preventing war. Collaboration with allies during World War II developed into full and sponsoring participation in the United Nations and a number of regional mutual-assistance agreements. Lend-Lease Aid to allies, begun in 1940, developed after the war into both military and economic aid to friendly and neutral countries.

Nuclear explosives and the great military power of the hostile Soviet Union have been the determining factors in US military policy since World War II. The relative decline of British and French economic and military power left the United States in the position of world leader against continued Communist-Soviet encroachment in Europe and elsewhere. In recent years the rising power of the People's Republic of China, and its development of nuclear weapons, have been an additional significant factor.

US policy on control and disarmament of nuclear weapons has been that such measures must be predicated on reliable inspection procedures; Soviet policy has been that all weapons should simply be destroyed, and that inspection would be an intolerable security threat to the Soviet Union. The little common ground between these positions yielded in 1963 the Treaty for a Partial Nuclear Test Ban and the Hot Line agreement providing a direct communications link between leaders of the two super-powers. The Nuclear Nonproliferation Treaty was ratified by the Senate in early 1969. Recent technological advances, including observation by man-made earth satellites, have eased the inspection controversy by making possible reasonable assurance that arms control agreements are being complied with, without necessity for on-site inspection. These advances, together with practical, and reasonably permanent, nuclear-weapon parity between the United States and the Soviet Union, seem to have opened the possibility of more fundamental strategic arms agreements. A new destabilizing force has appeared, however–MIRVs (multiple independently targeted warheads delivered by a single launcher).

"Massive retaliation," or instant response against aggression "by means and at places of our own choosing," was the strategic doctrine of the years from 1953 to about 1957. By the time Soviet testing of intercontinental ballistic missiles (ICBM) with thermonuclear warheads foreshadowed the end of the massive retaliation policy in 1957, the policy was already under thorough reevaluation.

Under the Kennedy administration, the policy of "flexible response," or "graduated response," became official US doctrine. All use of force was to be carefully controlled, with responses to aggression carefully selected to turn back the aggression at hand but not to trigger a nuclear reaction from the adversary power. Development of conventional forces, including special forces for counterinsurgency, was pushed. The country was to have the capability to fight limited war, so that it would not have to choose between survival and holocaust.

The Vietnam War demonstrated forcefully, however, that mere possession of a diversified array of weapons systems does not make it easy, or even necessarily feasible, to fight a limited war in the late 20th Century.

Production of long-range nuclear-warhead missiles, emphasized in the late Eisenhower administration to close the hypothetical missile gap with the Soviet Union, gave the United States a preponderance of nuclear offensive power. In the early 1960s efforts were concentrated on protecting (hardening) and dispersing the missile launching sites, thus resulting in relative invulnerability of missiles to enemy attack, without making them more provocative. The same purpose was served by the development of nuclear-powered submarines, with the ability to cruise under water at great speed, for long periods, and armed with long-range Polaris nuclear-warhead missiles.

During the early 1960s mutual nuclear deterrence of the United States and USSR became fairly stable, with each nation having enough striking power to survive a first nuclear strike by the other and still inflict unacceptable damage on its adversary. US policy then was that this condition was better than the instability, uncertainty, and consequent danger of nuclear war that might result from deployment of new weapons systems. More recently, technological improvements in ABMs (antiballistic missiles), some ABM deployment by the Soviet Union, and an approaching long-range nuclear capability of Communist China have brought reassessment. In September 1967 a limited ABM shield, stated to meet the kind of nuclear threat China could pose during the next 10 years, was proposed, but was never put into effect. In 1969 the Nixon administration proposed, and the Senate narrowly approved, the Safeguard ABM system, which was designed to protect a minimum nuclear deterrent force rather than attempting to protect any cities. Meanwhile, both the Johnson and Nixon administrations pushed for negotiations with the Soviet Union aimed at limiting the strategic arms race. The Strategic Arms Limitation Talks (SALT) began in 1969, and in May 1972 yielded two major agreements: (1) a treaty of unlimited duration limiting the installation of antiballistic missile sites in each country to two–one protecting the nation's capital and the other protecting a single ICBM site; (2) an interim executive agreement providing for a five-year moratorium on the deployment of strategic offensive rocket launchers. Its purpose was to freeze ICBM and SLBM (submarine-launched ballistic missile) deployment during the time necessary to work out a comprehensive agreement limiting strategic arms; its obvious weakness–perhaps unavoidable, for verification reasons–was the failure to limit the number of warheads per launcher, leaving the way open for deployment of MIRVs, the new destabilizing factor now threatening mutual deterrence.

A new development in 1974 was Secretary of Defense James R. Schlesinger's advocacy of a new, more flexible US targeting strategy for strategic missiles that would make it possible for the United States to strike at Soviet missile forces (that is, deliver counterforce strikes) as well as at Soviet cities. Critics of Schlesinger's approach consider it an attempt at building a US first-strike capability and thus a gravely destabilizing move. Schlesinger has asserted, however, that the Soviet Union's ccurrent missile projects have the "potential net throw weight for a major counterforce capability" and that the United States must not fall behind. The Schlesinger program passed a crucial test in summer 1974 when the Senate failed to delay funds for new projects to (1) increase the accuracy of the land-based intercontinental Minuteman missile, (2) double its nuclear yield, and (3) develop a terminally-guided warhead that would have almost perfect accuracy.

Evidence that the USSR has accelerated its efforts to strengthen its forces on land, in the air, and on the sea has caused further revision in US policy, to provide a more realistic deterrence. Involved are policies calling for improving strategic nuclear weapons, including submarine-launched missiles; the strengthening and modernization of the Navy; and increased research and development looking to the improvement of weapon systems for all services and the development of new ones. The observance of existing treaties is to be maintained, as is military assistance, but planning with our allies has the end of assuring that friendly countries increase their self defense efforts.

New factors in US politico-military policy include the detente with the Soviet Union and the end of hostile relations and establishment of diplomatic contact with the People's Republic of China, both accomplished in 1972. The end of US participation in the war in Indochina, in 1973, also removed a source of friction among the major powers.

Within the United States, despite the easing of anti-defense-establishment feelings brought by withdrawal from Vietnam, 1973 public opinion polls showed declining public support for defense spending. In 1973 it appeared that $5-6 billion would be cut from the President's FY 1975 defense budget of $79 billion, a figure he had stressed must not be cut at all. Congressional conservatives, usually strongly for defense, joined with liberals critical of the Pentagon to threaten the cuts. This attitude was a product of concern about inflation, anger at revelations that Defense officials had lied to Congress in official reports on bombing in Cambodia, and lessening of the President's political leverage as a result of the Watergate scandal, as well as of the drop in public support for defense spending. The October War in the Middle East, however, reversed the previous Congressional thinking, and the eventual cut was less than $3 billion.

Manpower for US armed forces is now obtained through voluntary service, with conscription legislation remaining in force should there not be enough volunteers to reach force level requirements. To implement the all-volunteer policy, determined efforts are being made to make military service attractive to young people.

STRATEGIC PROBLEMS

In the era of long-range nuclear bombing and nuclear-armed ICBMs, the nation's major strategic problem is security from possible attack by a hostile nuclear power. At present, only the USSR is a potential attacker, although China may soon achieve a limited ICBM capability. In addition to, and essential to, the policy of deterrence discussed above, is a realistic defense capability.

Air and aerospace defense of North America is the responsibility of the joint US-Canadian North American Air Defense Command (NORAD). The US component, more than 70 percent of NORAD's resources, is the US Air Force's Aerospace Defense Command (ADC). NORAD operational headquarters is under Cheyenne Mountain, near Colorado Springs, Colorado. When NORAD was established in 1958, the greatest danger was still from nuclear-armed bombers, and the NORAD force was composed largely of interceptor aircraft, plus some Bomarc and Nike missiles. A Distant Early Warning (DEW) line was established, stretching from the Aleutians to Greenland, with a radar, computer, and communications network that would immediately mobilize air defense to meet any threat from the north. It is recognized that the chief current threat is from missiles, and although the DEW line is maintained, NORAD's anti-bomber fighter and radar strengths are being reduced. A Ballistic Missile Early Warning System (BMEWS) was established in 1960, with stations in Alaska, the United Kingdom, and Greenland. NORAD's fighter-interceptor force of 530 aircraft (27 US and 3 Canadian squadrons) is to be cut to 336 aircraft by July 1975, and the 48 battery SAM force of US Army Nike-Hercules will be phased out. However, new missile warning systems and hardware are being integrated into NORAD, including Over-the-Horizon Forwardscatter early warning satellites and new phased array radar facing the southern approaches. Combined with BMEWS, DEW line and the network of SLBM warning radars there is a global air and space surveillance capability to prevent any kind of surprise attack on the United States.

The Panama Canal has had a crucial place in US strategy since its construction early in this century. With a two-ocean navy and the availability of massive air transport, the Canal has a less pivotal role in US national security. It is, however, still of great strategic and economic importance. A US garrison in the Canal Zone, the US base at Guantanamo, Cuba, and close surveillance of Caribbean regimes, are measures designed to protect the Canal and its approaches.

There is at present no serious threat to US national, state, or local government from internal subversion, although scattered outbreaks of civil disorder and isolated terroristic acts may be expected.

ALLIANCES

North Atlantic Treaty Organization (NATO). NATO members are pledged to consider an attack on one as an attack on all (see Western Europe, Regional Survey).

Organization of American States (OAS). The United States is signatory of the Inter-American Treaty of Reciprocal Assistance, approved for signature at Rio de Janeiro, September 2, 1947. Under the treaty the OAS Council can call a meeting of the Foreign Ministers of member nations to make decisions in crises (see Central America and West Indies Regional Survey).

The United States is a signatory of the Agreement for Mutual Defense Assistance in Indochina, signed at Saigon, December 23, 1950. Cambodia, France, Laos, the United States, and Vietnam are parties to the treaty.

ANZUS Pact. Security treaty signed at San Francisco, September 1, 1951. Australia, New Zealand, and the United

States are parties (see South and Southwest Pacific, Regional Survey).

Southeast Asia Collective Defense Treaty (SEATO). Signed at Manila, September 8, 1954. Australia, France, New Zealand, Pakistan, the Philippines, Thailand, and the United Kingdom are also parties (see South and Southeast Asia, Regional Survey).

The Pacific Charter. Signed at Manila, September 8, 1954. Australia, France, New Zealand, Pakistan, the Philippines, Thailand, and the United Kingdom are also parties.

The United States is not a member of the Central Treaty Organization of the Middle East (CENTO), formed in 1959 by Iran, Turkey, Pakistan, and the United Kingdom. The United States did, however, encourage the formation of CENTO, its representative sits as an observer at CENTO Council meetings, and the United States is a full member of CENTO committees. The US also has bilateral defense agreements with Turkey, Iran, and Pakistan, signed on March 5, 1959, in Ankara, pledging aid against aggression aimed at any of these countries.

The United States has bilateral alliances with the following nations: Japan, Republic of Korea (South Korea), Spain, and the Republic of China (Taiwan).

The United States has bilateral alliances or agreements, including military assistance agreements, with most of the other participants in the regional alliances listed above.

MILITARY ASSISTANCE

The table on p. 14 lists the nations which have received US military assistance since World War II under the Mutual Defense Act of 1949 and the Foreign Assistance Act of 1961.

ARMY

Personnel: 782,000

Organization:

- 2 commands in continental United States: Forces Command and Training and Doctrine Command (plus Materiel, Communications, etc.)
- 2 overseas armies: US Army Europe and US Army Pacific
- 3 armored divisions
- 2 airborne divisions
- 3 infantry divisions
- 4 mechanized infantry divisions
- 1 experimental division (air cavalry, airmobile, armored brigades)
- 3 independent infantry brigades
- 1 independent airborne brigade
- 1 independent armored cavalry brigade
- 30 SSM battalions
- 4 special forces groups
- 5 independent armored cavalry regiments
- independent artillery battalions (tube and missile)
- 200 independent aviation units
- independent SAM battalions

Deployment:

- Continental US: 1 airborne corps with 2 airborne divisions, 2 mechanized infantry divisions (less 1 brigade), 1 triple capacity division, 1 armored division, and 1 infantry division
- South Korea: 1 field army headquarters, 1 infantry division, and 1 missile command
- Hawaii: 1 infantry division
- Germany: 1 field army of 2 corps, 2 infantry divisions plus 1 brigade (mechanized), 2 armored divisions, 1 brigade (Berlin), 1 air defense command
- Italy: 1 task forces headquarters, 1 SSM (Sergeant) battalion

Major Equipment Inventory:

- M-60 medium tanks (M-60A1 with 105mm gun, M-60A1E2 with 152mm Shillelagh MGM-51A guided missile system)
- M-48 medium tanks (90mm gun)
- M-551 Sheridan assault vehicle (Shillelagh)
- M-41 light tanks (76mm gun)
- M-113 and M-114 armored personnel carriers
- MGM-31 Pershing SSM (about 250 in service)
- MGM-29A Sergeant SSM (about 500 in service)
- Lacrosse SSM
- MGR-1A/B Honest John SSM
- MGR-3A Little John SSM
- MGM-52A Lance SSM (replacing Honest John and Little John)
- MIM-23A Hawk SAM (2 battalions*)
- MIM-14A Nike-Hercules SAM (40 batteries* plus 36 National Guard batteries)
- Chaparral/Vulcan low-altitude air defense system
- Redeye man-portable SAM
- heavy artillery pieces (mostly M-107, M-109, and M-110 self-propelled guns and howitzers)

*Forming Army elements of the Air Defense Command.

VALUE OF MILITARY AID (Military Assistance Program) (Dollars in millions)*

Country	FY 1972	FY 1950-1972
East Asia		
Burma	0.3	80.7
Cambodia	129.2	310.2
China (Taiwan)	44.8	2,844.4
Indochina	-	716.9
Indonesia	8.5	98.4
Japan	-	913.4
Korea	174.2	3,421.9
Laos	-	347.6
Malaysia	0.1	1.3
Philippines	16.5	364.5
Thailand	-	610.6
Vietnam	-	1,544.4
Regional Costs	0.1	248.2
East Asia Total**	343.7	11,602.4
Near East and South Asia		
Afghanistan	0.2	4.4
Greece	43.9	1,717.1
India	0.2	101.3
Iran	6.3	853.7
Iraq	-	47.8
Jordan	23.4	96.2
Lebanon	0.4	10.2
Nepal	0.02	1.9
Pakistan	0.1	681.3
Saudi Arabia	0.4	36.7
Sri Lanka	0.6	1.5
Syria	-	0.1
Turkey	117.3	3,173.6
Regional Costs	0.02	19.3
NESA Total**	192.7	6,745.0
Europe		
Austria	0.01	100.2
Belgium	-	1,244.7
Denmark	-	624.9
Finland	0.01	0.1
France	-	4,249.7
Germany	-	901.0
Italy	-	2,361.8
Luxumbourg	-	8.3
Netherlands	-	1,231.7
Norway	-	908.2
Portugal	0.6	327.1
Spain	17.9	627.4
United Kingdom	-	1,058.8
Yugoslavia	-	703.0
Regional Costs	0.3	211.6
Europe Total**	18.9	14,558.4
Africa		
Cameroon	-	0.3
Dahomey	-	0.1
Ethiopia	11.7	171.7
Ghana	0.02	0.2
Guinea	-	0.9
Ivory Coast	-	0.1
Liberia	0.4	8.0
Libya	-	16.2
Mali	0.04	2.9
Morocco	1.4	42.7
Niger	-	0.1
Nigeria	0.1	1.5
Senegal	-	2.8
Sudan	-	0.7
Tunisia	2.4	33.5
Upper Volta	-	0.1
Zaire	0.4	27.4
Regional Costs	0.02	0.02
Africa Total**	16.5	309.8
Latin America		
Argentina	0.7	46.0
Bolivia	2.6	28.1
Brazil	0.9	248.2
Chile	2.2	102.6
Colombia	1.1	100.0
Costa Rica	-	1.9
Cuba	-	12.4
Dominican Republic	0.9	27.2
Ecuador	-	45.9
El Salvador	0.3	7.2
Guatemala	0.9	19.3
Haiti	-	3.3
Honduras	0.8	9.5
Jamaica	-	1.1
Mexico	0.1	2.0
Nicaragua	0.8	14.4
Panama	0.4	4.7
Paraguay	1.9	12.3
Peru	1.2	95.4
Uruguay	1.6	47.5
Venezuela	0.6	10.9
Regional Costs	0.2	15.8
Latin America Total**	17.1	855.6
Non-Regional Costs	-	100.8
General Costs	22.8	2,785.7
Grand Total**	641.7	36,957.8

*Department of Defense, Security Assistance Agency, *Military Assistance and Foreign Military Sales Facts*, May 1973.

**Rounding of items causes slight variations from these official regional totals.

medium artillery pieces
light artillery pieces
TOW antitank weapons
9,000 helicopters (including 1,100 UH-1)
3,900 fixed-wing aircraft

Reserves: The United States Army has two separate and independent reserve components. The Army National Guard has approximately 400,000 members, and the Army Reserve has about 260,000 members.

The Army National Guard is organized in eight combat divisions and 16 infantry, one airborne, one armored, one artillery, two engineer brigades, plus combat and combat service support units. The Army Reserve is organized in 19 Army Reserve Commands, 12 training divisions, and two maneuver area commands, 12 brigades (including 2 infantry and 1 mechanized infantry) plus combat and combat service support units. National Guard and Army Reserve units are to be ready for action five weeks after mobilization is ordered. Reserve units, in any number and combination, are mobilized by order of the President. Call up of individual reservists requires Presidential declaration of a national emergency or Congressional action. These provisions apply to all services.

NAVY

Personnel: 641,000 (not including Marine Corps)

Organization: The Chief of Naval Operations (CNO) commands the operating forces of the Navy. The Commandant of the Marine Corps (see below) is responsible to the Chief of Naval Operations for the readiness and performance of Marine Corps elements assigned to the operating forces of the Navy. Under the CNO are: The two major fleets (the Atlantic Fleet and the Pacific Fleet); the Naval Forces, Europe; the Military Sea Transportation Services; and, in time of war, the Coast Guard. There are four numbered fleets, Second, Third, Sixth, and Seventh. The two principal operational fleets are the Sixth Fleet in the Mediterranean, which is under the operational control of CINCNAVEUR, but which is administratively supported by CINCLANTFLT, and the Seventh Fleet, in the Western Pacific and South China Sea, under operational and administrative command of CINCPACFLT. MSTS provides sea transportation for military cargo and personnel of all services.

Major Units:

14 attack carriers (including the 76,000 ton nuclear-powered *Enterprise*; CVA/CVAN)
2 antisubmarine warfare (ASW) carriers (*Essex* class; CVS)
115 submarines (41 nuclear-powered ballistic missile submarines—10 with Poseidon missiles, 10 with Polaris undergoing conversion to Poseidon, and 21 with Polaris A-3, SSBN; 60 nuclear-powered attack submarines, SSN; 14 conventionally-powered attack submarines, SS, SSR, SSG)
6 guided missile cruisers (including 1 nuclear-powered; CG/CGN; CLG)
1 gun cruiser (CA)
28 guided missile frigates (including 4 nuclear-powered; DL, DLG/DLGN)
29 guided missile destroyers (DDG)
33 destroyers (DD, DDR)
63 escort ships (DEG, DER, DE, DH)
14 patrol craft (PG, PCER)
2 amphibious command ships (LCC)
14 transport dock ships (LPD)
65 amphibious assault ships (including 7 amphibious assault helicopter carriers)
20 tank landing ships (LST)
22 other amphibious ships
9 mine warfare ships (MSO, MSC, MM)
135 auxiliaries

There is a large Naval Reserve Training Command, with destroyers (DD), destroyer escorts (DE), ocean minesweepers (MSO), and coastal minesweepers (MSC), and a Training Fleet with submarines (AGSS), destroyers (DD), ocean minesweepers (MSO) and coastal minesweepers (MSC),

Naval Air Organization:

70 fighter/attack squadrons
10 reconnaissance squadrons
5 helicopter squadrons
24 patrol squadrons
16 ASW squadrons (fixed wing and helicopter)
33 other squadrons (training, etc.)

Naval Aircraft:

2,963 combat aircraft
38 F-14 Tomcat fighters

240 F-8 Crusader fighters
617 F-4 Phantom II fighter-bombers
521 A-7 Corsair II attack aircraft
401 A-4 Skyhawk attack aircraft
338 A-6 Intruder attack aircraft
226 other attack aircraft
582 shore- and carrier-based ASW, reconnaissance, ECM, and patrol aircraft (S-2, S-3, E-2, Tracker, P-3 Orion, SH-3 Sea King helicopters)
3,329 other aircraft
706 transport and support aircraft (C-130, KC-130)
1,179 other helicopters (AH-1, UH-1N)
1,444 trainer aircraft

Missiles:

656 SSM Polaris and Poseidon long-range ballis- missiles
ASROC anti-submarine
SUBROC submarine-launched anti-submarine
AAM Sparrow, Sidewinder
ASM Bullpup, Shrike, Standare ARM, Walleye
SAM Terrier, Tartar, Talos

Reserves: There are approximately 133,000 members of the Naval Reserve. In addition there are hundreds of reserve warships—mostly escort vessels, a few battleships and cruisers—in the so-called "mothball fleet." The major operational Naval Reserve units are naval aviation: 35 squadrons of fixed-wing aircraft and four squadrons of helicopters.

AIR FORCE

Personnel: 645,420

Organization:

Strategic Air Command (SAC: Commander in Chief, SAC, is responsible directly to the President, through the Secretary of Defense and the Joint Chiefs of Staff)
3 air forces (2 in United States, 1 in Guam), with 9 air divisions and 1 strategic areospace division, made up of:

23 bomb wings (B-52/KC-135)
2 bomb wings (FB-111/KC-135)
3 strategic missile wings (Titan II)
6 strategic missile wings (Minuteman)
1 strategic reconnaissance wing (SR-71)
1 strategic reconnaissance wing (RC/EC-135)
1 strategic reconnaissance wing (U-2, DC-130)
4 air refueling wings (KC-135)

Tactical Air Command (TAC: Commander TAC is also air commander of the joint US Readiness Command)
2 air forces, with 3 air divisions made up of:

13 tactical fighter wings (7 F-4, 3 F-111, 3 A-7)
2 tactical reconnaissance wings (RF-4, EB-66)
4 tactical airlift wings (C-130)
1 special operations wing (O-2, OV-10, UH-1, C-123, C-130, AC-130)
1 fighter weapons wing (F-4, F-111, F-105, A-7, T-38)

Aerospace Defense Command (ADC; the US element of North American Defense Command, NORAD, Joint US-Canadian defense command)

1 Aerospace Defense Force
6 air divisions
27 fighter-interceptor and squadrons, including 20 squadrons Air National Guards (6 F-101, 10 F-102, 4 F-106) and 7 squadrons Regular Air Force (F-106)

Pacific Air Forces (PACAF)
3 air forces (1 each in Thailand, Philippines, and Japan and Korea), with 4 air divisions, made up of:

6 tactical fighter wings (F-4, F-111, F-105, A-7)
1 tactical reconnaissance wing (RF-4)
1 special operations wing (CH-53, OV-10)
1 tactical airlift wing (C-130)

US Air Forces in Europe (USAFE)
3 air forces (1 each in England, Spain, and West Germany), with:

8 tactical fighter wings (7 F-4, 1 F-111)

2 tactical reconnaissance wings (RF-4)
2 tactical airlift wings (C-130)

US Air Forces, Southern Command (USAFSO)
Alaskan Air Command (AAC)
Military Airlift Command (MAC)
2 air forces, with 13 C-141, 4 C-5, and 3 VC-137 and VC-140 squadrons
Air Training Command
Air Force Systems Command
Air Force Logistics Command
(supporting services and special centers)

Major Equipment Inventory:
Missiles:
Surface-to-surface ICBMs (SAC)
54 Titan II (6 squadrons)
450 Minuteman II
550 Minuteman III (with MIRV warhead)
Surface-to-air
480 Nike-Hercules in NORAD (to be phased out)
Air-to-air
AIR-2 Genie rocket (ADC, Air National Guard)
AIM-4 Falcon (9 configurations, some nuclear, some conventional; TAC, ADC, PACAF, USAFE, Alaskan Air Command)
AIM-7 Sparrow III (TAC, PACAF, USAFE)
AIM-9 Sidewinder (TAC, ADC, PACAF, USAFE)
AIM-20 Quail (carried by SAC B-52s)
Air-to-surface
AGM-12 Bullpup (nuclear and conventional; TAC, PACAF, USAFE)
AGM-28 Hound Dog (SAC)
AGM-62 Walleye (TAC, PACAF)
AGM-45 Shrike (TAC, PACAF, USAFE)
AGM-65 Maverick (TAC, PACAF, USAFE)
AGM-69A SRAM (Short Range Attack Missile, on SAC B-52 and FB-111 aircraft)
AGM-78A Standard ARM (TAC, PACAF)

3,662 combat aircraft
350 B-52 long range heavy bombers
70 FB-111 long range bombers
75 F-105 fighter-bombers
1,500 F-4 fighter bombers
410 F-111 fighter-bombers
320 A-7 fighter-bombers
210 F-106 fighter-interceptors
375 electronic warfare/tactical reconnaissance aircraft (25 EB-66, 350 RF-4)
227 strategic/weather reconnaissance/electronic warfare aircraft (SR-71, EC/RC-135, EC-121, DC/WC-130, U-2, WB-57)
125 special operations aircraft (CH-53, UH-1, O-2, OV-10, C-123, C/AC-130)

4,518 other aircraft
657 KC-135 tankers
295 strategic and VIP airlift (72 C-5, 208 C-141, 4 VC-137, 11 VC-140)
272 C-130 tactical airlift transports
447 other transports (C-119, C-123, C-9)
56 HC-130 search and rescue aircraft
312 helicopters (UH-1, HH-3, HH-43, HH-1H, HH-53)
2,365 trainers (T-29, T-33, T-37, T-38, T-39, T-41, T-43)
114 utility/observation

Reserves: The Air National Guard has 92,000 paid personnel, organized in 92 squadrons, with 1,816 aircraft. They are committed as follows:

Tactical Air Command
27 fighter-bomber squadrons (18 F-100, 4 F-105, 1 F-104, 1 F-4, 3 A-7)
7 tactical reconnaissance squadrons (4 RF-101, 3 RF-4)
2 light ground attack squadrons (A-37)
9 tanker squadrons (KC-97)
3 special operations squadrons (C-119/U-10)
13 transport squadrons (C-123, C-130, C-7)
5 ground-air coordination squadrons (O-2)
1 early warning squadron (EC-121)

Aerospace Defense Command

20 interceptor squadrons (6 F-101, 10 F-102, 4 F-106)

2 electronic warfare squadrons (EB-57)

Military Airlift Command

3 airlift squadrons (C-124)

The Air Reserve has 56,000 paid and 101,000 unpaid personnel, organized in 37 squadrons with 427 aircraft. They are capable of immediate active service.

24 transport squadrons (2 C-7, 4 C-123, 18 C-130)

3 fighter-bomber squadrons (F-105)

4 light ground attack squadrons (A-37)

4 aerospace rescue squadrons (2 HC-130, 2 HH-1/3)

1 airborne early warning squadron (C-121)

1 special operations squadron (CH-3)

Personnel of an additional 18 squadrons fly with MAC in C-5, C-141, C-9 MAC squadrons.

MARINE CORPS

Personnel: 212,000

Organization:

3 Marine divisions (1st in California, 2d in North Carolina (elements in Mediterranean and Caribbean), 3d in Okinawa)

3 tank battalions (each associated with a division)

3 SAM battalions (24 missiles each; each associated with a division)

3 Marine Aircraft Wings (1st in Japan, 2d in North Carolina, 3d in California)

25 fighter-attack squadrons (F-4, A-4, A-6, AV-8)

3 composite reconnaissance squadrons (RF-4 and EA-6)

3 refueller/transport squadrons (KC-130)

3 observation squadrons (OV-10 and AH-1)

22 helicopter squadrons (CH-46, CH-53, UH-1)

Major Equipment Inventory:

M-103 heavy tanks
M-48 medium tanks
LVTP-5 amphibious APCs
M-113 APCs
Hawk SAMs
light artillery pieces
medium artillery pieces
heavy artillery pieces
550 combat aircraft
320 helicopters
100 other aircraft

Reserves: There are approximately 50,000 Marine Corps reservists, mostly in the 4th Marine Division and 4th Marine Aircraft Wing.

COAST GUARD

Personnel: 36,092

Organization: Under Department of Transportation. In time of war or by Presidential declaration, the Coast Guard is under the Navy Department.

Major Units:

44 high endurance cutters (WHEC)
19 medium endurance cutters (WMEC)
85 patrol craft (WPB)
4 training ships
8 icebreakers (WAGB)
98 buoy tenders
6 lightships
4 ferries
2 supply ships
18 tugs
2,054 non-commissioned boats
168 non-combat aircraft
110 helicopters
52 other aircraft

PARAMILITARY

There is no national police force or constabulary, nor is there any central law enforcement authority; this power is divided among the Federal, State, and local governments.

The Civil Air Patrol is an official auxiliary of the US Air Force. It numbers 85,000 volunteers, of which 25,000 are teen-age cadets, and operates 3,500 privately owned and 800 CAP-owned aircraft in more than 2,300 individual units, in eight regions. There is a wing in each state, the District of Columbia, and the Commonwealth of Puerto Rico. Missions include search and rescue, civil defense augmentation, disaster relief, and communications in support of emergency and civil defense activities and internal operations. More than 155,000 sorties have been flown, assisting over 16,000 people threatened by disaster and saving more than 1,250 lives.

The Office of Civil Defense under the Secretary of the Army directs the nation's civilian response to a nuclear attack. There are 10,000 civilian employees and about 20,000 part-time volunteers. The national organization is decentralized under State and local government. The program includes development of a nationwide fallout shelter system through dual-pupose use of available buildings, marking these shelters, stocking them with food, water, medical supplies, and radiological monitoring instruments. The program also includes some 3,000 protected Emergency Operating Centers (EOCs) for use by key State and local officials in directing emergency operations; the Emergency Broadcast System employing stations of the civilian boradcasting industry; a Broadcast Station Protection Program of fallout protection, emergency power, and radio links to the EOCs for over 600 radio stations; a warning system linking over 1,500 warning points to the North American Air Defense Command Center in Colorado; and a radiological monitoring system of more than 65,000 monitoring locations and communications, linking with US military communications, to tie all of these elements together.

APPENDIX LLL
MUTUAL AND BALANCED FORCE REDUCTIONS

[FROM: NATO Facts and Figures. Brussells, The North Atlantic Treaty Organization, Information Service, October 1971.]

MUTUAL AND BALANCED FORCE REDUCTIONS

DECLARATION ADOPTED BY FOREIGN MINISTERS AND REPRESENTATIVES OF COUNTRIES PARTICIPATING IN THE NATO DEFENCE PROGRAMME

Ministerial session, Reykjavik, 24-25 June, 1968

1. Meeting at Reykjavik on 24th and 25th June, 1968, the Ministers recalled the frequently expressed and strong desire of their countries to make progress in the field of disarmament and arms control.

2. Ministers recognized that the unresolved issues which still divide the European Continent must be settled by peaceful means, and are convinced that the ultimate goal of a lasting, peaceful order in Europe requires an atmosphere of trust and confidence and can only be reached by a step-by-step process. Mindful of the obvious and considerable interest of all European States in this goal, Ministers expressed their belief that measures in this field including balanced and mutual force reductions can contribute significantly to the lessening of tension and to further reducing the danger of war.

3. Ministers noted the important work undertaken within the North Atlantic Council by member governments in examining possible proposals for such reductions pursuant to paragraph 13 of the "Report on the Future Tasks of the Alliance", approved by the Ministers in December 1967. In particular, they have taken note of the work being done in the Committee of Political Advisers to establish bases of comparison and to analyse alternative ways of achieving a balanced reduction of forces, particularly in the Central part of Europe.

4. Ministers affirmed the need for the Alliance to maintain an effective military capability and to assure a balance of forces between NATO and the Warsaw Pact. Since the security of the NATO countries and the prospects for mutual force reductions would be weakened by NATO reductions alone, Ministers affirmed the proposition that the overall military capability of NATO should not be reduced except as part of a pattern of mutual force reductions balanced in scope and timing.

5. Accordingly, Ministers directed Permanent Representatives to continue and intensify their work in accordance with the following agreed principles:

a. Mutual force reductions should be reciprocal and balanced in scope and timing.

b. Mutual reductions should represent a substantial and significant step, which will serve to maintain the present degree of security at reduced cost, but should not be such as to risk de-stabilizing the situation in Europe.

c. Mutual reductions should be consonant with the aim of creating confidence in Europe generally and in the case of each party concerned.

d. To this end, any new arrangement regarding forces should be consistent with the vital security interests of all parties and capable of being carried out effectively.

6. Ministers affirmed the readiness of their governments to explore with other interested states specific and practical steps in the arms control field.

7. In particular, Ministers agreed that it was desirable that a process leading to mutual force reductions should be initiated. To that end they decided to make all necessary preparations for discussions on this subject with the Soviet Union and other countries of Eastern Europe and they call on them to join in this search for progress towards peace.

8. Ministers directed their Permanent Representatives to follow up on this declaration.

APPENDIX MMM

SOVIET MILITARY CAPABILITY*; [WARSAW PACT] TREATY OF FRIENDSHIP, COOPERATION, AND MUTUAL ASSISTANCE; AND ESTABLISHMENT OF A JOINT COMMAND

(TEXTS)

*[FROM: NATO Facts and Figures. Brussells, The North Atlantic Treaty Organization, Information Service, October 1971.]

SOVIET MILITARY CAPABILITY

The Soviet armed forces have been developed carefully and systematically. They are a modern and formidable, well-balanced and organized force, capable of conducting both defensive and aggressive offensive operations. A large proportion of the Soviet state budget is spent annually on defence and defence-related research and development.

The Warsaw Pact countries have improved the quality of their armed forces considerably. Their total strength is now estimated to be about 4.5 million men and their modern equipment is almost exclusively Soviet made. The Warsaw Pact nations, like the Soviets, have increased their military budgets.

Soviet Strategic Rocket Forces

The Soviet Strategic Rocket Forces consist of about 350,000 men. They have a total of approximately 1,400 operational Intercontinental Ballistic Missiles (ICBM) and about 550 Intermediate and Medium Range Ballistic Missiles (IRBM and MRBM). In addition there are more than 100 missiles with ICBM/IRBM/MRBM capability.

These missiles constitute the main strategic threat to NATO, ICBMs covering the most distant targets, including those in the United States and Canada, while IRBMS and MRBMS are primarily directed against targets in Western Europe. A new missile development, the "Multiple Re-Entry Vehicle" (MRV) has been in the trial stage for over two years and may now be available for deployment. This together with the "Fractional Orbital Bombardment System" (FOBS) which is to be used to overcome

the US ballistic missile warning system constitutes a further increase in Soviet strategic missile capability. Furthermore, a limited Anti Ballistic Missile (ABM) system has become operational.

Soviet Ground Forces

The Soviet ground forces have an estimated strength of 2,500,000 men, organized, so far as field units are concerned, in about 165 tank, motorized rifle and airborne divisions. Approximately 40 of these divisions are in the Sino-Soviet border area including 2 divisions in the People's Republic of Mongolia .Of the remaining divisions over 90 are located in Central USSR, West of the Ural mountains and North of the Caucasus and 31 in the other Warsaw Pact member countries: 20 in the German Democratic Republic, 2 in Poland, 5 in Czechoslovakia, and 4 in Hungary. These 31 divisions are combat ready. The divisions stationed in the USSR, however, are at different levels of combat readiness. About three-quarters of them would be almost immediately available for operations. The seven airborne divisions with approximately 50,000 men are combat ready and up to two of these divisions and their supporting elements could be air-dropped or air-landed simultaneously over medium ranges.
After World War II, the Soviets continued to modernize their ground forces. Particular emphasis has been placed on increased mobility, so that today the Soviets have only standardized armoured and motorized forces in addition to their airborne divisions. The cross-country and river-crossing capabilities of their units have been improved, as has their night-fighting ability. They have been equipped with heavier mobile weapons. One of the most important aspects of these modernizations has been a recent increase in conventional artillery and the equipping of ground forces with a variety of tactical nuclear weapons, some of which are mounted on tracked carriers to give them a higher degree of mobility. In general the Soviet forces are kept at a high level of proficiency from recruit training to advanced studies at military academies. They operate efficiently in both small and large-scale manœuvres. All these developments make the Soviet army a modern, well-equipped and efficient fighting force, geared to the realities of the nuclear age.

Other Warsaw Pact Ground Forces

Soviet strength is supplemented by forces provided by her allies totalling some 60 motorized rifle and tank divisions. There are about 6 East German, 15 Polish, 10 Czechoslovak, 6 Hungarian, 10 Rumanian and 13 Bulgarian divisions. These armies are constantly improving in the fields of equipment, training and co-ordination with Soviet forces. Almost all the divisions are combat ready. As far as their reliability is concerned, it is assumed that these forces will support the Soviet Union in case of a conflict with NATO.

Soviet Air Forces

The estimated strength of the Soviet Air Forces is at present of the order of about 7,000 fighters, 2,000 light, medium and heavy bombers, and 2,500 transport and other aircraft, totalling approximately 11,500 aircraft. About three-quarters of these, including some 3,000 air defence fighter aircraft, are likely to be of direct concern to the Alliance. The Soviet air forces are divided into five major components: Air Defence, Tactical, Long-Range, Transport and Naval Aviation. The quality of the aircraft is high and generally comparable with their Western counterparts. A large number of well protected airfields is available providing the Soviet air forces with a rapid redeployment capability and thus improving their flexibility and mobility. In view of this and the extensive air defence measures taken they also possess a high degree of survivability.

Other Warsaw Pact Air Forces

These air forces comprise a total of some 2,500 aircraft, most of them being air defence fighters and it can be assumed that the Soviets regard them as the forward element of their own air defence system.

Soviet Navy

The Soviet Navy consists of four fleets: The Pacific, Baltic, Black Sea and Northern Fleets. The Pacific Fleet is not of direct concern to NATO. The Baltic and Black Sea fleets share the problem of limited and difficult access to the open sea and, in wartime, would have to force a passage through narrow straits. During and since the Arab/Israeli conflict in the Middle East in 1967 the Soviets have established a greatly increased presence in the Mediterranean, reaching at times a total of 60 or more ships of all types.

The Northern Fleet, with direct access to the Atlantic Ocean, forms the main threat against the lines of communication between America and Europe.

A significant aspect of Soviet naval strength lies in its submarine fleet, comprising about 340 submarines, of which two-thirds are long-range ocean-going types, capable of operation almost anywhere in the Atlantic or Pacific. This impressive Soviet submarine force, like the rest of the fleet, has been undergoing extensive modernization and has rapidly increased in recent years. It probably now includes about 110 nuclear-propelled submarines, some of which are capable of firing missiles from underwater to range up to 1,500 miles. Many of the conventionally-powered submarines are also armed with missiles. The largest number of Soviet submarines belong to the Northern fleet and thus have access to areas of vital importance to the Alliance.

The pride of the Soviet surface fleet is now the cruiser-destroyer force, estimated at approximately 120 ships, including two helicopter cruisers. Many modernized ships or new classes of ships, fitted with surface-to-surface and surface-to-air missiles, have been sighted. The tendency to equip newly constructed ships with missiles rather than conventional weapons is also evident in quite small classes of vessels such as a fast patrol boat which has surface-to-surface missiles. Recently a larger craft of that kind with improved SSM armament became operational. Soviet Naval forces include an estimated 6 brigades of naval infantry, subordinate to the four Soviet fleets. Each of these fleets is backed up by its own Fleet Air Force consisting of strike/reconnaissance and anti-submarine aircraft, with a number of transport aircraft in support. Nearly all Soviet medium-range naval aircraft can carry anti-ship missiles with ranges of about 100 nautical miles.

The Soviet Union was for many years essentially a land power, and the fleet was regarded as an extension of the army. However, in 1962, the navy was accorded its own position as an individual service and is now required both to perform its own purely maritime tasks, and to co-operate in joint inter-service defence plans. This seems to indicate a growing appreciation of the proper application of seapower. Proof of this is to be found in the increasingly frequent appearances of Soviet fleet units in the Atlantic, in particular South of the Tropic of Cancer, and in the Indian Ocean far from their home bases, as well as in the continued Soviet build-up in the Mediterranean.

Soviet Merchant Fleet and Intelligence Collecting Vessels

Another threat which was not fully appreciated until recently lies in the growth of the Soviet merchant and fishing fleets. From very modest beginnings, both have grown spectacularly in recent years. The Soviet "fish factory" ships and trawlers now range over the world's oceans, and it is significant that a high proportion of them are equipped for intelligence gathering. They carry comprehensive monitoring equipment and highly sophisticated electronic gear. Their speed is often in excess of that usually associated with such craft. It is not unusual for such a trawler to attach itself to NATO formations during exercises as an uninvited and extremely persistent observer.

The Soviets are devoting considerable attention to merchant shipping. The target that has been set for their merchant fleet, which at present has a tonnage of approximately 14 million, has been announced as more than 22 million tons by 1980.

Other Warsaw Pact Navies

These navies are small and mainly equipped to assume responsibility for the defence of home waters. They include a naval infantry force of almost two divisions with adequate sealift capability. Combined Warsaw Pact exercises have been carried out in both the Baltic and Black Seas, and an improved operational capability has been demonstrated.

Conclusions

Although a military balance still exists between East and West when their military potential is viewed as a whole, the Warsaw Pact maintains a clear superiority of conventional Forces in the European region. This advantage is assumed to be kept in check by the deterrent effect of NATO's nuclear weapons and the inherent risks of escalation. Strategic nuclear parity or even superiority appears to be a Soviet objective. Should they reach this goal, the balance between NATO and the Warsaw Pact could swing in favour of the latter, thus enabling the USSR to take greater risks in trying to impose their will not only on their allies but on NATO countries and the rest of the world as well.

TREATY

of Friendship, Cooperation and Mutual Assistance

Between the People's Republic of Albania, the People's Republic of Bulgaria, the Hungarian People's Republic, the German Democratic Republic, the Polish People's Republic, the Rumanian People's Republic, the Union of Soviet Socialist Republics and the Czechoslovak Republic

The Contracting Parties,

reaffirming their desire for the establishment of a system of European collective security based on the participation of all European states irrespective of their social and political systems, which would make it possible to unite their efforts in safeguarding the peace of Europe;

mindful, at the same time, of the situation created in Europe by the ratification of the Paris agreements, which envisage the formation of a new military alignment in the shape of "Western European Union," with the participation of a remilitarized Western Germany and the integration of the latter in the North-Atlantic bloc, which increases the danger of another war and constitutes a threat to the national security of the peaceable states;

being persuaded that in these circumstances the peaceable European states must take the necessary measures to safeguard their security and in the interests of preserving peace in Europe;

guided by the objects and principles of the Charter of the United Nations Organization;

being desirous of further promoting and developing friendship, cooperation and mutual assistance in accordance with the principles of respect for the independence and sovereignty of states and of non-interference in their internal affairs,

have decided to conclude the present Treaty of Friendship, Cooperation and Mutual Assistance and have for that purpose appointed as their plenipotentiaries:

the Presidium of the People's Assembly of the People's Republic of Albania: Mehmet Shehu, Chairman of the Council of Ministers of the People's Republic of Albania;

the Presidium of the People's Assembly of the People's Republic of Bulgaria: Vylko Chervenkov, Chairman of the Council of Ministers of the People's Republic of Bulgaria;

the Presidium of the Hungarian People's Republic: Andras Hegedus, Chairman of the Council of Ministers of the Hungarian People's Republic;

the President of the German Democratic Republic: Otto Grotewohl, Prime Minister of the German Democratic Republic;

the State Council of the Polish People's Republic: Jozef Cyrankiewicz, Chairman of the Council of Ministers of the Polish People's Republic;

the Presidium of the Grand National Assembly of the Rumanian People's Republic: Gheorghe Gheorghiu-Dej, Chairman of the Council of Ministers of the Rumanian People's Republic;

the Presidium of the Supreme Soviet of the Union of Soviet Socialist Republics: Nikolai Alexandrovich Bulganin, Chairman of the Council of Ministers of the U.S.S.R.;

the President of the Czechoslovak Republic: Viliam Siroky, Prime Minister of the Czechoslovak Republic,

who, having presented their full powers, found in good and due form, have agreed as follows:

Article 1

The Contracting Parties undertake, in accordance with the Charter of the United Nations Organization, to refrain in their international relations from the threat or use of force, and to settle their international disputes peacefully and in such manner as will not jeopardize international peace and security.

Article 2

The Contracting Parties declare their readiness to participate in a spirit of sincere co-operation in all international actions designed to safeguard international peace and security, and will fully devote their energies to the attainment of this end.

The Contracting Parties will furthermore strive for the adoption, in agreement with other states which may desire to cooperate in this, of effective measures for universal reduction of armaments and prohibition of atomic, hydrogen and other weapons of mass destruction.

Article 3

The Contracting Parties shall consult with one another on all important international issues affecting their common interests, guided by the desire to strengthen international peace and security.

They shall immediately consult with one another whenever, in the opinion of any one of them, a threat of armed attack on one or more of the Parties to the Treaty has arisen, in order to ensure joint defence and the maintenance of peace and security.

Article 4

In the event of armed attack in Europe on one or more of the Parties to the Treaty by any state or group of states, each of the Parties to the Treaty, in the exercise of its right to individual or collective self-defence in accordance with Article 51 of the Charter of the United Nations Organization, shall immediately, either individually or in agreement with other Parties to the Treaty, come to the assistance of the state or states attacked with all such means as it deems necessary, including armed force. The Parties to the Treaty shall immediately consult concerning the necessary measures to be taken by them jointly in order to restore and maintain international peace and security.

Measures taken on the basis of this Article shall be reported to the Security Council in conformity with the provisions of the Charter of the United Nations Organization. These measures shall be discontinued immediately the Security Council adopts the necessary measures to restore and maintain international peace and security.

Article 5

The Contracting Parties have agreed to establish a Joint Command of the armed forces that by agreement among the Parties shall be assigned to the Command, which shall function on the basis of jointly established principles. They shall likewise adopt other agreed measures necessary to strengthen their defensive power, in order to protect the peaceful labours of their peoples, guarantee the inviolability of their frontiers and territories, and provide defence against possible aggression.

Article 6

For the purpose of the consultations among the Parties envisaged in the present Treaty, and also for the purpose of examining questions which may arise in the operation of the Treaty, a Political Consultative Committee shall be set up, in which each of the Parties to the Treaty shall be represented by a member of its Government or by another specifically pointed representative.

The Committee may set up such auxiliary bodies as may prove necessary.

Article 7

The Contracting Parties undertake not to participate in any coalitions or alliances and not to conclude any agreements whose objects conflict with the objects of the present Treaty.

The Contracting Parties declare that their commitments under existing international treaties do not conflict with the provisions of the present Treaty.

Article 8

The Contracting Parties declare that they will act in a spirit of friendship and cooperation with a view to further developing and fostering economic and cultural intercourse with one another, each adhering to the principle of respect for the independence and sovereignty of the others and non-interference in their internal affairs.

Article 9

The present Treaty is open to the accession of other states, irrespective of their social and political systems, which express their readiness by participation in the present Treaty to assist in uniting the efforts of the peaceable states in safeguarding the peace and security of the peoples. Such accession shall enter into force with the agreement of the Parties to the Treaty after the declaration of accession has been deposited with the Government of the Polish People's Republic.

Article 10

The present Treaty is subject to ratification, and the instruments of ratification shall be deposited with the Government of the Polish People's Republic.

The Treaty shall enter into force on the day the last instrument of ratification has been deposited. The Government of the Polish People's Republic shall notify the other Parties to the Treaty as each instrument of ratification is deposited.

Article 11

The present Treaty shall remain in force for twenty years. For such Contracting Parties as do not at least one year before the expiration of this period present to the Government of the Polish People's Republic a statement of denunciation of the Treaty, it shall remain in force for the next ten years.

Should a system of collective security be established in Europe, and a General European Treaty of Collective Security concluded for this purpose, for which the Contracting Parties will unswervingly strive, the present Treaty shall cease to be operative from the day the General European Treaty enters into force.

Done in Warsaw on May 14, 1955, in one copy each in the Russian, Polish, Czech and German languages, all texts being equally authentic. Certified copies of the present Treaty shall be sent by the Government of the Polish People's Republic to all the Parties to the Treaty.

In witness whereof the plenipotentiaries have signed the present Treaty and affixed their seals.

For the Presidium of the People's Assembly of the People's Republic of Albania

Mehmet Shehu

For the Presidium of the People's Assembly of the People's Republic of Bulgaria

Vylko Chervenkov

For the Presidium of the Hungarian People's Republic

Andras Hegedus

For the President of the German Democratic Republic

Otto Grotewohl

For the State Council of the Polish People's Republic

Jozef Cyrankiewicz

For the Presidium of the Grand National Assembly of the Rumanian People's Republic

Gheorghe Gheorghiu-Dej

For the Presidium of the Supreme Soviet of the Union of Soviet Socialist Republics

Nikolai Alexandrovich Bulganin

For the President of the Czechoslovak Republic

Viliam Siroky

ESTABLISHMENT OF A JOINT COMMAND

of the Armed Forces of the Signatories to the Treaty of Friendship, Cooperation and Mutual Assistance

In pursuance of the Treaty of Friendship, Cooperation and Mutual Assistance between the People's Republic of Albania, the People's Republic of Bulgaria, the Hungarian People's Republic, the German Democratic Republic, the Polish People's Republic, the Rumanian People's Republic, the Union of Soviet Socialist Republics and the Czechoslovak Republic, the signatory states have decided to establish a Joint Command of their armed forces.

The decision provides that general questions relating to the strengthening of the defensive power and the organization of the Joint Armed Forces of the signatory states shall be subject to examination by the Political Consultative Committee, which shall adopt the necessary decisions.

Marshal of the Soviet Union *I. S. Konev* has been appointed Commander-in-Chief of the Joint Armed Forces to be assigned by the signatory states.

The Ministers of Defence or other military leaders of the signatory states are to serve as Deputy Commanders-in-Chief of the Joint Armed Forces, and shall command the armed forces assigned by their respective states to the Joint Armed Forces.

The question of the participation of the German Democratic Republic in measures concerning the armed forces of the Joint Command will be examined at a later date.

A Staff of the Joint Armed Forces of the signatory states will be set up under the Commander-in-Chief of the Joint Armed Forces, and will include permanent representatives of the General Staffs of the signatory states.

The Staff will have its headquarters in *Moscow*.

The disposition of the Joint Armed Forces in the territories of the signatory states will be effected, by agreement among the states, in accordance with the requirements of their mutual defence.

APPENDIX NNN
ABBREVIATIONS IN COMMON USE

FROM: NATO Facts and Figures. Brussells, The North Atlantic Treaty Organization, Information Service, October 1971.]

ABBREVIATIONS IN COMMON USE

ABM	Anti-Ballistic Missile
ACCHAN	Allied Command Channel
ACE	Allied Command Europe
ACLANT	Allied Command Atlantic
ACSA	Allied Communications Security Agency
AFCENT	Allied Forces Central Europe
AFNORTH	Allied Forces Northern Europe
AFSOUTH	Allied Forces Southern Europe
AGARD	Advisory Group for Aerospace, Research and Development
ALLA	Allied Long Lines Agency
AMF	ACE Mobile Force
ANCA	Allied Naval Communications Agency
ARFA	Allied Radio Frequency Agency
ATA	Atlantic Treaty Association
BMEWS	Ballistic Missile Early Warning System
CCMS	Committee on Challenges of Modern Society
CEAC	Committee for European Airspace Co-ordination
CEOA	Central Europe Operating Agency
CEPO	Central Europe Pipeline Office
CES	Conference on European Security
CHANCOM	Channel Command
CINCEASTLANT	Commander-in-Chief Eastern Atlantic Area
CINCENT	Commander-in-Chief Allied Forces Central Europe
CINCHAN	Commander-in-Chief Channel and Southern North Sea
CINCIBERLANT	Commander-in-Chief Iberian Atlantic Area
CINCNORTH	Commander-in-Chief Allied Forces Northern Europe
CINCSOUTH	Commander-in-Chief Allied Forces Southern Europe
CINCWESTLANT	Commander-in-Chief Western Atlantic Area
CNAD	Conference of National Armaments Directors
CUSRPG	Canada-US Regional Planning Group
DPC	Defence Planning Committee
ECSC	European Coal and Steel Community
EDC	European Defence Community
EDIP	European Defence Improvement Programme
EEC	European Economic Community
ELDO	European Launcher Development Organization
ESRO	European Space Research Organization

IATA	International Air Transport Association
IBERLANT	Iberia-Atlantic Area
ICAO	International Civil Aviation Organization
ICBM	Intercontinental Ballistic Missile
IMS	International Military Staff
IRBM	Intermediate Range Ballistic Missile
MARAIRMED	Maritime Air Forces Mediterranean
MAS	Military Agency for Standardization
MBFR	Mutual and Balanced Force Reductions
MC	Military Committee
MILREP	Military Representative (to MC)
MLF	Multilateral Force
NAC	North Atlantic Council
NADGE	NATO Air Defence Ground Environment System
NAMFI	NATO Missile Firing Installation
NAMMO	NATO Multi-Role Combat Aircraft Development and Production Management Organization
NAMSA	NATO Maintenance and Supply Agency
NAMSO	NATO Maintenance and Supply Organization
NATO	North Atlantic Treaty Organization
NDAC	Nuclear Defence Affairs Committee
NDC	NATO Defence College
NIAG	NATO Industrial Advisory Group
NICS	NATO Integrated Communication System
NMR	National Military Representative (to SHAPE)
NORAD	North America Air Defence
NPG	Nuclear Planning Group
NPLO	NATO Production and Logistics Organization
NSC	NATO Supply Centre
OECD	Organization for Economic Co-operation and Development
SAC	Strategic Air Command
SACEUR	Supreme Allied Commander Europe
SACLANT	Supreme Allied Commander Atlantic
SACLANTCEN	SACLANT (Anti-Submarine Warfare Research) Centre
SALT	Strategic Arms Limitation Talks
SATCOM	Satellite Communications
SHAPE	Supreme Headquarters Allied Powers Europe
STANAVFORLANT	Standing Naval Force Atlantic
STC	SHAPE Technical Centre
TCC	Temporary Council Committee
WEU	Western European Union

☆ U.S. GOVERNMENT PRINTING OFFICE : 1976 O—591-085